Analysis of Panel Data

Panel data models have become increasingly popular among applied researchers due to their heightened capacity for capturing the complexity of human behavior as compared to cross-sectional or time-series data models. As a consequence, more and richer panel data sets also have become increasingly available. This second edition is a substantial revision of the highly successful first edition of 1986. Recent advances in panel data research are presented in a rigorous and accessible manner and are carefully integrated with the older material. The thorough discussion of theory and the judicious use of empirical examples will make this book useful to graduate students and advanced researchers in economics, business, sociology, political science, etc. Other specific revisions include the introduction of Bayes method and the notion of strict exogeneity with estimators presented in a generalized method of moments framework to link the identification of various models, intuitive explanations of semiparametric methods of estimating discrete choice models and methods of pairwise trimming for the estimation of panel sample selection models, etc.

Cheng Hsiao is Professor of Economics at the University of Southern California. His first edition of *Analysis of Panel Data* (Econometric Society Monograph 11, Cambridge University Press, 1986) has been the standard introduction for students to the subject in the economics literature. Professor Hsiao is also a coauthor of *Econometric Models, Techniques, and Applications*, Second Edition (Prentice Hall, 1996, with M. Intriligator and R. Bodkin), coeditor of *Analysis of Panels and Limited Dependent Variable Models* (Cambridge University Press, 1999, with K. Lahiri, L.F. Lee, and M.H. Pesaran), and coeditor of *Nonlinear Statistical Inference* (Cambridge University Press, 2001, with K. Morimune and J.L. Powell). He is a Fellow of the Econometric Society and coeditor and Fellow of the *Journal of Econometrics*.

Econometric Society Monographs No. 34

Editors:
Andrew Chesher, University College London
Matthew O. Jackson, California Institute of Technology

The Econometric Society is an international society for the advancement of economic theory in relation to statistics and mathematics. The Econometric Society Monograph Series is designed to promote the publication of original research contributions of high quality in mathematical economics and theoretical and applied econometrics.

Other titles in the series:

G. S. Maddala *Limited-dependent and qualitative variables in econometrics*, 0 521 33825 5
Gerard Debreu *Mathematical economics: Twenty papers of Gerard Debreu*, 0 521 33561 2
Jean-Michel Grandmont *Money and value: A reconsideration of classical and neoclassical monetary economics*, 0 521 31364 3
Franklin M. Fisher *Disequilibrium foundations of equilibrium economics*, 0 521 37856 7
Andreu Mas-Colell *The theory of general economic equilibrium: A differentiable approach*, 0 521 26514 2, 0 521 38870 8
Truman F. Bewley, Editor *Advances in econometrics – Fifth World Congress (Volume I)*, 0 521 46726 8
Truman F. Bewley, Editor *Advances in econometrics – Fifth World Congress (Volume II)*, 0 521 46725 X
Hervé Moulin *Axioms of cooperative decision making*, 0 521 36055 2, 0 521 42458 5
L. G. Godfrey *Misspecification tests in econometrics: The Lagrange multiplier principle and other approaches*, 0 521 42459 3
Tony Lancaster *The econometric analysis of transition data*, 0 521 43789 X
Alvin E. Roth and Marilda A. Oliviera Sotomayor, Editors *Two-sided matching: A study in game-theoretic modeling and analysis*, 0 521 43788 1
Wolfgang Härdle, *Applied nonparametric regression*, 0 521 42950 1
Jean-Jacques Laffont, Editor *Advances in economic theory – Sixth World Congress (Volume I)*, 0 521 48459 6
Jean-Jacques Laffont, Editor *Advances in economic theory – Sixth World Congress (Volume II)*, 0 521 48460 X
Halbert White *Estimation, inference and specification*, 0 521 25280 6, 0 521 57446 3
Christopher Sims, Editor *Advances in econometrics – Sixth World Congress (Volume I)*, 0 521 56610 X
Christopher Sims, Editor *Advances in econometrics – Sixth World Congress (Volume II)*, 0 521 56609 6
Roger Guesnerie *A contribution to the pure theory of taxation*, 0 521 23689 4, 0 521 62956 X
David M. Kreps and Kenneth F. Wallis, Editors *Advances in economics and econometrics – Seventh World Congress (Volume I)*, 0 521 58011 0, 0 521 58983 5
David M. Kreps and Kenneth F. Wallis, Editors *Advances in economics and econometrics – Seventh World Congress (Volume II)*, 0 521 58012 9, 0 521 58982 7
David M. Kreps and Kenneth F. Wallis, Editors *Advances in economics and econometrics – Seventh World Congress (Volume III)*, 0 521 58013 7, 0 521 58981 9
Donald P. Jacobs, Ehud Kalai, and Morton I. Kamien, Editors *Frontiers of research in economic theory: The Nancy L. Schwartz Memorial Lectures, 1983–1997*, 0 521 63222 6, 0 521 63538 1
A. Colin Cameron and Pravin K. Trivedi, *Regression analysis of count data*, 0 521 63201 3, 0 521 63567 5
Steinar Strøm, Editor *Econometrics and economic theory in the 20th century: The Ragnar Frisch Centennial Symposium*, 0 521 63323 0, 0 521 63365 6
Eric Ghysels, Norman R. Swanson, and Mark Watson, Editors *Essays in econometrics: Collected papers of Clive W. J. Granger (Volume I)*, 0 521 77496 9
Eric Ghysels, Norman R. Swanson, and Mark Watson, Editors *Essays in econometrics: Collected papers of Clive W. J. Granger (Volume II)*, 0 521 79649 0

Analysis of Panel Data

Second Edition

CHENG HSIAO
University of Southern California

PUBLISHED BY THE PRESS SYNDICATE OF THE UNIVERSITY OF CAMBRIDGE
The Pitt Building, Trumpington Street, Cambridge, United Kingdom

CAMBRIDGE UNIVERSITY PRESS
The Edinburgh Building, Cambridge CB2 2RU, UK
40 West 20th Street, New York, NY 10011-4211, USA
477 Williamstown Road, Port Melbourne, VIC 3207, Australia
Ruiz de Alarcón 13, 28014 Madrid, Spain
Dock House, The Waterfront, Cape Town 8001, South Africa

http://www.cambridge.org

First published 2003
Reprinted 2004

Printed in the United Kingdom at the University Press, Cambridge

Typeface Times Roman 10/12 pt. *System* LaTeX 2ε [TB]

A catalog record for this book is available from the British Library.

Library of Congress Cataloging in Publication Data

Hsiao, Cheng, 1943–

Analysis of panel data / Cheng Hsiao. – 2nd ed.

p. cm. – (Econometric Society monographs ; no. 34)

Includes bibliographical references and index.

ISBN 0-521-81855-9 – ISBN 0-521-52271-4 (pb.)

1. Econometrics. 2. Panel analysis. 3. Analysis of variance. I. Title. II. Series.

HB139 .H75 2002
330′.01′5195 – dc21 2002023348

ISBN 0 521 81855 9 hardback
ISBN 0 521 52271 4 paperback

To my wife, Amy Mei-Yun
and my children,
Irene Chiayun
Allen Chenwen
Michael Chenyee
Wendy Chiawen

Contents

Preface to the Second Edition

Since the publication of the first edition of this monograph in 1986, there has been a phenomenal growth of articles dealing with panel data. According to the *Social Science Citation Index*, there were 29 articles related to panel data in 1989. But in 1997 there were 518; in 1998, 553; and in 1999, 650. The increasing attention is partly due to the greater availability of panel data sets, which can better answer questions of substantial interest than a single set of cross-section or time series data can, and partly due to the rapid growth in computational power of the individual researcher. It is furthermore motivated by the internal methodological logic of the subject (e.g., Trognon (2000)).

The current version is a substantial revision of the first edition. The major additions are essentially on nonlinear panel data models of discrete choice (Chapter 7) and sample selection (Chapter 8); a new Chapter 10 on miscellaneous topics such as simulation techniques, large N and T theory, unit root and cointegration tests, multiple level structure, and cross-sectional dependence; and new sections on estimation of dynamic models (4.5–4.7), Bayesian treatment of models with fixed and random coefficients (6.6–6.8), and repeated cross-sectional data (or pseudopanels), etc. In addition, many of the discussions in old chapters have been updated. For instance, the notion of strict exogeneity is introduced, and estimators are also presented in a generalized method of moments framework to help link the assumptions that are required for the identification of various models. The discussion of fixed and random effects is updated in regard to restrictions on the assumption about unobserved specific effects, etc.

The goal of this revision remains the same as that of the first edition. It aims to bring up to date a comprehensive analytical framework for the analysis of a greater variety of data. The emphasis is on formulating appropriate statistical inference for issues shaped by important policy concerns. The revised edition of this monograph is intended neither as an encyclopedia nor as a history of panel data econometrics. I apologize for the omissions of many important contributions. A recount of the history of panel data econometrics can be found in Nerlove (2000). Some additional issues and references can also be found in a survey by Arellano and Honoré (2001) and in four recent edited volumes – Matyás and Sevester (1996); Hsiao, Lahiri, Lee, and Pesaran (1999); Hsiao, Morimune, and Powell (2001); and Krishnakumar and Ronchetti (2000). Software is reviewed by Blanchard (1996).

I would like to thank the editor, Scott Parris, for his encouragement and assistance in preparing the revision, and Andrew Chesher and two anonymous readers for helpful comments on an early draft. I am also very grateful to E. Kyriazidou for her careful and detailed comments on Chapters 7 and 8, S. Chen and J. Powell for their helpful comments and suggestions on Chapter 8, and H.R. Moon for the section on large panels, Sena Schlessinger for her expert typing of the manuscript except for Chapter 7, Yan Shen for carefully proofreading the manuscript and for expertly typing Chapter 7, and Siyan Wang for drawing the figures for Chapter 8. Of course, all remaining errors are mine. The kind permissions to reproduce parts of articles by James Heckman, C. Manski, Daniel McFadden, Ariel Pakes, *Econometrica, Journal of the American Statistical Association, Journal of Econometrics, Regional Science and Urban Economics, Review of Economic Studies*, The University of Chicago Press, and Elsevier Science are also gratefully acknowledged.

Preface to the First Edition

Recently, empirical research in economics has been enriched by the availability of a wealth of new sources of data: cross sections of individuals observed over time. These allow us to construct and test more realistic behavioral models that could not be identified using only a cross section or a single time series data set. Nevertheless, the availability of new data sources raises new issues. New methods are constantly being introduced, and points of view are changing. An author preparing an introductory monograph has to select the topics to be included. My selection involves controlling for unobserved individual and/or time characteristics to avoid specification bias and to improve the efficiency of the estimates. The more basic and more commonly used methods are treated here, although to some extent the coverage is a matter of taste. Some examples of applications of the methods are also given, and the uses, computational approaches, and interpretations are discussed.

I am very much indebted to C. Manski and to a reader for Cambridge University Press, as well as to G. Chamberlain and J. Ham, for helpful comments and suggestions. I am also grateful to Mario Tello Pacheco, who read through the manuscript and made numerous suggestions concerning matters of exposition and corrections of errors of every magnitude. My appreciation also goes to V. Bencivenga, A.C. Cameron, T. Crawley, A. Deaton, E. Kuh, B. Ma, D. McFadden, D. Mountain, G. Solon, G. Taylor, and K.Y. Tsui, for helpful comments, and Sophia Knapik and Jennifer Johnson, who patiently typed and retyped innumerable drafts and revisions. Of course, in material like this it is easy to generate errors, and the reader should put the blame on the author for any remaining errors.

Various parts of this monograph were written while I was associated with Bell Laboratories, Murray Hill, Princeton University, Stanford University, the University of Southern California, and the University of Toronto. I am grateful to these institutions for providing me with secretarial and research facilities and, most of all, stimulating colleagues. Financial support from the National Science Foundation, U.S.A., and from the Social Sciences and Humanities Research Council of Canada is gratefully acknowledged.

CHAPTER 1

Introduction

1.1 ADVANTAGES OF PANEL DATA

A longitudinal, or panel, data set is one that follows a given sample of individuals over time, and thus provides multiple observations on each individual in the sample. Panel data have become widely available in both the developed and developing countries. For instance, in the U.S., two of the most prominent panel data sets are the National Longitudinal Surveys of Labor Market Experience (NLS) and the University of Michigan's Panel Study of Income Dynamics (PSID).

The NLS began in the mid-1960s. It contains five separate longitudinal data bases covering distinct segments of the labor force: men whose ages were 45 to 59 in 1966, young men 14 to 24 in 1966, women 30 to 44 in 1967, young women 14 to 24 in 1968, and youth of both sexes 14 to 21 in 1979. In 1986, the NLS expanded to include surveys of the children born to women who participated in the National Longitudinal Survey of Youth 1979. The list of variables surveyed is running into the thousands, with the emphasis on the supply side of the labor market. Table 1.1 summarizes the NLS survey groups, the sizes of the original samples, the span of years each group has been interviewed, and the current interview status of each group (for detail, see *NLS Handbook 2000*, U.S. Department of Labor, Bureau of Labor Statistics).

The PSID began with collection of annual economic information from a representative national sample of about 6,000 families and 15,000 individuals in 1968 and has continued to the present. The data set contains over 5,000 variables, including employment, income, and human-capital variables, as well as information on housing, travel to work, and mobility. In addition to the NLS and PSID data sets there are several other panel data sets that are of interest to economists, and these have been cataloged and discussed by Borus (1981) and Juster (2000); also see Ashenfelter and Solon (1982) and Becketti et al. (1988).[1]

In Europe, various countries have their annual national or more frequent surveys – the Netherlands Socio-Economic Panel (SEP), the German Social Economics Panel (GSOEP), the Luxembourg Social Economic Panel (PSELL),

Table 1.1. *The NLS: Survey groups, sample sizes, interview years, and survey status*

Survey group	Age cohort	Birth year cohort	Original sample	Initial year/ latest year	Number of surveys	Number at last interview	Status
Older men	45–59	4/2/07–4/1/21	5,020	1966/1990	13	2,092[1]	Ended
Mature women	30–44	4/2/23–4/1/37	5,083	1967/1999	19	2,466[2]	Continuing
Young men	14–24	4/2/42–4/1/52	5,225	1966/1981	12	3,398	Ended
Young women	14–24	1944–1954	5,159	1968/1999	20	2,900[2]	Continuing
NLSY79	14–21	1957–1964	12,686[3]	1979/1998	18	8,399	Continuing
NLSY79 children	birth–14	—	—[4]	1986/1998	7	4,924	Continuing
NLSY79 young adults	15–22	—	—[4]	1994/1998	3	2,143	Continuing
NLSY97	12–16	1980–1984	8,984	1997/1999	3	8,386	Continuing

[1]Interviews in 1990 were also conducted with 2,206 widows or other next-of-kin of deceased respondents.
[2]Preliminary numbers.
[3]After dropping the military (in 1985) and economically disadvantaged non-Black, non-Hispanic oversamples (in 1991), the sample contains 9,964 respondents eligible for interview.
[4]The sizes of the NLSY79 children and young adult samples are dependent on the number of children born to female NLSY79 respondents, which is increasing over time.
Source: NLS Handbook, 2000, U.S. Department of Labor, Bureau of Labor Statistics.

the British Household Panel Survey (BHPS), etc. Starting in 1994, the National Data Collection Units (NDUs) of the Statistical Office of the European Communities, "in response to the increasing demand in the European Union for comparable information across the Member States on income, work and employment, poverty and social exclusion, housing, health, and many other diverse social indicators concerning living conditions of private households and persons" (Eurostat (1996)), have begun coordinating and linking existing national panels with centrally designed standardized multipurpose annual longitudinal surveys. For instance, the Manheim Innovation Panel (MIP) and the Manheim Innovation Panel – Service Sector (MIP-S) contain annual surveys of innovative activities (product innovations, expenditure on innovations, expenditure on R&D, factors hampering innovations, the stock of capital, wages, and skill structures of employees, etc.) of German firms with at least five employees in manufacturing and service sectors, started in 1993 and 1995, respectively. The survey methodology is closely related to the recommendations on innovation surveys manifested in the *OSLO Manual* of the OECD and Eurostat, thereby yielding international comparable data on innovation activities of German firms. The 1993 and 1997 surveys also become part of the European Community Innovation Surveys CIS I and CIS II (for detail, see Janz et al. (2001)). Similarly, the European Community Household Panel (ECHP) is to represent the population of the European Union (EU) at the household and individual levels. The ECHP contains information on demographics, labor-force behavior, income, health, education and training, housing, migration, etc. The ECHP now covers 14 of the 15 countries, the exception being Sweden (Peracchi (2000)). Detailed statistics from the ECHP are published in Eurostat's reference data base New Cronos in three domains, namely health, housing, and income and living conditions (ILC).[2]

Panel data have also become increasingly available in developing countries. In these countries, there may not have a long tradition of statistical collection. It is of special importance to obtain original survey data to answer many significant and important questions. The World Bank has sponsored and helped to design many panel surveys. For instance, the Development Research Institute of the Research Center for Rural Development of the State Council of China, in collaboration with the World Bank, undertook an annual survey of 200 large Chinese township and village enterprises from 1984 to 1990 (Hsiao et al. (1998)).

Panel data sets for economic research possess several major advantages over conventional cross-sectional or time-series data sets (e.g., Hsiao (1985a, 1995, 2000)). Panel data usually give the researcher a large number of data points, increasing the degrees of freedom and reducing the collinearity among explanatory variables – hence improving the efficiency of econometric estimates. More importantly, longitudinal data allow a researcher to analyze a number of important economic questions that cannot be addressed using cross-sectional or time-series data sets. For instance, consider the following example taken from Ben-Porath (1973): Suppose that a cross-sectional sample of married women is found to have an average yearly labor-force participation rate of 50 percent. At one extreme this might be interpreted as implying that each woman in a homogeneous population has a 50 percent chance of being in the labor force in any given year, while at the other extreme it might imply that 50 percent of the women in a heterogeneous population always work and 50 percent never work. In the first case, each woman would be expected to spend half of her married life in the labor force and half out of the labor force, and job turnover would be expected to be frequent, with an average job duration of two years. In the second case, there is no turnover, and current information about work status is a perfect predictor of future work status. To discriminate between these two models, we need to utilize individual labor-force histories to estimate the probability of participation in different subintervals of the life cycle. This is possible only if we have sequential observations for a number of individuals.

The difficulties of making inferences about the dynamics of change from cross-sectional evidence are seen as well in other labor-market situations. Consider the impact of unionism on economic behavior (e.g., Freeman and Medoff 1981). Those economists who tend to interpret the observed differences between union and nonunion firms or employees as largely real believe that unions and the collective-bargaining process fundamentally alter key aspects of the employment relationship: compensation, internal and external mobility of labor, work rules, and environment. Those economists who regard union effects as largely illusory tend to posit that the real world is close enough to satisfying the conditions of perfect competition; they believe that the observed union–nonunion differences are mainly due to differences between union and nonunion firms or workers prior to unionism or postunion sorting. Unions do not raise wages in the long run, because firms react to higher wages (forced by the union) by hiring better-quality workers. If one believes the former view, the coefficient of the dummy variable for union status in a wage or earning equation is a measure of the effect of unionism. If one believes the latter view, then the dummy variable for union status could be simply acting as a proxy for worker quality. A single cross-sectional data set usually cannot provide a direct choice between these two hypotheses, because the estimates are likely to reflect interindividual differences inherent in comparisons of *different* people or firms. However, if panel data are used, one can distinguish these two hypotheses by studying the wage differential for a worker moving from a nonunion firm to a union firm, or vice versa. If one accepts the view that unions have no effect, then a worker's wage should not be affected when he moves from a nonunion firm to a union firm, if the quality of this worker is constant over time. On the other hand, if unions truly do raise wages, then, holding worker quality constant, the worker's wage should rise as he moves to a union firm from a nonunion firm. By following given individuals or firms over time as they change status (say from nonunion to union, or vice versa), one can construct a proper recursive structure to study the before–after effect.

Whereas microdynamic and macrodynamic effects typically cannot be estimated using a cross-sectional data set, a single time-series data set usually cannot provide precise estimates of dynamic coefficients either. For instance, consider the estimation of a distributed-lag model:

$$y_t = \sum_{\tau=0}^{h} \beta_\tau x_{t-\tau} + u_t, \qquad t = 1, \ldots, T, \tag{1.1.1}$$

where x_t is an exogenous variable and u_t is a random disturbance term. In general, x_t is near x_{t-1}, and still nearer $2x_{t-1} - x_{t-2} = x_{t-1} + (x_{t-1} - x_{t-2})$; fairly strict multicollinearities appear among $h + 1$ explanatory variables, $x_1, x_{t-1}, \ldots, x_{t-h}$. Hence, there is not sufficient information to obtain precise estimates of any of the lag coefficients without specifying, a priori, that each of them is a function of only a very small number of parameters [e.g., Almon lag, rational distributed lag (Malinvaud (1970))]. If panel data are available, we can utilize the interindividual differences in x values to reduce the problem of collinearity; this allows us to drop the ad hoc conventional approach of constraining the lag coefficients $\{\beta_\tau\}$ and to impose a different prior restriction to estimate an unconstrained distributed-lag model.

Another example is that measurement errors can lead to unidentification of a model in the usual circumstance. However, the availability of multiple observations for a given individual or at a given time may allow a researcher to identify an otherwise unidentified model (e.g., Biørn (1992); Griliches and Hausman (1986); Hsiao (1991b); Hsiao and Taylor (1991); Wansbeek and Koning (1989)).

Besides the advantage that panel data allow us to construct and test more complicated behavioral models than purely cross-sectional or time-series data, the use of panel data also provides a means of resolving or reducing the magnitude of a key econometric problem that often arises in empirical studies, namely, the often heard assertion that the real reason one finds (or does not find) certain effects is the presence of omitted (mismeasured or unobserved) variables that are correlated with explanatory variables. By utilizing information on both the intertemporal dynamics and the individuality of the entities being investigated, one is better able to control in a more natural way for the effects of missing or unobserved variables. For instance, consider a simple regression model:

$$y_{it} = \alpha^* + \boldsymbol{\beta}'\mathbf{x}_{it} + \boldsymbol{\rho}'\mathbf{z}_{it} + u_{it}, \qquad \begin{array}{l} i = 1, \ldots, N, \\ t = 1, \ldots, T, \end{array} \tag{1.1.2}$$

where $\mathbf{x}_{it}$ and $\mathbf{z}_{it}$ are $k_1 \times 1$ and $k_2 \times 1$ vectors of exogenous variables; α^*, $\boldsymbol{\beta}$, and $\boldsymbol{\rho}$ are 1×1, $k_1 \times 1$, and $k_2 \times 1$ vectors of constants respectively; and the error term u_{it} is independently, identically distributed over i and t, with mean zero and variance σ_u^2. It is well known that the least-squares regression of y_{it} on $\mathbf{x}_{it}$ and $\mathbf{z}_{it}$ yields unbiased and consistent estimators of α^*, $\boldsymbol{\beta}$, and $\boldsymbol{\rho}$. Now suppose that $\mathbf{z}_{it}$ values are unobservable, and the covariances between $\mathbf{x}_{it}$ and $\mathbf{z}_{it}$ are nonzero. Then the least-squares regression coefficients of y_{it} on

$\mathbf{x}_{it}$ are biased. However, if repeated observations for a group of individuals are available, they may allow us to get rid of the effect of $\mathbf{z}$. For example, if $\mathbf{z}_{it} = \mathbf{z}_i$ for all t (i.e., $\mathbf{z}$ values stay constant through time for a given individual but vary across individuals), we can take the first difference of individual observations over time and obtain

$$y_{it} - y_{i,t-1} = \boldsymbol{\beta}'(\mathbf{x}_{it} - \mathbf{x}_{i,t-1}) + (u_{it} - u_{i,t-1}), \qquad i = 1, \ldots, N, \quad t = 2, \ldots, T. \tag{1.1.3}$$

Similarly, if $\mathbf{z}_{it} = \mathbf{z}_t$ for all i (i.e., $\mathbf{z}$ values stay constant across individuals at a given time, but exhibit variation through time), we can take the deviation from the mean across individuals at a given time and obtain

$$y_{it} - \bar{y}_t = \boldsymbol{\beta}'(\mathbf{x}_{it} - \bar{\mathbf{x}}_t) + (u_{it} - \bar{u}_t), \qquad i = 1, \ldots, N, \quad t = 1, \ldots, T, \tag{1.1.4}$$

where $\bar{y}_t = (1/N)\sum_{i=1}^N y_{it}$, $\bar{\mathbf{x}}_t = (1/N)\sum_{i=1}^N \mathbf{x}_{it}$, and $\bar{u}_t = (1/N)\sum_{i=1}^N u_{it}$. Least-squares regression of (1.1.3) or (1.1.4) now provides unbiased and consistent estimates of $\boldsymbol{\beta}$. Nevertheless if we have only a single cross-sectional data set ($T = 1$) for the former case ($\mathbf{z}_{it} = \mathbf{z}_i$), or a single time-series data set ($N = 1$) for the latter case ($\mathbf{z}_{it} = \mathbf{z}_t$), such transformations cannot be performed. We cannot get consistent estimates of $\boldsymbol{\beta}$ unless there exist instruments that are correlated with $\mathbf{x}$ but are uncorrelated with $\mathbf{z}$ and u.

MaCurdy's (1981) work on the life-cycle labor supply of prime-age males under certainty is an example of this approach. Under certain simplifying assumptions, MaCurdy shows that a worker's labor-supply function can be written as (1.1.2), where y is the logarithm of hours worked, x is the logarithm of the real wage rate, and z is the logarithm of the worker's (unobserved) marginal utility of initial wealth, which, as a summary measure of a worker's lifetime wages and property income, is assumed to stay constant through time but to vary across individuals (i.e., $z_{it} = z_i$). Given the economic problem, not only is x_{it} correlated with z_i, but every economic variable that could act as an instrument for x_{it} (such as education) is also correlated with z_i. Thus, in general, it is not possible to estimate $\boldsymbol{\beta}$ consistently from a cross-sectional data set,[3] but if panel data are available, one can consistently estimate $\boldsymbol{\beta}$ by first-differencing (1.1.2).

The "conditional convergence" of the growth rate is another example (e.g., Durlauf (2001); Temple (1999)). Given the role of transitional dynamics, it is widely agreed that growth regressions should control for the steady state level of income (e.g., Barro and Sala-i-Martin (1995); Mankiew, Romer, and Weil (1992)). Thus, a growth-rate regression model typically includes investment ratio, initial income, and measures of policy outcomes like school enrollment and the black-market exchange-rate premium as regressors. However, an important component, the initial level of a country's technical efficiency, z_{i0}, is omitted because this variable is unobserved. Since a country that is less efficient is also more likely to have lower investment rate or school enrollment, one can easily imagine that z_{i0} is correlated with the regressors and the resulting cross-sectional parameter estimates are subject to omitted-variable bias. However, with panel data one can eliminate the influence of initial efficiency by taking the first difference of individual country observations over time as in (1.1.3).

Panel data involve two dimensions: a cross-sectional dimension N, and a time-series dimension T. We would expect that the computation of panel data estimators would be more complicated than the analysis of cross-section data alone (where $T = 1$) or time series data alone (where $N = 1$). However, in certain cases the availability of panel data can actually simplify the computation and inference. For instance, consider a dynamic Tobit model of the form

$$y_{it}^* = \gamma y_{i,t-1}^* + \beta x_{it} + \epsilon_{it} \tag{1.1.5}$$

where y^* is unobservable, and what we observe is y, where $y_{it} = y_{it}^*$ if $y_{it}^* > 0$ and 0 otherwise. The conditional density of y_{it} given $y_{i,t-1} = 0$ is much more complicated than the case if $y_{i,t-1}^*$ is known, because the joint density of $(y_{it}, y_{i,t-1})$ involves the integration of $y_{i,t-1}^*$ from $-\infty$ to 0. Moreover, when there are a number of censored observations over time, the full implementation of the maximum likelihood principle is almost impossible. However, with panel data, the estimation of γ and β can be simplified considerably by simply focusing on the subset of data where $y_{i,t-1} > 0$, because the joint density of $f(y_{it}, y_{i,t-1})$ can be written as the product of the conditional density $f(y_{i,t} \mid y_{i,t-1})$ and the marginal density of $y_{i,t-1}$. But if $y_{i,t-1}^*$ is observable, the conditional density of y_{it} given $y_{i,t-1} = y_{i,t-1}^*$ is simply the density of ϵ_{it} (Arellano, Bover, and Labeager (1999)).

Another example is the time-series analysis of nonstationary data. The large-sample approximation of the distributions of the least-squares or maximum likelihood estimators when $T \to \infty$ are no longer normally distributed if the data are nonstationary (e.g., Dickey and Fuller (1979, 1981); Phillips and Durlauf (1986)). Hence, the behavior of the usual test statistics will often have to be inferred through computer simulations. But if panel data are available, and observations among cross-sectional units are independent, then one can invoke the central limit theorem across cross-sectional units to show that the limiting distributions of many estimators remain asymptotically normal and the Wald-type test statistics are asymptotically chi-square distributed (e.g., Binder, Hsiao, and Pesaran (2000); Levin and Lin (1993); Pesaran, Shin, and Smith (1999), Phillips and Moon (1999, 2000); Quah (1994)).

Panel data also provide the possibility of generating more accurate predictions for individual outcomes than time-series data alone. If individual behaviors are similar conditional on certain variables, panel data provide the possibility of learning an individual's behavior by observing the behavior of others, in addition to the information on that individual's behavior. Thus, a more accurate description of an individual's behavior can be obtained by pooling the data (e.g., Hsiao and Mountain (1994); Hsiao and Tahmiscioglu (1997); Hsiao et al. (1989); Hsiao, Applebe, and Dineen (1993)).

1.2 ISSUES INVOLVED IN UTILIZING PANEL DATA

1.2.1 Heterogeneity Bias

The oft-touted power of panel data derives from their theoretical ability to isolate the effects of specific actions, treatments, or more general policies. This theoretical ability is based on the assumption that economic data are generated from controlled experiments in which the outcomes are random variables with a probability distribution that is a smooth function of the various variables describing the conditions of the experiment. If the available data were in fact generated from simple controlled experiments, standard statistical methods could be applied. Unfortunately, most panel data come from the very complicated process of everyday economic life. In general, different individuals may be subject to the influences of different factors. In explaining individual behavior, one may extend the list of factors ad infinitum. It is neither feasible nor desirable to include all the factors affecting the outcome of all individuals in a model specification, since the purpose of modeling is not to mimic the reality but is to capture the essential forces affecting the outcome. It is typical to leave out those factors that are believed to have insignificant impacts or are peculiar to certain individuals.

However, when important factors peculiar to a given individual are left out, the typical assumption that economic variable y is generated by a parametric probability distribution function $P(y \mid \boldsymbol{\theta})$, where $\boldsymbol{\theta}$ is an m-dimensional real vector, identical for all individuals at all times, may not be a realistic one. Ignoring the individual or time-specific effects that exist among cross-sectional or time-series units but are not captured by the included explanatory variables can lead to parameter heterogeneity in the model specification. Ignoring such heterogeneity could lead to inconsistent or meaningless estimates of interesting parameters. For example, consider a simple model postulated as

$$y_{it} = \alpha_i^* + \beta_i x_{it} + u_{it}, \qquad \begin{array}{l} i = 1, \ldots, N, \\ t = 1, \ldots, T, \end{array} \tag{1.2.1}$$

where x is a scalar exogenous variable ($k_1 = 1$) and u_{it} is the error term with mean zero and constant variance σ_u^2. The parameters α_i^* and β_i may be different for different cross-sectional units, although they stay constant over time. Following this assumption, a variety of sampling distributions may occur. Such sampling distributions can seriously mislead the least-squares regression of y_{it} on x_{it} when all NT observations are used to estimate the model:

$$y_{it} = \alpha^* + \beta x_{it} + u_{it}, \qquad \begin{array}{l} i = 1, \ldots, N, \\ t = 1, \ldots, T. \end{array} \tag{1.2.2}$$

For instance, consider the situation that the data are generated as either in case 1 or case 2.

Case 1: Heterogeneous intercepts ($\alpha_i^* \neq \alpha_j^*$), homogeneous slope ($\beta_i = \beta_j$). We use graphs to illustrate the likely biases due to the assumption that $\alpha_i^* \neq \alpha_j^*$ and $\beta_i = \beta_j$. In these graphs, the broken-line ellipses represent the point scatter for an individual over time, and the broken straight lines represent the individual regressions. Solid lines serve the same purpose for the least-squares regression of (1.2.2) using all NT observations. A variety of circumstances may arise in this case, as shown in Figures 1.1, 1.2, and 1.3. All of these figures depict situations in which biases arise in pooled least-squares estimates of (1.2.2) because of heterogeneous intercepts. Obviously, in these cases, pooled regression ignoring heterogeneous intercepts should never be used. Moreover, the direction of the bias of the pooled slope estimates cannot be identified a priori; it can go either way.

Case 2: Heterogeneous intercepts and slopes ($\alpha_i^* \neq \alpha_j^*$, $\beta_i \neq \beta_j$). In Figures 1.4 and 1.5 the point scatters are not shown, and the circled numbers signify the individuals whose regressions have been included in the analysis. For the example depicted in Figure 1.4, a straightforward pooling of all NT observations, assuming identical parameters for all cross-sectional units, would lead to nonsensical results because it would represent an average of coefficients that differ greatly across individuals. Nor does the case of Figure 1.5 make any sense in pooling, because it gives rise to the false inference that the pooled relation is curvilinear. In either case, the classic paradigm of the "representative agent" simply does not hold, and pooling the data under homogeneity assumption makes no sense.

These are some of the likely biases when parameter heterogeneities among cross-sectional units are ignored. Similar patterns of bias will also arise if the intercepts and slopes vary through time, even though for a given time period they are identical for all individuals. More elaborate patterns than those depicted here are, of course, likely to occur (e.g., Chesher and Lancaster 1983; Kuh 1963).

1.2.2 Selectivity Bias

Another frequently observed source of bias in both cross-sectional and panel data is that the sample may not be randomly drawn from the population. For example, the New Jersey negative income tax experiment excluded all families in the geographic areas of the experiment who had incomes above 1.5 times the officially defined poverty level. When the truncation is based on earnings, uses of the data that treat components of earnings (specifically, wages or hours) as dependent variables will often create what is commonly referred to as selection bias (e.g., Hausman and Wise (1977); Heckman (1976a, 1979); Hsiao (1974b)).

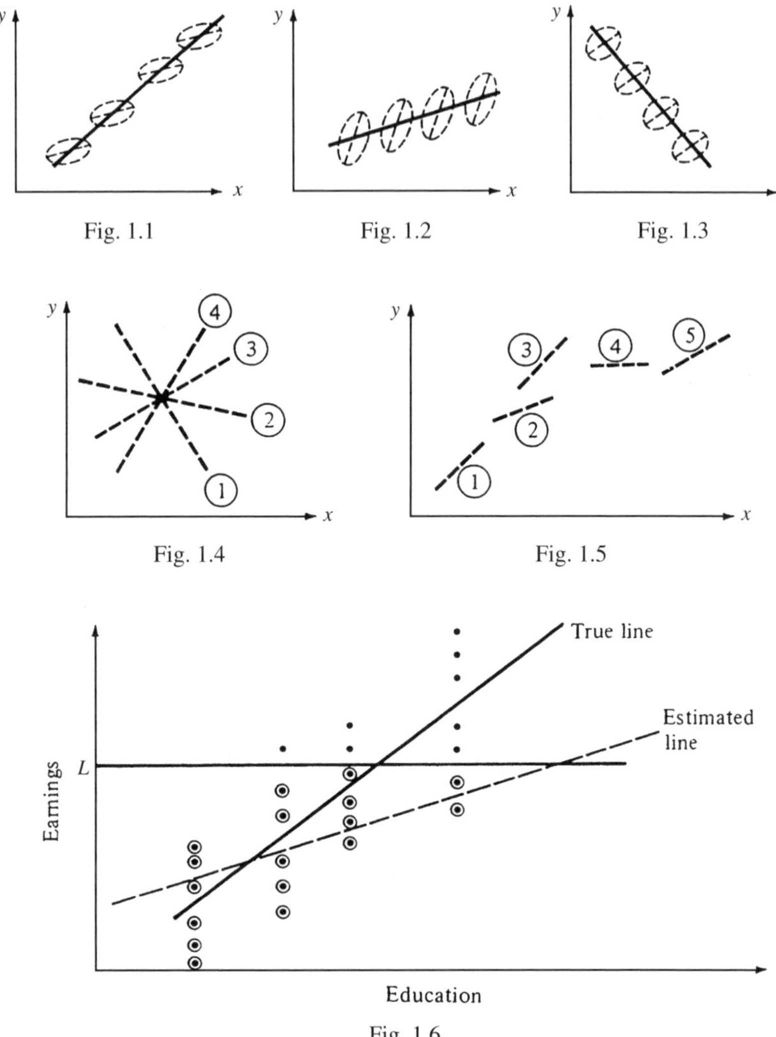

Fig. 1.1

Fig. 1.2

Fig. 1.3

Fig. 1.4

Fig. 1.5

Fig. 1.6

For ease of exposition, we shall consider a cross-sectional example to get some idea of how using a nonrandom sample may bias the least-squares estimates. We assume that in the population the relationship between earnings (y) and exogenous variables ($\mathbf{x}$), including education, intelligence, and so forth, is of the form

$$y_i = \boldsymbol{\beta}'\mathbf{x}_i + u_i, \qquad i = 1, \ldots, N, \tag{1.2.3}$$

where the disturbance term u_i is independently distributed with mean zero and variance σ_u^2. If the participants of an experiment are restricted to have earnings less than L, the selection criterion for families considered for inclusion in the experiment can be stated as follows:

$$\begin{aligned} y_i &= \boldsymbol{\beta}'\mathbf{x}_i + u_i \leq L, \quad \text{included,} \\ y_i &= \boldsymbol{\beta}'\mathbf{x}_i + u_i > L, \quad \text{excluded.} \end{aligned} \tag{1.2.4}$$

For simplicity, we assume that the values of exogenous variables, except for the education variable, are the same for each observation. In Figure 1.6, we let the upward-sloping solid line indicate the "average" relation between education and earnings and the dots represent the distribution of earnings around this mean for selected values of education. All individuals with earnings above a given level L, indicated by the horizontal line, would be eliminated from this experiment. In estimating the effect of education on earnings, we would observe only the points below the limit (circled) and thus would tend to underestimate the effect of education using ordinary least squares.[4] In other words, the sample selection procedure introduces correlation between right-hand variables and the error term, which leads to a downward-biased regression line, as the dashed line in Figure 1.6 indicates.

These examples demonstrate that despite the advantages panel data may possess, they are subject to their own potential experimental problems. It is only by taking proper account of selectivity and heterogeneity biases in the panel data that one can have confidence in the results obtained. The focus of this monograph will be on controlling for the effect of unobserved individual and/or time characteristics to draw proper inference about the characteristics of the population.

1.3 OUTLINE OF THE MONOGRAPH

Because the source of sample variation critically affects the formulation and estimation of many economic models, we shall first briefly review the classic analysis of covariance procedures in Chapter 2. We shall then relax the assumption that the parameters that characterize all temporal cross-sectional sample observations are identical and examine a number of specifications that allow for differences in behavior across individuals as well as over time. For instance, a single-equation model with observations of y depending on a vector of characteristics $\mathbf{x}$ can be written in the following form:

1. Slope coefficients are constant, and the intercept varies over individuals:

$$y_{it} = \alpha_i^* + \sum_{k=1}^{K} \beta_k x_{kit} + u_{it}, \qquad i = 1, \ldots, N, \quad t = 1, \ldots, T. \tag{1.3.1}$$

2. Slope coefficients are constant, and the intercept varies over individuals and time:

$$y_{it} = \alpha_{it}^{*} + \sum_{k=1}^{K} \beta_k x_{kit} + u_{it}, \qquad i = 1, \ldots, N, \quad t = 1, \ldots, T. \tag{1.3.2}$$

3. All coefficients vary over individuals:

$$y_{it} = \alpha_{i}^{*} + \sum_{k=1}^{K} \beta_{ki} x_{kit} + u_{it}, \qquad i = 1, \ldots, N, \quad t = 1, \ldots, T. \tag{1.3.3}$$

4. All coefficients vary over time and individuals:

$$y_{it} = \alpha_{it}^{*} + \sum_{k=1}^{K} \beta_{kit} x_{kit} + u_{it}, \qquad i = 1, \ldots, N, \quad t = 1, \ldots, T. \tag{1.3.4}$$

In each of these cases the model can be classified further, depending on whether the coefficients are assumed to be random or fixed.

Models with constant slopes and variable intercepts [such as (1.3.1) and (1.3.2)] are most widely used when analyzing panel data because they provide simple yet reasonably general alternatives to the assumption that parameters take values common to all agents at all times. We shall consequently devote the majority of this monograph to this type of model. Static models with variable intercepts will be discussed in Chapter 3, dynamic models in Chapter 4, simultaneous-equations models in Chapter 5, and discrete-data and sample selection models in Chapters 7 and 8, respectively. Basic issues in variable-coefficient models for linear models [such as (1.3.3) and (1.3.4)] will be discussed in Chapter 6. Chapter 9 discusses issues of incomplete panel models, such as estimating distributed-lag models in short panels, rotating samples, pooling of a series of independent cross sections (pseudopanels), and the pooling of data on a single cross section and a single time series. Miscellaneous topics such as simulation methods, measurement errors, panels with large N and large T, unit-root tests, cross-sectional dependence, and multilevel panels will be discussed in Chapter 10. A summary view of the issues involved in utilizing panel data will be presented in Chapter 11.

The challenge of panel data analysis has been, and will continue to be, the best way to formulate statistical models for inference motivated and shaped by substantive problems compatible with our understanding of the processes generating the data. The goal of this monograph is to summarize previous work in such a way as to provide the reader with the basic tools for analyzing and drawing inferences from panel data. Analyses of several important and advanced topics, such as continuous time-duration models (e.g., Florens, Fougére, and Mouchart (1996); Fougére and Kamionka (1996); Heckman and Singer (1984); Kiefer (1988); Lancaster (1990)), general nonlinear models (e.g., Abrevaya (1999); Amemiya (1983); Gourieroux and Jasiak (2000); Hsiao (1992c); Jorgenson and Stokes (1982); Lancaster (2001); Wooldridge (1999)),[5] count data (Cameron and Trevedi 1998), and econometric evaluation of social programs (e.g., Angrist and Hahn (1999); Hahn (1998); Heckman (2001); Heckman and Vytlacil (2001); Heckman, Ichimura, and Todd (1998); Hirano, Imbens, and Ridder (2000); Imbens and Angrist (1994)), are beyond the scope of this monograph.

CHAPTER 2

Analysis of Covariance

2.1 INTRODUCTION[1]

Suppose we have sample observations of characteristics of N individuals over T time periods denoted by $y_{it}, x_{kit}, i = 1, \ldots, N, t = 1, \ldots, T, k = 1, \ldots, K$. Conventionally, observations of y are assumed to be the random outcomes of some experiment with a probability distribution conditional on vectors of the characteristics $\mathbf{x}$ and a fixed number of parameters $\boldsymbol{\theta}$, $f(y \mid \mathbf{x}, \boldsymbol{\theta})$. When panel data are used, one of the ultimate goals is to use all available information to make inferences on $\boldsymbol{\theta}$. For instance, a simple model commonly postulated is that y is a linear function of $\mathbf{x}$. Yet to run a least-squares regression with all NT observations, we need to assume that the regression parameters take values common to all cross-sectional units for all time periods. If this assumption is not valid, as shown in Section 1.2, the pooled least-squares estimates may lead to false inferences. Thus, as a first step toward full exploitation of the data, we often test whether or not parameters characterizing the random outcome variable y stay constant across all i and t.

A widely used procedure to identify the source of sample variation is the analysis-of-covariance test. The name "analysis of variance" is often reserved for a particular category of linear hypotheses that stipulate that the expected value of a random variable y depends only on the class (defined by one or more factors) to which the individual considered belongs, but excludes tests relating to regressions. On the other hand, analysis-of-covariance models are of a mixed character involving genuine exogenous variables, as do regression models, and at the same time allowing the true relation for each individual to depend on the class to which the individual belongs, as do the usual analysis-of-variance models.

A linear model commonly used to assess the effects of both quantitative and qualitative factors is postulated as

$$y_{it} = \alpha_{it}^* + \boldsymbol{\beta}_{it}'\mathbf{x}_{it} + u_{it}, \qquad \begin{array}{l} i = 1, \ldots, N, \\ t = 1, \ldots, T, \end{array} \tag{2.1.1}$$

where α_{it}^* and $\boldsymbol{\beta}_{it}' = (\beta_{1it}, \beta_{2it}, \ldots, \beta_{Kit})$ are 1×1 and $1 \times K$ vectors of constants that vary across i and t, respectively, $\mathbf{x}'_{it} = (x_{1it}, \ldots, x_{Kit})$ is a $1 \times K$ vector of exogenous variables, and u_{it} is the error term. Two aspects of the estimated regression coefficients can be tested: first, the homogeneity of regression slope coefficients; second, the homogeneity of regression intercept coefficients. The test procedure has three main steps:

1. Test whether or not slopes and intercepts simultaneously are homogeneous among different individuals at different times.
2. Test whether or not the regression slopes collectively are the same.
3. Test whether or not the regression intercepts are the same.

It is obvious that if the hypothesis of overall homogeneity (step 1) is accepted, the testing procedure will go no further. However, should the overall homogeneity hypothesis be rejected, the second step of the analysis is to decide if the regression slopes are the same. If this hypothesis of homogeneity is not rejected, one then proceeds to the third and final test to determine the equality of regression intercepts. In principle, step 1 is separable from steps 2 and 3.[2]

Although this type of analysis can be performed on several dimensions, as described by Scheffé (1959) or Searle (1971), only one-way analysis of covariance has been widely used. Therefore, here we present only the procedures for performing one-way analysis of covariance.

2.2 ANALYSIS OF COVARIANCE

Model (2.1.1) only has descriptive value. It can neither be estimated nor be used to generate prediction, because the available degrees of freedom, NT, is less than the number of parameters, $NT(K+1)+$(number of parameters characterizing the distribution of u_{it}). A structure has to be imposed on (2.1.1) before any inference can be made. To start with, we assume that parameters are constant over time, but can vary across individuals. Thus, we can postulate a separate regression for each individual:

$$y_{it} = \alpha_i^* + \boldsymbol{\beta}_i'\mathbf{x}_{it} + u_{it}, \qquad i = 1, \ldots, N, \quad t = 1, \ldots, T. \tag{2.2.1}$$

Three types of restrictions can be imposed on (2.2.1). Namely:

H_1: Regression slope coefficients are identical, and intercepts are not. That is,

$$y_{it} = \alpha_i^* + \boldsymbol{\beta}'\mathbf{x}_{it} + u_{it}. \tag{2.2.2}$$

H_2: Regression intercepts are the same, and slope coefficients are not. That is,

$$y_{it} = \alpha^* + \boldsymbol{\beta}_i'\mathbf{x}_{it} + u_{it}. \tag{2.2.3}$$

H_3: Both slope and intercept coefficients are the same. That is,

$$y_{it} = \alpha^* + \boldsymbol{\beta}'\mathbf{x}_{it} + u_{it}. \tag{2.2.4}$$

Because it is seldom meaningful to ask if the intercepts are the same when the slopes are unequal, we shall ignore the type of restrictions postulated by (2.2.3). We shall refer to (2.2.1) as the unrestricted model, (2.2.2) as the individual-mean or cell-mean corrected regression model, and (2.2.4) as the pooled regression.

Let

$$\bar{y}_i = \frac{1}{T}\sum_{t=1}^{T} y_{it}, \tag{2.2.5}$$

$$\bar{\mathbf{x}}_i = \frac{1}{T}\sum_{t=1}^{T} \mathbf{x}_{it} \tag{2.2.6}$$

be the means of y and $\mathbf{x}$, respectively, for the ith individual. The least-squares estimates of $\boldsymbol{\beta}_i$ and α_i^* in the unrestricted model (2.2.1) are given by[3]

$$\hat{\boldsymbol{\beta}}_i = W_{xx,i}^{-1} W_{xy,i}, \quad \hat{\alpha}_i = \bar{y}_i - \hat{\boldsymbol{\beta}}_i' \bar{\mathbf{x}}_i, \qquad i = 1, \ldots, N, \tag{2.2.7}$$

where

$$\begin{aligned} W_{xx,i} &= \sum_{t=1}^{T} (\mathbf{x}_{it} - \bar{\mathbf{x}}_i)(\mathbf{x}_{it} - \bar{\mathbf{x}}_i)', \\ W_{xy,i} &= \sum_{t=1}^{T} (\mathbf{x}_{it} - \bar{\mathbf{x}}_i)(y_{it} - \bar{y}_i), \\ W_{yy,i} &= \sum_{t=1}^{T} (y_{it} - \bar{y}_i)^2. \end{aligned} \tag{2.2.8}$$

In the analysis-of-covariance terminology, equations (2.2.7) are called within-group estimates. The ith-group residual sum of squares is $\text{RSS}_i = W_{yy,i} - W_{xy,i}' W_{xx,i}^{-1} W_{xy,i}$. The unrestricted residual sum of squares is

$$S_1 = \sum_{i=1}^{N} \text{RSS}_i. \tag{2.2.9}$$

The least-squares regression of the individual-mean corrected model yields parameter estimates

$$\begin{aligned} \hat{\boldsymbol{\beta}}_w &= W_{xx}^{-1} W_{xy}, \\ \hat{\alpha}_i^* &= \bar{y}_i - \hat{\boldsymbol{\beta}}_w' \bar{\mathbf{x}}_i, \qquad i = 1, \ldots, N, \end{aligned} \tag{2.2.10}$$

where

$$W_{xx} = \sum_{i=1}^{N} W_{xx,i} \quad \text{and} \quad W_{xy} = \sum_{i=1}^{N} W_{xy,i}.$$

Let $W_{yy} = \sum_{i=1}^{N} W_{yy,i}$; the residual sum of squares of (2.2.2) is

$$S_2 = W_{yy} - W_{xy}' W_{xx}^{-1} W_{xy}. \tag{2.2.11}$$

The least-squares regression of the pooled model (2.2.4) yields parameter estimates

$$\hat{\boldsymbol{\beta}} = T_{xx}^{-1} T_{xy}, \qquad \hat{\alpha}^* = \bar{y} - \hat{\boldsymbol{\beta}}'\bar{\mathbf{x}}, \tag{2.2.12}$$

where

$$T_{xx} = \sum_{i=1}^{N} \sum_{t=1}^{T} (\mathbf{x}_{it} - \bar{\mathbf{x}})(\mathbf{x}_{it} - \bar{\mathbf{x}})',$$

$$T_{xy} = \sum_{i=1}^{N} \sum_{t=1}^{T} (\mathbf{x}_{it} - \bar{\mathbf{x}})(y_{it} - \bar{y}),$$

$$T_{yy} = \sum_{i=1}^{N} \sum_{t=1}^{T} (y_{it} - \bar{y})^2,$$

$$\bar{y} = \frac{1}{NT} \sum_{i=1}^{N} \sum_{t=1}^{T} y_{it}, \qquad \bar{\mathbf{x}} = \frac{1}{N} \sum_{i=1}^{N} \sum_{t=1}^{T} \mathbf{x}_{it}.$$

The (overall) residual sum of squares is

$$S_3 = T_{yy} - T_{xy}' T_{xx}^{-1} T_{xy}. \tag{2.2.13}$$

Under the assumption that the u_{it} are independently normally distributed over i and t with mean zero and variance σ_u^2, F tests can be used to test the restrictions postulated by (2.2.2) and (2.2.4). In effect, (2.2.2) and (2.2.4) can be viewed as (2.2.1) subject to various types of linear restrictions. For instance, the hypothesis of heterogeneous intercepts but homogeneous slopes [equation (2.2.2)] can be reformulated as (2.2.1) subject to $(N-1)K$ linear restrictions:

$$H_1 : \boldsymbol{\beta}_1 = \boldsymbol{\beta}_2 = \cdots = \boldsymbol{\beta}_N.$$

The hypothesis of common intercept and slope can be viewed as (2.2.1) subject to $(K+1)(N-1)$ linear restrictions:

$$H_3 : \alpha_1^* = \alpha_2^* = \cdots = \alpha_N^*,$$
$$\boldsymbol{\beta}_1 = \boldsymbol{\beta}_2 = \cdots = \boldsymbol{\beta}_N.$$

Thus, application of the analysis-of-covariance test is equivalent to the ordinary hypothesis test based on sums of squared residuals from linear-regression outputs.

The unrestricted residual sum of squares S_1 divided by σ_u^2 has a chi-square distribution with $NT - N(K+1)$ degrees of freedom. The increment in the explained sum of squares due to allowing for the parameters to vary across i is measured by $(S_3 - S_1)$. Under H_3, the restricted residual sum of squares S_3 divided by σ_u^2 has a chi-square distribution with $NT - (K+1)$ degrees of freedom, and $(S_3 - S_1)/\sigma_u^2$ has a chi-square distribution with $(N-1)(K+1)$ degrees of freedom. Because $(S_3 - S_1)/\sigma_u^2$ is independent of S_1/σ_u^2, the F

statistic

$$F_3 = \frac{(S_3 - S_1)/[(N-1)(K+1)]}{S_1/[NT - N(K+1)]} \tag{2.2.14}$$

can be used to test H_3. If F_3 with $(N-1)(K+1)$ and $N(T-K-1)$ degrees of freedom is not significant, we pool the data and estimate a single equation of (2.2.4). If the F ratio is significant, a further attempt is usually made to find out if the nonhomogeneity can be attributed to heterogeneous slopes or heterogeneous intercepts.

Under the hypothesis of heterogeneous intercepts but homogeneous slopes (H_1), the residual sum of squares of (2.2.2), $S_2 = W_{yy} - W'_{xy}W_{xx}^{-1}W_{xy}$, divided by σ_u^2 has a chi-square distribution with $N(T-1) - K$ degrees of freedom. The F test of H_1 is thus given by

$$F_1 = \frac{(S_2 - S_1)/[(N-1)K]}{S_1/[NT - N(K+1)]}. \tag{2.2.15}$$

If F_1 with $(N-1)K$ and $NT - N(K+1)$ degrees of freedom is significant, the test sequence is naturally halted and model (2.2.1) is treated as the maintained hypothesis. If F_1 is not significant, we can then determine the extent to which nonhomogeneities can arise in the intercepts.

If H_1 is accepted, one can also apply a conditional test for homogeneous intercepts, namely,

$$H_4 : \alpha_1^* = \alpha_2^* = \cdots = \alpha_N^* \qquad \text{given} \quad \boldsymbol{\beta}_1 = \cdots = \boldsymbol{\beta}_N.$$

The unrestricted residual sum of squares now is S_2, and the restricted residual sum of squares is S_3. The reduction in the residual sum of squares in moving from (2.2.4) to (2.2.2) is $(S_3 - S_2)$. Under H_4, S_3 divided by σ_u^2 is chi-square distributed with $NT - (K+1)$ degrees of freedom, and S_2 divided by σ_u^2 is chi-square distributed with $N(T-1) - K$ degrees of freedom. Because S_2/σ_u^2 is independent of $(S_3 - S_2)/\sigma_u^2$, which is chi-square distributed with $N-1$ degrees of freedom, the F test for H_4 is

$$F_4 = \frac{(S_3 - S_2)/(N-1)}{S_2/[N(T-1) - K]}. \tag{2.2.16}$$

We can summarize these tests in an analysis-of-covariance table (Table 2.1).

Alternatively, we can assume that coefficients are constant across individuals at a given time, but can vary over time. Hence, a separate regression can be postulated for each cross section:

$$y_{it} = \alpha_t^* + \boldsymbol{\beta}_t'\mathbf{x}_{it} + u_{it}, \qquad i = 1, \ldots, N, \quad t = 1, \ldots, T, \tag{2.2.17}$$

where we again assume that u_{it} is independently normally distributed with mean 0 and constant variance σ_u^2. Analogous analysis of covariance can then be performed to test the homogeneities of the cross-sectional parameters over

Table 2.1. *Covariance tests for homogeneity*

Source of variation	Residual sum of squares	Degrees of freedom	Mean squares
Within group with heterogeneous intercept and slope	$S_1 = \sum_{i=1}^{N} \left(W_{yy,i} - W'_{xy,i} W_{xx,i}^{-1} W_{xy,i} \right)$	$N(T - K - 1)$	$S_1/N(T - K - 1)$
Constant slope: heterogeneous intercept	$S_2 = W_{yy} - W'_{xy} W_{xx}^{-1} W_{xy}$	$N(T - 1) - K$	$S_2/[N(T - 1) - K]$
Common intercept and slope	$S_3 = T_{yy} - T'_{xy} T_{xx}^{-1} T_{xy}$	$NT - (K + 1)$	$S_3/[NT - (K + 1)]$

Notation:

Cells or groups (or individuals)	$i = 1, \ldots, N$
Observations within cell	$t = 1, \ldots, T$
Total sample size	NT
Within-cell (group) mean	$\bar{y}_i, \bar{\mathbf{x}}_i$
Overall mean	$\bar{y}, \bar{\mathbf{x}}$
Within-group covariance	$W_{yy,i}, W_{yx,i}, W_{xx,i}$
Total variation	T_{yy}, T_{yx}, T_{xx}

time. For instance, we can test for overall homogeneity ($H_3' : \alpha_1^* = \alpha_2^* = \cdots = \alpha_T^*, \boldsymbol{\beta}_1 = \boldsymbol{\beta}_2 = \cdots = \boldsymbol{\beta}_T$) by using the F statistic

$$F_3' = \frac{(S_3 - S_1')/[(T-1)(K+1)]}{S_1'/[NT - T(K+1)]} \tag{2.2.18}$$

with $(T-1)(K+1)$ and $NT - T(K+1)$ degrees of freedom, where

$$S_1' = \sum_{t=1}^{T} \left(W_{yy,t} - W_{xy,t}' W_{xx,t}^{-1} W_{xy,t}\right),$$

$$\begin{aligned} W_{yy,t} &= \sum_{i=1}^{N} (y_{it} - \bar{y}_t)^2, \qquad \bar{y}_t = \frac{1}{N}\sum_{i=1}^{N} y_{it}, \\ W_{xx,t} &= \sum_{i=1}^{N} (\mathbf{x}_{it} - \bar{\mathbf{x}}_t)(\mathbf{x}_{it} - \bar{\mathbf{x}}_t)', \qquad \bar{\mathbf{x}}_t = \frac{1}{N}\sum_{t=1}^{N} \mathbf{x}_{it}, \\ W_{xy,t} &= \sum_{i=1}^{N} (\mathbf{x}_{it} - \bar{\mathbf{x}}_t)(y_{it} - \bar{y}_t). \end{aligned} \tag{2.2.19}$$

Similarly, we can test the hypothesis of heterogeneous intercepts, but homogeneous slopes ($H_1' : \alpha_1^* \neq \alpha_2^* \neq \cdots \neq \alpha_T^*, \boldsymbol{\beta}_1 = \boldsymbol{\beta}_2 = \cdots = \boldsymbol{\beta}_T$), by using the F statistic

$$F_1' = \frac{(S_2' - S_1')/[(T-1)K]}{S_1'/[NT - T(K+1)]} \tag{2.2.20}$$

with $(T-1)K$ and $NT - T(K+1)$ degrees of freedom, where

$$S_2' = \sum_{t=1}^{T} W_{yy,t} - \left(\sum_{t=1}^{T} W_{xy,t}'\right)\left(\sum_{t=1}^{T} W_{xx,t}\right)^{-1}\left(\sum_{t=1}^{T} W_{xy,t}\right), \tag{2.2.21}$$

or test the hypothesis of homogeneous intercepts conditional on homogeneous slopes $\boldsymbol{\beta}_1 = \boldsymbol{\beta}_2 = \cdots = \boldsymbol{\beta}_T (H_4')$ by using the F statistic

$$F_4' = \frac{(S_3 - S_2')/(T-1)}{S_2'/[T(N-1) - K]} \tag{2.2.22}$$

with $T - 1$ and $T(N-1) - K$ degrees of freedom. In general, unless both cross-section and time-series analyses of covariance indicate the acceptance of homogeneity of regression coefficients, unconditional pooling (i.e., a single least-squares regression using all observations of cross-sectional units through time) may lead to serious bias.

Finally, it should be noted that the foregoing tests are not independent. For example, the uncomfortable possibility exists that according to F_3 (or F_3'), we might find homogeneous slopes and intercepts, and yet this finding could be compatible with opposite results according to $F_1(F_1')$ and $F_4(F_4')$, because the alternative or null hypotheses are somewhat different in the two cases. Worse still, we might reject the hypothesis of overall homogeneity using the test ratio $F_3(F_3')$, but then find according to $F_1(F_1')$ and $F_4(F_4')$ that we cannot reject the null hypothesis, so that the existence of heterogeneity indicated by F_3 (or F_3') cannot be traced. This outcome is quite proper at a formal statistical level, although at the less formal but important level of interpreting test statistics, it is an annoyance.

2.3 AN EXAMPLE[4]

With the aim of suggesting certain modifications to existing theories of investment behavior and providing estimates of the coefficients of principal interest, Kuh (1963) used data on 60 small and middle-sized firms in capital-goods-producing industries from 1935 to 1955, excluding the war years (1942 to 1945), to probe the proper specification for the investment function. He explored various models based on capacity accelerator behavior or internal funds flows, with various lags. For ease of illustration, we report here only functional specifications and results based on profit theories, capacity-utilization theories, financial restrictions, and long-run growth theories in arithmetic form (Table 2.2, part A), their logarithmic transformations (part B), and several ratio models (part C). The equations are summarized in Table 2.2.

There were two main reasons that Kuh resorted to using individual-firm data rather than economic aggregates. One was the expressed doubt about the quality of the aggregate data, together with the problems associated with estimating an aggregate time-series model when the explanatory variables are highly correlated. The other was the desire to construct and test more complicated behavioral models that require many degrees of freedom. However, as stated in Section 1.2, a single regression using all observations through time makes sense only when individual observations conditional on the explanatory variables can be viewed as random draws from the same universe. Kuh (1963) used the analysis-of-covariance techniques discussed in Section 2.2. to test for overall homogeneity (F_3 or F_3'), slope homogeneity (F_1 or F_1'), and homogeneous intercept conditional on acceptance of homogeneous slopes (F_4 or F_4') for both cross-sectional units and time-series units. The results for testing homogeneity of time-series estimates across cross-sectional units and homogeneity of cross-sectional estimates over time are reproduced in Tables 2.3 and 2.4, respectively.

A striking fact recorded from these statistics is that except for the time-series results for equations (2.3.1) and (2.3.3) (which are in first-difference form), all other specifications failed the overall homogeneity tests.[5] Furthermore, in most cases, with the exception of cross-sectional estimates of (2.3.17) and (2.3.18) (Table 2.4), the intercept and slope variabilities cannot be rigorously separated. Nor do the time-series results correspond closely to cross-sectional results for the same equation. Although analysis of covariance, like other statistics, is not a mill that will grind out results automatically, these results do suggest that the effects of excluded variables in both time series and cross sections may be

Table 2.2. *Investment equation forms estimated by Kuh (1963)*

Part A

$$\Delta I_{it} = \alpha_0 + \beta_1 C_i + \beta_2 \Delta K_{it} + \beta_3 \Delta S_{it} \quad (2.3.1)$$
$$\Delta I_{it} = \alpha_0 + \beta_1 C_i + \beta_2 \Delta K_{it} + \beta_4 \Delta P_{it} \quad (2.3.2)$$
$$\Delta I_{it} = \alpha_0 + \beta_1 C_i + \beta_2 \Delta K_{it} + \beta_3 \Delta S_{it} + \beta_4 \Delta P_{it} \quad (2.3.3)$$
$$I_{it} = \alpha_0 + \beta_1 C_i + \beta_2 K_{it} + \beta_3 S_{it} \quad (2.3.4)$$
$$I_{it} = \alpha_0 + \beta_1 C_i + \beta_2 K_{it} + \beta_4 P_{it} \quad (2.3.5)$$
$$I_{it} = \alpha_0 + \beta_1 C_i + \beta_2 K_{it} + \beta_3 S_{it} + \beta_4 P_{it} \quad (2.3.6)$$
$$I_{it} = \alpha_0 + \beta_1 C_i + \beta_2 K_{it} + \beta_3 S_{i,t-1} \quad (2.3.7)$$
$$I_{it} = \alpha_0 + \beta_1 C_i + \beta_2 K_{it} + \beta_4 P_{i,t-1} \quad (2.3.8)$$
$$I_{it} = \alpha_0 + \beta_1 C_i + \beta_2 K_{it} + \beta_3 S_{i,t-1} + \beta_4 P_{i,t-1} \quad (2.3.9)$$
$$I_{it} = \alpha_0 + \beta_1 C_i + \beta_2 K_{it} + \beta_3[(S_{it} + S_{i,t-1}) \div 2] \quad (2.3.10)$$
$$I_{it} = \alpha_0 + \beta_1 C_i + \beta_2 K_{it} + \beta_4[(P_{it} + P_{i,t-1}) \div 2] \quad (2.3.11)$$
$$I_{it} = \alpha_0 + \beta_1 C_i + \beta_2 K_{it} + \beta_3[(S_{it} + S_{i,t-1}) \div 2] + \beta_4[(P_{it} + P_{i,t-1}) \div 2] \quad (2.3.12)$$
$$[(I_{it} + I_{i,t-1}) \div 2] = \alpha_0 + \beta_1 C_i + \beta_2 K_{it} + \beta_3[(S_{it} + S_{i,t-1}) \div 2] \quad (2.3.13)$$
$$[(I_{it} + I_{i,t-1}) \div 2] = \alpha_0 + \beta_1 C_i + \beta_2 K_{it} + \beta_4[(P_{it} + P_{i,t-1}) \div 2] \quad (2.3.14)$$
$$[(I_{it} + I_{i,t-1}) \div 2] = \alpha_0 + \beta_1 C_i + \beta_2 K_{it} + \beta_3[(S_{it} + S_{i,t-1}) \div 2] + \beta_4[(P_{it} + P_{i,t-1}) \div 2] \quad (2.3.15)$$

Part B

$$\Delta \log I_{it} = \alpha_0 + \beta_1 \log C_i + \beta_2 \Delta \log K_{it} + \beta_3 \Delta \log S_{it} \quad (2.3.16)$$
$$\log I_{it} = \alpha_0 + \beta_1 \log C_i + \beta_2 \log K_{it} + \beta_3 \log S_{it} \quad (2.3.17)$$
$$\log I_{it} = \alpha_0 + \beta_1 \log C_i + \beta_2 \log K_{it} + \beta_3 \log S_{i,t-1} \quad (2.3.18)$$
$$\log I_{it} = \alpha_0 + \beta_1 \log C_i + \beta_2 \log[(K_{it} + K_{i,t-1}) \div 2] + \beta_3 \log[(S_{it} + S_{i,t-1}) \div 2] \quad (2.3.19)$$

Part C

$$\frac{I_{it}}{K_{it}} = \alpha_0 + \beta_1 \frac{P_{it}}{K_{it}} + \beta_2 \frac{S_{i,t-1}}{C_i \cdot K_{i,t-1}} \quad (2.3.20)$$
$$\frac{I_{it}}{K_{it}} = \alpha_0 + \beta_1 \frac{P_{it}}{K_{it}} + \beta_2 \frac{S_{i,t-1}}{C_i \cdot K_{i,t-1}} + \beta_3 \frac{S_{it}}{C_i \cdot K_{it}} \quad (2.3.21)$$
$$\frac{I_{it}}{K_{it}} = \alpha_0 + \beta_1 \frac{P_{it} + P_{i,t-1}}{K_{it} \cdot 2} + \beta_2 \frac{S_{i,t-1}}{C_i \cdot K_{i,t-1}} \quad (2.3.22)$$
$$\frac{I_{it}}{K_{it}} = \alpha_0 + \beta_1 \frac{P_{it} + P_{i,t-1}}{K_{it} \cdot 2} + \beta_2 \frac{S_{i,t-1}}{C_i \cdot K_{i,t-1}} + \beta_3 \frac{S_{it}}{C_i \cdot K_{it}} \quad (2.3.23)$$

Note: I = gross investment; C = capital-intensity index; K = capital stock; S = sales; P = gross retained profits.

very different. It would be quite careless not to explore the possible causes of discrepancies that give rise to the systematic interrelationships between different individuals at different periods of time.[6]

Kuh explored the sources of estimation discrepancies through decomposition of the error variances, comparison of individual coefficient behavior, assessment of the statistical influence of various lag structures, and so forth. He concluded that sales seem to include critical time-correlated elements common to a large number of firms and thus have a much greater capability of annihilating systematic, cyclical factors. In general, his results are more favorable to the acceleration sales model than to the internal-liquidity/profit hypothesis supported

Table 2.3. *Covariance tests for regression-coefficient homogeneity across cross-sectional units*[a]

	F_3 overall test			F_1 slope homogeneity			F_4 cell mean significance		
	Degrees of freedom			Degrees of freedom			Degrees of freedom		
Equation	Numerator	Denominator	Actual Fs	Numerator	Denominator	Actual Fs	Numerator	Denominator	Actual Fs
(2.3.1)	177	660	1.25	118	660	1.75[c]	57	660	0.12
(2.3.2)	177	660	1.40[b]	118	660	1.94[c]	57	660	0.11
(2.3.3)	236	600	1.13	177	600	1.42[b]	56	600	0.10
(2.3.4)	177	840	2.28[c]	118	840	1.58[c]	57	840	3.64[c]
(2.3.5)	177	840	2.34[c]	118	840	1.75[c]	57	840	3.23[c]
(2.3.6)	236	780	2.24[c]	177	780	1.76[c]	56	780	3.57[c]
(2.3.7)	177	720	2.46[c]	118	720	1.95[c]	57	720	3.57[c]
(2.3.8)	177	720	2.50[c]	118	720	1.97[c]	57	720	3.31[c]
(2.3.9)	236	660	2.49[c]	177	660	2.11[c]	56	660	3.69[c]
(2.3.10)	177	720	2.46[c]	118	720	1.75[c]	57	720	3.66[c]
(2.3.11)	177	720	2.60[c]	118	720	2.14[c]	57	720	3.57[c]
(2.3.12)	236	660	2.94[c]	177	660	2.49[c]	56	660	4.18[c]
(2.3.16)	177	720	1.92[c]	118	720	2.59[c]	57	720	0.55
(2.3.17)	177	840	4.04[c]	118	840	2.70[c]	57	840	0.39
(2.3.18)	177	720	5.45[c]	118	720	4.20[c]	57	720	6.32[c]
(2.3.19)	177	720	4.68[c]	118	720	3.17[c]	57	720	7.36[c]
(2.3.20)	177	720	3.64[c]	118	720	3.14[c]	57	720	3.66[c]
(2.3.21)	236	660	3.38[c]	177	660	2.71[c]	56	660	4.07[c]
(2.3.22)	177	600	3.11[c]	118	600	2.72[c]	57	600	3.22[c]
(2.3.23)	236	540	2.90[c]	177	540	2.40[c]	56	540	3.60[c]

[a]Critical F values were obtained from A.M. Mood, *Introduction to Statistics*, Table V, pp. 426–427. Linear interpolation was employed except for degrees of freedom exceeding 120. The critical F values in every case have been recorded for 120 degrees of freedom for each denominator sum of squares even though the actual degrees of freedom were at least four times as great. The approximation error in this case is negligible.

[b]Significant at the 5 percent level.

[c]Significant at the 1 percent level.

Source: Kuh (1963, pp. 141–142).

Table 2.4. *Covariance tests for homogeneity of cross-sectional estimates over time*[a]

	F_3' overall test			F_1' slope homogeneity			F_4' cell mean significance		
	Degrees of freedom			Degrees of freedom			Degrees of freedom		
Equation	Numerator	Denominator	Actual Fs	Numerator	Denominator	Actual Fs	Numerator	Denominator	Actual Fs
(2.3.1)	52	784	2.45^b	39	784	2.36^b	10	784	2.89^b
(2.3.2)	52	784	3.04^b	39	784	2.64^b	10	784	4.97^b
(2.3.3)	65	770	2.55^b	52	770	2.49^b	9	770	3.23^b
(2.3.4)	64	952	2.01^b	48	952	1.97^b	13	952	2.43^b
(2.3.5)	64	952	2.75^b	48	952	2.45^b	13	952	3.41^b
(2.3.6)	80	935	1.91^b	64	935	1.82^b	12	935	2.66^b
(2.3.7)	56	840	2.30^b	42	840	2.11^b	11	840	3.66^b
(2.3.8)	56	840	2.83^b	42	840	2.75^b	11	840	3.13^b
(2.3.9)	70	825	2.25^b	56	825	2.13^b	10	825	3.53^b
(2.3.10)	56	840	1.80^b	42	840	1.80^b	11	840	1.72^d
(2.3.11)	56	840	2.30^b	42	840	2.30^b	11	840	1.79^d
(2.3.12)	70	825	1.70^b	56	825	1.74^b	10	825	1.42

(2.3.13)	56	840	2.08[b]	42	840	2.11[b]	11	840	2.21[c]
(2.3.14)	56	840	2.66[b]	42	840	2.37[b]	11	840	2.87[b]
(2.3.15)	70	825	1.81[b]	56	825	1.76[b]	10	825	2.35[c]
(2.3.16)	56	840	3.67[b]	42	840	2.85[b]	11	840	3.10[b]
(2.3.17)	64	952	1.51[c]	48	952	1.14	13	952	0.80
(2.3.18)	56	840	2.34[b]	42	840	1.04	11	840	1.99[c]
(2.3.19)	56	840	2.29[b]	42	840	2.03[b]	11	840	2.05[c]
(2.3.20)	42	855	4.13[b]	28	855	5.01[b]	12	855	2.47[b]
(2.3.21)	56	840	2.88[b]	42	840	3.12[b]	11	840	2.56[b]
(2.3.22)	42	855	3.80[b]	28	855	4.62[b]	12	855	1.61[b]
(2.3.23)	56	840	3.51[b]	42	840	4.00[b]	11	840	1.71[b]

[a] Critical F values were obtained from A.M. Mood, *Introduction to Statistics*, Table V, pp. 426–427. Linear interpolation was employed except for degrees of freedom exceeding 120. The critical F values in every case have been recorded for 120 degrees of freedom for each denominator sum of squares even though the actual degrees of freedom were at least four times as great. The approximation error in this case is negligible.

[b] Significant at the 1 percent level.

[c] Significant at the 5 percent level.

[d] Significant at the 10 percent level.

Source: Kuh (1963, pp. 137–138).

by the results obtained using cross-sectional data (e.g., Meyer and Kuh (1957)). He found that the cash-flow effect is more important some time before the actual capital outlays are made than it is in actually restricting the outlays during the expenditure period. It appears more appropriate to view internal liquidity flows as a critical part of the budgeting process that later is modified, primarily in light of variations in levels of output and capacity utilization.

The policy implications of Kuh's conclusions are clear. Other things being equal, a small percentage increase in sales will have a greater effect on investment than will a small percentage increase in internal funds. If the government seeks to stimulate investment and the objective is magnitude, not qualitative composition, it inexorably follows that the greatest investment effect will come from measures that increase demand rather than from measures that increase internal funds.[7]

CHAPTER 3

Simple Regression with Variable Intercepts

3.1 INTRODUCTION

When the overall homogeneity hypothesis is rejected by the panel data while the specification of a model appears proper, a simple way to take account of the heterogeneity across individuals and/or through time is to use the variable-intercept models (1.3.1) and (1.3.2). The basic assumption of such models is that, conditional on the observed explanatory variables, the effects of all omitted (or excluded) variables are driven by three types of variables: individual time-invariant, period individual-invariant, and individual time-varying.[1] The individual time-invariant variables are variables that are the same for a given cross-sectional unit through time but that vary across cross-sectional units. Examples of these are attributes of individual-firm management, ability, sex, and socioeconomic-background variables. The period individual-invariant variables are variables that are the same for all cross-sectional units at a given point in time but that vary through time. Examples of these variables are prices, interest rates, and widespread optimism or pessimism. The individual time-varying variables are variables that vary across cross-sectional units at a given point in time and also exhibit variations through time. Examples of these variables are firm profits, sales, and capital stock. The variable-intercept models assume that the effects of the numerous omitted individual time-varying variables are each individually unimportant but are collectively significant, and possess the property of a random variable that is uncorrelated with (or independent of) all other included and excluded variables. On the other hand, because the effects of remaining omitted variables either stay constant through time for a given cross-sectional unit or are the same for all cross-sectional units at a given point in time, or a combination of both, they can be absorbed into the intercept term of a regression model as a means to allow explicitly for the individual and/or time heterogeneity contained in the temporal cross-sectional data. Moreover, when the individual- or time-specific effects are absorbed into the intercept term, there is no need to assume that those effects are uncorrelated with $\mathbf{x}$, although sometimes they are.

The variable-intercept models can provide a fairly useful specification for fitting regression models using panel data. For example, consider fitting a Cobb–Douglas production function

$$y_{it} = \mu + \beta_1 x_{1it} + \cdots + \beta_K x_{Kit} + v_{it}, \qquad \begin{array}{l} i = 1, \ldots, N, \\ t = 1, \ldots, T, \end{array} \tag{3.1.1}$$

where y is the logarithm of output and $x_1, \ldots, x_K$ are the logarithms of the inputs. The classic procedure is to assume that the effects of omitted variables are independent of $\mathbf{x}$ and are independently identically distributed. Thus, conditioning on $\mathbf{x}$, all observations are random variations of a representative firm. However, (3.1.1) has often been criticized for ignoring variables reflecting managerial and other technical differences between firms or variables that reflect general conditions affecting the productivity of all firms but that are fluctuating over time (such as weather in agriculture production); see, e.g., Hoch (1962); Mundlak (1961); Nerlove (1965). Ideally, such firm- and time-effects variables, say M_i and P_t, should be explicitly introduced into (3.1.1). Thus, v_{it} can be written as

$$v_{it} = \alpha M_i + \lambda P_t + u_{it}, \tag{3.1.2}$$

with u_{it} representing the effects of all remaining omitted variables. Unfortunately, there usually are no observations on M_i and P_t. It is impossible to estimate α and λ directly. A natural alternative would then be to consider the effects of the products, $\alpha_i = \alpha M_i$ and $\lambda_t = \lambda P_t$, which then leads to a variable-intercept model: (1.3.1) or (1.3.2).

Such a procedure was used by Hoch (1962) to estimate parameters of a Cobb–Douglas production function based on annual data for 63 Minnesota farms from 1946 to 1951. He treated output y as a function of labor x_1, real estate x_2, machinery x_3, and feed, fertilizer, and related expenses, x_4. However, because of the difficulties of measuring real-estate and machinery variables, he also tried an alternative specification that treated y as a function of x_1, x_4, a current-expenditures item x_5, and fixed capital x_6. Regression results for both specifications rejected the overall homogeneity hypothesis at the 5 percent significance level. The least-squares estimates under three assumptions ($\alpha_i = \lambda_t = 0$; $\alpha_i = 0$, $\lambda_t \neq 0$; and $\alpha_i \neq 0$, $\lambda_t \neq 0$) are summarized in Table 3.1. They exhibit an increase in the adjusted R^2 from 0.75 to about 0.88 when α_i and λ_t are introduced.

There are also some important changes in parameter estimates when we move from the assumption of identical α_is to the assumption that both α_i and λ_t differ from zero. There is a significant drop in the sum of the elasticities, mainly concentrated in the labor variable. If one interprets α_i as the firm scale effect, then this indicates that efficiency increases with scale. As demonstrated in Figure 1.1, when the production hyperplane of larger firms lies above the average production plane and the production plane of smaller firms below the average

Table 3.1. *Least-squares estimates of elasticity of Minnesota farm production function based on alternative assumptions*

Estimate of Elasticity: β_k	Assumption: α_i and λ_t are identically zero for all i and t	Assumption: α_i only is identically zero for all i	Assumption: α_i and λ_t different from zero
Variable set 1[a]			
$\hat{\beta}_1$, labor	0.256	0.166	0.043
$\hat{\beta}_2$, real estate	0.135	0.230	0.199
$\hat{\beta}_3$, machinery	0.163	0.261	0.194
$\hat{\beta}_4$, feed & fertilizer	0.349	0.311	0.289
Sum of $\hat{\beta}$'s	0.904	0.967	0.726
Adjusted R^2	0.721	0.813	0.884
Variable set 2			
$\hat{\beta}_1$, labor	0.241	0.218	0.057
$\hat{\beta}_5$, current expenses	0.121	0.185	0.170
$\hat{\beta}_6$, fixed capital	0.278	0.304	0.317
$\hat{\beta}_4$, feed & fertilizer	0.315	0.285	0.288
Sum of $\hat{\beta}$'s	0.954	0.991	0.832
Adjusted R^2	0.752	0.823	0.879

[a] All output and input variables are in service units, measured in dollars.
Source: Hoch (1962).

plane, the pooled estimates, neglecting firm differences, will have greater slope than the average plane. Some confirmation of this argument was provided by Hoch (1962).

Table 3.2 lists the characteristics of firms grouped on the basis of firm-specific effects α_i. The table suggests a fairly pronounced association between scale and efficiency.

This example demonstrates that by introducing the unit- and/or time-specific variables into the specification for panel data, it is possible to reduce or avoid the omitted-variable bias. In this chapter, we focus on the estimation and hypothesis testing of models (1.3.1) and (1.3.2) under the assumption that all explanatory variables, x_{kit}, are nonstochastic (or exogenous). In Section 3.2 we discuss estimation methods when the specific effects are treated as fixed constants. Section 3.3 discusses estimation methods when they are treated as random variables. Section 3.4 discusses the pros and cons of treating the specific effects as fixed or random. Tests for misspecification are discussed in Section 3.5. Some generalizations of the basic model are discussed in Sections 3.6 to 3.8. In Section 3.9, we use a multivariate setup of a single-equation model to provide a synthesis of the issues involved and to provide a link between the single-equation model and the linear simultaneous-equations model (see Chapter 5).

Table 3.2. *Characteristics of firms grouped on the basis of the firm constant*

Characteristics	All firms	Firms classified by value of $\exp(\alpha_i)^a$ <0.85	0.85–0.95	0.95–1.05	1.05–1.15	>1.15
Numbers of firms in group	63	6	17	19	14	7
Average value of:						
e^{α_i}, firm constant	1.00	0.81	0.92	1.00	1.11	1.26
Output (dollars)	15,602	10,000	15,570	14,690	16,500	24,140
Labor (dollars)	3,468	2,662	3,570	3,346	3,538	4,280
Feed & fertilizer (dollars)	3,217	2,457	3,681	3,064	2,621	5,014
Current expenses (dollars)	2,425	1,538	2,704	2,359	2,533	2,715
Fixed capital (dollars)	3,398	2,852	3,712	3,067	3,484	3,996
Profit (dollars)	3,094	491	1,903	2,854	4,324	8,135
Profit/output	0.20	0.05	0.12	0.19	0.26	0.33

[a] The mean of firm effects, α_i, is zero is invoked.
Source: Hoch (1962).

3.2 FIXED-EFFECTS MODELS: LEAST-SQUARES DUMMY-VARIABLE APPROACH

The obvious generalization of the constant-intercept-and-slope model for panel data is to introduce dummy variables to allow for the effects of those omitted variables that are specific to individual cross-sectional units but stay constant over time, and the effects that are specific to each time period but are the same for all cross-sectional units. For simplicity, in this section we assume no time-specific effects and focus only on individual-specific effects. Thus, the value of the dependent variable for the ith unit at time t, y_{it}, depends on K exogenous variables, $(x_{1it}, \ldots, x_{Kit}) = \mathbf{x}'_{it}$, that differ among individuals in a cross section at a given point in time and also exhibit variation through time, as well as on variables that are specific to the ith unit and that stay (more or less) constant over time. This is model (1.3.1), which we can rewrite as

$$y_{it} = \alpha_i^* + \underset{1\times K}{\boldsymbol{\beta}'}\,\underset{K\times 1}{\mathbf{x}_{it}} + u_{it}, \qquad i = 1, \ldots, N, \quad t = 1, \ldots, T, \tag{3.2.1}$$

where $\boldsymbol{\beta}'$ is a $1 \times K$ vector of constants and α_i^* is a 1×1 scalar constant representing the effects of those variables peculiar to the ith individual in more or less the same fashion over time. The error term, u_{it}, represents the effects of the omitted variables that are peculiar to both the individual units and time periods. We assume that u_{it} is uncorrelated with $(\mathbf{x}_{i1}, \ldots, \mathbf{x}_{iT})$ and can be characterized by an independently identically distributed random variable with mean zero and variance σ_u^2.

The model (3.2.1) is also called the analysis-of-covariance model. Without attempting to make the boundaries between regression analysis, analysis of variance, and analysis of covariance precise, we can say that regression model assumes that the expected value of y is a function of exogenous factors $\mathbf{x}$, while the conventional analysis-of-variance model stipulates that the expected value of y_{it} depends only on the class i to which the observation considered belongs and that the value of the measured quantity, y, satisfies the relation $y_{it} = \alpha_i^* + u_{it}$, where the other characteristics, u_{it}, are random and are in no way dependent on the class this individual belongs. But if y is also affected by other variables that we are not able to control and standardize within classes, the simple within-class sum of squares will be an overestimate of the stochastic component in y, and the differences between class means will reflect not only any class effect but also the effects of any differences in the values assumed by the uncontrolled variables in different classes. It was for this kind of problem that the analysis-of-covariance model of the form (3.2.1) was first developed. The models are of a mixed character, involving genuine exogenous variables $\mathbf{x}_{it}$, as do regression models, and at the same time allowing the true relation for each individual to depend on the class to which the individual belongs, α_i^*, as do the usual analysis-of-variance models. The regression model enables us to assess the effects of quantitative factors, the analysis-of-variance model those of qualitative factors; the analysis-of-covariance model covers both quantitative and qualitative factors.

Writing (3.2.1) in vector form, we have

$$Y = \begin{bmatrix} \mathbf{y}_1 \\ \vdots \\ \mathbf{y}_N \end{bmatrix} = \begin{bmatrix} \mathbf{e} \\ \mathbf{0} \\ \vdots \\ \mathbf{0} \end{bmatrix} \alpha_1^* + \begin{bmatrix} \mathbf{0} \\ \mathbf{e} \\ \vdots \\ \mathbf{0} \end{bmatrix} \alpha_2^* + \cdots + \begin{bmatrix} \mathbf{0} \\ \mathbf{0} \\ \vdots \\ \mathbf{e} \end{bmatrix} \alpha_N^* + \begin{bmatrix} X_1 \\ X_2 \\ \vdots \\ X_N \end{bmatrix} \boldsymbol{\beta} + \begin{bmatrix} \mathbf{u}_1 \\ \vdots \\ \mathbf{u}_N \end{bmatrix}, \tag{3.2.2}$$

where

$$\underset{T\times 1}{\mathbf{y}_i} = \begin{bmatrix} y_{i1} \\ y_{i2} \\ \vdots \\ y_{iT} \end{bmatrix}, \qquad \underset{T\times K}{X_i} = \begin{bmatrix} x_{1i1} & x_{2i1} & \cdots & x_{Ki1} \\ x_{1i2} & x_{2i2} & \cdots & x_{Ki2} \\ \vdots & \vdots & & \vdots \\ x_{1iT} & x_{2iT} & & x_{KiT} \end{bmatrix},$$

$$\underset{1\times T}{\mathbf{e}'} = (1, 1, \ldots, 1), \qquad \underset{1\times T}{\mathbf{u}_i'} = (u_{i1}, \ldots, u_{iT}),$$

$$E\mathbf{u}_i = \mathbf{0}, \qquad E\mathbf{u}_i\mathbf{u}_i' = \sigma_u^2 I_T, \qquad E\mathbf{u}_i\mathbf{u}_j' = \mathbf{0} \quad \text{if } i \neq j,$$

and I_T denotes the $T \times T$ identity matrix.

Given the assumed properties of u_{it}, we know that the ordinary-least-squares (OLS) estimator of (3.2.2) is the best linear unbiased estimator (BLUE). The

OLS estimators of α_i^* and $\boldsymbol{\beta}$ are obtained by minimizing

$$S = \sum_{i=1}^{N} \mathbf{u}_i'\mathbf{u}_i = \sum_{i=1}^{N} (\mathbf{y}_i - \mathbf{e}\alpha_i^* - X_i\boldsymbol{\beta})'(\mathbf{y}_i - \mathbf{e}\alpha_i^* - X_i\boldsymbol{\beta}). \tag{3.2.3}$$

Taking partial derivatives of S with respect to α_i^* and setting them equal to zero, we have

$$\hat{\alpha}_i^* = \bar{y}_i - \boldsymbol{\beta}'\bar{\mathbf{x}}_i, \qquad i = 1, \ldots, N, \tag{3.2.4}$$

where

$$\bar{y}_i = \frac{1}{T}\sum_{t=1}^{T} y_{it}, \qquad \bar{\mathbf{x}}_i = \frac{1}{T}\sum_{t=1}^{T} \mathbf{x}_{it}.$$

Substituting (3.2.4) into (3.2.3) and taking the partial derivative of S with respect to $\boldsymbol{\beta}$, we have[2]

$$\hat{\boldsymbol{\beta}}_{\text{CV}} = \left[\sum_{i=1}^{N}\sum_{t=1}^{T}(\mathbf{x}_{it} - \bar{\mathbf{x}}_i)(\mathbf{x}_{it} - \bar{\mathbf{x}}_i)'\right]^{-1}\left[\sum_{i=1}^{N}\sum_{t=1}^{T}(\mathbf{x}_{it} - \bar{\mathbf{x}}_i)(y_{it} - \bar{y}_i)\right]. \tag{3.2.5}$$

The OLS estimator (3.2.5) is called the least-squares dummy-variable (LSDV) estimator, because the observed values of the variable for the coefficient α_i^* takes the form of dummy variables. However, the computational procedure for estimating the slope parameters in this model does not require that the dummy variables for the individual (and/or time) effects actually be included in the matrix of explanatory variables. We need only find the means of time-series observations separately for each cross-sectional unit, transform the observed variables by subtracting out the appropriate time-series means, and then apply the least-squares method to the transformed data. Hence, we need only invert a matrix of order $K \times K$.

The foregoing procedure is equivalent to premultiplying the ith equation

$$\mathbf{y}_i = \mathbf{e}\alpha_i^* + X_i\boldsymbol{\beta} + \mathbf{u}_i$$

by a $T \times T$ idempotent (covariance) transformation matrix

$$Q = I_T - \frac{1}{T}\mathbf{e}\mathbf{e}' \tag{3.2.6}$$

to "sweep out" the individual effect α_i^* so that individual observations are measured as deviations from individual means (over time):

$$\begin{aligned} Q\mathbf{y}_i &= Q\mathbf{e}\alpha_i^* + QX_i\boldsymbol{\beta} + Q\mathbf{u}_i \\ &= QX_i\boldsymbol{\beta} + Q\mathbf{u}_i, \qquad i = 1, \ldots, N. \end{aligned} \tag{3.2.7}$$

Applying the OLS procedure to (3.2.7), we have[3]

$$\hat{\boldsymbol{\beta}}_{\text{CV}} = \left[\sum_{i=1}^{N} X_i' Q X_i \right]^{-1} \left[\sum_{i=1}^{N} X_i' Q \mathbf{y}_i \right], \tag{3.2.8}$$

which is identically equal to (3.2.5). Because (3.2.2) is called the analysis-of-covariance model, the LSDV estimator of $\boldsymbol{\beta}$ is sometimes called the covariance estimator. It is also called the within-group estimator, because only the variation within each group is utilized in forming this estimator.[4]

The covariance estimator $\hat{\beta}_{\text{CV}}$ is unbiased. It is also consistent when either N or T or both tend to infinity. Its variance–covariance matrix is

$$\text{Var}(\boldsymbol{\beta}_{\text{CV}}) = \sigma_u^2 \left[\sum_{t=1}^{N} X_i' Q X_i \right]^{-1}. \tag{3.2.9}$$

However, the estimator for the intercept, (3.2.4), although unbiased, is consistent only when $T \to \infty$.

It should be noted that an alternative and equivalent formulation of (3.2.1) is to introduce a "mean intercept," μ, so that

$$y_{it} = \mu + \boldsymbol{\beta}'\mathbf{x}_{it} + \alpha_i + u_{it}. \tag{3.2.10}$$

Because both μ and α_i are fixed constants, without additional restriction, they are not separately identifiable or estimable. One way to identify μ and α_i is to introduce the restriction $\sum_{i=1}^{N} \alpha_i = 0$. Then the individual effect α_i represents the deviation of the ith individual from the common mean μ.

Equations (3.2.10) and (3.2.1) lead to the same least-squares estimator for $\boldsymbol{\beta}$ [equation (3.2.5)]. This can easily be seen by noting that the BLUEs for μ, α_i, and $\boldsymbol{\beta}$ are obtained by minimizing

$$\sum_{i=1}^{N} \mathbf{u}_i'\mathbf{u}_i = \sum_{i=1}^{N} \sum_{t=1}^{T} u_{it}^2$$

subject to the restriction $\sum_{t=1}^{N} \alpha_i = 0$. Utilizing the restriction $\sum_{t=1}^{N} \alpha_i = 0$ in solving the marginal conditions, we have

$$\begin{aligned} \hat{\mu} = \bar{y} - \boldsymbol{\beta}'\bar{\mathbf{x}}, \quad \text{where } \bar{y} &= \frac{1}{NT} \sum_{i=1}^{N} \sum_{t=1}^{T} y_{it}, \\ \bar{\mathbf{x}} &= \frac{1}{NT} \sum_{i=1}^{N} \sum_{t=1}^{T} \mathbf{x}_{it}, \end{aligned} \tag{3.2.11}$$

$$\hat{\alpha}_i = \bar{y}_i - \hat{\mu} - \boldsymbol{\beta}'\bar{\mathbf{x}}_i. \tag{3.2.12}$$

Substituting (3.2.11) and (3.2.12) into (3.2.10) and solving the marginal condition for $\boldsymbol{\beta}$, we obtain (3.2.5).

3.3 RANDOM-EFFECTS MODELS: ESTIMATION OF VARIANCE-COMPONENTS MODELS

In Section 3.2, we discussed the estimation of linear-regression models when the effects of omitted individual-specific variables (α_i) are treated as fixed constants over time. In this section we treat the individual-specific effects, like u_{it}, as random variables.

It is a standard practice in the regression analysis to assume that the large number of factors that affect the value of the dependent variable, but that have not been explicitly included as independent variables, can be appropriately summarized by a random disturbance. When numerous individual units are observed over time, it is sometimes assumed that some of the omitted variables will represent factors peculiar to both the individual units and time periods for which observations are obtained, whereas other variables will reflect individual differences that tend to affect the observations for a given individual in more or less the same fashion over time. Still other variables may reflect factors peculiar to specific time periods, but affecting individual units more or less equally. Thus, the residual, v_{it}, is often assumed to consist of three components:[5]

$$v_{it} = \alpha_i + \lambda_t + u_{it}, \tag{3.3.1}$$

where

$$\begin{aligned}
&E\alpha_i = E\lambda_t = Eu_{it} = 0, \qquad E\alpha_i\lambda_t = E\alpha_i u_{it} = E\lambda_t u_{it} = 0,\\
&E\alpha_i\alpha_j = \begin{cases} \sigma_\alpha^2 & \text{if } i = j,\\ 0 & \text{if } i \neq j,\end{cases}\\
&E\lambda_t\lambda_s = \begin{cases} \sigma_\lambda^2 & \text{if } t = s,\\ 0 & \text{if } t \neq s,\end{cases}\\
&Eu_{it}u_{js} = \begin{cases} \sigma_u^2 & \text{if } i = j,\ t = s,\\ 0 & \text{otherwise,}\end{cases}
\end{aligned} \tag{3.3.2}$$

and

$$E\alpha_i\mathbf{x}'_{it} = E\lambda_t\mathbf{x}'_{it} = Eu_{it}\mathbf{x}'_{it} = \mathbf{0}'.$$

The variance of y_{it} conditional on $\mathbf{x}_{it}$ is, from (3.3.1) and (3.3.2), $\sigma_y^2 = \sigma_\alpha^2 + \sigma_\lambda^2 + \sigma_u^2$. The variances $\sigma_\alpha^2, \sigma_\lambda^2$, and σ_u^2 are accordingly called variance components; each is a variance in its own right and is a component of σ_y^2. Therefore, this kind of model is sometimes referred to as a variance-components (or error-components) model.

For ease of exposition we assume $\lambda_t = 0$ for all t in this and the following three sections. That is, we concentrate on models of the form (3.2.10).

Rewriting (3.2.10) in vector form, we have

$$\underset{T\times 1}{\mathbf{y}_i} = \underset{T\times(K+1)}{\tilde{X}_i}\ \underset{(K+1)\times 1}{\boldsymbol{\delta}} + \underset{T\times 1}{\mathbf{v}_i}, \qquad i = 1, 2, \ldots, N, \tag{3.3.3}$$

where $\tilde{X}_i = (\mathbf{e}, X_i)$, $\boldsymbol{\delta}' = (\mu, \boldsymbol{\beta}')$, $\mathbf{v}_i' = (v_{i1}, \ldots, v_{iT})$, and $v_{it} = \alpha_i + u_{it}$. The variance–covariance matrix of $\mathbf{v}_i$ is

$$E\mathbf{v}_i\mathbf{v}_i' = \sigma_u^2 I_T + \sigma_\alpha^2 \mathbf{ee}' = V. \tag{3.3.4}$$

Its inverse is (see Graybill (1969); Nerlove (1971b); Wallace and Hussain (1969))

$$V^{-1} = \frac{1}{\sigma_u^2}\left[I_T - \frac{\sigma_\alpha^2}{\sigma_u^2 + T\sigma_\alpha^2}\mathbf{ee}'\right]. \tag{3.3.5}$$

3.3.1 Covariance Estimation

The presence of α_i produces a correlation among residuals of the same cross-sectional unit, though the residuals from different cross-sectional units are independent. However, regardless of whether the α_is are treated as fixed or as random, the individual-specific effects for a given sample can be swept out by the idempotent (covariance) transformation matrix Q [equation (3.2.6)], because $Q\mathbf{e} = \mathbf{0}$, and hence $Q\mathbf{v}_i = Q\mathbf{u}_i$. Thus, premultiplying (3.3.3) by Q, we have

$$\begin{aligned} Q\mathbf{y}_i &= Q\mathbf{e}\mu + QX_i\boldsymbol{\beta} + Q\mathbf{e}\alpha_i + Q\mathbf{u}_i \\ &= QX_i\boldsymbol{\beta} + Q\mathbf{u}_i. \end{aligned} \tag{3.3.6}$$

Applying the least-squares method to (3.3.6), we obtain the covariance estimator (CV) (3.2.8) of $\boldsymbol{\beta}$. We estimate μ by $\hat{\mu} = \bar{y} - \hat{\boldsymbol{\beta}}_{\text{CV}}'\bar{\mathbf{x}}$.

Whether α_i are treated as fixed or random, the CV of $\boldsymbol{\beta}$ is unbiased and consistent either N or T or both tend to infinity. However, whereas the CV is the BLUE under the assumption that α_i are fixed constants, it is not the BLUE in finite samples when α_i are assumed random. The BLUE in the latter case is the generalized-least-squares (GLS) estimator.[6] Moreover, if the explanatory variables contain some time-invariant variables $\mathbf{z}_i$, their coefficients cannot be estimated by CV, because the covariance transformation eliminates $\mathbf{z}_i$ from (3.3.6).

3.3.2 Generalized-Least-Squares Estimation

Because v_{it} and v_{is} both contain α_i, the residuals of (3.3.3) are correlated. To get efficient estimates of $\boldsymbol{\delta}' = (\mu, \boldsymbol{\beta}')$, we have to use the GLS method. The normal equations for the GLS estimators are

$$\left[\sum_{i=1}^{N} \tilde{X}_i' V^{-1} \tilde{X}_i\right] \hat{\boldsymbol{\delta}}_{\text{GLS}} = \sum_{i=1}^{N} \tilde{X}_i' V^{-1} \mathbf{y}_i. \tag{3.3.7}$$

Following Maddala (1971a), we write V^{-1} [equation (3.3.5)] as

$$V^{-1} = \frac{1}{\sigma_u^2}\left[\left(I_T - \frac{1}{T}\mathbf{ee}'\right) + \psi \cdot \frac{1}{T}\mathbf{ee}'\right] = \frac{1}{\sigma_u^2}\left[Q + \psi \cdot \frac{1}{T}\mathbf{ee}'\right], \tag{3.3.8}$$

where

$$\psi = \frac{\sigma_u^2}{\sigma_u^2 + T\sigma_\alpha^2}. \tag{3.3.9}$$

Hence, (3.3.7) can conveniently be written as

$$[W_{\tilde{x}\tilde{x}} + \psi B_{\tilde{x}\tilde{x}}]\begin{bmatrix}\hat{\mu}\\ \hat{\boldsymbol{\beta}}\end{bmatrix}_{\text{GLS}} = W_{\tilde{x}y} + \psi B_{\tilde{x}y}, \tag{3.3.10}$$

where

$$\begin{aligned}
T_{\tilde{x}\tilde{x}} &= \sum_{i=1}^N \tilde{X}_i'\tilde{X}_i, & T_{\tilde{x}y} &= \sum_{i=1}^N \tilde{X}_i'\mathbf{y}_i,\\
B_{\tilde{x}\tilde{x}} &= \frac{1}{T}\sum_{i=1}^N (\tilde{X}_i'\mathbf{e}\mathbf{e}'\tilde{X}_i), & B_{\tilde{x}y} &= \frac{1}{T}\sum_{i=1}^N (\tilde{X}_i'\mathbf{e}\mathbf{e}'\mathbf{y}_i),\\
W_{\tilde{x}\tilde{x}} &= T_{\tilde{x}\tilde{x}} - B_{\tilde{x}\tilde{x}}, & W_{\tilde{x}y} &= T_{\tilde{x}y} - B_{\tilde{x}y}.
\end{aligned}$$

The matrices $B_{\tilde{x}\tilde{x}}$ and $B_{\tilde{x}y}$ contain the sums of squares and sums of cross products between groups, $W_{\tilde{x}\tilde{x}}$ and $W_{\tilde{x}y}$ are the corresponding matrices within groups, and $T_{\tilde{x}\tilde{x}}$ and $T_{\tilde{x}y}$ are the corresponding matrices for total variation.

Solving (3.3.10), we have

$$\begin{bmatrix} \psi NT & \psi T\sum_{i=1}^N \bar{\mathbf{x}}_i' \\ \psi T\sum_{i=1}^N \bar{\mathbf{x}}_i & \sum_{i=1}^N X_i'QX_i + \psi T\sum_{i=1}^N \bar{\mathbf{x}}_i\bar{\mathbf{x}}_i' \end{bmatrix}\begin{bmatrix}\hat{\mu}\\ \hat{\boldsymbol{\beta}}\end{bmatrix}_{\text{GLS}} = \begin{bmatrix} \psi NT\bar{y} \\ \sum_{i=1}^N X_i'Q\mathbf{y}_i + \psi T\sum_{i=1}^N \bar{\mathbf{x}}_i\bar{y}_i \end{bmatrix}. \tag{3.3.11}$$

Using the formula of the partitioned inverse, we obtain

$$\begin{aligned}
\hat{\boldsymbol{\beta}}_{\text{GLS}} &= \left[\frac{1}{T}\sum_{i=1}^N X_i'QX_i + \psi\sum_{i=1}^N (\bar{\mathbf{x}}_i - \bar{\mathbf{x}})(\bar{\mathbf{x}}_i - \bar{\mathbf{x}})'\right]^{-1}\\
&\quad\times\left[\frac{1}{T}\sum_{i=1}^N X_i'Q\mathbf{y}_i + \psi\sum_{i=1}^N (\bar{\mathbf{x}}_i - \bar{\mathbf{x}})(\bar{y}_i - \bar{y})\right] \qquad (3.3.12)\\
&= \Delta\hat{\boldsymbol{\beta}}_b + (I_K - \Delta)\hat{\boldsymbol{\beta}}_{\text{CV}},\\
\hat{\mu}_{\text{GLS}} &= \bar{y} - \hat{\boldsymbol{\beta}}_{\text{GLS}}'\bar{\mathbf{x}},
\end{aligned}$$

where

$$\Delta = \psi T\left[\sum_{i=1}^{N} X_i' Q X_i + \psi T \sum_{i=1}^{N}(\bar{\mathbf{x}}_i - \bar{\mathbf{x}})(\bar{\mathbf{x}}_i - \bar{\mathbf{x}})'\right]^{-1} \times \left[\sum_{i=1}^{N}(\bar{\mathbf{x}}_i - \bar{\mathbf{x}})(\bar{\mathbf{x}}_i - \bar{\mathbf{x}})'\right],$$

$$\hat{\boldsymbol{\beta}}_b = \left[\sum_{i=1}^{N}(\bar{\mathbf{x}}_i - \bar{\mathbf{x}})(\bar{\mathbf{x}}_i - \bar{\mathbf{x}})'\right]^{-1}\left[\sum_{i=1}^{N}(\bar{\mathbf{x}}_i - \bar{\mathbf{x}})(\bar{y}_i - \bar{y})\right].$$

The estimator $\hat{\boldsymbol{\beta}}_b$ is called the between-group estimator because it ignores variation within the group.

The GLS estimator (3.3.12) is a weighted average of the between-group and within-group estimators. If $\psi \to 1$, then $\boldsymbol{\delta}_{\text{GLS}}$ converges to the OLS estimator $T_{\tilde{x}\tilde{x}}^{-1} T_{\tilde{x}y}$. If $\psi \to 0$, the GLS estimator for $\boldsymbol{\beta}$ becomes the covariance estimator (LSDV) [equation (3.2.5)]. In essence, ψ measures the weight given to the between-group variation. In the LSDV (or fixed-effects model) procedure, this source of variation is completely ignored. The OLS procedure corresponds to $\psi = 1$. The between-group and within-group variations are just added up. Thus, one can view the OLS and LSDV as somewhat all-or-nothing ways of utilizing the between-group variation. The procedure of treating α_i as random provides a solution intermediate between treating them all as different and treating them all as equal as implied by the GLS estimator given in (3.3.12).

If $[W_{\tilde{x}\tilde{x}} + \psi B_{\tilde{x}\tilde{x}}]$ is nonsingular, the covariance matrix of GLS estimators of $\boldsymbol{\delta}$ can be written as

$$\begin{aligned}
\operatorname{Var}\begin{bmatrix}\hat{\mu}\\ \hat{\boldsymbol{\beta}}\end{bmatrix}_{\text{GLS}} &= \sigma_u^2 [W_{\tilde{x}\tilde{x}} + \psi B_{\tilde{x}\tilde{x}}]^{-1}\\
&= \sigma_u^2\left[\begin{pmatrix} 0 & \mathbf{0}' \\ \mathbf{0} & \sum_{i=1}^{N} X_i' Q X_i \end{pmatrix} + T\psi \begin{pmatrix} N & \sum_{i=1}^{N}\bar{\mathbf{x}}_i' \\ \sum_{i=1}^{N}\bar{\mathbf{x}}_i & \sum_{i=1}^{N}\bar{\mathbf{x}}_i\bar{\mathbf{x}}_i' \end{pmatrix}\right]^{-1}.
\end{aligned} \tag{3.3.13}$$

Using the formula for partitioned inversion (e.g., Rao (1973, Chapter 2); Theil (1971, Chapter 1)), we obtain

$$\operatorname{Var}(\hat{\boldsymbol{\beta}}_{\text{GLS}}) = \sigma_u^2\left[\sum_{i=1}^{N} X_i' Q X_i + T\psi \sum_{i=1}^{N}(\bar{\mathbf{x}}_i - \bar{\mathbf{x}})(\bar{\mathbf{x}}_i - \bar{\mathbf{x}})'\right]^{-1}. \tag{3.3.14}$$

Because $\psi > 0$, we see immediately that the difference between the covariance matrices of $\hat{\boldsymbol{\beta}}_{\text{CV}}$ and $\hat{\boldsymbol{\beta}}_{\text{GLS}}$ is a positive semidefinite matrix. However, for fixed N, as $T \to \infty$, $\psi \to 0$. Thus, under the assumption that $(1/NT)\sum_{i=1}^{N} X_i' X_i$ and $(1/NT)\sum_{i=1}^{N} X_i' Q X_i$ converge to finite positive definitive matrices when $T \to \infty$, we have $\hat{\beta}_{\text{GLS}} \to \hat{\beta}_{\text{CV}}$ and $\text{Var}(\sqrt{T}\hat{\boldsymbol{\beta}}_{\text{GLS}}) \to \text{Var}(\sqrt{T}\hat{\boldsymbol{\beta}}_{\text{CV}})$. This is because when $T \to \infty$, we have an infinite number of observations for each i. Therefore, we can consider each α_i as a random variable which has been drawn once and forever, so that for each i we can pretend that they are just like fixed parameters.

Computation of the GLS estimator can be simplified by noting the special form of V^{-1} (3.3.8). Let $P = [I_T - (1 - \psi^{1/2})(1/T)\mathbf{ee}']$; we have $V^{-1} = (1/\sigma_u^2)P'P$. Premultiplying (3.3.3) by the transformation matrix P, we obtain the GLS estimator (3.3.10) by applying the least-squares method to the transformed model (Theil (1971, Chapter 6)). This is equivalent to first transforming the data by subtracting a fraction $(1 - \psi^{1/2})$ of individual means $\bar{y}_i$ and $\bar{\mathbf{x}}_i$ from their corresponding y_{it} and $\mathbf{x}_{it}$, then regressing $[y_{it} - (1 - \psi^{1/2})\bar{y}_i]$ on a constant and $[\mathbf{x}_{it} - (1 - \psi^{1/2})\bar{\mathbf{x}}_i]$.

If the variance components σ_u^2 and σ_α^2 are unknown, we can use two-step GLS estimation. In the first step, we estimate the variance components using some consistent estimators. In the second step, we substitute their estimated values into (3.3.10) or its equivalent form. When the sample size is large (in the sense of either $N \to \infty$ or $T \to \infty$), the two-step GLS estimator will have the same asymptotic efficiency as the GLS procedure with known variance components (Fuller and Battese (1974)). Even for moderate sample size [for $T \geq 3$, $N - (K + 1) \geq 9$; for $T = 2$, $N - (K + 1) \geq 10$], the two-step procedure is still more efficient than the covariance (or within-group) estimator in the sense that the difference between the covariance matrices of the covariance estimator and the two-step estimator is nonnegative definite (Taylor (1980)).

Noting that $\bar{y}_i = \mu + \boldsymbol{\beta}'\bar{\mathbf{x}}_i + \alpha_i + \bar{u}_i$ and $(y_{it} - \bar{y}_i) = \boldsymbol{\beta}'(\mathbf{x}_{it} - \bar{\mathbf{x}}_i) + (u_{it} - \bar{u}_i)$, we can use the within- and between-group residuals to estimate σ_u^2 and σ_α^2 respectively, by[7]

$$\hat{\sigma}_u^2 = \frac{\sum_{i=1}^{N}\sum_{t=1}^{T}[(y_{it} - \bar{y}_i) - \hat{\boldsymbol{\beta}}_{\text{CV}}'(\mathbf{x}_{it} - \bar{\mathbf{x}}_i)]^2}{N(T-1) - K}, \tag{3.3.15}$$

and

$$\hat{\sigma}_\alpha^2 = \frac{\sum_{i=1}^{N}(\bar{y}_i - \tilde{\mu} - \tilde{\boldsymbol{\beta}}'\bar{\mathbf{x}}_i)^2}{N - (K+1)} - \frac{1}{T}\hat{\sigma}_u^2, \tag{3.3.16}$$

where $(\tilde{\mu}, \tilde{\boldsymbol{\beta}}')' = B_{\tilde{x}\tilde{x}}^{-1} B_{\tilde{x}\tilde{y}}$.

Amemiya (1971) has discussed efficient estimation of the variance components. However, substituting more efficiently estimated variance components into (3.3.9) need not lead to more efficient estimates of μ and $\boldsymbol{\beta}$ (Maddala and Mount (1973); Taylor (1980)).

3.3.3 Maximum Likelihood Estimation

When α_i and u_{it} are random and normally distributed, the logarithm of the likelihood function is

$$\begin{aligned}\log L = &-\frac{NT}{2}\log 2\pi - \frac{N}{2}\log|V| \\ &-\frac{1}{2}\sum_{i=1}^{N}(\mathbf{y}_i - \mathbf{e}\mu - X_i\boldsymbol{\beta})'V^{-1}(\mathbf{y}_i - \mathbf{e}\mu - X_i\boldsymbol{\beta}) \\ = &-\frac{NT}{2}\log 2\pi - \frac{N(T-1)}{2}\log\sigma_u^2 - \frac{N}{2}\log(\sigma_u^2 + T\sigma_\alpha^2) \\ &-\frac{1}{2\sigma_u^2}\sum_{i=1}^{N}(\mathbf{y}_i - \mathbf{e}\mu - X_i\boldsymbol{\beta})'Q(\mathbf{y}_i - \mathbf{e}\mu - X_i\boldsymbol{\beta}) \\ &-\frac{T}{2(\sigma_u^2 + T\sigma_\alpha^2)}\sum_{i=1}^{N}(\bar{y}_i - \mu - \boldsymbol{\beta}'\bar{\mathbf{x}}_i)^2, \end{aligned} \tag{3.3.17}$$

where the second equality follows from (3.3.8) and

$$|V| = \sigma_u^{2(T-1)}(\sigma_u^2 + T\sigma_\alpha^2). \tag{3.3.18}$$

The maximum likelihood estimator (MLE) of $(\mu, \boldsymbol{\beta}', \sigma_u^2, \sigma_\alpha^2) = \tilde{\boldsymbol{\delta}}'$ is obtained by solving the following first-order conditions simultaneously:

$$\frac{\partial \log L}{\partial \mu} = \frac{T}{\sigma_u^2 + T\sigma_\alpha^2}\sum_{i=1}^{N}(\bar{y}_i - \mu - \bar{\mathbf{x}}_i'\boldsymbol{\beta}) = 0, \tag{3.3.19}$$

$$\begin{aligned}\frac{\partial \log L}{\partial \boldsymbol{\beta}} = \frac{1}{\sigma_u^2}\Bigg[&\sum_{i=1}^{N}(\mathbf{y}_i - \mathbf{e}\mu - X_i\boldsymbol{\beta})'QX_i \\ &-\frac{T\sigma_u^2}{\sigma_u^2 + T\sigma_\alpha^2}\sum_{i=1}^{N}(\bar{y}_i - \mu - \bar{\mathbf{x}}_i'\boldsymbol{\beta})\bar{\mathbf{x}}_i'\Bigg] = \mathbf{0}, \end{aligned} \tag{3.3.20}$$

$$\begin{aligned}\frac{\partial \log L}{\partial \sigma_u^2} = &-\frac{N(T-1)}{2\sigma_u^2} - \frac{N}{2(\sigma_u^2 + T\sigma_\alpha^2)} \\ &+\frac{1}{2\sigma_u^4}\sum_{i=1}^{N}(\mathbf{y}_i - \mathbf{e}\mu - X_i\boldsymbol{\beta})'Q(\mathbf{y}_i - \mathbf{e}\mu - X_i\boldsymbol{\beta}) \\ &+\frac{T}{2(\sigma_u^2 + T\sigma_\alpha^2)^2}\sum_{i=1}^{N}(\bar{y}_i - \mu - \bar{\mathbf{x}}_i'\boldsymbol{\beta})^2 = 0, \end{aligned} \tag{3.3.21}$$

$$\frac{\partial \log L}{\partial \sigma_\alpha^2} = -\frac{NT}{2(\sigma_u^2 + T\sigma_\alpha^2)} + \frac{T^2}{2(\sigma_u^2 + T\sigma_\alpha^2)^2}\sum_{i=1}^{N}(\bar{y}_i - \mu - \bar{\mathbf{x}}_i'\boldsymbol{\beta})^2 = 0. \tag{3.3.22}$$

Simultaneous solution of (3.3.19)–(3.3.22) is complicated. The Newton–Raphson iterative procedure can be used to solve for the MLE. The procedure uses an initial trial value $\hat{\tilde{\boldsymbol{\delta}}}^{(1)}$ of $\tilde{\boldsymbol{\delta}}$ to start the iteration by substituting it into the formula

$$\hat{\tilde{\boldsymbol{\delta}}}^{(j)} = \hat{\tilde{\boldsymbol{\delta}}}^{(j-1)} - \left[\frac{\partial^2 \log L}{\partial \tilde{\boldsymbol{\delta}}\, \partial \tilde{\boldsymbol{\delta}}'}\right]^{-1}_{\tilde{\boldsymbol{\delta}}=\hat{\tilde{\boldsymbol{\delta}}}^{(j-1)}} \left.\frac{\partial \log L}{\partial \tilde{\boldsymbol{\delta}}}\right|_{\tilde{\boldsymbol{\delta}}=\hat{\tilde{\boldsymbol{\delta}}}^{(j-1)}} \tag{3.3.23}$$

to obtain a revised estimate of $\tilde{\boldsymbol{\delta}}$, $\hat{\tilde{\boldsymbol{\delta}}}^{(2)}$. The process is repeated until the jth iterative solution $\hat{\tilde{\boldsymbol{\delta}}}^{(j)}$ is close to the $(j-1)$th iterative solution $\hat{\tilde{\boldsymbol{\delta}}}^{(j-1)}$.

Alternatively, we can use a sequential iterative procedure to obtain the MLE. We note that from (3.3.19) and (3.3.20), we have

$$\begin{aligned}
\begin{bmatrix} \hat{\mu} \\ \hat{\boldsymbol{\beta}} \end{bmatrix} &= \left[\sum_{i=1}^{N} \tilde{X}_i' V^{-1} \tilde{X}_i\right]^{-1} \left[\sum_{i=1}^{N} \tilde{X}_i' V^{-1} \mathbf{y}_i\right] \\
&= \left\{\sum_{i=1}^{N} \begin{bmatrix} \mathbf{e}' \\ X_i' \end{bmatrix} \left[I_T - \frac{\sigma_\alpha^2}{\sigma_\alpha^2 + T\sigma_\alpha^2}\mathbf{ee}'\right](\mathbf{e}, X_i)\right\}^{-1} \\
&\quad \times \left\{\sum_{i=1}^{N} \begin{bmatrix} \mathbf{e}' \\ X_i' \end{bmatrix} \left[I_T - \frac{\sigma_\alpha^2}{\sigma_u^2 + T\sigma_\alpha^2}\mathbf{ee}'\right]\mathbf{y}_i\right\}.
\end{aligned} \tag{3.3.24}$$

Substituting (3.3.22) into (3.3.21), we have

$$\hat{\sigma}_u^2 = \frac{1}{N(T-1)} \sum_{i=1}^{N} (\mathbf{y}_i - \mathbf{e}\mu - X_i\boldsymbol{\beta})' Q (\mathbf{y}_i - \mathbf{e}\mu - X_i\boldsymbol{\beta}). \tag{3.3.25}$$

From (3.3.22), we have

$$\hat{\sigma}_\alpha^2 = \frac{1}{N} \sum_{i=1}^{N} (\bar{y}_i - \hat{\mu} - \bar{\mathbf{x}}_i'\hat{\boldsymbol{\beta}})^2 - \frac{1}{T}\hat{\sigma}_u^2. \tag{3.3.26}$$

Thus, we can obtain the MLE by first substituting an initial trial value of $\sigma_\alpha^2/(\sigma_u^2 + T\sigma_\alpha^2)$ into (3.3.24) to estimate μ and $\boldsymbol{\beta}'$, and then estimate σ_u^2 by (3.3.25) using the solution of (3.3.24). Substituting the solutions of (3.3.24) and (3.3.25) into (3.3.26), we obtain an estimate of σ_α^2. Then we repeat the process by substituting the new values of σ_u^2 and σ_α^2 into (3.3.24) to obtain new estimates of μ and $\boldsymbol{\beta}$, and so on until the solution converges.

When T is fixed and N goes to infinity, the MLE is consistent and asymptotically normally distributed with variance–covariance matrix

$$\operatorname{Var}(\sqrt{N}\hat{\tilde{\boldsymbol{\delta}}}_{\text{MLE}}) = NE\left[-\frac{\partial^2 \log L}{\partial\tilde{\boldsymbol{\delta}}\,\partial\tilde{\boldsymbol{\delta}}'}\right]^{-1}$$

$$= \begin{bmatrix} \dfrac{T}{\sigma^2} & \dfrac{T}{\sigma^2}\dfrac{1}{N}\displaystyle\sum_{i=1}^{N}\bar{\mathbf{x}}_i' & 0 & 0 \\ & \dfrac{1}{\sigma_u^2}\dfrac{1}{N}\displaystyle\sum_{i=1}^{N} X_i'\left(I_T - \dfrac{\sigma_\alpha^2}{\sigma^2}\mathbf{e}\mathbf{e}'\right)X_i & \mathbf{0} & \mathbf{0} \\ & & \dfrac{T-1}{2\sigma_u^2} + \dfrac{1}{2\sigma^4} & \dfrac{T}{2\sigma^4} \\ & & & \dfrac{T^2}{2\sigma^4} \end{bmatrix}^{-1}, \tag{3.3.27}$$

where $\sigma^2 = \sigma_u^2 + T\sigma_\alpha^2$. When N is fixed and T tends to infinity, the MLEs of μ, $\boldsymbol{\beta}$, and σ_u^2 converge to the covariance estimator and are consistent, but the MLE of σ_α^2 is inconsistent. This is because when N is fixed, there is not sufficient variation in α_i no matter how large T is; for details, see Anderson and Hsiao (1981, 1982).

Although the MLE is asymptotically efficient, sometimes simultaneous solution of (3.3.19)–(3.3.22) yields an estimated value of σ_α^2 that is negative.[8] When there is a unique solution to the partial-derivative equations (3.3.19)–(3.3.22), with $\sigma_u^2 > 0, \sigma_\alpha^2 > 0$, the solution is the MLE. However, when we constrain $\sigma_u^2 \geq 0$ and $\sigma_\alpha^2 \geq 0$, a boundary solution may occur. The solution then no longer satisfies all the derivative equations (3.3.19)–(3.3.22). Maddala (1971a) has shown that the boundary solution of $\sigma_u^2 = 0$ cannot occur, but the boundary solution of $\sigma_\alpha^2 = 0$ will occur when $T_{yy} - T_{\tilde{x}y}'T_{\tilde{x}\tilde{x}}^{-1}T_{\tilde{x}y} > T[B_{yy} - 2T_{\tilde{x}y}'T_{\tilde{x}\tilde{x}}^{-1}T_{\tilde{x}y} + T_{\tilde{x}y}'T_{\tilde{x}\tilde{x}}^{-1}B_{\tilde{x}\tilde{x}}T_{\tilde{x}\tilde{x}}^{-1}T_{\tilde{x}y}]$. However, the probability of occurrence of a boundary solution tends to zero when either T or N tends to infinity.

3.4 FIXED EFFECTS OR RANDOM EFFECTS

3.4.1 An Example

In previous sections we discussed the estimation of a linear-regression model (3.2.1) when the effects, α_i, are treated either as fixed or as random. Whether to treat the effects as fixed or random makes no difference when T is large, because both the LSDV estimator (3.2.8) and the generalized least-squares estimator (3.3.12) become the same estimator. When T is finite and N is large, whether to treat the effects as fixed or random is not an easy question to answer. It can make a surprising amount of difference in the estimates of the parameters.

Table 3.3. *Wage equations (dependent variable: log wage[a])*

Variable	Fixed effects	Random effects
1. Age 1 (20–35)	0.0557	0.0393
	(0.0042)	(0.0033)
2. Age 2 (35–45)	0.0351	0.0092
	(0.0051)	(0.0036)
3. Age 3 (45–55)	0.0209	−0.0007
	(0.0055)	(0.0042)
4. Age 4 (55–65)	0.0209	−0.0097
	(0.0078)	(0.0060)
5. Age 5 (65–)	−0.0171	−0.0423
	(0.0155)	(0.0121)
6. Unemployed previous year	−0.0042	−0.0277
	(0.0153)	(0.0151)
7. Poor health previous year	−0.0204	−0.0250
	(0.0221)	(0.0215)
8. Self-employment	−0.2190	−0.2670
	(0.0297)	(0.0263)
9. South	−0.1569	−0.0324
	(0.0656)	(0.0333)
10. Rural	−0.0101	−0.1215
	(0.0317)	(0.0237)
11. Constant	—	0.8499
	—	(0.0433)
s^2	0.0567	0.0694
Degrees of freedom	3,135	3,763

[a]3,774 observations; standard errors are in parentheses.
Source: Hausman (1978).

In fact, when only a few observations are available for different individuals over time, it is exceptionally important to make the best use of the lesser amount of information over time for the efficient estimation of the common behavioral relationship.

For example, Hausman (1978) found that using a fixed-effects specification produced significantly different results from a random-effects specification when estimating a wage equation using a sample of 629 high school graduates followed over six years by the Michigan income dynamics study. The explanatory variables in the Hausman wage equation include a piecewise-linear representation of age, the presence of unemployment or poor health in the previous year, and dummy variables for self-employment, living in the South, or living in a rural area. The fixed-effects specification was estimated using (3.2.5).[9] The random-effects specification was estimated using (3.3.10). The results are reproduced in Table 3.3. In comparing these two estimates, it is apparent that the effects of unemployment, self-employment, and geographical location differ widely (relative to their standard errors) in the two models.

3.4.2 Conditional Inference or Unconditional (Marginal) Inference

If the effects of omitted variables can be appropriately summarized by a random variable and the individual (or time) effects represent the ignorance of the investigator, it does not seem reasonable to treat one source of ignorance (α_i) as fixed and the other source of ignorance (u_{it}) as random. It appears that one way to unify the fixed-effects and random-effects models is to assume from the outset that the effects are random. The fixed-effects model is viewed as one in which investigators make inferences conditional on the effects that are in the sample. The random-effects model is viewed as one in which investigators make unconditional or marginal inferences with respect to the population of all effects. There is really no distinction in the "nature (of the effect)." It is up to the investigator to decide whether to make inference with respect to the population characteristics or only with respect to the effects that are in the sample.

In general, whether one wishes to consider the conditional-likelihood function or the marginal-likelihood function depends on the context of the data, the manner in which they were gathered, and the environment from which they came. For instance, consider an example in which several technicians care for machines. The effects of technicians can be assumed random if the technicians are all randomly drawn from a common population. But if the situation is not that each technician comes and goes, randomly sampled from all employees, but that all are available, and if we want to assess differences between those specific technicians, then the fixed-effects model is more appropriate. Similarly, if an experiment involves hundreds of individuals who are considered a random sample from some larger population, random effects are more appropriate. However, if the situation were one of analyzing just a few individuals, say five or six, and the sole interest lay in just these individuals, then individual effects would more appropriately be fixed, not random. The situation to which a model applies and the inferences based on it are the deciding factors in determining whether we should treat effects as random or fixed. When inferences are going to be confined to the effects in the model, the effects are more appropriately considered fixed. When inferences will be made about a population of effects from which those in the data are considered to be a random sample, then the effects should be considered random.[10]

If one accepts this view, then why do the fixed-effects and random-effects approaches sometimes yield vastly different estimates of the common slope coefficients that are not supposed to vary across individuals? It appears that in addition to the efficiency issue discussed earlier, there is also a different but important issue of whether or not the model is properly specified – that is, whether the differences in individual effects can be attributed to the chance mechanism.

In the random-effects framework of (3.3.1)–(3.3.3), there are two fundamental assumptions. One is that the unobserved individual effects α_i are random draws from a common population. The other is that the explanatory variables are strictly exogenous. That is, the error terms are uncorrelated with (or orthogonal to) the past, current, and future values of the regressors:

$$E(u_{it} \mid \mathbf{x}_{i1}, \ldots, \mathbf{x}_{iT}) = E(\alpha_i \mid \mathbf{x}_{i1}, \ldots, \mathbf{x}_{iT}) \\ = E(v_{it} \mid \mathbf{x}_{i1}, \ldots, \mathbf{x}_{iT}) = 0 \qquad \text{for} \quad t = 1, \ldots, T. \tag{3.4.1}$$

In the above example, if there are fundamental differences in the technicians (for instance, in their ability, age, years of experiences, etc.), then the difference in technicians cannot be attributed to a pure chance mechanism. It is more appropriate to view the technicians as drawn from heterogeneous populations and the individual effects $\alpha_i^* = \alpha_i + \mu$ as representing the fundamental difference among the heterogeneous populations. Thus, it would be more appropriate to treat α_i^* as fixed and different (Hsiao and Sun (2000)). If the difference in technicians captured by α_i^* is ignored, the least-squares estimator of (3.3.3) yields

$$\hat{\boldsymbol{\beta}}_{\text{LS}} = \left[\sum_{i=1}^{N}\sum_{t=1}^{T}(\mathbf{x}_{it} - \bar{\mathbf{x}})(\mathbf{x}_{it} - \bar{\mathbf{x}})'\right]^{-1}\left[\sum_{i=1}^{N}\sum_{t=1}^{T}(\mathbf{x}_{it} - \bar{\mathbf{x}})(y_{it} - \bar{y})\right] \\ = \boldsymbol{\beta} + \left[\sum_{i=1}^{N}\sum_{t=1}^{T}(\mathbf{x}_{it} - \bar{\mathbf{x}})(\mathbf{x}_{it} - \bar{\mathbf{x}})'\right]^{-1}\left\{T\sum_{i=1}^{N}(\bar{\mathbf{x}}_i - \bar{\mathbf{x}})(\alpha_i^* - \bar{\alpha})\right\}, \tag{3.4.2}$$

where $\bar{\alpha} = \frac{1}{N}\sum_{i=1}^{N}\alpha_i^*$. It is clear that unless $\frac{1}{N}\sum_{i=1}^{N}(\bar{\mathbf{x}}_i - \bar{\mathbf{x}})(\alpha_i^* - \bar{\alpha})$ converges to zero as $N \to \infty$, the least-squares estimator of $\boldsymbol{\beta}$ is inconsistent. The bias of $\hat{\boldsymbol{\beta}}_{\text{LS}}$ depends on the correlation between $\mathbf{x}_{it}$ and α_i^*.

3.4.2.a Mundlak's Formulation

Mundlak (1978a) criticized the random-effects formulation (3.3.2) on the grounds that it neglects the correlation that may exist between the effects α_i and the explanatory variables $\mathbf{x}_{it}$. There are reasons to believe that in many circumstances α_i and $\mathbf{x}_{it}$ are indeed correlated. For instance, consider the estimation of a production function using firm data. The output of each firm, y_{it}, may be affected by unobservable managerial ability α_i. Firms with more efficient management tend to produce more and use more inputs X_i. Less efficient firms tend to produce less and use fewer inputs. In this situation, α_i and X_i cannot be independent. Ignoring this correlation can lead to biased estimation.

The properties of various estimators we have discussed thus far depend on the existence and extent of the relations between the X's and the effects. Therefore, we have to consider the joint distribution of these variables. However, α_i are unobservable. Mundlak (1978a) suggested that we approximate $E(\alpha_i \mid X_i)$ by a linear function. He introduced the auxiliary regression

$$\alpha_i = \sum_t \mathbf{x}_{it}'\mathbf{a}_t + \omega_i, \qquad \omega_i \sim N\big(0, \sigma_\omega^2\big). \tag{3.4.3a}$$

A simple approximation to (3.4.3a) is to let

$$\alpha_i = \bar{\mathbf{x}}_i'\mathbf{a} + \omega_i, \qquad \omega_i \sim N\big(0, \sigma_\omega^2\big). \tag{3.4.3b}$$

Clearly, $\mathbf{a}$ will be equal to zero (and $\sigma_\omega^2 = \sigma_\alpha^2$) if (and only if) the explanatory variables are uncorrelated with the effects.

Substituting (3.4.3b) into (3.3.3), and stacking equations over t and i, we have

$$\begin{bmatrix} \mathbf{y}_1 \\ \mathbf{y}_2 \\ \vdots \\ \mathbf{y}_N \end{bmatrix} = \begin{bmatrix} \tilde{X}_1 \\ \tilde{X}_2 \\ \vdots \\ \tilde{X}_N \end{bmatrix} \boldsymbol{\delta} + \begin{bmatrix} \mathbf{e}\bar{\mathbf{x}}_1' \\ \mathbf{e}\bar{\mathbf{x}}_2' \\ \vdots \\ \mathbf{e}\bar{\mathbf{x}}_N' \end{bmatrix} \mathbf{a} + \begin{bmatrix} \mathbf{e} \\ \mathbf{0} \\ \vdots \\ \mathbf{0} \end{bmatrix} \omega_1$$

$$+ \begin{bmatrix} \mathbf{0} \\ \mathbf{e} \\ \vdots \\ \mathbf{0} \end{bmatrix} \omega_2 + \cdots + \begin{bmatrix} \mathbf{0} \\ \mathbf{0} \\ \vdots \\ \mathbf{e}_N \end{bmatrix} \omega_N + \begin{bmatrix} \mathbf{u}_1 \\ \mathbf{u}_2 \\ \vdots \\ \mathbf{u}_N \end{bmatrix}, \tag{3.4.4}$$

where, conditional on $\mathbf{x}_i$,

$$E(\mathbf{u}_i + \mathbf{e}\omega_i) = \mathbf{0},$$

$$E(\mathbf{u}_i + \mathbf{e}\omega_i)(\mathbf{u}_j + \mathbf{e}\omega_j)' = \begin{cases} \sigma_u^2 I_T + \sigma_\omega^2 \mathbf{e}\mathbf{e}' = \tilde{V} & \text{if } i = j, \\ \mathbf{0} & \text{if } i \neq j, \end{cases}$$

$$\tilde{V}^{-1} = \frac{1}{\sigma_u^2}\left[I_T - \frac{\sigma_\omega^2}{\sigma_u^2 + T\sigma_\omega^2}\mathbf{e}\mathbf{e}' \right].$$

Utilizing the expression for the inverse of a partitioned matrix (Theil (1971, Chapter 1)), we obtain the GLS of $(\mu, \boldsymbol{\beta}', \mathbf{a}')$ as

$$\hat{\mu}^*_{\text{GLS}} = \bar{y} - \bar{\mathbf{x}}'\hat{\boldsymbol{\beta}}_b, \tag{3.4.5}$$

$$\hat{\boldsymbol{\beta}}^*_{\text{GLS}} = \hat{\boldsymbol{\beta}}_{\text{CV}}, \tag{3.4.6}$$

$$\hat{\mathbf{a}}^*_{\text{GLS}} = \hat{\boldsymbol{\beta}}_b - \hat{\boldsymbol{\beta}}_{\text{CV}}. \tag{3.4.7}$$

Thus, in the present framework, the BLUE of $\boldsymbol{\beta}$ is the covariance estimator of (3.2.1) or (3.2.10). It does not depend on knowledge of the variance components. Therefore, Mundlak (1978a) maintained that the imaginary difference between the fixed-effects and random-effects approaches is based on an incorrect specification. In fact, applying GLS to (3.2.10) yields a biased estimator. This can be seen by noting that the GLS estimate of $\boldsymbol{\beta}$ for (3.3.3), that is, (3.3.10), can be viewed as the GLS estimate of (3.4.4) after imposing the restriction $\mathbf{a} = \mathbf{0}$. As shown in (3.3.12),

$$\hat{\boldsymbol{\beta}}_{\text{GLS}} = \Delta\hat{\boldsymbol{\beta}}_b + (I_K - \Delta)\hat{\boldsymbol{\beta}}_{\text{CV}}. \tag{3.4.8}$$

If (3.4.4) is the correct specification, then $E\hat{\boldsymbol{\beta}}_b$ is equal to $\boldsymbol{\beta} + \mathbf{a}$, and $E\hat{\boldsymbol{\beta}}_{\text{CV}} = \boldsymbol{\beta}$, so that

$$E\hat{\boldsymbol{\beta}}_{\text{GLS}} = \boldsymbol{\beta} + \Delta \mathbf{a}. \tag{3.4.9}$$

This is a biased estimator if $\mathbf{a} \neq \mathbf{0}$. However, when T tends to infinity, Δ tends to zero, and $\hat{\boldsymbol{\beta}}_{\text{GLS}}$ tends to $\hat{\boldsymbol{\beta}}_{\text{CV}}$ and is asymptotically unbiased. But in the more relevant situation in which T is fixed and N tends to infinity, $\text{plim}_{N\to\infty} \hat{\boldsymbol{\beta}}_{\text{GLS}} \neq \boldsymbol{\beta}$ in Mundlak's formulation.

While it is important to recognize the possible correlation between the effects and the explanatory variables, Mundlak's claim (1978a) that there is only one estimator and that efficiency is not a consideration in distinguishing between the random-effects and fixed-effects approaches is perhaps a bit strong. In fact, in the dynamic, random-coefficient, and discrete-choice models to be discussed later, one can show that the two approaches do not lead to the same estimator even when one allows for the correlation between α_i and X_i. Moreover, in the linear static model if $\mathbf{a} = \mathbf{0}$, the efficient estimator is (3.3.12), not the covariance estimator (3.2.8).

3.4.2.b Conditional and Unconditional Inferences in the Presence or Absence of Correlation between Individual Effects and Attributes

To gain further intuition about the differences between models (3.3.3) and (3.4.4) within the conditional- and unconditional-inference frameworks, we consider the following two experiments. Let a population be made up of a certain composition of red and black balls. The first experiment consists in N individuals, each picking a fixed number of balls randomly from this population to form his person-specific urn. Each individual then makes T independent trials of drawing a ball from his specific urn and putting it back. The second experiment assumes that individuals have different preferences for the compositions of red and black balls for their specific urns and allows personal attributes to affect the compositions. Specifically, prior to making T independent trials with replacement from their respective urns, individuals are allowed to take any number of balls from the population until their compositions reach the desired proportions.

If one is interested in making inferences regarding an individual urn's composition of red and black balls, a fixed-effects model should be used, whether the sample comes from the first or the second experiment. On the other hand, if one is interested in the population composition, a marginal or unconditional inference should be used. However, the marginal distributions are different for these two cases. In the first experiment, differences in individual urns are outcomes of random sampling. The subscript i is purely a labeling device, with no substantive content. A conventional random-effects model assuming independence between α_i and $\mathbf{x}_{it}$ would be appropriate. In the second experiment, the differences in individual urns reflect differences in personal attributes. A proper marginal inference has to allow for these nonrandom effects. It so happens that, for the Mundlak's formulation a marginal inference that properly allows for the correlation between individual effects (α_i) and the attributes ($\mathbf{x}_i$) generating the process gives rise to the same estimator as when the individual effects are treated as fixed. It is not that in making inferences about population characteristics we should assume a fixed-effects model.

Formally, let u_{it} and α_i be independent normal processes that are mutually independent. In the case of the first experiment, α_i are independently distributed and independent of individual attributes $\mathbf{x}_i$, so the distribution of α_i must be expressible as random sampling from a univariate distribution (Box and Tiao (1968); Chamberlain (1980)). Thus, the conditional distribution of $\{(u_i + \mathbf{e}\alpha_i)', \alpha_i \mid X_i\}$ is identical with the marginal distribution of $\{(\mathbf{u}_i + \mathbf{e}\alpha_i)', \alpha_i\}$,

$$\begin{bmatrix} u_{i1} + \alpha_i \\ \vdots \\ u_{iT} + \alpha_i \\ \cdots\cdots\cdots \\ \alpha_i \end{bmatrix} = \left[\begin{array}{c|c} u_{i1} + \alpha_i & \\ \vdots & \\ u_{iT} + \alpha_i & X_i \\ \cdots\cdots\cdots & \\ \alpha_i & \end{array}\right] \sim N\left[\begin{bmatrix} \mathbf{0} \\ \cdots \\ 0 \end{bmatrix}, \begin{bmatrix} \sigma_u^2 I_T + \sigma_\alpha^2 \mathbf{e}\mathbf{e}' & \vdots & \sigma_\alpha^2 \mathbf{e} \\ \cdots\cdots\cdots\cdots & \vdots & \cdots \\ \sigma_\alpha^2 \mathbf{e}' & \vdots & \sigma_\alpha^2 \end{bmatrix}\right]. \tag{3.4.10a}$$

In the second experiment, α_i may be viewed as a random draw from heterogeneous populations with mean a_i^* and variance $\sigma_{\omega i}^2$ (Mundlak's (1978a) formulation may be viewed as a special case of this in which $E(\alpha_i \mid X_i) = a_i^* = \mathbf{a}'\bar{\mathbf{x}}_i$, and $\sigma_{\omega i}^2 = \sigma_\omega^2$ for all i). Then the conditional distribution of $\{(\mathbf{u}_i + \mathbf{e}\alpha_i)' \vdots\, \alpha_i \mid X_i\}$ is

$$\left[\begin{array}{c|c} u_{i1} + \alpha_i & \\ \vdots & \\ u_{iT} + \alpha_i & X_i \\ \cdots\cdots\cdots & \\ \alpha_i & \end{array}\right] \sim N\left[\begin{bmatrix} \mathbf{e}a_i^* \\ \cdots \\ a_i^* \end{bmatrix}, \begin{bmatrix} \sigma_u^2 I_T + \sigma_{\omega i}^2 \mathbf{e}\mathbf{e}' & \vdots & \sigma_{\omega i}^2 \mathbf{e} \\ \cdots\cdots\cdots\cdots & \vdots & \cdots \\ \sigma_{\omega i}^2 \mathbf{e}' & \vdots & \sigma_{\omega i}^2 \end{bmatrix}\right]. \tag{3.4.10b}$$

In both cases, the conditional density of $\mathbf{u}_i + \mathbf{e}\alpha_i$, given α_i, is[11]

$$\left(2\pi\sigma_u^2\right)^{T/2} \exp\left\{-\frac{1}{2\sigma_u^2}\mathbf{u}_i'\mathbf{u}_i\right\}. \tag{3.4.11}$$

But the marginal density of $\mathbf{u}_i + \mathbf{e}\alpha_i$, given X_i, are different [(3.4.10a) and (3.4.10b), respectively]. Under the independence assumption, $\{\mathbf{u}_i + \mathbf{e}\alpha_i \mid X_i\}$ has a common mean of zero for $i = 1, \ldots, N$. Under the assumption that α_i and X_i are correlated or α_i is a draw from a heterogeneous population, $\{\mathbf{u}_i + \mathbf{e}\alpha_i \mid X_i\}$ has a different mean $\mathbf{e}a_i^*$ for different i.

In the linear regression model, conditional on α_i the Jacobian of transformation from $\mathbf{u}_i + \mathbf{e}\alpha_i$ to $\mathbf{y}_i$ is 1. Maximizing the conditional-likelihood function of $(\mathbf{y}_1 \mid \alpha_1, X_1), \ldots, (\mathbf{y}_N \mid \alpha_N, X_N)$, treating α_i as unknown parameters, yields the covariance (or within-group) estimators for both cases. Maximizing the marginal-likelihood function of $(y_1, \ldots, y_N \mid X_1, \ldots, X_N)$ yields the GLS estimator (3.3.12) for (3.4.10a) if σ_u^2 and σ_α^2 are known, and it happens to yield the covariance estimator for (3.4.10b) in the linear case. In other words, there is no loss of information using a conditional approach for the case of (3.4.10b). However, there is a loss in efficiency in maximizing the conditional-likelihood function for the former case [i.e., (3.4.10a)] because of the loss of degrees of freedom in estimating additional unknown parameters $(\alpha_1, \ldots, \alpha_N)$, which leads to ignoring the information contained in the between-group variation.

The advantage of the unconditional inference is that the likelihood function may only depend on a finite number of parameters and hence can often lead to efficient inference. The disadvantage is that the correct specification of the conditional density of $\mathbf{y}_i$ given $\mathbf{X}_i$,

$$f(\mathbf{y}_i \mid X_i) = \int f(\mathbf{y}_i \mid X_i, \alpha_i) f(\alpha_i \mid X_i)\, d\alpha_i, \tag{3.4.12}$$

depends on the correct specification of $f(\alpha_i \mid X_i)$. A misspecified $f(\alpha_i \mid X_i)$ can lead to a misspecified $f(\mathbf{y}_i \mid X_i)$. Maximizing the wrong $f(\mathbf{y}_i \mid X_i)$ can lead to biased and inconsistent estimators. The bias of the GLS estimator (3.3.12) in the case that $\alpha_i \sim N(a_i^*, \sigma_{\omega i}^2)$ is not due to any fallacy of the unconditional inference, but due to the misspecification of $f(\alpha_i \mid X_i)$.

The advantage of the conditional inference is that there is no need to specify $f(\alpha_i \mid X_i)$. Therefore, if the distribution of effects cannot be represented by a simple parametric functional form (say bimodal), or one is not sure of the correlation pattern between the effects and X_i, there may be an advantage in basing one's inference conditionally. In the situation that there are fundamental differences between the effects (for instance, if there are fundamental differences in the ability, years of experiences, etc., as in the previous of example of technicians), then it is more appropriate to treat the technicians' effects as fixed.

The disadvantage of the conditional inference is that not only there is a loss of efficiency due to the loss of degrees of freedom of estimating the effects, there is also an issue of incidental parameters if T is finite (Neyman and Scott (1948)). A typical panel contains a large number of individuals observed over a short time period; the number of individual effects parameters (α_i^*) increases with the number of cross-sectional dimension, N. Because increase in N provides no information on a particular α_i^* apart from that already contained in $\mathbf{y}_i$, α_i^* cannot be consistently estimated with finite T. The condition that, in general,

$$E(u_{it} \mid \mathbf{x}_{it}) = 0 \tag{3.4.13}$$

is not informative about the common parameters $\boldsymbol{\beta}$ in the absence of any knowledge about α_i^*. If the estimation of the incidental parameters α_i^* is not asymptotically independent of the estimation of the common parameters (called structural parameters in the statistical literature), the conditional inference of the common parameter $\boldsymbol{\beta}$ conditional on the inconsistently estimated α_i^*, in general, will be inconsistent.

In the case of a linear static model (3.2.1) or (3.2.10), the strict exogeneity of $\mathbf{x}_{it}$ to u_{it},

$$E(u_{it} \mid \mathbf{x}_i) = 0, \qquad t = 1, 2, \ldots, T, \tag{3.4.14}$$

where $\mathbf{x}_i' = (\mathbf{x}_{i1}', \ldots, \mathbf{x}_{iT}')$, implies that

$$E(u_{it} - \bar{u}_i \mid \mathbf{x}_i) = E[(y_{it} - \bar{y}_i) - (\mathbf{x}_{it} - \bar{\mathbf{x}}_i)'\boldsymbol{\beta}] = 0, \qquad \begin{aligned} t &= 1, 2, \ldots, T, \\ i &= 1, \ldots, N. \end{aligned} \tag{3.4.15}$$

Since $\boldsymbol{\beta}$ can be identified from the moment conditions of the form (3.4.15) in the linear static model and (3.4.15) no longer involves α_i^*, consistent estimators of $\boldsymbol{\beta}$ can be proposed by making use of these moment conditions (e.g., (3.2.8)). Unfortunately, for nonlinear panel data models, it is in general not possible to find moment conditions that are independent of α_i^* to provide consistent estimators of common parameters.

The advantage of fixed-effects inference is that there is no need to assume that the effects are independent of $\mathbf{x}_i$. The disadvantage is that it introduces the issue of incidental parameters. The advantage of random-effects inference is that the number of parameters is fixed and efficient estimation methods can be derived. The disadvantage is that one has to make specific assumptions about the pattern of correlation (or no correlation) between the effects and the included explanatory variables.

Finally, it should be noted that the assumption of randomness does not carry with it the assumption of normality. Often this assumption is made for random effects, but it is a separate assumption made subsequent to the randomness assumption. Most estimation procedures do not require normality, although if distributional properties of the resulting estimators are to be investigated, then normality is often assumed.

3.5 TESTS FOR MISSPECIFICATION

As discussed in Section 3.4, the issue is not whether α_i is fixed or random. The issue is whether or not α_i can be viewed as random draws from a common population or whether the conditional distribution of α_i given $\mathbf{x}_i$ can be viewed as identical across i. In the linear-regression framework, treating α_i as fixed in (3.2.10) leads to the identical estimator of $\boldsymbol{\beta}$ whether α_i is correlated with $\mathbf{x}_i$ as in (3.4.3) or is from a heterogeneous population. Hence, for ease of reference, when α_i is correlated with $\mathbf{x}_i$, we shall follow the convention and call (3.2.10) a fixed-effects model, and when α_i is uncorrelated with $\mathbf{x}_i$, we shall call it a random-effects model.

Thus, one way to decide whether to use a fixed-effects or a random-effects model is to test for misspecification of (3.3.3), where α_i is assumed random and uncorrelated with $\mathbf{x}_i$. Using Mundlak's formulation, (3.4.3a) or (3.4.3b), this test can be reduced to a test of

$$H_0 : \mathbf{a} = \mathbf{0}$$

against

$$H_1 : \mathbf{a} \neq \mathbf{0}.$$

If the alternative hypothesis H_1 holds, we use the fixed-effects model (3.2.1). If the null hypothesis H_0 holds, we use the random-effects model (3.3.3). The ratio

$$F = \frac{\left(\dfrac{\sum_{i=1}^N (\mathbf{y}_i - \tilde{X}_i \hat{\boldsymbol{\delta}}_{\text{GLS}})' V^{*-1} (\mathbf{y}_i - \tilde{X}_i \hat{\boldsymbol{\delta}}_{\text{GLS}}) - \sum_{i=1}^N (\mathbf{y}_i - \tilde{X}_i \hat{\boldsymbol{\delta}}^*_{\text{GLS}} - \mathbf{e}\bar{\mathbf{x}}'_i \hat{\mathbf{a}}^*_{\text{GLS}})' V^{*-1} \cdot (\mathbf{y}_i - \tilde{X}_i \hat{\boldsymbol{\delta}}^*_{\text{GLS}} - \mathbf{e}\bar{\mathbf{x}}'_i \hat{\mathbf{a}}^*_{\text{GLS}})}{K} \right)}{\left(\dfrac{\sum_{i=1}^N (\mathbf{y}_i - \tilde{X}_i \hat{\boldsymbol{\delta}}^*_{\text{GLS}} - \mathbf{e}\bar{\mathbf{x}}'_i \hat{\mathbf{a}}^*_{\text{GLS}})' V^{*-1} (\mathbf{y}_i - \tilde{X}_i \hat{\boldsymbol{\delta}}^*_{\text{GLS}} - \mathbf{e}\bar{\mathbf{x}}'_i \hat{\mathbf{a}}^*_{\text{GLS}})}{NT - (2K+1)} \right)} \tag{3.5.1}$$

under H_0 has a central F distribution with K and $NT - (2K+1)$ degrees of freedom, where $V^{*-1} = (1/\sigma_u^2)[Q + \psi^*(1/T)\mathbf{e}\mathbf{e}']$, $\psi^* = \sigma_u^2/(\sigma_u^2 + T\sigma_\omega^2)$. Hence, (3.5.1) can be used to test H_0 against H_1.[12]

An alternative testing procedure suggested by Hausman (1978) notes that under H_0 the GLS for (3.3.3) achieves the Cramer–Rao lower bounds, but under H_1, the GLS is a biased estimator. In contrast, the CV of $\boldsymbol{\beta}$ is consistent under both H_0 and H_1. Hence, the Hausman test basically asks if the CV and GLS estimates of $\boldsymbol{\beta}$ are significantly different.

To derive the asymptotic distribution of the differences of the two estimates, Hausman makes use of the following lemma:[13]

Lemma 3.5.1. *Based on a sample of N observations, consider two estimates $\hat{\boldsymbol{\beta}}_0$ and $\hat{\boldsymbol{\beta}}_1$ that are both consistent and asymptotically normally distributed, with $\hat{\boldsymbol{\beta}}_0$ attaining the asymptotic Cramer–Rao bound so that $\sqrt{N}(\hat{\boldsymbol{\beta}}_0 - \boldsymbol{\beta})$ is asymptotically normally distributed with variance–covariance matrix V_0. Suppose $\sqrt{N}(\hat{\boldsymbol{\beta}}_1 - \boldsymbol{\beta})$ is asymptotically normally distributed, with mean zero and variance–covariance matrix V_1. Let $\hat{\mathbf{q}} = \hat{\boldsymbol{\beta}}_1 - \hat{\boldsymbol{\beta}}_0$. Then the limiting distribution of $\sqrt{N}(\hat{\boldsymbol{\beta}}_0 - \boldsymbol{\beta})$ and $\sqrt{N}\hat{\mathbf{q}}$ has zero covariance: $C(\hat{\boldsymbol{\beta}}_0, \hat{\mathbf{q}}) = \mathbf{0}$, a zero matrix.*

From this lemma, it follows that $\text{Var}(\hat{\mathbf{q}}) = \text{Var}(\hat{\boldsymbol{\beta}}_1) - \text{Var}(\hat{\boldsymbol{\beta}}_0)$. Thus, Hausman suggests using the statistic[14]

$$m = \hat{\mathbf{q}}' \,\text{Var}(\hat{\mathbf{q}})^{-1} \hat{\mathbf{q}}, \tag{3.5.2}$$

where $\hat{\mathbf{q}} = \hat{\boldsymbol{\beta}}_{\text{CV}} - \hat{\boldsymbol{\beta}}_{\text{GLS}}$, $\text{Var}(\hat{\mathbf{q}}) = \text{Var}(\hat{\boldsymbol{\beta}}_{\text{CV}}) - \text{Var}(\hat{\boldsymbol{\beta}}_{\text{GLS}})$, to test the null hypothesis $E(\alpha_i \mid X_i) = 0$ against the alternative $E(\alpha_i \mid X_i) \neq 0$. Under the null hypothesis, this statistic is distributed asymptotically as central chi-square, with K degrees of freedom. Under the alternative, it has a noncentral chi-square distribution with noncentrality parameter $\bar{\mathbf{q}}' \operatorname{Var}(\hat{\mathbf{q}})^{-1}\bar{\mathbf{q}}$, where $\bar{\mathbf{q}} = \operatorname{plim}(\hat{\boldsymbol{\beta}}_{CV} - \hat{\boldsymbol{\beta}}_{GLS})$.

When N is fixed and T tends to infinity, $\hat{\boldsymbol{\beta}}_{CV}$ and $\hat{\boldsymbol{\beta}}_{GLS}$ become identical. However, it was shown by Ahn and Moon (2001) that the numerator and denominator of (3.5.2) approach zero at the same speed. Therefore the ratio remains chi-square distributed. However, in this situation the fixed-effects and random-effects models become indistinguishable for all practical purposes. The more typical case in practice is that N is large relative to T, so that differences between the two estimators or two approaches are important problems.

We can use either (3.5.1) or (3.5.2) to test whether a fixed-effects or a random-effects formulation is more appropriate for the wage equation cited at the beginning of Section 3.4 (Table 3.3). The chi-square statistic for (3.5.2) computed by Hausman (1978) is 129.9. The critical value for the 1 percent significance level at 10 degrees of freedom is 23.2, a very strong indication of misspecification in the conventional random-effects model (3.3.3). Similar conclusions are also obtained by using (3.5.1). The F value computed by Hausman (1978) is 139.7, which well exceeds the 1 percent critical value. These tests imply that in the Michigan survey, important individual effects are present that are correlated with the right-hand variables. Because the random-effects estimates appear to be significantly biased with high probability, it may well be important to take account of permanent unobserved differences across individuals in estimating earnings equations using panel data.

3.6 MODELS WITH SPECIFIC VARIABLES AND BOTH INDIVIDUAL- AND TIME-SPECIFIC EFFECTS

3.6.1 Estimation of Models with Individual-Specific Variables

Model (3.2.10) can be generalized in a number of different directions with no fundamental change in the analysis. For instance, we can include a $1 \times p$ vector $\mathbf{z}_i'$ of individual-specific variables (such as sex, race, socioeconomic-background variables, which vary across individual units but do not vary over time) in the specification of the equation for y_{it} and consider

$$\begin{aligned}\underset{T\times 1}{\mathbf{y}_i} &= \underset{T\times 1}{\mathbf{e}}\,\underset{1\times 1}{\mu} + \underset{T\times p}{Z_i}\,\underset{p\times 1}{\boldsymbol{\gamma}} + \underset{T\times K}{X_i}\,\underset{K\times 1}{\boldsymbol{\beta}} \\ &\quad + \underset{T\times 1}{\mathbf{e}}\,\underset{1\times 1}{\alpha_i} + \underset{T\times 1}{\mathbf{u}_i}, \qquad i = 1, \ldots, N, \end{aligned} \tag{3.6.1}$$

where

$$Z_i = \underset{T\times 1}{\mathbf{e}}\,\underset{1\times p}{\mathbf{z}_i'}.$$

If we assume that the α_i are fixed constants, model (3.6.1) is subject to perfect multicollinearity because $Z = (Z_1', \ldots, Z_N')'$ and $(I_N \otimes \mathbf{e})$ are perfectly correlated.[15] Hence, $\boldsymbol{\gamma}$, μ, and α_i are not separately estimable. However, $\boldsymbol{\beta}$ may still be estimated by the covariance method (provided $\sum_{i=1}^{N} X_i' Q X_i$ is of full rank). Premultiplying (3.6.1) by the (covariance) transformation matrix Q [(3.2.6)], we sweep out Z_i, $\mathbf{e}\mu$, and $\mathbf{e}\alpha_i$ from (3.6.1), so that

$$Q\mathbf{y}_i = QX_i\boldsymbol{\beta} + Q\mathbf{u}_i, \qquad i = 1, \ldots, N. \tag{3.6.2}$$

Applying OLS to (3.6.2), we obtain the CV estimate of $\boldsymbol{\beta}$, (3.2.8).

When the α_i are assumed random and uncorrelated with X_i and Z_i, CV uses the same method to estimate $\boldsymbol{\beta}$ (3.2.8). To estimate $\boldsymbol{\gamma}$, we note that the individual mean over time satisfies

$$\bar{y}_i - \bar{\mathbf{x}}_i'\boldsymbol{\beta} = \mu + \mathbf{z}_i'\boldsymbol{\gamma} + \alpha_i + \bar{u}_i, \qquad i = 1, \ldots, N. \tag{3.6.3}$$

Treating $(\alpha_i + \bar{u}_i)$ as the error term and minimizing $\sum_{i=1}^{N}(\alpha_i + \bar{u}_i)^2$, we obtain

$$\hat{\boldsymbol{\gamma}} = \left[\sum_{i=1}^{N}(\mathbf{z}_i - \bar{\mathbf{z}})(\mathbf{z}_i - \bar{\mathbf{z}})'\right]^{-1} \left\{\sum_{i=1}^{N}(\mathbf{z}_i - \bar{\mathbf{z}})[(\bar{y}_i - \bar{y}) - (\bar{\mathbf{x}}_i - \bar{\mathbf{x}})'\boldsymbol{\beta}]\right\}, \tag{3.6.4}$$

$$\hat{\mu} = \bar{y} - \bar{\mathbf{x}}'\boldsymbol{\beta} - \bar{\mathbf{z}}'\hat{\boldsymbol{\gamma}}, \tag{3.6.5}$$

where

$$\bar{\mathbf{z}} = \frac{1}{N}\sum_{i=1}^{N}\mathbf{z}_i, \qquad \bar{\mathbf{x}} = \frac{1}{N}\sum_{i=1}^{N}\bar{\mathbf{x}}_i, \qquad \bar{y} = \frac{1}{N}\sum_{i=1}^{N}\bar{y}_i.$$

Substituting the CV estimate of $\boldsymbol{\beta}$ into (3.6.4) and (3.6.5), we obtain estimators of $\boldsymbol{\gamma}$ and μ. When N tends to infinity, this two-step procedure is consistent. When N is fixed and T tends to infinity, $\boldsymbol{\beta}$ can still be consistently estimated by (3.2.8). But $\boldsymbol{\gamma}$ can no longer be consistently estimated, because when N is fixed, we have a limited amount of information on α_i and $\mathbf{z}_i$. To see this, note that the OLS estimate of (3.6.3) after substituting $\text{plim}_{T\to\infty}\hat{\boldsymbol{\beta}}_{\text{CV}} = \boldsymbol{\beta}$ converges to

$$\begin{aligned}\hat{\boldsymbol{\gamma}}_{\text{OLS}} = \boldsymbol{\gamma} &+ \left[\sum_{i=1}^{N}(\mathbf{z}_i - \bar{\mathbf{z}})(\mathbf{z}_i - \bar{\mathbf{z}})'\right]^{-1}\left[\sum_{i=1}^{N}(\mathbf{z}_i - \bar{\mathbf{z}})(\alpha_i - \bar{\alpha})\right] \\ &+ \left[T\sum_{i=1}^{N}(\mathbf{z}_i - \bar{\mathbf{z}})(\mathbf{z}_i - \bar{\mathbf{z}})'\right]^{-1}\left[\sum_{i=1}^{N}\sum_{t=1}^{T}(\mathbf{z}_i - \bar{\mathbf{z}})(u_{it} - \bar{u})\right],\end{aligned} \tag{3.6.6}$$

where

$$\bar{u} = \frac{1}{NT}\sum_{i=1}^{N}\sum_{t=1}^{T}u_{it}, \qquad \bar{\alpha} = \frac{1}{N}\sum_{i=1}^{N}\alpha_i.$$

It is clear that

$$\underset{T\to\infty}{\text{plim}}\frac{1}{N}\sum_{i=1}^{N}(\mathbf{z}_i - \bar{\mathbf{z}})\frac{1}{T}\sum_{t=1}^{T}(u_{it} - \bar{u}) = 0,$$

but $(1/N)\sum_{i=1}^{N}(\mathbf{z}_i - \bar{\mathbf{z}})(\alpha_i - \bar{\alpha})$ is a random variable, with mean zero and covariance $\sigma_\alpha^2[\sum_{i=1}^{N}(\mathbf{z}_i - \bar{\mathbf{z}})(\mathbf{z}_i - \bar{\mathbf{z}})'/N^2] \neq 0$ for finite N, so that the second term in (3.6.6) does not have zero plim.

When α_i are random and uncorrelated with X_i and Z_i, the CV is not the BLUE. The BLUE of (3.6.1) is the GLS estimator

$$\begin{bmatrix} \hat{\mu} \\ \hat{\boldsymbol{\gamma}} \\ \hat{\boldsymbol{\beta}} \end{bmatrix} = \begin{bmatrix} NT\psi & NT\psi\bar{\mathbf{z}}' & NT\psi\bar{\mathbf{x}}' \\ NT\psi\bar{\mathbf{z}} & T\psi\sum_{i=1}^{N}\mathbf{z}_i\mathbf{z}_i' & T\psi\sum_{i=1}^{N}\mathbf{z}_i\bar{\mathbf{x}}_i' \\ NT\psi\bar{\mathbf{x}} & T\psi\sum_{i=1}^{N}\bar{\mathbf{x}}_i\mathbf{z}_i' & \sum_{i=1}^{N}X_i'QX_i + \psi T\sum_{i=1}^{N}\bar{\mathbf{x}}_i\bar{\mathbf{x}}_i' \end{bmatrix}^{-1} \times \begin{bmatrix} NT\psi\bar{y} \\ \psi T\sum_{i=1}^{N}\mathbf{z}_i\bar{y}_i \\ \sum_{i=1}^{N}X_i'Q\mathbf{y}_i + \psi T\sum_{i=1}^{N}\bar{\mathbf{x}}_i\bar{\mathbf{y}}_i \end{bmatrix}. \tag{3.6.7}$$

If ψ in (3.6.7) is unknown, we can substitute a consistent estimate for it. When T is fixed, the GLS is more efficient than the CV. When T tends to infinity, the GLS estimator of $\boldsymbol{\beta}$ converges to the CV estimator; for details, see Lee (1978b).

One way to view (3.6.1) is that by explicitly incorporating time-invariant explanatory variables $\mathbf{z}_i$ we can eliminate or reduce the correlation between α_i and $\mathbf{x}_{it}$. However, if α_i remains correlated with $\mathbf{x}_{it}$ or $\mathbf{z}_i$, the GLS will be a biased estimator. The CV will produce an unbiased estimate of $\boldsymbol{\beta}$, but the OLS estimates of $\boldsymbol{\gamma}$ and μ in (3.6.3) are inconsistent even when N tends to infinity if α_i is correlated with $\mathbf{z}_i$.[16] Thus, Hausman and Taylor (1981) suggested estimating $\boldsymbol{\gamma}$ in (3.6.3) by two-stage least squares, using those elements of $\bar{\mathbf{x}}_i$ that are uncorrelated with α_i as instruments for $\mathbf{z}_i$. A necessary condition to implement this method is that the number of elements of $\bar{\mathbf{x}}_i$ that are uncorrelated with α_i must be greater than the number of elements of $\mathbf{z}_i$ that are correlated with α_i.

3.6.2 Estimation of Models with Both Individual and Time Effects

We can further generalize model (3.6.1) to include time-specific variables and effects. Let

$$y_{it} = \mu + \underset{1\times p}{\mathbf{z}_i'}\underset{p\times 1}{\boldsymbol{\gamma}} + \underset{1\times l}{\mathbf{r}_t'}\underset{l\times 1}{\boldsymbol{\rho}} + \underset{1\times K}{\mathbf{x}_{it}'}\underset{K\times 1}{\boldsymbol{\beta}} + \alpha_i + \lambda_t + u_{it}, \qquad \begin{array}{l} i = 1, \ldots, N, \\ t = 1, \ldots, T, \end{array} \tag{3.6.8}$$

where $\mathbf{r}_t$ and λ_t denote $l \times 1$ and 1×1 time-specific variables and effects. Stacking (3.6.8) over i and t, we have

$$\underset{NT\times 1}{Y} = \begin{bmatrix} \mathbf{y}_1 \\ \mathbf{y}_2 \\ \vdots \\ \mathbf{y}_N \end{bmatrix} = \begin{bmatrix} \mathbf{e} & Z_1 & R & X_1 \\ \mathbf{e} & Z_2 & R & X_2 \\ \vdots & \vdots & \vdots & \vdots \\ \mathbf{e} & Z_N & R & X_N \end{bmatrix} \begin{bmatrix} \mu \\ \boldsymbol{\gamma} \\ \boldsymbol{\rho} \\ \boldsymbol{\beta} \end{bmatrix} + (I_N \otimes \mathbf{e})\boldsymbol{\alpha} + (\mathbf{e}_N \otimes I_T)\boldsymbol{\lambda} + \begin{bmatrix} \mathbf{u}_1 \\ \mathbf{u}_2 \\ \vdots \\ \mathbf{u}_N \end{bmatrix}, \tag{3.6.9}$$

where $\boldsymbol{\alpha}' = (\alpha_1, \ldots, \alpha_N)$, $\boldsymbol{\lambda}' = (\lambda_1 \ldots, \lambda_T)$, $R' = (\mathbf{r}_1, \mathbf{r}_2, \ldots, \mathbf{r}_T)$, $\mathbf{e}_N$ is an $N \times 1$ vector of ones, and $\otimes$ denotes the Kronecker product.

If $\boldsymbol{\alpha}$ and $\boldsymbol{\lambda}$ are treated as fixed constants, there is a multicollinearity problem, for the same reasons stated in Section 3.6.1. The coefficients $\boldsymbol{\alpha}$, $\boldsymbol{\lambda}$, $\boldsymbol{\gamma}$, $\boldsymbol{\rho}$, and μ cannot be separately estimated. The coefficient $\boldsymbol{\beta}$ can still be estimated by the covariance method. Using the $NT \times NT$ (covariance) transformation matrix

$$\tilde{Q} = I_{NT} - I_N \otimes \frac{1}{T}\mathbf{e}\mathbf{e}' - \frac{1}{N}\mathbf{e}_N\mathbf{e}_N' \otimes I_T + \frac{1}{NT}J, \tag{3.6.10}$$

where J is an $NT \times NT$ matrix of ones, we can sweep out μ, $\mathbf{z}_i$, $\mathbf{r}_t$, α_i, and λ_t and estimate $\boldsymbol{\beta}$ by

$$\hat{\boldsymbol{\beta}}_{\text{CV}} = [(X_1', \ldots, X_N')\tilde{Q}(X_1', \ldots, X_N')']^{-1}[(X_1', \ldots, X_N')\tilde{Q}Y]. \tag{3.6.11}$$

If α_i and λ_t are random, we can still estimate $\boldsymbol{\beta}$ by the covariance method. To estimate μ, $\boldsymbol{\gamma}$, and $\boldsymbol{\rho}$, we note that the individual-mean (over time) and time-mean (over individuals) equations are of the form

$$\bar{y}_i - \bar{\mathbf{x}}_i'\boldsymbol{\beta} = \mu_c^* + \mathbf{z}_i'\boldsymbol{\gamma} + \alpha_i + \bar{u}_i, \qquad i = 1, \ldots, N, \tag{3.6.12}$$

$$\bar{y}_t - \bar{\mathbf{x}}_t'\boldsymbol{\beta} = \mu_T^* + \mathbf{r}_t'\boldsymbol{\rho} + \lambda_t + \bar{u}_t, \qquad t = 1, \ldots, T, \tag{3.6.13}$$

where

$$\mu_c^* = \mu + \bar{\mathbf{r}}'\boldsymbol{\rho} + \bar{\lambda}, \tag{3.6.14}$$

$$\mu_T^* = \mu + \bar{\mathbf{z}}'\boldsymbol{\gamma} + \bar{\alpha}, \tag{3.6.15}$$

and

$$\bar{\mathbf{r}} = \frac{1}{T}\sum_{t=1}^{T}\mathbf{r}_t, \quad \bar{\mathbf{z}} = \frac{1}{N}\sum_{i=1}^{N}\mathbf{z}_i, \quad \bar{\lambda} = \frac{1}{T}\sum_{t=1}^{T}\lambda_t, \quad \bar{\alpha} = \frac{1}{N}\sum_{i=1}^{N}\alpha_i,$$

$$\bar{y}_t = \frac{1}{N}\sum_{i=1}^{N}y_{it}, \quad \bar{\mathbf{x}}_t = \frac{1}{N}\sum_{i=1}^{N}\mathbf{x}_{it}, \quad \bar{u}_t = \frac{1}{N}\sum_{i=1}^{N}u_{it}.$$

Replacing $\boldsymbol{\beta}$ by $\hat{\boldsymbol{\beta}}_{\text{CV}}$, we can estimate $(\mu_c^*, \boldsymbol{\gamma}')$ and $(\mu_T^*, \boldsymbol{\rho}')$ by applying OLS to (3.6.12) and (3.6.13) over i and t, respectively, if α_i and λ_t are uncorrelated with $\mathbf{z}_i$, $\mathbf{r}_t$, and $\mathbf{x}_{it}$. To estimate μ, we can substitute estimated values of $\boldsymbol{\gamma}$, $\boldsymbol{\rho}$, and $\boldsymbol{\beta}$ into any of

$$\hat{\mu} = \hat{\mu}_c^* - \bar{\mathbf{r}}'\hat{\boldsymbol{\rho}}, \tag{3.6.16}$$

$$\hat{\mu} = \hat{\mu}_T^* - \bar{\mathbf{z}}'\hat{\boldsymbol{\gamma}}, \tag{3.6.17}$$

$$\hat{\mu} = \bar{y} - \bar{\mathbf{z}}'\hat{\boldsymbol{\gamma}} - \bar{\mathbf{r}}'\hat{\boldsymbol{\rho}} - \bar{\mathbf{x}}'\hat{\boldsymbol{\beta}}, \tag{3.6.18}$$

or apply the least-squares method to the combined equations (3.6.16)–(3.6.18). When both N and T go to infinity, $\hat{\mu}$ is consistent.

If α_i and λ_t are random and uncorrelated with $\mathbf{z}_i$, $\mathbf{r}_t$, and $\mathbf{x}_{it}$, the BLUE is the GLS estimator. Assuming α_i and λ_t satisfy (3.3.2), the $NT \times NT$ variance–covariance matrix of the error term, $\mathbf{u} + (I_N \otimes \mathbf{e})\boldsymbol{\alpha} + (\mathbf{e}_N \otimes I_T)\boldsymbol{\lambda}$, is

$$\tilde{V} = \sigma_u^2 I_{NT} + \sigma_\alpha^2 I_N \otimes \mathbf{e}\mathbf{e}' + \sigma_\lambda^2 \mathbf{e}_N \mathbf{e}_N' \otimes I_T. \tag{3.6.19}$$

Its inverse (Henderson (1971); Nerlove (1971b); Wallace and Hussain (1969)) (see Appendix 3B) is

$$\tilde{V}^{-1} = \frac{1}{\sigma_u^2}[I_{NT} - \eta_1 I_N \otimes \mathbf{e}\mathbf{e}' - \eta_2 \mathbf{e}_N \mathbf{e}_N' \otimes I_T + \eta_3 J], \tag{3.6.20}$$

where

$$\eta_1 = \frac{\sigma_\alpha^2}{\sigma_u^2 + T\sigma_\alpha^2}, \qquad \eta_2 = \frac{\sigma_\lambda^2}{\sigma_u^2 + N\sigma_\lambda^2},$$

$$\eta_3 = \frac{\sigma_\alpha^2 \sigma_\lambda^2}{(\sigma_u^2 + T\sigma_\alpha^2)(\sigma_u^2 + N\sigma_\lambda^2)} \left(\frac{2\sigma_u^2 + T\sigma_\alpha^2 + N\sigma_\lambda^2}{\sigma_u^2 + T\sigma_\alpha^2 + N\sigma_\lambda^2} \right).$$

When $N \to \infty$, $T \to \infty$, and the ratio N/T tends to a nonzero constant, Wallace and Hussain (1969) have shown that the GLS estimator converges to the CV estimator. It should also be noted that, contrary to the conventional linear-regression model without specific effects, the speed of convergence of $\boldsymbol{\beta}_{\text{GLS}}$ to $\boldsymbol{\beta}$ is $(NT)^{1/2}$, whereas the speed of convergence for μ is $N^{1/2}$. This is because the effect of a random component can be averaged out only in the direction of that random component. For details, see Kelejian and Stephan (1983).

For the discussion of the MLE of the two-way error components models, see Baltagi (1995) and Baltagi and Li (1992).

3.7 HETEROSCEDASTICITY

So far we have confined our discussion to the assumption that the variances of the errors across individuals are identical. However, many panel studies involve cross-sectional units of varying size. In an error-components setup, heteroscedasticity can arise because the variance $\sigma_{\alpha i}^2$ of α_i varies with i

(e.g., Mazodier and Trognon (1978); Baltagi and Griffin (1983)), or the variance σ_{ui}^2 of u_{it} varies with i, or both $\sigma_{\alpha i}^2$ and σ_{ui}^2 vary with i. Then

$$E\mathbf{v}_i\mathbf{v}_i' = \sigma_{ui}^2 I_T + \sigma_{\alpha i}^2 \mathbf{e}\mathbf{e}' = V_i. \tag{3.7.1}$$

The V_i^{-1} is of the same form as (3.3.5) with σ_{ui}^2 and $\sigma_{\alpha i}^2$ in place of σ_u^2 and σ_α^2. The GLS estimator of $\boldsymbol{\delta}$ is obtained by replacing V by V_i in (3.3.7).

When σ_{ui}^2 and $\sigma_{\alpha i}^2$ are unknown, by replacing the unknown true values with their estimates, a feasible (or two-step) GLS estimator can be implemented. Unfortunately, with a single realization of α_i, there is no way one can get a consistent estimator for $\sigma_{\alpha i}^2$ even when $T \to \infty$. The conventional formula

$$\hat{\sigma}_{\alpha i}^2 = \hat{\bar{v}}_i^2 - \frac{1}{T}\hat{\sigma}_{ui}^2, \qquad i = 1, \ldots, N, \tag{3.7.2}$$

where $\hat{v}_{it}$ is the initial estimate of v_{it} (say, the least-squares or CV estimated residual of (3.3.3)), converges to α_i^2, not $\sigma_{\alpha i}^2$. However, σ_{ui}^2 can be consistently estimated by

$$\hat{\sigma}_{ui}^2 = \frac{1}{T-1}\sum_{t=1}^{T}(\hat{v}_{it} - \hat{\bar{v}}_i)^2, \tag{3.7.3}$$

as T tends to infinity. In the event that $\sigma_{\alpha i}^2 = \sigma_\alpha^2$ for all i, we can estimate σ_α^2 by taking the average of (3.7.2) across i as their estimates.

It should be noted that when T is finite, there is no way we can get consistent estimates of σ_{ui}^2 and $\sigma_{\alpha i}^2$ even when N tends to infinity. This is the classical incidental-parameter problem of Neyman and Scott (1948). However, if $\sigma_{\alpha i}^2 = \sigma_\alpha^2$ for all i, then we can get consistent estimates of σ_{ui}^2 and σ_α^2 when both N and T tend to infinity. Substituting $\hat{\sigma}_{ui}^2$ and $\hat{\sigma}_\alpha^2$ for σ_{ui}^2 and σ_α^2 in V_i, we obtain its estimation $\hat{V}_i$. Alternatively, one may assume that the conditional variance of α_i conditional on $\mathbf{x}_i$ has the same functional form across individuals, $\text{Var}(\alpha_i \mid \mathbf{x}_i) = \sigma^2(\mathbf{x}_i)$, to allow for the consistent estimation of heteroscedastic variance, $\sigma_{\alpha i}^2$. The feasible GLS estimator of $\boldsymbol{\delta}$,

$$\hat{\boldsymbol{\delta}}_{\text{FGLS}} = \left[\sum_{i=1}^{N}\tilde{X}_i'\hat{V}_i^{-1}\tilde{X}_i\right]^{-1}\left[\sum_{i=1}^{N}\tilde{X}_i'\hat{V}_i^{-1}\mathbf{y}_i\right] \tag{3.7.4}$$

is asymptotically equivalent to the GLS estimator when both N and T approach to infinity. The asymptotic variance–covariance matrix of the $\hat{\boldsymbol{\delta}}_{\text{FGLS}}$ can be approximated by $(\sum_{i=1}^{N}\tilde{X}_i'\hat{V}_i^{-1}\tilde{X}_i)^{-1}$.

In the case that both $\sigma_{\alpha i}^2$ and σ_{ui}^2 vary across i, another way to estimate the model is to treat α_i as fixed by taking the covariance transformation to eliminate the effect of α_i, then apply feasible weighted least squares method. That is, we first weight each individual observation by the reciprocal of σ_{ui},

$$\mathbf{y}_i^* = \frac{1}{\sigma_{ui}}\mathbf{y}_i, \qquad X_i^* = \frac{1}{\sigma_{ui}}X_i,$$

then apply the covariance estimator to the transformed data

$$\hat{\boldsymbol{\beta}}_{\text{CV}} = \left[\sum_{i=1}^{N} X_i^{*'} Q X_i^*\right]^{-1} \left[\sum_{i=1}^{N} X_i^{*'} Q \mathbf{y}_i^*\right]. \tag{3.7.5}$$

3.8 MODELS WITH SERIALLY CORRELATED ERRORS

The fundamental assumption we made with regard to the variable-intercept model was that the error term is serially uncorrelated conditional on the individual effects α_i. But there are cases in which the effects of unobserved variables vary systematically over time, such as the effect of serially correlated omitted variables or the effects of transitory variables whose effects last more than one period. The existence of these variables is not well described by an error term that is either constant or independently distributed over time periods. To provide for a more general autocorrelation scheme, one can relax the restriction that u_{it} are serially uncorrelated (e.g., Lillard and Weiss (1978, 1979??)).[17] Anderson and Hsiao (1982) have considered the MLE of the model (3.3.3) with u_{it} following a first-order autoregressive process,

$$u_{it} = \rho u_{i,t-1} + \epsilon_{it}, \tag{3.8.1}$$

where ϵ_{it} are independently, identically distributed, with zero mean and variance σ_ϵ^2. However, computation of the MLE is complicated. But if we know ρ, we can transform the model into a standard variance-components model,

$$y_{it} - \rho y_{i,t-1} = \mu(1-\rho) + \boldsymbol{\beta}'(\mathbf{x}_{it} - \rho \mathbf{x}_{i,t-1}) + (1-\rho)\alpha_i + \epsilon_{it}. \tag{3.8.2}$$

Therefore, we can obtain an asymptotically efficient estimator of $\boldsymbol{\beta}$ by the following multistep procedure:

Step 1. Eliminate the individual effect α_i by subtracting the individual mean from (3.3.3). We have

$$y_{it} - \bar{y}_i = \boldsymbol{\beta}'(\mathbf{x}_{it} - \bar{\mathbf{x}}_i) + (u_{it} - \bar{u}_i). \tag{3.8.3}$$

Step 2. Use the least-squares residual of (3.8.3) to estimate the serial correlation coefficient ρ, or use the Durbin (1960) method by regressing $(y_{it} - \bar{y}_i)$ on $(y_{i,t-1} - \bar{y}_{i,-1})$, and $(\mathbf{x}_{i,t-1} - \bar{\mathbf{x}}_{i,-1})$, and treat the coefficient of $(y_{i,t-1} - \bar{y}_{i,-1})$ as the estimated value of ρ, where $\bar{y}_{i,-1} = (1/T)\sum_{t=1}^{T} y_{i,t-1}$ and $\bar{\mathbf{x}}_{i,-1} = (1/T)\sum_{t=1}^{T} \mathbf{x}_{i,t-1}$. (For simplicity, we assume that y_{i0} and x_{i0} are observable.)

Step 3. Estimate σ_ϵ^2 and σ_α^2 by

$$\hat{\sigma}_\epsilon^2 = \frac{1}{NT}\sum_{i=1}^{N}\sum_{t=1}^{T}\{(y_{it}-\bar{y}_i) -(1-\hat{\rho})\hat{\mu} - \hat{\rho}(y_{i,t-1}-\bar{y}_{i,-1}) -\hat{\boldsymbol{\beta}}'[(\mathbf{x}_{it}-\bar{\mathbf{x}}_i)-(\mathbf{x}_{i,t-1}-\bar{\mathbf{x}}_{i,-1})\hat{\rho}]\}^2, \quad (3.8.4)$$

and

$$\hat{\sigma}_\alpha^2 = \frac{1}{(1-\hat{\rho})^2}\cdot\frac{1}{N}\sum_{i=1}^{N}[\bar{y}_i - \hat{\mu}(1-\hat{\rho}) - \hat{\rho}\bar{y}_{i,-1} - \hat{\boldsymbol{\beta}}'(\bar{\mathbf{x}}_i - \bar{\mathbf{x}}_{i,-1}\hat{\rho})]^2 - \frac{1}{T}\hat{\sigma}_\epsilon^2. \quad (3.8.5)$$

Step 4. Substituting $\hat{\rho}$, (3.8.4), and (3.8.5) for ρ, σ_ϵ^2, and σ_α^2 in the variance–covariance matrix of $\epsilon_{it} + (1-\rho)\alpha_i$, we estimate (3.8.2) by the GLS method.

The above multistep or feasible generalized least-squares procedure treats the initial u_{i1} as fixed constants. A more efficient, but computationally more burdensome, feasible GLS is to treat initial u_{i1} as random variables with mean 0 and variance $\sigma_\epsilon^2/(1-\rho^2)$ (e.g., Baltagi and Li (1991)). Premultiplying (3.3.3) by the $T\times T$ transformation matrix

$$R = \begin{pmatrix} (1-\rho^2)^{1/2} & 0 & 0 & \cdots & 0 & 0 \\ -\rho & 1 & 0 & \cdots & 0 & 0 \\ 0 & -\rho & 1 & \cdots & 0 & 0 \\ 0 & 0 & -\rho & \ddots & \vdots & \vdots \\ \vdots & \vdots & \vdots & \ddots & 1 & 0 \\ 0 & 0 & 0 & \cdots & -\rho & 1 \end{pmatrix}$$

transforms $\mathbf{u}_i$ into serially uncorrelated homoscedastic error terms, but also transforms $\mathbf{e}_T\alpha_i$ into $(1-\rho)\boldsymbol{\ell}_T\alpha_i$, where

$$\boldsymbol{\ell}_T = \left[\left(\frac{1+\rho}{1-\rho}\right)^{1/2}, 1, \ldots, 1\right]'.$$

Therefore, the transformed error terms will have covariance matrix

$$V^* = \sigma_\epsilon^2 I_T + (1-\rho)^2\sigma_\alpha^2 \boldsymbol{\ell}_T\boldsymbol{\ell}_T', \quad (3.8.6)$$

with inverse

$$V^{*-1} = \frac{1}{\sigma_\epsilon^2}\left[I_T - \frac{(1-\rho)^2\sigma_\alpha^2}{[T-(T-1)\rho-\rho^2]\sigma_\alpha^2+\sigma_\epsilon^2}\boldsymbol{\ell}_T\boldsymbol{\ell}_T'\right]. \quad (3.8.7)$$

Substituting initial estimates of ρ, σ_α^2, and σ_ϵ^2 into (3.8.7), one can apply the GLS procedure using (3.8.7) to estimate $\boldsymbol{\delta}$.

When T tends to infinity, the GLS estimator of $\boldsymbol{\beta}$ converges to the covariance estimator of the transformed model (3.8.2). In other words, an asymptotically efficient estimator of $\boldsymbol{\beta}$ is obtained by finding a consistent estimate of ρ, transforming the model to eliminate the serial correlation, and then applying the covariance method to the transformed model (3.8.2).

MaCurdy (1982) has considered a similar estimation procedure for (3.3.3) with a more general time-series process of u_{it}. His procedure essentially involves eliminating α_i by first-differencing and treating $y_{it} - y_{i,t-1}$ as the dependent variable. He then modeled the variance–covariance matrix of $\mathbf{u}_i$ by using a standard Box–Jenkins (1970) procedure to model the least-squares predictor of $u_{it} - u_{i,t-1}$, and estimated the parameters by an efficient algorithm.

Kiefer (1980) considered estimation of fixed-effects models of (3.2.1) with arbitrary intertemporal correlations for u_{it}. When T is fixed, the individual effects cannot be consistently estimated. He suggested that we first eliminate the individual effects by transforming the model to the form (3.8.3) using the transformation matrix $Q = I_T - (1/T)\mathbf{ee}'$. Then estimate the intertemporal covariance matrix of $Q\mathbf{u}_i$ by

$$\hat{\Sigma}^* = \frac{1}{N}\sum_{i=1}^{N}[Q(\mathbf{y}_i - X_i\hat{\boldsymbol{\beta}})][Q(\mathbf{y}_i - X_i\hat{\boldsymbol{\beta}})]', \tag{3.8.8}$$

where $\hat{\boldsymbol{\beta}}$ is any arbitrary consistent estimator of $\boldsymbol{\beta}$ (e.g., CV of $\boldsymbol{\beta}$). Given an estimate of $\hat{\Sigma}^*$, one can estimate $\boldsymbol{\beta}$ by the GLS method,

$$\hat{\boldsymbol{\beta}}^* = \left[\sum_{i=1}^{N} X_i' Q\hat{\Sigma}^{*-} QX_i\right]^{-1}\left[\sum_{i=1}^{N} X_i' Q\hat{\Sigma}^{*-} Q\mathbf{y}_i\right], \tag{3.8.9}$$

where $\hat{\Sigma}^{*-}$ is a generalized inverse of Σ^*, because Σ^* has only rank $T-1$. The asymptotic variance–covariance matrix of $\hat{\boldsymbol{\beta}}^*$ is

$$\text{Var}(\hat{\boldsymbol{\beta}}^*) = \left[\sum_{i=1}^{N} X_i' Q\hat{\Sigma}^{*-} QX_i\right]^{-1}. \tag{3.8.10}$$

Although any generalized inverse can be used for $\hat{\Sigma}^*$, a particularly attractive choice is

$$\hat{\Sigma}^{*-} = \begin{bmatrix} \hat{\Sigma}_{T-1}^{*-1} & \mathbf{0} \\ \mathbf{0}' & 0 \end{bmatrix},$$

where $\hat{\Sigma}_{T-1}^*$ is the $(T-1) \times (T-1)$ full-rank submatrix of $\hat{\Sigma}^*$ obtained by deleting the last row and column from $\hat{\Sigma}^*$. Using this generalized inverse simply amounts to deleting the Tth observation from the transformed observations $Q\mathbf{y}_i$ and QX_i, and then applying GLS to the remaining subsample. However, it should be noted that this is not the GLS estimator that would be used if the variance–covariance matrix of $\mathbf{u}_i$ were known.

3.9 MODELS WITH ARBITRARY ERROR STRUCTURE – CHAMBERLAIN π APPROACH

The focus of this chapter is formulation and estimation of linear-regression models when there exist time-invariant and/or individual-invariant omitted (latent) variables. In Sections 3.1–3.7 we have been assuming that the variance–covariance matrix of the error term possesses a known structure. In fact, when N tends to infinity, the characteristics of short panels allow us to exploit the unknown structure of the error process. Chamberlain (1982, 1984) has proposed to treat each period as an equation in a multivariate setup to transform the problems of estimating a single-equation model involving two dimensions (cross sections and time series) into a one-dimensional problem of estimating a T-variate regression model with cross-sectional data. This formulation avoids imposing restrictions a priori on the variance–covariance matrix, so that serial correlation and certain forms of heteroscedasticity in the error process, which covers certain kinds of random-coefficient models (see Chapter 6), can be incorporated. The multivariate setup also provides a link between the single-equation and simultaneous-equations models (see Chapter 5). Moreover, the extended view of the Chamberlain method can also be reinterpreted in terms of the generalized method of moments (GMM) method to be discussed in Chapter 4 (Crépon and Mairesse (1996)).

For simplicity, consider the following model:

$$y_{it} = \alpha_i^* + \boldsymbol{\beta}'\mathbf{x}_{it} + u_{it}, \qquad i = 1, \ldots, N, \quad t = 1, \ldots, T, \tag{3.9.1}$$

and

$$E(u_{it} \mid \mathbf{x}_{i1}, \ldots, \mathbf{x}_{iT}, \alpha_i^*) = 0. \tag{3.9.2}$$

When T is fixed and N tends to infinity, we can stack the T time-period observations of the ith individual's characteristics into a vector $(\mathbf{y}_i', \mathbf{x}_i')$, where $\mathbf{y}_i' = (y_{i1}, \ldots, y_{iT})$ and $\mathbf{x}_i' = (\mathbf{x}_{i1}', \ldots, \mathbf{x}_{iT}')$ are $1 \times T$ and $1 \times KT$ vectors, respectively. We assume that $(\mathbf{y}_i', \mathbf{x}_i')$ is an independent draw from a common (unknown) multivariate distribution function with finite fourth-order moments and with $E\mathbf{x}_i\mathbf{x}_i' = \Sigma_{xx}$ positive definite. Then each individual observation vector corresponds to a T-variate regression

$$\underset{T\times 1}{\mathbf{y}_i} = \mathbf{e}\alpha_i^* + (I_T \otimes \boldsymbol{\beta}')\mathbf{x}_i + \mathbf{u}_i, \qquad i = 1, \ldots, N. \tag{3.9.3}$$

To allow for the possible correlation between α_i^* and $\mathbf{x}_i$, Chamberlain, following the idea of Mundlak (1978a), assumes that

$$E(\alpha_i^* \mid \mathbf{x}_i) = \mu + \sum_{t=1}^{T} \mathbf{a}_t'\mathbf{x}_{it} = \mu + \mathbf{a}'\mathbf{x}_i, \tag{3.9.4}$$

where $\mathbf{a}' = (\mathbf{a}_1', \ldots, \mathbf{a}_T')$. While $E(\mathbf{y}_i \mid \mathbf{x}_i, \alpha_i^*)$ is assumed linear, it is possible to relax the assumption of $E(\alpha_i^* \mid \mathbf{x}_i)$ being linear for the linear model. In the case in which $E(\alpha_i^* \mid \mathbf{x}_i)$ is not linear, Chamberlain (1984) replaces (3.9.4) by

$$E^*(\alpha_i^* \mid \mathbf{x}_i) = \mu + \mathbf{a}'\mathbf{x}_i, \tag{3.9.5}$$

where $E^*(\alpha_i^* \mid \mathbf{x}_i)$ refers to the (minimum-mean-squared-error) linear predictor (or the projection) of α_i^* onto $\mathbf{x}_i$. Then,[18]

$$\begin{aligned} E^*(\mathbf{y}_i \mid \mathbf{x}_i) &= E^*\{E^*(\mathbf{y}_i \mid \mathbf{x}_i, \alpha_i^*) \mid \mathbf{x}_i\} \\ &= E^*\{\mathbf{e}\alpha_i^* + (I_T \otimes \boldsymbol{\beta}')\mathbf{x}_i \mid \mathbf{x}_i\} \\ &= \mathbf{e}\mu + \Pi \mathbf{x}_i, \end{aligned} \tag{3.9.6}$$

where

$$\underset{T\times KT}{\Pi} = I_T \otimes \boldsymbol{\beta}' + \mathbf{e}\mathbf{a}'. \tag{3.9.7}$$

Rewrite equations (3.9.3) and (3.9.6) as

$$\mathbf{y}_i = \mathbf{e}\mu + [I_T \otimes \mathbf{x}_i']\boldsymbol{\pi} + \boldsymbol{\nu}_i, \qquad i = 1, \ldots, N, \tag{3.9.8}$$

where $\boldsymbol{\nu}_i = \mathbf{y}_i - E^*(\mathbf{y}_i \mid \mathbf{x}_i)$ and $\boldsymbol{\pi}' = \text{vec}(\Pi^{*\prime})' = [\boldsymbol{\pi}_1', \ldots, \boldsymbol{\pi}_T']$ is a $1 \times KT^2$ vector with $\boldsymbol{\pi}_t'$ denoting the tth row of Π. Treating the coefficients of (3.9.8) as if they were unconstrained, we regress $(\mathbf{y}_i - \bar{\mathbf{y}})$ on $[I_T \otimes (\mathbf{x}_i - \bar{\mathbf{x}}^*)']$ and obtain the least-squares estimate of $\boldsymbol{\pi}$ as[19]

$$\begin{aligned} \hat{\boldsymbol{\pi}} &= \left\{\sum_{i=1}^{N}[I_T \otimes (\mathbf{x}_i - \bar{\mathbf{x}}^*)][I_T \otimes (\mathbf{x}_i - \bar{\mathbf{x}}^*)']\right\}^{-1} \\ &\quad \times \left\{\sum_{i=1}^{N}[I_T \otimes (\mathbf{x}_i - \bar{\mathbf{x}}^*)](\mathbf{y}_i - \bar{\mathbf{y}})\right\} \\ &= \boldsymbol{\pi} + \left\{\frac{1}{N}\sum_{i=1}^{N}[I_T \otimes (\mathbf{x}_i - \bar{\mathbf{x}}^*)][I_T \otimes (\mathbf{x}_i - \bar{\mathbf{x}}^*)']\right\}^{-1} \\ &\quad \times \left\{\frac{1}{N}\sum_{i=1}^{N}[I_T \otimes (\mathbf{x}_i - \bar{\mathbf{x}}^*)]\boldsymbol{\nu}_i\right\}, \end{aligned} \tag{3.9.9}$$

where $\bar{\mathbf{y}} = (1/N)\sum_{i=1}^{N}\mathbf{y}_i$ and $\bar{\mathbf{x}}^* = (1/N)\sum_{i=1}^{N}\mathbf{x}_i$.

By construction, $E(\boldsymbol{\nu}_i \mid \mathbf{x}_i) = 0$, and $E(\boldsymbol{\nu}_i \otimes \mathbf{x}_i) = 0$. The law of large numbers implies that $\hat{\boldsymbol{\pi}}$ is a consistent estimator of $\boldsymbol{\pi}$ when T is fixed and N tends to infinity (Rao (1973, Chapter 2)). Moreover, because

$$\begin{aligned} \underset{N\to\infty}{\text{plim}}\frac{1}{N}\sum_{i=1}^{N}(\mathbf{x}_i - \bar{\mathbf{x}}^*)(\mathbf{x}_i - \bar{\mathbf{x}}^*)' &= E[\mathbf{x}_i - E\mathbf{x}_i][\mathbf{x}_i - E\mathbf{x}_i]' \\ &= \Sigma_{xx} - (E\mathbf{x})(E\mathbf{x})' = \Phi_{xx}, \end{aligned}$$

we have $\sqrt{N}(\hat{\boldsymbol{\pi}} - \boldsymbol{\pi})$ converging in distribution to (Rao (1973, Chapter 2))

$$\left[I_T \otimes \Phi_{xx}^{-1}\right]\left\{\frac{1}{\sqrt{N}}\sum_{i=1}^{N}[I_T \otimes (\mathbf{x}_i - \bar{\mathbf{x}}^*)]\boldsymbol{\nu}_i\right\}$$

$$= \left[I_T \otimes \Phi_{xx}^{-1}\right]\left\{\frac{1}{\sqrt{N}}\sum_{i=1}^{N}[\boldsymbol{\nu}_i \otimes (\mathbf{x}_i - \bar{\mathbf{x}}^*)]\right\}. \tag{3.9.10}$$

So the central limit theorem implies that $\sqrt{N}(\hat{\boldsymbol{\pi}} - \boldsymbol{\pi})$ is asymptotically normally distributed, with mean zero and variance–covariance matrix Ω, where[20]

$$\Omega = E\big[(\mathbf{y}_i - \mathbf{e}\mu - \Pi\mathbf{x}_i)(\mathbf{y}_i - \mathbf{e}\mu - \Pi\mathbf{x}_i)' \\ \otimes \Phi_{xx}^{-1}(\mathbf{x}_i - E\mathbf{x})(\mathbf{x}_i - E\mathbf{x})'\Phi_{xx}^{-1}\big]. \tag{3.9.11}$$

A consistent estimator of Ω is readily available from the corresponding sample moments,

$$\hat{\Omega} = \frac{1}{N}\sum_{i=1}^{N}\{[(\mathbf{y}_i - \bar{\mathbf{y}}) - \hat{\Pi}(\mathbf{x}_i - \bar{\mathbf{x}}^*)][(\mathbf{y}_i - \bar{\mathbf{y}}) \\ - \hat{\Pi}(\mathbf{x}_i - \bar{\mathbf{x}}^*)]' \otimes S_{xx}^{-1}(\mathbf{x}_i - \bar{\mathbf{x}}^*)(\mathbf{x}_i - \bar{\mathbf{x}}^*)'S_{xx}^{-1}\}, \tag{3.9.12}$$

where

$$S_{xx} = \frac{1}{N}\sum_{i=1}^{N}(\mathbf{x}_i - \bar{\mathbf{x}}^*)(\mathbf{x}_i - \bar{\mathbf{x}}^*)'.$$

Equation (3.9.7) implies that Π is subject to restrictions. Let $\boldsymbol{\theta} = (\boldsymbol{\beta}', \mathbf{a}')$. We specify the restrictions on Π [equation (3.9.7)] by the conditions that

$$\boldsymbol{\pi} = \mathbf{f}(\boldsymbol{\theta}). \tag{3.9.13}$$

We can impose these restrictions by using a minimum-distance estimator. Namely, choose $\hat{\boldsymbol{\theta}}$ to minimize

$$[\hat{\boldsymbol{\pi}} - \mathbf{f}(\boldsymbol{\theta})]'\hat{\Omega}^{-1}[\hat{\boldsymbol{\pi}} - \mathbf{f}(\boldsymbol{\theta})]. \tag{3.9.14}$$

Under the assumptions that $\mathbf{f}$ possesses continuous second partial derivatives, and the matrix of first partial derivatives

$$F = \frac{\partial \mathbf{f}}{\partial \boldsymbol{\theta}'} \tag{3.9.15}$$

has full column rank in an open neighborhood containing the true parameter $\boldsymbol{\theta}$, the minimum-distance estimator $\hat{\boldsymbol{\theta}}$ of (3.9.14) is consistent, and $\sqrt{N}(\hat{\boldsymbol{\theta}} - \boldsymbol{\theta})$ is asymptotically normally distributed, with mean zero and variance–covariance matrix

$$(F'\Omega^{-1}F)^{-1}. \tag{3.9.16}$$

The quadratic form

$$N[\hat{\boldsymbol{\pi}} - \mathbf{f}(\boldsymbol{\theta})]'\hat{\Omega}^{-1}[\hat{\boldsymbol{\pi}} - \mathbf{f}(\boldsymbol{\theta})] \tag{3.9.17}$$

converges to a chi-square distribution with $KT^2 - K(1+T)$ degrees of freedom.[21]

The advantage of the multivariate setup is that we need only to assume that the T period observations of the characteristics of the ith individual are independently distributed across cross-sectional units with finite fourth-order moments. We do not need to make specific assumptions about the error process. Nor do we need to assume that $E(\alpha_i^* \mid \mathbf{x}_i)$ is linear.[22] In the more restrictive case that $E(\alpha_i^* \mid \mathbf{x}_i)$ is indeed linear, [then the regression function is linear, that is, $E(\mathbf{y}_i \mid \mathbf{x}_i) = \mathbf{e}\mu + \Pi\mathbf{x}_i$] and $\text{Var}(\mathbf{y}_i \mid \mathbf{x}_i)$ is uncorrelated with $\mathbf{x}_i\mathbf{x}_i'$, (3.9.12) will converge to

$$E[\text{Var}(\mathbf{y}_i \mid \mathbf{x}_i)] \otimes \Phi_{xx}^{-1}. \tag{3.9.18}$$

If the conditional variance–covariance matrix is homoscedastic, so that $\text{Var}(\mathbf{y}_i \mid \mathbf{x}_i) = \Sigma$ does not depend on $\mathbf{x}_i$, then (3.9.12) will converge to

$$\Sigma \otimes \Phi_{xx}^{-1}. \tag{3.9.19}$$

The Chamberlain procedure of combining all T equations for a single individual into one system, obtaining the matrix of unconstrained linear-predictor coefficients, and then imposing restrictions by using a minimum-distance estimator also has a direct analog in the linear simultaneous-equations model, in which an efficient estimator is provided by applying a minimum-distance procedure to the reduced form (Malinvaud (1970, Chapter 19)). We demonstrate this by considering the standard simultaneous-equations model for the time-series data,[23]

$$\Gamma\mathbf{y}_t + B\mathbf{x}_t = \mathbf{u}_t, \qquad t = 1, \ldots, T, \tag{3.9.20}$$

and its reduced form

$$\mathbf{y}_t = \Pi\mathbf{x}_t + \mathbf{v}_t, \qquad \Pi = -\Gamma^{-1}B, \qquad \mathbf{v}_t = \Gamma^{-1}\mathbf{u}_t, \tag{3.9.21}$$

where Γ, B, and Π are $G \times G$, $G \times K$, and $G \times K$ matrices of coefficients, $\mathbf{y}_t$ and $\mathbf{u}_t$ are $G \times 1$ vectors of observed endogenous variables and unobserved disturbances, respectively, and $\mathbf{x}_t$ is a $K \times 1$ vector of observed exogenous variables. The $\mathbf{u}_t$ are assumed to be serially independent, with bounded variances and covariances.

In general, there are restrictions on Γ and B. We assume that the model (3.9.20) is identified by zero restrictions (e.g., Hsiao (1983)), so that the gth structural equation is of the form

$$y_{gt} = \mathbf{w}_{gt}'\boldsymbol{\theta}_g + v_{gt}, \tag{3.9.22}$$

where the components of $\mathbf{w}_{gt}$ are the variables in $\mathbf{y}_t$ and $\mathbf{x}_t$ that appear in the gth equation with unknown coefficients. Let $\Gamma(\boldsymbol{\theta})$ and $B(\boldsymbol{\theta})$ be parametric representations of Γ and B that satisfy the zero restrictions and the normalization rule, where $\boldsymbol{\theta}' = (\boldsymbol{\theta}'_1, \ldots, \boldsymbol{\theta}'_G)$. Then $\boldsymbol{\pi} = \mathbf{f}(\boldsymbol{\theta}) = \text{vec}\{[-\Gamma^{-1}(\boldsymbol{\theta})B(\boldsymbol{\theta})]'\}$.

Let $\hat{\Pi}$ be the least-squares estimate of Π, and

$$\tilde{\Omega} = \frac{1}{T}\sum_{t=1}^{T}\left[(\mathbf{y}_t - \hat{\Pi}\mathbf{x}_t)(\mathbf{y}_t - \hat{\Pi}\mathbf{x}_t)' \otimes S_x^{*-1}(\mathbf{x}_t\mathbf{x}_t')S_x^{*-1}\right], \tag{3.9.23}$$

where $S_x^* = (1/T)\sum_{t=1}^{T}\mathbf{x}_t\mathbf{x}_t'$. The generalization of the Malinvaud (1970) minimum-distance estimator is to choose $\hat{\boldsymbol{\theta}}$ to

$$\min[\hat{\boldsymbol{\pi}} - \mathbf{f}(\boldsymbol{\theta})]'\tilde{\Omega}^{-1}[\hat{\boldsymbol{\pi}} - \mathbf{f}(\boldsymbol{\theta})]. \tag{3.9.24}$$

Then we have $\sqrt{T}(\hat{\boldsymbol{\theta}} - \boldsymbol{\theta})$ being asymptotically normally distributed, with mean zero and variance–covariance matrix $(F'\tilde{\Omega}^{-1}F)^{-1}$, where $F = \partial\mathbf{f}(\boldsymbol{\theta})/\partial\boldsymbol{\theta}'$.

The formula for $\partial\boldsymbol{\pi}/\partial\boldsymbol{\theta}'$ is given in Rothenberg (1973, p. 69):

$$F = \frac{\partial\boldsymbol{\pi}}{\partial\boldsymbol{\theta}'} = -(\Gamma^{-1} \otimes I_K)\left[\Sigma_{wx}\left(I_G \otimes \Sigma_{xx}^{-1}\right)\right]', \tag{3.9.25}$$

where Σ_{wx} is block-diagonal: $\Sigma_{wx} = \text{diag}\{E(\mathbf{w}_{1t}\mathbf{x}_t'), \ldots, E(\mathbf{w}_{Gt}\mathbf{x}_t')\}$ and $\Sigma_{xx} = E(\mathbf{x}_t\mathbf{x}_t')$. So we have

$$(F'\tilde{\Omega}^{-1}F)^{-1} = \{\Sigma_{wx}[E(\mathbf{u}_t\mathbf{u}_t' \otimes \mathbf{x}_t\mathbf{x}_t')]^{-1}\Sigma_{wx}'\}^{-1}, \tag{3.9.26}$$

If $\mathbf{u}_t\mathbf{u}_t'$ is uncorrelated with $\mathbf{x}_t\mathbf{x}_t'$, then (3.9.26) reduces to

$$\left\{\Sigma_{wx}\left[[E(\mathbf{u}_t\mathbf{u}_t')]^{-1} \otimes \Sigma_{xx}^{-1}\right]\Sigma_{xw}'\right\}^{-1}, \tag{3.9.27}$$

which is the conventional asymptotic covariance matrix for the three-stage least-squares (3SLS) estimator (Zellner and Theil (1962)). If $\mathbf{u}_t\mathbf{u}_t'$ is correlated with $\mathbf{x}_t\mathbf{x}_t'$, then the minimum-distance estimator of $\hat{\boldsymbol{\theta}}$ is asymptotically equivalent to the Chamberlain (1982) generalized 3SLS estimator,

$$\hat{\boldsymbol{\theta}}_{\text{G3SLS}} = (S_{wx}\hat{\Psi}^{-1}S_{wx}')^{-1}(S_{wx}\hat{\Psi}^{-1}\mathbf{s}_{xy}), \tag{3.9.28}$$

where

$$S_{wx} = \text{diag}\left\{\frac{1}{T}\sum_{t=1}^{T}\mathbf{w}_{1t}\mathbf{x}_t', \ldots, \frac{1}{T}\sum_{t=1}^{T}\mathbf{w}_{Gt}\mathbf{x}_t'\right\},$$

$$\hat{\Psi} = \frac{1}{T}\sum_{t=1}^{T}\{\hat{\mathbf{u}}_t\hat{\mathbf{u}}_t' \otimes \mathbf{x}_t\mathbf{x}_t'\}, \qquad \mathbf{s}_{xy} = \frac{1}{T}\sum_{t=1}^{T}\mathbf{y}_t \otimes \mathbf{x}_t,$$

and

$$\hat{\mathbf{u}}_t = \hat{\Gamma}\mathbf{y}_t + \hat{B}\mathbf{x}_t,$$

where $\hat{\Gamma}$ and $\hat{B}$ are any consistent estimators for Γ and B. When certain equations are exactly identified, then just as in the conventional 3SLS case, applying the generalized 3SLS estimator to the system of equations, excluding the exactly identified equations, yields the same asymptotic covariance matrix as the estimator obtained by applying the generalized 3SLS estimator to the full set of G equations.[24]

However, as with any generalization, there is a cost associated with it. The minimum-distance estimator is efficient only relative to the class of estimators that do not impose a priori restrictions on the variance–covariance matrix of the error process. If the error process is known to have an error-component structure, as assumed in previous sections, then the least-squares estimate of Π is not efficient (see Section 5.2), and hence the minimum-distance estimator, ignoring the specific structure of the error process, cannot be efficient, although it remains consistent.[25] The efficient estimator is the GLS estimator. Moreover, computation of the minimum-distance estimator can be quite tedious, whereas the two-step GLS estimation procedure is fairly easy to implement.

APPENDIX 3A: CONSISTENCY AND ASYMPTOTIC NORMALITY OF THE MINIMUM-DISTANCE ESTIMATOR[26]

In this appendix we briefly sketch the proof of consistency and asymptotic normality of the minimum-distance estimator. For completeness we shall state the set of conditions and properties that they imply in general forms.

Let

$$S_N = [\hat{\boldsymbol{\pi}}_N - \mathbf{f}(\boldsymbol{\theta})]' A_N [\hat{\boldsymbol{\pi}}_N - \mathbf{f}(\boldsymbol{\theta})]. \tag{3A.1}$$

Assumption 3A.1. The vector $\hat{\boldsymbol{\pi}}_N$ converges to $\boldsymbol{\pi} = f(\boldsymbol{\theta})$ in probability.[27] The matrix A_N converges to Ψ in probability, where Ψ is positive definite.

Assumption 3A.2. The vector $\boldsymbol{\theta}$ belongs to a compact subset of p-dimensional space. The functions $\mathbf{f}(\boldsymbol{\theta})$ possess continuous second partial derivatives, and the matrix of the first partial derivatives [equation (3.9.15)] has full column rank p in an open neighborhood containing the true parameter $\boldsymbol{\theta}$.

Assumption 3A.3. $\sqrt{N}[\hat{\boldsymbol{\pi}}_N - \mathbf{f}(\boldsymbol{\theta})]$ is asymptotically normally distributed with mean zero and variance–covariance matrix Δ.

The minimum-distance estimator chooses $\hat{\boldsymbol{\theta}}$ to minimize S_N.

Proposition 3A.1. *If Assumptions 3A.1 and 3A.2 are satisfied, $\hat{\boldsymbol{\theta}}$ converges to $\boldsymbol{\theta}$ in probability.*

Proof. Assumption 3A.1 implies that S_N converges to $S = [\mathbf{f}(\boldsymbol{\theta}) - \mathbf{f}(\hat{\boldsymbol{\theta}})]'\Psi \times [\mathbf{f}(\boldsymbol{\theta}) - \mathbf{f}(\hat{\boldsymbol{\theta}})] = h \geq 0$. Because $\min S = 0$ and the rank condition [Assumption 3A.2 or (3.9.15)] implies that in the neighborhood of the true $\boldsymbol{\theta}$, $\mathbf{f}(\boldsymbol{\theta}) = \mathbf{f}(\boldsymbol{\theta}^*)$ if and only if $\boldsymbol{\theta} = \boldsymbol{\theta}^*$ (Hsiao (1983, p. 256)), $\hat{\boldsymbol{\theta}}$ must converge to $\boldsymbol{\theta}$ in probability. Q.E.D.

Proposition 3A.2. *If Assumptions 3A.1–3A.3 are satisfied, $\sqrt{N}(\hat{\boldsymbol{\theta}} - \boldsymbol{\theta})$ is asymptotically normally distributed, with mean zero and variance–covariance matrix*

$$(F'\Psi F)^{-1} F'\Psi\Delta\Psi F(F'\Psi F)^{-1}. \tag{3A.2}$$

Proof. $\hat{\boldsymbol{\theta}}$ is the solution of

$$\mathbf{d}_N(\hat{\boldsymbol{\theta}}) = \frac{\partial S_N}{\partial \boldsymbol{\theta}} = -2\left(\frac{\partial \mathbf{f}'}{\partial \hat{\boldsymbol{\theta}}}\right) A_N[\hat{\boldsymbol{\pi}}_N - \mathbf{f}(\hat{\boldsymbol{\theta}})] = \mathbf{0}. \tag{3A.3}$$

The mean-value theorem implies that

$$\mathbf{d}_N(\hat{\boldsymbol{\theta}}) = \mathbf{d}_N(\boldsymbol{\theta}) + \left(\frac{\partial d_N(\boldsymbol{\theta}^*)}{\partial \boldsymbol{\theta}'}\right)(\hat{\boldsymbol{\theta}} - \boldsymbol{\theta}), \tag{3A.4}$$

where $\boldsymbol{\theta}^*$ is on the line segment connecting $\hat{\boldsymbol{\theta}}$ and $\boldsymbol{\theta}$. Because $\hat{\boldsymbol{\theta}}$ converges to $\boldsymbol{\theta}$, direct evaluation shows that $\partial d_N(\boldsymbol{\theta}^*)/\partial \boldsymbol{\theta}'$ converges to

$$\frac{\partial d_N(\boldsymbol{\theta})}{\partial \boldsymbol{\theta}'} = 2\left(\frac{\partial \mathbf{f}(\boldsymbol{\theta})}{\partial \boldsymbol{\theta}'}\right)' \Psi \left(\frac{\partial \mathbf{f}(\boldsymbol{\theta})}{\partial \boldsymbol{\theta}'}\right) = 2F'\Psi F.$$

Hence, $\sqrt{N}(\hat{\boldsymbol{\theta}} - \boldsymbol{\theta})$ has the same limiting distribution as

$$-\left[\frac{\partial d_N(\boldsymbol{\theta})}{\partial \boldsymbol{\theta}'}\right]^{-1} \cdot \sqrt{N}\mathbf{d}_N(\boldsymbol{\theta}) = (F'\Psi F)^{-1}F'\Psi \cdot \sqrt{N}[\hat{\boldsymbol{\pi}}_N - \mathbf{f}(\boldsymbol{\theta})]. \tag{3A.5}$$

Assumption 3A.3 says that $\sqrt{N}[\hat{\boldsymbol{\pi}} - \mathbf{f}(\boldsymbol{\theta})]$ is asymptotically normally distributed, with mean zero and variance–covariance Δ. Therefore, $\sqrt{N}(\hat{\boldsymbol{\theta}} - \boldsymbol{\theta})$ is asymptotically normally distributed, with mean zero and variance–covariance matrix given by (3A.2). Q.E.D.

Proposition 3A.3. *If Δ is positive definite, then*

$$(F'\Psi F)^{-1}F'\Psi\Delta\Psi F(F'\Psi F)^{-1} - (F'\Delta^{-1}F)^{-1} \tag{3A.6}$$

is positive semidefinite; hence, an optimal choice for Ψ is Δ^{-1}.

Proof. Because Δ is positive definite, there is a nonsingular matrix $\tilde{C}$ such that $\Delta = \tilde{C}\tilde{C}'$. Let $\tilde{F} = \tilde{C}^{-1}F$ and $\tilde{B} = (F'\Psi F)^{-1}F'\Psi\tilde{C}$. Then (3A.6) becomes $\tilde{B}[I - \tilde{F}(\tilde{F}'\tilde{F})^{-1}\tilde{F}']\tilde{B}'$, which is positive semidefinite. Q.E.D.

Proposition 3A.4. *If Assumptions 3A.1–3A.3 are satisfied, if Δ is positive definite, and if A_N converges to Δ^{-1} in probability, then*

$$N[\hat{\boldsymbol{\pi}} - \mathbf{f}(\hat{\boldsymbol{\theta}})]'A_N[\hat{\boldsymbol{\pi}} - \mathbf{f}(\hat{\boldsymbol{\theta}})] \tag{3A.7}$$

converges to a chi-square distribution with $KT^2 - p$ degrees of freedom.

Proof. Taking a Taylor series expansion of $\mathbf{f}(\boldsymbol{\theta})$ around $\boldsymbol{\theta}$, we have

$$\mathbf{f}(\hat{\boldsymbol{\theta}}) \simeq \mathbf{f}(\boldsymbol{\theta}) + \frac{\partial \mathbf{f}(\boldsymbol{\theta})}{\partial \boldsymbol{\theta}'}(\hat{\boldsymbol{\theta}} - \boldsymbol{\theta}). \tag{3A.8}$$

Therefore, for sufficiently large N, $\sqrt{N}[\mathbf{f}(\hat{\boldsymbol{\theta}}) - \mathbf{f}(\boldsymbol{\theta})]$ has the same limiting distribution as $F \cdot \sqrt{N}(\hat{\boldsymbol{\theta}} - \boldsymbol{\theta})$. Thus,

$$\sqrt{N}[\hat{\boldsymbol{\pi}} - \mathbf{f}(\hat{\boldsymbol{\theta}})] = \sqrt{N}[\hat{\boldsymbol{\pi}}_N - \mathbf{f}(\boldsymbol{\theta})] - \sqrt{N}[\mathbf{f}(\hat{\boldsymbol{\theta}}) - \mathbf{f}(\boldsymbol{\theta})] \tag{3A.9}$$

converges in distribution to $Q^*\tilde{C}u^*$, where $Q^* = I_{KT^2} - F(F'\Delta^{-1}F)^{-1} \times F'\Delta^{-1}$, $\tilde{C}$ is a nonsingular matrix such that $\tilde{C}\tilde{C}' = \Delta$, and $\mathbf{u}^*$ is normally distributed, with mean zero and variance–covariance matrix I_{KT^2}. Then the quadratic form (3A.7) converges in distribution to $\mathbf{u}^{*'}\tilde{C}'Q^{*'}\Delta^{-1}Q^*\tilde{C}\mathbf{u}^*$. Let $\tilde{F} = \tilde{C}^{-1}F$ and $M = I_{KT^2} - \tilde{F}(\tilde{F}'\tilde{F})^{-1}\tilde{F}'$; then M is a symmetric idempotent matrix with rank $KT^2 - p$, and $\tilde{C}'Q^{*'}\Delta^{-1}Q^*\tilde{C} = M^2 = M$; hence, (3A.7) converges in distribution to $\mathbf{u}^{*'}M\mathbf{u}^*$, which is chi-square, with $KT^2 - p$ degrees of freedom. Q.E.D.

APPENDIX 3B: CHARACTERISTIC VECTORS AND THE INVERSE OF THE VARIANCE–COVARIANCE MATRIX OF A THREE-COMPONENT MODEL

In this appendix we derive the inverse of the variance–covariance matrix for a three-component model (3.6.19) by means of its characteristic roots and vectors. The material is drawn from the work of Nerlove (1971b).

The matrix $\tilde{V}$ (3.6.19) has three terms, one in I_{NT}, one in $I_N \otimes \mathbf{e}\mathbf{e}'$, and one in $\mathbf{e}_N\mathbf{e}_N' \otimes I_T$. Thus, the vector $(\mathbf{e}_N/\sqrt{N}) \otimes (\mathbf{e}/\sqrt{T})$ is a characteristic vector, with the associated root $\sigma_u^2 + T\sigma_\alpha^2 + N\sigma_\lambda^2$. To find $NT - 1$ other characteristic vectors, we note that we can always find $N - 1$ vectors, $\boldsymbol{\psi}_j$, $j = 1, \ldots, N - 1$, each $N \times 1$, that are orthonormal and orthogonal to $\mathbf{e}_N$:

$$\begin{aligned} \mathbf{e}_N'\boldsymbol{\psi}_j &= 0, \\ \boldsymbol{\psi}_j'\boldsymbol{\psi}_{j'} &= \begin{cases} 1 & \text{if } j = j', \\ 0 & \text{if } j \neq j', \quad j = 1, \ldots, N-1, \end{cases} \end{aligned} \tag{3B.1}$$

and $T - 1$ vectors Φ_k, $k = 1, \ldots, T - 1$, each $T \times 1$, that are orthonormal and orthogonal to $\mathbf{e}$:

$$\begin{aligned} \mathbf{e}'\Phi_k &= 0, \\ \Phi_k'\Phi_{k'} &= \begin{cases} 1 & \text{if } k = k', \\ 0, & \text{if } k \neq k', \quad k = 1, \ldots, T-1. \end{cases} \end{aligned} \tag{3B.2}$$

Then the $(N - 1)(T - 1)$ vectors $\boldsymbol{\psi}_j \otimes \Phi_k$, $j = 1, \ldots, N - 1$, $k = 1, \ldots, T - 1$, the $N - 1$ vectors $\boldsymbol{\psi}_j \otimes (\mathbf{e}/\sqrt{T})$, $j = 1, \ldots, N - 1$, and the $T - 1$ vectors $\mathbf{e}_N/\sqrt{N} \otimes \Phi_k$, $k = 1, \ldots, T - 1$, are also characteristic vectors of $\tilde{V}$, with the associated roots σ_u^2, $\sigma_u^2 + T\sigma_\alpha^2$ and $\sigma_u^2 + N\sigma_\lambda^2$, which are of multiplicity $(N - 1)(T - 1)$, $(N - 1)$, and $(T - 1)$, respectively.

Let

$$\begin{aligned} C_1 &= \frac{1}{\sqrt{T}}[\boldsymbol{\psi}_1 \otimes \mathbf{e}, \ldots, \boldsymbol{\psi}_{N-1} \otimes \mathbf{e}], \\ C_2 &= \frac{1}{\sqrt{N}}[\mathbf{e}_N \otimes \Phi_1, \ldots, \mathbf{e}_N \otimes \Phi_{T-1}], \\ C_3 &= [\boldsymbol{\psi}_1 \otimes \Phi_1, \boldsymbol{\psi}_1 \otimes \Phi_2, \ldots, \boldsymbol{\psi}_{N-1} \otimes \Phi_{T-1}], \\ C_4 &= (\mathbf{e}_N/\sqrt{N}) \otimes (\mathbf{e}/\sqrt{T}) = \frac{1}{\sqrt{NT}}\mathbf{e}_{NT}, \end{aligned} \tag{3B.3}$$

and

$$C = [C_1 \quad C_2 \quad C_3 \quad C_4]. \tag{3B.4}$$

Then,

$$CC' = C_1C_1' + C_2C_2' + C_3C_3' + C_4C_4' = I_{NT}, \tag{3B.5}$$

$$C\tilde{V}C' = \begin{bmatrix} (\sigma_u^2 + T\sigma_\alpha^2)I_{N-1} & \mathbf{0} & \mathbf{0} & \mathbf{0} \\ \mathbf{0} & (\sigma_u^2 + N\sigma_\lambda^2)\,I_{T-1} & \mathbf{0} & \mathbf{0} \\ \mathbf{0} & \mathbf{0} & \sigma_u^2 I_{(N-1)(T-1)} & \mathbf{0} \\ \mathbf{0} & \mathbf{0} & \mathbf{0} & \sigma_u^2 + T\sigma_\alpha^2 + N\sigma_\lambda^2 \end{bmatrix}$$

$$= \Lambda, \tag{3B.6}$$

and

$$\hat{V} = C\Lambda C'.$$

Let $A = I_N \otimes \mathbf{ee}'$, $D = \mathbf{e}_N\mathbf{e}_N' \otimes I_T$, and $J = \mathbf{e}_{NT}\mathbf{e}_{NT}'$. From

$$C_4C_4' = \frac{1}{NT}J, \tag{3B.7}$$

Nerlove (1971b) showed that by premultiplying (3B.5) by A, we have

$$C_1C_1' = \frac{1}{T}A - \frac{1}{NT}J, \tag{3B.8}$$

and premultiplying (3B.5) by D,

$$C_2C_2' = \frac{1}{N}D - \frac{1}{NT}J. \tag{3B.9}$$

Premultiplying (3B.5) by A and D and using the relations (3B.5), (3B.7), (3B.8), and (3B.9), we have

$$C_3C_3' = I_{NT} - \frac{1}{T}A - \frac{1}{N}D + \frac{1}{NT}J = \tilde{Q}. \tag{3B.10}$$

Because $\tilde{V}^{-1} = C\Lambda^{-1}C'$, it follows that

$$\tilde{V}^{-1} = \frac{1}{\sigma_u^2 + T\sigma_\alpha^2}\left(\frac{1}{T}A - \frac{1}{NT}J\right) + \frac{1}{\sigma_u^2 + N\sigma_\lambda^2}\left(\frac{1}{N}D - \frac{1}{NT}J\right)$$
$$+ \frac{1}{\sigma_u^2}\tilde{Q} + \frac{1}{\sigma_u^2 + T\sigma_\alpha^2 + N\sigma_\lambda^2}\left(\frac{1}{NT}J\right). \tag{3B.11}$$

CHAPTER 4

Dynamic Models with Variable Intercepts

4.1 INTRODUCTION

In the last chapter we discussed the implications of treating the specific effects as fixed or random and the associated estimation methods for the linear static model

$$y_{it} = \boldsymbol{\beta}'\mathbf{x}_{it} + \alpha_i^* + \lambda_t + u_{it}, \qquad \begin{array}{l} i = 1, \ldots, N, \\ t = 1, \ldots, T, \end{array} \tag{4.1.1}$$

where $\mathbf{x}_{it}$ is a $K \times 1$ vector of explanatory variables, including the constant term; $\boldsymbol{\beta}$ is a $K \times 1$ vector of constants; α_i^* and λ_t are the (unobserved) individual- and time-specific effects, which are assumed to stay constant for given i over t and for given t over i, respectively; and u_{it} represents the effects of those unobserved variables that vary over i and t. Very often we also wish to use panel data to estimate behavioral relationships that are dynamic in character, namely, models containing lagged dependent variables such as[1]

$$y_{it} = \gamma y_{i,t-1} + \boldsymbol{\beta}'\mathbf{x}_{it} + \alpha_i^* + \lambda_t + u_{it}, \qquad \begin{array}{l} i = 1, \ldots, N, \\ t = 1, \ldots, T, \end{array} \tag{4.1.2}$$

where $Eu_{it} = 0$, and $Eu_{it}u_{js} = \sigma_u^2$ if $i = j$ and $t = s$, and $Eu_{it}u_{js} = 0$ otherwise. It turns out that in this circumstance the choice between a fixed-effects formulation and a random-effects formulation has implications for estimation that are of a different nature than those associated with the static model.

Roughly speaking, two issues have been raised in the literature regarding whether the effects, α_i^* and λ_t, should be treated as random or as fixed for a linear static model, namely, the efficiency of the estimates and the independence between the effects and the regressors [i.e., the validity of the strict exogeneity assumption of the regressors (equation (3.4.1))]; (see, e.g., Maddala (1971a), Mundlak (1978a) and Chapter 3). When all the explanatory variables are exogenous, the covariance estimator is the best linear unbiased estimator under the fixed-effects assumption and a consistent and unbiased estimator under the random-effects assumption, even though it is not efficient when T is fixed.

However, when there exist omitted individual attributes that are correlated with the included exogenous variables, the covariance estimator does not suffer from bias due to omission of these relevant individual attributes, because their effects have been differenced out; but a generalized least-squares estimator for the random-effects model under the assumption of independence between the effects and explanatory variables will be biased. Furthermore, in a linear static model, if the effects are correlated with the explanatory variables, a correctly formulated random-effects model leads to the same covariance estimator (CV) as the fixed-effects model (Mundlak (1978a), also see Section 3.4). Thus, the fixed-effects model has assumed paramount importance in empirical studies (e.g., Ashenfelter (1978); Hausman (1978); Kiefer (1979)).

However, if lagged dependent variables also appear as explanatory variables, strict exogeneity of the regressors no longer holds. The maximum-likelihood estimator (MLE) or the CV under the fixed-effects formulation is no longer consistent in the typical situation in which a panel involves a large number of individuals, but over only a short period of time. The initial values of a dynamic process raise another problem. It turns out that with a random-effects formulation, the interpretation of a model depends on the assumption of initial observation. The consistency property of the MLE and the generalized least-squares estimator (GLS) also depends on this assumption and on the way in which the number of time-series observations (T) and the number of cross-sectional units (N) tend to infinity.

In Section 4.2, we show that the CV (or the least-squares dummy variable) estimator is inconsistent for a panel-dynamic model, whether the effects are treated as fixed or random. Section 4.3 discusses the random-effects model. We discuss the implications of various formulation and methods of estimation. We show that the ordinary least-squares estimator is inconsistent but the MLE, the instrumental variable (IV), and the generalized method of moments (GMM) estimator are consistent. Procedures to test initial conditions are also discussed. In Section 4.4, we use Balestra and Nerlove's model (1966) of demand for natural gas to illustrate the consequences of various assumptions for the estimated coefficients.

Section 4.5 discusses the estimation of fixed-effects dynamic model. We show that although the conventional MLE and CV estimators are inconsistent when T is fixed and N tends to infinity, there exists a transformed likelihood approach that does not involve the incidental parameter and is consistent and efficient under proper formulation of initial conditions. We also discuss the IV and GMM estimators that do not need the formulation of initial conditions. Procedures to test fixed versus random effects are also suggested.

In Section 4.6, we relax the assumption on the specific serial-correlation structure of the error term and propose a system approach to estimating dynamic models. Section 4.7 discusses the estimation of fixed effects vector autoregressive models. For ease of exposition, we assume that the time-specific effects λ_t do not appear.

4.2 THE COVARIANCE ESTIMATOR

The CV estimator is consistent for the static model whether the effects are fixed or random. In this section we show that the CV (or LSDV) is inconsistent for a dynamic panel data model with individual effects, whether the effects are fixed or random.

Consider[2]

$$y_{it} = \gamma y_{i,t-1} + \alpha_i^* + u_{it}, \qquad |\gamma| < 1, \quad \begin{array}{l} i = 1, \ldots, N, \\ t = 1, \ldots, T, \end{array} \tag{4.2.1}$$

where for simplicity we let $\alpha_i^* = \alpha_i + \mu$ to avoid imposing the restriction that $\sum_{i=1}^N \alpha_i = 0$. We also assume that y_{i0} are observable, $Eu_{it} = 0$, and $Eu_{it}u_{js} = \sigma_u^2$ if $i = j$ and $t = s$, and $Eu_{it}u_{js} = 0$ otherwise.

Let $\bar{y}_i = \sum_{t=1}^T y_{it}/T$, $\bar{y}_{i,-1} = \sum_{t=1}^T y_{i,t-1}/T$, and $\bar{u}_i = \sum_{t=1}^T u_{it}/T$. The LSDV estimators for α_i^* and γ are

$$\hat{\alpha}_i^* = \bar{y}_i - \hat{\gamma}_{\text{CV}} \bar{y}_{i,-1}, \qquad i = 1, \ldots, N, \tag{4.2.2}$$

$$\begin{aligned} \hat{\gamma}_{\text{CV}} &= \frac{\sum_{i=1}^N \sum_{t=1}^T (y_{it} - \bar{y}_i)(y_{i,t-1} - \bar{y}_{i,-1})}{\sum_{i=1}^N \sum_{t=1}^T (y_{i,t-1} - \bar{y}_{i,-1})^2} \\ &= \gamma + \frac{\sum_{i=1}^N \sum_{t=1}^T (y_{i,t-1} - \bar{y}_{i,-1})(u_{it} - \bar{u}_i)/NT}{\sum_{i=1}^N \sum_{t=1}^T (y_{i,t-1} - \bar{y}_{i,-1})^2/NT}. \end{aligned} \tag{4.2.3}$$

The CV exists if the denominator of the second term of (4.2.3) is nonzero. It is consistent if the numerator of the second term of (4.2.3) converges to zero.

By continuous substitution, we have

$$y_{it} = u_{it} + \gamma u_{i,t-1} + \cdots + \gamma^{t-1} u_{i1} + \frac{1 - \gamma^t}{1 - \gamma} \alpha_i^* + \gamma^t y_{i0}. \tag{4.2.4}$$

Summing $y_{i,t-1}$ over t, we have

$$\begin{aligned} \sum_{t=1}^T y_{i,t-1} = {} & \frac{1 - \gamma^T}{1 - \gamma} y_{i0} + \frac{(T-1) - T\gamma + \gamma^T}{(1-\gamma)^2} \alpha_i^* \\ & + \frac{1 - \gamma^{T-1}}{1 - \gamma} u_{i1} + \frac{1 - \gamma^{T-2}}{1 - \gamma} u_{i2} + \cdots + u_{i,T-1}. \end{aligned} \tag{4.2.5}$$

Because u_{it} are uncorrelated with α_i^* and are independently and identically distributed, by a law of large numbers (Rao (1973)), and using (4.2.5), we can show that when N tends to infinity,

$$\begin{aligned}\operatorname*{plim}_{N\to\infty} \frac{1}{NT}\sum_{i=1}^{N}\sum_{t=1}^{T}(y_{i,t-1}-\bar{y}_{i,-1})(u_{it}-\bar{u}_i) &= -\operatorname*{plim}_{N\to\infty}\frac{1}{N}\sum_{i=1}^{N}\bar{y}_{i,-1}\bar{u}_i \\ &= -\frac{\sigma_u^2}{T^2}\cdot\frac{(T-1)-T\gamma+\gamma^T}{(1-\gamma)^2}. \end{aligned} \tag{4.2.6}$$

By similar manipulations we can show that the denominator of (4.2.3) converges to

$$\frac{\sigma_u^2}{1-\gamma^2}\left\{1-\frac{1}{T}-\frac{2\gamma}{(1-\gamma)^2}\cdot\frac{(T-1)-T\gamma+\gamma^T}{T^2}\right\}. \tag{4.2.7}$$

If T also tends to infinity, then (4.2.6) converges to zero, and (4.2.7) converges to a nonzero constant $\sigma_u^2/(1-\gamma^2)$; hence, (4.2.2) and (4.2.3) are consistent estimators of α_i^* and γ. If T is fixed, then (4.2.6) is a nonzero constant, and (4.2.2) and (4.2.3) are inconsistent estimators no matter how large N is. The asymptotic bias of the CV of γ is

$$\begin{aligned}\operatorname*{plim}_{N\to\infty}(\hat{\gamma}_{\mathrm{CV}}-\gamma) = &-\frac{1+\gamma}{T-1}\left(1-\frac{1}{T}\frac{1-\gamma^T}{1-\gamma}\right)\\ &\times\left\{1-\frac{2\gamma}{(1-\gamma)(T-1)}\left[1-\frac{1-\gamma^T}{T(1-\gamma)}\right]\right\}^{-1}.\end{aligned} \tag{4.2.8}$$

The bias of $\hat{\gamma}$ is caused by having to eliminate the unknown individual effects α_i^* from each observation, which creates a correlation of order $(1/T)$ between the explanatory variables and the residuals in the transformed model $(y_{it}-\bar{y}_i)=\gamma(y_{i,t-1}-\bar{y}_{i,-1})+(u_{it}-\bar{u}_i)$. When T is large, the right-hand-side variables become asymptotically uncorrelated. For small T, this bias is always negative if $\gamma>0$. Nor does the bias go to zero as γ goes to zero. Because a typical panel usually contains a small number of time-series observations, this bias can hardly be ignored. For instance, when $T=2$, the asymptotic bias is equal to $-(1+\gamma)/2$, and when $T=3$, it is equal to $-(2+\gamma)(1+\gamma)/2$. Even with $T=10$ and $\gamma=0.5$, the asymptotic bias is -0.167.

The CV for dynamic fixed-effects model remains biased with the introduction of exogenous variables if T is small; for details of the derivation, see Anderson and Hsiao (1982) and Nickell (1981); for Monte Carlo studies, see Nerlove (1971a). Fortunately, if the existence of the consistent (or asymptotic unbiased) estimator of the common slope coefficient is a concern, a consistent estimator of γ can be obtained by using instrumental-variable methods or a properly formulated likelihood approach, to be discussed in the following sections.

4.3 RANDOM-EFFECTS MODELS

When the specific effects are treated as random, they can be considered to be either correlated or not correlated with the explanatory variables. In the case in which the effects are correlated with the explanatory variables, ignoring this correlation and simply using the covariance estimator no longer yields the desirable properties as in the case of static regression models. Thus, a more appealing approach here would be to take explicit account of the linear dependence between the effects and the exogenous variables by letting $\alpha_i = \mathbf{a}'\bar{\mathbf{x}}_i + \omega_i$ (Mundlak (1978a)) (see Section 3.4) and use a random-effects framework of the model

$$\mathbf{y}_i = \mathbf{y}_{i,-1}\gamma + X_i\boldsymbol{\beta} + \mathbf{e}\bar{\mathbf{x}}_i'\mathbf{a} + \mathbf{e}\omega_i + \mathbf{u}_i, \tag{4.3.1}$$

where now $E(\mathbf{x}_{it}\omega_i) = \mathbf{0}$, and $E(\mathbf{x}_{it}u_{it}) = \mathbf{0}$. However, because $\bar{\mathbf{x}}_i$ is time-invariant and the (residual) individual effect ω_i possesses the same property as α_i when the assumption $E\alpha_i\mathbf{x}_{it}' = \mathbf{0}'$ holds, the estimation of (4.3.1) is formally equivalent to the estimation of the model

$$\mathbf{y}_i = \mathbf{y}_{i,-1}\gamma + X_i\boldsymbol{\beta} + \mathbf{e}\mathbf{z}_i'\boldsymbol{\rho} + \mathbf{e}\alpha_i + \mathbf{u}_i, \tag{4.3.2}$$

with X_i now denoting the $T \times K_1$ time-varying explanatory variables, $\mathbf{z}_i'$ being the $1 \times K_2$ time-invariant explanatory variables including the intercept term, and $E\alpha_i = 0$, $E\alpha_i\mathbf{z}_i' = \mathbf{0}'$, and $E\alpha_i\mathbf{x}_{it}' = \mathbf{0}'$. So, for ease of exposition, we assume in this section that the effects are uncorrelated with the exogenous variables.[3]

We first show that the ordinary-least-squares (OLS) estimator for dynamic error-component models is biased. We then discuss how the assumption about the initial observations affects interpretation of a model. Finally we discuss estimation methods and their asymptotic properties under various assumptions about initial conditions and sampling schemes.

4.3.1 Bias in the OLS Estimator

In the static case in which all the explanatory variables are exogenous and are uncorrelated with the effects, we can ignore the error-component structure and apply the OLS method. The OLS estimator, although less efficient, is still unbiased and consistent. But this is no longer true for dynamic error-component models. The correlation between the lagged dependent variable and individual-specific effects would seriously bias the OLS estimator.

We use the following simple model to illustrate the extent of bias. Let

$$y_{it} = \gamma y_{i,t-1} + \alpha_i + u_{it}, \qquad |\gamma| < 1, \quad \begin{array}{l} i = 1, \ldots, N, \\ t = 1, \ldots, T, \end{array} \tag{4.3.3}$$

where u_{it} is independently, identically distributed over i and t. The OLS estimator of γ is

$$\hat{\gamma}_{\text{LS}} = \frac{\sum_{i=1}^N \sum_{t=1}^T y_{it} \cdot y_{i,t-1}}{\sum_{i=1}^N \sum_{t=1}^T y_{i,t-1}^2} = \gamma + \frac{\sum_{i=1}^N \sum_{t=1}^T (\alpha_i + u_{it}) y_{i,t-1}}{\sum_{i=1}^N \sum_{t=1}^T y_{i,t-1}^2}. \tag{4.3.4}$$

The asymptotic bias of the OLS estimator is given by the probability limit of the second term on the right-hand side of (4.3.4). Using a manipulation similar to that in Section 4.2, we can show that

$$\begin{aligned} &\operatorname*{plim}_{N\to\infty} \frac{1}{NT} \sum_{i=1}^N \sum_{t=1}^T (\alpha_i + u_{it}) y_{i,t-1} \\ &\quad = \frac{1}{T} \frac{1-\gamma^T}{1-\gamma} \operatorname{Cov}(y_{i0}, \alpha_i) + \frac{1}{T} \frac{\sigma_\alpha^2}{(1-\gamma)^2} [(T-1) - T\gamma + \gamma^T], \end{aligned} \tag{4.3.5}$$

$$\begin{aligned} &\operatorname*{plim}_{N\to\infty} \frac{1}{NT} \sum_{i=1}^N \sum_{t=1}^T y_{i,t-1}^2 \\ &\quad = \frac{1-\gamma^{2T}}{T(1-\gamma^2)} \cdot \frac{\sum_{i=1}^N y_{i0}^2}{N} \\ &\qquad + \frac{\sigma_\alpha^2}{(1-\gamma)^2} \cdot \frac{1}{T} \left(T - 2\frac{1-\gamma^T}{1-\gamma} + \frac{1-\gamma^{2T}}{1-\gamma^2} \right) \\ &\qquad + \frac{2}{T(1-\gamma)} \left(\frac{1-\gamma^T}{1-\gamma} - \frac{1-\gamma^{2T}}{1-\gamma^2} \right) \operatorname{Cov}(\alpha_i, y_{i0}) \\ &\qquad + \frac{\sigma_u^2}{T(1-\gamma^2)^2} [(T-1) - T\gamma^2 + \gamma^{2T}]. \end{aligned} \tag{4.3.6}$$

Usually, y_{i0} are assumed either to be arbitrary constants or to be generated by the same process as any other y_{it}, so that $\operatorname{Cov}(y_{i0}, \alpha_i)$ is either zero or positive.[4] Under the assumption that the initial values are bounded, namely, that $\operatorname{plim}_{N\to\infty} \sum_{i=1}^N y_{i0}^2/N$ is finite, the OLS method overestimates the true autocorrelation coefficient γ when N or T or both tend to infinity. The overestimation is more pronounced the greater the variance of the individual effects, σ_α^2. This asymptotic result also tends to hold in finite samples according to the Monte Carlo studies conducted by Nerlove (1967) ($N = 25$, $T = 10$).

The addition of exogenous variables to a first-order autoregressive process does not alter the direction of bias of the estimator of the coefficient of the lagged dependent variable, although its magnitude is somewhat reduced. The estimator of the coefficient of the lagged dependent variable remains biased upward, and the coefficients of the exogenous variables are biased toward zero.

Formulas for the asymptotic bias of the OLS estimator for a pth-order autoregressive process and for a model also containing exogenous variables were given by Trognon (1978). The direction of the asymptotic bias for a higher-order autoregressive process is difficult to identify a priori.

4.3.2 Model Formulation

When T is fixed, the interpretation of a model depends on the assumption about the behavior of the initial values y_{i0}. The statistical properties of the maximum likelihood and generalized least squares (GLS) estimation methods also depend on the assumption about y_{i0}, but not those of the IV or the GMM methods.

Consider a model of the form[5]

$$y_{it} = \gamma y_{i,t-1} + \boldsymbol{\rho}'\mathbf{z}_i + \boldsymbol{\beta}'\mathbf{x}_{it} + v_{it}, \qquad \begin{array}{l} i = 1, \ldots, N, \\ t = 1, \ldots, T, \end{array} \tag{4.3.7}$$

where $|\gamma| < 1$, $v_{it} = \alpha_i + u_{it}$,

$$\begin{aligned}
E\alpha_i &= Eu_{it} = 0, \\
E\alpha_i\mathbf{z}_i' &= \mathbf{0}', \qquad E\alpha_i\mathbf{x}_{it}' = \mathbf{0}', \\
E\alpha_i u_{jt} &= 0, \\
E\alpha_i\alpha_j &= \begin{cases} \sigma_\alpha^2 & \text{if } i = j, \\ 0 & \text{otherwise,} \end{cases} \\
Eu_{it}u_{js} &= \begin{cases} \sigma_u^2 & \text{if } i = j,\ t = s, \\ 0 & \text{otherwise,} \end{cases}
\end{aligned}$$

and where $\mathbf{z}_i$ is a $K_2 \times 1$ vector of time-invariant exogenous variables such as the constant term or an individual's sex or race, $\mathbf{x}_{it}$ is a $K_1 \times 1$ vector of time-varying exogenous variables, γ is 1×1, and $\boldsymbol{\rho}$ and $\boldsymbol{\beta}$ are $K_2 \times 1$ and $K_1 \times 1$ vectors of parameters, respectively. Equation (4.3.7) can also be written in the form

$$w_{it} = \gamma w_{i,t-1} + \boldsymbol{\rho}'\mathbf{z}_i + \boldsymbol{\beta}'\mathbf{x}_{it} + u_{it}, \tag{4.3.8}$$

$$y_{it} = w_{it} + \eta_i, \tag{4.3.9}$$

where

$$\alpha_i = (1-\gamma)\eta_i, \qquad E\eta_i = 0, \qquad \text{Var}(\eta_i) = \sigma_\eta^2 = \sigma_\alpha^2/(1-\gamma)^2. \tag{4.3.10}$$

Algebraically, (4.3.7) is identical to (4.3.8) and (4.3.9). However, the interpretation of how y_{it} is generated is not the same. Equation (4.3.7) implies that apart from a common response to its own lagged value and the exogenous variables, each individual process is also driven by the unobserved characteristics α_i, which are different for different individuals. Equations (4.3.8) and (4.3.9) imply that the dynamic process $\{w_{it}\}$ is independent of the individual effect η_i. Conditional on the exogenous variables, individuals are driven by an identical stochastic process with independent (and different) shocks that are random draws from a common population [equation (4.3.8)]. It is the observed value of the latent variable w_{it}, y_{it}, that is shifted by the individual time-invariant random variable η_i [equation (4.3.9)]. This difference in means can be interpreted as a difference in individual endowments or a common measurement error for the ith process.

If we observed w_{it}, we could distinguish (4.3.7) from (4.3.8) and (4.3.9). Unfortunately, w_{it} are unobservable. However, knowledge of initial observations can provide information to distinguish these two processes. Standard assumptions about initial observations are either that they are fixed or that they are random. If (4.3.7) is viewed as the model, we have two fundamental cases: (I) y_{i0} fixed and (II) y_{i0} random. If (4.3.8) and (4.3.9) are viewed as the basic model, we have (III) w_{i0} fixed and (IV) w_{i0} random.

Case I: y_{i0} fixed. A cross-sectional unit may start at some arbitrary position y_{i0} and gradually move toward a level $(\alpha_i + \boldsymbol{\rho}'\mathbf{z}_i)/(1-\gamma) + \boldsymbol{\beta}' \sum_{j=0} \mathbf{x}_{i,t-j}\gamma^j$. This level is determined jointly by the unobservable effect (characteristic) α_i, observable time-invariant characteristics $\mathbf{z}_i$, and time-varying variables $\mathbf{x}_{it}$. The individual effect, α_i, is a random draw from a population with mean zero and variance σ_α^2. This appears to be a reasonable model. But if the decision about when to start sampling is arbitrary and independent of the values of y_{i0}, treating y_{i0} as fixed might be questionable because the assumption $E\alpha_i y_{i0} = 0$ implies that the individual effects, α_i, are not brought into the model at time 0, but affect the process at time 1 and later. If the process has been going on for some time, there is no particular reason to believe that y_{i0} should be viewed differently than y_{it}.

Case II: y_{i0} random. We can assume that the initial observations are random, with a common mean μ_0 and variance σ_{y0}^2. Namely, let

$$y_{i0} = \mu_{y0} + \epsilon_i. \tag{4.3.11}$$

A rationalization of this assumption is that we can treat y_{it} as a state. We do not care how the initial state is reached, as long as we know that it has a distribution with finite mean and variance. Or, alternatively, we can view ϵ_i as representing the effect of initial individual endowments (after correction for the mean). Depending on the assumption with regard to the correlation between y_{i0} and α_i, we can divide this case into two subcases:

Case IIa: y_{i0} independent of α_i; that is, $\text{Cov}(\epsilon_i, \alpha_i) = 0$. In this case the impact of initial endowments gradually diminishes over time and eventually vanishes. The model is somewhat like case I, in which the starting value and the effect α_i are independent, except that now the starting observable value is not a fixed constant but a random draw from a population with mean μ_{y0} and variance σ_{y0}^2.

Case IIb: y_{i0} correlated with α_i. We denote the covariance between y_{i0} and α_i by $\phi\sigma_{y0}^2$. Then, as time goes on, the impact of initial endowments (ϵ_i) affects all future values of y_{it} through its correlation with α_i and eventually reaches a level $[\phi\epsilon_i/$

$(1-\gamma)] = \lim_{t\to\infty} E[y_{it} - \boldsymbol{\rho}'\mathbf{z}_i/(1-\gamma) - \boldsymbol{\beta}' \sum_{j=0}^{t-1} \mathbf{x}_{i,t-j}\gamma^j \mid \epsilon_i]$. In the special case that $\phi\sigma_{y0}^2 = \sigma_\alpha^2$, namely, $\epsilon_i = \alpha_i$, the individual effect can be viewed as completely characterized by the differences in initial endowments. The eventual impact of this initial endowment equals $[\alpha_i/(1-\gamma)] = \eta_i$.

Case III: w_{i0} fixed. Here the unobserved individual process $\{w_{it}\}$ has an arbitrary starting value. In this respect, this case is similar to case I. However, the observed cross-sectional units, y_{it}, are correlated with the individual effects η_i. That is, each of the observed cross-sectional units may start at some arbitrary position y_{i0} and gradually move toward a level $\eta_i + \boldsymbol{\rho}'\mathbf{z}_i/(1-\gamma) + \boldsymbol{\beta}' \sum_{j=0}^{t-1} \mathbf{x}_{i,t-j}\gamma^j$. Nevertheless, we allow for the possibility that the starting period of the sample observations need not coincide with the beginning of a stochastic process by letting the individual effect η_i affect all sample observations, including y_{i0}.

Case IV: w_{i0} random. Depending on whether or not the w_{i0} are viewed as having common mean, we have four subcases:

Case IVa: w_{i0} random, with common mean μ_w and variance $\sigma_u^2/(1-\gamma^2)$.

Case IVb: w_{i0} random, with common mean μ_w and arbitrary variance σ_{w0}^2.

Case IVc: w_{i0} random, with mean θ_{i0} and variance $\sigma_u^2/(1-\gamma^2)$.

Case IVd: w_{i0} random, with mean θ_{i0} and arbitrary variance σ_{w0}^2.

In each of these four subcases we allow correlation between y_{i0} and η_i. In other words, η_i affects y_{it} in all periods, including y_{i0}. Cases IVa and IVb are similar to the state-space representation discussed in case IIa, in which the initial states are random draws from a distribution with finite mean. Case IVa assumes that the initial state has the same variance as the latter states. Case IVb allows the initial state to be nonstationary (with arbitrary variance). Cases IVc and IVd take a different view in that they assume that the individual states are random draws from different populations with different means. A rationalization for this can be seen through successive substitution of (4.3.8), yielding

$$w_{i0} = \frac{1}{1-\gamma}\boldsymbol{\rho}'\mathbf{z}_i + \boldsymbol{\beta}' \sum_{j=0}^{\infty} \mathbf{x}_{i,-j}\gamma^j + u_{i0} + \gamma u_{i,-1} + \gamma^2 u_{i,-2} + \cdots. \tag{4.3.12}$$

Because $\mathbf{x}_{i0}, \mathbf{x}_{i,-1}, \ldots$ are not observable, we can treat the combined cumulative effects of nonrandom variables for the ith individual as an unknown parameter and let

$$\theta_{i0} = \frac{1}{1-\gamma}\boldsymbol{\rho}'\mathbf{z}_i + \boldsymbol{\beta}' \sum_{j=0}^{\infty} \mathbf{x}_{i,-j}\gamma^j. \tag{4.3.13}$$

Case IVc assumes that the process $\{w_{it}\}$ was generated from the infinite past and has achieved stationarity of its second moments after conditioning on the exogenous variables (i.e., w_{i0} has the same variance as any other w_{it}). Case IVd relaxes this assumption by allowing the variance of w_{i0} to be arbitrary.

4.3.3 Estimation of Random-Effects Models

There are various ways to estimate the unknown parameters. Here we discuss four methods: the MLE, the GLS, the IV, and the GMM methods.

4.3.3.a Maximum Likelihood Estimator

Different assumptions about the initial conditions imply different forms of the likelihood functions. Under the assumption that α_i and u_{it} are normally distributed, the likelihood function for case I is[6]

$$\begin{aligned} L_1 &= (2\pi)^{-\frac{NT}{2}} |V|^{-\frac{N}{2}} \\ &\quad \times \exp\left\{ -\frac{1}{2} \sum_{i=1}^{N} (\mathbf{y}_i - \mathbf{y}_{i,-1}\gamma - Z_i\boldsymbol{\rho} - X_i\boldsymbol{\beta})' \cdot V^{-1} (\mathbf{y}_i - \mathbf{y}_{i,-1}\gamma \right. \\ &\quad \left. - Z_i\boldsymbol{\rho} - X_i\boldsymbol{\beta}) \right\}, \end{aligned} \tag{4.3.14}$$

where $\mathbf{y}_i = (y_{i1}, \ldots, \mathbf{y}_{iT})'$, $\mathbf{y}_{i,-1} = (y_{i0}, \ldots, y_{i,T-1})'$, $Z_i = \mathbf{e}\mathbf{z}_i'$, $\mathbf{e} = (1, \ldots, 1)'$, $X_i = (\mathbf{x}_{i1}, \ldots, \mathbf{x}_{iT})'$, and $V = \sigma_u^2 I_T + \sigma_\alpha^2 \mathbf{e}\mathbf{e}'$. The likelihood function for case IIa is

$$L_{2a} = L_1 \cdot (2\pi)^{-\frac{N}{2}} \left(\sigma_{y0}^2\right)^{-\frac{N}{2}} \exp\left\{ -\frac{1}{2\sigma_{y0}^2} \sum_{i=1}^{N} (y_{i0} - \mu_{y0})^2 \right\}. \tag{4.3.15}$$

For case IIb, it is of the form

$$\begin{aligned} L_{2b} &= (2\pi)^{-\frac{NT}{2}} \left(\sigma_u^2\right)^{-\frac{N(T-1)}{2}} \left(\sigma_u^2 + Ta\right)^{-\frac{N}{2}} \\ &\quad \times \exp\left\{ -\frac{1}{2\sigma_u^2} \sum_{i=1}^{N} \sum_{t=1}^{T} [y_{it} - \gamma y_{i,t-1} - \boldsymbol{\rho}'\mathbf{z}_i - \boldsymbol{\beta}'\mathbf{x}_{it} - \phi(y_{i0} - \mu_{y0})]^2 \right. \\ &\qquad + \frac{\mathrm{a}}{2\sigma_u^2(\sigma_u^2 + Ta)} \\ &\quad \left. \times \sum_{i=1}^{N} \left\{ \sum_{t=1}^{T} [y_{it} - \gamma y_{i,t-1} - \boldsymbol{\rho}'\mathbf{z}_i - \boldsymbol{\beta}'\mathbf{x}_{it} - \phi(y_{i0} - \mu_{y0})] \right\}^2 \right\} \\ &\quad \times (2\pi)^{-\frac{N}{2}} \left(\sigma_{y0}^2\right)^{-\frac{N}{2}} \exp\left\{ -\frac{1}{2\sigma_{y0}^2} \sum_{i=1}^{N} (y_{i0} - \mu_{y0})^2 \right\}, \end{aligned} \tag{4.3.16}$$

where $a = \sigma_\alpha^2 - \phi^2\sigma_{y0}^2$. The likelihood function for case III is

$$\begin{aligned} L_3 = {} & (2\pi)^{-\frac{NT}{2}} \left(\sigma_u^2\right)^{-\frac{NT}{2}} \\ & \times \exp\left\{ -\frac{1}{2\sigma_u^2} \sum_{i=1}^{N} \sum_{t=1}^{T} [(y_{it} - y_{i0} + w_{i0}) - \gamma(y_{i,t-1} - y_{i0} + w_{i0}) \right. \\ & \left. - \boldsymbol{\rho}'\mathbf{z}_i - \boldsymbol{\beta}'\mathbf{x}_{it}]^2 \right\} \cdot (2\pi)^{-\frac{N}{2}} \left(\sigma_\eta^2\right)^{-\frac{N}{2}} \\ & \times \exp\left\{ -\frac{1}{2\sigma_\eta^2} \sum_{i=1}^{N} (y_{i0} - w_{i0})^2 \right\}, \end{aligned} \tag{4.3.17}$$

and for case IVa it is

$$\begin{aligned} L_{4\text{a}} = {} & (2\pi)^{-\frac{N(T+1)}{2}} |\Omega|^{-\frac{N}{2}} \\ & \times \exp\left\{ -\frac{1}{2} \sum_{i=1}^{N} (y_{i0} - \mu_w, y_{i1} - \gamma y_{i0} - \boldsymbol{\rho}'\mathbf{z}_i - \boldsymbol{\beta}'\mathbf{x}_{i1}, \ldots, \right. \\ & \qquad y_{iT} - \gamma y_{i,T-1} - \boldsymbol{\rho}'\mathbf{z}_i - \boldsymbol{\beta}'\mathbf{x}_{iT}) \\ & \left. \times \Omega^{-1} (y_{i0} - \mu_w, \ldots, y_{iT} - \gamma y_{i,T-1} - \boldsymbol{\rho}'\mathbf{z}_i - \boldsymbol{\beta}'\mathbf{x}_{iT})' \right\}, \end{aligned} \tag{4.3.18}$$

where

$$\begin{aligned} \underset{(T+1)\times(T+1)}{\Omega} &= \sigma_u^2 \begin{bmatrix} \frac{1}{1-\gamma^2} & \mathbf{0}' \\ \mathbf{0} & I_T \end{bmatrix} + \sigma_\alpha^2 \begin{bmatrix} \frac{1}{1-\gamma} \\ \mathbf{e} \end{bmatrix} \left(\frac{1}{1-\gamma}, \mathbf{e}' \right), \\ |\Omega| &= \frac{\sigma_u^{2T}}{1-\gamma^2} \left(\sigma_u^2 + T\sigma_\alpha^2 + \frac{1+\gamma}{1-\gamma}\sigma_\alpha^2 \right), \\ \Omega^{-1} &= \frac{1}{\sigma_u^2} \left[\begin{bmatrix} 1-\gamma^2 & \mathbf{0}' \\ \mathbf{0} & I_T \end{bmatrix} \right. \\ & \qquad \left. - \left(\frac{\sigma_u^2}{\sigma_\alpha^2} + T + \frac{1+\gamma}{1-\gamma} \right)^{-1} \begin{bmatrix} 1+\gamma \\ \mathbf{e} \end{bmatrix} (1+\gamma, \mathbf{e}') \right]. \end{aligned} \tag{4.3.19}$$

The likelihood function for case IVb, $L_{4\text{b}}$, is of the form (4.3.18), except that Ω is replaced by Λ, where Λ differs from Ω only in that the upper left element of the first term, $1/(1-\gamma^2)$, is replaced by σ_{w0}^2/σ_u^2. The likelihood function for case IVc, $L_{4\text{c}}$, is similar to that for case IVa, except that the mean of y_{i0} in the exponential term is replaced by θ_{i0}. The likelihood function for case IVd, $L_{4\text{d}}$, is of the form (4.3.16), with θ_{i0}, $(1-\gamma)\sigma_\eta^2/(\sigma_\eta^2 + \sigma_{w0}^2)$, and $\sigma_\eta^2 + \sigma_{w0}^2$ replacing μ_{y0}, ϕ, and σ_{y0}^2, respectively.

Maximizing the likelihood function with respect to unknown parameters yields the MLE. The consistency of the MLE depends on the initial conditions and on the way in which the numbers of time-series observations (T) and of cross-sectional units (N) tend to infinity. For cases III and IVd, the MLEs do not exist. By letting y_{i0} equal w_{i0} or θ_{i0}, the exponential term of the second function of their respective likelihood function becomes 1. If we let the variances σ_η^2 or $\sigma_\eta^2 + \sigma_{w0}^2$ approach zero, the likelihood functions become unbounded. However, we can still take partial derivatives of these likelihood functions and solve for the first-order conditions. For simplicity of exposition, we shall refer to these interior solutions as the MLEs and examine their consistency properties in the same way as in other cases in which the MLEs exist.

When N is fixed, a necessary condition for $\boldsymbol{\rho}$ being identifiable is that $N \geq K_2$. Otherwise, the model is subject to strict multicollinearity. However, when T tends to infinity, even with N greater than K_2, the MLEs for $\boldsymbol{\rho}$ and σ_α^2 remain inconsistent because of insufficient variation across individuals. On the other hand, the MLEs of γ, $\boldsymbol{\beta}$, and σ_u^2 are consistent for all these different cases. When T becomes large, the weight of the initial observations becomes increasingly negligible, and the MLEs for different cases all converge to the same covariance estimator.

Table 4.1. *Consistency properties of the MLEs for dynamic random-effects models*[a]

Case		N fixed, $T \to \infty$	T fixed, $N \to \infty$
Case I: y_{i0} fixed	$\gamma, \boldsymbol{\beta}, \sigma_u^2$	Consistent	Consistent
	$\boldsymbol{\rho}, \sigma_\alpha^2$	Inconsistent	Consistent
Case II: y_{i0} random			
IIa: y_{i0} independent of α_i	$\gamma, \boldsymbol{\beta}, \sigma_u^2$	Consistent	Consistent
	$\mu_{y0}, \boldsymbol{\rho}, \sigma_\alpha^2, \sigma_{y0}^2$	Inconsistent	Consistent
IIb: y_{i0} correlated	$\gamma, \boldsymbol{\beta}, \sigma_u^2$	Consistent	Consistent
with α_i	$\mu_{y0}, \boldsymbol{\rho}, \sigma_\alpha^2, \sigma_{y0}^2, \phi$	Inconsistent	Consistent
Case III: w_{i0} fixed	$\gamma, \boldsymbol{\beta}, \sigma_u^2$	Consistent	Inconsistent
	$w_{i0}, \boldsymbol{\rho}, \sigma_\eta^2$	Inconsistent	Inconsistent
Case IV: w_{i0} random			
IVa: mean μ_w			
and variance	$\gamma, \boldsymbol{\beta}, \sigma_u^2$	Consistent	Consistent
$\sigma_u^2/(1-\gamma^2)$	$\mu_w, \boldsymbol{\rho}, \sigma_\eta^2$	Inconsistent	Consistent
IVb: mean μ_w	$\gamma, \boldsymbol{\beta}, \sigma_u^2$	Consistent	Consistent
and variance σ_{w0}^2	$\sigma_{w0}^2, \boldsymbol{\rho}, \sigma_\eta^2, \mu_w$	Inconsistent	Consistent
IVc: mean θ_{i0}	$\gamma, \boldsymbol{\beta}, \sigma_u^2$	Consistent	Inconsistent
and variance $\sigma_u^2/(1-\gamma^2)$	$\theta_{i0}, \boldsymbol{\rho}, \sigma_\eta^2$	Inconsistent	Inconsistent
IVd: mean θ_{i0}	$\gamma, \boldsymbol{\beta}, \sigma_u^2$	Consistent	Inconsistent
and variance σ_{w0}^2	$\theta_{i0}, \boldsymbol{\sigma}_\eta^2, \sigma_{w0}^2$	Inconsistent	Inconsistent

[a]If an MLE does not exist, we replace it by the interior solution.
Source: Anderson and Hsiao (1982).

For cases IVc and IVd, where w_{i0} have means θ_{i0}, Bhargava and Sargan (1983) suggest predicting θ_{i0} by all the observed $\mathbf{x}_{it}$ and $\mathbf{z}_i$ as a way to get around the incidental-parameters problem.[7] If $\mathbf{x}_{it}$ is generated by a homogeneous stochastic process

$$\mathbf{x}_{it} = \mathbf{c} + \sum_{j=0}^{\infty} \mathbf{b}_j \boldsymbol{\xi}_{i,t-j}, \tag{4.3.20}$$

where $\boldsymbol{\xi}_{it}$ is independently, identically distributed, then conditional on $\mathbf{x}_{it}$ and $\mathbf{z}_i$, we have

$$y_{i0} = \sum_{t=1}^{T} \boldsymbol{\pi}'_{0t}\mathbf{x}_{it} + \boldsymbol{\rho}^{*\prime}\mathbf{z}_i + v_{i0}, \tag{4.3.21}$$

and

$$v_{i0} = \epsilon_{i0} + u^*_{i0} + \eta_i, \qquad i = 1, \ldots, N. \tag{4.3.22}$$

The coefficients $\boldsymbol{\pi}_{0t}$ are identical across i (Hsiao, Pesaran, and Tahmiscioglu (2002)). The error term v_{i0} is the sum of three components: the prediction error of θ_{i0}, ϵ_{i0}, the cumulative shocks before time zero, $u^*_{i0} = u_{i0} + \gamma u_{i,-1} + \gamma^2 u_{i,-2} + \cdots$, and the individual effects η_i. The prediction error ϵ_{i0} is independent of u_{it} and η_i, with mean zero and variance $\sigma^2_{\epsilon 0}$. Depending on whether or not the error process of w_{i0} conditional on the exogenous variables has achieved stationarity (i.e., whether or not the variance of w_{i0} is the same as any other w_{it}), we have[8] case IVc′,

$$\begin{aligned} \operatorname{Var}(v_{i0}) &= \sigma^2_{\epsilon 0} + \frac{\sigma^2_u}{1-\gamma^2} + \frac{\sigma^2_\alpha}{(1-\gamma)^2}, \\ \operatorname{Cov}(v_{i0}, v_{it}) &= \frac{\sigma^2_\alpha}{(1-\gamma)}, \qquad t = 1, \ldots, T, \end{aligned} \tag{4.3.23}$$

or case IVd′,

$$\operatorname{Var}(v_{i0}) = \sigma^2_{w0} \quad \text{and} \quad \operatorname{Cov}(v_{i0}, v_{it}) = \sigma^2_\tau, \qquad t = 1, \ldots, T. \tag{4.3.24}$$

Cases IVc′ and IVd′ transform cases IVc and IVd, in which the number of parameters increases with the number of observations, into a situation in which N independently distributed $(T+1)$-component vectors depend only on a fixed number of parameters. Therefore, the MLE is consistent when $N \to \infty$.

The MLE is obtained by solving the first-order conditions of the likelihood function with respect to unknown parameters. If there is a unique solution to these partial-derivative equations with $\sigma^2_\alpha > 0$, the solution is the MLE. However, just as in the static case discussed in Section 3.3, a boundary solution with $\sigma^2_\alpha = 0$ may occur for dynamic error-components models as well. Anderson and Hsiao (1981) have derived the conditions under which the boundary solution will occur for various cases. Trognon (1978) has provided analytic explanations based on asymptotic approximations where the number of time periods tends to infinity. Nerlove (1967, 1971a) has conducted Monte Carlo experiments to explore the properties of the MLE. These results show that the autocorrelation structure of the exogenous variables is a criterion for the existence of boundary solutions. In general, the more autocorrelated the exogenous variables or the more important the weight of the exogenous variables, the less likely it is that a boundary solution will occur.

The solution for the MLE is complicated. We can apply the Newton–Raphson iterative procedure or the sequential iterative procedure suggested by Anderson and Hsiao (1982) to obtain a solution. Alternatively, because we have a cross section of size N repeated successively in T time periods, we can regard the problems of estimation (and testing) of (4.3.7) as akin to those for a simultaneous-equations system with T or $T+1$ structural equations with N observations available on each of the equations. That is, the dynamic relationship (4.3.7) in a given time period is written as an equation in a system of simultaneous equations,

$$\Gamma Y' + BX' + PZ' = U', \tag{4.3.25}$$

where we now let[9]

$$\underset{N\times(T+1)}{Y} = \begin{bmatrix} y_{10} & y_{11} & \cdots & y_{1T} \\ y_{20} & y_{21} & \cdots & y_{2T} \\ \vdots & \vdots & & \vdots \\ y_{N0} & y_{N1} & \cdots & y_{NT} \end{bmatrix},$$

$$\underset{N\times TK_1}{X} = \begin{bmatrix} \mathbf{x}'_{11} & \mathbf{x}'_{12} & \cdots & \mathbf{x}'_{1T} \\ \mathbf{x}'_{21} & \mathbf{x}'_{22} & \cdots & \mathbf{x}'_{2T} \\ \vdots & \vdots & & \vdots \\ \mathbf{x}'_{N1} & \mathbf{x}'_{N2} & \cdots & \mathbf{x}'_{NT} \end{bmatrix},$$

$$\underset{N\times K_2}{Z} = \begin{bmatrix} \mathbf{z}'_1 \\ \mathbf{z}'_2 \\ \vdots \\ \mathbf{z}'_N \end{bmatrix}, \qquad i = 1\ldots, N,$$

and U is the $N \times T$ matrix of the errors if the initial values y_{i0} are treated as constants, and the $N \times (T+1)$ matrix of errors if the initial values are treated as stochastic. The structural-form coefficient matrix $A = [\Gamma \;\; B \;\; P]$ is $T \times [(T+1) + TK_1 + K_2]$ or $(T+1) \times [(T+1) + TK_1 + K_2]$, depending on whether the initial values are treated as fixed or random. The earlier serial covariance matrix [e.g., (3.3.4), (4.3.19), (4.3.23), or (4.3.24)] now becomes the variance–covariance matrix of the errors on T or $(T+1)$ structural equations. We can then use the algorithm for solving the full-information maximum-likelihood estimator to obtain the MLE.

There are cross-equation linear restrictions on the structural-form coefficient matrix, and restrictions on the variance–covariance matrix. For instances, in case

I, where y_{i0} are treated as fixed constants, we have

$$A = \begin{bmatrix} -\gamma & 1 & 0 & \cdots & 0 & 0 & \boldsymbol{\beta}' & \mathbf{0}' & \cdots & \mathbf{0}' & \mathbf{0}' & \boldsymbol{\rho}' \\ 0 & -\gamma & 1 & \cdots & 0 & 0 & \mathbf{0}' & \boldsymbol{\beta}' & \cdots & \mathbf{0}' & \mathbf{0}' & \boldsymbol{\rho}' \\ \vdots & \vdots & \ddots & \ddots & \vdots & \vdots & \vdots & \vdots & \ddots & \vdots & \vdots & \vdots \\ 0 & 0 & \cdots & & 1 & 0 & \mathbf{0}' & \mathbf{0}' & \cdots & \boldsymbol{\beta}' & \mathbf{0}' & \boldsymbol{\rho}' \\ 0 & 0 & \cdots & & -\gamma & 1 & \mathbf{0}' & \mathbf{0}' & \cdots & \mathbf{0}' & \boldsymbol{\beta}' & \boldsymbol{\rho}' \end{bmatrix}. \tag{4.3.26}$$

The variance–covariance matrix of U is block-diagonal, with the diagonal blocks equal to V [equation (3.3.4)]. In case IVd′, where y_{i0} are treated as stochastic, the structural-form coefficient matrix A is a $(T+1) \times [(T+1) + TK_1 + K_2]$ matrix of the form

$$A = \begin{bmatrix} 1 & 0 & \cdots & 0 & 0 & \boldsymbol{\pi}'_{01} & \boldsymbol{\pi}'_{02} & \cdots & \boldsymbol{\pi}'_{0T} & \boldsymbol{\rho}^{*\prime} \\ -\gamma & 1 & \cdots & 0 & 0 & \boldsymbol{\beta}' & \mathbf{0}' & \cdots & \mathbf{0}' & \boldsymbol{\rho}' \\ 0 & -\gamma & \cdots & 0 & 0 & \mathbf{0}' & \boldsymbol{\beta}' & \cdots & \mathbf{0}' & \boldsymbol{\rho}' \\ \vdots & \vdots & \ddots & \vdots & \vdots & \vdots & \vdots & \ddots & \vdots & \vdots \\ 0 & 0 & \cdots & -\gamma & 1 & \mathbf{0}' & \cdots & \boldsymbol{\beta}' & \boldsymbol{\rho}' & \end{bmatrix}, \tag{4.3.27}$$

and the variance–covariance matrix of U is block-diagonal, with each diagonal block a $(T+1) \times (T+1)$ matrix of the form

$$\begin{bmatrix} \sigma^2_{w0} & \sigma^2_\tau \mathbf{e}' \\ \sigma^2_\tau \mathbf{e} & V \end{bmatrix}. \tag{4.3.28}$$

Bhargava and Sargan (1983) suggest maximizing the likelihood function of (4.3.25) by directly substituting the restrictions into the structural-form coefficient matrix A and the variance–covariance matrix of U'.

Alternatively, we can ignore the restrictions on the variance–covariance matrix of U' and use three-stage least-squares (3SLS) methods. Because the restrictions on A are linear, it is easy to obtain the constrained 3SLS estimator of γ, $\boldsymbol{\beta}$, $\boldsymbol{\rho}$, and $\boldsymbol{\rho}^*$ from the unconstrained 3SLS estimator.[10] Or we can use the Chamberlain (1982, 1984) minimum-distance estimator by first obtaining the unconstrained reduced-form coefficient matrix Π, then solving for the structural-form parameters (see Section 3.9.). The Chamberlain minimum-distance estimator has the same limiting distribution as the constrained generalized 3SLS estimator (see Chapter 5). However, because the maintained hypothesis in the model implies that the covariance matrix of U' is constrained and in some cases dependent on the parameter γ occurring in the structural form, the constrained 3SLS or the constrained generalized 3SLS is inefficient in comparison with the (full-information) MLE.[11] But if the restrictions on the variance–covariance matrix are not true, the (full-information) MLE imposing the wrong restrictions will in general be inconsistent. But the (constrained) 3SLS or the Chamberlain minimum-distance estimator, because it does not impose any restriction on the covariance matrix of U', remains consistent and is efficient within the class of estimators that do not impose restrictions on the variance–covariance matrix.

4.3.3.b Generalized Least-Squares Estimator

We note that except for cases III, IVc, and IVd, the likelihood function only depends on a fixed number of parameters. Furthermore, conditional on Ω or σ_u^2, σ_α^2, σ_{y0}^2 and ϕ, the MLE is equivalent to the GLS estimator. For instance, under case I, the covariance matrix of $(y_{i1}, \ldots, y_{iT})$ is the usual error-components form (3.3.4). Under cases IIa,b, and under cases IVa,b or cases IVc,d when the conditional mean of θ_{i0} can be represented in the form of (4.3.21), the covariance matrix $\tilde{V}$ of $\mathbf{v}_i = (v_{i0}, v_{i1}, \ldots, v_{iT})$ is of similar form to (4.3.28). Therefore, a GLS estimator of $\boldsymbol{\delta}' = (\boldsymbol{\pi}', \boldsymbol{\rho}^{*\prime}, \gamma, \boldsymbol{\beta}', \boldsymbol{\rho}')$, can be applied:

$$\hat{\boldsymbol{\delta}}_{\text{GLS}} = \left(\sum_{i=1}^{N} \tilde{X}_i' \tilde{V}^{-1} \tilde{X}_i\right)^{-1} \left(\sum_{i=1}^{N} \tilde{X}_i' \tilde{V}^{-1} \tilde{\mathbf{y}}_i\right), \tag{4.3.29}$$

where $\tilde{\mathbf{y}}_i' = (y_{i0}, \ldots, y_{iT})$, and

$$\tilde{X}_i = \begin{pmatrix} \mathbf{x}_{i1}' & \mathbf{x}_{i2}' & \cdots & \mathbf{x}_{iT}' & \mathbf{z}_i' & 0 & \mathbf{0}' & \mathbf{0} \\ \mathbf{0}' & \cdots & \cdots & \cdots & \mathbf{0}' & y_{i0} & \mathbf{x}_{i1}' & \mathbf{z}_i' \\ \vdots & & & & \vdots & y_{i1} & \mathbf{x}_{i2}' & \mathbf{z}_i' \\ \vdots & & & & \vdots & \vdots & \vdots & \vdots \\ \mathbf{0}' & \cdots & \cdots & \cdots & \mathbf{0}' & y_{i,T-1} & \mathbf{x}_{iT}' & \mathbf{z}_i' \end{pmatrix}.$$

The estimator is consistent and asymptotically normally distributed as $N \to \infty$.

Blundell and Smith (1991) suggest a conditional GLS procedure by conditioning $(y_{i1}, \ldots, y_{iT})$ on $v_{i0} = y_{i0} - E(y_{i0} \mid \mathbf{x}_i', \mathbf{z}_i)$:

$$\mathbf{y}_i = \mathbf{y}_{i,-1}\gamma + Z_i\boldsymbol{\rho} + X_i\boldsymbol{\beta} + \boldsymbol{\tau} v_{i0} + \mathbf{v}_i^*, \tag{4.3.30}$$

where $\mathbf{v}_i^* = (v_{i1}^*, \ldots, v_{iT}^*)'$, and $\boldsymbol{\tau}$ is a $T \times 1$ vector of constants with the values depending on the correlation pattern between y_{i0} and α_i. For case IIa, $\boldsymbol{\tau} = \mathbf{0}$, case IIb, $\boldsymbol{\tau} = \mathbf{e}_T \cdot \phi$. When the covariances between y_{i0} and $(y_{i1}, \ldots, y_{iT})$ are arbitrary, $\boldsymbol{\tau}$ is a $T \times 1$ vector of unrestricted constants. Application of the GLS to (4.3.30) is consistent as $N \to \infty$.

When the covariance matrix of $\mathbf{v}_i$ or $\mathbf{v}_i^*$ is unknown, a feasible GLS estimator can be applied. In the first step, we obtain some consistent estimates of the covariance matrix from the estimated $\mathbf{v}_i$ or $\mathbf{v}_i^*$. For instance, we can use the IV estimator, to be discussed in Section 4.3.3.c, to obtain consistent estimators of γ and $\boldsymbol{\beta}$, then substitute them into $y_{it} - \gamma y_{i,t-1} - \boldsymbol{\beta}'\mathbf{x}_{it}$, and regress the resulting value on $\mathbf{z}_i$ across individuals to obtain a consistent estimate of $\boldsymbol{\rho}$. Substituting estimated γ, $\boldsymbol{\beta}$, and $\boldsymbol{\rho}$ into (4.3.2), we obtain estimates of v_{it} for $t = 1, \ldots, T$. The estimates of v_{i0} can be obtained as the residuals of the cross-section regression of (4.3.21). The covariance matrix of $\mathbf{v}_i$ can then be estimated using the procedures discussed in Chapter 3. The estimated $\mathbf{v}_i^*$ can also be obtained as the residuals of the cross-sectional regression of $\mathbf{y}_i - \mathbf{y}_{i,-1}\gamma - X_i\boldsymbol{\beta}$ on Z_i and $\mathbf{e}\hat{v}_{i0}$. In the second step, we treat the estimated covariance matrix of

$\mathbf{v}_i$ or $\mathbf{v}_i^*$ as if it were known, and apply the GLS to the system composed of (4.3.2) and (4.3.21) or the conditional system (4.3.30).

It should be noted that if $\text{Cov}(y_{i0}, \alpha_i) \neq 0$, the GLS applied to the system (4.3.2) is inconsistent when T is fixed and $N \to \infty$. This is easily seen by noting that conditional on y_{i0}, the system is of the form (4.3.30). Applying GLS to (4.3.2) is therefore subject to omitted-variable bias. However, the asymptotic bias of the GLS of (4.3.2) is still smaller than that of the OLS or the within estimator of (4.3.2) (Sevestre and Trognon (1982)). When T tends to infinity, GLS of (4.3.2) is again consistent because GLS converges to the within (or LSDV) estimator, which becomes consistent.

It should also be noted that contrary to the static case, the feasible GLS is asymptotically less efficient than the GLS knowing the true covariance matrix, because when a lagged dependent variable appears as one of the regressors, the estimation of slope coefficients is no longer asymptotically independent of the estimation of the parameters of the covariance matrix (Amemiya and Fuller (1967); Hsiao, Pesaran, and Tahmiscioglu (2002); or Appendix 4A).

4.3.3.c Instrumental-Variable Estimator

Because the likelihood functions under different initial conditions are different when dealing with panels involving large numbers of individuals over a short period of time, mistaken choices of initial conditions will yield estimators that are not asymptotically equivalent to the correct one, and hence may not be consistent. Sometimes we have little information to rely on in making a correct choice about the initial conditions. A simple consistent estimator that is independent of the initial conditions is appealing in its own right and in addition can be used to obtain initial values for the iterative process that yields the MLE. One estimation method consists of the following procedure.[12]

Step 1: Taking the first difference of (4.3.7), we obtain

$$y_{it} - y_{i,t-1} = \gamma(y_{i,t-1} - y_{i,t-2}) + \boldsymbol{\beta}'(\mathbf{x}_{it} - \mathbf{x}_{i,t-1}) + u_{it} - u_{i,t-1}, \quad \text{for} \quad t = 2, \ldots, T. \tag{4.3.31}$$

Because $y_{i,t-2}$ or $(y_{i,t-2} - y_{i,t-3})$ are correlated with $(y_{i,t-1} - y_{i,t-2})$ but are uncorrelated with $(u_{it} - u_{i,t-1})$ they can be used as an instrument for $(y_{i,t-1} - y_{i,t-2})$ and estimate γ and $\boldsymbol{\beta}$ by the instrumental-variable method. Both

$$\begin{pmatrix} \hat{\gamma}_{iv} \\ \hat{\boldsymbol{\beta}}_{iv} \end{pmatrix} = \left[\sum_{i=1}^{N} \sum_{t=3}^{T} \times \begin{pmatrix} (y_{i,t-1} - y_{i,t-2})(y_{i,t-2} - y_{i,t-3}) & (y_{i,t-2} - y_{it-3})(\mathbf{x}_{it} - \mathbf{x}_{i,t-1})' \\ (\mathbf{x}_{it} - \mathbf{x}_{i,t-1})(y_{i,t-2} - y_{i,t-3}) & (\mathbf{x}_{it} - \mathbf{x}_{i,t-1})(\mathbf{x}_{it} - \mathbf{x}_{i,t-1})' \end{pmatrix} \right]^{-1} \times \left[\sum_{i=1}^{N} \sum_{t=3}^{T} \begin{pmatrix} y_{i,t-2} - y_{i,t-3} \\ \mathbf{x}_{it} - \mathbf{x}_{i,t-1} \end{pmatrix} (y_{it} - y_{i,t-1}) \right], \tag{4.3.32}$$

and

$$\begin{pmatrix} \tilde{\gamma}_{iv} \\ \tilde{\boldsymbol{\beta}}_{iv} \end{pmatrix} = \left[\sum_{i=1}^{N} \sum_{t=2}^{T} \begin{pmatrix} y_{i,t-2}(y_{i,t-1} - y_{i,t-2}) & y_{i,t-2}(\mathbf{x}_{it} - \mathbf{x}_{i,t-1})' \\ (\mathbf{x}_{it} - \mathbf{x}_{i,t-1})y_{i,t-2} & (\mathbf{x}_{it} - \mathbf{x}_{i,t-1})(\mathbf{x}_{it} - \mathbf{x}_{i,t-1})' \end{pmatrix} \right]^{-1} \times \left[\sum_{i=1}^{N} \sum_{t=2}^{T} \begin{pmatrix} y_{i,t-2} \\ \mathbf{x}_{it} - \mathbf{x}_{i,t-1} \end{pmatrix} (y_{i,t} - y_{i,t-1}) \right] \quad (4.3.33)$$

are consistent. The estimator (4.3.33) has an advantage over (4.3.32) in that the minimum number of time periods required is two, whereas (4.3.33) requires $T \geq 3$. In practice, if $T \geq 3$, the choice between (4.3.33) and (4.3.32) depends on the correlations between $(y_{i,t-1} - y_{i,t-2})$ and $y_{i,t-2}$ or $(y_{i,t-2} - y_{i,t-3})$. For a comparison of asymptotic efficiencies of the instruments $y_{i,t-2}$ or $(y_{i,t-2} - y_{i,t-3})$, see Anderson and Hsiao (1981).

Step 2: Substitute the estimated $\boldsymbol{\beta}$ and γ into the equation

$$\bar{y}_i - \gamma \bar{y}_{i,-1} - \boldsymbol{\beta}' \bar{\mathbf{x}}_i = \boldsymbol{\rho}' \mathbf{z}_i + \alpha_i + \bar{u}_i, \qquad i = 1, \ldots, N, \quad (4.3.34)$$

where $\bar{y}_i = \sum_{t=1}^{T} y_{it}/T$, $\bar{y}_{i,-1} = \sum_{t=1}^{T} y_{i,t-1}/T$, $\bar{\mathbf{x}}_i = \sum_{t=1}^{T} \mathbf{x}_{it}/T$, and $\bar{u}_i = \sum_{t=1}^{T} u_{it}/T$. Estimate $\boldsymbol{\rho}$ by the OLS method.

Step 3: Estimate σ_u^2 and σ_α^2 by

$$\hat{\sigma}_u^2 = \frac{\sum_{i=1}^{N} \sum_{t=2}^{T} [(y_{it} - y_{i,t-1}) - \hat{\gamma}(y_{i,t-1} - y_{i,t-2}) - \hat{\boldsymbol{\beta}}'(\mathbf{x}_{it} - \mathbf{x}_{i,t-1})]^2}{2N(T-1)}, \quad (4.3.35)$$

$$\hat{\sigma}_\alpha^2 = \frac{\sum_{i=1}^{N} (\bar{y}_i - \hat{\gamma} \bar{y}_{i,-1} - \hat{\boldsymbol{\rho}}' \mathbf{z}_i - \hat{\boldsymbol{\beta}}' \bar{\mathbf{x}}_i)^2}{N} - \frac{1}{T} \hat{\sigma}_u^2. \quad (4.3.36)$$

The consistency of these estimators is independent of initial conditions. The instrumental-variable estimators of γ, $\boldsymbol{\beta}$, and σ_u^2 are consistent when N or T or both tend to infinity. The estimators of $\boldsymbol{\rho}$ and σ_α^2 are consistent only when N goes to infinity. They are inconsistent if N is fixed and T tends to infinity. The instrumental-variable method is simple to implement. But if we also wish to test the maintained hypothesis on initial conditions in the random-effects model, it would seem more appropriate to rely on maximum likelihood methods.

4.3.3.d Generalized Method of Moments Estimator

We note that $y_{i,t-2}$ or $(y_{i,t-2} - y_{i,t-3})$ is not the only instrument for $(y_{i,t-1} - y_{i,t-2})$. In fact, it is noted by Amemiya and MaCurdy (1986), Arellano and Bond (1991), Breusch, Mizon, and Schmidt (1989), etc. that all $y_{i,t-2-j}$, $j = 0, 1, \ldots,$ satisfy the conditions $E[y_{i,t-2-j}(y_{i,t-1} - y_{i,t-2})] \neq 0$ and $E[y_{i,t-2-j}(u_{it} - u_{i,t-1})] = 0$. Therefore, they all are legitimate instruments for $(y_{i,t-1} - y_{i,t-2})$. Letting $\Delta = (1 - L)$ where L denotes the lag operator and $\mathbf{q}_{it} = (y_{i0}, y_{i1}, \ldots, y_{i,t-2}, \mathbf{x}_i')'$, where $\mathbf{x}_i' = (\mathbf{x}_{i1}', \ldots, \mathbf{x}_{iT}')$, we have

$$E\mathbf{q}_{it} \Delta u_{it} = 0, \qquad t = 2, \ldots, T. \quad (4.3.37)$$

Stacking the $(T-1)$ first-differenced equations of (4.3.31) in matrix form, we have

$$\Delta \mathbf{y}_i = \Delta \mathbf{y}_{i,-1}\gamma + \Delta X_i \boldsymbol{\beta} + \Delta \mathbf{u}_i, \qquad i = 1, \ldots, N, \tag{4.3.38}$$

where $\Delta \mathbf{y}_i$, $\Delta \mathbf{y}_{i,-1}$, and $\Delta \mathbf{u}_i$ are $(T-1) \times 1$ vectors of the form $(y_{i2} - y_{i1}, \ldots, y_{iT} - y_{i,T-1})'$, $(y_{i1} - y_{i0}, \ldots, y_{i,T-1} - y_{i,T-2})'$, $(u_{i2} - u_{i1}, \ldots, u_{iT} - u_{i,T-1})'$, respectively, and ΔX_i is the $(T-1) \times K$ matrix of $(\mathbf{x}_{i2} - \mathbf{x}_{i1}, \ldots, \mathbf{x}_{iT} - \mathbf{x}_{i,T-1})'$. The $T(T-1)[K_1 + \frac{1}{2}]$ orthogonality (or moment) conditions of (4.3.37) can be represented as

$$E W_i \Delta \mathbf{u}_i = \mathbf{0}, \tag{4.3.39}$$

where

$$W_i = \begin{pmatrix} \mathbf{q}_{i2} & \mathbf{0} & \cdots & \mathbf{0} \\ \mathbf{0} & \mathbf{q}_{i3} & \cdots & \mathbf{0} \\ \vdots & \vdots & \ddots & \vdots \\ \mathbf{0} & \mathbf{0} & \cdots & \mathbf{q}_{iT} \end{pmatrix} \tag{4.3.40}$$

is of dimension $[T(T-1)(K_1 + \frac{1}{2})] \times (T-1)$. The dimension of (4.3.40) in general is much larger than $K_1 + 1$. Thus, Arellano and Bond (1991) suggest a generalized method of moments (GMM) estimator.

The standard method of moments estimator consists of solving the unknown parameter vector $\boldsymbol{\theta}$ by equating the theoretical moments with their empirical counterparts or estimates. For instance, suppose that $\mathbf{m}(\mathbf{y}, \mathbf{x}; \boldsymbol{\theta})$ denotes some population moments of $\mathbf{y}$ and/or $\mathbf{x}$ (say the first and second moments), which are functions of the unknown parameter vector $\boldsymbol{\theta}$ and are supposed to equal some known constants, say zero. Let $\hat{\mathbf{m}}(\mathbf{y}, \mathbf{x}; \boldsymbol{\theta}) = \frac{1}{N}\sum_{i=1}^{N} \mathbf{m}(\mathbf{y}_i, \mathbf{x}_i; \boldsymbol{\theta})$ be their sample estimates based on N independent samples of $(\mathbf{y}_i, \mathbf{x}_i)$. Then the method of moments estimator of $\boldsymbol{\theta}$ is $\hat{\boldsymbol{\theta}}_{\text{mm}}$, such that

$$\mathbf{m}(\mathbf{y}, \mathbf{x}; \boldsymbol{\theta}) = \hat{\mathbf{m}}(\mathbf{y}, \mathbf{x}; \hat{\boldsymbol{\theta}}_{\text{mm}}) = \mathbf{0}. \tag{4.3.41}$$

For instance, the orthogonality conditions between QX_i and $Q\mathbf{u}_i$ for the fixed-effects linear static model (3.2.2), $E(X_i'Q\mathbf{u}_i) = E[X_i'Q(\mathbf{y}_i - \mathbf{e}\alpha_i^* - X_i\boldsymbol{\beta})] = \mathbf{0}$, lead to the LSDV estimator (3.2.8). In this sense, the method of moments estimator may be viewed as descendents of the IV method.

If the number of equations in (4.3.41) is equal to the dimension of $\boldsymbol{\theta}$, it is in general possible to solve for $\hat{\boldsymbol{\theta}}_{\text{mm}}$ uniquely. If the number of equations is greater than the dimension of $\boldsymbol{\theta}$, (4.3.41) in general has no solution. It is then necessary to minimize some norm (or distance measure) of $\hat{\mathbf{m}}(\mathbf{y}, \mathbf{x}; \boldsymbol{\theta}) - \mathbf{m}(\mathbf{y}, \mathbf{x}; \boldsymbol{\theta})$, say

$$[\hat{\mathbf{m}}(\mathbf{y}, \mathbf{x}; \boldsymbol{\theta}) - \mathbf{m}(\mathbf{y}, \mathbf{x}; \boldsymbol{\theta})]' A [\hat{\mathbf{m}}(\mathbf{y}, \mathbf{x}; \boldsymbol{\theta}) - \mathbf{m}(\mathbf{y}, \mathbf{x}; \boldsymbol{\theta})], \tag{4.3.42}$$

where A is some positive definite matrix.

The property of the estimator thus obtained depends on A. The optimal choice of A turns out to be

$$A^* = \{E[\hat{\mathbf{m}}(\mathbf{y}, \mathbf{x}; \boldsymbol{\theta}) - m(\mathbf{y}, \mathbf{x}; \boldsymbol{\theta})][\hat{\mathbf{m}}(\mathbf{y}, \mathbf{x}; \boldsymbol{\theta}) - \mathbf{m}(\mathbf{y}, \mathbf{x}; \boldsymbol{\theta})]'\}^{-1} \tag{4.3.43}$$

(Hansen (1982)). The GMM estimation of $\boldsymbol{\theta}$ is to choose $\hat{\boldsymbol{\theta}}_{\text{GMM}}$ such that it minimizes (4.3.42) when $A = A^*$.

The Arellano and Bond GMM estimator of $\boldsymbol{\theta} = (\gamma, \boldsymbol{\beta}')'$ is obtained by minimizing

$$\left(\frac{1}{N}\sum_{i=1}^{N} \Delta\mathbf{u}_i' \, W_i'\right) \Psi^{-1} \left(\frac{1}{N}\sum_{i=1}^{N} W_i \Delta\mathbf{u}_i\right), \tag{4.3.44}$$

where $\Psi = E[1/N^2 \sum_{i=1}^{N} W_i \Delta\mathbf{u}_i \Delta\mathbf{u}_i' \, W_i']$. Under the assumption that u_{it} is i.i.d. with mean zero and variance σ_u^2, Ψ can be approximated by $(\sigma_u^2/N^2) \sum_{i=1}^{N} W_i \tilde{A} W_i'$, where

$$\underset{(T-1)\times(T-1)}{\tilde{A}} = \begin{bmatrix} 2 & -1 & 0 & \cdots & 0 \\ -1 & 2 & -1 & \cdots & 0 \\ 0 & \ddots & \ddots & \ddots & \vdots \\ \vdots & \ddots & \ddots & 2 & -1 \\ 0 & \cdots & 0 & -1 & 2 \end{bmatrix}. \tag{4.3.45}$$

Thus, the Arellano–Bover GMM estimator takes the form

$$\begin{aligned} \hat{\boldsymbol{\theta}}_{\text{GMM,AB}} = & \left\{ \left[\sum_{i=1}^{N} \begin{pmatrix} \Delta\mathbf{y}_{i,-1}' \\ \Delta X_i' \end{pmatrix} W_i' \right] \left[\sum_{i=1}^{N} W_i \tilde{A} W_i'\right]^{-1} \left[\sum_{i=1}^{N} W_i (\Delta\mathbf{y}_{i,-1}, \Delta X_i)\right] \right\}^{-1} \\ & \times \left\{ \left[\sum_{i=1}^{N} \begin{pmatrix} \Delta\mathbf{y}_{i,-1}' \\ \Delta X_i' \end{pmatrix} W_i' \right] \left[\sum_{i=1}^{N} W_i \tilde{A} W_i'\right]^{-1} \left[\sum_{i=1}^{N} W_i \Delta\mathbf{y}_i\right] \right\}, \end{aligned} \tag{4.3.46}$$

with asymptotic covariance matrix

$$\begin{aligned} &\text{Cov}(\hat{\boldsymbol{\theta}}_{\text{GMM,AB}}) \\ &= \boldsymbol{\sigma}_u^2 \left\{ \left[\sum_{i=1}^{N} \begin{pmatrix} \Delta\mathbf{y}_{i,-1}' \\ \Delta X_i' \end{pmatrix} W_i' \right] \left[\sum_{i=1}^{N} W_i \tilde{A} W_i'\right]^{-1} \left[\sum_{i=1}^{N} W_i (\Delta\mathbf{y}_{i,-1}, \Delta X_i)\right] \right\}^{-1}. \end{aligned} \tag{4.3.47}$$

In addition to the moment conditions (4.3.38), Arellano and Bover (1995) also note that $E\bar{v}_i = 0$, where $\bar{v}_i = \bar{y}_i - \bar{y}_{i,-1}\gamma - \bar{\mathbf{x}}_i'\boldsymbol{\beta} - \boldsymbol{\rho}'\mathbf{z}_i$.[13] Therefore, if instruments $\tilde{\mathbf{q}}_i$ exist (for instance, the constant 1 is a valid instrument) such that

$$E\tilde{\mathbf{q}}_i\bar{v}_i = \mathbf{0}, \tag{4.3.48}$$

then a more efficient GMM estimator can be derived by incorporating this additional moment condition.

Apart from the linear moment conditions (4.3.39) and (4.3.48), Ahn and Schmidt (1995) note that the homoscedasticity condition on $E(v_{it}^2)$ implies the following $T-2$ linear conditions:

$$E(y_{it}\Delta u_{i,t+1} - y_{i,t+1}\Delta u_{i,t+2}) = \mathbf{0}, \qquad t = 1, \ldots, T-2. \quad (4.3.49)$$

Combining (4.3.39), (4.3.48), and (4.3.49), a more efficient GMM estimator can be derived by minimizing[14]

$$\left(\frac{1}{N}\sum_{i=1}^{N}\mathbf{u}_i^{+\prime}W_i^{+\prime}\right)\Psi^{+-1}\left(\frac{1}{N}\sum_{i=1}^{N}W_i^{+}\mathbf{u}_i^{+}\right) \quad (4.3.50)$$

with respect to $\boldsymbol{\theta}$, where $\mathbf{u}_i^+ = (\Delta\mathbf{u}_i', \bar{v}_i)'$, $\Psi^+ = E((1/N^2)\sum_{i=1}^N W_i^+\mathbf{u}_i^+ \times \mathbf{u}_i^{+\prime}W_i^{+\prime})$, and

$$W_i^{+\prime} = \begin{pmatrix} W_i' & W_i^{*\prime} & \mathbf{0} \\ \mathbf{0}' & \mathbf{0}' & \tilde{\mathbf{q}}_i' \end{pmatrix},$$

where

$$\underset{(T-2)\times(T-1)}{W_i^*} = \begin{pmatrix} y_{i1} & -y_{i2} & 0 & 0 & \cdots & 0 & 0 \\ 0 & y_{i2} & -y_{i3} & 0 & \cdots & 0 & 0 \\ \vdots & \vdots & \ddots & \ddots & \ddots & \vdots & \vdots \\ 0 & 0 & \cdots & y_{i,T-3} & -y_{i,T-2} & 0 & 0 \\ 0 & 0 & \cdots & 0 & y_{i,T-2} & -y_{i,T-1} & 0 \end{pmatrix}.$$

However, because the covariance matrix (4.3.49) depends on the unknown $\boldsymbol{\theta}$, it is impractical to implement the GMM. A less efficient, but computationally feasible GMM estimation is to ignore the information that Ψ^+ also depends on $\boldsymbol{\theta}$ and simply replace Ψ by its consistent estimator

$$\hat{\Psi}^+ = \left(\frac{1}{N^2}\sum_{i=1}^{N}W_i^+\hat{\mathbf{u}}_i^+\hat{\mathbf{u}}_i^{+\prime}W_i^{+\prime}\right) \quad (4.3.51)$$

in the objective function (4.3.50) to derive a linear estimator of form (4.3.46), where $\hat{\mathbf{u}}_i^+$ is derived by using some simple consistent estimator of γ and $\boldsymbol{\beta}$, say the IV discussed in Section 4.3.3.c, into (4.3.38) and the $\bar{v}_i$ equation.

In principle, one can improve the asymptotic efficiency of the GMM estimator by adding more moment conditions. For instance, Ahn and Schmidt (1995) note that in addition to the linear moment conditions of (4.3.39), (4.3.48), and (4.3.49), there exist $(T-1)$ nonlinear moment conditions of the form $E((\bar{y}_i - \gamma\bar{y}_{i,-1} - \boldsymbol{\beta}'\bar{\mathbf{x}}_i)\Delta u_{it}) = 0$, $t = 2, \ldots, T$, implied by the homoscedasticity conditions of Ev_{it}^2. Under the additional assumption that $E(\alpha_i y_{it})$ is the same for all t, this condition and condition (4.3.49) can be transformed into the $(2T-2)$ linear moment conditions

$$E[(y_{iT} - \gamma y_{i,T-1} - \boldsymbol{\beta}'\mathbf{x}_{iT})\Delta y_{it}] = 0, \quad t = 1, \ldots, T-1, \quad (4.3.52)$$

and

$$E[(y_{it} - \gamma y_{i,t-1} - \boldsymbol{\beta}'\mathbf{x}_{it})y_{it} - (y_{i,t-1} - \gamma y_{i,t-2} - \boldsymbol{\beta}'\mathbf{x}_{i,t-1})y_{i,t-1}] = 0, \quad t = 2, \ldots, T. \quad (4.3.53)$$

While theoretically it is possible to add additional moment conditions to improve the asymptotic efficiency of GMM, it is doubtful how much efficiency gain one can achieve by using a huge number of moment conditions in a finite sample. Moreover, if higher-moment conditions are used, the estimator can be very sensitive to outlying observations. Through a simulation study, Ziliak (1997) has found that the downward bias in GMM is quite severe as the number of moment conditions expands, outweighing the gains in efficiency. The strategy of exploiting all the moment conditions for estimation is actually not recommended for panel data applications. For further discussions, see Judson and Owen (1999), Kiviet (1995), and Wansbeek and Bekker (1996).

4.3.4 Testing Some Maintained Hypotheses on Initial Conditions

As discussed in Sections 4.3.2 and 4.3.3, the interpretation and consistency property for the MLE and GLS of a random-effects model depend on the initial conditions. Unfortunately, in practice we have very little information on the characteristics of the initial observations. Because some of these hypotheses are nested, Bhargava and Sargan (1983) suggest relying on the likelihood principle to test them. For instance, when y_{i0} are exogenous (case I), we can test the validity of the error-components formulation by maximizing L_1 with or without the restrictions on the covariance matrix V. Let L_1^* denote the maximum of log L_1 subject to the restriction of model (4.3.7), and let L_1^{**} denote the maximum of log L_1 with V being an arbitrary positive definite matrix. Under the null hypothesis, the resulting test statistic $2(L_1^{**} - L_1^*)$ is asymptotically chi-square distributed, with $[T(T+1)/2 - 2]$ degrees of freedom.

Similarly, we can test the validity of the error-components formulation under the assumption that y_{i0} are endogenous. Let the maximum of the log likelihood function under case IVa and case IVc$'$ be denoted by $L_{4\text{a}}^*$ and $L_{4\text{c}'}^*$, respectively. Let the maximum of the log likelihood function under case IVa or IVc$'$ without the restriction (4.3.19) or (4.3.23) [namely, the $(T+1) \times (T+1)$ covariance matrix is arbitrary] be denoted by $L_{4\text{a}}^{**}$ or $L_{4\text{c}'}^{**}$, respectively. Then, under the null, $2(L_{4\text{a}}^{**} - L_{4\text{a}}^*)$ and $2(L_{4\text{c}'}^{**} - L_{4\text{c}'}^*)$ are asymptotically chi-square, with $[(T+1)(T+2)/2 - 2]$ and $[(T+1)(T+2)/2 - 3]$ degrees of freedom, respectively.

To test the stationarity assumption, we denote the maximum of the log likelihood function for case IVb and case IVd$'$ as $L_{4\text{b}}^*$ and $L_{4\text{d}'}^*$, respectively. Then $2(L_{4\text{b}}^* - L_{4\text{a}}^*)$ and $2(L_{4\text{d}'}^* - L_{4\text{c}'}^*)$ are asymptotically chi-square, with one degree of freedom. The statistics $2(L_{4\text{a}}^{**} - L_{4\text{b}}^*)$ and $2(L_{4\text{c}'}^{**} - L_{4\text{d}'}^*)$ can also be used to test the validity of case IVb and case IVd$'$, respectively. They are asymptotically chi-square distributed, with $[(T+1)(T+2)/2 - 3]$ and $[(T+1)(T+2)/2 - 4]$ degrees of freedom, respectively.

We can also generalize Bhargava and Sargan's principle to test the assumption that the initial observations have a common mean μ_w or have different means θ_{i0} under various assumptions about the error process. The statistics $2[L^*_{4c'} - L^*_{4a}]$, $2[L^{**}_{4c'} - L^{**}_{4a}]$, and $2[L^*_{4d'} - L^*_{4b}]$ are asymptotically chi-square distributed, with q, $(q-1)$, and $(q-1)$ degrees of freedom, respectively, where q is the number of unknown coefficients in (4.3.21). We can also test the combined assumption of a common mean and a variance-components formulation by using the statistic $2[L^{**}_{4c'} - L^*_{4a}]$ or $2[L^{**}_{4c'} - L^*_{4b}]$, which are asymptotically chi-square distributed, with $q + (T+1)(T+2)/2 - 3$ and $q + (T+1)(T+2)/2 - 4$ degrees of freedom, respectively.

With regard to the test that y_{i0} are exogenous, unfortunately it is not possible to compare L_1 directly with the likelihood functions of various forms of case IV, because in the former case we are considering the density of $(y_{i1}, \ldots, y_{iT})$ assuming y_{i0} to be exogenous, whereas in the latter case it is the joint density of $(y_{i0}, \ldots, y_{iT})$. However, we can write the joint likelihood function of (4.3.7) and (4.3.21) under the restriction that v_{i0} are independent of η_i (or α_i) and have variance $\sigma^2_{\epsilon 0}$. Namely, we impose the restriction that $\text{Cov}(v_{i0}, v_{it}) = 0$, $t = 1, \ldots, T$, in the $(T+1) \times (T+1)$ variance–covariance matrix of $(y_{i0}, \ldots, y_{iT})$. We denote this likelihood function by L_5. Let L^{**}_5 denote the maximum of log L_5 with unrestricted variance–covariance matrix for $(v_{i0}, \ldots, v_{iT})$. Then we can test the exogeneity of y_{i0} using $2(L^{**}_{4c'} - L^{**}_5)$, which is asymptotically chi-square with T degrees of freedom under the null.

It is also possible to test the exogeneity of y_{i0} by constraining the error terms to have a variance-components structure. Suppose the variance–covariance matrix of $(v_{i1}, \ldots, v_{iT})$ is of the form V [equation (3.3.4)]. Let L^*_5 denote the maximum of the log likelihood function L_5 under this restriction. Let $L^*_{4d'}$ denote the maximum of the log likelihood function of $(y_{i0}, \ldots, y_{iT})$ under the restriction that $E\mathbf{v}_i\mathbf{v}'_i = \tilde{V}^*$, but allowing the variance of v_{i0} and the covariance between v_{i0} and v_{it}, $t = 1, \ldots, T$, to be arbitrary constants σ^2_{w0} and σ^2_τ. The statistic $2(L^*_{4d'} - L^*_5)$ is asymptotically chi-square with one degree of freedom if y_{i0} are exogenous. In practice, however, it may not even be necessary to calculate $L^*_{4d'}$, because $L^*_{4d'} \geq L^*_{4c'}$, and if the null is rejected using $2(L^*_{4c'} - L^*_5)$ against the critical value of chi-square with one degree of freedom, then $2(L^*_{4d'} - L^{**}_5)$ must also reject the null.

4.3.5 Simulation Evidence

In order to investigate the performance of maximum likelihood estimators under various assumptions about the initial conditions, Bhargava and Sargan (1983) conducted Monte Carlo studies. Their true model was generated by

$$y_{it} = 1 + 0.5 y_{i,t-1} - 0.16 z_i + 0.35 x_{it} + \alpha_i + u_{it}, \quad i = 1, \ldots, 100, \quad t = 1, \ldots, 20, \tag{4.3.54}$$

where α_i and u_{it} were independently normally distributed, with means zero and variances 0.09 and 0.4225, respectively. The time-varying exogenous variables x_{it} were generated by

$$x_{it} = 0.1t + \phi_i x_{i,t-1} + \omega_{it}, \qquad \begin{aligned} i &= 1, \ldots, 100, \\ t &= 1, \ldots, 20, \end{aligned} \tag{4.3.55}$$

with ϕ_i and ω_{it} independently normally distributed, with means zero and variances 0.01 and 1, respectively. The time-invariant exogenous variables z_i were generated by

$$z_i = -0.2x_{i4} + \omega_i^*, \qquad i = 1, \ldots, 100, \tag{4.3.56}$$

and ω_i^* were independently normally distributed, with mean zero and variance 1. The z and the x were held fixed over the replications, and the first 10 observations were discarded. Thus, the y_{i0} are in fact stochastic and are correlated with the individual effects α_i. Table 4.2 reproduces the results on the biases in the estimates for various models obtained in 50 replications.

In cases where the y_{i0} are treated as endogenous, the MLE performs extremely well, and the biases in the parameters are almost negligible. But this is not so for the MLE where y_{i0} are treated as exogenous. The magnitude of the bias is about one standard error. The boundary solution of $\sigma_\alpha^2 = 0$ occurs in a number of replications for the error components formulation as well. The likelihood-ratio statistics also rejected the exogeneity of y_{i0} 46 and 50 times, respectively, using the tests $2[L_{4c'}^{**} - L_5^{**}]$ and $2[L_{4c'}^{*} - L_5^{*}]$. Under the endogeneity assumption, the likelihood-ratio statistic $2(L_{4c'}^{**} - L_{4c'}^{*})$ rejected the error-components formulation 4 times (out of 50), whereas under the exogeneity assumption, the statistic $2(L_1^{**} - L_1^{*})$ rejected the error-components formulation 7 times.[15]

4.4 AN EXAMPLE

We have discussed the properties of various estimators for dynamic models with individual-specific effects. In this section we report results from the study of demand for natural gas conducted by Balestra and Nerlove (1966) to illustrate the specific issues involved in estimating dynamic models using observations drawn from a time series of cross sections.

Balestra and Nerlove (1966) assumed that the new demand for gas (inclusive of demand due to the replacement of gas appliances and the demand due to net increases in the stock of such appliances), G^*, was a linear function of the relative price of gas, P, and the total new requirements for all types of fuel, F^*. Let the depreciation rate for gas appliances be r, and assume that the rate of utilization of the stock of appliances is constant; the new demand for gas and the gas consumption at year t, G_t, follow the relation

$$G_t^* = G_t - (1 - r)G_{t-1}. \tag{4.4.1}$$

They also postulated a similar relation between the total new demand for all

Table 4.2. *Simulation results for the biases of the MLEs for dynamic random-effects models*

Coefficient of	y_{i0} exogenous, unrestricted covariance matrix	y_{i0} exogenous, error-components formulation	y_{i0} endogenous, unrestricted covariance matrix	y_{i0} endogenous, error-components formulation
Intercept	−0.1993	−0.1156	−0.0221	0.0045
	(0.142)[a]	(0.1155)	(0.1582)	(0.105)
z_i	0.0203	0.0108	0.0007	−0.0036
	(0.0365)	(0.0354)	(0.0398)	(0.0392)
x_{it}	0.0028	0.0044	0.0046	0.0044
	(0.0214)	(0.0214)	(0.0210)	(0.0214)
$y_{i,t-1}$	0.0674	0.0377	0.0072	−0.0028
	(0.0463)	(0.0355)	(0.0507)	(0.0312)
$\sigma_\alpha^2/\sigma_u^2$		−0.0499		0.0011
		(0.0591)		(0.0588)

[a]Means of the estimated standard errors in parentheses.
Source: Bhargava and Sargan (1983).

types of fuel and the total fuel consumption F, with F approximated by a linear function of the total population N and per capita income I. Substituting these relations into (4.4.1), they obtained

$$G_t = \beta_0 + \beta_1 P_t + \beta_2 \Delta N_t + \beta_3 N_{t-1} + \beta_4 \Delta I_t + \beta_5 I_{t-1} + \beta_6 G_{t-1} + v_t, \tag{4.4.2}$$

where $\Delta N_t = N_t - N_{t-1}$, $\Delta I_t = I_t - I_{t-1}$, and $\beta_6 = 1 - r$.

Balestra and Nerlove used annual U.S. data from 36 states over the period 1957–1962 to estimate the model (4.4.2) for residential and commercial demand for natural gas. Because the average age of the stock of gas appliances during this period was relatively young, it was expected that the coefficient of the lagged gas-consumption variable, β_6, would be less than 1, but not by much. The OLS estimates of (4.4.2) are reported in the second column of Table 4.3. The estimated coefficient of G_{t-1} is 1.01. It is clearly incompatible with a priori theoretical expectations, as it implies a negative depreciation rate for gas appliances.

One possible explanation for the foregoing result is that when cross-sectional and time-series data are combined in the estimation of (4.4.2), certain effects specific to the individual state may be present in the data. To account for such effects, dummy variables corresponding to the 36 different states were introduced into the model. The resulting dummy-variable estimates are shown in the third column of Table 4.3. The estimated coefficient of the lagged endogenous

Table 4.3. *Various estimates of the parameters of Balestra and Nerlove's demand-for-gas model (4.4.2) from the pooled sample, 1957–1962*

Coefficient	OLS	LSDV	GLS
β_0	−3.650	—	−4.091
	(3.316)[a]		(11.544)
β_1	−0.0451	−0.2026	−0.0879
	(0.0270)	(0.0532)	(0.0468)
β_2	0.0174	−0.0135	−0.00122
	(0.0093)	(0.0215)	(0.0190)
β_3	0.00111	0.0327	0.00360
	(0.00041)	(0.0046)	(0.00129)
β_4	0.0183	0.0131	0.0170
	(0.0080)	(0.0084)	(0.0080)
β_5	0.00326	0.0044	0.00354
	(0.00197)	(0.0101)	(0.00622)
β_6	1.010	0.6799	0.9546
	(0.014)	(0.0633)	(0.0372)

[a]Figures in parentheses are standard errors for the corresponding coefficients.
Source: Balestra and Nerlove (1966).

variable is drastically reduced; in fact, it is reduced to such a low level that it implies a depreciation rate of gas appliances of over 30 percent – again highly implausible.

Instead of assuming the regional effect to be fixed, they again estimated (4.4.2) by explicitly incorporating individual state-effects variables into the error term, so that $v_{it} = \alpha_i + u_{it}$, where α_i and u_{it} are independent random variables. The two-step GLS estimates under the assumption that the initial observations are fixed are shown in the fourth column of Table 4.3. The estimated coefficient of lagged consumption is 0.9546. The implied depreciation rate is approximately 4.5 percent, which is in agreement with a priori expectation.

The foregoing results illustrate that by properly taking account of the unobserved heterogeneity in the panel data, Balestra and Nerlove were able to obtain results that were reasonable on the basis of a priori theoretical considerations that they were not able to obtain through attempts to incorporate other variables into the equation by conventional procedures. Moreover, the least-squares and the least-squares dummy-variables estimates of the coefficient of the lagged gas-consumption variable were 1.01 and 0.6799, respectively. In previous sections we showed that for dynamic models with individual-specific effects, the least-squares estimate of the coefficient of the lagged dependent variable is biased upward and the least-squares dummy-variable estimate is biased downward if T is small. Their estimates are in agreement with these theoretical results.[16]

4.5 FIXED-EFFECTS MODELS

If individual effects are considered fixed and different across individuals, then because of the strict multicollinearity between the effects and other time-invariant variables, there is no way one can disentangle the effects from those of other time-invariant variables. We shall therefore assume $\mathbf{z}_i \equiv \mathbf{0}$. When T tends to infinity, even though lagged y does not satisfy the strict exogeneity condition for the regressors, it does satisfy the weak exogeneity condition $E(u_{it} \mid y_{i,t-1}, y_{i,t-2}, .; \alpha_i) = 0$; hence the least-squares regression of y_{it} on lagged $y_{i,t}$ and $\mathbf{x}_{it}$ and the individual specific constant yields consistent estimator. In the case that T is fixed and N tends to infinity, the number of parameters in a fixed-effects specification increases with the number of cross-sectional observations. This is the classical incidental-parameters problem (Neyman and Scott (1948)). In a static model with strict exogeneity assumption, the presence of individual specific constants does not affect the consistency of the CV or MLE estimator of the slope coefficients (see Chapter 3). However, the result no longer holds if lagged dependent variables also appear as explanatory variables. The regularity conditions for the consistency of the MLE is violated. In fact, if u_{it} are normally distributed and y_{i0} are given constants, the MLE of (4.2.1) is the CV of (4.2.2) and (4.2.3). The asymptotic bias is given by (4.2.8).

While the MLE is inconsistent, the IV estimator of (4.3.31) or the GMM estimator (4.3.42) remains consistent and asymptotically normally distributed with fixed α_i^*. The transformed equation (4.3.38) does not involve the incidental parameters α_i^*. The orthogonality condition (4.3.39) remains valid.

In addition to the IV type estimator, a likelihood-based approach based on a transformed likelihood function can also yield a consistent and asymptotically normally distributed estimator.

4.5.1 Transformed Likelihood Approach

The first-difference equation (4.3.31) no longer contains the individual effects α_i^* and is well defined for $t = 2, 3, \ldots, T$, under the assumption that the initial observations y_{i0} and $\mathbf{x}_{i0}$ are available. But (4.3.31) is not defined for $\Delta y_{i1} = (y_{i1} - y_{i0})$, because Δy_{i0} and $\Delta \mathbf{x}_{i0}$ are missing. However, by continuous substitution, we can write Δy_{i1} as

$$\Delta y_{i1} = a_{i1} + \sum_{j=0}^{\infty} \gamma^j \Delta u_{i,1-j}, \tag{4.5.1}$$

where $a_{i1} = \boldsymbol{\beta}' \sum_{j=0}^{\infty} \Delta \mathbf{x}_{i,1-j} \gamma^j$. Since $\Delta \mathbf{x}_{i,1-j}$, $j = 1, 2, \ldots,$ are unavailable, a_{i1} is unknown. Treating a_{i1} as a free parameter to be estimated will again introduce the incidental-parameters problem. To get around this problem, the expected value of a_{i1}, conditional on the observables, has to be a function of a finite number of parameters of the form

$$E(a_{i1} \mid \Delta \mathbf{x}_i) = c^* + \boldsymbol{\pi}' \Delta \mathbf{x}_i, \qquad i = 1, \ldots, N, \tag{4.5.2}$$

where $\boldsymbol{\pi}$ is a $TK_1 \times 1$ vector of constants, and $\Delta \mathbf{x}_i$ is the $TK_1 \times 1$ vector $(\Delta \mathbf{x}_{i1}', \ldots, \Delta \mathbf{x}_{iT}')'$. Hsiao, Pesaran, and Tahmiscioglu (2002) have shown that if $\mathbf{x}_{it}$ are generated by

$$\mathbf{x}_{it} = \boldsymbol{\mu}_i + \mathbf{g}t + \sum_{j=0}^{\infty} \mathbf{b}_j \boldsymbol{\xi}_{i,t-j}, \qquad \sum_{j=0}^{\infty} |\mathbf{b}_j| < \infty, \tag{4.5.3}$$

where $\boldsymbol{\xi}_{it}$ are assumed to be i.i.d. with mean zero and constant covariance matrix, then (4.5.2) holds. The data-generating process of the exogenous variables $\mathbf{x}_{it}$ (4.5.3) can allow fixed and different intercepts $\boldsymbol{\mu}_i$ across i, or $\boldsymbol{\mu}_i$ randomly distributed with a common mean. However, if there exists a trend term in the data generating process of $\mathbf{x}_{it}$, then they must be identical across i.

Given (4.5.2), Δy_{i1} can be written as

$$\Delta y_{i1} = c^* + \boldsymbol{\pi}' \Delta \mathbf{x}_i + v_{i1}^*, \tag{4.5.4}$$

where $v_{i1}^* = \sum_{j=0}^{\infty} \gamma^j \Delta u_{i,1-j} + [a_{i1} - E(a_{i1} \mid \Delta \mathbf{x}_i)]$. By construction, $E(v_{i1}^* \mid \Delta \mathbf{x}_i) = 0$, $E(v_{i1}^{*2}) = \sigma_{v^*}^2$, $E(v_{i1}^* \Delta u_{i2}) = -\sigma_u^2$, and $E(v_{i1}^* \Delta u_{it}) = 0$, for $t = 3, 4, \ldots, T$. It follows that the covariance matrix of $\Delta \mathbf{u}_i^* = (v_{i1}^*, \Delta \mathbf{u}_i')'$ has the form

$$\Omega^* = \sigma_u^2 \begin{bmatrix} h & -1 & 0 & \cdots & 0 \\ -1 & 2 & -1 & \cdots & 0 \\ 0 & \ddots & \ddots & \ddots & \vdots \\ \vdots & \ddots & \ddots & \ddots & -1 \\ 0 & \cdots & 0 & -1 & 2 \end{bmatrix} = \sigma_u^2 \tilde{\Omega}^*, \tag{4.5.5}$$

where $h = \sigma_{v^*}^2 / \sigma_u^2$.

Combining (4.3.31) and (4.5.4), we can write the likelihood function of $\Delta \mathbf{y}_i^* = (\Delta y_{i1}, \ldots, \Delta y_{iT})$, $i = 1, \ldots, N$, in the form

$$(2\pi)^{-\frac{NT}{2}} |\Omega^*|^{-\frac{N}{2}} \exp\left\{ -\frac{1}{2} \sum_{i=1}^{N} \Delta \mathbf{u}_i^{*\prime} \, \Omega^{*-1} \Delta \mathbf{u}_i^* \right\} \tag{4.5.6}$$

if $\Delta \mathbf{u}_i^*$ is normally distributed, where

$$\begin{aligned} \Delta \mathbf{u}_i^* = [&\Delta y_{i1} - c^* - \boldsymbol{\pi}' \Delta \mathbf{x}_i, \Delta y_{i2} - \gamma \Delta y_{i1} \\ &- \boldsymbol{\beta}' \Delta \mathbf{x}_{i2}, \ldots, \Delta y_{iT} - \gamma \Delta y_{i,T-1} - \boldsymbol{\beta}' \Delta \mathbf{x}_{iT}]'. \end{aligned}$$

The likelihood function again only depends on a fixed number of parameters and satisfies the standard regularity conditions, so that the MLE is consistent and asymptotically normally distributed as $N \to \infty$.

Since $|\tilde{\Omega}^*| = 1 + T(h-1)$ and

$$\tilde{\Omega}^{*-1} = [1 + T(h-1)]^{-1} \times \begin{bmatrix} T & T-1 & \cdots & 2 & 1 \\ T-1 & (T-1)h & \cdots & 2h & h \\ \vdots & \vdots & & \vdots & \vdots \\ 2 & 2h & \cdots & 2[(T-2)h-(T-3)] & (T-2)h-(T-3) \\ 1 & h & \cdots & (T-2)h-(T-3) & (T-1)h-(T-2) \end{bmatrix}, \tag{4.5.7}$$

the logarithm of the likelihood function (4.5.6) is

$$\begin{aligned} \log L = &-\frac{NT}{2} \log 2\pi - \frac{NT}{2} \log \sigma_u^2 - \frac{N}{2} \log [1 + T(h-1)] \\ &- \frac{1}{2} \sum_{i=1}^{N} [(\Delta \mathbf{y}_i^* - H_i \boldsymbol{\psi})' \Omega^{*-1} (\Delta \mathbf{y}_i^* - H_i \boldsymbol{\psi})], \end{aligned} \tag{4.5.8}$$

where $\Delta \mathbf{y}_i^* = (\Delta y_{i1}, \ldots, \Delta y_{iT})'$, $\boldsymbol{\psi} = (c^*, \boldsymbol{\pi}', \gamma, \boldsymbol{\beta}')'$, and

$$H_i = \begin{bmatrix} 1 & \Delta \mathbf{x}_i' & 0 & \mathbf{0}' \\ 0 & \mathbf{0}' & \Delta y_{i1} & \Delta \mathbf{x}_{i2}' \\ \vdots & \vdots & \vdots & \vdots \\ 0 & \mathbf{0}' & \Delta y_{i,T-1} & \Delta \mathbf{x}_{iT}' \end{bmatrix}.$$

The MLE is obtained by solving the following equations simultaneously:

$$\hat{\boldsymbol{\psi}} = \left(\sum_{i=1}^{N} H_i' \hat{\tilde{\Omega}}^{*-1} H_i\right)^{-1} \left(\sum_{i=1}^{N} H_i' \hat{\tilde{\Omega}}^{*-1} \Delta \mathbf{y}_i^*\right), \tag{4.5.9}$$

$$\hat{\sigma}_u^2 = \frac{1}{NT} \sum_{i=1}^{N} [(\Delta \mathbf{y}_i^* - H_i \hat{\boldsymbol{\psi}})' (\hat{\tilde{\Omega}}^*)^{-1} (\Delta \mathbf{y}_i^* - H_i \hat{\boldsymbol{\psi}})], \tag{4.5.10}$$

$$\hat{h} = \frac{T-1}{T} + \frac{1}{\hat{\sigma}_u^2 N T^2} \sum_{i=1}^{N} [(\Delta \mathbf{y}_i^* - H_i \hat{\boldsymbol{\psi}})' (\mathbf{J}\mathbf{J}') (\Delta \mathbf{y}_i^* - H_i \hat{\boldsymbol{\psi}})], \tag{4.5.11}$$

where $\mathbf{J}' = (T, T-1, \ldots, 2, 1)$. One way to obtain the MLE is to iterate among (4.5.9)–(4.5.11) conditionally on the early round estimates of the other parameters until the solution converges, or to use a Newton–Raphson iterative scheme (Hsiao, Pesaran, and Tahmiscioglu (2002)).

4.5.2 Minimum-Distance Estimator

Conditional on Ω^*, the MLE is the minimum-distance estimator (MDE) of the form

$$\min \sum_{i=1}^{N} \Delta \mathbf{u}_i^{*\prime} \, \Omega^{*-1} \Delta \mathbf{u}_i^*. \tag{4.5.12}$$

In the case that Ω^* is unknown, a two-step feasible MDE can be implemented. In the first step we obtain consistent estimators of σ_u^2 and σ_{v*}^2. For instance, we can regress (4.5.4) across i to obtain the least-squares residuals $\hat{v}_{i1}^*$, then estimate

$$\hat{\sigma}_{v*}^2 = \frac{1}{N - TK_1 - 1} \sum_{i=1}^{N} \hat{v}_{i1}^{*2}. \tag{4.5.13}$$

Similarly, we can apply the IV to (4.3.31) and obtain the estimated residuals $\Delta \hat{u}_{it}$ and

$$\hat{\sigma}_u^2 = \frac{1}{N(T-1)} \sum_{i=1}^{N} \Delta \hat{\mathbf{u}}_i' \, \tilde{A}^{-1} \Delta \hat{\mathbf{u}}_i, \tag{4.5.14}$$

where $\tilde{A}$ is defined in (4.3.45).

In the second step, we substitute estimated σ_u^2 and σ_{v*}^2 into (4.5.5) and treat them as if they were known, and use (4.5.9) to obtain the MDE of $\boldsymbol{\psi}$, $\hat{\boldsymbol{\psi}}_{\text{MDE}}$.

The asymptotic covariance matrix of the MDE, $\text{Var}(\hat{\boldsymbol{\psi}}_{\text{MDE}})$, using the true Ω^* as the weighting matrix, is equal to $(\sum_{i=1}^{N} H_i' \Omega^{*-1} H_i)^{-1}$. The asymptotic covariance of the feasible MDE using a consistently estimated Ω^*, $\text{Var}(\hat{\boldsymbol{\psi}}_{\text{FMDE}})$, contrary to the static case, is equal to (Hsiao, Pesaran and Tahmiscioglu (2002))

$$\left(\sum_{i=1}^{N} H_i'\Omega^{*-1}H_i\right)^{-1} + \left(\sum_{i=1}^{N} H_i'\Omega^{*-1}H_i\right)^{-1} \begin{bmatrix} 0 & \mathbf{0}' & 0 & \mathbf{0}' \\ \mathbf{0} & \mathbf{0} & \mathbf{0} & \mathbf{0} \\ 0 & \mathbf{0}' & d & \mathbf{0}' \\ \mathbf{0} & \mathbf{0} & \mathbf{0} & \mathbf{0} \end{bmatrix} \left(\frac{1}{N}\sum_{i=1}^{N} H_i'\Omega^{*-1}H_i\right)^{-1}, \tag{4.5.15}$$

where

$$d = \frac{[\gamma^{T-2} + 2\gamma^{T-3} + \cdots + (T-1)]^2}{[1 + T(h-1)]^2\sigma_u^4} \times \left(\sigma_u^4 \operatorname{Var}\left(\hat{\sigma}_{v*}^2\right) + \sigma_{v*}^4 \operatorname{Var}\left(\hat{\sigma}_u^2\right) - 2\sigma_u^2\sigma_{v*}^2 \operatorname{Cov}\left(\hat{\sigma}_{v*}^2, \hat{\sigma}_u^2\right)\right).$$

The second term of (4.5.15) arises because the estimation of $\boldsymbol{\psi}$ and Ω^* are not asymptotically independent when the lagged dependent variables also appear as regressors.

4.5.3 Relations between the Likelihood-Based Estimator and the Generalized Method of Moments Estimated (GMM)

Although normality is assumed to derive the transformed MLE and MDE, it is not required. Both estimators remain consistent and asymptotically normally distributed, even though the errors are not normally distributed. Under normality, the transformed MLE achieves the Cramér–Rao lower bound for the transformed model, and hence is fully efficient. Even without normality, the transformed MLE or MDE is more efficient than the GMM that only uses second-moment restrictions if Ω^* is known.

Using the formula of the partitioned inverse (e.g., Amemiya (1985)), the covariance matrix of the MDE of $(\gamma, \boldsymbol{\beta})$ is of the form

$$\operatorname{Cov}\begin{pmatrix} \hat{\gamma}_{\text{MDE}} \\ \hat{\boldsymbol{\beta}}_{\text{MDE}} \end{pmatrix} = \sigma_u^2 \left[\sum_{i=1}^{N} \begin{pmatrix} \Delta\mathbf{y}_{i,-1}' \\ \Delta X_i' \end{pmatrix} \left(\tilde{A} - \frac{1}{h}\mathbf{g}\mathbf{g}'\right)^{-1} (\Delta\mathbf{y}_{i,-1},\ \Delta X_i)\right]^{-1}, \tag{4.5.16}$$

where $\mathbf{g}' = (-1, 0, \ldots, 0)$. We note that (4.5.16) is smaller than

$$\sigma_u^2 \left[\sum_{i=1}^{N} \begin{pmatrix} \Delta\mathbf{y}_{i,-1}' \\ \Delta X_i' \end{pmatrix} \tilde{A}^{-1} (\Delta\mathbf{y}_{i,-1}, \Delta X_i)\right]^{-1}, \tag{4.5.17}$$

in the sense that the difference between the two matrices is a negative semidefinite matrix, because $\tilde{A} - (\tilde{A} - \frac{1}{h}\mathbf{g}\mathbf{g}')$ is a positive semidefinite matrix.

Furthermore,

$$\sum_{i=1}^{N} \begin{pmatrix} \Delta \mathbf{y}'_{i,-1} \\ \Delta X'_i \end{pmatrix} \tilde{A}^{-1}(\Delta \mathbf{y}_{i,-1}, \Delta X_i) \\ - \left[\sum_{i=1}^{N} \begin{pmatrix} \Delta \mathbf{y}'_{i,-1} \\ \Delta X'_i \end{pmatrix} W'_i \right] \left(\sum_{i=1}^{N} W_i \tilde{A} W'_i \right)^{-1} \left[\sum_{i=1}^{N} W_i (\Delta y_{i,-1}, \Delta X_i) \right] \\ = D'[I - Q(Q'Q)^{-1}Q]D, \quad (4.5.18)$$

is a positive semidefinite matrix, where $D = (D'_1, \ldots, D'_N)'$, $Q = (Q'_1, Q'_2, \ldots, Q'_N)'$, $D_i = \Lambda'(\Delta \mathbf{y}_{i,-1}, \Delta X_i)$, $Q_i = \Lambda^{-1} W_i$, and $\Lambda \Lambda' = \tilde{A}^{-1}$. Therefore, the asymptotic covariance matrix (4.3.47) of the GMM estimator (4.3.46) is greater than (4.5.17), which is greater than (4.5.16) in the sense that the difference of the two covariance matrix is a positive semidefinite matrix.

When $\tilde{\Omega}^*$ is unknown, the asymptotic covariance matrix of (4.3.46) remains (4.3.47). But the asymptotic covariance matrix of the feasible MDE is (4.5.15). Although the first term of (4.5.15) is smaller than (4.3.47), it is not clear that with the addition of the second term it will remain smaller. However, it is very likely that it will, for several reasons. First, additional information due to the Δy_{i1} equation is utilized, which can be substantial (e.g., see Hahn (1999)). Second, the GMM method uses the $(t-1)$ instruments $(y_{i0}, \ldots, y_{i,t-2})$ for the Δy_{it} equation for $t = 2, 3, \ldots, T$. The likelihood-based approach uses the t instruments $(y_{i0}, y_{i1}, \ldots, y_{i,t-1})$. Third, the likelihood approach uses the condition $E(\Delta \mathbf{u}_i^*) = \mathbf{0}$, and the GMM method uses the condition $E(\frac{1}{N} \sum_{i=1}^{N} W_i \Delta \mathbf{u}_i) = \mathbf{0}$. The grouping of observations in general will lead to a loss of information.[17]

Hsiao, Pesaran, and Tahmiscioglu (2002) have conducted Monte Carlo studies to compare the performance of the IV of (4.3.31), the GMM of (4.3.43), the MLE, and the MDE. They generate y_{it} by

$$y_{it} = \alpha_i + \gamma y_{i,t-1} + \beta x_{it} + u_{it}, \quad (4.5.19)$$

where the error term u_{it} is generated from two schemes. One is $N(0, \sigma_u^2)$. The other is the mean adjusted chi-square with two degrees of freedom. The regressor x_{it} is generated according to

$$x_{it} = \mu_i + gt + \xi_{it}, \quad (4.5.20)$$

where ξ_{it} follows an autoregressive moving average process

$$\xi_{it} - \phi \xi_{i,t-1} = \epsilon_{it} + \theta \epsilon_{i,t-1}, \quad (4.5.21)$$

and $\epsilon_{it} \sim N(0, \sigma_\epsilon^2)$. The fixed effects μ_i and α_i are generated from a variety of schemes such as being correlated with x_{it} or uncorrelated with x_{it} but from a mixture of different distributions. Table 4.4 gives a summary of the different designs of the Monte Carlo study.

In generating y_{it} and x_{it}, both are assumed to start from zero. But the first 50 observations are discarded. The bias and root mean square error (RMSE)

Table 4.4. *Monte Carlo design*

Design number	γ	β	ϕ	θ	g	$R^2_{\Delta y}$	σ_ϵ
1	0.4	0.6	0.5	0.5	0.01	0.2	0.800
2	0.4	0.6	0.9	0.5	0.01	0.2	0.731
3	0.4	0.6	1	0.5	0.01	0.2	0.711
4	0.4	0.6	0.5	0.5	0.01	0.4	1.307
5	0.4	0.6	0.9	0.5	0.01	0.4	1.194
6	0.4	0.6	1	0.5	0.01	0.4	1.161
7	0.8	0.2	0.5	0.5	0.01	0.2	1.875
8	0.8	0.2	0.9	0.5	0.01	0.2	1.302
9	0.8	0.2	1	0.5	0.01	0.2	1.104
10	0.8	0.2	0.5	0.5	0.01	0.4	3.062
11	0.8	0.2	0.9	0.5	0.01	0.4	2.127
12	0.8	0.2	1	0.5	0.01	0.4	1.803

Source: Hsiao, Pesaran, and Tahmiscioglu (2002, Table 1).

of various estimators of γ and β when $T = 5$ and $N = 50$ based on 2500 replications are reported in Tables 4.5 and 4.6 respectively. The results show that the bias of the MLE of γ as a percentage of the true value is smaller than 1 percent in most cases. The bias of the IV of γ can be significant for certain data-generating processes. The MDE and GMM of γ also have substantial downward biases in all designs. The bias of the GMM estimator of γ can be as large as 15 to 20 percent in many cases and is larger than the bias of the MDE. The MLE also has the smallest RMSE, followed by the MDE and then the GMM. The IV has the largest RMSE.

4.5.4 Random- versus Fixed-Effects Specification

When α_i are random, the MLE of the transformed likelihood function (4.5.6) or the MDE (4.5.12) remains consistent and asymptotically normally distributed. However, comparing the likelihood function of (4.3.25) with (4.5.6), it is obvious that first-differencing reduces the number of time-series observations by one per cross-sectional unit, and hence will not be as efficient as the MLE of (4.3.25) when α_i are indeed random. However, if α_i are fixed, then the MLE of (4.3.25) yields an inconsistent estimator.

The transformed MLE or MDE is consistent under a more general data-generating process of $\mathbf{x}_{it}$ than the MLE of (4.3.25) or the GLS (4.3.29). In order for the Bhargava–Sargan (1983) MLE of the random-effects model to be consistent, we shall have to assume that the $\mathbf{x}_{it}$ are generated from the same stationary process with common means (equation (4.3.20)). Otherwise, $E(y_{i0} \mid \mathbf{x}_i) = \mathbf{c}_i + \boldsymbol{\pi}_i'\mathbf{x}_i$, where $\mathbf{c}_i$ and $\boldsymbol{\pi}_i$ vary across i, and we have the incidental-parameters problem again. On the other hand, the transformed likelihood approach allows $\mathbf{x}_{it}$ to have different means (or intercepts) (equation (4.5.3)). Therefore it appears that if one is not sure about the assumption on the effects α_i, or the

Table 4.5. *Bias of estimators ($T = 5$ and $N = 50$)*

		Bias			
Design	Coeff.	IVE	MDE	MLE	GMM
1	$\gamma = 0.4$	0.0076201	−0.050757	−0.000617	−0.069804
	$\beta = 0.6$	−0.001426	0.0120812	0.0023605	0.0161645
2	$\gamma = 0.4$	0.0220038	−0.052165	−0.004063	−0.072216
	$\beta = 0.6$	−0.007492	0.0232612	0.0027946	0.0321212
3	$\gamma = 0.4$	1.3986691	−0.054404	−0.003206	−0.075655
	$\beta = 0.6$	−0.386998	0.0257393	0.0002997	0.0365942
4	$\gamma = 0.4$	0.0040637	−0.026051	−0.001936	−0.03616
	$\beta = 0.6$	0.0004229	0.0066165	0.0019218	0.0087369
5	$\gamma = 0.4$	0.1253257	−0.023365	−0.000211	−0.033046
	$\beta = 0.6$	−0.031759	0.0113724	0.0016388	0.0155831
6	$\gamma = 0.4$	−0.310397	−0.028377	−0.00351	−0.040491
	$\beta = 0.6$	0.0640605	0.0146638	0.0022274	0.0209054
7	$\gamma = 0.8$	−0.629171	−0.108539	0.009826	−0.130115
	$\beta = 0.2$	−0.018477	0.0007923	0.0026593	0.0007962
8	$\gamma = 0.8$	−1.724137	−0.101727	0.0027668	−0.128013
	$\beta = 0.2$	0.0612431	0.0109865	−0.000011	0.013986
9	$\gamma = 0.8$	−0.755159	−0.102658	0.00624	−0.133843
	$\beta = 0.2$	−0.160613	0.0220208	0.0002624	0.0284606
10	$\gamma = 0.8$	0.1550445	−0.045889	0.001683	−0.05537
	$\beta = 0.2$	0.0096871	0.0000148	0.0007889	−0.000041
11	$\gamma = 0.8$	−0.141257	−0.038216	−0.000313	−0.050427
	$\beta = 0.2$	0.0207338	0.0048828	0.0007621	0.0063229
12	$\gamma = 0.8$	0.5458734	−0.039023	0.0005702	−0.053747
	$\beta = 0.2$	−0.069023	0.0079627	0.0003263	0.010902

Source: Hsiao, Pesaran, and Tahmiscioglu (2002, Table 2).

homogeneity assumption about the data-generating process for $\mathbf{x}_{it}$, one should work with the transformed likelihood function (4.5.6) or the MDE (4.5.12), despite the fact that one may lose efficiency under the ideal condition.

The use of the transformed likelihood approach also offers the possibility of using a Hausman (1978) test for fixed- versus random-effects specification, or of testing the homogeneity and stationarity assumption about the $\mathbf{x}_{it}$ process under the assumption that α_i are random. Under the null of random effects and homogeneity of the $\mathbf{x}_{it}$ process, the MLE of (4.3.25) is asymptotically efficient. The transformed MLE of (4.5.6) is consistent, but not efficient. On the other hand, if α_i are fixed or $\mathbf{x}_{it}$ is not generated by a homogeneous process but satisfies (4.5.3), the transformed MLE of (4.5.6) is consistent, but the MLE of (4.3.25) is inconsistent. Therefore, a Hausman type test statistic (3.5.2) can be constructed by using the difference between the two estimators.

Table 4.6. *Root mean square error ($T = 5$ and $N = 50$)*

		Root Mean Square Error			
Design	Coeff.	IVE	MDE	MLE	GMM
1	$\gamma = 0.4$	0.1861035	0.086524	0.0768626	0.1124465
	$\beta = 0.6$	0.1032755	0.0784007	0.0778179	0.0800119
2	$\gamma = 0.4$	0.5386099	0.0877669	0.0767981	0.11512
	$\beta = 0.6$	0.1514231	0.0855346	0.0838699	0.091124
3	$\gamma = 0.4$	51.487282	0.0889483	0.0787108	0.1177141
	$\beta = 0.6$	15.089928	0.0867431	0.0848715	0.0946891
4	$\gamma = 0.4$	0.1611908	0.0607957	0.0572515	0.0726422
	$\beta = 0.6$	0.0633505	0.0490314	0.0489283	0.0497323
5	$\gamma = 0.4$	2.3226456	0.0597076	0.0574316	0.0711803
	$\beta = 0.6$	0.6097378	0.0529131	0.0523433	0.0556706
6	$\gamma = 0.4$	14.473198	0.0620045	0.0571656	0.0767767
	$\beta = 0.6$	2.9170627	0.0562023	0.0550687	0.0607588
7	$\gamma = 0.8$	27.299614	0.1327602	0.116387	0.1654403
	$\beta = 0.2$	1.2424372	0.0331008	0.0340688	0.0332449
8	$\gamma = 0.8$	65.526156	0.1254994	0.1041461	0.1631983
	$\beta = 0.2$	3.2974597	0.043206	0.0435698	0.0450143
9	$\gamma = 0.8$	89.83669	0.1271169	0.104646	0.1706031
	$\beta = 0.2$	5.2252014	0.0535363	0.0523473	0.0582538
10	$\gamma = 0.8$	12.201019	0.074464	0.0715665	0.0884389
	$\beta = 0.2$	0.6729934	0.0203195	0.020523	0.0203621
11	$\gamma = 0.8$	17.408874	0.0661821	0.0642971	0.0822454
	$\beta = 0.2$	1.2541247	0.0268981	0.026975	0.02756742
12	$\gamma = 0.8$	26.439613	0.0674678	0.0645253	0.0852814
	$\beta = 0.2$	2.8278901	0.0323355	0.0323402	0.0338716

Source: Hsiao, Pesaran, and Tahmiscioglu (2002, Table 5).

4.6 ESTIMATION OF DYNAMIC MODELS WITH ARBITRARY CORRELATIONS IN THE RESIDUALS

In previous sections we discussed estimation of the dynamic model

$$y_{it} = \gamma y_{i,t-1} + \boldsymbol{\beta}'\mathbf{x}_{it} + \alpha_i^* + u_{it}, \qquad \begin{aligned} i &= 1, \dots, N, \\ t &= 1, \dots, T, \end{aligned} \tag{4.6.1}$$

under the assumption that u_{it} are serially uncorrelated, where we now again let $\mathbf{x}_{it}$ stand for a $K \times 1$ vector of time-varying exogenous variables. When T is fixed and N tends to infinity, we can relax the restrictions on the serial correlation structure of u_{it} and still obtain efficient estimates of γ and $\boldsymbol{\beta}$.

Taking the first difference of (4.6.1) to eliminate the individual effect α_i^*, and stacking all equations for a single individual, we have a system of $(T - 1)$

equations,

$$\begin{aligned}
y_{i2} - y_{i1} &= \gamma(y_{i1} - y_{i0}) + \boldsymbol{\beta}'(\mathbf{x}_{i2} - \mathbf{x}_{i1}) + (u_{i2} - u_{i1}),\\
y_{i3} - y_{i2} &= \gamma(y_{i2} - y_{i1}) + \boldsymbol{\beta}'(\mathbf{x}_{i3} - \mathbf{x}_{i2}) + (u_{i3} - u_{i2}),\\
&\vdots\\
y_{iT} - y_{i,T-1} &= \gamma(y_{i,T-1} - y_{i,T-2}) + \boldsymbol{\beta}'(\mathbf{x}_{iT} - \mathbf{x}_{i,T-1})\\
&\quad + (u_{iT} - u_{i,T-1}), \qquad i = 1, \dots, N,
\end{aligned} \tag{4.6.2}$$

We complete the system (4.6.2) with the identities

$$\begin{aligned}
y_{i0} &= E^*(y_{i0} \mid \mathbf{x}_{i1}, \dots, \mathbf{x}_{iT}) + [y_{i0} - E^*(y_{i0} \mid \mathbf{x}_{i1}, \dots, \mathbf{x}_{iT})]\\
&= a_0 + \sum_{t=1}^{T} \boldsymbol{\pi}'_{0t}\mathbf{x}_{it} + \epsilon_{i0},
\end{aligned} \tag{4.6.3}$$

and

$$\begin{aligned}
y_{i1} &= E^*(y_{i1} \mid \mathbf{x}_{i1}, \dots, \mathbf{x}_{iT}) + [y_{i1} - E^*(y_{i1} \mid \mathbf{x}_{i1}, \dots, \mathbf{x}_{iT})]\\
&= a_1 + \sum_{t=1}^{T} \boldsymbol{\pi}'_{1t}\mathbf{x}_{it} + \epsilon_{i1}, \qquad i = 1, \dots, N,
\end{aligned} \tag{4.6.4}$$

where E^* denotes the projection operator. Because (4.6.3) and (4.6.4) are exactly identified equations, we can ignore them and apply the three-stage least-squares (3SLS) or generalized 3SLS (see Chapter 5) to the system (4.6.2) only. With regard to the cross-equation constraints in (4.6.2), one can either directly substitute them out or first obtain unknown nonzero coefficients of each equation ignoring the cross-equation linear constraints, then impose the constraints and use the constrained estimation formula [Theil (1971, p. 281, equation (8.5))].

Because the system (4.6.2) does not involve the individual effects α_i^*, nor does the estimation method rely on specific restrictions on the serial-correlation structure of u_{it}, the method is applicable whether α_i^* are treated as fixed or random or as being correlated with $\mathbf{x}_{it}$. However, in order to implement simultaneous-equations estimation methods to (4.6.2) without imposing restrictions on the serial-correlation structure of u_{it}, there must exist strictly exogenous variables $\mathbf{x}_{it}$ such that

$$E(u_{it} \mid \mathbf{x}_{i1}, \dots, \mathbf{x}_{iT}) = 0. \tag{4.6.5}$$

Otherwise, the coefficient γ and the serial correlations of u_{it} cannot be disentangled (e.g., Binder, Hsiao, and Pesaran (2000)).

4.7 FIXED-EFFECTS VECTOR AUTOREGRESSIVE MODELS

4.7.1 Model Formulation

Vector autoregressive (VAR) models have become a widely used modeling tool in economics (e.g., Hsiao (1979a,b, 1982); Sims (1980)). To provide more flexibility to the VAR modeling for panel data, it is common to assume that fixed individual specific effects $\boldsymbol{\alpha}_i^*$ are present for the panel VAR (PVAR) models (Holtz-Eakin, Newey, and Rosen (1988)):

$$\Phi(L)\mathbf{y}_{it} = \mathbf{y}_{it} - \Phi_1\mathbf{y}_{i,t-1} - \cdots - \Phi_p\mathbf{y}_{i,t-p} = \boldsymbol{\alpha}_i^* + \boldsymbol{\epsilon}_{it}, \quad i = 1, \ldots, N, \quad t = 1, \ldots, T, \tag{4.7.1}$$

where $\mathbf{y}_{it}$ is an $m \times 1$ vector of observed random variables, $\boldsymbol{\alpha}_i^*$ is an $m \times 1$ vector of individual specific constants that vary with i, $\boldsymbol{\epsilon}_{it}$ is an $m \times 1$ vector of random variables that is independently, identically distributed with mean zero and covariance matrix Ω, and $\Phi(L) = I_m - \Phi_1 L - \cdots - \Phi_p L^p$ is a pth-order polynomial of the lag operator L, $L^s\mathbf{y}_t = \mathbf{y}_{t-s}$.

It is well known that time-series inference on VARs critically depends on whether the underlying processes are (trend) stationary, or integrated, or cointegrated, and, if they are cointegrated, on the rank of cointegration[18] (e.g., Sims, Stock, and Watson (1990); Phillips (1991); Johansen (1995); Pesaran, Shin, and Smith (2000)). To simplify the analysis, instead of considering (4.7.1) directly, we consider

$$\Phi(L)(\mathbf{y}_{it} - \boldsymbol{\eta}_i - \boldsymbol{\delta}t) = \boldsymbol{\epsilon}_{it}, \tag{4.7.2}$$

where the roots of the determinant equation

$$|\Phi(\rho)| = 0 \tag{4.7.3}$$

either are equal to unity or fall outside the unit circle. Under the assumption that $E\boldsymbol{\epsilon}_{it} = \mathbf{0}$, it follows that

$$E(\mathbf{y}_{it} - \boldsymbol{\eta}_i - \boldsymbol{\delta}t) = \mathbf{0}. \tag{4.7.4}$$

To allow for the possibility of the presence of unit roots, we assume that

$$E(\mathbf{y}_{it} - \boldsymbol{\eta}_i - \boldsymbol{\delta}t)(\mathbf{y}_{it} - \boldsymbol{\eta}_i - \boldsymbol{\delta}t)' = \Psi_t. \tag{4.7.5}$$

Model (4.7.2)–(4.7.5) encompasses many well-known PVAR models as special cases. For instance:

Case 1: *Stationary PVAR with fixed effects.* Let $\boldsymbol{\delta} = \mathbf{0}_{m\times 1}$. If all roots of (4.7.3) fall outside the unit circle, (4.7.2) becomes (4.7.1) with

$\boldsymbol{\alpha}_i^* = -\Pi\boldsymbol{\eta}_i$, and

$$\Pi = -\left(I_m - \sum_{j=1}^{p} \Phi_j\right). \tag{4.7.6}$$

Case 2: *Trend-stationary PVAR with fixed effects.* If all roots of (4.7.3) fall outside the unit circle and $\boldsymbol{\delta} \neq \mathbf{0}$, we have

$$\Phi(L)\mathbf{y}_{it} = \mathbf{a}_{i0} + \mathbf{a}_1 t + \epsilon_{it}, \tag{4.7.7}$$

where $\mathbf{a}_{i0} = -\Pi\boldsymbol{\eta}_i + (\Gamma + \Pi)\boldsymbol{\delta}$,

$$\Gamma = -\Pi + \sum_{j=1}^{p} j\Phi_j, \tag{4.7.8}$$

and $\mathbf{a}_1 = -\Pi\boldsymbol{\delta}$.

Case 3: *PVAR with unit roots (but noncointegrated).*

$$\Phi^*(L)\Delta\mathbf{y}_{it} = -\Pi^*\boldsymbol{\delta} + \boldsymbol{\epsilon}_{it}, \tag{4.7.9}$$

where $\Delta = (1 - L)$,

$$\Phi^*(L) = I_m - \sum_{j=1}^{p-1} \Phi_j^* L^j, \tag{4.7.10}$$

$\Phi_j^* = -(I_m - \sum_{\ell=1}^{j} \Phi_\ell)$, $j = 1, 2. \ldots, p-1$, and $\Pi^* = -(I_m - \sum_{j=1}^{p-1} \Phi_j^*)$.

Case 4: *Cointegrated PVAR with fixed effects.* If some roots of (4.7.3) are equal to unity and $\text{rank}(\Pi) = r$, $0 < r < m$, then (4.7.2) may be rewritten in the form of a panel vector error-corrections model

$$\Delta\mathbf{y}_{it} = \boldsymbol{\alpha}_i^* + (\Gamma + \Pi)\boldsymbol{\delta} + \mathbf{a}_1 t + \Pi\mathbf{y}_{i,t-1} + \sum_{j=1}^{p-1} \Gamma_j \Delta\mathbf{y}_{i,t-j} + \boldsymbol{\epsilon}_{it}, \tag{4.7.11}$$

where $\Gamma_j = -\sum_{s=j+1}^{p} \Phi_s$, $j = 1, \ldots, p-1$, and Π can be decomposed as the product $\Pi = J\boldsymbol{\beta}$ of two $m \times r$ matrices J and $\boldsymbol{\beta}$, with rank r, and $J_\perp' \beta_\perp$ is of rank $m - r$, where $J_\perp$ and $\beta_\perp$ are $m \times (m - r)$ matrices of full column rank such that $J' J_\perp = \mathbf{0}$ and $\boldsymbol{\beta}'\boldsymbol{\beta}_\perp = \mathbf{0}$ (Johansen (1995)).

The reason for formulating the fixed-effects VAR model in terms of (4.7.2)–(4.7.5) rather than (4.7.1) is that it puts restrictions on the model intercepts and trend term so that the time-series properties of $\mathbf{y}_{it}$ remain the same in the presence of unit roots and cointegration. For instance, when $\boldsymbol{\delta} = 0$, whether the roots of (4.7.3) all fall outside the unit circle or one or more roots are equal to unity, $\mathbf{y}_{it}$ exhibit no trend growth. However, if $\boldsymbol{\alpha}_i^*$ is unrestricted, then $\mathbf{y}_{it}$ will exhibit differential trend growth if unit roots are present. If $\boldsymbol{\delta} \neq \mathbf{0}$, (4.7.2) ensures that the trend growth of $\mathbf{y}_{it}$ is linear whether the roots of (4.7.3) are all outside the unit circle or some or all are unity. But if the trend term is unrestricted, then $\mathbf{y}_{it}$ exhibit linear trends if the roots of (4.7.3) all fall outside the unit circle and exhibit quadratic trends if one or more roots of (4.7.3) are equal to unity (e.g. Pesaran, Shin, and Smith (2000)).

When the time dimension of the panel is short, just as in the single-equation fixed-effects dynamic panel data model (Section 4.5), (4.7.2) raises the classical incidental-parameters problem and the issue of modeling initial observations. For ease of exposition, we shall illustrate the estimation and inference by considering $p = 1$, namely, the model

$$(I - \Phi L)(\mathbf{y}_{it} - \boldsymbol{\eta}_i - \boldsymbol{\delta} t) = \boldsymbol{\epsilon}_{it}, \qquad \begin{array}{l} i = 1.\ldots, N, \\ t = 1, \ldots, T. \end{array} \tag{4.7.12}$$

We also assume that $\mathbf{y}_{i0}$ are available.

4.7.2 GMM Estimation

Just as in the single-equation case, the individual effects $\boldsymbol{\eta}_i$ can be eliminated by first-differencing (4.7.12):

$$\Delta \mathbf{y}_{it} - \boldsymbol{\delta} = \Phi(\Delta \mathbf{y}_{i,t-1} - \boldsymbol{\delta}) + \Delta \boldsymbol{\epsilon}_{it}, \qquad t = 2, \ldots, T. \tag{4.7.13}$$

Thus, we have the orthogonality conditions

$$E\{[(\Delta \mathbf{y}_{it} - \boldsymbol{\delta}) - \Phi(\Delta \mathbf{y}_{i,t-1} - \boldsymbol{\delta})]\mathbf{q}'_{it}\} = \mathbf{0}, \qquad t = 2, \ldots, T, \tag{4.7.14}$$

where

$$\mathbf{q}_{it} = (1, \mathbf{y}'_{i0}, \ldots, \mathbf{y}'_{i,t-2})'. \tag{4.7.15}$$

Stacking the $(T - 1)$ (4.7.13) together yields

$$S_i = R_i \Lambda + E_i, \qquad i = 1, 2, \ldots, N, \tag{4.7.16}$$

where

$$\begin{aligned} &S_i = (\Delta \mathbf{y}_{i2}, \Delta \mathbf{y}_{i3}, \ldots, \Delta \mathbf{y}_{iT})', \qquad E_i = (\Delta \boldsymbol{\epsilon}_{i2}, \ldots, \Delta \boldsymbol{\epsilon}_{iT})' \\ &R_i = (S_{i,-1}, \mathbf{e}_{T-1}), \qquad S_{i,-1} = (\Delta \mathbf{y}_{i1}, \ldots, \Delta \mathbf{y}_{i,T-1})', \\ &\Lambda = (\Phi, \mathbf{a}_1), \qquad \mathbf{a}_1 = (I_m - \Phi)\boldsymbol{\delta}, \end{aligned} \tag{4.7.17}$$

and $\mathbf{e}_{T-1}$ denotes a $(T - 1) \times 1$ vector of ones. Premultiplying (4.7.16) by the $(MT/2 + 1)(T - 1) \times (T - 1)$ block-diagonal instrumental variable matrix

$$Q_i = \begin{pmatrix} \mathbf{q}_{i2} & \mathbf{0} & \cdots & \mathbf{0} \\ \mathbf{0} & \mathbf{q}_{is} & \cdots & \mathbf{0} \\ \vdots & \vdots & \ddots & \vdots \\ \mathbf{0} & \mathbf{0} & \cdots & \mathbf{q}_{iT} \end{pmatrix}, \tag{4.7.18}$$

one obtains

$$Q_i S_i = Q_i R_i \Lambda + Q_i E_i, \tag{4.7.19}$$

the transpose of which in vectorized form becomes[19]

$$(Q_i \otimes I_m)\,\text{vec}(S_i') = (Q_i R_i \otimes I_m)\boldsymbol{\lambda} + (Q_i \otimes I_m)\,\text{vec}(E_i'), \tag{4.7.20}$$

where $\lambda = \text{vec}(\Lambda')$, and $\text{vec}(\cdot)$ is the operator that transforms a matrix into a vector by stacking the columns of the matrix one underneath the other. Thus, the GMM estimator of $\boldsymbol{\lambda}$ can be obtained by minimizing (Binder, Hsiao, and Pesaran (2000))

$$\left[\sum_{i=1}^{N}((Q_i \otimes I_m)\,\text{vec}(S_i') - (Q_i R_i \otimes I_m)\boldsymbol{\lambda})\right]' \times \left[\sum_{i=1}^{N}(Q_i \otimes I_m)\Sigma(Q_i \otimes I_m)'\right]^{-1} \times \left[\sum_{i=1}^{N}((Q_i \otimes I_m)\,\text{vec}(S_i') - (Q_i R_i \otimes I_m)\boldsymbol{\lambda})\right], \tag{4.7.21}$$

where

$$\Sigma = \begin{bmatrix} 2\Omega & -\Omega & \mathbf{0} & \cdots & \mathbf{0} \\ -\Omega & 2\Omega & -\Omega & \cdots & \mathbf{0} \\ \mathbf{0} & -\Omega & 2\Omega & \cdots & \mathbf{0} \\ \vdots & \vdots & \vdots & \ddots & \vdots \\ \mathbf{0} & \mathbf{0} & \mathbf{0} & \cdots & 2\Omega \end{bmatrix}. \tag{4.7.22}$$

The moment conditions relevant to the estimation of Ω are given by

$$E\{[\Delta\mathbf{y}_{it} - \boldsymbol{\delta} - \Phi(\Delta\mathbf{y}_{i,t-1} - \boldsymbol{\delta})][\Delta\mathbf{y}_{it} - \boldsymbol{\delta} - \Phi(\Delta\mathbf{y}_{i,t-1} - \boldsymbol{\delta})]' - 2\Omega\} = \mathbf{0}, \qquad t = 2, 3, \ldots, T. \tag{4.7.23}$$

Also, in the trend-stationary case, upon estimation of $\mathbf{a}_1$, $\boldsymbol{\delta}$ may be obtained as

$$\hat{\boldsymbol{\delta}} = (I_m - \hat{\Phi})^{-1}\hat{\mathbf{a}}_1. \tag{4.7.24}$$

The GMM estimator is consistent and asymptotically normally distributed as $N \to \infty$ if all the roots of (4.7.3) fall outside the unit circle, but breaks down if some roots are equal to unity. To see this, note that a necessary condition for the GMM estimator (4.7.21) to exist is that $\text{rank}(N^{-1}\sum_{i=1}^{N} Q_i R_i) = m + 1$ as $N \to \infty$. In the case where $\Phi = I_m$, we have $\Delta\mathbf{y}_{it} = \boldsymbol{\delta} + \boldsymbol{\epsilon}_{it}$ and $\mathbf{y}_{it} = \mathbf{y}_{i0} + \boldsymbol{\delta}t + \sum_{\ell=1}^{t}\boldsymbol{\epsilon}_{i\ell}$. Thus it follows that for $t = 2, 3, \ldots, T,\ j = 0, 1, \ldots, t-2$, as $N \to \infty$,

$$\frac{1}{N}\sum_{i=1}^{N}\Delta\mathbf{y}_{i,t-1}\mathbf{y}_{ij}' \to \boldsymbol{\delta}(\mathbf{y}_{i0} + \boldsymbol{\delta}j)', \tag{4.7.25}$$

which is of rank one. In other words, when $\Phi = I_m$, the elements of $\mathbf{q}_{it}$ are not legitimate instruments.

4.7.3 (Transformed) Maximum Likelihood Estimator

We note that, conditional on $\Delta\mathbf{y}_{i-1}$, (4.7.13) is well defined for $t = 2, \ldots, T$. For $\Delta\mathbf{y}_{i1}$, from (4.7.12), we have

$$\Delta\mathbf{y}_{i1} - \boldsymbol{\delta} = -(I - \Phi)(\mathbf{y}_{i0} - \boldsymbol{\eta}_i) + \boldsymbol{\epsilon}_{i1}. \tag{4.7.26}$$

We note that by (4.7.4) and (4.7.5), $E(\Delta\mathbf{y}_{i1} - \boldsymbol{\delta}) = -(I - \Phi)E(\mathbf{y}_{i0} - \boldsymbol{\eta}_i) + E\boldsymbol{\epsilon}_{i1} = \mathbf{0}$ and $E(\Delta\mathbf{y}_{i1} - \boldsymbol{\delta})(\Delta\mathbf{y}_{i1} - \boldsymbol{\delta})' = -(I - \Phi)\Psi_0(I - \Phi)' + \Omega = \Psi_1$. Therefore, the joint likelihood of $\Delta\mathbf{y}_i' = (\Delta\mathbf{y}_{i1}', \ldots, \Delta\mathbf{y}_{iT}')$ is well defined and does not involve incidental parameters. Under the assumption that $\boldsymbol{\epsilon}_{it}$ is normally distributed, the likelihood function is given by

$$\sum_{i=1}^{N}(2\pi)^{-\frac{NT}{2}}\,|\Sigma^*|^{-\frac{1}{2}}\exp\left[-\tfrac{1}{2}(\mathbf{r}_i - H_i\boldsymbol{\phi})'\Sigma^{*-1}(\mathbf{r}_i - H_i\boldsymbol{\phi})\right], \tag{4.7.27}$$

where

$$\begin{aligned} H_i &= G_i' \otimes I_m, \\ G_i &= (\mathbf{0}, \Delta\mathbf{y}_{i1} - \boldsymbol{\delta}, \ldots, \Delta\mathbf{y}_{iT-1} - \boldsymbol{\delta}), \\ \boldsymbol{\phi} &= \operatorname{vec}(\Phi), \end{aligned}$$

and

$$\Sigma^* = \begin{pmatrix} \Psi_1 & -\Omega & \mathbf{0} & \cdots & \cdots & \mathbf{0} & \mathbf{0} \\ -\Omega & 2\Omega & -\Omega & & \cdots & \mathbf{0} & \mathbf{0} \\ \mathbf{0} & -\Omega & 2\Omega & & \ddots & \mathbf{0} & \mathbf{0} \\ \vdots & \vdots & & \ddots & \ddots & \ddots & \vdots \\ \mathbf{0} & \mathbf{0} & & \cdots & -\Omega & 2\Omega & -\Omega \\ \mathbf{0} & \mathbf{0} & & \cdots & \mathbf{0} & -\Omega & 2\Omega \end{pmatrix}. \tag{4.7.28}$$

Maximizing the logarithm of (4.7.27), $\ell(\boldsymbol{\theta})$, with respect to $\boldsymbol{\theta}' = (\boldsymbol{\delta}', \boldsymbol{\phi}', \boldsymbol{\sigma}')'$, where $\boldsymbol{\sigma}$ denotes the unknown element of Σ^*, yields the (transformed) MLE that is consistent and asymptotically normally distributed with asymptotic covariance matrix given by $-E\left(\partial^2\ell(\boldsymbol{\theta})/\partial\boldsymbol{\theta}\,\partial\boldsymbol{\theta}'\right)^{-1}$ as $N \to \infty$, independent of whether $\mathbf{y}_{it}$ contains unit roots or is cointegrated.

4.7.4 Minimum-Distance Estimator

We note that conditional on Σ^*, the MLE of Φ and $\boldsymbol{\delta}$ is equivalent to the MDE that minimizes

$$\sum_{i=1}^{N}(\mathbf{r}_i - H_i\boldsymbol{\phi})'\Sigma^{*-1}(\mathbf{r}_i - H_i\boldsymbol{\phi}). \tag{4.7.29}$$

Furthermore, conditional on $\boldsymbol{\delta}$ and Σ^*, the MDE of Φ is given by

$$\hat{\boldsymbol{\phi}} = \left(\sum_{i=1}^{N} H_i' \Sigma^{*-1} H_i\right)^{-1} \left(\sum_{i=1}^{N} H_i' \Sigma^{*-1} \mathbf{r}_i\right). \tag{4.7.30}$$

Conditional on Φ and Σ^*, the MDE of $\boldsymbol{\delta}$ is equal to

$$\hat{\boldsymbol{\delta}} = (N P \Sigma^{*-1} P')^{-1} \left[\sum_{i=1}^{N} P \Sigma^{*-1} (\Delta \mathbf{y}_i - L_i \boldsymbol{\phi})\right], \tag{4.7.31}$$

where

$$P = (I_m, I_m - \Phi', I_m - \Phi', \ldots, I_m - \Phi'), \tag{4.7.32}$$

and

$$L_i = K_i' \otimes I_m \quad \text{and} \quad K_i = (\mathbf{0}, \Delta \mathbf{y}_{i1}, \ldots, \Delta \mathbf{y}_{i,T-1}).$$

Conditional on $\boldsymbol{\delta}$,

$$\hat{\Psi}_1 = \frac{1}{N} \sum_{i=1}^{N} (\Delta \mathbf{y}_{i1} - \boldsymbol{\delta})(\Delta \mathbf{y}_{i1} - \boldsymbol{\delta})', \tag{4.7.33}$$

and conditional on $\boldsymbol{\delta}$, Φ,

$$\hat{\Omega} = \frac{1}{N(T-1)} \sum_{i=1}^{N} \sum_{t=2}^{T} [\Delta \mathbf{y}_{it} - \boldsymbol{\delta} - \Phi(\Delta \mathbf{y}_{i,t-1} - \boldsymbol{\delta})] \times [\Delta \mathbf{y}_{it} - \boldsymbol{\delta} - \Phi(\Delta y_{i,t-1} - \boldsymbol{\delta})]'. \tag{4.7.34}$$

We may iterate between (4.7.30) and (4.7.34) to obtained the feasible MDE, using

$$\hat{\boldsymbol{\delta}}^{(0)} = \frac{1}{NT} \sum_{i=1}^{N} \sum_{t=1}^{T} \Delta \mathbf{y}_{it}, \tag{4.7.35}$$

and

$$\hat{\Phi}^{(0)} = \left[\sum_{i=1}^{N} \sum_{t=3}^{T} (\Delta \mathbf{y}_{it} - \boldsymbol{\delta})(\Delta \mathbf{y}_{i,t-2} - \boldsymbol{\delta})'\right] \times \left[\sum_{i=1}^{N} \sum_{t=3}^{T} (\Delta \mathbf{y}_{i,t-1} - \boldsymbol{\delta})(\Delta \mathbf{y}_{i,t-2} - \boldsymbol{\delta})'\right]^{-1} \tag{4.7.36}$$

to start the iteration.

Conditional on Σ^*, the MDE of $\boldsymbol{\phi}$ and $\boldsymbol{\delta}$ is identical to the MLE. When $\boldsymbol{\delta} = 0$ (no trend term), conditional on Σ^*, the asymptotic covariance matrix of the MLE or MDE of $\boldsymbol{\phi}$ is equal to

$$\left[\sum_{i=1}^{N}(K_i \otimes I_m)\Sigma^{*-1}(K_i' \otimes I_m)\right]^{-1}. \tag{4.7.37}$$

When Σ^* is unknown, the asymptotic variance–covariance matrices of the MLE and MDE of $\boldsymbol{\phi}$ do not converge to (4.7.37), because when lagged dependent variables appear as regressors, the estimation of Φ and Σ^* is not asymptotically independent. The asymptotic variance–covariance matrix of the feasible MDE is equal to the sum of (4.7.37) and a positive semidefinite matrix attributable to the estimation error of Σ^* (Hsiao, Pesaran, and Tahmiscioglu (2002)).

Both the MLE and MDE always exist, whether $\mathbf{y}_{it}$ contains unit roots or not. The MLE and MDE are asymptotically normally distributed, independent of whether $\mathbf{y}_{it}$ is (trend) stationary, integrated, or cointegrated as $N \to \infty$. Therefore, the conventional likelihood-ratio test statistic or Wald test statistic of the unit root or the rank of cointegration can be approximated by chi-square statistics. Moreover, the limited Monte Carlo studies conducted by Binder, Hsiao, and Pesaran (2000) show that both the MLE and MDE perform very well in finite samples and dominate the conventional GMM, in particular, if the roots of (4.7.3) are near unity.

APPENDIX 4A: DERIVATION OF THE ASYMPTOTIC COVARIANCE MATRIX OF THE FEASIBLE MDE

The estimation error of $\hat{\boldsymbol{\psi}}_{\text{MDE}}$ is equal to

$$\sqrt{N}(\hat{\boldsymbol{\psi}}_{\text{MDE}} - \boldsymbol{\psi}) = \left(\frac{1}{N}\sum_{i=1}^{N} H_i' \hat{\tilde{\Omega}}^{*-1} H_i\right)^{-1}\left(\frac{1}{\sqrt{N}}\sum_{i=1}^{N} H_i'\hat{\tilde{\Omega}}^{*-1}\Delta\mathbf{u}_i^*\right). \tag{4A.1}$$

When $N \to \infty$,

$$\frac{1}{N}\sum_{i=1}^{N} H_i'\hat{\tilde{\Omega}}^{*-1} H_i \to \frac{1}{N}\sum_{i=1}^{N} H_i'\tilde{\Omega}^{*-1} H_i, \tag{4A.2}$$

but

$$\frac{1}{\sqrt{N}}\sum_{i=1}^{N} H_i'\hat{\tilde{\Omega}}^{*-1}\Delta\mathbf{u}_i^* \simeq \frac{1}{\sqrt{N}}\sum_{i=1}^{N} H_i'\tilde{\Omega}^{*-1}\Delta\mathbf{u}_i^* + \left[\frac{1}{N}\sum_{i=1}^{N} H_i'\left(\frac{\partial}{\partial h}\tilde{\Omega}^{*-1}\right)\Delta\mathbf{u}_i^*\right]\cdot\sqrt{N}(\hat{h} - h), \tag{4A.3}$$

where the right-hand side follows from taking the Taylor series expansion of $\hat{\tilde{\Omega}}^{*-1}$ around $\tilde{\Omega}^{*-1}$. By (4.5.7),

$$\frac{\partial}{\partial h}\tilde{\Omega}^{*-1} = \frac{-T}{[1+T(h-1)]^2}\tilde{\Omega}^{*-1} + \frac{1}{1+T(h-1)} \times \begin{bmatrix} 0 & 0 & \dots & 0 & 0 \\ 0 & T-1 & \dots & 2 & 1 \\ \vdots & \vdots & & \vdots & \vdots \\ 0 & 2 & \dots & 2T & T-2 \\ 0 & 1 & \dots & T-2 & T-1 \end{bmatrix}. \tag{4A.4}$$

We have

$$\frac{1}{N}\sum_{i=1}^{N} H_i'\tilde{\Omega}^{*-1}\Delta\mathbf{u}_i^* \to \mathbf{0},$$

$$\frac{1}{N}\sum_{i=1}^{N}\begin{bmatrix} 1 & \Delta\mathbf{x}_i' & \mathbf{0}' \\ \mathbf{0} & \mathbf{0} & \Delta X_i \end{bmatrix}' \cdot \frac{\partial}{\partial h}\tilde{\Omega}^{*-1}\Delta\mathbf{u}_i^* \to \mathbf{0},$$

$$\frac{1}{N}\sum_{i=1}^{N}\Delta\mathbf{y}_{i,-1}'\begin{bmatrix} T-1 & \dots & 1 \\ \vdots & & \vdots \\ 2 & \dots & T-2 \\ 1 & \dots & T-1 \end{bmatrix}\Delta\mathbf{u}_i^* \to [\gamma^{T-2} + 2\gamma^{T-3} + \dots + (T-1)]\sigma_u^2.$$

Since plim $\hat{\sigma}_u^2 = \sigma_u^2$, and

$$\sqrt{N}(\hat{h}-h) = \sqrt{N}\left[\frac{\hat{\sigma}_{v*}^2}{\hat{\sigma}_u^2} - \frac{\sigma_{v*}^2}{\sigma_u^2}\right] = \sqrt{N}\frac{\sigma_u^2(\hat{\sigma}_{v*}^2 - \sigma_{v*}^2) - \sigma_{v*}^2(\hat{\sigma}_u^2 - \sigma_u^2)}{\hat{\sigma}_u^2\sigma_u^2},$$

it follows that the limiting distribution of the feasible MDE converges to

$$\begin{aligned} &\sqrt{N}(\hat{\boldsymbol{\psi}}_{\text{MDE}} - \boldsymbol{\psi}) \\ &\to \left(\frac{1}{N}\sum_{i=1}^{N} H_i'\Omega^{*-1}H_i\right)^{-1} \\ &\quad \times \left\{\frac{1}{\sqrt{N}}\sum_{i=1}^{N} H_i'\Omega^{*-1}\Delta\mathbf{u}_i^* - \begin{bmatrix} 0 \\ \mathbf{0} \\ 1 \\ \mathbf{0} \end{bmatrix}\frac{[\gamma^{T-2} + 2\gamma^{T-3} + \dots + (T-1)]}{[1+T(h-1)]\sigma_u^2}\right. \\ &\quad \left. \times \left[\sigma_u^2 \cdot \sqrt{N}(\hat{\sigma}_{v*}^2 - \sigma_{v*}^2) - \sigma_{v*}^2 \cdot \sqrt{N}(\hat{\sigma}_u^2 - \sigma_u^2)\right]\right\}, \end{aligned} \tag{4A.5}$$

with the asymptotic covariance matrix equal to (4.5.15).

CHAPTER 5

Simultaneous-Equations Models

5.1 INTRODUCTION

In Chapters 3 and 4, we discussed the approach of decomposing the effect of a large number of factors that affect the dependent variables, but are not explicitly included as explanatory variables, into effects specific to individual units, to time periods, and to both individual units and time periods as a means to take account of the heterogeneity in panel data in estimating single-equation models. However, the consistency or asymptotic efficiency of various estimators discussed in previous chapters depends on the validity of the single-equation model assumptions. If they are not true, this approach may solve one problem, but aggravate other problems.

For instance, consider the income-schooling model,

$$y = \beta_0 + \beta_1 S + \beta_2 A + u, \tag{5.1.1}$$

where y is a measure of income, earnings, or wage rate, S is a measure of schooling, and A is an unmeasured ability variable that is assumed to be positively related to S. The coefficients β_1 and β_2 are assumed positive. Under the assumption that S and A are uncorrelated with u, the least-squares estimate of β_1 that ignores A is biased upward. The standard left-out-variable formula gives the size of this bias as

$$E(\hat{\beta}_{1,\mathrm{LS}}) = \beta_1 + \beta_2 \frac{\sigma_{AS}}{\sigma_S^2}, \tag{5.1.2}$$

where σ_S^2 is the variance of S, and σ_{AS} is the covariance between A and S.

If the omitted variable A is a purely "family" one,[1] that is, if siblings have exactly the same level of A, then estimating β_1 from within-family data (i.e., from differences between the brothers' earnings and differences between the brothers' education) will eliminate this bias. But if ability, apart from having a family component, also has an individual component, and this individual component is not independent of the schooling variable, the within-family estimates are not necessarily less biased.

Suppose

$$A_{it} = \alpha_i + \omega_{it}, \tag{5.1.3}$$

where i denotes the family, and t denotes members of the family. If ω_{it} is uncorrelated with S_{it}, the combination of (5.1.1) and (5.1.3) is basically of the same form as (3.3.3). The expected value of the within (or LSDV) estimator is unbiased. On the other hand, if the within-family covariance between A and S, $\sigma_{s\omega}$, is not equal to zero, the expected value of the within estimator is

$$E(\hat{\beta}_{1,w}) = \beta_1 + \beta_2 \frac{\sigma_{S\omega}}{\sigma^2_{S|w}}, \tag{5.1.4}$$

where $\sigma^2_{S|w}$ is the within-family variance of S. The estimator remains biased. Furthermore, if the reasons for the correlation between A and S are largely individual rather than familial, then going to within data will drastically reduce $\sigma^2_{S|w}$, with little change to σ_{AS} (or $\sigma_{S\omega}$), which would make this source of bias even more serious.

Moreover, if S is also a function of A and other social–economic variables, (5.1.1) is only one behavioral equation in a simultaneous-equations model. Then the probability limit of the least-squares estimate, $\hat{\beta}_{1,\text{LS}}$, is no longer (5.1.2) but is of the form

$$\text{plim}\, \hat{\beta}_{1,\text{LS}} = \beta_1 + \beta_2 \frac{\sigma_{AS}}{\sigma^2_S} + \frac{\sigma_{uS}}{\sigma^2_S}, \tag{5.1.5}$$

where σ_{uS} is the covariance between u and S. If, as argued by Griliches (1977, 1979), schooling is the result, at least in part, of optimizing behavior by individuals and their family, σ_{uS} could be negative. This opens the possibility that the least-squares estimates of the schooling coefficient may be biased downward rather than upward. Furthermore, if the reasons for σ_{uS} being negative are again largely individual rather than familial, and the within-family covariance between A and S reduces σ_{AS} by roughly the same proportion as $\sigma^2_{S|w}$ is to σ^2_S, there will be a significant decline in the $\hat{\beta}_{1,w}$ relative to $\hat{\beta}_{1,\text{LS}}$. The size of this decline will be attributed to the importance of ability and "family background," but in fact it reflects nothing more than the simultaneity problems associated with the schooling variable itself. In short, the simultaneity problem could reverse the single-equation conclusions.

In this chapter we focus on estimating simultaneous-equations models from a time series of cross sections. Suppose the model is[2]

$$\Gamma \mathbf{y}_{it} + \mathbf{B}\mathbf{x}_{it} + \boldsymbol{\mu} = \mathbf{v}_{it}, \qquad i = 1, \dots, N, \quad t = 1, \dots, T, \tag{5.1.6}$$

where Γ and $\mathbf{B}$ are $G \times G$ and $G \times K$ matrices of coefficients; $\mathbf{y}_{it}$ is a $G \times 1$ vector of observed endogenous variables, $\mathbf{x}_{it}$ is a $K \times 1$ vector of observed exogenous variables; $\boldsymbol{\mu}$ is the $G \times 1$ vector of intercepts, $\mathbf{v}_{it}$ is a $G \times 1$ vector of unobserved disturbances, with

$$\mathbf{v}_{it} = \boldsymbol{\alpha}_i + \boldsymbol{\lambda}_t + \mathbf{u}_{it}, \tag{5.1.7}$$

where $\boldsymbol{\alpha}_i$, $\boldsymbol{\lambda}_t$, and $\mathbf{u}_{it}$ are each $G \times 1$ random vectors that have zero means and are independent of one another, and

$$\begin{aligned}
&E\mathbf{x}_{it}\mathbf{v}'_{js} = \mathbf{0},\\
&E\boldsymbol{\alpha}_i\boldsymbol{\alpha}'_j = \begin{cases}\Omega_\alpha = (\sigma^2_{\alpha g\ell}) & \text{if } i = j,\\ \mathbf{0} & \text{if } i \neq j,\end{cases}\\
&E\boldsymbol{\lambda}_t\boldsymbol{\lambda}'_s = \begin{cases}\Omega_\lambda = (\sigma^2_{\lambda g\ell}) & \text{if } t = s,\\ \mathbf{0} & \text{if } t \neq s,\end{cases}\\
&E\mathbf{u}_{it}\mathbf{u}'_{js} = \begin{cases}\Omega_u = (\sigma^2_{ug\ell}) & \text{if } i = j, \quad \text{and} \quad t = s,\\ \mathbf{0} & \text{otherwise.}\end{cases}
\end{aligned} \tag{5.1.8}$$

Multiplying (5.1.6) by Γ^{-1}, we have the reduced form

$$\mathbf{y}_{it} = \boldsymbol{\mu}^* + \Pi\mathbf{x}_{it} + \boldsymbol{\epsilon}_{it}, \tag{5.1.9}$$

where $\boldsymbol{\mu}^* = -\Gamma^{-1}\boldsymbol{\mu}$, $\Pi = -\Gamma^{-1}\mathbf{B}$, and $\boldsymbol{\epsilon}_{it} = \Gamma^{-1}\mathbf{v}_{it}$. The reduced-form error term $\boldsymbol{\epsilon}_{it}$ again has an error-component structure[3]

$$\boldsymbol{\epsilon}_{it} = \boldsymbol{\alpha}^*_i + \boldsymbol{\lambda}^*_t + \mathbf{u}^*_{it}, \tag{5.1.10}$$

with

$$\begin{aligned}
&E\boldsymbol{\alpha}^*_i = E\boldsymbol{\lambda}^*_t = E\mathbf{u}^*_{it} = \mathbf{0}, \qquad E\boldsymbol{\alpha}^*_i\boldsymbol{\lambda}^{*\prime}_t = E\boldsymbol{\alpha}^*_i\mathbf{u}^{*\prime}_{it} = E\boldsymbol{\lambda}^*_t\mathbf{u}^{*\prime}_{it} = \mathbf{0},\\
&E\boldsymbol{\alpha}^*_i\boldsymbol{\alpha}^{*\prime}_j = \begin{cases}\Omega^*_\alpha = (\sigma^{*2}_{\alpha g\ell}) & \text{if } i = j,\\ \mathbf{0} & \text{if } i \neq j,\end{cases}\\
&E\boldsymbol{\lambda}^*_t\boldsymbol{\lambda}^{*\prime}_s = \begin{cases}\Omega^*_\lambda = (\sigma^{*2}_{\lambda g\ell}) & \text{if } t = s,\\ \mathbf{0} & \text{if } t \neq s,\end{cases}\\
&E\mathbf{u}^*_{it}\mathbf{u}^{*\prime}_{js} = \begin{cases}\Omega^*_u = (\sigma^{*2}_{ug\ell}) & \text{if } i = j \quad \text{and} \quad t = s,\\ \mathbf{0} & \text{otherwise.}\end{cases}
\end{aligned} \tag{5.1.11}$$

If the $G \times G$ covariance matrices Ω_α, Ω_λ, and Ω_u are unrestricted, there are no restrictions on the variance–covariance matrix. The usual order and rank conditions are the necessary and sufficient conditions for identifying a particular equation in the system (e.g., Hsiao (1983)). If there are restrictions on Ω_α, Ω_λ, or Ω_u, we can combine these covariance restrictions with the restrictions on the coefficient matrices to identify a model and obtain efficient estimates of the parameters. We shall first discuss estimation of the simultaneous-equations model under the assumption that there are no restrictions on the variance–covariance matrix, but the rank condition for identification holds. Estimation of reduced-form or stacked equations will be discussed in Section 5.2, and estimation of the structural form will be dealt with in Section 5.3. We then discuss the case in which there are restrictions on the variance–covariance matrix in Section 5.4. Because a widely used structure for longitudinal microdata is the triangular structure (e.g., Chamberlain (1976, 1977a, 1977b); Chamberlain and Griliches (1975)), we shall use this special case to illustrate how the covariance restrictions can be used to identify an otherwise unidentified model and to improve the efficiency of the estimates.

5.2 JOINT GENERALIZED-LEAST-SQUARES ESTIMATION TECHNIQUE

We can write an equation of a reduced form (5.1.9) in the more general form in which the explanatory variables in each equation can be different[4]:

$$\mathbf{y}_g = \mathbf{e}_{NT}\boldsymbol{\mu}_g^* + X_g\boldsymbol{\pi}_g + \boldsymbol{\epsilon}_g, \qquad g = 1, \ldots, G, \tag{5.2.1}$$

where $\mathbf{y}_g$ and $\mathbf{e}_{NT}$ are $NT \times 1$, X_g is $NT \times K_g$, $\boldsymbol{\mu}_g^*$ is the 1×1 intercept term for the gth equation, $\boldsymbol{\pi}_g$ *is* $K_g \times 1$, and $\boldsymbol{\epsilon}_g = (I_N \otimes \mathbf{e}_T)\boldsymbol{\alpha}_g^* + (\mathbf{e}_N \otimes I_T)\boldsymbol{\lambda}_g^* + \mathbf{u}_g^*$, where $\boldsymbol{\alpha}_g^* = (\boldsymbol{\alpha}_{1g}^*, \boldsymbol{\alpha}_{2g}^*, \ldots, \boldsymbol{\alpha}_{Ng}^*)'$, $\boldsymbol{\lambda}_g^* = (\lambda_{1g}^*, \lambda_{2g}^*, \ldots, \lambda_{Tg}^*)'$, and $\mathbf{u}_g^* = (u_{11g}^*, u_{12g}^*, \ldots, u_{1Tg}^*, u_{21g}^*, \ldots, u_{NTg}^*)'$ are $N \times 1$, $T \times 1$, and $NT \times 1$ random vectors, respectively. Stacking the set of G equations, we get

$$\underset{GNT\times 1}{\mathbf{y}} = (I_G \otimes \mathbf{e}_{NT})\boldsymbol{\mu}^* + X\boldsymbol{\pi} + \boldsymbol{\epsilon}, \tag{5.2.2}$$

where

$$\underset{GNT\times 1}{\mathbf{y}} = \begin{bmatrix} \mathbf{y}_1 \\ \vdots \\ \mathbf{y}_G \end{bmatrix}, \qquad \underset{GNT\times(\sum_{g=1}^G K_g)}{X} = \begin{bmatrix} X_1 & \mathbf{0} & \cdots & \mathbf{0} \\ \mathbf{0} & X_2 & & \vdots \\ \vdots & & \ddots & \mathbf{0} \\ \mathbf{0} & \cdots & \mathbf{0} & X_G \end{bmatrix},$$

$$\underset{G\times 1}{\boldsymbol{\mu}^*} = \begin{bmatrix} \boldsymbol{\mu}_1^* \\ \boldsymbol{\mu}_2^* \\ \vdots \\ \boldsymbol{\mu}_G^* \end{bmatrix}, \qquad \underset{(\sum_{g=1}^G K_g)\times 1}{\boldsymbol{\pi}} = \begin{bmatrix} \boldsymbol{\pi}_1 \\ \vdots \\ \boldsymbol{\pi}_G \end{bmatrix}, \qquad \boldsymbol{\epsilon} = \begin{bmatrix} \boldsymbol{\epsilon}_1 \\ \vdots \\ \boldsymbol{\epsilon}_G \end{bmatrix},$$

with

$$V = E(\boldsymbol{\epsilon}\boldsymbol{\epsilon}') = [V_{g\ell}], \tag{5.2.3}$$

where $V_{g\ell}$ denotes the $g\ell$th block submatrix of V, which is given by

$$\underset{NT\times NT}{V_{g\ell}} = E(\boldsymbol{\epsilon}_g\boldsymbol{\epsilon}_\ell') = \sigma_{\alpha_{g\ell}}^{*2} A + \sigma_{\lambda_{g\ell}}^{*2} D + \sigma_{u_{g\ell}}^{*2} I_{NT}, \tag{5.2.4}$$

where $A = I_N \otimes \mathbf{e}_T\mathbf{e}_T'$ and $D = \mathbf{e}_N\mathbf{e}_N' \otimes I_T$. Equation (5.2.4) can also be written as

$$V_{g\ell} = \sigma_{1_{g\ell}}^{*2}\left(\frac{1}{T}A - \frac{1}{NT}J\right) + \sigma_{2_{g\ell}}^{*2}\left(\frac{1}{N}D - \frac{1}{NT}J\right) + \sigma_{u_{g\ell}}^{*2}\tilde{Q} + \sigma_{4_{g\ell}}^{*2}\left(\frac{1}{NT}J\right), \tag{5.2.5}$$

where $J = \mathbf{e}_{NT}\mathbf{e}'_{NT}$, $\tilde{Q} = I_{NT} - (1/T)A - (1/N)D + (1/NT)J$, $\sigma^{*2}_{1_{g\ell}} = \sigma^{*2}_{u_{g\ell}} + T\sigma^{*2}_{\alpha_{g\ell}}$, $\sigma^{*2}_{2_{g\ell}} = \sigma^{*2}_{u_{g\ell}} + N\sigma^{*2}_{\lambda_{g\ell}}$, and $\sigma^{*2}_{4_{g\ell}} = \sigma^{*2}_{u_{g\ell}} + T\sigma^{*2}_{\alpha_{g\ell}} + N\sigma^{*2}_{\lambda_{g\ell}}$. It was shown in Appendix 3B that $\sigma^{*2}_{1_{g\ell}}$, $\sigma^{*2}_{2_{g\ell}}$, $\sigma^{*2}_{u_{g\ell}}$, and $\sigma^{*2}_{4_{g\ell}}$ are the distinct characteristic roots of $V_{g\ell}$ of multiplicity $N-1$, $T-1$, $(N-1)(T-1)$, and 1, with C_1, C_2, C_3, and C_4 as the matrices of their corresponding characteristic vectors.

We can rewrite V as

$$V = V_1 \otimes \left(\frac{1}{T}A - \frac{1}{NT}J\right) + V_2 \otimes \left(\frac{1}{N}D - \frac{1}{NT}J\right) + \Omega^*_u \otimes \tilde{Q} + V_4 \otimes \left(\frac{1}{NT}J\right), \tag{5.2.6}$$

where $V_1 = (\sigma^{*2}_{1_{g\ell}})$, $V_2 = (\sigma^{*2}_{2_{g\ell}})$, and $V_4 = (\sigma^{*2}_{4_{g\ell}})$ all of dimension $G \times G$. Using the fact that $[(1/T)A - (1/NT)J]$, $[(1/N)D - (1/NT)J]$, $\tilde{Q}$, and $[(1/NT)J]$ are symmetric idempotent matrices, mutually orthogonal, and sum to the identity matrix I_{NT}, we can write down the inverse of V explicitly as (Avery (1977); Baltagi (1980))[5]

$$V^{-1} = V_1^{-1} \otimes \left(\frac{1}{T}A - \frac{1}{NT}J\right) + V_2^{-1} \otimes \left(\frac{1}{N}D - \frac{1}{NT}J\right) + \Omega_u^{*-1} \otimes \tilde{Q} + V_4^{-1} \otimes \left(\frac{1}{NT}J\right). \tag{5.2.7}$$

The GLS estimators of $\boldsymbol{\mu}^*$ and $\boldsymbol{\pi}$ are obtained by minimizing the distance function

$$[\mathbf{y} - (I_G \otimes \mathbf{e}_{NT})\boldsymbol{\mu}^* - X\boldsymbol{\pi}]'V^{-1}[\mathbf{y} - (I_G \otimes \mathbf{e}_{NT})\boldsymbol{\mu}^* - X\boldsymbol{\pi}]. \tag{5.2.8}$$

Taking partial derivatives of (5.2.8) with respect to $\boldsymbol{\mu}^*$ and $\boldsymbol{\pi}$, we obtain the first-order conditions

$$(I_G \otimes \mathbf{e}_{NT})'V^{-1}[\mathbf{y} - (I_G \otimes \mathbf{e}_{NT})\boldsymbol{\mu}^* - X\boldsymbol{\pi}] = \mathbf{0}, \tag{5.2.9}$$

$$-X'V^{-1}[\mathbf{y} - (I_G \otimes \mathbf{e}_{NT})\boldsymbol{\mu}^* - X\boldsymbol{\pi}] = \mathbf{0}. \tag{5.2.10}$$

Solving (5.2.9) and making use of the relations $[(1/T)A - (1/NT)J]\mathbf{e}_{NT} = \mathbf{0}$, $[(1/N)D - (1/NT)J]\mathbf{e}_{NT} = \mathbf{0}$, $\tilde{Q}\mathbf{e}_{NT} = \mathbf{0}$, and $(1/NT)J\mathbf{e}_{NT} = \mathbf{e}_{\text{NT}}$, we have

$$\hat{\boldsymbol{\mu}}^* = \left(I_G \otimes \frac{1}{NT}\mathbf{e}'_{NT}\right)(\mathbf{y} - X\boldsymbol{\pi}). \tag{5.2.11}$$

Substituting (5.2.11) into (5.2.10), we have the GLS estimator of $\boldsymbol{\pi}$ as[6]

$$\hat{\boldsymbol{\pi}}_{\text{GLS}} = [X'\tilde{V}^{-1}X]^{-1}(X'\tilde{V}^{-1}\mathbf{y}), \tag{5.2.12}$$

where

$$\tilde{V}^{-1} = V_1^{-1} \otimes \left(\frac{1}{T}A - \frac{1}{NT}J\right) + V_2^{-1} \otimes \left(\frac{1}{N}D - \frac{1}{NT}J\right) + \Omega_u^{*-1} \otimes \tilde{Q}. \tag{5.2.13}$$

If $E(\boldsymbol{\epsilon}_g \boldsymbol{\epsilon}_\ell') = \mathbf{0}$ for $g \neq \ell$ then V is block-diagonal, and equation (5.2.12) is reduced to applying the GLS estimation method to each equation separately. If both N and T tend to infinity and N/T tends to a nonzero constant, then $\lim V_1^{-1} = \mathbf{0}$, $\lim V_2^{-1} = \mathbf{0}$, and $\lim V_4^{-1} = \mathbf{0}$. Equation (5.2.12) becomes the least-squares dummy-variable (or fixed-effects) estimator for the seemingly unrelated regression case,

$$\text{plim}\ \hat{\boldsymbol{\pi}}_{\text{GLS}} = \underset{\substack{N\to\infty \\ T\to\infty}}{\text{plim}} \left[\frac{1}{N} X'(\Omega_u^{*-1} \otimes \tilde{Q})X\right]^{-1} \times \left[\frac{1}{NT} X'(\Omega_u^{*-1} \otimes \tilde{Q})\mathbf{y}\right]. \tag{5.2.14}$$

In the case of the standard reduced form, $X_1 = X_2 = \cdots = X_G = \bar{X}$,

$$\begin{aligned}\hat{\boldsymbol{\pi}}_{\text{GLS}} = \Bigg[& V_1^{-1} \otimes \bar{X}'\left(\frac{1}{T}A - \frac{1}{NT}J\right)\bar{X} \\ & + V_2^{-1} \otimes \bar{X}'\left(\frac{1}{N}D - \frac{1}{NT}J\right)\bar{X} + \Omega_u^{*-1} \otimes \bar{X}'\tilde{Q}\bar{X}\Bigg]^{-1} \\ & \times \left\{\left[V_1^{-1} \otimes \bar{X}'\left(\frac{1}{T}A - \frac{1}{NT}J\right)\right]\mathbf{y} \right. \\ & \left. + \left[V_2^{-1} \otimes \bar{X}'\left(\frac{1}{N}D - \frac{1}{NT}J\right)\right]\mathbf{y} + [\Omega_u^{*-1} \otimes \bar{X}'\tilde{Q}]\mathbf{y}\right\}.\end{aligned} \tag{5.2.15}$$

We know that in the conventional case when no restriction is imposed on the reduced-form coefficients vector $\boldsymbol{\pi}$, estimating each equation by the least-squares method yields the best linear unbiased estimate. Equation (5.2.15) shows that in a seemingly unrelated regression model with error components, the fact that each equation has an identical set of explanatory variables is not a sufficient condition for the GLS performed on the whole system to be equivalent to estimating each equation separately.

Intuitively, by stacking different equations together we shall gain efficiency in the estimates, because knowing the residual of the ℓth equation helps in predicting the gth equation when the covariance terms between different equations are nonzero. For instance, if the residuals are normally distributed, $E(\boldsymbol{\epsilon}_g \mid \boldsymbol{\epsilon}_\ell) = \text{Cov}(\boldsymbol{\epsilon}_g, \boldsymbol{\epsilon}_\ell)\text{Var}(\boldsymbol{\epsilon}_\ell)^{-1}\boldsymbol{\epsilon}_\ell \neq \mathbf{0}$. To adjust for this nonzero mean, it would be appropriate to regress $\mathbf{y}_g - \text{Cov}(\boldsymbol{\epsilon}_g, \boldsymbol{\epsilon}_\ell)\text{Var}(\boldsymbol{\epsilon}_\ell)^{-1}\boldsymbol{\epsilon}_\ell$ on $(\mathbf{e}_{NT}, X_g)$. Although in general $\boldsymbol{\epsilon}_\ell$ is unknown, asymptotically there is no difference if we replace it by the least-squares residual, $\hat{\boldsymbol{\epsilon}}_\ell$. However, if the explanatory variables in different equations are identical, namely, $X_g = X_\ell = \bar{X}$, there is no gain in efficiency by bringing different equations together when the cross-equation covariances are unrestricted; because $\text{Cov}(\boldsymbol{\epsilon}_g, \boldsymbol{\epsilon}_\ell) = \sigma_{\epsilon_{g\ell}} I_{NT}$, $\text{Var}(\boldsymbol{\epsilon}_\ell) = \sigma_{\epsilon_{\ell\ell}} I_{NT}$, and $\hat{\boldsymbol{\epsilon}}_\ell$ is orthogonal to $(\mathbf{e}_{NT}, X_g)$ by construction, the variable $\sigma_{\epsilon_\ell}\sigma_{\epsilon_{\ell\ell}}^{-1}\hat{\boldsymbol{\epsilon}}_\ell$ can have no effect on the estimate of $(\mu_g, \boldsymbol{\pi}'_g)$ when it is subtracted from $\mathbf{y}_g$. But the same cannot be said for the error-components case, because $\text{Cov}(\boldsymbol{\epsilon}_g, \boldsymbol{\epsilon}_\ell)\text{Var}(\boldsymbol{\epsilon}_\ell)^{-1}$ is not proportional to an identity matrix. The weighted variable $\text{Cov}(\boldsymbol{\epsilon}_g, \boldsymbol{\epsilon}_\ell)\text{Var}(\boldsymbol{\epsilon}_\ell)^{-1}\hat{\boldsymbol{\epsilon}}_\ell$ is no longer orthogonal to $(\mathbf{e}_{NT}, \bar{X})$. Therefore, in the error-components case it remains fruitful to exploit the covariances between different equations to improve the accuracy of the estimates.

When V_1, V_2, and Ω_u^* are unknown, we can replace them by their consistent estimates. In Chapter 3, we discussed methods of estimating variance components. These techniques can be straightforwardly applied to the multiple-equations model as well (Avery (1977); Baltagi (1980)).

The model discussed earlier assumes the existence of both individual and time effects. Suppose we believe that the covariances of some of the components are zero. The same procedure can be applied to the simpler model with some slight modifications. For example, if the covariance of the residuals between equations g and ℓ is composed of only two components (an individual effect and overall effect), then $\sigma^2_{\lambda_{g\ell}} = 0$. Hence, $\sigma^{*2}_{1_{g\ell}} = \sigma^{*2}_{4_{g\ell}}$, and $\sigma^{*2}_{2_{g\ell}} = \sigma^{*2}_{u_{g\ell}}$. These adjusted roots can be substituted into the appropriate positions in (5.2.6) and (5.2.7), with coefficient estimates following directly from (5.2.12).

5.3 ESTIMATION OF STRUCTURAL EQUATIONS

5.3.1 Estimation of a Single Equation in the Structural Model

As (5.2.12) shows, the generalized least-squares estimator of the slope coefficients is invariant against centering the data around overall sample means; so for ease of exposition we shall assume that there is an intercept term and that all sample observations are measured as deviations from their respective overall means and consider the gth structural equation as

$$\begin{aligned}\underset{NT\times 1}{\mathbf{y}_g} &= \mathbf{Y}_g\boldsymbol{\gamma}_g + X_g\boldsymbol{\beta}_g + \mathbf{v}_g \\ &= W_g\boldsymbol{\theta}_g + \mathbf{v}_g, \quad g = 1, \ldots, G, \end{aligned} \tag{5.3.1}$$

where Y_g is an $NT \times (G_g - 1)$ matrix of NT observations of $G_g - 1$ included joint dependent variables, X_g is an $NT \times K_g$ matrix of NT observations of K_g included exogenous variables, $W_g = (Y_g, X_g)$, and $\boldsymbol{\theta}_g = (\boldsymbol{\gamma}'_g, \boldsymbol{\beta}'_g)'$, The $\mathbf{v}_g$ is an $NT \times 1$ vector of error terms,

$$\mathbf{v}_g = (I_N \otimes \mathbf{e}_T)\boldsymbol{\alpha}_g + (\mathbf{e}_N \otimes I_T)\boldsymbol{\lambda}_g + \mathbf{u}_g, \tag{5.3.2}$$

with $\boldsymbol{\alpha}_g = (\alpha_{1g}, \ldots, \alpha_{Ng})'$, $\boldsymbol{\lambda}_g = (\lambda_{1g}, \ldots, \lambda_{Tg})'$, and $\mathbf{u}_g = (u_{11g}, \ldots, u_{1Tg}, u_{21g}, \ldots, u_{NTg})'$ satisfying assumption (5.1.3). So the covariance matrix between the gth and the ℓth structural equations is

$$\begin{aligned}\Sigma_{g\ell} &= E(\mathbf{v}_g\mathbf{v}_\ell') = \sigma^2_{\alpha_{g\ell}} A + \sigma^2_{\lambda_{g\ell}} D + \sigma^2_{u_{g\ell}} I_{NT} \\ &= \sigma^2_{1_{g\ell}}\left(\frac{1}{T}A - \frac{1}{NT}J\right) + \sigma^2_{2_{g\ell}}\left(\frac{1}{N}D - \frac{1}{NT}J\right) \\ &\quad + \sigma^2_{3_{g\ell}}\tilde{Q} + \sigma^2_{4_{g\ell}}\left(\frac{1}{NT}J\right),\end{aligned} \tag{5.3.3}$$

where $\sigma^2_{1_{g\ell}} = \sigma^2_{u_{g\ell}} + T\sigma^2_{\alpha_{g\ell}}$, $\sigma^2_{2_{g\ell}} = \sigma^2_{u_{g\ell}} + N\sigma^2_{\lambda_{g\ell}}$, $\sigma^2_{3_{g\ell}} = \sigma^2_{u_{g\ell}}$, and $\sigma^2_{4_{g\ell}} = \sigma^2_{u_{g\ell}} + T\sigma^2_{\alpha_{g\ell}} + N\sigma^2_{\lambda_{g\ell}}$. We also assume that each equation in (5.3.1) satisfies the rank condition for identification with $K \geq G_g + K_g - 1$, $g = 1, \ldots, G$.

We first consider estimation of a single equation in the structural model. To estimate the gth structural equation, we take account only of the a priori restrictions affecting that equation and ignore the restrictions affecting all other equations. Therefore, suppose we are interested in estimating the first equation. The *limited-information* principle of estimating this equation is equivalent to the full-information estimation of the system

$$\begin{aligned} y_{1_{it}} &= \mathbf{w}'_{1_{it}}\boldsymbol{\theta}_1 + v_{1_{it}}, \\ y_{2_{it}} &= \mathbf{x}'_{it}\boldsymbol{\pi}_2 + \epsilon_{2_{it}}, \\ &\vdots \\ y_{G_{it}} &= \mathbf{x}'_{it}\boldsymbol{\pi}_G + \epsilon_{G_{it}}, \qquad i = 1, \ldots, N, \\ & \qquad\qquad\qquad\qquad\quad t = 1, \ldots, T, \end{aligned} \tag{5.3.4}$$

where there are no restrictions on $\boldsymbol{\pi}_2, \ldots, \boldsymbol{\pi}_G$.

We can apply the usual two-stage least-squares (2SLS) method to estimate the first equation in (5.3.4). The 2SLS estimator is consistent. However, if the $v_{1_{it}}$ are not independently identically distributed over i and t, the 2SLS estimator is not efficient even within the limited-information context. To allow for arbitrary heteroscedasticity and serial correlation in the residuals, we can generalize Chamberlain's (1982, 1984) minimum-distance or generalized 2SLS estimator.

We first consider the minimum-distance estimator. Suppose T is fixed and N tends to infinity. Stacking the T period equations for a single individual's behavioral equation into one system, we create a model of GT equations,

$$\begin{aligned} \underset{T\times 1}{\mathbf{y}_{1_i}} &= W_{1_i}\boldsymbol{\theta}_1 + \mathbf{v}_{1_i}, \\ \underset{T\times 1}{\mathbf{y}_{2_i}} &= X_i\boldsymbol{\pi}_2 + \boldsymbol{\epsilon}_{2_i}, \\ &\vdots \\ \mathbf{y}_{G_i} &= X_i\boldsymbol{\pi}_G + \boldsymbol{\epsilon}_{G_i}, \qquad i = 1, \ldots, N. \end{aligned} \tag{5.3.5}$$

Let $\mathbf{y}_i' = (\mathbf{y}_{1_i}', \ldots, \mathbf{y}_{G_i}')$. The reduced form of $\mathbf{y}_i$ is

$$\mathbf{y}_i = \begin{bmatrix} \mathbf{y}_{1_i} \\ \mathbf{y}_{2_i} \\ \vdots \\ \mathbf{y}_{G_i} \end{bmatrix} = (I_G \otimes \tilde{X}_i)\tilde{\boldsymbol{\pi}} + \boldsymbol{\epsilon}_i, \qquad i = 1, \ldots, N, \tag{5.3.6}$$

where

$$\underset{T \times TK}{\tilde{X}_i} = \begin{bmatrix} \mathbf{x}_{i1}' & & & \mathbf{0} \\ & \mathbf{x}_{i2}' & & \\ & & \ddots & \\ \mathbf{0} & & & \mathbf{x}_{iT}' \end{bmatrix},$$

$$\tilde{\boldsymbol{\pi}} = \text{vec}(\tilde{\Pi}'), \tag{5.3.7}$$

$$\underset{GT \times K}{\tilde{\Pi}} = \Pi \otimes \mathbf{e}_T, \quad \text{and} \quad \Pi = E(\mathbf{y}_{it} \mid \mathbf{x}_{it}). \tag{5.3.8}$$

The unconstrained least-squares regression of $\mathbf{y}_i$ on $(I_G \otimes \tilde{X}_i)$ yields a consistent estimate of $\tilde{\boldsymbol{\pi}}$, $\hat{\tilde{\boldsymbol{\pi}}}$. If $\boldsymbol{\epsilon}_i$ are independently distributed over i, then $\sqrt{N}(\hat{\tilde{\boldsymbol{\pi}}} - \tilde{\boldsymbol{\pi}})$ is asymptotically normally distributed, with mean zero and variance–covariance matrix

$$\underset{GTK \times GTK}{\tilde{\Omega}} = \left(I_G \otimes \Phi_{xx}^{-1}\right)\tilde{V}\left(I_G \otimes \Phi_{xx}^{-1}\right), \tag{5.3.9}$$

where $\Phi_{xx} = E\tilde{X}_i'\tilde{X}_i = \text{diag}\{E(\mathbf{x}_{i1}\mathbf{x}_{i1}'), \ldots, E(\mathbf{x}_{iT}\mathbf{x}_{iT}')\}$, and $\tilde{V}$ is a $GTK \times GTK$ matrix, with the $g\ell$th block a $TK \times TK$ matrix of the form

$$\tilde{V}_{g\ell} = E \begin{bmatrix} \boldsymbol{\epsilon}_{g_{i1}}\boldsymbol{\epsilon}_{\ell_{i1}}\mathbf{x}_{i1}\mathbf{x}_{i1}' & \boldsymbol{\epsilon}_{g_{i1}}\boldsymbol{\epsilon}_{\ell_{i2}}\mathbf{x}_{i1}\mathbf{x}_{i2}' & \cdots & \boldsymbol{\epsilon}_{g_{i1}}\boldsymbol{\epsilon}_{\ell_{iT}}\mathbf{x}_{i1}\mathbf{x}_{iT}' \\ \boldsymbol{\epsilon}_{g_{i2}}\boldsymbol{\epsilon}_{\ell_{i1}}\mathbf{x}_{i2}\mathbf{x}_{i1}' & \boldsymbol{\epsilon}_{g_{i2}}\boldsymbol{\epsilon}_{\ell_{i2}}\mathbf{x}_{i2}\mathbf{x}_{i2}' & \cdots & \boldsymbol{\epsilon}_{g_{i2}}\boldsymbol{\epsilon}_{\ell_{iT}}\mathbf{x}_{i2}\mathbf{x}_{iT}' \\ \vdots & \vdots & & \vdots \\ \boldsymbol{\epsilon}_{g_{iT}}\boldsymbol{\epsilon}_{\ell_{i1}}\mathbf{x}_{iT}\mathbf{x}_{i1}' & \boldsymbol{\epsilon}_{g_{iT}}\boldsymbol{\epsilon}_{\ell_{i2}}\mathbf{x}_{iT}\mathbf{x}_{i2}' & \cdots & \boldsymbol{\epsilon}_{g_{iT}}\boldsymbol{\epsilon}_{\ell_{iT}}\mathbf{x}_{iT}\mathbf{x}_{iT}' \end{bmatrix}. \tag{5.3.10}$$

One can obtain a consistent estimator of $\tilde{\Omega}$ by replacing the population moments in $\tilde{\Omega}$ by the corresponding sample moments (e.g., $E\mathbf{x}_{i1}\mathbf{x}_{i1}'$ is replaced by $\sum_{i=1}^{N} \mathbf{x}_{i1}\mathbf{x}_{i1}'/N$).

Let $\boldsymbol{\theta}' = (\boldsymbol{\theta}_1', \boldsymbol{\pi}_2', \ldots, \pi_G')$, and specify the restrictions on $\tilde{\boldsymbol{\pi}}$ by the condition that $\tilde{\boldsymbol{\pi}} = \mathbf{f}(\boldsymbol{\theta})$. Choose $\boldsymbol{\theta}$ to minimize the following distance function:

$$[\hat{\tilde{\boldsymbol{\pi}}} - \tilde{\mathbf{f}}(\boldsymbol{\theta})]'\hat{\tilde{\Omega}}^{-1}[\hat{\tilde{\boldsymbol{\pi}}} - \tilde{\mathbf{f}}(\boldsymbol{\theta})]. \tag{5.3.11}$$

Then $\sqrt{N}(\hat{\boldsymbol{\theta}} - \boldsymbol{\theta})$ is asymptotically normally distributed with mean zero and variance–covariance matrix $(\tilde{F}'\tilde{\Omega}^{-1}\tilde{F})^{-1}$, where $\tilde{F} = \partial\tilde{\mathbf{f}}/\partial\boldsymbol{\theta}'$. Noting that $\tilde{\Pi} = \Pi \otimes \mathbf{e}_T$, and evaluating the partitioned inverse, we obtain the asymptotic variance–covariance matrix of $\sqrt{N}(\hat{\boldsymbol{\theta}}_1 - \boldsymbol{\theta}_1)$ as

$$\left\{\tilde{\Phi}_{w_1x}\Psi_{11}^{-1}\tilde{\Phi}_{w_1x}'\right\}^{-1}, \tag{5.3.12}$$

where $\tilde{\Phi}_{w_1x} = [E(\mathbf{w}_{1_{i1}}\mathbf{x}'_{i1}), E(\mathbf{w}_{1_{i2}}\mathbf{x}'_{i2}), \ldots, E(\mathbf{w}_{1_{iT}}\mathbf{x}'_{iT})]$, and

$$\Psi_{11} = E\begin{bmatrix} v_{1_{i1}}^2\mathbf{x}_{i1}\mathbf{x}'_{i1} & v_{1_{i1}}v_{1_{i2}}\mathbf{x}_{i1}\mathbf{x}'_{i2} & \cdots & v_{1_{i1}}v_{1_{i1}}\mathbf{x}_{i1}\mathbf{x}'_{iT} \\ v_{1_{i2}}v_{1_{i1}}\mathbf{x}_{i2}\mathbf{x}'_{i1} & v_{1_{i2}}^2\mathbf{x}_{i2}\mathbf{x}'_{i2} & \cdots & v_{1_{i2}}v_{1_{iT}}\mathbf{x}_{i2}\mathbf{x}'_{iT} \\ \vdots & \vdots & & \vdots \\ v_{1_{iT}}v_{1_{i1}}\mathbf{x}_{iT}\mathbf{x}'_{i1} & v_{1_{iT}}v_{1_{i2}}\mathbf{x}_{iT}\mathbf{x}'_{i2} & \cdots & v_{1_{iT}}v_{1_{iT}}\mathbf{x}_{iT}\mathbf{x}'_{iT} \end{bmatrix}. \tag{5.3.13}$$

The limited-information minimum-distance estimator of (5.3.11) is asymptotically equivalent to the following generalization of the 2SLS estimator:

$$\hat{\boldsymbol{\theta}}_{1,\text{G2SLS}} = \left(\tilde{\mathbf{S}}_{w_1x}\hat{\Psi}_{11}^{-1}\tilde{S}'_{w_1x}\right)^{-1}\left(\tilde{S}_{w_1x}\hat{\Psi}_{11}^{-1}\mathbf{s}_{xy_1}\right), \tag{5.3.14}$$

where

$$\tilde{\mathbf{S}}_{w_1x} = \left[\frac{1}{N}\sum_{i=1}^{N}\mathbf{w}_{1_{i1}}\mathbf{x}'_{i1}, \frac{1}{N}\sum_{i=1}^{N}\mathbf{w}_{1_{i2}}\mathbf{x}'_{i2}, \ldots, \frac{1}{N}\sum_{i=1}^{N}\mathbf{w}_{1_{iT}}\mathbf{x}'_{iT}\right],$$

$$\mathbf{s}_{xy_1} = \begin{bmatrix} \frac{1}{N}\sum_{i=1}^{N}\mathbf{x}_{i1}y_{1_{i1}} \\ \frac{1}{N}\sum_{i=1}^{N}\mathbf{x}_{i2}y_{1_{i2}} \\ \vdots \\ \frac{1}{N}\sum_{i=1}^{N}\mathbf{x}_{iT}y_{1_{iT}} \end{bmatrix},$$

$$\hat{\Psi}_{11} = \frac{1}{N}\begin{bmatrix} \sum_{i=1}^{N}\hat{v}_{1_{i1}}^2\mathbf{x}_{i1}\mathbf{x}'_{i1} & \sum_{i=1}^{N}\hat{v}_{1_{i1}}\hat{v}_{1_{i2}}\mathbf{x}_{i1}\mathbf{x}'_{i2} & \cdots & \sum_{i=1}^{N}\hat{v}_{1_{i1}}\hat{v}_{1_{iT}}\mathbf{x}_{i1}\mathbf{x}'_{iT} \\ \vdots & \vdots & & \vdots \\ \sum_{i=1}^{N}\hat{v}_{1_{iT}}\hat{v}_{1_{i1}}\mathbf{x}_{iT}\mathbf{x}'_{i1} & \sum_{i=1}^{N}\hat{v}_{1iT}\hat{v}_{1i2}\mathbf{x}_{iT}\mathbf{x}_{i2} & \cdots & \sum_{i=1}^{N}\hat{v}_{1_{iT}}\hat{v}_{1_{iT}}\mathbf{x}_{iT}\mathbf{x}'_{iT} \end{bmatrix},$$

and $\hat{v}_{1_{iT}} = y_{1_{it}} - \mathbf{w}'_{1_{it}}\hat{\boldsymbol{\theta}}_1$, with $\hat{\boldsymbol{\theta}}_1$ any consistent estimator of $\boldsymbol{\theta}_1$. The generalized 2SLS coverges to the 2SLS if $v_{1_{it}}$ is independently identically distributed over i and t and $E\mathbf{x}_{it}\mathbf{x}'_{it} = E\mathbf{x}_{is}\mathbf{x}'_{is}$. But the generalized 2SLS, like the minimum-distance estimator of (5.3.11), makes allowance for the heteroscedasticity and arbitrary serial correlation in $v_{1_{it}}$, whereas the 2SLS does not.

When the variance–covariance matrix $\sum_{gg}$ possesses an error-component structure as specified in (5.3.3), although both the 2SLS estimator and the minimum-distance estimator of (5.3.11) (or the generalized 2SLS estimator) remain consistent, they are no longer efficient even within a limited-information framework, because, as shown in the last section, when there are restrictions on the variance–covariance matrix the least-squares estimator of the unconstrained Π is not as efficient as the generalized least-squares estimator[7]. An efficient estimation method has to exploit the known restrictions on the error structure.

Baltagi (1981a) has suggested using the following error-component two-stage least-squares (EC2SLS) method to obtain a more efficient estimator of the unknown parameters in the gth equation.

Transforming (5.3.1) by the eigenvectors of $\sum_{gg}$, C_1', C_2', and C_3', we have[8]

$$\mathbf{y}_g^{(h)} = Y_g^{(h)}\boldsymbol{\gamma}_g + X_g^{(h)}\boldsymbol{\beta}_g + \mathbf{v}_g^{(h)} = W_g^{(h)}\boldsymbol{\theta}_g + \mathbf{v}_g^{(h)}, \tag{5.3.15}$$

where $\mathbf{y}_g^{(h)} = C_h'\mathbf{y}_g$, $W_g^{(h)} = C_h'W_g$, $\mathbf{v}_g^{(h)} = C_h'\mathbf{v}_g$ for $h = 1, 2, 3$, and C_1', C_2', and C_3' are as defined in Appendix 3B. The transformed disturbance term $\mathbf{v}_g^{(h)}$ is mutually orthogonal and has a covariance matrix proportional to an identity matrix. We can therefore use $X^{(h)} = C_h'X$ as the instruments and apply the Aitken estimation procedure to the system of equations

$$\begin{bmatrix} X^{(1)\prime}\mathbf{y}_g^{(1)} \\ X^{(2)\prime}\mathbf{y}_g^{(2)} \\ X^{(3)\prime}\mathbf{y}_g^{(3)} \end{bmatrix} = \begin{bmatrix} X^{(1)\prime}W_g^{(1)} \\ X^{(2)\prime}W_g^{(2)} \\ X^{(3)\prime}W_g^{(3)} \end{bmatrix} \begin{bmatrix} \boldsymbol{\gamma}_g \\ \boldsymbol{\beta}_g \end{bmatrix} + \begin{bmatrix} X^{(1)\prime}\mathbf{v}_g^{(1)} \\ X^{(2)\prime}\mathbf{v}_g^{(2)} \\ X^{(3)\prime}\mathbf{v}_g^{(3)} \end{bmatrix}. \tag{5.3.16}$$

The resulting Aitken estimator of $(\boldsymbol{\gamma}_g', \boldsymbol{\beta}_g')$ is

$$\begin{aligned} \hat{\boldsymbol{\theta}}_{g,\text{EC2SLS}} = {} & \left\{ \sum_{h=1}^{3} \left[\frac{1}{\sigma_{hgg}^2} W_g^{(h)\prime} P_X(h) W_g^{(h)} \right] \right\}^{-1} \\ & \left\{ \sum_{h=1}^{3} \left[\frac{1}{\sigma_{hgg}^2} W_g^{(h)\prime} P_X(H) \mathbf{y}_g^{(h)} \right] \right\}, \end{aligned} \tag{5.3.17}$$

where $P_X(h) = X^{(h)}(X^{(h)\prime}X^{(h)})^{-1}X^{(h)\prime}$. It is a weighted combination of the between-groups, between-time-periods, and within-groups 2SLS estimators of $(\boldsymbol{\gamma}_g', \boldsymbol{\beta}_g')$. The weights σ_{hgg}^2 can be estimated by substituting the transformed 2SLS residuals in the usual variance formula,

$$\hat{\sigma}_{hgg}^2 = \left(\mathbf{y}_g^{(h)} - W_g^{(h)}\hat{\boldsymbol{\theta}}_{g,2\text{SLS}}^{(h)}\right)'\left(\mathbf{y}_g^{(h)} - W_g^{(h)}\hat{\boldsymbol{\theta}}_{g,2\text{SLS}}^{(h)}\right)\big/n(h), \tag{5.3.18}$$

where $\hat{\boldsymbol{\theta}}_{g,2\text{SLS}}^{(h)} = [W_g^{(h)\prime}P_X(h)W_g^{(h)}]^{-1}[W_g^{(h)\prime}P_X(h)\mathbf{y}_g^{(h)}]$, and $n(1) = N - 1$, $n(2) = T - 1$, $n(3) = (N-1)(T-1)$. If $N \to \infty$, $T \to \infty$, and N/T tends to a nonzero constant, then the probability limit of the EC2SLS tends to the 2SLS estimator based on the within-groups variation alone.

In the special case in which the source of correlation between some of the regressors and residuals comes from the unobserved time-invariant individual effects alone, the correlations between them can be removed by removing the time-invariant component from the corresponding variables. Thus, instruments for the correlated regressors can be chosen from "inside" the equation, as opposed to the conventional method of being chosen from "outside" the equation. Hausman and Taylor (1981) noted that for variables that are time-varying and are correlated with α_{ig}, transforming them into deviations from their corresponding time means provides legitimate instruments, because they will no longer be correlated with α_{ig}. For variables that are time-invariant, the time means of those variables that are uncorrelated with α_{ig} can be used as instruments. Hence, a necessary condition for identification of all the parameters within a single-equation framework is that the number of time-varying variables that are uncorrelated with α_{ig} be at least as great as the number of time-invariant variables that are correlated with α_{ig}. They further showed that when the variance-component structure of the disturbance term is taken account of, the instrumental-variable estimator with instruments chosen this way is efficient among the single-equation estimators.

5.3.2 Estimation of the Complete Structural System

The single-equation estimation method considered earlier ignores restrictions in all equations in the structural system except the one being estimated. In general, we expect to get more efficient estimates if we consider the additional information contained in the other equations. In this subsection we consider the full-information estimation methods.

Let $\mathbf{y} = (\mathbf{y}_1', \ldots, \mathbf{y}_G')'$, $\mathbf{v} = (\mathbf{v}_1', \ldots, \mathbf{v}_G')'$,

$$W = \begin{bmatrix} W_1 & \mathbf{0} & \cdots & \mathbf{0} \\ \mathbf{0} & W_2 & \cdots & \mathbf{0} \\ \vdots & \vdots & & \vdots \\ \mathbf{0} & \mathbf{0} & \cdots & W_G \end{bmatrix}, \quad \text{and} \quad \boldsymbol{\theta} = \begin{bmatrix} \boldsymbol{\theta}_1 \\ \vdots \\ \boldsymbol{\theta}_G \end{bmatrix}.$$

We write the set of G structural equations as

$$\mathbf{y} = W\boldsymbol{\theta} + \mathbf{v}. \tag{5.3.19}$$

We can estimate the system (5.3.19) by the three-stage least-squares (3SLS) method. But just as in the limited-information case, the 3SLS estimator is efficient only if $(v_{1_{it}}, v_{2_{it}}, \ldots, v_{G_{it}})$ are independently identically distributed over i and t. To allow for arbitrary heteroscedasticity or serial correlation, we can use the full-information minimum-distance estimator or the generalized 3SLS estimator.

We first consider the minimum-distance estimator. When T is fixed and N tends to infinity, we can stack the T period equations for an individual's behavioral equation into a system to create a model of GT equations,

$$\begin{aligned} \underset{T\times 1}{\mathbf{y}_{1_i}} &= W_{1_i}\boldsymbol{\theta}_1 + \mathbf{v}_{1_i}, \\ \mathbf{y}_{2_i} &= W_{2i}\boldsymbol{\theta}_2 + \mathbf{v}_{2_i}, \\ &\vdots \\ \mathbf{y}_{G_i} &= W_{G_i}\boldsymbol{\theta}_G + \mathbf{v}_{G_i}, \qquad i = 1, \ldots, N. \end{aligned} \tag{5.3.20}$$

We obtain a minimum-distance estimator of $\boldsymbol{\theta}$ by choosing $\hat{\boldsymbol{\theta}}$ to minimize $[\hat{\tilde{\boldsymbol{\pi}}} - \tilde{\mathbf{f}}(\boldsymbol{\theta})]'\hat{\tilde{\Omega}}^{-1}[\hat{\tilde{\boldsymbol{\pi}}} - \tilde{\mathbf{f}}(\boldsymbol{\theta})]$, where $\hat{\tilde{\boldsymbol{\pi}}}$ is the unconstrained least-squares estimator of regressing $\mathbf{y}_i$ on $(I_G \otimes \tilde{X}_i)$, and $\hat{\tilde{\Omega}}$ is a consistent estimate of $\tilde{\Omega}$ [equation (5.3.9)]. Noting that $\tilde{\Pi} = \Pi \otimes \mathbf{e}_T$ and $\text{vec}(\Pi') = \boldsymbol{\pi} = \text{vec}[-\Gamma^{-1}B]'$ for all elements of Γ and B not known a priori, and making use of the formula $\partial\boldsymbol{\pi}/\partial\boldsymbol{\theta}'$

[equation (3.8.25)], we can show that if $\mathbf{v}_i$ are independently distributed over i, then $\sqrt{N}(\hat{\boldsymbol{\theta}} - \boldsymbol{\theta})$ is asymptotically normally distributed, with mean zero and variance–covariance matrix

$$\{\Phi_{wx}\Psi^{-1}\Phi'_{wx}\}^{-1}, \tag{5.3.21}$$

where

$$\Phi_{wx} = \begin{bmatrix} \tilde{\Phi}_{w_1x} & \mathbf{0} & \cdots & \mathbf{0} \\ \mathbf{0} & \tilde{\Phi}_{w_2x} & & \mathbf{0} \\ \vdots & & \ddots & \vdots \\ \mathbf{0} & \mathbf{0} & \cdots & \tilde{\Phi}_{w_Gx} \end{bmatrix},$$

$$\tilde{\Phi}_{w_gx} = [E(\mathbf{w}_{g_{i1}}\mathbf{x}'_{i1}), E(\mathbf{w}_{g_{i2}}\mathbf{x}'_{i2}), \ldots, E(\mathbf{w}_{g_{iT}}\mathbf{x}'_{iT})],$$

$$\underset{GTK\times GTK}{\Psi} = \begin{bmatrix} \Psi_{11} & \Psi_{12} & \cdots & \Psi_{1G} \\ \Psi_{21} & \Psi_{22} & \cdots & \Psi_{2G} \\ \vdots & \vdots & & \vdots \\ \Psi_{G1} & \Psi_{G2} & \cdots & \Psi_{GG} \end{bmatrix}, \tag{5.3.22}$$

$$\underset{TK\times TK}{\Psi_{g\ell}} = E\begin{bmatrix} v_{g_{i1}}v_{\ell_{i1}}\mathbf{x}_{i1}\mathbf{x}'_{i1} & v_{g_{i1}}v_{\ell_{i2}}\mathbf{x}_{i1}\mathbf{x}'_{i2} & \cdots & v_{g_{i1}}v_{\ell_{iT}}\mathbf{x}_{i1}\mathbf{x}'_{iT} \\ \vdots & \vdots & & \vdots \\ v_{g_{iT}}v_{\ell i1}\,\mathbf{x}_{iT}\mathbf{x}'_{i1} & v_{g_{iT}}v_{\ell_{i2}}\mathbf{x}_{iT}\mathbf{x}'{}_{i2} & \cdots & v_{g_{iT}}v_{\ell_{iT}}\mathbf{x}_{iT}\mathbf{x}'_{iT} \end{bmatrix}.$$

We can also estimate (5.3.20) by using a generalized 3SLS estimator,

$$\hat{\boldsymbol{\theta}}_{\text{G3SLS}} = (S_{wx}\hat{\Psi}^{-1}S'_{wx})^{-1}(S_{wx}\hat{\Psi}^{-1}S_{xy}), \tag{5.3.23}$$

where

$$S_{wx} = \begin{bmatrix} \tilde{S}_{w_1x} & \mathbf{0} & \cdots & \mathbf{0} \\ \mathbf{0} & \tilde{S}_{w_2x} & & \mathbf{0} \\ \vdots & \vdots & \ddots & \vdots \\ \mathbf{0} & \mathbf{0} & \cdots & \tilde{S}_{w_Gx} \end{bmatrix},$$

$$\tilde{S}_{w_gx} = \left[\frac{1}{N}\sum_{i=1}^{N}\mathbf{w}_{g_{i1}}\mathbf{x}'_{i1}, \frac{1}{N}\sum_{i=1}^{N}\mathbf{w}_{g_{i2}}\mathbf{x}'_{i2}, \ldots, \frac{1}{N}\sum_{i=1}^{N}\mathbf{w}_{g_{iT}}\mathbf{x}'_{iT}\right],$$

$$S_{xy} = \begin{bmatrix} \mathbf{s}_{xy_1} \\ \mathbf{s}_{xy_2} \\ \vdots \\ \mathbf{s}_{xy_G} \end{bmatrix},$$

$$\underset{TK\times 1}{\mathbf{s}_{xy_g}} = \begin{bmatrix} \dfrac{1}{N}\displaystyle\sum_{i=1}^{N}\mathbf{x}_{i1}y_{g_{i1}} \\ \vdots \\ \dfrac{1}{N}\displaystyle\sum_{i=1}^{N}\mathbf{x}_{iT}y_{g_{iT}}, \end{bmatrix},$$

and $\hat{\Psi}$ is Ψ [equation (5.3.22)] with $\mathbf{v}_{it}$ replaced by $\hat{\mathbf{v}}_{it} = \hat{\Gamma}\mathbf{y}_{it} + \hat{B}\mathbf{x}_{it}$, where $\hat{\Gamma}$ and $\hat{B}$ are any consistent estimates of Γ and B. The generalized 3SLS is asymptotically equivalent to the minimum-distance estimator.

Both the 3SLS and the generalized 3SLS are consistent. But just as in the limited-information case, if the variance–covariance matrix possesses an error-component structure, they are not fully efficient. To take advantage of the known structure of the covariance matrix, Baltagi (1981a) suggested the following error-component three-stage least-squares estimator (EC3SLS).

The $g\ell$th block of the covariance matrix Σ is of the form (5.3.3). A key point that is evident from Appendix 3B is that the set of eigenvectors C_1, C_2, C_3, and C_4 of (5.3.3) is invariant with respect to changes in the parameters $\sigma^2_{\lambda_{g\ell}}$, $\sigma^2_{\alpha_{g\ell}}$, and $\sigma^2_{u_{g\ell}}$. Therefore, premultiplying (5.3.19) by $I_G \otimes C'_h$, we have[9]

$$\mathbf{y}^{(h)} = W^{(h)}\boldsymbol{\theta} + \mathbf{v}^{(h)}, \qquad h = 1, 2, 3, \tag{5.3.24}$$

where $\mathbf{y}^{(h)} = (I_G \otimes C'_h)\mathbf{y}$, $W^{(h)} = (I_G \otimes C'_h)W$, $\mathbf{v}^{(h)} = (I_G \otimes C'_h)\mathbf{v}$, with $E(\mathbf{v}^{(h)}\mathbf{v}^{(h)\prime}) = \Sigma^{(h)} \otimes I_{n(h)}$, where $\Sigma^{(h)} = (\sigma^2_{h_{g\ell}})$ for $h = 1$, 2, and 3. Because $W^{(h)}$ contains endogenous variables that are correlated with $\mathbf{v}^{(h)}$, we first premultiply (5.3.24) by $(I_G \otimes X^{(h)})'$ to purge the correlation between $W^{(h)}$ and $\mathbf{v}^{(h)}$. Then apply the GLS estimation procedure to the resulting systems of equations to obtain

$$\hat{\boldsymbol{\theta}}_{\text{GLS}} = \left[\sum_{h=1}^{3}\{W^{(h)\prime}[(\Sigma^{(h)})^{-1} \otimes P_X(h)]W^{(h)}\}\right]^{-1} \times \left[\sum_{h=1}^{3}\{W^{(h)\prime}[(\Sigma^{(h)})^{-1} \otimes P_X(h)]\mathbf{y}^{(h)}\right]. \tag{5.3.25}$$

Usually we do not know $\Sigma^{(h)}$. Therefore, the following three-stage procedure is suggested:

1. Estimate the $\hat{\boldsymbol{\theta}}_g^{(h)}$ by 2SLS.
2. Use the residuals from the hth 2SLS estimate to estimate $\hat{\sigma}^2_{h_{g\ell}}$ [equation (5.3.18)].
3. Replace $\Sigma^{(h)}$ by the estimated covariance matrix. Estimate $\boldsymbol{\theta}$ by (5.3.25).

The resulting estimator is called the EC3SLS estimator. It is a weighted combination of three 3SLS (within, between-groups, and between-time-periods) estimators of the structural parameters (Baltagi (1981a)).

The EC3SLS estimator is asymptotically equivalent to the full-information maximum-likelihood estimator. In the case in which Σ is block-diagonal, the EC3SLS reduces to the EC2SLS. But, contrary to the usual simultaneous-equations models, when the error terms have an error-component structure, the EC3SLS does not necessarily reduce to the EC2SLS, even if all the structural equations are just identified. For details, see Baltagi (1981a).

5.4 TRIANGULAR SYSTEM

The model discussed earlier assumes that residuals of different equations in a multiequation model have an unrestricted variance-component structure. Under this assumption, the panel data only improve the precision of the estimates by providing a large number of sample observations. It does not offer additional opportunities that are not standard. However, quite often the residual correlations may simply be due to one or two common omitted or unobservable variables (Chamberlain (1976, 1977a, 1977b); Chamberlain and Griliches (1975); Goldberger (1972); Zellner (1970). For instance, in the estimation of income and schooling relations or individual-firm production and factor-demand relations, it is sometimes postulated that the biases in different equations are caused by a common left-out "ability" or "managerial-differences" variable. When panel data are used, this common omitted variable is again assumed to have a within- and between-group structure. The combination of this factor-analytic structure with error-components formulations puts restrictions on the residual covariance matrix that can be used to identify an otherwise unidentified model and improve the efficiency of the estimates. Because a widely used structure for longitudinal microdata is the triangular structure, and because its connection with the general simultaneous-equations model in which the residuals have a factor-analytic structure holds in general, in this section we focus on the triangular structure to illustrate how such information can be used to identify and estimate a model.

5.4.1 Identification

A convenient way to model correlations across equations, as well as the correlation of a given individual at different times (or different members of a group), is to use latent variables to connect the residuals. Let $y_{g_{it}}$ denote the value of the variable y_g for the ith individual (or group) at time t (or tth member). We can assume that

$$v_{g_{it}} = d_g h_{it} + u_{g_{it}}, \tag{5.4.1}$$

where the u_g are uncorrelated across equations and across i and t. The correlations across equations are all generated by the common omitted variable h, which is assumed to have a variance-component structure:

$$h_{it} = \alpha_i + \omega_{it}, \tag{5.4.2}$$

where α_i is invariant over t but is independently identically distributed across i (groups), with mean zero and variance σ_α^2, and ω_{it} is independently identically distributed across i and t, with mean zero and variance σ_ω^2 and is uncorrelated with α_i.

An example of the model with $\mathbf{\Gamma}$ lower-triangular and $\mathbf{v}$ of the form (5.4.1) is (Chamberlain (1977a, 1977b); Chamberlain and Griliches (1975); Griliches

(1979))

$$
\begin{aligned}
y_{1_{it}} &= \boldsymbol{\beta}_1'\mathbf{x}_{it} + d_1 h_{it} + u_{1_{it}},\\
y_{2_{it}} &= -\gamma_{21} y_{1_{it}} + \boldsymbol{\beta}_2'\mathbf{x}_{it} + d_2 h_{it} + u_{2_{it}}, \qquad (5.4.3)\\
y_{3_{it}} &= -\gamma_{31} y_{1_{it}} - \gamma_{32} y_{2_{it}} + \boldsymbol{\beta}_3'\mathbf{x}_{it} + d_3 h_{it} + u_{3_{it}},
\end{aligned}
$$

where y_1, y_2, and y_3 denote years of schooling, a late (postschool) test score, and earnings, respectively, and $\mathbf{x}_{it}$ are exogenous variables (which may differ from equation to equation via restrictions on $\boldsymbol{\beta}_g$). The unobservable h can be interpreted as early "ability," and u_2 as measurement error in the test. The index i indicates groups (or families), and t indicates members in each group (or family).

Without the h variables, or if $d_g = 0$, equation (5.4.3) would be only a simple recursive system that could be estimated by applying least squares separately to each equation. The simultaneity problem arises when we admit the possibility that $d_g \neq 0$. In general, if there were enough exogenous variables in the first (schooling) equation that did not appear again in the other equations, the system could be estimated using 2SLS or EC2SLS procedures. Unfortunately, in the income–schooling–ability model using sibling data [e.g., see the survey by Griliches (1979)] there usually are not enough distinct $\mathbf{x}$'s to identify all the parameters. Thus, restrictions imposed on the variance–covariance matrix of the residuals will have to be used.

Given that h is unobservable, we have an indeterminate scale

$$d_g^2(\sigma_\alpha^2 + \sigma_\omega^2) = c d_g^2\left(\frac{1}{c}\sigma_\alpha^2 + \frac{1}{c}\sigma_\omega^2\right). \qquad (5.4.4)$$

So we normalize h by letting $\sigma_\alpha^2 = 1$. Then

$$E\mathbf{v}_{it}\mathbf{v}_{it}' = (1 + \sigma_\omega^2)\mathbf{d}\mathbf{d}' + \text{diag}(\sigma_1^2, \ldots, \sigma_G^2) = \Omega, \qquad (5.4.5)$$

$$E\mathbf{v}_{it}\mathbf{v}_{is}' = \mathbf{d}\mathbf{d}' = \Omega_w \qquad \text{if } t \neq s, \qquad (5.4.6)$$

$$E\mathbf{v}_{it}\mathbf{v}_{js}' = \mathbf{0} \qquad \text{if } i \neq j, \qquad (5.4.7)$$

where $\mathbf{d} = (d_1, \ldots, d_G)$, and $\text{diag}(\sigma_1^2, \ldots, \sigma_G^2)$ denotes a $G \times G$ diagonal matrix with $\sigma_1^2, \sigma_2^2, \ldots, \sigma_G^2$ on the diagonal.

Under the assumption that α_i, ω_{it}, and $u_{g_{it}}$ are normally distributed, or if we limit our attention to second-order moments, all the information with regard to the distribution of $\mathbf{y}$ is contained in

$$C_{y_{tt}} = \boldsymbol{\Gamma}^{-1}\mathbf{B}C_{x_{tt}}\mathbf{B}'\boldsymbol{\Gamma}'^{-1} + \boldsymbol{\Gamma}^{-1}\Omega\boldsymbol{\Gamma}'^{-1}, \qquad (5.4.8)$$

$$C_{y_{ts}} = \boldsymbol{\Gamma}^{-1}\mathbf{B}C_{x_{ts}}\mathbf{B}'\boldsymbol{\Gamma}'^{-1} + \boldsymbol{\Gamma}^{-1}\Omega_w\boldsymbol{\Gamma}'^{-1}, \qquad t \neq s, \qquad (5.4.9)$$

$$C_{yx_{ts}} = -\boldsymbol{\Gamma}^{-1}\mathbf{B}C_{x_{ts}}, \qquad (5.4.10)$$

where $C_{y_{ts}} = E\mathbf{y}_{it}\mathbf{y}_{is}'$, $C_{yx_{ts}} = E\mathbf{y}_{it}\mathbf{x}_{is}'$, and $C_{x_{ts}} = E\mathbf{x}_{it}\mathbf{x}_{is}'$.

Stack the coefficient matrices Γ and $\mathbf{B}$ into a $1 \times G(G+K)$ vector $\boldsymbol{\theta}' = (\boldsymbol{\gamma}_1', \ldots, \boldsymbol{\gamma}_G', \boldsymbol{\beta}_1', \ldots, \boldsymbol{\beta}_G')$. Suppose $\boldsymbol{\theta}$ is subject to M a priori constraints:

$$\Phi(\boldsymbol{\theta}) = \boldsymbol{\phi}, \qquad (5.4.11)$$

where $\boldsymbol{\phi}$ is an $M \times 1$ vector of constants. Then a necessary and sufficient condition for local identification of $\boldsymbol{\Gamma}, \mathbf{B}, \mathbf{d}, \sigma_\omega^2$, and $\sigma_1^2, \ldots, \sigma_G^2$ is that the rank of the Jacobian formed by taking partial derivatives of (5.4.8)–(5.4.11) with respect to the unknowns is equal to $G(G+K)+2G+1$ (e.g., Hsiao (1983)).

Suppose there is no restriction on the matrix $\mathbf{B}$. The GK equations (5.4.10) can be used to identify $\mathbf{B}$ provided that $\boldsymbol{\Gamma}$ is identifiable. Hence, we can concentrate on

$$\boldsymbol{\Gamma}\left(C_{y_{tt}} - C_{yx_{tt}} C_{x_{tt}}^{-1} C'_{yx_{tt}}\right)\boldsymbol{\Gamma}' = \Omega, \tag{5.4.12}$$

$$\boldsymbol{\Gamma}\left(C_{y_{ts}} - C_{yx_{ts}} C_{x_{ts}}^{-1} C'_{yx_{ts}}\right)\boldsymbol{\Gamma}' = \Omega_w, \qquad t \neq s, \tag{5.4.13}$$

We note that Ω is symmetric, and we have $G(G+1)/2$ independent equations from (5.4.12). But Ω_w is of rank 1; therefore, we can derive only G independent equations from (5.4.13). Suppose $\boldsymbol{\Gamma}$ is lower-triangular and the diagonal elements of $\boldsymbol{\Gamma}$ are normalized to be unity; there are $G(G-1)/2$ unknowns in $\boldsymbol{\Gamma}$, and $2G+1$ unknowns of $(\mathrm{d}_1, \ldots, d_G)$, $(\sigma_1^2, \ldots, \sigma_G^2)$, and σ_ω^2. We have one less equation than the number of unknowns. In order for the Jacobian matrix formed by (5.4.12), (5.4.13), and a priori restrictions to be nonsingular, we need at least one additional a priori restriction. Thus, for the system

$$\boldsymbol{\Gamma}\mathbf{y}_{it} + \mathbf{B}\mathbf{x}_{it} = \mathbf{v}_{it}, \tag{5.4.14}$$

where $\boldsymbol{\Gamma}$ is lower-triangular, $\mathbf{B}$ is unrestricted, and $\mathbf{v}_{it}$ satisfies (5.4.1) and (5.4.2), a necessary condition for the identification under exclusion restrictions is that at least one $\gamma_{g\ell} = 0$ for $g > \ell$. [For details, see Chamberlain (1976) or Hsiao (1983).]

5.4.2 Estimation

We have discussed how the restrictions in the variance–covariance matrix can help identify the model. We now turn to the issues of estimation. Two methods are discussed: the purged-instrumental-variable method (Chamberlain (1977a)) and the maximum-likelihood method (Chamberlain and Griliches 1975)). The latter method is efficient, but computationally complicated. The former method is inefficient, but it is simple and consistent. It also helps to clarify the previous results on the sources of identification.

For simplicity, we assume that there is no restriction on the coefficients of exogenous variables. Under this assumption we can further ignore the existence of exogenous variables without loss of generality, because there are no excluded exogenous variables that can legitimately be used as instruments for the endogenous variables appearing in the equation. The instruments have to come from the group structure of the model. We illustrate this point by considering the following triangular system:

$$\begin{aligned}
y_{1_{it}} &= && + v_{1_{it}},\\
y_{2_{it}} &= \gamma_{21} y_{1_{it}} && + v_{2_{it}},\\
&\ \vdots \\
y_{G_{it}} &= \gamma_{G1} y_{1_{it}} + \cdots + \gamma_{G,G-1} y_{G-1_{it}} && + v_{G_{it}},
\end{aligned} \tag{5.4.15}$$

where $v_{g_{it}}$ satisfy (5.4.1) and (5.4.2). We assume one additional $\gamma_{\ell k} = 0$ for some ℓ and k, $\ell > k$, for identification.

The reduced form of (5.4.15) is

$$y_{g_{it}} = a_g h_{it} + \epsilon_{g_{it}}, \qquad g = 1, \ldots, G, \tag{5.4.16}$$

where

$$\mathbf{a} = \begin{bmatrix} a_1 \\ a_2 \\ a_3 \\ \vdots \\ a_G \end{bmatrix} = \begin{bmatrix} d_1 \\ d_2 + \gamma_{21} d_1 \\ d_3 + \gamma_{31} d_1 + \gamma_{32}(d_2 + \gamma_{21} d_1) \\ \vdots \end{bmatrix}, \tag{5.4.17}$$

$$\boldsymbol{\epsilon}_{it} = \begin{bmatrix} \epsilon_{1_{it}} \\ \epsilon_{2_{it}} \\ \epsilon_{3_{it}} \\ \vdots \\ \epsilon_{g_{it}} \\ \vdots \end{bmatrix} = \begin{bmatrix} u_{1_{it}} \\ u_{2_{it}} + \gamma_{21} u_{1_{it}} \\ u_{3_{it}} + \gamma_{31} u_{1_{it}} + \gamma_{32}(u_{2_{it}} + \gamma_{21} u_{1_{it}}) \\ \vdots \\ u_{g_{it}} + \sum_{k=1}^{g-1} \gamma_{gk}^{*} u_{k_{it}} \\ \vdots \end{bmatrix}, \tag{5.4.18}$$

where $\gamma_{gk}^{*} = \gamma_{gk} + \sum_{i=k+1}^{g-1} \gamma_{gi} \gamma_{ik}^{*}$ if $g > 1$ and $k + 1 < g$, and $\gamma_{gk}^{*} = \gamma_{gk}$ if $k + 1 = g$.

5.4.2.a *Instrumental-Variable Method*

The trick of the purged instrumental-variable (IV) method is to leave h in the residual and construct instruments that are uncorrelated with h. Before going to the general formula, we use several simple examples to show where the instruments come from.

Consider the case that $G = 3$. Suppose $\gamma_{21} = \gamma_{31} = 0$. Using y_1 as a proxy for h in the y_3 equation, we have

$$y_{3_{it}} = \gamma_{32} y_{2_{it}} + \frac{d_3}{d_1} y_{1_{it}} + u_{3_{it}} - \frac{d_3}{d_1} u_{1_{it}}. \tag{5.4.19}$$

If $T \geq 2$ then $y_{1_{is}}$, $s \neq t$, is a legitimate instrument for $y_{1_{it}}$, because it is uncorrelated with $u_{3_{it}} - (d_3/d_1) u_{1_{it}}$ but it is correlated with $y_{1_{it}}$ provided that $d_1 \sigma_\alpha^2 \neq 0$. Therefore, we can use $(y_{2_{it}}, y_{1_{is}})$ as instruments to estimate (5.4.19).

Next, suppose that only $\gamma_{32} = 0$. The reduced form of the model becomes

$$\begin{bmatrix} y_1 \\ y_2 \\ y_3 \end{bmatrix} = \begin{bmatrix} d_1 \\ d_2 + \gamma_{21} d_1 \\ d_3 + \gamma_{31} d_1 \end{bmatrix} h_{it} + \begin{bmatrix} u_{1_{it}} \\ u_{2_{it}} + \gamma_{21} u_{1_{it}} \\ u_{3_{it}} + \gamma_{31} u_{1_{it}} \end{bmatrix}$$
$$= \begin{bmatrix} a_1 \\ a_2 \\ a_3 \end{bmatrix} h_{it} + \begin{bmatrix} \epsilon_{1_{it}} \\ \epsilon_{2_{it}} \\ \epsilon_{3_{it}} \end{bmatrix}. \qquad (5.4.20)$$

In this case, the construction of valid instruments is more complicated. It requires two stages. The first stage is to use y_1 as a proxy for h in the reduced-form equation for y_2:

$$y_{2_{it}} = \frac{a_2}{a_1} y_{1_{it}} + \epsilon_{2_{it}} - \frac{a_2}{a_1} \epsilon_{1_{it}}. \qquad (5.4.21)$$

Equation (5.4.21) can be estimated by using $y_{1_{is}}$, $s \neq t$, as an instrument for $y_{1_{it}}$, provided that $d_1 \sigma_\alpha^2 \neq 0$. Then form the residual, thereby purging y_2 of its dependence on h:

$$z_{2_{it}} = y_{2_{it}} - \frac{a_2}{a_1} y_{1_{it}} = \epsilon_{2_{it}} - \frac{a_2}{a_1} \epsilon_{1_{it}}. \qquad (5.4.22)$$

The second stage is to use z_2 as an instrument for y_1 in the structural equation y_3:

$$y_{3_{it}} = \gamma_{31} y_{1_{it}} + d_3 h_{it} + u_{3_{it}}. \qquad (5.4.23)$$

The variable z_2 is an appropriate IV because it is uncorrelated with h and u_3, but it is correlated with y_1, provided $d_2 \sigma_1^2 \neq 0$. (If $d_2 = 0$, then $z_2 = y_2 - \gamma_{21} y_1 = u_2$. It is no longer correlated with y_1.) Therefore, we require that h appear directly in the y_2 equation and that y_1 not be proportional to h – otherwise we could never separate the effects of y_1 and h.

In order to identify the y_2 equation

$$y_{2_{it}} = \gamma_{21} y_{1_{it}} + d_2 h_{it} + u_{2_{it}}, \qquad (5.4.24)$$

we can interchange the reduced-form y_2 and y_3 equations and repeat the two stages. With γ_{21} and γ_{31} identified, in the third stage we form the residuals

$$\begin{aligned} v_{2_{it}} &= y_{2_{it}} - \gamma_{21} y_{1_{it}} = d_2 h_{it} + u_{2_{it}}, \\ v_{3_{it}} &= y_{3_{it}} - \gamma_{31} y_{1_{it}} = d_3 h_{it} + u_{3_{it}}. \end{aligned} \qquad (5.4.25)$$

Then use y_1 as a proxy for h:

$$\begin{aligned} v_{2_{it}} &= \frac{d_2}{d_1} y_{1_{it}} + u_{2_{it}} - \frac{d_2}{d_1} u_{1_{it}}, \\ v_{3_{it}} &= \frac{d_3}{d_1} y_{1_{it}} + u_{3_{it}} - \frac{d_3}{d_1} u_{1_{it}}. \end{aligned} \qquad (5.4.26)$$

Now d_2/d_1 and d_3/d_1 can be identified by a third application of instrumental variables, using $y_{1_{is}}$, $s \neq t$, as an instrument for $y_{1_{it}}$. (Note that only the ratio of the d's is identified, because of the indeterminate scale of the latent variable.)

Now come back to the construction of IVs for the general system (5.4.15)–(5.4.18). We assume that $T \geq 2$. The instruments are constructed over several stages. At the first stage, let y_1 be a proxy for h. Then the reduced-form equation for y_g becomes

$$y_{g_{it}} = \frac{a_g}{a_1} y_{1_{it}} + \epsilon_{g_{it}} - \frac{a_g}{a_1}\epsilon_{1_{it}}, \qquad g = 2, \ldots, \ell - 1. \tag{5.4.27}$$

If $T \geq 2$, a_g/a_1 can be consistently estimated by using different members in the same group (e.g., $y_{1_{is}}$ and $y_{1_{it}}$, $t \neq s$) as instruments for the y_g equation (5.4.27) when $d_1\sigma_\alpha^2 \neq 0$. Once a_g/a_1 is consistently estimated, we form the residual

$$z_{g_{it}} = y_{g_{it}} - \frac{a_g}{a_1} y_{1_{it}} = \epsilon_{g_{it}} - \frac{a_g}{a_1}\epsilon_{1_{it}}, \qquad g = 2, \ldots, \ell - 1. \tag{5.4.28}$$

The z_g are uncorrelated with h. They are valid instruments for y_g provided $d_g\sigma_1^2 \neq 0$. There are $\ell - 2$ IVs for the $\ell - 2$ variables that remain on the right-hand side of the ℓth structural equation after y_k has been excluded.

To estimate the equations that follow y_ℓ, we form the transformed variables

$$\begin{aligned} y_{2_{it}}^* &= y_{2_{it}} - \gamma_{21} y_{1_{it}}, \\ y_{3_{it}}^* &= y_{3_{it}} - \gamma_{31} y_{1_{it}} - \gamma_{32} y_{2_{it}}, \\ &\vdots \\ y_{\ell_{it}}^* &= y_{\ell_{it}} - \gamma_{\ell 1} y_{1_{it}} - \cdots - \gamma_{\ell,\ell-1} y_{\ell-1_{it}}, \end{aligned} \tag{5.4.29}$$

and rewrite the $y_{\ell+1}$ equation as

$$\begin{aligned} y_{\ell+1_{it}} &= \gamma_{\ell+1,1}^* y_{1_{it}} + \gamma_{\ell+1,2}^* y_{2_{it}}^* + \cdots + \gamma_{\ell+1,\ell-1}^* y_{\ell-1_{it}}^* + \gamma_{\ell+1,\ell} y_{\ell_{it}}^* \\ &\quad + d_{\ell+1} h_{it} + u_{\ell+1_{it}}, \end{aligned} \tag{5.4.30}$$

where $\gamma_{\ell+1,j}^* = \gamma_{\ell+1,j} + \sum_{m=j+1}^{\ell} \gamma_{\ell+1,m}\gamma_{mj}^*$ for $j < \ell$. Using y_1 as a proxy for h, we have

$$\begin{aligned} y_{\ell+1_{it}} &= \gamma_{\ell+1,2}^* y_{2_{it}}^* + \cdots + \gamma_{\ell+1,\ell} y_{\ell_{it}}^* \\ &\quad + \left(\gamma_{\ell+1,1}^* + \frac{d_{\ell+1}}{d_1}\right) y_{1_{it}} + u_{\ell+1_{it}} - \frac{d_{\ell+1}}{d_1} u_{1_{it}}, \end{aligned} \tag{5.4.31}$$

Because u_1 is uncorrelated with y_g^* for $2 \leq g \leq \ell$, we can use $y_{g_{it}}^*$ together with $y_{1_{is}}$, $s \neq t$ as instruments to identify $\gamma_{\ell+1,j}$. Once $\gamma_{\ell+1,j}$ are identified, we can form $y_{\ell+1}^* = y_{\ell+1} - \gamma_{\ell+1,1} y_1 - \cdots - \gamma_{\ell+1,\ell} y_\ell$ and proceed in a similar fashion to identify the $y_{\ell+2}$ equation, and so on.

Once all the γ are identified, we can form the estimated residuals, $\hat{\mathbf{v}}_{it}$. From $\hat{\mathbf{v}}_{it}$ we can estimate d_g/d_1 by the same procedure as (5.4.26). Or we can form the matrix $\hat{\Omega}$ of variance–covariances of the residuals, and the matrix $\hat{\bar{\Omega}}$ of variance–covariances of averaged residuals $(1/T)\sum_{t=1}^{T} \hat{\mathbf{v}}_{it}$, then solve for $\mathbf{d}$,

$(\sigma_1^2, \ldots, \sigma_G^2)$, and σ_ω^2 from the relations

$$\hat{\Omega} = \left(1 + \sigma_\omega^2\right)\mathbf{dd}' + \text{diag}\left(\sigma_1^2, \ldots, \sigma_G^2\right), \tag{5.4.32}$$

$$\hat{\hat{\Omega}} = \left(1 + \sigma_\omega^2\right)\mathbf{dd}' + \frac{1}{T}\text{diag}\left(\sigma_1^2, \ldots, \sigma_G^2\right). \tag{5.4.33}$$

The purged IV estimator is consistent. It also will often indicate quickly if a new model is identified. For instance to see the necessity of having at least one more $\gamma_{g\ell} = 0$ for $g > \ell$ to identify the foregoing system, we can check if the instruments formed by the foregoing procedure satisfy the required rank condition. Consider the example where $G = 3$ and all $\gamma_{g\ell} \neq 0$ for $g > \ell$. In order to follow the strategy of allowing h to remain in the residual, in the third equation we need IVs for y_1 and y_2 that are uncorrelated with h. As indicated earlier, we can purge y_2 of its dependence on h by forming $z_2 = y_2 - (a_2/a_1)y_1$. A similar procedure can be applied to y_1. We use y_2 as a proxy for h, with $y_{2_{is}}$ as an IV for $y_{2_{it}}$. Then form the residual $z_1 = y_1 - (a_1/a_2)y_2$. Again z_1 is uncorrelated with h and u_3. But $z_1 = -(a_1/a_2)z_2$, and so an attempt to use both z_2 and z_1 as IVs fails to meet the rank condition.

5.4.2.b Maximum-Likelihood Method

Although the purged IV method is simple to use, it is likely to be inefficient, because the correlations between the endogenous variables and the purged IVs will probably be small. Also, the restriction that (5.4.6) is of rank 1 is not being utilized. To obtain efficient estimates of the unknown parameters, it is necessary to estimate the covariance matrices simultaneously with the equation coefficients. Under the normality assumptions for α_i, ω_{it} and u_{it}, we can obtain efficient estimates of (5.4.15) by maximizing the log likelihood function

$$\begin{aligned} \log L = &-\frac{N}{2}\log|V| \\ &-\frac{1}{2}\sum_{i=1}^{N}(\mathbf{y}_{1i}', \mathbf{y}_{2i}', \ldots, \mathbf{y}_{Gi}')V^{-1}(\mathbf{y}_{1i}', \ldots, \mathbf{y}_{Gi}')', \end{aligned} \tag{5.4.34}$$

where

$$\begin{aligned} \underset{T\times 1}{\mathbf{y}_{gi}} &= (y_{g_{i1}}, \ldots, y_{g_{iT}})', \qquad g = 1, \ldots, G, \\ \underset{GT\times GT}{V} &= \Lambda \otimes I_T + \mathbf{aa}' \otimes \mathbf{e}_T\mathbf{e}_T', \\ \underset{G\times G}{\Lambda} &= E(\boldsymbol{\epsilon}_{it}\boldsymbol{\epsilon}_{it}') + \sigma_\omega^2\mathbf{aa}'. \end{aligned} \tag{5.4.35}$$

Using the relations[10]

$$V^{-1} = \Lambda^{-1} \otimes I_T - \mathbf{cc}' \otimes \mathbf{e}_T\mathbf{e}_T', \tag{5.4.36}$$

$$|V| = |\Lambda|^T|1 - T\mathbf{c}'\Lambda\mathbf{c}|^{-1}, \tag{5.4.37}$$

we can simplify the log likelihood function as[11]

$$\log L = -\frac{NT}{2}\log|\Lambda| + \frac{N}{2}\log(1 - T\mathbf{c}'\Lambda\mathbf{c}) - \frac{NT}{2}\operatorname{tr}(\Lambda^{-1}R) + \frac{NT^2}{2}\mathbf{c}'\bar{R}\mathbf{c}, \tag{5.4.38}$$

where $\mathbf{c}$ is a $G \times 1$ vector proportional to $\Lambda^{-1}\mathbf{a}$, R is the matrix of the sums of the squares and cross-products of the residuals divided by NT, and $\bar{R}$ is the matrix of sums of squares and cross-products of the averaged residuals (over t for i) divided by N. In other words, we simplify the log likelihood function (5.4.34) by reparameterizing it in terms of $\mathbf{c}$ and Λ.

Taking partial derivatives of (5.4.38), we obtain the first-order conditions[12]

$$\frac{\partial \log L}{\partial \Lambda^{-1}} = \frac{NT}{2}\Lambda + \frac{NT}{2}\frac{1}{(1 - T\mathbf{c}'\Lambda\mathbf{c})}\Lambda\mathbf{c}\mathbf{c}'\Lambda - \frac{NT}{2}R = \mathbf{0}, \tag{5.4.39}$$

$$\frac{\partial \log L}{\partial \mathbf{c}} = -\frac{NT}{1 - T\mathbf{c}'\Lambda\mathbf{c}}\Lambda\mathbf{c} + NT^2\bar{R}\mathbf{c} = \mathbf{0}. \tag{5.4.40}$$

Postmultiplying (5.4.39) by $\mathbf{c}$ and regrouping the terms, we have

$$\Lambda\mathbf{c} = \frac{1 - T\mathbf{c}'\Lambda\mathbf{c}}{1 - (T-1)\mathbf{c}'\Lambda\mathbf{c}}R\mathbf{c}. \tag{5.4.41}$$

Combining (5.4.40) and (5.4.41), we obtain

$$\left[\bar{R} - \frac{1}{T[1 - (T-1)\mathbf{c}'\Lambda\mathbf{c}]}R\right]\mathbf{c} = \mathbf{0}. \tag{5.4.42}$$

Hence, the MLE of $\mathbf{c}$ is a characteristic vector corresponding to a root of

$$|\bar{R} - \lambda R| = 0. \tag{5.4.43}$$

The determinate equation (5.4.43) has G roots. To find which root to use, substitute (5.4.39) and (5.4.40) into (5.4.38):

$$\begin{aligned}\log L &= -\frac{NT}{2}\log|\Lambda| + \frac{N}{2}\log(1 - T\mathbf{c}'\Lambda\mathbf{c}) \\ &\quad - \frac{NT}{2}(G + T\operatorname{tr}\mathbf{c}'\bar{R}\mathbf{c}) + \frac{NT^2}{2}\operatorname{tr}(\mathbf{c}'\bar{R}\mathbf{c}) \\ &= -\frac{NT}{2}\log|\Lambda| + \frac{N}{2}\log(1 - T\mathbf{c}'\Lambda\mathbf{c}) - \frac{NTG}{2}.\end{aligned} \tag{5.4.44}$$

Let the G characteristic vectors corresponding to the G roots of (5.4.43) be denoted as $\mathbf{c}_1(=\mathbf{c}), \mathbf{c}_2, \ldots, \mathbf{c}_G$. These characteristic vectors are determined only up to a scalar. Choose the normalization $\mathbf{c}_g^{*\prime}R\mathbf{c}_g^* = 1$, $g = 1, \ldots, G$, where $\mathbf{c}_g^* = (\mathbf{c}_g' R\mathbf{c}_g)^{-1/2}\mathbf{c}_g$. Let $C^* = [\mathbf{c}_1^*, \ldots, \mathbf{c}_G^*]$; then $C^{*\prime}RC^* = I_G$. From (5.4.39) and (5.4.41) we have

$$C^{*\prime}\Lambda C^{*} = C^{*\prime}RC^{*} - \frac{1 - T\mathbf{c}'\Lambda\mathbf{c}}{[1-(T-1)\mathbf{c}'\Lambda\mathbf{c}]^2}C^{*\prime}R\mathbf{c}\mathbf{c}'RC^{*}$$
$$= I_G - \frac{1 - T\mathbf{c}'\Lambda\mathbf{c}}{[1-(T-1)\mathbf{c}'\Lambda\mathbf{c}]^2}$$
$$\times \begin{bmatrix} (\mathbf{c}'R\mathbf{c})^{1/2} \\ 0 \\ \vdots \\ 0 \end{bmatrix} [(\mathbf{c}'R\mathbf{c})^{1/2} \quad 0 \quad \cdots \quad 0]. \qquad (5.4.45)$$

Equation (5.4.41) implies that $(\mathbf{c}'R\mathbf{c}) = \{[1-(T-1)\mathbf{c}'\Lambda\mathbf{c}]/[1-T\mathbf{c}'\Lambda\mathbf{c}]\}\mathbf{c}'\Lambda\mathbf{c}$. Therefore, the determinant of (5.4.45) is $\{[1-T\mathbf{c}'\Lambda\mathbf{c}]/[1-(T-1)\mathbf{c}'\Lambda\mathbf{c}]\}$. Using $C^{*\prime-1}C^{*-1} = R$, we have $|\Lambda| = \{[1-T\mathbf{c}'\Lambda\mathbf{c}]/[1-(T-1)\mathbf{c}'\Lambda\mathbf{c}]\}|R|$. Substituting this into (5.4.44), the log likelihood function becomes

$$\log L = -\frac{NT}{2}\{\log|R| + \log(1 - T\mathbf{c}'\Lambda\mathbf{c})$$
$$- \log[1-(T-1)\mathbf{c}'\Lambda\mathbf{c}]\}$$
$$+ \frac{N}{2}\log[1 - T\mathbf{c}'\Lambda\mathbf{c}] - \frac{NTG}{2}, \qquad (5.4.46)$$

which is positively related to $\mathbf{c}'\Lambda\mathbf{c}$ within the admissible range $(0, 1/T)$.[13] So the MLE of $\mathbf{c}$ is the characteristic vector corresponding to the largest root of (5.4.43). Once $\mathbf{c}$ is obtained, from Appendix 5A and (5.4.39) and (5.4.40) we can estimate $\mathbf{a}$ and Λ by

$$\mathbf{a}' = T(1 + T^2\mathbf{c}'\bar{R}\mathbf{c})^{-1/2}\mathbf{c}'\bar{R}, \qquad (5.4.47)$$

and

$$\Lambda = R - \mathbf{a}\mathbf{a}'. \qquad (5.4.48)$$

Knowing $\mathbf{a}$ and Λ, we can solve for the coefficients of the joint dependent variables Γ.

When exogenous variables also appear in the equation, and with no restrictions on the coefficients of exogenous variables, we need only replace the exponential term of the likelihood function (5.4.34),

$$-\frac{1}{2}\sum_{i=1}^{N}(\mathbf{y}'_{1i},\ldots,\mathbf{y}'_{Gi})V^{-1}(\mathbf{y}'_{1i},\ldots,\mathbf{y}'_{Gi})',$$

with

$$-\frac{1}{2}\sum_{i=1}^{N}(\mathbf{y}'_{1i} - \boldsymbol{\pi}'_1X'_i,\ldots,\mathbf{y}'_{Gi} - \boldsymbol{\pi}'_GX'_i)$$
$$\times V^{-1}(\mathbf{y}'_{1i} - \boldsymbol{\pi}'_1X'_i,\ldots,\mathbf{y}'_{Gi} - \boldsymbol{\pi}'_GX'_i)'.$$

The MLEs of $\mathbf{c}$, $\mathbf{a}$, and Λ remain the solutions of (5.4.43), (5.4.47), and (5.4.48). From knowledge of Λ and $\mathbf{a}$ we can solve for Γ and σ_ω^2. The MLE of Π conditional on V is the GLS of Π. Knowing Π and Γ, we can solve for $B = -\Gamma\Pi$.

Thus, Chamberlain and Griliches (1975) suggested the following iterative algorithm to solve for the MLE. Starting from the least-squares reduced-form estimates, we can form consistent estimates of R and $\bar{R}$. Then estimate $\mathbf{c}$ by maximizing[14]

$$\frac{\mathbf{c}'\bar{R}\mathbf{c}}{\mathbf{c}'R\mathbf{c}}. \tag{5.4.49}$$

Once $\mathbf{c}$ is obtained, we solve for $\mathbf{a}$ and Λ by (5.4.47) and (5.4.48). After obtaining Λ and $\mathbf{a}$, the MLE of the reduced-form parameters is just the generalized least-squares estimate. With these estimated reduced-form coefficients, one can form new estimates of R and $\bar{R}$ and continue the iteration until the solution converges. The structural-form parameters are then solved from the convergent reduced-form parameters.

5.4.3 An Example

Chamberlain and Griliches (1975) used the Gorseline (1932) data of the highest grade of schooling attained (y_1), the logarithm of the occupational (Duncan's SES) standing (y_2), and the logarithm of 1927 income (y_3) for 156 pairs of brothers from Indiana (U.S.) to fit a model of the type (5.4.1)–(5.4.3). Specifically, they let

$$\begin{aligned}
y_{1_{it}} &= \boldsymbol{\beta}_1'\mathbf{x}_{it} + d_1 h_{it} + u_{1_{it}},\\
y_{2_{it}} &= \gamma_{21} y_{1_{it}} + \boldsymbol{\beta}_2'\mathbf{x}_{it} + d_2 h_{it} + u_{2_{it}},\\
y_{3_{it}} &= \gamma_{31} y_{1_{it}} + \boldsymbol{\beta}_3'\mathbf{x}_{it} + d_3 h_{it} + u_{3_{it}}.
\end{aligned} \tag{5.4.50}$$

The set X contains a constant, age, and age squared, with age squared appearing only in the income equation.

The reduced form of (5.4.50) is

$$\mathbf{y}_{it} = \Pi\mathbf{x}_{it} + \mathbf{a}h_{it} + \boldsymbol{\epsilon}_{it}, \tag{5.4.51}$$

where

$$\begin{aligned}
\Pi &= \begin{bmatrix} \boldsymbol{\beta}_1' \\ \gamma_{21}\boldsymbol{\beta}_1' + \boldsymbol{\beta}_2' \\ \gamma_{31}\boldsymbol{\beta}_1' + \boldsymbol{\beta}_3' \end{bmatrix},\\
\mathbf{a} &= \begin{bmatrix} d_1 \\ d_2 + \gamma_{21}d_1 \\ d_3 + \gamma_{31}d_1 \end{bmatrix},\\
\boldsymbol{\epsilon}_{it} &= \begin{bmatrix} u_{1_{it}} \\ u_{2_{it}} + \gamma_{21}u_{1_{it}} \\ u_{3_{it}} + \gamma_{31}u_{1_{it}} \end{bmatrix}.
\end{aligned} \tag{5.4.52}$$

Therefore,

$$E\boldsymbol{\epsilon}_{it}\boldsymbol{\epsilon}_{it}' = \begin{bmatrix} \sigma_{u1}^2 & \gamma_{21}\sigma_{u1}^2 & \gamma_{31}\sigma_{u1}^2 \\ & \sigma_{u2}^2 + \gamma_{21}^2\sigma_{u1}^2 & \gamma_{21}\gamma_{31}\sigma_{u1}^2 \\ & & \sigma_{u3}^2 + \gamma_{31}^2\sigma_{u1}^2 \end{bmatrix}, \tag{5.4.53}$$

and

$$\Lambda = \begin{bmatrix} \sigma_{11} & \sigma_{12} & \sigma_{13} \\ & \sigma_{22} & \sigma_{23} \\ & & \sigma_{33} \end{bmatrix} = E(\boldsymbol{\epsilon}_{it}\boldsymbol{\epsilon}_{it}') + \sigma_{\omega}^2\mathbf{a}\mathbf{a}'. \tag{5.4.54}$$

We show that knowing $\mathbf{a}$ and Λ identifies the structural coefficients of the joint dependent variables as follows: For a given value of σ_{ω}^2, we can solve for

$$\sigma_{u1}^2 = \sigma_{11} - \sigma_{\omega}^2 a_1^2, \tag{5.4.55}$$

$$\gamma_{21} = \frac{\sigma_{12} - \sigma_{\omega}^2 a_1 a_2}{\sigma_{u1}^2}, \tag{5.4.56}$$

$$\gamma_{31} = \frac{\sigma_{13} - \sigma_{\omega}^2 a_1 a_3}{\sigma_{u1}^2}. \tag{5.4.57}$$

Equating

$$\gamma_{21}\gamma_{31} = \frac{\sigma_{23} - \sigma_{\omega}^2 a_2 a_3}{\sigma_{u1}^2} \tag{5.4.58}$$

with the product of (5.4.56) and (5.4.57), and making use of (5.4.55), we have

$$\sigma_{\omega}^2 = \frac{\sigma_{12}\sigma_{13} - \sigma_{11}\sigma_{23}}{\sigma_{12}a_1a_3 + \sigma_{13}a_1a_2 - \sigma_{11}a_2a_3 - \sigma_{23}a_1^2}. \tag{5.4.59}$$

The problem then becomes one of estimating $\mathbf{a}$ and Λ. Table 5.1 presents the MLE of Chamberlain and Griliches (1975) for the coefficients of schooling and (unobservable) ability variables with σ_{α}^2 normalized to equal 1. Their least-squares estimates ignore the familial information, and the covariance estimates in which each brother's characteristics (his income, occupation, schooling, and age) are measured around his own family's mean are also presented in Table 5.1.

The covariance estimate of the coefficient-of-schooling variable in the income equation is smaller than the least-squares estimate. However, the simultaneous-equations model estimate of the coefficient for the ability variable is negative in the schooling equation. As discussed in Section 5.1, if schooling and ability are negatively correlated, the single-equation within-family estimate of the schooling coefficient could be less than the least-squares estimate (here 0.080 versus 0.082). To attribute this decline to "ability" or "family background" is erroneous. In fact, when schooling and ability were treated symmetrically, the coefficient-of-schooling variable (0.088) became greater than the least-squares estimate 0.082.

Table 5.1. *Parameter estimates and their standard errors for the income–occupation–schooling model*

	Method		
Coefficients of the structural equations	Least-squares estimate	Covariance estimate	MLE
Schooling in the:			
Income equation	0.082 (0.010)[a]	0.080 (0.011)	0.088 (0.009)
Occupation equation	0.104 (0.010)	0.135 (0.015)	0.107 (0.010)
"Ability" in the:			
Income equation			0.416 (0.038)
Occupation equation			0.214 (0.046)
Schooling equation			−0.092 (0.178)

[a] Standard errors in parentheses.
Source: Chamberlain and Griliches (1975, p. 429).

APPENDIX 5A

Let

$$V = \Lambda \otimes I_T + \mathbf{aa}' \otimes \mathbf{e}_T\mathbf{e}_T'. \tag{5A.1}$$

Because Λ is positive definite and $\mathbf{aa}'$ is positive semidefinite, there exists a $G \times G$ nonsingular matrix F such that (Anderson (1958, p. 341))

$$F'\Lambda F = I_G \quad \text{and} \quad F'\mathbf{aa}'F = \begin{bmatrix} \psi_1 & & & \mathbf{0} \\ & 0 & & \\ & & \ddots & \\ \mathbf{0} & & & 0 \end{bmatrix},$$

where ψ_1 is the root of

$$|\mathbf{aa}' - \lambda\Lambda| = 0. \tag{5A.2}$$

Next, choose a $T \times T$ orthogonal matrix E, with the first column of E being the vector $(1/\sqrt{T})\mathbf{e}_T$. Then

$$E'E = I_T \quad \text{and} \quad E'\mathbf{e}_T\mathbf{e}_T'E = \begin{bmatrix} T & \mathbf{0}' \\ \mathbf{0} & \mathbf{0} \end{bmatrix}. \tag{5A.3}$$

Now $F \otimes E$ can be used to diagonalize V,

$$(F \otimes E)' V (F \otimes E) = I_{GT} + \underset{G\times G}{\begin{bmatrix} \psi_1 & \mathbf{0}' \\ \mathbf{0} & \mathbf{0} \end{bmatrix}} \otimes \underset{T\times T}{\begin{bmatrix} T & \mathbf{0}' \\ \mathbf{0} & \mathbf{0} \end{bmatrix}}, \tag{5A.4}$$

and factor V^{-1},

$$\begin{aligned} V^{-1} &= \Lambda^{-1} \otimes I_T - F' \underset{G\times G}{\begin{bmatrix} \dfrac{\psi_1}{1+T\psi_1} & \mathbf{0}' \\ \mathbf{0} & \mathbf{0} \end{bmatrix}} F \otimes \mathbf{e}_T \mathbf{e}_T' \\ &= \Lambda^{-1} \otimes I_T - \mathbf{c}\mathbf{c}' \otimes \mathbf{e}_T \mathbf{e}_T', \end{aligned} \tag{5A.5}$$

where $\mathbf{c}' = [\psi_1/(1+T\psi_1)]^{1/2}\mathbf{f}_1'$, and $\mathbf{f}_1$ is the first column of F.

The determinant of V can be obtained from (5A.4):

$$|V| = |\Lambda|^T \cdot (1 + T\psi_1). \tag{5A.6}$$

This can be expressed in terms of $\mathbf{c}$ and Λ by noting that

$$\mathbf{c}'\Lambda\mathbf{c} = \frac{\psi_1}{1+T\psi_1}. \tag{5A.7}$$

Thus, we have

$$1 - T\mathbf{c}'\Lambda\mathbf{c} = \frac{1}{1+T\psi_1}, \tag{5A.8}$$

and

$$|V| = |\Lambda|^T \cdot |1 - T\mathbf{c}'\Lambda\mathbf{c}|^{-1}. \tag{5A.9}$$

From $V \cdot V^{-1} = I_{GT}$ it is implied that

$$-\Lambda\mathbf{c}\mathbf{c}' + \mathbf{a}\mathbf{a}'\Lambda^{-1} - T\mathbf{a}\mathbf{a}'\mathbf{c}\mathbf{c}' = 0. \tag{5A.10}$$

Premultiplying (5A.10) by $\mathbf{c}'$, we obtain

$$\mathbf{a} = \frac{\mathbf{c}'\mathbf{a}}{[\mathbf{c}'\Lambda\mathbf{c} + (\mathbf{c}'\mathbf{a})^2]}\Lambda\mathbf{c}. \tag{5A.11}$$

Also, from $\mathbf{f}_1'\mathbf{a} = \psi^{1/2}$ and $\mathbf{a}$ proportional to $\mathbf{c}_1$ [equation (5A.11)], and hence $\mathbf{f}_1$, we have

$$\mathbf{a} = \frac{\psi^{1/2}}{\mathbf{f}_1'\mathbf{f}_1}\mathbf{f}_1 = \frac{1}{(1+T\psi_1)^{1/2}(\mathbf{c}'\mathbf{c})}\mathbf{c}. \tag{5A.12}$$

Premultiplying (5.4.40) by $\mathbf{c}'$, we obtain

$$\mathbf{c}'\bar{R}\mathbf{c} = \frac{\mathbf{c}'\Lambda\mathbf{c}}{T(1 - T\mathbf{c}'\Lambda\mathbf{c})} = \frac{1}{T}\psi_1. \tag{5A.13}$$

Combining (5.4.40) with (5A.8), (5A.12), and (5A.13), and using $\Lambda \mathbf{f}_1 = (1/\mathbf{f}_1'\mathbf{f}_1)\mathbf{f}_1$, we obtain

$$\begin{aligned}\bar{R}\mathbf{c} &= \frac{1}{T}(1 + T\psi_1)\Lambda\mathbf{c} \\ &= \frac{1}{T}(1 + T\psi_1)^{1/2}\mathbf{a} \\ &= \frac{1}{T}(1 + T^2\mathbf{c}'\bar{R}\mathbf{c})^{1/2}\mathbf{a}. \qquad (5A.14)\end{aligned}$$

From (5.4.39) and (5A.12), we have

$$\begin{aligned}\Lambda &= R - \frac{1}{(1 - T\mathbf{c}'\Lambda\mathbf{c})}\Lambda\mathbf{c}\mathbf{c}'\Lambda \\ &= R - \mathbf{a}\mathbf{a}' \qquad (5A.15)\end{aligned}$$

CHAPTER 6

Variable-Coefficient Models

6.1 INTRODUCTION

So far we have confined our discussion to models in which the effects of omitted variables are either individual-specific or time-specific or both. But there are cases in which there are changing economic structures or different socioeconomic and demographic background factors that imply that the response parameters may be varying over time and/or may be different for different cross-sectional units. For example, in Chapter 2 we reported a study (Kuh (1963)) on investment expenditures of 60 small and middle-sized firms in capital-goods-producing industries from 1935 to 1955, excluding the war years (1942–1945). In a majority of the cases Kuh investigated, the hypothesis of common intercept and slope coefficients for all firms, as well as that of variable intercept but common slope, was rejected (Tables 2.3 and 2.4). Similar results were found by Swamy (1970), who used the annual data on 11 U.S. corporations from 1935 to 1954 to fit the Grunfeld (1958) investment functions. His preliminary test of a variable intercept but common coefficients for the value of a firm's outstanding shares at the beginning of the year and its beginning-of-year capital stock yielded an F value of 14.4521. That is well above the 5 percent value of an F distribution with 27 and 187 degrees of freedom.[1]

When data do not support the hypothesis of coefficients being the same, yet the specification of the relationships among variables appears proper or it is not feasible to include additional conditional variables, then it would seem reasonable to allow variations in parameters across cross-sectional units and/or over time as a means to take account of the interindividual and/or interperiod heterogeneity. A single-equation model in its most general form can be written as

$$y_{it} = \sum_{k=1}^{K} \beta_{kit} x_{kit} + u_{it}, \qquad i = 1, \ldots, N, \quad t = 1, \ldots, T, \tag{6.1.1}$$

where, in contrast to previous chapters, we no longer treat the intercept differently than other explanatory variables and let $x_{1it} = 1$. However, if all the coefficients are treated as fixed and different for different cross-sectional units in different time periods, there are NKT parameters with only NT observations. Obviously, there is no way we can obtain any meaningful estimates of β_{kit}. We are thus led to search for an approach that allows the coefficients of interest to differ, but provides some method of modeling the cross-sectional units as a group rather than individually.

One possibility would be to introduce dummy variables into the model that would indicate differences in the coefficients across individual units and/or over time, that is, to develop an approach similar to the least-squares dummy-variable approach. In the case in which only cross-sectional differences are present, this approach is equivalent to postulating a separate regression for each cross-sectional unit,[2]

$$y_{it} = \boldsymbol{\beta}_i'\mathbf{x}_{it} + u_{it}, \qquad \begin{array}{l} i = 1, \ldots, N, \\ t = 1, \ldots, T, \end{array} \tag{6.1.2}$$

where $\boldsymbol{\beta}_i$ and $\mathbf{x}_{it}$ are $K \times 1$ vectors of parameters and explanatory variables.

Alternatively, each regression coefficient can be viewed as a random variable with a probability distribution (e.g., Hurwicz (1950); Klein (1953); Theil and Mennes (1959); Zellner (1966)). The random-coefficient specification reduces the number of parameters to be estimated substantially, while still allowing the coefficients to differ from unit to unit and/or from time to time. Depending on the type of assumption about the parameter variation, it can be further classified into one of two categories: stationary and nonstationary random-coefficient models.

Stationary random-coefficient models regard the coefficients as having constant means and variance–covariances. Namely, the $K \times 1$ vector of parameters $\boldsymbol{\beta}_{it}$ is specified as

$$\boldsymbol{\beta}_{it} = \bar{\boldsymbol{\beta}} + \boldsymbol{\xi}_{it}, \qquad \begin{array}{l} i = 1, \ldots, N, \\ t = 1, \ldots, T, \end{array} \tag{6.1.3}$$

where $\bar{\boldsymbol{\beta}}$ is a $K \times 1$ vector of constants, and $\boldsymbol{\xi}_{it}$ is a $K \times 1$ vector of stationary random variables with zero means and constant variance–covariances. For this type of model we are interested in (1) estimating the mean coefficient vector $\bar{\boldsymbol{\beta}}$, (2) predicting each individual component $\boldsymbol{\xi}_{it}$, (3) estimating the dispersion of the individual-parameter vector, and (4) testing the hypothesis that the variances of $\boldsymbol{\xi}_{it}$ are zero.

The nonstationary random-coefficient models do not regard the coefficient vector as having constant mean or variance. Changes in coefficients from one observation to the next can be the result of the realization of a nonstationary stochastic process or can be a function of exogenous variables. In this case we are interested in (1) estimating the parameters characterizing the time-evolving process, (2) estimating the initial value and the history of parameter realizations, (3) predicting the future evolutions, and (4) testing the hypothesis of random variation.

Because of the computational complexities, variable-coefficient models have not gained as wide acceptance in empirical work as has the variable-intercept model. However, that does not mean that there is less need for taking account of parameter heterogeneity in pooling the data. For instance, take the empirical studies of economic growth as an example, the per capita output growth rates are assumed to depend over a common horizon on two sets of variables. One set of variables consists of the initial per capita output and the savings and population growth rates, variables that are suggested by the Solow growth model. The second set of variables consists of control variables that correspond to whatever additional determinants of growth a researcher wishes to examine (e.g., Durlauf (2001); Durlauf and Quah (1999)). However, there is nothing in growth theory which would lead one to think that the marginal effect of a change in high school enrollment percentages on the per capita growth of the U.S. should be the same as the effect on a country in SubSaharan Africa. In fact, any parsimonious regression will necessarily leave out many factors that from the perspective of economic theory would be likely to affect the parameters of the included variables (e.g., Canova (1999); Durlauf and Johnson (1995)).

In this chapter we shall survey some of the popular single-equation varying-coefficient models. We shall first discuss the single-equation model with exogenous explanatory variables, then discuss models involving lagged dependent variables (e.g., Hsiao and Mountain (1994); Hsiao and Tahmiscioglu (1997); Hsiao, Pesaran, and Tahmiscioglu (1999); Liu and Tiao (1980) Nicholls and Quinn (1982); and Swamy (1974)). We shall not discuss simultaneous-equations models with random coefficients (e.g., see Chow (1983); Kelejian (1977); and Raj and Ullah (1981)). Further discussion of the subject of this chapter can also be found in Amemiya (1983), Chow (1983), Judge et al. (1980), and Raj and Ullah (1981).

In Section 6.2, we discuss models with coefficients varying over individuals, and in Section 6.3, we discuss models with coefficients varying over individuals and time. Section 6.4 concerns models with time-evolving coefficients. Models with coefficients that are functions of other exogenous variables will be discussed in Section 6.5. Section 6.6 proposes a mixed fixed- and random-coefficient model as a unifying framework for various approaches to controlling unobserved heterogeneity. Section 6.7 discusses issues of dynamic models. Section 6.8 provides an analysis of liquidity constraints and firm investment expenditure.

6.2 COEFFICIENTS THAT VARY OVER CROSS-SECTIONAL UNITS

When regression coefficients are viewed as invariant over time, but varying from one unit to another, we can write the model as

$$
\begin{aligned}
y_{it} &= \sum_{k=1}^{K} \beta_{ki} x_{kit} + u_{it} \\
&= \sum_{k=1}^{K} (\bar{\beta}_k + \alpha_{ki}) x_{kit} + u_{it}, \qquad i = 1, \ldots, N, \\
&\qquad\qquad\qquad\qquad\qquad\qquad\quad t = 1, \ldots, T,
\end{aligned}
\tag{6.2.1}
$$

where $\bar{\boldsymbol{\beta}} = (\bar{\beta}_1, \ldots, \bar{\beta}_K)'$ can be viewed as the common-mean-coefficient vector, and $\boldsymbol{\alpha}_i = (\alpha_{1i}, \ldots, \alpha_{Ki})'$ as the individual deviation from the common mean $\bar{\boldsymbol{\beta}}$. If individual observations are heterogeneous or the performance of individual units from the data base is of interest, then $\boldsymbol{\alpha}_i$ are treated as fixed constants. If conditional on x_{kit}, individual units can be viewed as random draws from a common population or the population characteristics are of interest, then α_{ki} are generally treated as random variables having zero means and constant variances and covariances.

6.2.1 Fixed-Coefficient Model

When $\boldsymbol{\beta}_i$ are treated as fixed and different constants, we can stack the NT observations in the form of the Zellner (1962) seemingly unrelated regression model

$$\begin{bmatrix} \mathbf{y}_1 \\ \mathbf{y}_2 \\ \vdots \\ \mathbf{y}_N \end{bmatrix} = \begin{bmatrix} X_1 & & & \mathbf{0} \\ & X_2 & & \\ & & \ddots & \\ \mathbf{0} & & & X_N \end{bmatrix} \begin{bmatrix} \boldsymbol{\beta}_1 \\ \boldsymbol{\beta}_2 \\ \vdots \\ \boldsymbol{\beta}_N \end{bmatrix} + \begin{bmatrix} \mathbf{u}_1 \\ \mathbf{u}_2 \\ \vdots \\ \mathbf{u}_N \end{bmatrix}, \tag{6.2.2}$$

where $\mathbf{y}_i$ and $\mathbf{u}_i$ are $T \times 1$ vectors $(y_{i1}, \ldots, y_{iT})'$ and $(u_{i1}, \ldots, u_{iT})'$, and X_i is the $T \times K$ matrix of the time-series observations of the ith individual's explanatory variables with the tth row equal to $\mathbf{x}'_{it}$. If the covariances between different cross-sectional units are not zero ($E\mathbf{u}_i\mathbf{u}'_j \neq \mathbf{0}$), the GLS estimator of $(\boldsymbol{\beta}'_1, \ldots, \boldsymbol{\beta}'_N)$ is more efficient than the single-equation estimator of $\boldsymbol{\beta}_i$ for each cross-sectional unit. If X_i are identical for all i or $E\mathbf{u}_i\mathbf{u}'_i = \sigma_i^2 I$ and $E\mathbf{u}_i\mathbf{u}'_j = \mathbf{0}$ for $i \neq j$, the GLS estimator for $(\boldsymbol{\beta}'_1, \ldots, \boldsymbol{\beta}'_N)$ is the same as applying least squares separately to the time-series observations of each cross-sectional unit.

6.2.2 Random-Coefficient Model

6.2.2.a The Model

When $\boldsymbol{\beta}_i = \bar{\boldsymbol{\beta}} + \boldsymbol{\alpha}_i$ are treated as random, with common mean $\bar{\boldsymbol{\beta}}$, Swamy (1970) assumed that[3]

$$\begin{aligned} E\boldsymbol{\alpha}_i &= \mathbf{0}, \\ \underset{K\times K}{E\boldsymbol{\alpha}_i\boldsymbol{\alpha}'_j} &= \begin{cases} \Delta & \text{if } i = j, \\ \mathbf{0} & \text{if } i \neq j, \end{cases} \\ E\mathbf{x}_{it}\boldsymbol{\alpha}'_j &= \mathbf{0}, \qquad E\boldsymbol{\alpha}_i\mathbf{u}'_j = \mathbf{0}, \\ E\mathbf{u}_i\mathbf{u}'_j &= \begin{cases} \sigma_i^2 I_T & \text{if } i = j, \\ \mathbf{0} & \text{if } i \neq j. \end{cases} \end{aligned} \tag{6.2.3}$$

Stacking all NT observations, we have

$$\mathbf{y} = X\bar{\boldsymbol{\beta}} + \tilde{X}\boldsymbol{\alpha} + \mathbf{u}, \tag{6.2.4}$$

where

$$\underset{NT\times 1}{\mathbf{y}} = (\mathbf{y}_1', \ldots, \mathbf{y}_N')',$$

$$\underset{NT\times K}{X} = \begin{bmatrix} X_1 \\ X_2 \\ \vdots \\ X_N \end{bmatrix}, \qquad \underset{NT\times NK}{\tilde{X}} = \begin{bmatrix} X_1 & & & \mathbf{0} \\ & X_2 & & \\ & & \ddots & \\ \mathbf{0} & & & X_N \end{bmatrix} = \text{diag}(X_1, \ldots, X_N),$$

$\mathbf{u} = (\mathbf{u}_1', \ldots, \mathbf{u}_N')'$, and $\boldsymbol{\alpha} = (\boldsymbol{\alpha}_1', \ldots, \boldsymbol{\alpha}_N')'$. The covariance matrix for the composite disturbance term $\tilde{X}\boldsymbol{\alpha} + \mathbf{u}$ is block-diagonal, with the ith diagonal block given by

$$\Phi_i = X_i \Delta X_i' + \sigma_i^2 I_T. \tag{6.2.5}$$

6.2.2.b *Estimation*

Under Swamy's assumption, the simple regression of $\mathbf{y}$ on X will yield an unbiased and consistent estimator of $\boldsymbol{\beta}$ if $(1/NT)X'X$ converges to a nonzero constant matrix. But the estimator is inefficient, and the usual least-squares formula for computing the variance–covariance matrix of the estimator is incorrect, often leading to misleading statistical inferences. Moreover, when the pattern of parameter variation is of interest in its own right, an estimator ignoring parameter variation is incapable of shedding light on this aspect of the economic process.

The best linear unbiased estimator of $\bar{\boldsymbol{\beta}}$ for (6.2.4) is the GLS estimator[4]

$$\begin{aligned} \hat{\bar{\boldsymbol{\beta}}}_{\text{GLS}} &= \left(\sum_{i=1}^{N} X_i' \Phi_i^{-1} X_i\right)^{-1} \left(\sum_{i=1}^{N} X_i' \Phi_i^{-1} \mathbf{y}_i\right) \\ &= \sum_{i=1}^{N} W_i \hat{\boldsymbol{\beta}}_i, \end{aligned} \tag{6.2.6}$$

where

$$W_i = \left\{\sum_{i=1}^{N} \left[\Delta + \sigma_i^2 (X_i' X_i)^{-1}\right]^{-1}\right\}^{-1} \left[\Delta + \sigma_i^2 (X_i' X_i)^{-1}\right]^{-1},$$

and

$$\hat{\boldsymbol{\beta}}_i = (X_i' X_i)^{-1} X_i' \mathbf{y}_i.$$

The last expression of (6.2.6) shows that the GLS estimator is a matrix-weighted average of the least-squares estimator for each cross-sectional unit, with the weights inversely proportional to their covariance matrices. It also shows that the GLS estimator requires only a matrix inversion of order K, and so it is not much more complicated to compute than the simple least-squares estimator.

The covariance matrix for the GLS estimator is

$$\begin{aligned}\operatorname{Var}(\hat{\bar{\boldsymbol{\beta}}}_{\text{GLS}}) &= \left(\sum_{i=1}^{N} X_i'\Phi_i^{-1}X_i\right)^{-1} \\ &= \left\{\sum_{i=1}^{N}[\Delta + \sigma_i^2(X_i'X_i)^{-1}]^{-1}\right\}^{-1}. \end{aligned} \tag{6.2.7}$$

Swamy proposed using the least-squares estimators $\hat{\boldsymbol{\beta}}_i = (X_i'X_i)^{-1}X_i'\mathbf{y}_i$ and their residuals $\hat{\mathbf{u}}_i = \mathbf{y}_i - X_i\hat{\boldsymbol{\beta}}_i$ to obtain[5] unbiased estimators of σ_i^2 and Δ,

$$\begin{aligned}\hat{\sigma}_i^2 &= \frac{\hat{\mathbf{u}}_i'\hat{\mathbf{u}}_i}{T-K} \\ &= \frac{1}{T-K}\mathbf{y}_i'[I - X_i(X_i'X_i)^{-1}X_i']\mathbf{y}_i, \end{aligned} \tag{6.2.8}$$

$$\begin{aligned}\hat{\Delta} &= \frac{1}{N-1}\sum_{i=1}^{N}\left(\hat{\boldsymbol{\beta}}_i - N^{-1}\sum_{i=1}^{N}\hat{\boldsymbol{\beta}}_i\right)\left(\hat{\boldsymbol{\beta}}_i - N^{-1}\sum_{i=1}^{N}\hat{\boldsymbol{\beta}}_i\right)' \\ &\quad - \frac{1}{N}\sum_{i=1}^{N}\hat{\sigma}_i^2(X_i'X_i)^{-1}. \end{aligned} \tag{6.2.9}$$

Again, just as in the error-component model, the estimator (6.2.9) is not necessarily nonnegative definite. In this situation, Swamy [see also Judge et al. (1980)] has suggested replacing (6.2.9) by

$$\hat{\Delta} = \frac{1}{N-1}\sum_{i=1}^{N}\left(\hat{\boldsymbol{\beta}}_i - N^{-1}\sum_{i=1}^{N}\hat{\boldsymbol{\beta}}_i\right)\left(\hat{\boldsymbol{\beta}}_i - N^{-1}\sum_{i=1}^{N}\hat{\boldsymbol{\beta}}_i\right)'. \tag{6.2.10}$$

This estimator, although not unbiased, is nonnegative definite and is consistent when T tends to infinity. Alternatively, we can use the Bayes mode estimator suggested by Lindley and Smith (1972) and Smith (1973),

$$\Delta^* = \frac{\{R + (N-1)\hat{\Delta}\}}{(N + \rho - K - 2)}, \tag{6.2.11}$$

where R and ρ are prior parameters, assuming that Δ^{-1} has a Wishart distribution with ρ degrees of freedom and matrix R. For instance, we may let $R = \hat{\Delta}$ and $\rho = 2$ as in Hsiao, Pesaran, and Tahmiscioglu (2002).

Swamy proved that substituting $\hat{\sigma}_i^2$ and $\hat{\Delta}$ for σ_i^2 and Δ in (6.2.6) yields an asymptotically normal and efficient estimator of $\bar{\boldsymbol{\beta}}$. The speed of convergence of the GLS estimator is $N^{1/2}$. This can be seen by noting that the inverse of the covariance matrix for the GLS estimator [equation (6.2.7)] is[6]

$$\begin{aligned}\operatorname{Var}(\hat{\bar{\boldsymbol{\beta}}}_{\text{GLS}})^{-1} &= N\Delta^{-1} - \Delta^{-1}\left[\sum_{i=1}^{N}\left(\Delta^{-1} + \frac{1}{\sigma_i^2}X_i'X_i\right)^{-1}\right]\Delta^{-1} \\ &= O(N) - O(N/T). \end{aligned} \quad (6.2.12)$$

Swamy (1970) used the model (6.2.3) and (6.2.4) to reestimate the Grunfeld investment function with the annual data of 11 U.S. corporations. His GLS estimates of the common-mean coefficients of the firms' beginning-of-year value of outstanding shares and capital stock are 0.0843 and 0.1961, with asymptotic standard errors 0.014 and 0.0412, respectively. The estimated dispersion measure of these coefficients is

$$\hat{\Delta} = \begin{bmatrix} 0.0011 & -0.0002 \\ & 0.0187 \end{bmatrix}. \quad (6.2.13)$$

Zellner (1966) has shown that when each $\boldsymbol{\beta}_i$ can be viewed as a random variable with a constant mean, and $\boldsymbol{\beta}_i$ and $\mathbf{x}_i$ are uncorrelated, thereby satisfying Swamy's assumption, the model will not possess an aggregation bias. In this sense, Swamy's estimate can also be interpreted as an average relationship indicating that in general the value of a firm's outstanding shares is an important variable explaining the investment.

6.2.2.c *Predicting Individual Coefficients*

Sometimes one may wish to predict the individual component $\boldsymbol{\beta}_i$, because it provides information on the behavior of each individual and also because it provides a basis for predicting future values of the dependent variable for a given individual. Swamy (1970, 1971) has shown that the best linear unbiased predictor, conditional on given $\boldsymbol{\beta}_i$, is the least-squares estimator $\hat{\boldsymbol{\beta}}_i$. However, if the sampling properties of the class of predictors are considered in terms of repeated sampling over both time and individuals, Lee and Griffiths (1979) [also see Lindley and Smith (1972) or Section 6.6] have suggested predicting $\boldsymbol{\beta}_i$ by

$$\hat{\boldsymbol{\beta}}_i^* = \hat{\bar{\boldsymbol{\beta}}}_{\text{GLS}} + \Delta X_i'\left(X_i\Delta X_i' + \sigma_i^2 I_T\right)^{-1}(\mathbf{y}_i - X_i\hat{\bar{\boldsymbol{\beta}}}_{\text{GLS}}). \quad (6.2.14)$$

This predictor is the best linear unbiased estimator in the sense that $E(\hat{\boldsymbol{\beta}}_i^* - \boldsymbol{\beta}_i) = \mathbf{0}$, where the expectation is an unconditional one.

6.2.2.d *Testing for Coefficient Variation*

An important question in empirical investigation is whether or not the regression coefficients are indeed varying across cross-sectional units. Because the effect of introducing random coefficient variation is to give the dependent variable a different variance at each observation, models with this feature can be transformed into a particular heteroscedastic formulation, and likelihood-ratio tests can be used to detect departure from the constant-parameter assumption.

However, computation of the likelihood-ratio test statistic can be complicated. To avoid the iterative calculations necessary to obtain maximum likelihood estimates of the parameters in the full model, Breusch and Pagan (1979) have proposed a Lagrange-multiplier test for heteroscedasticity. Their test has the same asymptotic properties as the likelihood-ratio test in standard situations, but it is computationally much simpler. It can be computed simply by repeatedly applying least-squares regressions.

Dividing the individual-mean-over-time equation by σ_i^{-1}, we have

$$\frac{1}{\sigma_i}\bar{y}_i = \frac{1}{\sigma_i}\bar{\mathbf{x}}_i'\bar{\boldsymbol{\beta}} + \omega_i, \qquad i = 1, \ldots, N, \tag{6.2.15}$$

where

$$\omega_i = \frac{1}{\sigma_i}\bar{\mathbf{x}}_i'\boldsymbol{\alpha}_i + \frac{1}{\sigma_i}\bar{u}_i.$$

When the assumption (6.2.3) holds, (6.2.15) is a model with heteroscedastic variances, $\text{Var}(\omega_i) = (1/T) + (1/\sigma_i^2)\bar{\mathbf{x}}_i'\Delta\bar{\mathbf{x}}_i$, $i = 1, \ldots, N$. Under the null hypothesis that $\Delta = \mathbf{0}$, (6.2.15) has homoscedastic variances, $\text{Var}(\omega_i) = 1/T$, $i = 1, \ldots, N$. Thus, we can generalize Breusch and Pagan's (1979) test of heteroscedasticity to test for random-coefficient variation here.

Following the procedures of Rao (1973, pp. 418–419) we can show that the transformed Lagrange-multiplier statistic[7] for testing the null hypothesis leads to computing one-half the predicted sum of squares in a regression of

$$\left(T\omega_i^2 - 1\right) = \frac{1}{\sigma_i^2}\left[\sum_{k=1}^{K}\sum_{k'=1}^{K}\bar{x}_{ki}\bar{x}_{k'i}\sigma_{\alpha_{kk'}}^2\right] + \epsilon_i, \qquad i = 1, \ldots, N, \tag{6.2.16}$$

where $\sigma_{\alpha_{kk'}}^2 = E(\alpha_{ki}\alpha_{k'i})$.[8] Because ω_i and σ_i^2 usually are unknown, we can replace them by their estimated values $\hat{\omega}_i$ and $\hat{\sigma}_i^2$, where $\hat{\omega}_i$ is the least-squares residual of (6.2.15) and $\hat{\sigma}_i^2$ is given by (6.2.8). When both N and T tend to infinity, the transformed Lagrange-multiplier statistic has the same limiting distribution as chi-square with $[K(K+1)]/2$ degrees of freedom under the null hypothesis of $\Delta = \mathbf{0}$.

Breusch and Pagan's (1979) Lagrange-multiplier test can be put into the framework of the White (1980) information-matrix test. Chesher (1984) has shown that the many variants of varying parameters of the same general type of model under consideration can be tested using the statistic

$$\begin{aligned} D_N(\hat{\boldsymbol{\theta}}_N) = {} & \frac{1}{N}\sum_{i=1}^{N}\sum_{t=1}^{T}\frac{\partial^2 \log f(y_{it} \mid \mathbf{x}_{it}, \hat{\boldsymbol{\theta}}_N)}{\partial\boldsymbol{\theta}\,\partial\boldsymbol{\theta}'} \\ & + \frac{1}{N}\sum_{i=1}^{N}\left[\sum_{t=1}^{T}\frac{\partial \log f(y_{it} \mid \mathbf{x}_{it}, \hat{\theta}_N)}{\partial\boldsymbol{\theta}}\right]\left[\sum_{t=1}^{T}\frac{\partial \log f(y_{it} \mid \mathbf{x}_{it}; \hat{\boldsymbol{\theta}}_N)}{\partial\boldsymbol{\theta}'}\right], \end{aligned} \tag{6.2.17}$$

where $f(y_{it} \mid \mathbf{x}_{it}, \boldsymbol{\theta})$ denotes the conditional density of y_{it} given $\mathbf{x}_{it}$ and $\boldsymbol{\theta}$ under the null of no parameter variation, and $\hat{\boldsymbol{\theta}}_N$ denotes the maximum likelihood estimator of $\boldsymbol{\theta}$. The elements of $\sqrt{N} D_N(\hat{\boldsymbol{\theta}}_N)$ are asymptotically jointly normal with mean zero and the covariance matrix given by White (1980) and simplified by Chesher (1983) and Lancaster (1984).

Alternatively, because $\boldsymbol{\alpha}_i$ is fixed for given i, we can test for random variation indirectly by testing whether or not the fixed-coefficient vectors $\boldsymbol{\beta}_i$ are all equal. That is, we form the null hypothesis

$$H_0 : \boldsymbol{\beta}_1 = \boldsymbol{\beta}_2 = \cdots = \boldsymbol{\beta}_N = \bar{\boldsymbol{\beta}}.$$

If different cross-sectional units have the same variance, $\sigma_i^2 = \sigma^2$, $i = 1, \ldots, N$, the conventional analysis-of-covariance test for homogeneity discussed in Chapter 2 (F_3) can be applied. If σ_i^2 are assumed different, as postulated by Swamy (1970, 1971), we can apply the modified test statistic

$$F_3^* = \sum_{i=1}^{N} \frac{(\hat{\boldsymbol{\beta}}_i - \hat{\bar{\boldsymbol{\beta}}}^*)' X_i' X_i (\hat{\boldsymbol{\beta}}_i - \hat{\bar{\boldsymbol{\beta}}}^*)}{\hat{\sigma}_i^2}, \tag{6.2.18}$$

where

$$\hat{\bar{\boldsymbol{\beta}}}^* = \left[\sum_{i=1}^{N} \frac{1}{\hat{\sigma}_i^2} X_i' X_i \right]^{-1} \left[\sum_{i=1}^{N} \frac{1}{\hat{\sigma}_i^2} X_i' \mathbf{y}_i \right].$$

Under H_0, (6.2.18) is asymptotically chi-square-distributed, with $K(N-1)$ degrees of freedom, as T tends to infinity and N is fixed.

6.2.2.e *Fixed or Random Coefficients*

The question whether $\boldsymbol{\beta}_i$ should be assumed fixed and different or random and different depends on whether $\boldsymbol{\beta}_i$ can be viewed as coming from a heterogeneous population or as random draws from a common population, and on whether we are making inferences conditional on the individual characteristics or making unconditional inferences on the population characteristics. If $\boldsymbol{\beta}_i$ are heterogeneous or we are making inferences conditional on the individual characteristics, the fixed-coefficient model should be used. If $\boldsymbol{\beta}_i$ can be viewed as random draws from a common population and inference is on the population characteristics, the random-coefficient model should be used. However, extending his work on the variable-intercept model, Mundlak (1978b) has raised the issue of whether or not the variable coefficients are correlated with the explanatory variables. If they are, the assumptions of the Swamy random-coefficient model are unreasonable, and the GLS estimator of the mean coefficient vector will be biased. To correct this bias, Mundlak (1978b) suggested that the inferences of $f(\mathbf{y}_i \mid X_i, \boldsymbol{\beta})$ be viewed as $\int f(\mathbf{y}_i \mid X_i, \bar{\boldsymbol{\beta}}, \boldsymbol{\alpha}_i) f(\boldsymbol{\alpha}_i \mid X_i)\, d\boldsymbol{\alpha}_i$, where $f(\mathbf{y}_i \mid X_i, \bar{\boldsymbol{\beta}}, \boldsymbol{\alpha}_i)$ denotes the conditional density of y_i given X_i, $\bar{\boldsymbol{\beta}}$, and $\boldsymbol{\alpha}_i$, and $f(\boldsymbol{\alpha}_i \mid X_i)$ denotes the conditional density of $\boldsymbol{\alpha}_i$ given X_i, which provides auxiliary equations for the coefficient vector $\boldsymbol{\alpha}_i$ as a function of the ith individual's observed explanatory variables. Because this framework can be viewed as a special case of a random-coefficient model with the coefficients being functions of other explanatory variables, we shall maintain the assumption that the random coefficients are not correlated with the explanatory variables, and we shall discuss estimation of the random coefficients that are functions of other explanatory variables in Section 6.5.

6.2.2.f An Example

To illustrate the specific issues involved in estimating a behavioral equation using temporal cross-sectional observations when the data do not support the hypothesis that the coefficients are the same for all cross-sectional units, we report a study conducted by Barth, Kraft, and Kraft (1979). They used quarterly observations on output prices, wages, materials prices, inventories, and sales for 17 manufacturing industries for the period from 1959 (I) to 1971 (II) to estimate a price equation for the U.S. manufacturing sector. Assuming heteroscedastic disturbance, but common intercept and slope coefficients across industries, and using the two-step Aitken estimator, they obtained

$$\hat{y} = \underset{(0.0003)}{0.0005} + \underset{(0.0304)}{0.2853}x_2 + \underset{(0.005)}{0.0068}x_3 + \underset{(0.0017)}{0.0024}x_4, \tag{6.2.19}$$

where y_t is the quarterly change in output price, x_2 is labor costs, x_3 is materials input prices, and x_4 is a proxy variable for demand, constructed from the ratio of finished inventory to sales. The standard errors of the estimates are in parentheses.

The findings (6.2.19) are somewhat unsettling. The contribution of materials input costs is extremely small, less than 1 percent. Furthermore, the proxy variable has the wrong sign. As the inventory-to-sales ratio increases, one would expect the resulting inventory buildup to exert a downward pressure on prices.

There are many reasons that (6.2.19) can go wrong. For instance, pricing behavior across industries is likely to vary, because input combinations are different, labor markets are not homogeneous, and demand may be more elastic or inelastic in one industry than another. In fact, a modified one-way analysis-of-covariance test for the common intercept and slope coefficients,

$$H_0: \boldsymbol{\beta}_1 = \boldsymbol{\beta}_2 = \cdots = \boldsymbol{\beta}_N, \qquad N = 17,$$

using the statistic (6.2.18), has a value of 449.28. That is well above the chi-square critical value of 92.841 for the 1 percent significance level with 64 $((N-1)K)$ degrees of freedom.

The rejection of the hypothesis of homogeneous price behavior across industries suggests a need to modify the model to allow for heterogeneous behavior across industries. However, previous studies have found that output prices are affected mainly by unit labor and materials input costs, and only secondarily, if at all, by demand factors. Thus, to account for heterogeneous behavior, one can assume that the relationships among variables are proper, but the coefficients are different across industries. But if these coefficients are treated as fixed and different, this will imply a complicated aggregation problem for the price behavior of the U.S. manufacturing sector (e.g., Theil (1954)). On the other hand, if the coefficients are treated as random, with common means, there is no aggregation bias (Zellner (1966)). The random-coefficient formulation will provide a microeconomic foundation for aggregation, as well as permit the aggregate-price equation to capture more fully the disaggregated industry behavior.

Therefore, Barth, Kraft, and Kraft (1979) used the Swamy random-coefficient formulation, (6.2.3) and (6.2.4), to reestimate the price equation. Their new estimates, with standard errors in parentheses, are

$$\hat{y} = \underset{(0.0005)}{-0.0006} + \underset{(0.0432)}{0.3093}x_2 + \underset{(0.0577)}{0.2687}x_3 - \underset{(0.0101)}{0.0082}x_4. \tag{6.2.20}$$

The estimated dispersion of these coefficients is

$$\hat{\Delta} = \begin{bmatrix} \overset{\beta_1}{0.0000} & \overset{\beta_2}{-0.0002} & \overset{\beta_3}{0.0000} & \overset{\beta_4}{-0.0001} \\ & 0.0020 & 0.0003 & 0.0081 \\ & & 0.0320 & 0.0030 \\ & & & 0.0014 \end{bmatrix}. \tag{6.2.21}$$

The results of the Swamy random-coefficient formulation appear more plausible than the previous aggregate price specification [equation (6.2.19), which ignores variation across industries] from several points of view: (1) both labor costs and materials costs are now dominant in determining output prices; (2) the proxy variable for demand has the correct sign, although it plays only a small and insignificant role in the determination of manufacturing prices; (3) productivity, as captured in the intercept term, appears to be increasing.

This example suggests that one must be careful about drawing conclusions on the basis of aggregate data or pooled estimates that do not allow for individual heterogeneity. Such estimates can be misleading with regard to both the size of coefficients and the significance of variables.

6.3 COEFFICIENTS THAT VARY OVER TIME AND CROSS-SECTIONAL UNITS

6.3.1 The Model

Just as in the variable-intercept models, it is possible to assume that the coefficient of the explanatory variable has a component specific to an individual unit and a component specific to a given time period such that

$$y_{it} = \sum_{k=1}^{K} (\bar{\beta}_k + \alpha_{ki} + \lambda_{kt}) x_{kit} + u_{it}, \qquad i = 1, \ldots, N, \quad t = 1, \ldots, T. \tag{6.3.1}$$

Stacking all NT observations, we can rewrite (6.3.1) as

$$\mathbf{y} = X\bar{\boldsymbol{\beta}} + \tilde{X}\boldsymbol{\alpha} + \underset{\sim}{X}\boldsymbol{\lambda} + \mathbf{u}, \tag{6.3.2}$$

where $\mathbf{y}$, X, $\tilde{X}$, $\mathbf{u}$, and $\boldsymbol{\alpha}$ are defined in Section 6.2,

$$\underset{NT\times TK}{\underset{\sim}{\mathbf{X}}} = \begin{bmatrix} \underset{\sim}{\mathbf{X}}_1 \\ \underset{\sim}{\mathbf{X}}_2 \\ \vdots \\ \underset{\sim}{\mathbf{X}}_N \end{bmatrix}, \qquad \underset{T\times TK}{\underset{\sim}{\mathbf{X}}_i} = \begin{bmatrix} \mathbf{x}'_{i1} & & & \mathbf{0}' \\ & \mathbf{x}'_{i2} & & \\ & & \ddots & \\ \mathbf{0} & & & \mathbf{x}'_{iT} \end{bmatrix},$$

and

$$\underset{KT\times 1}{\boldsymbol{\lambda}} = (\boldsymbol{\lambda}'_1, \ldots, \boldsymbol{\lambda}'_T)', \qquad \underset{K\times 1}{\boldsymbol{\lambda}_t} = (\lambda_{1t}, \ldots, \lambda_{Kt})'.$$

We can also rewrite (6.3.2) as

$$\begin{aligned} \mathbf{y} = {} & X\bar{\boldsymbol{\beta}} + U_1\boldsymbol{\alpha}_1 + U_2\boldsymbol{\alpha}_2 + \cdots + U_K\boldsymbol{\alpha}_K \\ & + U_{K+1}\boldsymbol{\lambda}_1 + \cdots + U_{2K}\boldsymbol{\lambda}_K + U_{2K+1}\mathbf{u}, \end{aligned} \tag{6.3.3}$$

where

$$\underset{NT\times N}{U_k} = \begin{bmatrix} x_{k11} & & & \\ \vdots & & & \mathbf{0} \\ x_{k1T} & & & \\ & x_{k21} & & \\ & \vdots & & \\ & x_{k2T} & & \\ & & \ddots & \\ & & & x_{kN1} \\ \mathbf{0} & & & \vdots \\ & & & x_{kNT} \end{bmatrix}, \qquad k = 1, \ldots, K, \tag{6.3.4a}$$

$$\underset{NT\times T}{U_{K+k}} = \begin{bmatrix} x_{k11} & & & \mathbf{0} \\ & x_{k12} & & \\ & & \vdots & \\ \mathbf{0} & & & x_{k1T} \\ x_{k21} & & & \mathbf{0} \\ & x_{k22} & & \\ & & \ddots & \\ \mathbf{0} & & & x_{k2T} \\ \cdot & \cdot & \cdots & \cdot \\ x_{kN1} & & & \mathbf{0} \\ & \ddots & & \\ \mathbf{0} & & & x_{kNT} \end{bmatrix}, \qquad k = 1. \ldots, K, \tag{6.3.4b}$$

$$U_{2K+1} = I_{NT}, \tag{6.3.4c}$$

$$\underset{N\times 1}{\boldsymbol{\alpha}_k} = (\alpha_{k1}, \ldots, \alpha_{kN})', \qquad \underset{T\times 1}{\boldsymbol{\lambda}_k} = (\lambda_{k1}, \ldots, \lambda_{kT})'. \tag{6.3.4d}$$

When $\boldsymbol{\alpha}_k$ and $\boldsymbol{\lambda}_k$ as well as $\bar{\boldsymbol{\beta}}$ are considered fixed, it is a fixed-effects model; when $\boldsymbol{\alpha}_k$ and $\boldsymbol{\lambda}_k$ are considered random, with $\bar{\boldsymbol{\beta}}$ fixed, equation (6.3.3) corresponds to the mixed analysis-of-variance model (Hartley and Rao (1967), Miller (1977)). Thus, model (6.3.1) and its special case (6.2.1) fall within the general analysis-of-variance framework.

6.3.2 Fixed-Coefficient Model

When $\boldsymbol{\alpha}_k$ and $\boldsymbol{\lambda}_k$ are treated as fixed, as mentioned earlier, (6.3.1) can be viewed as a fixed-effects analysis-of-variance model. However, the matrix of explanatory variables is $NT \times (T+N+1)K$, but its rank is only $(T+N-1)K$; so we must impose $2K$ independent linear restrictions on the coefficients $\boldsymbol{\alpha}_k$ and $\boldsymbol{\lambda}_k$ for estimation of $\bar{\boldsymbol{\beta}}$, $\boldsymbol{\alpha}$, and $\boldsymbol{\lambda}$. A natural way of imposing the constraints in this case is to let[9]

$$\sum_{i=1}^{N} \alpha_{ik} = 0, \tag{6.3.5}$$

and

$$\sum_{t=1}^{T} \lambda_{kt} = 0, \qquad k = 1, \ldots, K. \tag{6.3.6}$$

Then the best linear unbiased estimators (BLUEs) of $\boldsymbol{\beta}$, $\boldsymbol{\alpha}$, and $\boldsymbol{\lambda}$ are the solutions of

$$\min(\mathbf{y} - X\bar{\boldsymbol{\beta}} - \tilde{X}\boldsymbol{\alpha} - \underset{\sim}{X}\boldsymbol{\lambda})'(\mathbf{y} - X\bar{\boldsymbol{\beta}} - \tilde{X}\boldsymbol{\alpha} - \underset{\sim}{X}\boldsymbol{\lambda}) \tag{6.3.7}$$

subject to (6.3.5) and (6.3.6).

6.3.3 Random-Coefficient Model

When $\boldsymbol{\alpha}_i$ and $\boldsymbol{\lambda}_t$ are treated as random, Hsiao (1974a, 1975) assumes that

$$\begin{aligned} &\underset{K\times K}{E\boldsymbol{\alpha}_i\boldsymbol{\alpha}_j'} = \begin{cases} \Delta & \text{if } i = j, \\ \mathbf{0} & \text{if } i \neq j, \end{cases} \\ &\underset{K\times K}{E\boldsymbol{\lambda}_t\boldsymbol{\lambda}_s'} = \begin{cases} \Lambda & \text{if } t = s, \\ \mathbf{0} & \text{if } t \neq s, \end{cases} \\ &E\boldsymbol{\alpha}_i\boldsymbol{\lambda}_t' = \mathbf{0}, \qquad E\boldsymbol{\alpha}_i\mathbf{x}_{it}' = \mathbf{0}, \qquad E\boldsymbol{\lambda}_t\mathbf{x}_{it}' = \mathbf{0}, \end{aligned} \tag{6.3.8}$$

and

$$E\mathbf{u}_i\mathbf{u}_j' = \begin{cases} \sigma_u^2 I_T & \text{if } i = j, \\ \mathbf{0} & \text{if } i \neq j. \end{cases}$$

Then the composite error term,

$$\mathbf{v} = \tilde{X}\boldsymbol{\alpha} + \underset{\sim}{X}\boldsymbol{\lambda} + \mathbf{u}, \tag{6.3.9}$$

has a variance–covariance matrix

$$\Omega = E\mathbf{v}\mathbf{v}' = \begin{bmatrix} X_1\Delta X_1' & & & \mathbf{0} \\ & X_2\Delta X_2' & & \\ & & \ddots & \\ \mathbf{0} & & & X_N\Delta X_N' \end{bmatrix} + \begin{bmatrix} D(X_1\Lambda X_1') & D(X_1\Lambda X_2') & \cdots & D(X_1\Lambda X_N') \\ D(X_2\Lambda X_1') & D(X_2\Lambda X_2') & \dots & D(X_2\Lambda X_N') \\ \vdots & \vdots & \ddots & \vdots \\ D(X_N\Lambda X_1') & D(X_N\Lambda X_2') & \cdots & D(X_N\Lambda X_N') \end{bmatrix} + \sigma_u^2 I_{NT}, \tag{6.3.10}$$

where

$$\underset{T\times T}{D(X_i\Lambda X_j')} = \begin{bmatrix} \mathbf{x}_{i1}'\Lambda\mathbf{x}_{j1} & & & \mathbf{0} \\ & \mathbf{x}_{i2}'\Lambda\mathbf{x}_{j2} & & \\ & & \ddots & \\ \mathbf{0} & & & \mathbf{x}_{iT}'\Lambda\mathbf{x}_{jT} \end{bmatrix}.$$

We can estimate $\bar{\boldsymbol{\beta}}$ by the least-squares method, but as discussed in Section 6.2.2.b, it is not efficient. Moreover, the associated sampling theory is misleading.

If Ω is known, the BLUE of $\bar{\boldsymbol{\beta}}$ is the GLS estimator,

$$\hat{\bar{\boldsymbol{\beta}}}_{\text{GLS}} = (X'\Omega^{-1}X)^{-1}(X'\Omega^{-1}\mathbf{y}). \tag{6.3.11}$$

The variance–covariance matrix of the GLS estimator is

$$\text{Var}(\hat{\bar{\boldsymbol{\beta}}}_{\text{GLS}}) = (X'\Omega^{-1}X)^{-1}. \tag{6.3.12}$$

Without knowledge of Ω, we can estimate $\bar{\boldsymbol{\beta}}$ and Ω simultaneously by the maximum likelihood method. However, because of the computational difficulty, a natural alternative is to first estimate Ω, then substitute the estimated Ω in (6.3.11).

When Δ and Λ are diagonal, it is easy to see from (6.3.3) that Ω is a linear combination of known matrices with unknown weights. So the problem of estimating the unknown covariance matrix is actually the problem of estimating the variance components. Statistical methods developed for estimating the variance (and covariance) components can be applied here (e.g., Anderson (1969, 1970); Rao (1970, 1972)). In this section we shall describe only a method due to Hildreth and Houck (1968).[10]

Consider the time-series equation for the ith individual,

$$\mathbf{y}_i = X_i(\bar{\boldsymbol{\beta}} + \boldsymbol{\alpha}_i) + \underline{\mathbf{X}}_i\boldsymbol{\lambda} + \mathbf{u}_i. \tag{6.3.13}$$

We can treat $\boldsymbol{\alpha}_i$ as if it is a vector of constants. Then (6.3.13) is a linear model with heteroscedastic variance. The variance of the error term

$r_{it} = \sum_{k=1}^{K} \lambda_{kt} x_{kit} + u_{it}$ is

$$\theta_{it} = E\left[r_{it}^2\right] = \sum_{k=1}^{K} \sigma_{\lambda k}^2 x_{kit}^2 + \sigma_u^2. \tag{6.3.14}$$

Let $\boldsymbol{\theta}_i = (\theta_{i1}, \ldots, \theta_{iT})'$; then

$$\boldsymbol{\theta}_i = \dot{X}_i \boldsymbol{\sigma}_\lambda^2, \tag{6.3.15}$$

where $\dot{X}_i$ is X_i with each of its elements squared, and $\boldsymbol{\sigma}_\lambda^2 = (\sigma_{\lambda 1}^2 + \sigma_u^2, \sigma_{\lambda 2}^2, \ldots, \sigma_{\lambda K}^2)'$.

An estimate of $\mathbf{r}_i$ can be obtained as the least-squares residual, $\hat{\mathbf{r}}_i = \mathbf{y}_i - X_i \hat{\boldsymbol{\beta}}_i = M_i \mathbf{y}_i$, where $\hat{\boldsymbol{\beta}}_i = (X_i' X_i)^{-1} X_i' \mathbf{y}_i$ and $M_i = I_T - X_i (X_i' X_i)^{-1} X_i'$. Squaring each element of $\hat{\mathbf{r}}_i$ and denoting it by $\dot{\hat{\mathbf{r}}}_i$, we have

$$E(\dot{\hat{\mathbf{r}}}_i) = \dot{M}_i \boldsymbol{\theta}_i = F_i \boldsymbol{\sigma}_\lambda^2, \tag{6.3.16}$$

where $\dot{M}_i$ is M_i with each of its elements squared, and $F_i = \dot{M}_i \dot{X}_i$.

Repeating the foregoing process for all i gives

$$E(\dot{\hat{\mathbf{r}}}) = F \boldsymbol{\sigma}_\lambda^2, \tag{6.3.17}$$

where $\dot{\hat{\mathbf{r}}} = (\dot{\hat{\mathbf{r}}}_1, \ldots, \dot{\hat{\mathbf{r}}}_N)'$, and $F = (F_1', \ldots, F_N')'$. Application of least squares to (6.3.17) yields a consistent estimator of $\boldsymbol{\sigma}_\lambda^2$,

$$\hat{\boldsymbol{\sigma}}_\lambda^2 = (F'F)^{-1} F' \dot{\hat{\mathbf{r}}}. \tag{6.3.18}$$

Similarly, we can apply the same procedure with respect to each time period to yield a consistent estimator of $\boldsymbol{\sigma}_\alpha^2 = (\sigma_{\alpha_1}^2 + \sigma_u^2, \sigma_{\alpha_2}^2, \ldots, \sigma_{\alpha_K}^2)'$. To obtain separate estimates of σ_u^2, $\sigma_{\alpha_1}^2$, and $\sigma_{\lambda_1}^2$, we note that $E(\mathbf{x}_{it}' \boldsymbol{\alpha}_i + u_{it})(\mathbf{x}_{it}' \boldsymbol{\lambda}_t + u_{it}) = \sigma_u^2$. So, letting $\hat{s}_{it}$ denote the residual obtained by applying least squares separately to each time period, we can consistently estimate σ_u^2 by

$$\hat{\sigma}_u^2 = \frac{1}{NT} \sum_{i=1}^{N} \sum_{t=1}^{T} \hat{r}_{it} \hat{s}_{it}. \tag{6.3.19}$$

Subtracting (6.3.19) from an estimated $\sigma_{\alpha_1}^2 + \sigma_u^2$ and $\sigma_{\lambda_1}^2 + \sigma_u^2$, we obtain consistent estimates of $\sigma_{\alpha_1}^2$, and $\sigma_{\lambda_1}^2$, respectively.

Substituting consistently estimated values of $\boldsymbol{\sigma}_\alpha^2$, $\boldsymbol{\sigma}_\lambda^2$, and σ_u^2 into (6.3.11), one can show that when N and T both tend to infinity and N/T tends to a nonzero constant, the two-stage Aitken estimator is asymptotically as efficient as if one knew the true Ω. Also, Kelejian and Stephan (1983) have pointed out that, contrary to the conventional regression model, the speed of convergence of $\hat{\hat{\boldsymbol{\beta}}}_{\text{GLS}}$ here is not $(NT)^{1/2}$, but $\max(N^{1/2}, T^{1/2})$.

If one is interested in predicting the random components associated with an individual, Lee and Griffiths (1979) have shown that the predictor

$$\hat{\boldsymbol{\alpha}} = (I_N \otimes \Delta) X' \Omega^{-1} (\mathbf{y} - X \hat{\hat{\boldsymbol{\beta}}}_{\text{GLS}}) \tag{6.3.20}$$

is the BLUE.

To test for the random variation of the coefficients, we can again apply the Breusch–Pagan (1979) Lagrange-multiplier test for heteroscedasticity. Because, for given i, $\boldsymbol{\alpha}_i$ is fixed, the error term $\mathbf{x}_{it}'\boldsymbol{\lambda}_t + u_{it}$ will be homoscedastic if the coefficients are not varying over time. Therefore, under the null, one-half the explained sum of squares in a regression[11]

$$\frac{\hat{u}_{it}^2}{\hat{\sigma}_u^2} = \dot{\mathbf{x}}_{it}'\boldsymbol{\sigma}_\lambda^2 + \epsilon_{it}, \qquad \begin{aligned} i &= 1, \ldots, N, \\ t &= 1, \ldots, T, \end{aligned} \tag{6.3.21}$$

is distributed asymptotically as chi-square, with $K - 1$ degrees of freedom, where $\hat{u}_{it} = y_{it} - \hat{\boldsymbol{\beta}}_i'\mathbf{x}_{it}$, $\hat{\sigma}_u^2 = \sum_{i=1}^N \sum_{t=1}^T (y_{it} - \hat{\boldsymbol{\beta}}_i'\mathbf{x}_{it})^2/NT$, and $\dot{\mathbf{x}}_{it}$ is $\mathbf{x}_{it}$ with each element squared.[12]

Similarly, we can test for random variation across cross-sectional units by regressing

$$\frac{\hat{u}_{it}^{*2}}{\hat{\sigma}_u^{*2}} = \dot{\mathbf{x}}_{it}'\boldsymbol{\sigma}_\alpha^2 + \epsilon_{it}^*, \qquad \begin{aligned} i &= 1, \ldots, N, \\ t &= 1, \ldots, T, \end{aligned} \tag{6.3.22}$$

where $\hat{u}_{it}^* = y_{it} - \hat{\boldsymbol{\beta}}_t'\mathbf{x}_{it}$, $\hat{\sigma}_u^{*2} = \sum_{i=1}^N \sum_{t=1}^T \hat{u}_{it}^{*2}/NT$, and $\hat{\boldsymbol{\beta}}_t$ is the least-squares estimate of $\boldsymbol{\beta}_t = \bar{\boldsymbol{\beta}} + \boldsymbol{\lambda}_t$ across cross-sectional units for a given t. Under the null hypothesis of no random variation across cross-sectional units, one-half the explained sum of squares of (6.3.22) is asymptotically chi-square-distributed, with $K - 1$ degrees of freedom.

We can also test the random variation indirectly by applying the classic analysis-of-covariance test. For details, see Hsiao (1974a).

Swamy and Mehta (1977) have proposed a more general type of time-varying-component model by allowing $E\boldsymbol{\lambda}_t\boldsymbol{\lambda}_t' = \Lambda_t$ to vary over t. However, models with the coefficients varying randomly across cross-sectional units and over time have not gained much acceptance in empirical investigation. Part of the reason is that the inversion of Ω is at least of order $\max(NK, TK)$ (Hsiao (1974a)). For any panel data of reasonable size, this would be a computationally demanding problem.

6.4 COEFFICIENTS THAT EVOLVE OVER TIME[13]

6.4.1 The Model

In most models with coefficients evolving over time it is assumed that there is no individual heterogeneity (e.g., Zellner, Hong, and Min (1991)). At a given t, the coefficient vectors $\boldsymbol{\beta}_t$ are identical for all cross-sectional units. For this reason we shall discuss the main issues of time-varying-parameter models assuming that $N = 1$, then indicate how this analysis can be modified when $N > 1$.

As shown by Chow (1983, Chapter 10), a wide variety of time-varying-parameter models can be put in the general form

$$y_t = \boldsymbol{\beta}_t'\mathbf{x}_t + u_t, \tag{6.4.1}$$

and

$$\boldsymbol{\beta}_t = H\boldsymbol{\beta}_{t-1} + \boldsymbol{\eta}_t, \qquad t = 1, \ldots, T, \tag{6.4.2}$$

where $\mathbf{x}_t$ is a $K \times 1$ vector of exogenous variables, u_t is independent normal with mean zero and variance σ_u^2, $\boldsymbol{\eta}_t$ is a K-variant independent normal random variable with mean zero and covariance matrix Ψ, and $\boldsymbol{\eta}$ and u are independent. For instance, when $H = I_K$, it is the random-walk model of Cooley and Prescott (1976). When $H = I_K$ and $\Psi = \mathbf{0}$, this model is reduced to the standard regression model.

The Rosenberg (1972, 1973) return-to-normality model can also be put in this form. The model corresponds to replacing $\boldsymbol{\beta}_t$ and $\boldsymbol{\beta}_{t-1}$ in (6.4.2) by $(\boldsymbol{\beta}_t - \bar{\boldsymbol{\beta}})$ and $(\boldsymbol{\beta}_{t-1} - \bar{\boldsymbol{\beta}})$ and restricting the absolute value of the characteristic roots of H to less than 1. Although this somewhat changes the formulation, if we define $\boldsymbol{\beta}_t^* = \boldsymbol{\beta}_t - \bar{\boldsymbol{\beta}}$ and $\boldsymbol{\beta}_t = \bar{\boldsymbol{\beta}}$, the return-to-normality model can be rewritten as

$$\begin{aligned} y_t &= (\mathbf{x}_t', \mathbf{x}_t') \begin{bmatrix} \boldsymbol{\beta}_t \\ \boldsymbol{\beta}_t^* \end{bmatrix} + u_t, \\ \begin{bmatrix} \boldsymbol{\beta}_t \\ \boldsymbol{\beta}_t^* \end{bmatrix} &= \begin{bmatrix} I & \mathbf{0} \\ \mathbf{0} & H \end{bmatrix} \begin{bmatrix} \boldsymbol{\beta}_{t-1} \\ \boldsymbol{\beta}_{t-1}^* \end{bmatrix} + \begin{bmatrix} \mathbf{0} \\ \boldsymbol{\eta}_t \end{bmatrix}, \end{aligned} \tag{6.4.3}$$

which is a special case of (6.4.1) and (6.4.2).

Similarly, we can allow $\boldsymbol{\beta}_t$ to be stationary, with constant mean $\bar{\boldsymbol{\beta}}$ (Pagan (1980)). Suppose

$$\begin{aligned} y_t &= \mathbf{x}_t'\bar{\boldsymbol{\beta}} + \mathbf{x}_t'\boldsymbol{\beta}_t^* + u_t, \\ \boldsymbol{\beta}_t^* &= \boldsymbol{\beta}_t - \bar{\boldsymbol{\beta}} = A^{-1}(\mathcal{L})\boldsymbol{\epsilon}_t, \end{aligned} \tag{6.4.4}$$

where $A(\mathcal{L})$ is a ratio of polynomials of orders p and q in the lag operator $\mathcal{L}\,(\mathcal{L}\boldsymbol{\epsilon}_t = \boldsymbol{\epsilon}_{t-1})$, and $\boldsymbol{\epsilon}$ is independent normal, so that $\boldsymbol{\beta}_t^*$ follows an autoregressive moving-average (ARMA) (p, q) process. Because an ARMA of order p and q can be written as a first-order autoregressive process, this model can again be put in the form of (6.4.1) and (6.4.2). For example,

$$\boldsymbol{\beta}_t^* = B_1\boldsymbol{\beta}_{t-1}^* + B_2\boldsymbol{\beta}_{t-2}^* + \boldsymbol{\epsilon}_t + B_3\boldsymbol{\epsilon}_{t-1} \tag{6.4.5}$$

can be written as

$$\tilde{\boldsymbol{\beta}}_t^* = \begin{bmatrix} \boldsymbol{\beta}_t^* \\ \boldsymbol{\beta}_{t-1}^* \\ \boldsymbol{\epsilon}_t \end{bmatrix} = \begin{bmatrix} B_1 & B_2 & B_3 \\ I & \mathbf{0} & \mathbf{0} \\ \mathbf{0} & \mathbf{0} & \mathbf{0} \end{bmatrix} \begin{bmatrix} \boldsymbol{\beta}_{t-1}^* \\ \boldsymbol{\beta}_{t-2}^* \\ \boldsymbol{\epsilon}_{t-1} \end{bmatrix} + \begin{bmatrix} \boldsymbol{\epsilon}_t \\ \mathbf{0} \\ \boldsymbol{\epsilon}_t \end{bmatrix} = H\tilde{\boldsymbol{\beta}}_{t-1}^* + \boldsymbol{\eta}_t. \tag{6.4.6}$$

Thus, we can write Pagan's model in the form

$$y_t = (\mathbf{x}'_t, \tilde{\mathbf{x}}'_t) \begin{bmatrix} \boldsymbol{\beta}_t \\ \tilde{\boldsymbol{\beta}}^*_t \end{bmatrix} + u_t, \tag{6.4.4a}$$

where $\tilde{x}'_t = (\mathbf{x}'_t, \mathbf{0}', \mathbf{0}')$. Equation (6.4.4a) is then formally equivalent to (6.4.3).

The Kalman filter (Kalman (1960)) provides a basis for computing the maximum likelihood estimators and predicting the evolution of the time path of $\boldsymbol{\beta}_t$ for this type of model. In this section we first consider the problem of estimating $\boldsymbol{\beta}_t$ using information $\mathcal{I}_s$, up to the time s, assuming that σ_u^2, Ψ, and H are known. We denote the conditional expectation of $\boldsymbol{\beta}_t$, given $\mathcal{I}_s$, as $E(\boldsymbol{\beta}_t \mid \mathcal{I}_s) = \boldsymbol{\beta}_{t|s}$. The evaluation of $\boldsymbol{\beta}_{t|s}$ is called *filtering* when $t = s$; it is called *smoothing* when $s > t$; it is called *prediction* when $s < t$. We then study the problem of estimating σ_u^2, Ψ, and H by the method of maximum likelihood. Finally, we consider the problem of testing for constancy of the parameters.

6.4.2 Predicting $\boldsymbol{\beta}_t$ by the Kalman Filter

Denote $(y_1, \ldots, y_t)$ by Y_t. By definition, the conditional mean of $\boldsymbol{\beta}_t$, given Y_t, is

$$\begin{aligned} \boldsymbol{\beta}_{t|t} &= E(\boldsymbol{\beta}_t \mid y_t, Y_{t-1}) \\ &= E(\boldsymbol{\beta}_t \mid Y_{t-1}) + L_t[y_t - E(y_t \mid Y_{t-1})] \\ &= \boldsymbol{\beta}_{t|t-1} + L_t[y_t - \mathbf{x}'_t \boldsymbol{\beta}_{t|t-1}], \end{aligned} \tag{6.4.7}$$

where $y_t - E(y_t \mid Y_{t-1})$ denotes the additional information of y_t not contained in Y_{t-1}, and L_t denotes the adjustment of $\boldsymbol{\beta}_{t|t-1}$ due to this additional information. If L_t is known, (6.4.7) can be used to update our estimate $\boldsymbol{\beta}_{t|t-1}$ to form $\boldsymbol{\beta}_{t|t}$.

To derive L_t, we know from our assumption on $\boldsymbol{\eta}_t$ and u_t that, conditional on $\mathbf{x}_t$, y_t and $\boldsymbol{\beta}_t$ are jointly normally distributed. The normal-distribution theory (Anderson (1958, Chapter 2)) states that, conditional on Y_{t-1} (and X_t), the mean of $\boldsymbol{\beta}_t$, given y_t, is $E(\boldsymbol{\beta}_t \mid Y_{t-1}) + \text{Cov}(\boldsymbol{\beta}_t, y_t \mid Y_{t-1}) \,\text{Var}(y_t \mid Y_{t-1})^{-1}[y_t - E(y_t \mid Y_{t-1})]$. Therefore,

$$L_t = [E(\boldsymbol{\beta}_t - \boldsymbol{\beta}_{t|t-1})(y_t - y_{t|t-1})] \,\text{Var}(y_t \mid Y_{t-1})^{-1}, \tag{6.4.8}$$

where $y_{t|t-1} = E(y_t \mid Y_{t-1}) = \mathbf{x}'_t \boldsymbol{\beta}_{t|t-1}$. Denoting the covariance matrix $\text{Cov}(\boldsymbol{\beta}_t \mid Y_{t-1}) = E(\boldsymbol{\beta}_t - \boldsymbol{\beta}_{t|t-1})(\boldsymbol{\beta}_t - \boldsymbol{\beta}_{t|t-1})'$ by $\Sigma_{t|t-1}$, we have

$$\begin{aligned} &E(\boldsymbol{\beta}_t - \boldsymbol{\beta}_{t|t-1})(y_t - y_{t|t-1}) \\ &\quad = E\{(\boldsymbol{\beta}_t - \boldsymbol{\beta}_{t|t-1})[(\boldsymbol{\beta}_t - \boldsymbol{\beta}_{t|t-1})'\mathbf{x}_t + u_t]\} = \Sigma_{t|t-1}\mathbf{x}_t, \end{aligned} \tag{6.4.9}$$

and

$$\begin{aligned} \text{Var}(y_t \mid Y_{t-1}) &= E[\mathbf{x}'_t(\boldsymbol{\beta}_t - \boldsymbol{\beta}_{t|t-1}) + u_t][(\boldsymbol{\beta}_t - \boldsymbol{\beta}_{t|t-1})'\mathbf{x}_t + u_t] \\ &= \mathbf{x}'_t \Sigma_{t|t-1}\mathbf{x}_t + \sigma_u^2. \end{aligned} \tag{6.4.10}$$

Hence, (6.4.8) becomes

$$L_t = \Sigma_{t|t-1}\mathbf{x}_t\left(\mathbf{x}_t'\Sigma_{t|t-1}\mathbf{x}_t + \sigma_u^2\right)^{-1}. \tag{6.4.11}$$

From (6.4.2) we have

$$\boldsymbol{\beta}_{t|t-1} = H\boldsymbol{\beta}_{t-1\,|\,t-1}. \tag{6.4.12}$$

Thus, we can compute $\Sigma_{t|t-1}$ recursively by

$$\begin{aligned}\Sigma_{t|t-1} &= E(\boldsymbol{\beta}_t - H\boldsymbol{\beta}_{t-1|t-1})(\boldsymbol{\beta}_t - H\boldsymbol{\beta}_{t-1|t-1})' \\ &= E[H(\boldsymbol{\beta}_{t-1} - \boldsymbol{\beta}_{t-1|t-1}) + \boldsymbol{\eta}_t] \\ &\quad \times [H(\boldsymbol{\beta}_{t-1} - \boldsymbol{\beta}_{t-1|t-1}) + \boldsymbol{\eta}_t]' \\ &= H\Sigma_{t-1|t-1}H' + \Psi.\end{aligned} \tag{6.4.13}$$

Next, from (6.4.1) and (6.4.7) we can write

$$\boldsymbol{\beta}_t - \boldsymbol{\beta}_{t|t} = \boldsymbol{\beta}_t - \boldsymbol{\beta}_{t|t-1} - L_t[\mathbf{x}_t'(\boldsymbol{\beta}_t - \boldsymbol{\beta}_{t|t-1}) + u_t]. \tag{6.4.14}$$

Taking the expectation of the product of (6.4.14) and its transpose, and using (6.4.11), we obtain

$$\begin{aligned}\Sigma_{t|t} &= \Sigma_{t|t-1} - L_t\left(\mathbf{x}_t'\Sigma_{t|t-1}\mathbf{x}_t + \sigma_u^2\right)L_t' \\ &= \Sigma_{t|t-1} - \Sigma_{t|t-1}\mathbf{x}_t\left(\mathbf{x}_t'\Sigma_{t|t-1}\mathbf{x}_t + \sigma_u^2\right)^{-1}\mathbf{x}_t'\Sigma_{t|t-1}.\end{aligned} \tag{6.4.15}$$

Equations (6.4.13) and (6.4.15) can be used to compute $\Sigma_{t|t}$ $(t = 1, 2, \ldots)$ successively, given $\Sigma_{0|0}$. Having computed $\Sigma_{t|t-1}$, we can use (6.4.11) to compute L_t. Given L_t, (6.4.7) and (6.4.12) can be used to compute $\boldsymbol{\beta}_{t|t}$ from $\boldsymbol{\beta}_{t-1|t-1}$ if $\boldsymbol{\beta}_{0|0}$ is known.

Similarly, we can predict $\boldsymbol{\beta}_t$ using future observations $y_{t+1}, y_{t+2}, \ldots, y_{t+n}$. We first consider the regression of $\boldsymbol{\beta}_t$ on y_{t+1}, conditional on Y_t. Analogous to (6.4.7) and (6.4.11) are

$$\boldsymbol{\beta}_{t|t+1} = \boldsymbol{\beta}_{t|t} + F_{t|t+1}(y_{t+1} - y_{t+1|t}), \tag{6.4.16}$$

and

$$F_{t|t+1} = [E(\boldsymbol{\beta}_t - \boldsymbol{\beta}_{t|t})(y_{t+1} - y_{t+1|t})'][\mathrm{Cov}(y_{t+1} \mid Y_t)]^{-1}. \tag{6.4.17}$$

To derive the matrix $F_{t|t+1}$ of regression coefficients, we use (6.4.1) and (6.4.2) to write

$$\begin{aligned}y_{t+1} - y_{t+1|t} &= \mathbf{x}_{t+1}'(\boldsymbol{\beta}_{t+1} - \boldsymbol{\beta}_{t+1|t}) + u_{t+1} \\ &= \mathbf{x}_{t+1}'H(\boldsymbol{\beta}_t - \boldsymbol{\beta}_{t|t}) + \mathbf{x}_{t+1}'\boldsymbol{\eta}_{t+1} + u_{t+1}.\end{aligned} \tag{6.4.18}$$

Combining (6.4.17), (6.4.18), (6.4.10), and (6.4.11), we have

$$\begin{aligned}F_{t|t+1} &= \Sigma_{t|t}H'\mathbf{x}_{t+1}\left(\mathbf{x}_{t+1}'\Sigma_{t+1|t}\mathbf{x}_{t+1} + \sigma_u^2\right)^{-1} \\ &= \Sigma_{t|t}H'\Sigma_{t+1|t}^{-1}L_{t+1}.\end{aligned} \tag{6.4.19}$$

Therefore, from (6.4.19) and (6.4.14), we can rewrite (6.4.16) as

$$\boldsymbol{\beta}_{t|t+1} = \boldsymbol{\beta}_{t|t} + \Sigma_{t|t} H' \Sigma_{t+1|t}^{-1} (\boldsymbol{\beta}_{t+1|t+1} - \boldsymbol{\beta}_{t+1|t}). \tag{6.4.20}$$

Equation (6.4.20) can be generalized to predict $\boldsymbol{\beta}_t$ using future observations $y_{t+1}, \ldots, y_{t+n}$:

$$\boldsymbol{\beta}_{t|t+n} = \boldsymbol{\beta}_{t|t+n-1} + F_t^* (\boldsymbol{\beta}_{t+1|t+n} - \boldsymbol{\beta}_{t+1|t+n-1}), \tag{6.4.21}$$

where $F_t^* = \Sigma_{t|t} H' \Sigma_{t+1|t}^{-1}$. The proof of this is given by Chow (1983, Chapter 10).

When H, Ψ, and σ_u^2 are known, (6.4.7) and (6.4.21) trace out the time path of $\boldsymbol{\beta}_t$ and provide the minimum-mean-squared-error forecast of the future values of the dependent variable, given the initial values $\boldsymbol{\beta}_{0|0}$ and $\Sigma_{0|0}$. To obtain the initial values of $\boldsymbol{\beta}_{0|0}$ and $\Sigma_{0|0}$, Sant (1977) suggested using the generalized least-squares method on the first K observations of y_t and $\mathbf{x}_t$. Noting that

$$\begin{aligned}
\boldsymbol{\beta}_t &= H\boldsymbol{\beta}_{t-1} + \boldsymbol{\eta}_t \\
&= H^2 \boldsymbol{\beta}_{t-2} + \boldsymbol{\eta}_t + H\boldsymbol{\eta}_{t-1} \\
&= H^{t-j} \boldsymbol{\beta}_j + \boldsymbol{\eta}_t + H\boldsymbol{\eta}_{t-1} + \cdots + H^{t-j-1} \boldsymbol{\eta}_j,
\end{aligned} \tag{6.4.22}$$

and assuming that H^{-1} exists, we can also write y_k in the form

$$\begin{aligned}
y_k &= \mathbf{x}_k' \boldsymbol{\beta}_k + u_k \\
&= \mathbf{x}_k' [H^{-K+k} \boldsymbol{\beta}_K - H^{-K+k} \boldsymbol{\eta}_K - \cdots - H^{-1} \boldsymbol{\eta}_{k+1}] + u_k.
\end{aligned}$$

Thus, $(y_1, \ldots, y_K)$ can be written as

$$\begin{bmatrix} y_1 \\ y_2 \\ \vdots \\ y_K \end{bmatrix} = \begin{bmatrix} \mathbf{x}_1' H^{-K+1} \\ \mathbf{x}_2' H^{-K+2} \\ \vdots \\ \mathbf{x}_K' \end{bmatrix} \boldsymbol{\beta}_K + \begin{bmatrix} u_1 \\ u_2 \\ \vdots \\ u_K \end{bmatrix}$$
$$- \begin{bmatrix} \mathbf{x}_1' H^{-1} & \mathbf{x}_1' H^{-2} & \ldots & \mathbf{x}_1' H^{-K+1} \\ \mathbf{0}' & \mathbf{x}_2' H^{-1} & \ldots & \mathbf{x}_2' H^{-K+2} \\ & & \ddots & \vdots \\ & & & \mathbf{x}_{K-1}' H^{-1} \\ & & & \mathbf{0}' \end{bmatrix} \begin{bmatrix} \boldsymbol{\eta}_2 \\ \boldsymbol{\eta}_3 \\ \vdots \\ \boldsymbol{\eta}_K \end{bmatrix}. \tag{6.4.23}$$

Applying GLS to (6.4.23) gives

$$\begin{aligned}
\Sigma_{K|K} = \sigma_u^2 \{ & [H'^{-K+1} \mathbf{x}_1, H'^{-K+2} \mathbf{x}_2, \ldots, \mathbf{x}_K] \\
& \times [I_K + A_K (I_{K-1} \otimes P) A_K']^{-1} [H^{-K+1} \mathbf{x}_1, \ldots, \mathbf{x}_K]' \}^{-1},
\end{aligned} \tag{6.4.24}$$

and

$$\boldsymbol{\beta}_{K|K} = \frac{1}{\sigma_u^2}\Sigma_{K|K}[H'^{-K+1}\mathbf{x}_1, H'^{-K+2}\mathbf{x}_2, \ldots, \mathbf{x}_K] \times [I_K + A_K(I_{K-1} \otimes P)A_K']^{-1} \begin{bmatrix} y_1 \\ \vdots \\ y_K \end{bmatrix}, \tag{6.4.25}$$

where $P = \sigma_u^{-2}\Psi$, and A_K is the coefficient matrix of $(\boldsymbol{\eta}_2, \ldots, \boldsymbol{\eta}_K)'$ in (6.4.23). The initial estimators, $\boldsymbol{\beta}_{K|K}$ and $\Sigma_{K|K}$, are functions of σ_u^2, Ψ, and H.

6.4.3 Maximum Likelihood Estimation

When H, Ψ, and σ_u^2 are unknown, (6.4.7) opens the way for maximum likelihood estimation without the need for repeated inversions of covariance matrices of large dimensions. To form the likelihood function, we note that

$$y_t - y_{t|t} = \mathbf{x}_t'(\boldsymbol{\beta}_t - \boldsymbol{\beta}_{t|t-1}) + u_t = y_t - x_t'\boldsymbol{\beta}_{t|t-1} \tag{6.4.26}$$

is normal and serially uncorrelated. Hence, the joint density of $(y_1, \ldots, y_T)$ can be written as the product of the conditional density of $(y_{K+1}, \ldots, y_T \mid y_1, \ldots, y_K)$ and the marginal density of $(y_1, \ldots, y_K)$. The log likelihood function of $(y_{K+1}, \ldots, y_T)$, given $(y_1, \ldots, y_K)$, is

$$\log L = -\frac{T-K}{2}\log 2\pi - \frac{1}{2}\sum_{t=K+1}^{T}\log\left(\mathbf{x}_t'\Sigma_{t|t-1}\mathbf{x}_t + \sigma_u^2\right) - \frac{1}{2}\sum_{t=K+1}^{T}\frac{(y_t - \mathbf{x}_t'\boldsymbol{\beta}_{t|t-1})^2}{\mathbf{x}_t'\Sigma_{t|t-1}\mathbf{x}_t + \sigma_u^2}. \tag{6.4.27}$$

The first K observations are used to compute $\Sigma_{K|K}$ and $\boldsymbol{\beta}_{K|K}$ [equations (6.4.24) and (6.4.25)] as functions of σ_u^2, Ψ, and H. Hence, the data $\boldsymbol{\beta}_{t|t-1}$ and $\Sigma_{t|t-1}$ $(t = K+1, \ldots, T)$ required to evaluate $\log L$ are functions of σ_u^2, Ψ, and H, as given by (6.4.13), (6.4.15), (6.4.12), and (6.4.11). To find the maximum of (6.4.27), numerical methods will have to be used.

When we estimate the model (6.4.1) and (6.4.2) using panel data, all the derivations in Section 6.4.2 remain valid if we replace y_t, $\mathbf{x}_t$, $\mathbf{u}_t$, and σ_u^2 by the $N \times 1$ vector $\mathbf{y}_t = (y_{1t}, \ldots, y_{Nt})'$, the $N \times K$ matrix $X_t = (\mathbf{x}_{1t}, \ldots, \mathbf{x}_{NT})'$, the $N \times 1$ vector $\mathbf{u}_t = (u_{1t}, \ldots, u_{Nt})'$, and $\sigma_u^2 I_N$ in appropriate places. The MLE can be carried out in the same way as outlined in this section, except that the likelihood function (6.4.27) is replaced by

$$\log L = \text{const} - \frac{1}{2}\sum_t \log\left|X_t'\Sigma_{t|t-1}X_t + \sigma_u^2 I_N\right| - \frac{1}{2}\sum_t(\mathbf{y}_t - X_t\boldsymbol{\beta}_{t|t-1})' \times \left(X_t\Sigma_{t|t-1}X_t' + \sigma_u^2 I_N\right)^{-1}(\mathbf{y}_t - X_t\boldsymbol{\beta}_{t|t-1}). \tag{6.4.27$'$}$$

However, we no longer need to use the first K period observations to start the iteration. If $N > K$, we need to use only the first-period cross-sectional data to obtain $\boldsymbol{\beta}_{1|1}$ and $\Sigma_{1|1}$. Additional details with regard to the computation can be found in Harvey (1978) and Harvey and Phillips (1982).

6.4.4 Tests for Parameter Constancy

A simple alternative to the null hypothesis of constancy of regression coefficients over time is

$$\boldsymbol{\beta}_t = \boldsymbol{\beta}_{t-1} + \boldsymbol{\eta}_t, \tag{6.4.28}$$

where $\boldsymbol{\eta}_t$ is assumed independently normally distributed, with mean zero and a diagonal covariance matrix Ψ. Regarding $\boldsymbol{\beta}_0$ as fixed, we have

$$\boldsymbol{\beta}_t = \boldsymbol{\beta}_0 + \sum_{s=1}^{t} \boldsymbol{\eta}_s. \tag{6.4.29}$$

Thus, the regression model becomes

$$\begin{aligned} y_t = \mathbf{x}_t'\boldsymbol{\beta}_t + u_t &= \mathbf{x}_t'\boldsymbol{\beta}_0 + u_t + \mathbf{x}_t'\left(\sum_{s=1}^{t} \boldsymbol{\eta}_s\right) \\ &= \mathbf{x}_t'\boldsymbol{\beta}_0 + u_t^*, \end{aligned} \tag{6.4.30}$$

where $u_t^* = u_t + \mathbf{x}_t'(\sum_{s=1}^{t} \boldsymbol{\eta}_s)$ has variance

$$Eu_t^{*2} = \sigma_u^2 + t\mathbf{x}_t'\Psi\mathbf{x}_t. \tag{6.4.31}$$

For $\Psi = \text{diag}\{\psi_{kk}\}$, (6.4.31) becomes

$$Eu_t^{*2} = \sigma_u^2 + t\sum_{k=1}^{K} x_{kt}^2\psi_{kk}, \qquad t = 1.\dots, T. \tag{6.4.32}$$

The null hypothesis states that $\Psi = \mathbf{0}$. Hence, the Breusch–Pagan (1979) Lagrange-multiplier test applied here is to regress $\hat{u}_t^2/\hat{\sigma}_u^2$ on $t(1, x_{2t}^2, \dots, x_{Kt}^2)$, $t = 1, \dots, T$, where $\hat{u}_t$ is the least-squares residual $\hat{u}_t = y_t - \hat{\boldsymbol{\beta}}'\mathbf{x}_t$, $\hat{\boldsymbol{\beta}} = (\sum_{t=1}^{T} \mathbf{x}_t\mathbf{x}_t')^{-1}(\sum_{t=1}^{T} \mathbf{x}_t y_t)$, and $\hat{\sigma}_u^2 = \sum_{t=1}^{T} \hat{u}_t^2/T$. Under the null hypothesis, one-half the explained sum of squares of this regression is asymptotically chi-square-distributed, with K degrees of freedom.[14]

When panel data are available, it is possible to test for parameter constancy indirectly using the classic analysis-of-covariance test. By the assumption that the parameter vector $\boldsymbol{\beta}_t$ is constant over cross-sectional units in the sample period, an indirect test is to postulate the null hypothesis

$$H_0 : \boldsymbol{\beta}_1 = \boldsymbol{\beta}_2 = \cdots = \boldsymbol{\beta}_T = \boldsymbol{\beta}.$$

If the disturbances of the regression model $y_{it} = \boldsymbol{\beta}_t'\mathbf{x}_{it} + u_{it}$ are independently normally distributed over i and t, then the test statistic F_3' from Chapter 2 has an F distribution with $(T-1)K$ and $N(T-K)$ degrees of freedom under the null.

If the null hypothesis is rejected, we can use the information that under mild regularity conditions $\text{plim}_{N\to\infty}\hat{\boldsymbol{\beta}}_t = \boldsymbol{\beta}_t$, $t = 1, \ldots, T$, to investigate the nature of variation in the parameters over time. We can apply the Box–Jenkins (1970) method on $\hat{\boldsymbol{\beta}}_t$ to identify a suitable stochastic process with which to model the parameter variation.

6.5 COEFFICIENTS THAT ARE FUNCTIONS OF OTHER EXOGENOUS VARIABLES

Sometimes, instead of assuming that parameters are random draws from a common distribution, an investigation of possible dependence of $\boldsymbol{\beta}_{it}$ on characteristics of the individuals or time is of considerable interest (e.g., Amemiya (1978b); Hendricks, Koenker, and Poirier (1979); Singh et al. (1976); Swamy and Tinsley (1977); Wachter (1970)). A general formulation of stochastic-parameter models with systematic components can be expressed within the context of the linear model. Suppose that

$$\mathbf{y}_i = X_{i1}\boldsymbol{\beta}_1 + X_{i2}\boldsymbol{\beta}_{2i} + \mathbf{u}_i, \qquad i = 1, \ldots, N, \tag{6.5.1}$$

and

$$\boldsymbol{\beta}_{2i} = Z_i\boldsymbol{\gamma} + \boldsymbol{\eta}_{2i} \tag{6.5.2}$$

where X_{i1} and X_{i2} denote the $T \times K_1$ and $T \times K_2$ matrices of the time-series observations of the first K_1 and last $K_2 (= K - K_1)$ exogenous variables for the ith individual, $\boldsymbol{\beta}_1$ is a $K_1 \times 1$ vector of fixed constants, $\boldsymbol{\beta}_{2i}$ is a $K_2 \times 1$ vector that varies according to (6.5.2), Z_i and $\boldsymbol{\gamma}$ are a $K_2 \times M$ matrix of known constants and a $M \times 1$ vector of unknown constants, respectively, and $\mathbf{u}_i$ and $\boldsymbol{\eta}_{2i}$ are $T \times 1$ and $K_2 \times 1$ vectors of unobservable random variables. For example, in Wachter (1970), $\mathbf{y}_i$ is a vector of time-series observations on the logarithm of the relative wage rate in the ith industry. X_{i1} contains the logarithms of such variables as the relative value added in the ith industry and the change in the consumer price, X_{i2} consists of a single vector of time-series observations on the logarithm of unemployment, and Z_i contains the degree of concentration and the degree of unionization in the ith industry.

For simplicity, we assume that $\mathbf{u}_i$ and $\boldsymbol{\eta}_{2i}$ are uncorrelated with each other and have zero means. The variance–covariance matrices of $\mathbf{u}_i$ and $\boldsymbol{\eta}_{2i}$ are given by

$$E\mathbf{u}_i\mathbf{u}_j' = \sigma_{ij}I_T, \tag{6.5.3}$$

and

$$E\boldsymbol{\eta}_{2i}\boldsymbol{\eta}_{2j}' = \begin{cases} \Lambda & \text{if } i = j, \\ \mathbf{0} & \text{if } i \neq j. \end{cases} \tag{6.5.4}$$

Let $\Sigma = (\sigma_{ij})$. We can write the variance–covariance matrices of $\mathbf{u} = (\mathbf{u}_1', \ldots, \mathbf{u}_N')'$ and $\boldsymbol{\eta}_2 = (\boldsymbol{\eta}_{21}', \ldots, \boldsymbol{\eta}_{2N}')'$ as

$$E\mathbf{u}\mathbf{u}' = \Sigma \otimes I_T, \tag{6.5.5}$$

and

$$E\boldsymbol{\eta}_2\boldsymbol{\eta}_2' = \begin{bmatrix} \Lambda & & \mathbf{0} \\ & \ddots & \\ \mathbf{0} & & \Lambda \end{bmatrix} = \tilde{\Lambda}. \tag{6.5.6}$$

Combining (6.5.1) and (6.5.2), we have

$$\mathbf{y} = X_1\boldsymbol{\beta}_1 + \mathbf{W}\boldsymbol{\gamma} + \tilde{X}_2\boldsymbol{\eta}_2 + \mathbf{u}, \tag{6.5.7}$$

where

$$\underset{NT\times 1}{\mathbf{y}} = (\mathbf{y}_1', \ldots, \mathbf{y}_N')',$$

$$\underset{NT\times K_1}{X_1} = (X_{11}', \ldots, X_{N1}')',$$

$$\underset{NT\times M}{\mathbf{W}} = (Z_1'X_{12}', Z_2'X_{22}', \ldots, Z_N'X_{N2}')',$$

$$\underset{NT\times NK_2}{\tilde{X}_2} = \begin{bmatrix} X_{12} & & & \mathbf{0} \\ & X_{22} & & \\ & & \ddots & \\ \mathbf{0} & & & X_{N2} \end{bmatrix},$$

and

$$\underset{NK_2\times 1}{\boldsymbol{\eta}_2} = (\boldsymbol{\eta}_{21}', \ldots, \boldsymbol{\eta}_{2N}')'.$$

The BLUE of $\boldsymbol{\beta}_1$ and $\boldsymbol{\gamma}$ of (6.5.7) is the GLS estimator

$$\begin{bmatrix} \hat{\boldsymbol{\beta}}_1 \\ \hat{\boldsymbol{\gamma}} \end{bmatrix}_{\text{GLS}} = \left\{ \begin{bmatrix} X_1' \\ W' \end{bmatrix} [\Sigma \otimes I_T + \tilde{X}_2\tilde{\Lambda}\tilde{X}_2']^{-1}(X_1, W) \right\}^{-1} \times \left\{ \begin{bmatrix} X_1' \\ W' \end{bmatrix} [\Sigma \otimes I_T + \tilde{X}_2\tilde{\Lambda}\tilde{X}_2']^{-1}\mathbf{y} \right\}. \tag{6.5.8}$$

If Σ is diagonal, the variance–covariance matrix of the stochastic term of (6.5.7) is block-diagonal, with the ith diagonal block equal to

$$\Omega_i = X_{i2}\Lambda X_{i2}' + \sigma_{ii} I_T. \tag{6.5.9}$$

The GLS estimator (6.5.8) can be simplified as

$$\begin{bmatrix} \hat{\boldsymbol{\beta}}_1 \\ \hat{\boldsymbol{\gamma}} \end{bmatrix}_{\text{GLS}} = \left[\sum_{i=1}^{N} \begin{bmatrix} X_{i1}' \\ Z_i'X_{i2}' \end{bmatrix} \Omega_i^{-1}(X_{i1}, X_{2i}Z_i) \right]^{-1} \times \left[\sum_{i=1}^{N} \begin{bmatrix} X_{i1}' \\ Z_i'X_{i2}' \end{bmatrix} \Omega_i^{-1}\mathbf{y}_i \right]. \tag{6.5.10}$$

Amemiya (1978b) suggested estimating Λ and σ_{ij} as follows. Let

$$\begin{bmatrix} \mathbf{y}_1 \\ \vdots \\ \mathbf{y}_N \end{bmatrix} = \begin{bmatrix} X_{11} \\ \vdots \\ X_{N1} \end{bmatrix} \boldsymbol{\beta}_1 + \begin{bmatrix} X_{12} \\ \mathbf{0} \\ \vdots \\ \mathbf{0} \end{bmatrix} \boldsymbol{\beta}_{21} + \begin{bmatrix} \mathbf{0} \\ X_{22} \\ \vdots \\ \mathbf{0} \end{bmatrix} \boldsymbol{\beta}_{22}$$

$$+ \cdots + \begin{bmatrix} \mathbf{0} \\ \vdots \\ X_{N2} \end{bmatrix} \boldsymbol{\beta}_{2N} + \begin{bmatrix} \mathbf{u}_1 \\ \vdots \\ \mathbf{u}_N \end{bmatrix}. \tag{6.5.11}$$

Apply the least-squares method to (6.5.11). Denote the resulting estimates by $\hat{\boldsymbol{\beta}}_1$ and $\hat{\boldsymbol{\beta}}_{2i}$, $i = 1, \ldots, N$. Then σ_{ij} can be estimated by

$$\hat{\sigma}_{ij} = \frac{1}{T}(\mathbf{y}_i - X_{i1}\hat{\boldsymbol{\beta}}_1 - \mathbf{X}_{i2}\hat{\boldsymbol{\beta}}_{2i})'(\mathbf{y}_j - \mathbf{X}_{j1}\hat{\boldsymbol{\beta}}_1 - \mathbf{X}_{j2}\hat{\boldsymbol{\beta}}_{2j}), \tag{6.5.12}$$

and $\boldsymbol{\gamma}$ can be estimated by

$$\hat{\boldsymbol{\gamma}} = \left(\sum_{i=1}^{N} Z_i' Z_i\right)^{-1} \left(\sum_{i=1}^{N} Z_i' \hat{\boldsymbol{\beta}}_{2i}\right). \tag{6.5.13}$$

We then estimate Λ by

$$\hat{\Lambda} = \frac{1}{N}\sum_{i=1}^{N}(\hat{\boldsymbol{\beta}}_{2i} - Z_i\hat{\boldsymbol{\gamma}})(\hat{\boldsymbol{\beta}}_{2i} - Z_i\hat{\boldsymbol{\gamma}})'. \tag{6.5.14}$$

Once consistent estimates of σ_{ij} and Λ are obtained (as both N and T approach infinity), we can substitute them into (6.5.8). The resulting two-stage Aitken estimator of $(\boldsymbol{\beta}_1', \boldsymbol{\gamma}')$ is consistent and asymptotically normally distributed under general conditions. A test of the hypothesis that $\boldsymbol{\gamma} = 0$ can be performed in the usual regression framework using

$$\text{Var}(\hat{\boldsymbol{\gamma}}_{\text{GLS}}) = [W'\tilde{\Omega}^{-1}W - W'\tilde{\Omega}^{-1}X_1(X_1'\tilde{\Omega}^{-1}X_1)^{-1}X_1'\tilde{\Omega}^{-1}W]^{-1}, \tag{6.5.15}$$

where

$$\tilde{\Omega} = \tilde{X}_2\tilde{\Lambda}\tilde{X}_2' + \Sigma \otimes I_T.$$

6.6 A MIXED FIXED- AND RANDOM-COEFFICIENTS MODEL

6.6.1 Model Formulation

Many of the previously discussed models can be treated as special cases of a general mixed fixed- and random-coefficients model. For ease of exposition, we shall assume that only time-invariant cross-sectional heterogeneity exists.

Suppose that each cross-sectional unit is postulated to be different, so that

$$y_{it} = \sum_{k=1}^{K} \beta_{ki} x_{kit} + \sum_{\ell=1}^{m} \gamma_{\ell i} w_{\ell it} + u_{it}, \qquad \begin{array}{l} i = 1, \ldots, N, \\ t = 1, \ldots, T, \end{array} \tag{6.6.1}$$

where $\mathbf{x}_{it}$ and $\mathbf{w}_{it}$ are each a $K \times 1$ and an $m \times 1$ vector of explanatory variables that are independent of the error of the equation, u_{it}. Stacking the NT observations together, we have

$$\mathbf{y} = X\boldsymbol{\beta} + W\boldsymbol{\gamma} + \mathbf{u}, \tag{6.6.2}$$

where

$$\underset{NT \times NK}{X} = \begin{pmatrix} X_1 & \mathbf{0} & \cdots & \mathbf{0} \\ \mathbf{0} & X_2 & \cdots & \mathbf{0} \\ \vdots & & \ddots & \vdots \\ \mathbf{0} & & & X_N \end{pmatrix},$$

$$\underset{NT \times Nm}{W} = \begin{pmatrix} W_1 & \mathbf{0} & \cdots & \mathbf{0} \\ \mathbf{0} & W_2 & \cdots & \mathbf{0} \\ \vdots & & \ddots & \vdots \\ \mathbf{0} & & & W_N \end{pmatrix},$$

$$\underset{NT \times 1}{\mathbf{u}} = (\mathbf{u}_1', \ldots, \mathbf{u}_N'),$$

$$\underset{NK \times 1}{\boldsymbol{\beta}} = (\boldsymbol{\beta}_1', \ldots, \boldsymbol{\beta}_N')' \quad \text{and} \quad \underset{Nm \times 1}{\boldsymbol{\gamma}} = (\boldsymbol{\gamma}_1', \ldots, \boldsymbol{\gamma}_N')'.$$

Equation (6.6.1), just like (6.2.2), assumes a different behavioral-equation relation for each cross-sectional unit. In this situation, the only advantage of pooling is to put the model (6.6.2) in Zellner's (1962) seemingly unrelated regression framework to obtain efficiency of the estimates of the individual behavioral equation.

The motivation of a mixed fixed- and random-coefficients model is that while there may be fundamental differences among cross-sectional units, by conditioning on these individual specific effects one may still be able to draw inferences on certain population characteristics through the imposition of a priori constraints on the coefficients of $\mathbf{x}_{it}$ and $\mathbf{w}_{it}$. We assume that there exist two kinds of restrictions, stochastic and fixed (e.g., Hsiao (1991a); Hsiao, Appelbe, and Dineen (1993)), in the following form:

A.6.6.1. The coefficients of $\mathbf{x}_{it}$ are assumed to be subject to stochastic restrictions of the form

$$\boldsymbol{\beta} = A_1 \bar{\boldsymbol{\beta}} + \boldsymbol{\alpha}, \tag{6.6.3}$$

where A_1 is an $NK \times L$ matrix with known elements, $\bar{\boldsymbol{\beta}}$ is an $L \times 1$ vector of constants, and $\boldsymbol{\alpha}$ is assumed to be (normally distributed) random variables with mean $\mathbf{0}$ and nonsingular constant covariance matrix C and is independent of $\mathbf{x}_{it}$.

A.6.6.2. The coefficients of $\mathbf{w}_{it}$ are assumed to be subject to

$$\boldsymbol{\gamma} = A_2 \bar{\boldsymbol{\gamma}}, \tag{6.6.4}$$

where A_2 is an $Nm \times n$ matrix with known elements, and $\bar{\boldsymbol{\gamma}}$ is an $n \times 1$ vector of constants.

Since A_2 is known, we may substitute (6.6.4) into (6.6.2) and write the model as

$$\mathbf{y} = X\boldsymbol{\beta} + \tilde{W}\bar{\boldsymbol{\gamma}} + \mathbf{u} \tag{6.6.5}$$

subject to (6.6.3), where $\tilde{W} = WA_2$.

A.6.6.2 allows for various possible fixed parameter configurations. For instance, if $\boldsymbol{\gamma}$ is different across cross-sectional units, we can let $A_2 = I_N \otimes I_m$. On the other hand, if we wish to constrain $\boldsymbol{\gamma}_i = \boldsymbol{\gamma}_j$, we can let $A_2 = \mathbf{e}_N \otimes I_m$.

Many of the linear panel data models with unobserved individual specific but time-invariant heterogeneity can be treated as special cases of the model (6.6.2)–(6.6.4). These include:

i. A common model for all cross-sectional units. If there is no interindividual difference in behavioral patterns, we may let $X = \mathbf{0}$, $A_2 = \mathbf{e}_N \otimes I_m$, so (6.6.2) becomes

$$y_{it} = \mathbf{w}_{it}'\bar{\boldsymbol{\gamma}} + u_{it}. \tag{6.6.6}$$

ii. Different models for different cross-sectional units. When each individual is considered different, then $X = \mathbf{0}$, $A_2 = I_N \otimes I_m$, and (6.6.2) becomes

$$y_{it} = \mathbf{w}_{it}'\boldsymbol{\gamma}_i + u_{it}. \tag{6.6.7}$$

iii. Variable-intercept model (e.g., Kuh (1963, Section 3.2)). If conditional on the observed exogenous variables, the interindividual differences stay constant through time. Let $X = \mathbf{0}$, and

$$A_2 = (I_N \otimes \mathbf{i}_m \vdots \mathbf{e}_N \otimes I_{m-1}^*), \qquad \bar{\boldsymbol{\gamma}} = (\gamma_{11}, \ldots, \gamma_{N1}, \bar{\gamma}_2, \ldots, \bar{\gamma}_m)',$$

where we arrange $W_i = (\mathbf{e}_T, \mathbf{w}_{i2}, \ldots, \mathbf{w}_{im})$, $i = 1, \ldots, N$, $\mathbf{i}_m = (1, 0, \ldots, 0)'$, and

$$\underset{m \times (m-1)}{I_{m-1}^*} = (\mathbf{0} \vdots I_{m-1})'.$$

Then (6.6.2) becomes

$$y_{it} = \gamma_{i1} + \bar{\gamma}_2 w_{it2} + \cdots + \bar{\gamma}_m w_{itm} + u_{it}. \tag{6.6.8}$$

iv. Error-components model (e.g., Balestra and Nerlove (1966); Wallace and Hussain (1969); or Section 3.3). When the effects of the individual-specific, time-invariant omitted variables are treated as random variables just as in the assumption on the effects of other omitted variables, we can let $X_i = \mathbf{e}_T, \boldsymbol{\alpha}' = (\alpha_1, \ldots, \alpha_N), A_1 = \mathbf{e}_N, C = \sigma_\alpha^2 I_N, \bar{\beta}$ be an unknown constant, and $\mathbf{w}_{it}$ not contain an intercept term. Then (6.4.2) becomes

$$y_{it} = \bar{\beta} + \bar{\boldsymbol{\gamma}}'\mathbf{w}_{it} + \alpha_i + u_{it}. \tag{6.6.9}$$

v. Random-coefficients model (Swamy (1970), or Section 6.2.2). Let $Z = \mathbf{0}$, $A_1 = \mathbf{e}_N \otimes I_K$, and $C = I_N \otimes \Delta$. Then we have model (6.2.4).

6.6.2 A Bayes Solution

The formulation of (6.6.5) subject to (6.6.3) can be viewed from a Bayesian perspective, as there exists an informative prior on $\boldsymbol{\beta}$ (6.6.3), but not on $\bar{\boldsymbol{\gamma}}$. In the classical sampling approach, inferences are made typically by assuming that the probability law $f(\mathbf{y}, \boldsymbol{\theta})$ generating the observations $\mathbf{y}$ is known, but not the vector of constant parameters $\boldsymbol{\theta}$. Estimators $\hat{\boldsymbol{\theta}}(\mathbf{y})$ of the parameters $\boldsymbol{\theta}$ are chosen as functions of $\mathbf{y}$ so that their sampling distributions, in repeated experiments, are, in some sense, concentrated as closely as possible about the true values of $\boldsymbol{\theta}$. In the Bayesian approach, a different line is taken. First, all quantities, including the parameters, are considered random variables. Second, all probability statements are conditional, so that in making a probability statement it is necessary to refer to the conditioning event as well as the event whose probability is being discussed. Therefore, as part of the model, a prior distribution $p(\boldsymbol{\theta})$ of the parameter $\boldsymbol{\theta}$ is introduced. The prior distribution is supposed to express a state of knowledge (or ignorance) about $\boldsymbol{\theta}$ before the data are obtained. Given the probability model $f(y; \boldsymbol{\theta})$, the prior distribution, and the data $\mathbf{y}$, the probability distribution of $\boldsymbol{\theta}$ is revised to $p(\boldsymbol{\theta} \mid \mathbf{y})$, which is called the posterior distribution of $\boldsymbol{\theta}$, according to Bayes' theorem (e.g., Kaufman (1977), Intriligator, Bodkin, and Hsiao (1996)):[15]

$$P(\boldsymbol{\theta} \mid \mathbf{y}) \propto p(\boldsymbol{\theta}) f(\mathbf{y} \mid \boldsymbol{\theta}), \tag{6.6.10}$$

where the sign "$\propto$" denotes "is proportional to," with the factor of proportionality being a normalizing constant.

Under the assumption that

A.6.6.3. $\mathbf{u} \sim N(\mathbf{0}, \Omega)$,

we may write the model (6.6.5) as follows:

A.1. Conditional on X, $\tilde{W}$, $\boldsymbol{\beta}$, and $\bar{\boldsymbol{\gamma}}$,

$$\mathbf{y} \sim N(X\boldsymbol{\beta} + \tilde{W}\bar{\boldsymbol{\gamma}}, \Omega). \tag{6.6.11}$$

A.2. The prior distributions of $\boldsymbol{\beta}$ and $\bar{\boldsymbol{\gamma}}$ are independent:

$$P(\boldsymbol{\beta}, \bar{\boldsymbol{\gamma}}) = P(\boldsymbol{\beta}) \cdot P(\bar{\boldsymbol{\gamma}}). \tag{6.6.12}$$

A.3. $P(\boldsymbol{\beta}) \sim N(A_1\bar{\boldsymbol{\beta}}, C)$.

A.4. There is no information about $\bar{\boldsymbol{\beta}}$ and $\bar{\boldsymbol{\gamma}}$; therefore $P(\bar{\boldsymbol{\beta}})$ and $P(\bar{\boldsymbol{\gamma}})$ are independent and

$$P(\bar{\boldsymbol{\beta}}) \propto \text{constant},$$
$$P(\bar{\boldsymbol{\gamma}}) \propto \text{constant}.$$

Conditional on Ω and C, repeatedly applying the formulas in Appendix 6A yields (Hsiao, Appelbe, and Dineen (1993)):

i. The posterior distribution of $\bar{\boldsymbol{\beta}}$ and $\bar{\boldsymbol{\gamma}}$ given $\mathbf{y}$ is

$$N\left(\begin{pmatrix} \bar{\beta}^* \\ \bar{\boldsymbol{\gamma}}^* \end{pmatrix}, D_1\right), \tag{6.6.13}$$

where

$$D_1 = \left[\begin{pmatrix} A_1'X' \\ \tilde{W}' \end{pmatrix} (\Omega + XCX')^{-1}(XA_1, \tilde{W})\right]^{-1}, \tag{6.6.14}$$

and

$$\begin{pmatrix} \bar{\boldsymbol{\beta}}^* \\ \bar{\boldsymbol{\gamma}}^* \end{pmatrix} = D_1 \begin{bmatrix} A_1'X' \\ \tilde{W}' \end{bmatrix} (\Omega + XCX')^{-1}\mathbf{y}. \tag{6.6.15}$$

ii. The posterior distribution of $\boldsymbol{\beta}$ given $\bar{\boldsymbol{\beta}}$ and $\mathbf{y}$ is $N(\boldsymbol{\beta}^*, D_2)$, where

$$D_2 = \{X'[\Omega^{-1} - \Omega^{-1}\tilde{W}(\tilde{W}'\Omega^{-1}\tilde{W})^{-1}\tilde{W}'\Omega^{-1}]X + C^{-1}\}^{-1}, \tag{6.6.16}$$

$$\boldsymbol{\beta}^* = D_2\{X'[\Omega^{-1} - \Omega^{-1}\tilde{W}(\tilde{W}'\Omega^{-1}\tilde{W})^{-1}\tilde{W}'\Omega^{-1}]\mathbf{y} + C^{-1}A_1\bar{\boldsymbol{\beta}}\}. \tag{6.6.17}$$

iii. The (unconditional) posterior distribution of $\boldsymbol{\beta}$ is $N(\boldsymbol{\beta}^{**}, D_3)$, where

$$\begin{aligned} D_3 = \{&X'[\Omega^{-1} - \Omega^{-1}\tilde{W}(\tilde{W}'\Omega^{-1}\tilde{W})^{-1}\tilde{W}'\Omega^{-1}]X + C^{-1} \\ &- C^{-1}A_1(A_1'C^{-1}A_1)^{-1}A_1'C^{-1}\}^{-1}, \end{aligned} \tag{6.6.18}$$

$$\begin{aligned} \boldsymbol{\beta}^{**} &= D_3\{X'[\Omega^{-1} - \Omega^{-1}\tilde{W}(\tilde{W}'\Omega^{-1}\tilde{W})^{-1}\tilde{W}'\Omega^{-1}]\mathbf{y}\} \\ &= D_2\{X'[\Omega^{-1} - \Omega^{-1}\tilde{W}(\tilde{W}'\Omega^{-1}\tilde{W})^{-1}\tilde{W}'\Omega^{-1}]X\hat{\boldsymbol{\beta}} + C^{-1}A_1\bar{\boldsymbol{\beta}}^*\}, \end{aligned} \tag{6.6.19}$$

where $\hat{\boldsymbol{\beta}}$ is the GLS estimate of (6.6.5),

$$\begin{aligned} \hat{\boldsymbol{\beta}} = \{&X'[\Omega^{-1} - \Omega^{-1}\tilde{W}(\tilde{W}'\Omega^{-1}\tilde{W})^{-1}\tilde{W}'\Omega^{-1}]X\}^{-1} \\ &\times \{X'[\Omega^{-1} - \Omega^{-1}\tilde{W}(\tilde{W}'\Omega^{-1}\tilde{W})^{-1}\tilde{W}'\Omega^{-1}]\mathbf{y}\}. \end{aligned} \tag{6.6.20}$$

Given a quadratic loss function of the error of the estimation, a Bayes point estimate is the posterior mean. The posterior mean of $\bar{\boldsymbol{\beta}}$ and $\bar{\boldsymbol{\gamma}}$ (6.6.15) is the GLS estimator of the model (6.6.5) after substituting the restriction (6.6.3),

$$\mathbf{y} = XA_1\bar{\boldsymbol{\beta}} + \tilde{W}\bar{\boldsymbol{\gamma}} + \mathbf{v}, \tag{6.6.21}$$

where $\mathbf{v} = X\boldsymbol{\alpha} + \mathbf{u}$. However, the posterior mean of $\boldsymbol{\beta}$ is not the GLS estimator of (6.6.5). It is the weighted average between the GLS estimator of $\boldsymbol{\beta}$ and the overall mean $\bar{\boldsymbol{\beta}}$ (6.6.17) or $\bar{\boldsymbol{\beta}}^*$ (6.6.19) with the weights proportional to the inverse of the precision of respective estimates. The reason is that although both (6.2.2) and (6.6.5) allow the coefficients to be different across cross-sectional units, (6.6.3) has imposed the additional prior information that $\boldsymbol{\beta}$ are randomly distributed with mean $A_1\bar{\boldsymbol{\beta}}$. For (6.2.2), the best linear predictor for an individual outcome is to substitute the best linear unbiased estimator of the individual coefficients into the individual equation. For model of (6.6.5) and (6.6.3), because the expected $\boldsymbol{\beta}_i$ is the same across i and the actual difference can be attributed to a chance outcome, additional information about $\boldsymbol{\beta}_i$ may be obtained by examining the behavior of others, hence (6.6.17) or (6.6.19).

In the special case of the error-components model (6.6.9), $X = I_N \otimes \mathbf{e}_T$. Under the assumption that $\mathbf{w}_{it}$ contains an intercept term (i.e., $\bar{\beta} = 0$) and u_{it} is i.i.d., the Bayes estimator ((6.6.15)) of $\bar{\boldsymbol{\gamma}}$ is simply the GLS estimator of (6.6.21) $\bar{\boldsymbol{\gamma}}^*$. The Bayes estimator of α_i (6.6.17) is

$$\alpha_i^{**} = \left(\frac{T\sigma_\alpha^2}{T\sigma_\alpha^2 + \sigma_u^2}\right)\hat{\bar{v}}_i, \qquad (6.6.22)$$

where $\hat{\bar{v}}_i = \frac{1}{T}\sum_{t=1}^{T}\hat{v}_{it}$ and $\hat{v}_{it} = y_{it} - \bar{\boldsymbol{\gamma}}^*\mathbf{w}_{it}$. Substituting $\bar{\boldsymbol{\gamma}}^*$, and α_i^{**} for the unknown $\bar{\boldsymbol{\gamma}}$, and α_i in (6.6.9), Wansbeek and Kapteyn (1978) and Taub (1979) show that

$$\hat{y}_{i,T+S} = \bar{\boldsymbol{\gamma}}^{*'}\mathbf{w}_{i,t+s} + \alpha_i^{**} \qquad (6.6.23)$$

is the best linear unbiased predictor (BLUP) for the ith individual s periods ahead.[16]

6.6.3 An Example

In a classical framework, it makes no sense to predict the independently drawn random variable $\boldsymbol{\beta}_i$ (or $\boldsymbol{\alpha}_i$). However, in panel data, we actually operate with two dimensions – a cross-sectional dimension and a time-series dimension. Even though $\boldsymbol{\beta}_i$ is an independently distributed random variable across i, once a particular $\boldsymbol{\beta}_i$ is drawn, it stays constant over time. Therefore, it makes sense to predict $\boldsymbol{\beta}_i$. The classical predictor of $\boldsymbol{\beta}_i$ is the generalized least-squares estimator of the model (6.6.5). The Bayes predictor (6.6.19) is the weighted average between the generalized least-squares estimator of $\boldsymbol{\beta}$ for the model (6.6.5) and the overall mean $A_1\bar{\boldsymbol{\beta}}$ if $\bar{\boldsymbol{\beta}}$ is known, or $A_1\bar{\boldsymbol{\beta}}^*$ if $\bar{\boldsymbol{\beta}}$ is unknown, with the weights proportional to the inverse of the precisions of respective estimates. The Bayes estimator of the individual coefficients, $\boldsymbol{\beta}_i$, "shrinks" the GLS estimator of $\boldsymbol{\beta}_i$ toward the grand mean $\bar{\boldsymbol{\beta}}$ or $\bar{\boldsymbol{\beta}}^*$. The reason for doing so stems from DeFinetti's (1964) exchangeability assumption. When there are not enough time-series observations to allow for precise estimation of individual $\boldsymbol{\beta}_i$ (namely, T is small), additional information about $\boldsymbol{\beta}_i$ may be obtained by

Table 6.1. *Long-haul regression coefficients*[a]

Route	Price coefficient, unconstrained	Mixed coefficients
1	−0.0712(−0.15)	−0.2875(N/A)
2	0.1694(0.44)	−0.0220(N/A)
3	−1.0142(−5.22)	−0.7743(N/A)
4	−0.4874(−2.29)	−0.1686(N/A)
5	−0.3190(−2.71)	−0.2925(N/A)
6	0.0365(0.20)	−0.0568(N/A)
7	−0.3996(−3.92)	−0.3881(N/A)
8	−0.1033(−0.95)	−0.2504(N/A)
9	−0.3965(−4.22)	−0.2821(N/A)
10	−0.6187(−4.82)	−0.5934(N/A)
Average	N/A	−0.3116
Route	Income coefficient	
1	1.4301(3.07)	0.4740(N/A)
2	−0.348(−0.09)	0.2679(N/A)
3	0.3698(1.95)	0.3394(N/A)
4	0.2497(0.70)	0.3145(N/A)
5	0.5556(2.71)	0.3501(N/A)
6	0.1119(0.95)	0.1344(N/A)
7	0.9197(8.10)	0.5342(N/A)
8	0.3886(3.88)	0.5255(N/A)
9	0.6688(6.16)	0.5648(N/A)
10	0.1928(2.39)	0.2574(N/A)
Average	N/A	0.3762

[a] t-statistics in parentheses.
Source: Hsiao, Appelbe, and Dineen (1993, Table 3).

examining the behavior of others because the expected response is assumed the same and the actual differences in response among individuals are the work of a chance mechanism.

Table 6.1 presents Canadian route-specific estimates of the demand for customer-dialed long-haul long-distance service (>920 miles) based on quarterly data from 1980 (I) to 1989 (IV) (Hsiao, Appelbe, and Dineen (1993)). Some of the point-to-point individual route estimates (unconstrained model) of the price and income coefficients have the wrong signs (Table 6.1, column 2) perhaps because of multicollinearity. However, if one invokes the representative-consumer argument by assuming that consumers respond in more or less the same way to price and income changes (thus considering the coefficients of these variables across routes as random draws from a common population with constant mean and variance–covariance matrix), but also allows route-specific effects to exist by assuming that the coefficients of the intercept and seasonal dummies are fixed and different for different routes, then all the estimated route-specific price and income coefficients have the correct signs (Table 6.1, column 3).

6.6.4 Random or Fixed Parameters

6.6.4.a An Example

When homogeneity is rejected by the data, whether to treat unobserved heterogeneity as fixed or random has paramount importance in panel data modeling. For instance, in a study of Ontario, Canada regional electricity demand, Hsiao et al. (1989) estimate a model of the form

$$y_{it} = \gamma_i y_{i,t-1} + \boldsymbol{\delta}_i'\mathbf{d}_{it} + \boldsymbol{\beta}_i'\mathbf{x}_{it} + u_{it}, \tag{6.6.24}$$

where y_{it} denotes the logarithm of monthly kilowatt-hour or kilowatt demand for region i at time t, $\mathbf{d}_{it}$ denotes 12 monthly dummies, and $\mathbf{x}_{it}$ denotes the climatic factor and the logarithm of income, own price, and price of its close substitutes, all measured in real terms. Four different specifications are considered:

1. The coefficients $\boldsymbol{\theta}_i' = (\gamma_i, \boldsymbol{\delta}_i', \boldsymbol{\beta}_i')$ are fixed and different for different regions.
2. The coefficients $\boldsymbol{\theta}_i = \boldsymbol{\theta}' = (\gamma, \boldsymbol{\delta}', \boldsymbol{\beta}')$ for all i.
3. The coefficients vectors $\boldsymbol{\theta}_i$ are randomly distributed with common mean $\boldsymbol{\theta}$ and covariance matrix Δ.
4. The coefficients $\boldsymbol{\beta}_i$ are randomly distributed with common mean $\bar{\boldsymbol{\beta}}$ and covariance matrix Δ_{11}, and the coefficients γ_i and $\boldsymbol{\delta}_i$ are fixed and different for different i.

Monthly data for Hamilton, Kitchener–Waterloo, London, Ottawa, St. Catherines, Sudbury, Thunder Bay, Toronto, and Windsor from January 1967 to December 1982 are used to estimate these four different specifications. Comparisons of the one-period-ahead root-mean-square prediction error

$$\sqrt{\sum_{t=T+1}^{T+f} (y_{it} - \hat{y}_{it})^2 / f}$$

from January 1983 to December 1986 are summarized in Tables 6.2 and 6.3. As one can see from these tables, the simple pooling (model 2) and random-coefficients (model 3) formulations on average yield less precise prediction for regional demand. The mixed fixed- and random-coefficient model (model 4) performs the best. It is interesting to note that combining information across regions together with a proper account of region-specific factors is capable of yielding better predictions for regional demand than the approach of simply using region-specific data (model 1).

Table 6.2. *Root-mean-square prediction error of log kilowatt-hours (one-period-ahead forecast)*

	Root Mean Square Error			
Municipality	Region-specific	Pooled	Random coefficients	Mixed
Hamilton	0.0865	0.0535	0.0825	0.0830
Kitchener–Waterloo	0.0406	0.0382	0.0409	0.0395
London	0.0466	0.0494	0.0467	0.0464
Ottawa	0.0697	0.0523	0.0669	0.0680
St. Catharines	0.0796	0.0724	0.0680	0.0802
Sudbury	0.0454	0.0857	0.0454	0.0460
Thunder Bay	0.0468	0.0615	0.0477	0.0473
Toronto	0.0362	0.0497	0.0631	0.0359
Windsor	0.0506	0.0650	0.0501	0.0438
Unweighted average	0.0558	0.0586	0.0568	0.0545
Weighted average[a]	0.0499	0.0525	0.0628	0.0487

[a]The weight is kilowatt-hours of demand in the municipality in June 1985.
Source: Hsiao et al. (1989, p. 584).

6.6.4.b Model Selection

The above example demonstrates that the way in which individual heterogeneity is taken into account makes a difference in the accuracy of inference. The various estimation methods discussed so far presuppose that we know which coefficients

Table 6.3. *Root-mean-square prediction error of log kilowatts (one-period-ahead forecast)*

	Root Mean Square Error			
Municipality	Regional specific	Pooled	Random coefficients	Mixed
Hamilton	0.0783	0.0474	0.0893	0.0768
Kitchener–Waterloo	0.0873	0.0440	0.0843	0.0803
London	0.0588	0.0747	0.0639	0.0586
Ottawa	0.0824	0.0648	0.0846	0.0768
St. Catharines	0.0531	0.0547	0.0511	0.0534
Sudbury	0.0607	0.0943	0.0608	0.0614
Thunder Bay	0.0524	0.0597	0.0521	0.0530
Toronto	0.0429	0.0628	0.0609	0.0421
Windsor	0.0550	0.0868	0.0595	0.0543
Unweighted average	0.0634	0.0655	0.0674	0.0619
Weighted average[a]	0.0558	0.0623	0.0673	0.0540

[a]The weight is kilowatt-hours of demand in the municipality in June 1985.
Source: Hsiao et al. (1989, p. 584).

should be treated as fixed (and different) and which coefficients should be treated as random. In practice, we have very little prior information for selecting the appropriate specifications. Various statistical tests have been suggested to select an appropriate formulation (e.g., Breusch and Pagan (1979); Hausman (1978); or Section 6.2.2.d). However, all these tests essentially exploit the implications of a certain formulation in a specific framework. They are indirect in nature. The distribution of a test statistic is derived under a specific null, but the alternative is composite. The rejection of a null does not automatically imply the acceptance of a specific alternative. It would appear more appropriate to treat the fixed-coefficient, random-coefficient, or various forms of mixed fixed- and random-coefficient models as different models and use model selection criteria to select an appropriate specification (Hsiao and Sun (2000)). For instance, one can use a well-known model selection criterion such as Akaike's (1973) information criterion, or Schwarz's (1978) Bayesian information criterion that selects the model H_j among $j = 1, \ldots, J$ different specifications if it yields the smallest value of

$$-2 \log f(\mathbf{y} \mid H_j) + 2m_j, \qquad j = 1, \ldots, J, \tag{6.6.25}$$

or

$$-2 \log f(\mathbf{y} \mid H_j) + m_j \log NT, \qquad j = 1, \ldots, J, \tag{6.6.26}$$

where $\log f(\mathbf{y} \mid H_j)$ and m_j denote the log likelihood values of $\mathbf{y}$ and the number of unknown parameters of the model H_j. Alternatively, Hsiao (1995) and Min and Zellner (1993) suggest selecting the model that yields the highest predictive density. In this framework, time-series observations are divided into two periods: 1 to T_1, denoted by $\mathbf{y}^1$, and $T_1 + 1$ to T, denoted by $\mathbf{y}^2$. The first T_1 observations are used to obtain the probability distribution $P(\boldsymbol{\theta}^j \mid \mathbf{y}^1)$ of the parameters $\boldsymbol{\theta}^j$ associated with H_j. The predictive density is then evaluated as

$$\int f(\mathbf{y}^2 \mid \boldsymbol{\theta}^j) p(\boldsymbol{\theta}^j \mid \mathbf{y}^1)\, d\boldsymbol{\theta}^j, \tag{6.6.27}$$

where $f(\mathbf{y}^2 \mid \boldsymbol{\theta}^j)$ is the density of $\mathbf{y}^2$ conditional on $\boldsymbol{\theta}^j$. Given the sensitivity of the Bayesian approach to the choice of prior, the advantage of using (6.6.27) is that the choice of a model does not have to depend on the prior. One can use the noninformative (or diffuse) prior to derive $P(\boldsymbol{\theta}^j \mid \mathbf{y}^1)$. It is also consistent with the theme that "a severe test for an economic theory, the only test and the ultimate test is its ability to predict" (Klein (1988, p. 21); see also Friedman (1953)).

When $\mathbf{y}^2$ only contains a limited number of observations, the choice of model in terms of predictive density may become heavily sample-dependent. If too many observations are put in $\mathbf{y}^2$, then a lot of sample information is not utilized to estimate unknown parameters. One compromise is to modify (6.6.27) by recursively updating the estimates,

$$\int f(\mathbf{y}_T \mid \boldsymbol{\theta}^j, \mathbf{y}^{T-1}) P(\boldsymbol{\theta}^j \mid \mathbf{y}^{T-1})\, d\boldsymbol{\theta}^j \times \int f(\mathbf{y}_{T-1} \mid \boldsymbol{\theta}^j, \mathbf{y}^{T-2}) P(\boldsymbol{\theta}^j \mid \mathbf{y}^{T-2})\, d\boldsymbol{\theta}^j \cdots \times \int f(\mathbf{y}_{T_1+1} \mid \boldsymbol{\theta}^j, \mathbf{y}^{1}) P(\boldsymbol{\theta}^j \mid \mathbf{y}^{1})\, d\boldsymbol{\theta}^j, \tag{6.6.28}$$

where $P(\boldsymbol{\theta}^j \mid y^T)$ denotes the posterior distribution of $\boldsymbol{\theta}$ given observations from 1 to T. While the formula may look formidable, it turns out that the Bayes updating formula is fairly straightforward to compute. For instance, consider the model (6.6.5). Let $\boldsymbol{\theta} = (\boldsymbol{\beta}, \bar{\boldsymbol{\gamma}})$, $\boldsymbol{\theta}_t$, and V_t denote the posterior mean and variance of $\boldsymbol{\theta}$ based on the first t observations. Then

$$\boldsymbol{\theta}_t = V_{t-1}\left(Q_t'\Omega^{-1}\mathbf{y}_t + V_{t-1}^{-1}\boldsymbol{\theta}_{t-1}\right), \tag{6.6.29}$$

$$V_t = \left(Q_t'\Omega^{-1}Q_t + V_{t-1}^{-1}\right)^{-1}, \qquad t = T_1 + 1, \ldots, T, \tag{6.6.30}$$

and

$$P(\mathbf{y}_{t+1} \mid \mathbf{y}^t) = \int P(\mathbf{y}_{t+1} \mid \boldsymbol{\theta}, \mathbf{y}^t) P(\boldsymbol{\theta} \mid \mathbf{y}^t)\, d\boldsymbol{\theta} \sim N(Q_{t+1}\boldsymbol{\theta}_t, \Omega + Q_{t+1}V_tQ_{t+1}'), \tag{6.6.31}$$

where $\mathbf{y}_t' = (y_{1t}, y_{2t}, \ldots, y_{Nt})$, $Q_t = (\mathbf{x}_t', \mathbf{w}_t')$, $\mathbf{x}_t = (\mathbf{x}_{1t}, \ldots, \mathbf{x}_{Nt})$, $\mathbf{w}_t = (\mathbf{w}_{1t}, \ldots, \mathbf{w}_{Nt})$, $\Omega = E\mathbf{u}_t\mathbf{u}_t'$, and $\mathbf{u}_t' = (u_{1t}, \ldots, u_{Nt})$ (Hsiao, Appelbe, and Dineen (1993)).

Hsiao and Sun (2000) have conducted limited Monte Carlo studies to evaluate the performance of these model selection criteria in selecting the random-, fixed-, and mixed random–fixed-coefficient specification. They all appear to have very good performance in selecting the correct specification.

6.7 DYNAMIC RANDOM-COEFFICIENT MODELS

For ease of exposition and without loss of the essentials, instead of considering generalizing (6.6.5) to the dynamic model, in this section we consider the generalization of the random-coefficient model (6.2.1) to the dynamic model of the form[17]

$$y_{it} = \gamma_i y_{i,t-1} + \beta_i'\mathbf{x}_{it} + u_{it}, \qquad |\gamma_i| < 1, \quad i = 1, \ldots, N, \quad t = 1, \ldots, T, \tag{6.7.1}$$

where $\mathbf{x}_{it}$ is a $k \times 1$ vector of exogenous variables, and the error term u_{it} is assumed to be independently, identically distributed over t with mean zero and variance $\sigma_{u_i}^2$ and is independent across i. The coefficients $\boldsymbol{\theta}_i = (\gamma_i, \boldsymbol{\beta}_i')'$ are assumed to be independently distributed across i with mean $\bar{\boldsymbol{\theta}} = (\bar{\gamma}, \bar{\boldsymbol{\beta}}')'$ and covariance matrix Δ. Let

$$\boldsymbol{\theta}_i = \bar{\boldsymbol{\theta}} + \boldsymbol{\alpha}_i, \tag{6.7.2}$$

where $\boldsymbol{\alpha}_i = (\alpha_{i1}, \boldsymbol{\alpha}'_{i2})$. We have

$$E\boldsymbol{\alpha}_i = \mathbf{0}, \qquad E\boldsymbol{\alpha}_i\boldsymbol{\alpha}'_j = \begin{cases} \Delta & \text{if } i = j, \\ \mathbf{0} & \text{otherwise,} \end{cases} \tag{6.7.3}$$

and[18]

$$E\boldsymbol{\alpha}_i\mathbf{x}'_{jt} = \mathbf{0}. \tag{6.7.4}$$

Stacking the T time-series observations of the ith individuals in matrix form yields

$$\underset{T\times 1}{\mathbf{y}_i} = Q_i\boldsymbol{\theta}_i + \mathbf{u}_i, \qquad i = 1, \ldots, N, \tag{6.7.5}$$

where $\mathbf{y}_i = (y_{i1}, \ldots, y_{it})'$, $Q_i = (\mathbf{y}_{i,-1}, X_i)$, $\mathbf{y}_{i,-1} = (y_{i0}, \ldots, y_{i,T-1})'$, $X_i = (\mathbf{x}_{i1}, \ldots, \mathbf{x}_{it})'$, $\mathbf{u}_i = (u_{i1}, \ldots, u_{it})'$, and for ease of exposition we assume that y_{i0} are observable.[19]

We note that because $y_{i,t-1}$ depends on γ_i, we have $EQ_i\boldsymbol{\alpha}'_i \neq \mathbf{0}$, i.e., the independence between the explanatory variables and $\boldsymbol{\alpha}_i$ (equation (6.2.3)) is violated. Substituting $\boldsymbol{\theta}_i = \bar{\boldsymbol{\theta}} + \boldsymbol{\alpha}_i$ into (6.7.5) yields

$$\mathbf{y}_i = Q_i\bar{\boldsymbol{\theta}} + \mathbf{v}_i, \qquad i = 1, \ldots, N, \tag{6.7.6}$$

where

$$\mathbf{v}_i = Q_i\boldsymbol{\alpha}_i + \mathbf{u}_i. \tag{6.7.7}$$

Since

$$y_{i,t-1} = \sum_{j=0}^{\infty}(\bar{\gamma} + \alpha_{i1})^j\mathbf{x}'_{i,t-j-1}(\bar{\boldsymbol{\beta}} + \boldsymbol{\alpha}_{i2}) + \sum_{j=0}^{\infty}(\bar{\gamma} + \alpha_{i1})^j u_{i,t-j-1}, \tag{6.7.8}$$

it follows that $E(\mathbf{v}_i \mid Q_i) \neq \mathbf{0}$. Therefore, contrary to the static case, the least-squares estimator of the common mean, $\bar{\boldsymbol{\theta}}$, is inconsistent.

Equations (6.7.7) and (6.7.8) also demonstrate that the covariance matrix V of $\mathbf{v}_i$ is not easily derivable. Thus, the procedure of premultiplying (6.7.6) by $V^{-1/2}$ to transform the model into one with serially uncorrelated error is not implementable. Neither does the instrumental-variable method appear implementable, because the instruments that are uncorrelated with $\mathbf{v}_i$ are most likely uncorrelated with Q_i as well.

Pesaran and Smith (1995) have noted that as $T \to \infty$, the least-squares regression of $\mathbf{y}_i$ on Q_i yields a consistent estimator $\hat{\boldsymbol{\theta}}_i$ of $\boldsymbol{\theta}_i$. They suggest finding a mean group estimator of $\bar{\boldsymbol{\theta}}$ by taking the average of $\hat{\boldsymbol{\theta}}_i$ across i,

$$\hat{\bar{\boldsymbol{\theta}}} = \frac{1}{N}\sum_{i=1}^{N}\hat{\boldsymbol{\theta}}_i. \tag{6.7.9}$$

The mean group estimator (6.7.9) is consistent and asymptotically normally distributed so long as $\sqrt{N}/T \to 0$ as both N and $T \to \infty$ (Hsiao, Pesaran, and Tahmiscioglu (1999)).

Panels with large T are the exception in economics. Nevertheless, under the assumption that y_{i0} are fixed and known and $\boldsymbol{\alpha}_i$ and u_{it} are independently normally distributed, we can implement the Bayes estimator of $\bar{\boldsymbol{\theta}}$ conditional on σ_i^2 and Δ using the formula (6.6.19), just as in the mixed-model case discussed in Section 6.6. The Bayes estimator condition on Δ and σ_i^2 is equal to

$$\hat{\bar{\boldsymbol{\theta}}}_B = \left\{ \sum_{i=1}^{N} \left[\sigma_i^2 (Q_i' Q_i)^{-1} + \Delta \right]^{-1} \right\}^{-1} \sum_{i=1}^{N} \left[\sigma_i^2 (Q_i' Q_i)^{-1} + \Delta \right]^{-1} \hat{\boldsymbol{\theta}}_i, \tag{6.7.10}$$

which is a weighted average of the least-squares estimator of individual units with the weights being inversely proportional to individual variances. When $T \to \infty$, $N \to \infty$, and $\sqrt{N}/T^{3/2} \to 0$, the Bayes estimator is asymptotically equivalent to the mean group estimator (6.7.9) (Hsiao, Pesaran, and Tahmiscioglu (1999)).

In practice, the variance components, σ_i^2 and Δ, are rarely known, so the Bayes estimator (6.7.10) is rarely calculable. One approach is to substitute the consistently estimated σ_i^2 and Δ, say (6.2.8) and (6.2.9), into the formula (6.7.10), and treat them as if they were known. For ease of reference, we shall call (6.7.10) with known σ_i^2 and Δ the *infeasible* Bayes estimator. We shall call the estimator obtained by replacing σ_i^2 and Δ in (6.7.10) with their consistent estimates, say (6.2.8) and (6.2.9), the *empirical* Bayes estimator.

The other approach is to follow Lindley and Smith (1972) and assume that the prior distributions of σ_i^2 and Δ are independent and are distributed as

$$P\left(\Delta^{-1}, \sigma_1^2, \ldots, \sigma_N^2\right) = W(\Delta^{-1} \mid (\rho R)^{-1}, \rho) \prod_{i=1}^{N} \sigma_i^{-1}, \tag{6.7.11}$$

where W represents the Wishart distribution with scale matrix (ρR) and degrees of freedom ρ (e.g., Anderson (1958)). Incorporating this prior into the model (6.7.1)–(6.7.2), we can obtain the marginal posterior densities of the parameters of interest by integrating out σ_i^2 and Δ from the joint posterior density. However, the required integrations do not yield closed-form solutions. Hsiao, Pesaran, and Tahmiscioglu (1999) have suggested using Gibbs sampler to calculate marginal densities.

The Gibbs sampler is an iterative Markov-chain Monte Carlo method which only requires the knowledge of the full conditional densities of the parameter vector (e.g., Gelfand and Smith (1990)). Starting from some arbitrary initial values, say $(\boldsymbol{\theta}_1^{(0)}, \boldsymbol{\theta}_2^{(0)}, \ldots, \boldsymbol{\theta}_k^{(0)})$, for a parameter vector $\boldsymbol{\theta} = (\boldsymbol{\theta}_1, \ldots, \boldsymbol{\theta}_k)$, it samples alternatively from the conditional density of each component of the parameter vector, conditional on the values of other components sampled in the latest iteration. That is:

1. sample $\boldsymbol{\theta}_1^{(j+1)}$ from $P(\boldsymbol{\theta}_1 \mid \boldsymbol{\theta}_2^{(j)}, \boldsymbol{\theta}_3^{(j)}, \ldots, \boldsymbol{\theta}_k^{(j)}, \mathbf{y})$,
2. sample $\boldsymbol{\theta}_2^{(j+1)}$ from $P(\boldsymbol{\theta}_2 \mid \boldsymbol{\theta}_1^{(j+1)}, \boldsymbol{\theta}_3^{(j)}, \ldots, \boldsymbol{\theta}_k^{(j)}, \mathbf{y})$,

   $\vdots$

k. sample $\boldsymbol{\theta}_k^{(j+1)}$ from $P(\boldsymbol{\theta}_k \mid \boldsymbol{\theta}_1^{(j+1)}, \ldots, \boldsymbol{\theta}_{k-1}^{(j+1)}, \mathbf{y})$.

The vectors $\boldsymbol{\theta}^{(0)}, \boldsymbol{\theta}^{(1)}, \ldots, \boldsymbol{\theta}^{(k)}$ forms a Markov chain with the transition probability from stage $\boldsymbol{\theta}^{(j)}$ to the next stage $\boldsymbol{\theta}^{(j+1)}$ given by

$$K\left(\boldsymbol{\theta}^{(j)}, \boldsymbol{\theta}^{(j+1)}\right) = P\left(\boldsymbol{\theta}_1 \mid \boldsymbol{\theta}_2^{(j)}, \ldots, \boldsymbol{\theta}_k^{(j)}, \mathbf{y}\right) P\left(\boldsymbol{\theta}_2 \mid \boldsymbol{\theta}_1^{(j+1)}, \boldsymbol{\theta}_3^{(j)}, \ldots, \boldsymbol{\theta}_k^{(j)}, \mathbf{y}\right) \times \cdots \times P\left(\boldsymbol{\theta}_k \mid \boldsymbol{\theta}_1^{(j+1)}, \ldots, \boldsymbol{\theta}_{k-1}^{(j+1)}, \mathbf{y}\right).$$

As the number of iterations j approaches infinity, the sampled values in effect can be regarded as drawing from true joint and marginal posterior densities. Moreover, the ergodic averages of functions of the sample values will be consistent estimates of their expected values.

Under the assumption that the prior of $\bar{\boldsymbol{\theta}}$ is $N(\bar{\boldsymbol{\theta}}^*, \Psi)$, the relevant conditional distributions that are needed to implement the Gibbs sampler for (6.7.1)–(6.7.2) are easily obtained from

$$P\left(\boldsymbol{\theta}_i \mid \mathbf{y}, \bar{\boldsymbol{\theta}}, \Delta^{-1}, \sigma_1^2, \ldots, \sigma_N^2\right) \sim N\left\{A_i\left(\sigma_i^{-2} Q_i' \mathbf{y}_i + \Delta^{-1}\bar{\boldsymbol{\theta}}\right), A_i\right\}, \quad i = 1, \ldots, N,$$

$$P\left(\bar{\boldsymbol{\theta}} \mid \mathbf{y}, \boldsymbol{\theta}_1, \ldots, \boldsymbol{\theta}_N, \Delta^{-1}, \sigma_1^2, \ldots, \sigma_N^2\right) \sim N\{D(N\Delta^{-1}\hat{\bar{\boldsymbol{\theta}}} + \Psi^{-1}\boldsymbol{\theta}^*), B\},$$

$$P\left(\Delta^{-1} \mid \mathbf{y}, \boldsymbol{\theta}_1, \ldots, \boldsymbol{\theta}_N, \bar{\boldsymbol{\theta}}, \sigma_1^2, \ldots, \sigma_N^2\right) \sim W\left[\left(\sum_{i=1}^N (\boldsymbol{\theta}_i - \bar{\boldsymbol{\theta}}) \times (\boldsymbol{\theta}_i - \bar{\boldsymbol{\theta}})' + \rho R\right)^{-1}, \rho + N\right],$$

$$P\left(\sigma_i^2 \mid \mathbf{y}_i, \boldsymbol{\theta}_1, \ldots, \boldsymbol{\theta}_N, \bar{\boldsymbol{\theta}}, \Delta^{-1}\right) \sim \mathrm{IG}[T/2, (\mathbf{y}_i - Q_i\boldsymbol{\theta}_i)'(\mathbf{y}_i - Q_i\boldsymbol{\theta}_i)/2], \quad i = 1, \ldots, N,$$

where $A_i = (\sigma_i^{-2} Q_i' Q_i + \Delta^{-1})^{-1}$, $D = (N\Delta^{-1} + \Psi^{-1})^{-1}$, $\hat{\bar{\boldsymbol{\theta}}} = \frac{1}{N}\sum_{i=1}^N \boldsymbol{\theta}_i$, and IG denotes the inverse gamma distribution.

Hsiao, Pesaran, and Tahmiscioglu (1999) have conducted Monte Carlo experiments to study the finite-sample properties of (6.7.10), referred to as the infeasible Bayes estimator; the Bayes estimator using (6.7.11) as prior for Δ and σ_i^2 obtained through the Gibbs sampler, referred to as the hierarchical Bayes estimator; the empirical Bayes estimator; the group-mean estimator (6.7.8); the bias-corrected group-mean estimator obtained by directly correcting the finite-T bias of the least-squares estimator $\hat{\boldsymbol{\theta}}_i$, using the formula of Kiviet (1995) and Kiviet and Phillips (1993), then taking the average; and the pooled least-squares estimator. Table 6.4 presents the bias of the different estimators of $\bar{\gamma}$ for $N = 50$

Table 6.4. *Bias of the short-run coefficient $\bar{\gamma}$*

			Bias					
T		$\bar{\gamma}$	Pooled OLS	Mean group	Bias-corrected mean group	Infeasible Bayes	Empirical Bayes	Hierarchical Bayes
5	1	0.3	0.36859	−0.23613	−0.14068	0.05120	−0.12054	−0.02500
	2	0.3	0.41116	−0.23564	−0.14007	0.04740	−0.11151	−0.01500
	3	0.6	1.28029	−0.17924	−0.10969	0.05751	−0.02874	0.02884
	4	0.6	1.29490	−0.18339	−0.10830	0.06879	−0.00704	0.06465
	5	0.3	0.06347	−0.26087	−0.15550	0.01016	−0.18724	−0.10068
	6	0.3	0.08352	−0.26039	−0.15486	0.01141	−0.18073	−0.09544
	7	0.6	0.54756	−0.28781	−0.17283	0.05441	−0.12731	−0.02997
	8	0.6	0.57606	−0.28198	−0.16935	0.06258	−0.10366	−0.01012
20	9	0.3	0.44268	−0.07174	−0.01365	0.00340	−0.00238	0.00621
	10	0.3	0.49006	−0.06910	−0.01230	0.00498	−0.00106	0.00694
	11	0.35	0.25755	−0.06847	−0.01209	−0.00172	−0.01004	−0.00011
	12	0.35	0.25869	−0.06644	−0.01189	−0.00229	−0.00842	0.00116
	13	0.3	0.07199	−0.07966	−0.01508	−0.00054	−0.01637	−0.00494
	14	0.3	0.09342	−0.07659	−0.01282	0.00244	−0.01262	−0.00107
	15	0.55	0.26997	−0.09700	−0.02224	−0.00062	−0.01630	0.00011
	16	0.55	0.29863	−0.09448	−0.02174	−0.00053	−0.01352	0.00198

Source: Hsiao, Pesaran, and Tahmiscioglu (1999).

and $T = 5$ or 20. The infeasible Bayes estimator performs very well. It has small bias even for $T = 5$. For $T = 5$, its bias falls within the range of 3 to 17 percent. For $T = 20$, the bias is at most about 2 percent. The hierarchical Bayes estimator also performs well,[20] followed by the empirical Bayes estimator when T is small; but the latter improves quickly as T increases. The empirical Bayes estimator gives very good results even for $T = 5$ in some cases, but the bias also appears to be quite large in certain other cases. As T gets larger its bias decreases considerably. The mean-group and the bias-corrected mean-group estimator both have large bias when T is small, with the bias-corrected estimator performing slightly better. However, the performance of both improves as T increases, and both are still much better than the least-squares estimator. The least-squares estimator yields significant bias, and its bias persists as T increases.

The Bayes estimator is derived under the assumption that the initial observations y_{i0} are fixed constants. As discussed in Chapter 4 or Anderson and Hsiao (1981, 1982), this assumption is clearly unjustifiable for a panel with finite T. However, contrary to the sampling approach, where the correct modeling of initial observations is quite important, Bayesian approach appears to perform fairly well in the estimation of the mean coefficients for dynamic random-coefficient models even the initial observations are treated as fixed constants. The Monte Carlo study also cautions against the practice of justifying the use of certain estimators on the basis of their asymptotic properties. Both the mean-group and the corrected mean-group estimator perform poorly in panels with very small T. The hierarchical Bayes estimator appears preferable to the other consistent estimators unless the time dimension of the panel is sufficiently large.

6.8 AN EXAMPLE – LIQUIDITY CONSTRAINTS AND FIRM INVESTMENT EXPENDITURE

The effects of financial constraints on company investment have been subject to intensive debate by economists. At one extreme, Jorgenson (1971) claims that "the evidence clearly favors the Modigliani–Miller theory [Modigliani and Miller (1958), Miller and Modigliani (1961)]. Internal liquidity is not an important determinant of the investment, given the level of output and external funds." At the other extreme, Stiglitz and Weiss (1981) argue that because of imperfections in the capital markets, costs of internal and external funds generally will diverge, and internal and external funds generally will not be perfect substitutes for each other. Fazzari, Hubbard, and Petersen (1988), Bond and Meghir (1994), etc. tested for the importance of internal finance by studying the effects of cash flow across different groups of companies – identified, e.g., according to company retention practices. If the null hypothesis of a perfect capital market is correct, then no difference should be found in the coefficient of the cash-flow variable across groups. However, these authors find that the cash-flow coefficient is large for companies with low dividend payout rates.

However, there is no sound theoretical basis for assuming that only low-dividend-payout companies are subject to financial constraints. The finding that larger companies have larger cash-flow coefficients is inconsistent with both the transaction-costs and asymmetric-information explanations of liquidity constraints. Whether firm heterogeneity can be captured by grouping firms according to some indicators remains open to question.

Hsiao and Tahmiscioglu (1997) use COMPUSTAT annual industrial files of 561 firms in the manufacturing sector for the period 1971–1992 to estimate the following five different investment expenditure models with and without using liquidity models:

$$\left(\frac{I}{K}\right)_{it} = \alpha_i^* + \gamma_i \left(\frac{I}{K}\right)_{i,t-1} + \beta_{i1} \left(\frac{\text{LIQ}}{K}\right)_{i,t-1} + \epsilon_{it}, \tag{6.8.1}$$

$$\left(\frac{I}{K}\right)_{it} = \alpha_i^* + \gamma_i \left(\frac{I}{K}\right)_{i,t-1} + \beta_{i1} \left(\frac{\text{LIQ}}{K}\right)_{i,t-1} + \beta_{i2} q_{it} + \epsilon_{it}, \tag{6.8.2}$$

$$\left(\frac{I}{K}\right)_{it} = \alpha_i^* + \gamma_i \left(\frac{I}{K}\right)_{i,t-1} + \beta_{i1} \left(\frac{\text{LIQ}}{K}\right)_{i,t-1} + \beta_{i2} \left(\frac{S}{K}\right)_{i,t-1} + \epsilon_{it}, \tag{6.8.3}$$

$$\left(\frac{I}{K}\right)_{it} = \alpha_i^* + \gamma_i \left(\frac{I}{K}\right)_{i,t-1} + \beta_{i2} q_{it} + \epsilon_{it}, \tag{6.8.4}$$

$$\left(\frac{I}{K}\right)_{it} = \alpha_i^* + \gamma_i \left(\frac{I}{K}\right)_{i,t-1} + \beta_{i2} \left(\frac{S}{K}\right)_{i,t-1} + \epsilon_{it}. \tag{6.8.5}$$

where I_{it} is firm i's capital investment at time t; LIQ_{it} is a liquidity variable (defined as cash flow minus dividends); S_{it} is sales, q_{it} is Tobin's q (Brainard and Tobin (1968), Tobin (1969)), defined as the ratio of the market value of the firm to the replacement value of capital; and K_{it} is the beginning-of-period capital stock. The coefficient β_{i1} measures the short-run effect of the liquidity variable on firm i's investment in each of these three specifications. Models 4 and 5 ((6.8.4) and (6.8.5)) are two popular variants of investment equations that do not use the liquidity variable as an explanatory variable – the Tobin q model (e.g., Hayashi (1982), Summers (1981)) and the sales capacity model (e.g., Kuh (1963)). The sales variable can be regarded as a proxy for future demand for the firm's output. The q theory relates investment to marginal q, which is defined as the ratio of the market value of new investment goods to their replacement cost. If a firm has unexploited profit opportunities, then an increase of its capital stock of \$1 will increase its market value by more than \$1. Therefore, firm managers can be expected to increase investment until marginal q equals 1. Thus, investment will be an increasing function of marginal q. Because marginal q is unobservable, it is common in empirical work to replace it with the average or Tobin's q.

Tables 6.5 and 6.6 present some summary information from the firm-by-firm regressions of these five models. Table 6.5 shows the percentage of significant coefficients at the 5 percent significance level for a one-tailed test. Table 6.6 shows the first and third quartiles of the estimated coefficients. The estimated

Table 6.5. *Individual firm regressions (percentage of firms with significant coefficients)*

	Percentage of firms				
	Model 1	2	3	4	5
Coefficient for:					
$(\text{LIQ}/K)_{t-1}$	46	36	31		
q		31		38	
$(S/K)_{t-1}$			27		44
Percentage of firms with significant autocorrelation	14	12	13	20	15
Actual F	2.47	2.98	2.01	2.66	2.11
Critical F	1.08	1.08	1.08	1.06	1.06

Note: The number of firms is 561. The significance level is 5 percent for a one-tailed test. Actual F is the F statistic for testing the equality of slope coefficients across firms. For the F test, the 5 percent significance level is chosen. To detect serial correlation, Durbin's t-test at the 5 percent significance level is used.
Source: Hsiao and Tahmiscioglu (1997, Table 1).

coefficients vary widely from firm to firm. The F test of slope homogeneity across firms while allowing for firm-specific intercepts is also rejected (see Table 6.5).

The approach of relating the variation of β_{i1} to firm characteristics such as dividend payout rate, company size, sales growth, capital intensity, standard deviation of retained earnings, debt–equity ratio, measures of liquidity stocks from the balance sheet, number of shareholders, and industry dummies is unsuccessful. These variables as a whole do not explain the variation of estimated $\boldsymbol{\beta}_{i1}$ well. The maximum $\bar{R}^2$ is only 0.113. Many of the estimated coefficients are not significant under various specifications. Neither can one substitute functions of the form (6.5.2) into (6.8.1)–(6.8.5) and estimate the coefficients directly, because of perfect multicollinearity. So Hsiao and Tahmiscioglu (1997) classify

Table 6.6. *Coefficient heterogeneity: slope estimates at first and third quartiles across a sample of 561 firms*

	Slope estimates			
Model	$(I/K)_{i,t-1}$	$(\text{LIQ}/K)_{i,t-1}$	q_{it}	$(S/K)_{i,t-1}$
1	.026, .405	.127, .529		
2	−.028, .359	.062, .464	0, .039	
3	.100, .295	.020, .488		−.005, .057
4	.110, .459		.007, .048	
5	−.935, .367			.012, .077

Source: Hsiao and Tahmiscioglu (1997, Table 2).

Table 6.7. *Variable intercept estimation of models for less- and more-capital-intensive firms*

	Variable intercept estimate					
Variable	Less-capital-intensive firms			More-capital-intensive firms		
$(I/K)_{i,t-1}$	.265	.198	.248	.392	.363	.364
	(.011)	(.012)	(.011)	(.022)	(.023)	(.022)
$(\text{LIQ}/K)_{i,t-1}$	.161	.110	.119	.308	.253	.278
	(.007)	(.007)	(.007)	(.024)	(.027)	(.025)
$(S/K)_{i,t-1}$		.023			.025	
		(.001)			(.006)	
q_{it}			.011			.009
			(.0006)			(.002)
Actual F	2.04	1.84	2.22	2.50	2.19	2.10
Critical F	1.09	1.07	1.07	1.20	1.17	1.17
Numerator d.f.	834	1,251	1,251	170	255	255
Denominator d.f.	6,592	6,174	6,174	1,368	1,282	1,282
Number of firms	418	418	418	86	86	86

Note: The dependent variable is $(I/K)_{it}$. Less-capital-intensive firms are those with minimum (K/S) between 0.15 and 0.55 over the sample period. For more-capital-intensive firms, the minimum (K/S) is greater than 0.55. The regressions include company-specific intercepts. Actual F is the F statistic for testing the homogeneity of slope coefficients. For the F test, a 5 percent significance level is chosen. The estimation period is 1974–1992. Standard errors are in parentheses.
Source: Hsiao and Tahmiscioglu (1997, Table 5).

firms into reasonably homogeneous groups using the capital intensity ratio of 0.55 as a cutoff point. Capital intensity is defined as the minimum value of the ratio of capital stock to sales over the sample period. It is the most statistically significant and most stable variable under different specifications.

Table 6.7 presents the variable intercept estimates for the groups of less- and more-capital-intensive firms. The liquidity variable is highly significant in all three variants of the liquidity model. There are also significant differences in the coefficients of the liquidity variable across the two groups. However, Table 6.7 also shows that the null hypothesis of the equality of slope coefficients conditioning on the firm-specific effects is strongly rejected for all specifications for both groups. In other words, using the capital intensity ratio of 0.55 as a cutoff point, there is still substantial heterogeneity within the groups.

Since neither does there appear to be a set of explanatory variables that adequately explains the variation of β_{i1}, nor can homogeneity be achieved by classifying firms into groups, one is left with either treating $\boldsymbol{\beta}_i$ as fixed and different or treating $\boldsymbol{\beta}_i$ as random draws from a common distribution. Within the random-effects framework, individual differences are viewed as random draws from a population with constant mean and variance. Therefore, it is appropriate to pool the data and try to draw some generalization about the population. On the other hand, if individual differences reflect fundamental heterogeneity or if individual response coefficients depend on the values of

Table 6.8. *Estimation of mixed fixed- and random-coefficient models for less- and more-capital-intensive firms*

Variable	Estimate					
	Less-capital-intensive firms			More-capital-intensive firms		
$(I/K)_{i,t-1}$	.230 (.018)	.183 (.017)	.121 (.019)	.321 (.036)	.302 (.037)	.236 (.041)
$(\mathrm{LIQ}/K)_{i,t-1}$	.306 (.021)	.252 (.023)	.239 (.027)	.488 (.065)	.449 (.067)	.416 (.079)
$(S/K)_{i,t-1}$		.024 (.003)			.038 (.015)	
q_{it}		.019 (.003)			.022 (.008)	
Number of firms	418	418	418	86	86	86

Note: The dependent variable is $(I/K)_{it}$. The regressions include fixed firm-specific effects. The estimation period is 1974–1992. Standard errors are in parentheses.
Source: Hsiao and Tahmiscioglu (1997, Table 7).

the included explanatory variables, estimation of the model parameters based on the conventional random-effects formulation can be misleading. To avoid this bias, heterogeneity among individuals must be treated as fixed. In other words, one must investigate investment behavior firm by firm, and there is no advantage in pooling. Without pooling, the shortage of degrees of freedom and multicollinearity can render the resulting estimates meaningless and make drawing general conclusions difficult.

Table 6.8 presents the estimates of the mixed fixed- and random-coefficient model of the form (6.6.24) by assuming that, conditional on company-specific effects, the remaining slope coefficients are randomly distributed around a certain mean within the less- and the more-capital-intensive groups. To evaluate the appropriateness of these specifications, Table 6.9 presents the comparison of the recursive predictive density of the mixed fixed- and random-coefficients model and the fixed-coefficient model, assuming that each company has different coefficients for the three variants of the liquidity model, by dividing the sample into pre- and post-1989 periods. The numbers reported in the table are the logarithms of (6.6.28). The results indicate that the mixed fixed- and random-coefficient model is favored over the fixed-coefficient model for both groups. Similar comparison between the liquidity model, Tobin's q, and sales accelerator models also favor liquidity as an important explanatory variable.

Table 6.8 shows that the estimated liquidity coefficients are highly significant and there are significant differences between different classes of companies. The mean coefficient of the liquidity variable turns out to be 60–80 percent larger for the more-capital-intensive group than for the less-capital-intensive group. The implied long-run relationships between the liquidity variable and the fixed investment variable are also statistically significant. For instance,

Table 6.9. *Prediction comparison of fixed-coefficient and mixed fixed- and random-coefficient models for Less- and more-capital-intensive firms (recursive predictive density)*

Sample	Model	Liquidity	Liquidity with q	Liquidity with sales
Less-capital-intensive firms	Fixed-slope coefficients	2,244	2,178	2,172
	Random-slope coefficients	2,299	2,272	2,266
More-capital-intensive firms	Fixed-slope coefficients	587	544	557
	Random-slope coefficients	589	556	576

Note: The recursive predictive density is the logarithm of (6.6.28). Columns 3, 4, and 5 correspond to models 1, 2 and 3. The fixed-coefficient model assumes different coefficients for each firm. The random-coefficient model assumes randomly distributed slope coefficients with constant mean conditional on fixed firm-specific effects. The prediction period is 1990–1992.
Source: Hsiao and Tahmiscioglu (1997, Table 6).

for model (6.8.1), a 10 percent increase in liquidity capital ratio leads to a 4 percent increase in fixed investment capital ratio in the long run for the less-capital-intensive group, compared to a 7 percent increase in the ratio for the more-capital-intensive group. The mixed model also yields substantially larger coefficient estimates of the liquidity variable than those obtained from the variable-intercept model. If the coefficients are indeed randomly distributed and the explanatory variables are positively autocorrelated, the downward bias is precisely what one would expect from the within-group estimates (Pesaran and Smith (1995)).

In short, there are substantial differences in investment behavior across firms. When these differences are ignored by constraining the parameters to be identical across firms, the effect of liquidity variable on firm investment is seriously underestimated. The mixed fixed- and random-coefficient model appears to fit the data well. The mixed model allows pooling and allows some general conclusions to be drawn about a group of firms. The estimation results and prediction tests appear to show that financial constraints are the most important factor affecting actual investment expenditure, at least for a subset U.S. manufacturing companies.

APPENDIX 6A: COMBINATION OF TWO NORMAL DISTRIBUTIONS

Suppose that, conditional on X, $\boldsymbol{\beta}$, we have $\mathbf{y} \sim N(X\boldsymbol{\beta}, \Omega)$ and $\boldsymbol{\beta} \sim N(A\bar{\boldsymbol{\beta}}, C)$. Then the posterior of $\boldsymbol{\beta}$ and $\bar{\boldsymbol{\beta}}$ given $\mathbf{y}$ is

$$
\begin{aligned}
&P(\boldsymbol{\beta}, \bar{\boldsymbol{\beta}} \mid \mathbf{y}) \\
&\quad \propto \exp -\frac{1}{2}\{(\mathbf{y} - X\boldsymbol{\beta})'\Omega^{-1}(\mathbf{y} - X\boldsymbol{\beta}) \\
&\qquad\qquad + (\boldsymbol{\beta} - A\bar{\boldsymbol{\beta}})'C^{-1}(\boldsymbol{\beta} - A\bar{\boldsymbol{\beta}})\},
\end{aligned}
\tag{6A.1}
$$

where $\propto$ denotes proportionality. Using the identities (e.g., Rao (1973, p. 33)

$$(D+BFB')^{-1}=D^{-1}-D^{-1}B(B'D^{-1}B+F^{-1})^{-1}B'D^{-1}, \quad (6A.2)$$

and

$$(D+F)^{-1}=D^{-1}-D^{-1}(D^{-1}+F^{-1})^{-1}D^{-1}, \quad (6A.3)$$

we can complete the squares of

$$\begin{aligned}(\boldsymbol{\beta}-A\bar{\boldsymbol{\beta}})'C^{-1}(\boldsymbol{\beta}-A\bar{\boldsymbol{\beta}})&+(\mathbf{y}-X\boldsymbol{\beta})'\Omega^{-1}(\mathbf{y}-X\boldsymbol{\beta})\\ &=\boldsymbol{\beta}'C^{-1}\boldsymbol{\beta}+\bar{\boldsymbol{\beta}}'A'C^{-1}A\bar{\boldsymbol{\beta}}-2\boldsymbol{\beta}'C^{-1}A\bar{\boldsymbol{\beta}}\\ &\quad+\mathbf{y}'\Omega^{-1}\mathbf{y}+\boldsymbol{\beta}'X'\Omega^{-1}X\boldsymbol{\beta}-2\boldsymbol{\beta}'X'\Omega^{-1}\mathbf{y}. \end{aligned} \quad (6A.4)$$

Let

$$\begin{aligned}Q_1=[\boldsymbol{\beta}&-(X'\Omega^{-1}X+C^{-1})^{-1}(X\Omega^{-1}\mathbf{y}+C^{-1}A\bar{\boldsymbol{\beta}})]'\\ &\times(C^{-1}+X'\Omega^{-1}X)[\boldsymbol{\beta}-(X'\Omega^{-1}X+C^{-1})^{-1}\\ &\times(X'\Omega^{-1}\mathbf{y}+C^{-1}A\bar{\boldsymbol{\beta}})]. \end{aligned} \quad (6A.5)$$

Then

$$\begin{aligned}\boldsymbol{\beta}'C^{-1}\boldsymbol{\beta}&+\boldsymbol{\beta}'X'\Omega^{-1}X\boldsymbol{\beta}-2\boldsymbol{\beta}'C^{-1}A\bar{\boldsymbol{\beta}}-2\boldsymbol{\beta}'X'\Omega^{-1}\mathbf{y}\\ &=Q_1-(X'\Omega^{-1}\mathbf{y}+C^{-1}A\bar{\boldsymbol{\beta}})'(X'\Omega^{-1}X+C^{-1})^{-1}\\ &\quad\times(X'\Omega^{-1}\mathbf{y}+C^{-1}A\bar{\boldsymbol{\beta}}). \end{aligned} \quad (6A.6)$$

Substituting (6A.6) into (6A.4) yields

$$\begin{aligned}Q_1&+\mathbf{y}'[\Omega^{-1}-\Omega^{-1}X(X'\Omega^{-1}X+C^{-1})^{-1}X'\Omega^{-1}]\mathbf{y}\\ &+\bar{\boldsymbol{\beta}}'A'[C^{-1}-C^{-1}(X'\Omega^{-1}X+C^{-1})^{-1}C^{-1}]A\bar{\boldsymbol{\beta}}\\ &-2\bar{\boldsymbol{\beta}}'A'C^{-1}(X'\Omega^{-1}X+C^{-1})^{-1}X'\Omega^{-1}\mathbf{y}\\ &\qquad=Q_1+\mathbf{y}'(XCX'+\Omega)^{-1}\mathbf{y}+\bar{\boldsymbol{\beta}}'A'X'(XCX'+\Omega)^{-1}XA\bar{\boldsymbol{\beta}}\\ &\qquad\quad-2\bar{\boldsymbol{\beta}}'A'X'(XCX'+\Omega)^{-1}\mathbf{y}\\ &\qquad=Q_1+Q_2+Q_3, \end{aligned} \quad (6A.7)$$

where

$$\begin{aligned}Q_2=\{\bar{\boldsymbol{\beta}}&-[A'X'(XCX'+\Omega)^{-1}XA]^{-1}[A'X'(XCX'+\Omega)^{-1}y]\}'\\ &\times[A'X'(XCX'+\Omega)^{-1}XA]\{\bar{\boldsymbol{\beta}}-[A'X'(XCX'+\Omega)^{-1}XA]^{-1}\\ &\times[A'X'(XCX'+\Omega)^{-1}\mathbf{y}]\}, \end{aligned} \quad (6A.8)$$

$$\begin{aligned}Q_3=\mathbf{y}'\{&(XCX'+\Omega)^{-1}\\ &-(XCX'+\Omega)^{-1}XA[A'X(XCX'+\Omega)^{-1}XA]^{-1}\\ &\times A'X'(XCX'+\Omega)^{-1}\}\,\mathbf{y}. \end{aligned} \quad (6A.9)$$

Since Q_3 is a constant independent of $\boldsymbol{\beta}$ and $\bar{\boldsymbol{\beta}}$, we can write $P(\boldsymbol{\beta}, \bar{\boldsymbol{\beta}} \mid \mathbf{y})$ in the form $P(\boldsymbol{\beta} \mid \bar{\boldsymbol{\beta}}, \mathbf{y})P(\bar{\boldsymbol{\beta}} \mid \mathbf{y})$, which becomes

$$P\{\boldsymbol{\beta}, \bar{\boldsymbol{\beta}} \mid \mathbf{y}\} \propto \exp\left\{-\tfrac{1}{2}Q_1\right\}\exp\left\{-\tfrac{1}{2}Q_2\right\}, \tag{6A.10}$$

where $\exp\{-\frac{1}{2}Q_1\}$ is proportional to $P(\boldsymbol{\beta} \mid \bar{\boldsymbol{\beta}}, \mathbf{y})$ and $\exp\{-\frac{1}{2}Q_2\}$ is proportional to $P(\bar{\boldsymbol{\beta}} \mid \mathbf{y})$. That is, $P(\boldsymbol{\beta} \mid \bar{\boldsymbol{\beta}}, \mathbf{y})$ is $N\{(X'\Omega^{-1}X + C^{-1})^{-1}(X'\Omega^{-1}\mathbf{y} + C^{-1}A\bar{\boldsymbol{\beta}}), (C^{-1} + X'\Omega^{-1}X)^{-1}\}$, and $P(\bar{\boldsymbol{\beta}} \mid \mathbf{y})$ is $N\{[A'X'(XCX' + \Omega)^{-1}XA]^{-1} \times [A'X'(XCX' + \Omega)^{-1}\mathbf{y}], [A'X'(XCX' + \Omega)^{-1}XA]^{-1}\}$.

Alternatively, we may complete the square of the left side of (6A.4) with the aim of writing $P(\boldsymbol{\beta}, \bar{\boldsymbol{\beta}} \mid \mathbf{y})$ in the form $P(\bar{\boldsymbol{\beta}} \mid \boldsymbol{\beta}, \mathbf{y})P(\boldsymbol{\beta} \mid \mathbf{y})$:

$$\begin{aligned} &Q_4 + \boldsymbol{\beta}'[X'\Omega^{-1}X + C^{-1} - C^{-1}A(A'CA)^{-1}A'C^{-1}]\boldsymbol{\beta} \\ &\quad - 2\boldsymbol{\beta}'X'\Omega^{-1}\mathbf{y} + \mathbf{y}'\Omega^{-1}\mathbf{y} \\ &\qquad = Q_4 + Q_5 + Q_3, \end{aligned} \tag{6A.11}$$

where

$$\begin{aligned} Q_4 = {} & [\bar{\boldsymbol{\beta}} - (A'C^{-1}A)^{-1}A'C^{-1}\boldsymbol{\beta}]'(A'C^{-1}A) \\ & \times [\bar{\boldsymbol{\beta}} - (A'C^{-1}A)^{-1}A'C^{-1}\boldsymbol{\beta}], \end{aligned} \tag{6A.12}$$

$$Q_5 = [\boldsymbol{\beta} - D^{-1}X'\Omega^{-1}\mathbf{y}]'D[\boldsymbol{\beta} - D^{-1}X'\Omega^{-1}\mathbf{y}], \tag{6A.13}$$

and

$$D = X'\Omega^{-1}X + C^{-1} - C^{-1}A(A'C^{-1}A)^{-1}A'C^{-1}. \tag{6A.14}$$

Therefore, $P(\bar{\boldsymbol{\beta}} \mid \boldsymbol{\beta}, \mathbf{y}) \sim N\{(A'C^{-1}A)^{-1}C^{-1}\boldsymbol{\beta}, (A'C^{-1}A)^{-1}\}$, and $P(\boldsymbol{\beta} \mid \mathbf{y}) \sim N\{D^{-1}X'\Omega^{-1}\,\mathbf{y}, D^{-1}\}$.

CHAPTER 7

Discrete Data

7.1 INTRODUCTION

In this chapter, we consider situations in which an analyst has at his disposal a random sample of N individuals, having recorded histories indicating the presence or absence of an event in each of T equally spaced discrete time periods. Statistical models in which the endogenous random variables take only discrete values are known as discrete, categorical, qualitative-choice, or quantal-response models. The literature, both applied and theoretical, on this subject is vast. Amemiya (1981), Maddala (1983), and McFadden (1976, 1984) have provided excellent surveys. Thus, the focus of this chapter will be only on controlling for unobserved characteristics of individual units to avoid specification bias. Many important and more advanced topics are omitted, such as continuous-time and duration-dependence models (Chamberlain (1978b); Flinn and Heckman (1982); Heckman and Borjas (1980); Heckman and Singer (1982); Lancaster (1990); Nickell (1979); Singer and Spilerman (1976)).

7.2 SOME DISCRETE-RESPONSE MODELS

In this section, we briefly review some widely used discrete-response models. We first consider the case in which the dependent variable y can assume only two values, which for convenience and without any loss of generality will be the value 1 if an event occurs and 0 if it does not. Examples of this include purchases of durables in a given year, participation in the labor force, the decision to enter college, and the decision to marry.

The discrete outcome of y can be viewed as the observed counterpart of a latent continuous random variable crossing a threshold. Suppose that the continuous latent random variable, y^*, is a linear function of a vector of explanatory variables, $\mathbf{x}$,

$$y^* = \boldsymbol{\beta}'\mathbf{x} + v, \tag{7.2.1}$$

where the error term v is independent of $\mathbf{x}$ with mean zero. Suppose, instead of observing y^*, we observe y, where

$$y = \begin{cases} 1 & \text{if } y^* > 0, \\ 0 & \text{if } y^* \leq 0. \end{cases} \tag{7.2.2}$$

Then the expected value of y_i is the probability that the event will occur,

$$\begin{aligned} E(y \mid \mathbf{x}) &= 1 \cdot \Pr(v > -\boldsymbol{\beta}'\mathbf{x}) + 0 \cdot \Pr(v \leq -\boldsymbol{\beta}'\mathbf{x}) \\ &= \Pr(v > -\boldsymbol{\beta}'\mathbf{x}) \\ &= \Pr(y = 1 \mid \mathbf{x}). \end{aligned} \tag{7.2.3}$$

When the probability law for generating v follows a two-point distribution $(1 - \boldsymbol{\beta}'\mathbf{x})$ and $(-\boldsymbol{\beta}'\mathbf{x})$, with probabilities $\boldsymbol{\beta}'\mathbf{x}$ and $(1 - \boldsymbol{\beta}'\mathbf{x})$, respectively, we have the linear-probability model

$$y = \boldsymbol{\beta}'\mathbf{x} + v, \tag{7.2.4}$$

with $Ev = \boldsymbol{\beta}'\mathbf{x}(1 - \boldsymbol{\beta}'\mathbf{x}) + (1 - \boldsymbol{\beta}'\mathbf{x})(-\boldsymbol{\beta}'\mathbf{x}) = 0$. When the probability density function of v is a standard normal density function, $(1/\sqrt{2\pi}) \times \exp(-v^2/2) = \phi(v)$, we have the probit model,

$$\begin{aligned} \Pr(y = 1 \mid \mathbf{x}) &= \int_{-\boldsymbol{\beta}'\mathbf{x}}^{\infty} \phi(v)\, dv \\ &= \int_{-\infty}^{\boldsymbol{\beta}'\mathbf{x}} \phi(v)\, dv = \Phi(\boldsymbol{\beta}'\mathbf{x}). \end{aligned} \tag{7.2.5}$$

When the probability density function is a standard logistic,

$$\frac{\exp(v)}{(1 + \exp(v))^2} = [(1 + \exp(v))(1 + \exp(-v))]^{-1},$$

we have the logit model

$$\Pr(y = 1 \mid \mathbf{x}) = \int_{-\boldsymbol{\beta}'\mathbf{x}}^{\infty} \frac{\exp(v)}{(1 + \exp(v))^2}\, dv_i = \frac{\exp(\boldsymbol{\beta}'\mathbf{x})}{1 + \exp(\boldsymbol{\beta}'\mathbf{x})}. \tag{7.2.6}$$

Let $F(\boldsymbol{\beta}'\mathbf{x}) = E(y_i \mid \mathbf{x})$. Then the three commonly used parametric models for the binary choice may be summarized with a single index w as follows:

Linear-probability model,

$$F(w) = w. \tag{7.2.7}$$

Probit model,

$$F(w) = \int_{-\infty}^{w} \frac{1}{\sqrt{2\pi}} e^{-\frac{u^2}{2}}\, du = \Phi(w). \tag{7.2.8}$$

Logit model,

$$F(w) = \frac{e^w}{1 + e^w}. \tag{7.2.9}$$

The linear-probability model is a special case of the linear regression model with heteroscadastic variance, $\boldsymbol{\beta}'\mathbf{x}(1-\boldsymbol{\beta}'\mathbf{x})$. It can be estimated by least squares or weighted least squares (Goldberger (1964)). But it has an obvious defect in that $\boldsymbol{\beta}'\mathbf{x}$ is not constrained to lie between 0 and 1 as a probability should, whereas in the probit and logit models it is.

The probability functions used for the probit and logit models are the standard normal distribution and the logistic distribution, respectively. We use cumulative standard normal because in the dichotomy case there is no way to identify the variance of a normal density. The logit probability density function is symmetric around 0 and has a variance of $\pi^2/3$. Because they are distribution functions, the probit and logit models are bounded between 0 and 1.

The cumulative normal distribution and the logistic distribution are very close to each other; the logistic distribution has sightly heavier tails (Cox (1970)). Moreover, the cumulative normal distribution Φ is reasonably well approximated by a linear function for the range of probabilities between 0.3 and 0.7. Amemiya (1981) has suggested an approximate conversion rule for the coefficients of these models. Let the coefficients for the linear-probability, probit, and logit models be denoted as $\hat{\boldsymbol{\beta}}_{\text{LP}}, \hat{\boldsymbol{\beta}}_{\Phi}, \hat{\boldsymbol{\beta}}_L$, respectively. Then

$$\begin{aligned} &\hat{\boldsymbol{\beta}}_L \simeq 1.6\hat{\boldsymbol{\beta}}_{\Phi}, \\ &\hat{\boldsymbol{\beta}}_{\text{LP}} \simeq 0.4\hat{\boldsymbol{\beta}}_{\Phi} \text{ except for the constant term,} \end{aligned} \tag{7.2.10}$$

and

$$\hat{\boldsymbol{\beta}}_{\text{LP}} \simeq 0.4\hat{\boldsymbol{\beta}}_{\Phi} + 0.5 \text{ for the constant term.}$$

For a random sample of N individuals, $(y_i, \mathbf{x}_i)$, $i = 1, \ldots, N$, the likelihood function for these three models can be written in general form as

$$L = \prod_{i=1}^{N} F(\boldsymbol{\beta}'\mathbf{x}_i)^{y_i}[1 - F(\boldsymbol{\beta}'\mathbf{x}_i)]^{1-y_i}. \tag{7.2.11}$$

Differentiating the logarithm of the likelihood function yields the vector of first derivatives and the matrix of second-order derivatives as

$$\frac{\partial \log L}{\partial \boldsymbol{\beta}} = \sum_{i=1}^{N} \frac{y_i - F(\boldsymbol{\beta}'\mathbf{x}_i)}{F(\boldsymbol{\beta}'\mathbf{x}_i)[1 - F(\boldsymbol{\beta}'\mathbf{x}_i)]} F'(\boldsymbol{\beta}'\mathbf{x}_i)\mathbf{x}_i, \tag{7.2.12}$$

and

$$\begin{aligned} \frac{\partial^2 \log L}{\partial \boldsymbol{\beta}\partial \boldsymbol{\beta}'} = &\left\{ -\sum_{i=1}^{N} \left[\frac{y_i}{F^2(\boldsymbol{\beta}'\mathbf{x}_i)} + \frac{1 - y_i}{[1 - F(\boldsymbol{\beta}'\mathbf{x}_i)]^2} \right] [F'(\boldsymbol{\beta}'\mathbf{x}_i)]^2 \right. \\ &\left. + \sum_{i=1}^{N} \left[\frac{y_i - F(\boldsymbol{\beta}'\mathbf{x}_i)}{F(\boldsymbol{\beta}'\mathbf{x}_i)[1 - F(\boldsymbol{\beta}'\mathbf{x}_i)]} \right] F''(\boldsymbol{\beta}'\mathbf{x}_i) \right\} \mathbf{x}_i\mathbf{x}_i', \end{aligned} \tag{7.2.13}$$

where $F'(\boldsymbol{\beta}'\mathbf{x}_i)$ and $F''(\boldsymbol{\beta}'\mathbf{x}_i)$ denote the first and second derivatives of $F(\boldsymbol{\beta}'\mathbf{x}_i)$ with respect to $\boldsymbol{\beta}'\mathbf{x}_i$. If the likelihood function (7.2.11) is concave, as in the models discussed here (e.g., Amemiya (1985, p. 273)), then a Newton–Raphson method,

$$\hat{\boldsymbol{\beta}}^{(j)} = \hat{\boldsymbol{\beta}}^{(j-1)} - \left(\frac{\partial^2 \log L}{\partial \boldsymbol{\beta}\, \partial \boldsymbol{\beta}'}\right)^{-1}_{\boldsymbol{\beta}=\hat{\boldsymbol{\beta}}^{(j-1)}} \left(\frac{\partial \log L}{\partial \boldsymbol{\beta}}\right)_{\boldsymbol{\beta}=\hat{\boldsymbol{\beta}}^{(j-1)}}, \tag{7.2.14}$$

or a method of scoring,

$$\hat{\boldsymbol{\beta}}^{(j)} = \hat{\boldsymbol{\beta}}^{(j-1)} - \left[E\frac{\partial^2 \log L}{\partial \boldsymbol{\beta}\, \partial \boldsymbol{\beta}'}\right]^{-1}_{\boldsymbol{\beta}=\hat{\boldsymbol{\beta}}^{(j-1)}} \left(\frac{\partial \log L}{\partial \boldsymbol{\beta}}\right)_{\boldsymbol{\beta}=\hat{\boldsymbol{\beta}}^{(j-1)}}, \tag{7.2.15}$$

can be used to find the maximum likelihood estimator (MLE) of $\boldsymbol{\beta}$ with arbitrary initial values $\hat{\boldsymbol{\beta}}^{(0)}$, where $\hat{\boldsymbol{\beta}}^{(j)}$ denotes the jth iterative solution.

In the case in which there are repeated observations of y for a specific value of $\mathbf{x}$, the proportion of $y = 1$ for individuals with the same characteristic $\mathbf{x}$ is a consistent estimator of $p = F(\boldsymbol{\beta}'\mathbf{x})$. Taking the inverse of this function yields $F^{-1}(p) = \boldsymbol{\beta}'\mathbf{x}$. Substituting $\hat{p}$ for p, we have $F^{-1}(\hat{p}) = \boldsymbol{\beta}'\mathbf{x} + \zeta$, where ζ denotes the approximation error of using $F^{-1}(\hat{p})$ for $F^{-1}(p)$. Since ζ has a nonscalar covariance matrix, we can apply the weighted least-squares method to estimate $\boldsymbol{\beta}$. The resulting estimator, which is generally referred to as the minimum-chi-square estimator, has the same asymptotic efficiency as the MLE and computationally may be simpler than the MLE. Moreover, in finite samples, the minimum-chi-square estimator may even have a smaller mean squared error than the MLE (e.g., Amemiya (1974, 1976, 1980b); Berkson (1944, 1955, 1957, 1980); Ferguson (1958); Neyman (1949)). However, despite its statistical attractiveness, the minimum-chi-square method is probably less useful than the maximum likelihood method in analyzing survey data than it is in the laboratory setting. Application of the minimum-chi-square method requires repeated observations for each value of the vector of explanatory variables. In survey data, most explanatory variables are continuous. The survey sample size has to be extremely large for the possible configurations of explanatory variables. Furthermore, if the proportion of $y = 1$ is 0 or 1 for a given $\mathbf{x}$, the minimum-chi-square method is not defined, but the maximum likelihood method can still be applied. For this reason, we shall confine our attention to the maximum likelihood method.[1]

When the dependent variable y_i can assume more than two values, things are more complicated. We can classify these cases into ordered and unordered variables. An example of ordered variables is

$$y_i = \begin{cases} 0 & \text{if the price of a home bought} < \$49{,}999, \\ 1 & \text{if the price of a home bought is } \$50{,}000\text{–}\$99{,}999, \\ 2 & \text{if the price of a home bought} > \$100{,}000. \end{cases}$$

An example of unordered variables is

$$y_i = \begin{cases} 1 & \text{if mode of transport is car,} \\ 2 & \text{if mode of transport is bus,} \\ 3 & \text{if mode of transport is train.} \end{cases}$$

In general, ordered models are used whenever the values taken by the discrete random variable y_i correspond to the intervals within which a continuous latent random variable y_i^* falls. Unordered models are used when more than one latent continuous random variable is needed to characterize the responses of y_i.

Assume that the dependent variable y_i takes $m_i + 1$ values $0, 1, 2, \ldots, m_i$ for the ith unit. To simplify the exposition without having to distinguish ordered from unordered models, we define $\sum_{i=1}^{N}(m_i + 1)$ binary variables as

$$y_{ij} = \begin{cases} 1 & \text{if} \quad y_i = j, \quad i = 1, \ldots, N, \\ 0 & \text{if} \quad y_i \neq j, \quad j = 0, 1, \ldots, m_i. \end{cases} \tag{7.2.16}$$

Let $\text{Prob}(y_{ij} = 1 \mid \mathbf{x}_i) = F_{ij}$. We can write the likelihood function as

$$L = \prod_{i=1}^{N} \prod_{j=0}^{m_i} F_{ij}^{y_{ij}}. \tag{7.2.17}$$

The complication in the multivariate case is in the specification of F_{ij}. Once F_{ij} is specified, general results concerning the methods of estimation and their asymptotic distributions for the dichotomous case also apply here. However, contrary to the univariate case, the similarity between the probit and logit specifications no longer holds. In general, they will lead to different inferences.

The multivariate probit model follows from the assumption that the errors of the latent response functions across alternatives are multivariate normally distributed. Its advantage is that it allows the choice among alternatives to have arbitrary correlation. Its disadvantage is that the evaluation of $\text{Prob}(y_i = j)$ involves multiple integrations, which can be computationally infeasible.

The conditional logit model follows from the assumption that the errors of the latent response functions across alternatives are independently, identically distributed with type I extreme value distribution (McFadden (1974)). Its advantage is that the evaluation of $\text{Prob}(y_i = j)$ does not involve multiple integration. Its disadvantage is that the relative odds between two alternatives are independent of the presence or absence of the other alternatives – the so-called independence of irrelevant alternatives. If the errors among alternatives are not independently distributed, this can lead to grossly false predictions of the outcomes. For discussion of model specification tests, see Hausman and McFadden (1984), Hsiao (1992b), Lee (1982, 1987), and Small and Hsiao (1985).

Because in many cases a multiresponse model can be transformed into a dichotomous model characterized by the $\sum_{i=1}^{N}(m_i + 1)$ binary variables as in (7.2.16),[2] for ease of exposition we shall concentrate on the dichotomous model.[3]

When there is no information about the probability laws for generating v_i, a semiparametric approach can be used to estimate $\boldsymbol{\beta}$ subject to a certain normalization rule (e.g., Klein and Spady (1993); Manski (1985); Powell, Stock, and Stoker (1989)). However, whether an investigator takes a parametric or semiparametric approach, the cross-sectional model assumes that the error term v_i in the latent response function (7.2.1) is independently, identically distributed and is independent of $\mathbf{x}_i$. In other words, conditional on $\mathbf{x}_i$, everyone has the same probability that an event will occur. It does not allow the possibility that the average behavior given **x** can be different from individual probabilities, that is, that it does not allow $\Pr(y_i = 1 \mid \mathbf{x}) \neq \Pr(y_j = 1 \mid \mathbf{x})$. The availability of panel data provides the possibility of distinguishing average behavior from individual behavior by decomposing the error term v_{it} into

$$v_{it} = \alpha_i + \lambda_t + u_{it}, \tag{7.2.18}$$

where α_i and λ_t denote the effects of omitted individual-specific and time-specific variables, respectively. In this chapter we shall demonstrate the misspecifications that can arise because of failure to control for unobserved characteristics of the individuals in panel data, and discuss possible remedies.

7.3 PARAMETRIC APPROACH TO STATIC MODELS WITH HETEROGENEITY

Statistical models developed for analyzing cross-sectional data essentially ignore individual differences and treat the aggregate of the individual effect and the omitted-variable effect as a pure chance event. However, as stated in Chapter 1, a discovery of a group of married women having an average yearly labor participation rate of 50 percent could lead to diametrically opposite inferences. At one extreme, each woman in a homogeneous population could have a 50 percent chance of being in the labor force in any given year, whereas at the other extreme 50 percent of women in a heterogeneous population might always work and 50 percent never work. Either explanation is consistent with the given cross-sectional data. To discriminate among the many possible explanations, we need information on individual labor-force histories in different subintervals of the life cycle. Panel data, through their information on intertemporal dynamics of individual entities, provide the possibility of separating a model of individual behavior from a model of the average behavior of a group of individuals.

For simplicity, we shall assume that the heterogeneity across cross-sectional units is time-invariant,[4] and these individual-specific effects are captured by decomposing the error term v_{it} in (7.2.1) as $\alpha_i + u_{it}$. When the α_i are treated as fixed, $\text{Var}(v_{it} \mid \alpha_i) = \text{Var}(u_{it}) = \sigma_u^2$. When they are treated as random, we assume that $E\alpha_i = Eu_{it} = E\alpha_i u_{it} = 0$ and $\text{Var}(v_{it}) = \sigma_u^2 + \sigma_\alpha^2$. However, as discussed earlier, when the dependent variables are binary, the scale factor is not identifiable. Thus, for ease of exposition, we normalize the variance σ_u^2 of u to be equal to 1 for the specifications discussed in the rest of this chapter.

The existence of such unobserved permanent components allows individuals who are homogeneous in their observed characteristics to be heterogeneous in their response probabilities $F(\boldsymbol{\beta}'\mathbf{x}_{it} + \alpha_i)$. For example, heterogeneity will imply that the sequential-participation behavior of a woman, $F(\boldsymbol{\beta}'\mathbf{x} + \alpha_i)$, within a group of observationally identical women differs systematically from $F(\boldsymbol{\beta}'\mathbf{x})$ or the average behavior of the group, $\int F(\boldsymbol{\beta}'\mathbf{x} + \alpha)\, dH(\alpha \mid \mathbf{x})$, where $H(\alpha \mid \mathbf{x})$ gives the population probability (or empirical distribution) for α conditional on **x**.[5] In this section, we discuss statistical inference of the common parameters $\boldsymbol{\beta}$ based on a parametric specification of $F(\cdot)$.

7.3.1 Fixed-Effects Models

7.3.1.a Maximum Likelihood Estimator

If the individual-specific effect, α_i, is assumed to be fixed,[6] then both α_i and $\boldsymbol{\beta}$ are unknown parameters to be estimated for the model $\text{Prob}(y_{it} = 1 \mid \mathbf{x}_{it}, \alpha_i) = F(\boldsymbol{\beta}'\mathbf{x}_{it} + \alpha_i)$. When T tends to infinity, the MLE is consistent. However, T is usually small for panel data. There are only a limited number of observations to estimate α_i. Thus, we have the familiar incidental-parameter problem (Neyman and Scott (1948)). Any estimation of the α_i is meaningless if we intend to judge the estimators by their large-sample properties. We shall therefore concentrate on estimation of the common parameters, $\boldsymbol{\beta}$.

Unfortunately, contrary to the linear-regression case where the individual effects α_i can be eliminated by taking a linear transformation such as the first difference, in general no simple transformation exists to eliminate the incidental parameters from a nonlinear model. The MLEs for α_i and $\boldsymbol{\beta}$ are not independent of each other for the discrete-choice models. When T is fixed, the inconsistency of $\hat{\alpha}_i$ is transmitted into the MLE for $\boldsymbol{\beta}$. Hence, even if N tends to infinity, the MLE of $\boldsymbol{\beta}$ remains inconsistent.

We demonstrate the inconsistency of the MLE for $\boldsymbol{\beta}$ by considering a logit model. The log likelihood function for this model is

$$\log L = -\sum_{i=1}^{N}\sum_{t=1}^{T} \log[1 + \exp(\boldsymbol{\beta}'\mathbf{x}_{it} + \alpha_i)] + \sum_{i=1}^{N}\sum_{t=1}^{T} y_{it}(\boldsymbol{\beta}'\mathbf{x}_{it} + \alpha_i). \tag{7.3.1}$$

For ease of illustration, we consider the special case of $T = 2$ and one explanatory variable, with $x_{i1} = 0$ and $x_{i2} = 1$. Then the first-derivative equations are

$$\begin{aligned} \frac{\partial \log L}{\partial \beta} &= \sum_{i=1}^{N}\sum_{t=1}^{2}\left[-\frac{e^{\beta x_{it}+\alpha_i}}{1+e^{\beta x_{it}+\alpha_i}} + y_{it}\right]x_{it} \\ &= \sum_{i=1}^{N}\left[-\frac{e^{\beta+\alpha_i}}{1+e^{\beta+\alpha_i}} + y_{i2}\right] = 0, \end{aligned} \tag{7.3.2}$$

$$\frac{\partial \log L}{\partial \alpha_i} = \sum_{t=1}^{2}\left[-\frac{e^{\beta x_{it}+\alpha_i}}{1+e^{\beta x_{it}+\alpha_i}} + y_{it}\right] = 0. \tag{7.3.3}$$

Solving (7.3.3), we have

$$\hat{\alpha}_i = \begin{cases} \infty & \text{if } y_{i1} + y_{i2} = 2, \\ -\infty & \text{if } y_{i1} + y_{i2} = 0, \\ -\dfrac{\beta}{2} & \text{if } y_{i1} + y_{i2} = 1. \end{cases} \tag{7.3.4}$$

Inserting (7.3.4) into (7.3.2), and letting n_1 denote the number of individuals with $y_{i1} + y_{i2} = 1$ and n_2 the number of individuals with $y_{i1} + y_{i2} = 2$, we have[7]

$$\sum_{i=1}^{N} \frac{e^{\beta+\alpha_i}}{1+e^{\beta+\alpha_i}} = n_1 \frac{e^{\beta/2}}{1+e^{\beta/2}} + n_2 = \sum_{i=1}^{N} y_{i2}. \tag{7.3.5}$$

Therefore,

$$\hat{\beta} = 2\left\{\log\left(\sum_{i=1}^{N} y_{i2} - n_2\right) - \log\left(n_1 + n_2 - \sum_{i=1}^{N} y_{i2}\right)\right\}. \tag{7.3.6}$$

By a law of large numbers (Rao (1973, Chapter 2)),

$$\begin{aligned} \operatorname*{plim}_{N\to\infty} \frac{1}{N}\left(\sum_{i=1}^{N} y_{i2} - n_2\right) &= \frac{1}{N}\sum_{i=1}^{N} \text{Prob}(y_{i1} = 0,\, y_{i2} = 1 \mid \beta, \alpha_i) \\ &= \frac{1}{N}\sum_{i=1}^{N} \frac{e^{\beta+\alpha_i}}{(1+e^{\alpha_i})(1+e^{\beta+\alpha_i})}, \end{aligned} \tag{7.3.7}$$

$$\begin{aligned} \operatorname*{plim}_{N\to\infty} \frac{1}{N}\left(n_1 + n_2 - \sum_{i=1}^{N} y_{i2}\right) &= \frac{1}{N}\sum_{i=1}^{N} \text{Prob}(y_{i1} = 1,\, y_{i2} = 0 \mid \beta, \alpha_i) \\ &= \frac{1}{N}\sum_{i=1}^{N} \frac{e^{\alpha_i}}{(1+e^{\alpha_i})(1+e^{\beta+\alpha_i})}. \end{aligned} \tag{7.3.8}$$

Substituting $\hat{\alpha}_i = -\frac{\beta}{2}$ into (7.3.7) and (7.3.8), we obtain

$$\operatorname*{plim}_{N\to\infty} \hat{\beta} = 2\beta, \tag{7.3.9}$$

which is not consistent.

7.3.1.b Conditions for the Existence of a Consistent Estimator

Neyman and Scott (1948) suggested a general principle to find a consistent estimator for the (structural) parameter $\boldsymbol{\beta}$ in the presence of the incidental parameters α_i.[8] Their idea is to find K functions

$$\Psi_{Nj}(\mathbf{y}_1, \ldots, \mathbf{y}_N \mid \boldsymbol{\beta}), \qquad j = 1, \ldots, K, \tag{7.3.10}$$

that are independent of the incidental parameters α_i and have the property that when $\boldsymbol{\beta}$ are the true values, $\Psi_{Nj}(\mathbf{y}_1, \ldots, \mathbf{y}_N \mid \boldsymbol{\beta})$ converges to zero in probability as N tends to infinity. Then an estimator $\hat{\boldsymbol{\beta}}$ derived by solving $\Psi_{Nj}(\mathbf{y}_1, \ldots, \mathbf{y}_N \mid \hat{\boldsymbol{\beta}}) = 0$ is consistent under suitable regularity conditions. For instance, $\hat{\beta}^* = (\frac{1}{2})\hat{\beta}$ for the foregoing example of a fixed-effect logit model (7.3.1)–(7.3.3) is such an estimator.

In the case of a linear-probability model, either taking first differences over time or taking differences with respect to the individual mean eliminates the individual-specific effect. The least-squares regression of the differenced equations yields a consistent estimator for $\boldsymbol{\beta}$ when N tends to infinity.

But in the general nonlinear models, simple functions for Ψ are not always easy to find. For instance, in general we do not know the probability limit of the MLE of a fixed-effects logit model. However, if a minimum sufficient statistic τ_i for the incidental parameter α_i exists and is not dependent on the structural parameter $\boldsymbol{\beta}$, then the conditional density,

$$f^*(\mathbf{y}_i \mid \boldsymbol{\beta}, \tau_i) = \frac{f(\mathbf{y}_i \mid \boldsymbol{\beta}, \alpha_i)}{g(\tau_i \mid \boldsymbol{\beta}, \alpha_i)} \qquad \text{for } g(\tau_i \mid \boldsymbol{\beta}, \alpha_i) > 0, \tag{7.3.11}$$

no longer depends on α_i.[9] Andersen (1970, 1973) has shown that maximizing the conditional density of $\mathbf{y}_1, \ldots, \mathbf{y}_N$ given $\tau_1, \ldots, \tau_N$,

$$\prod_{i=1}^{N} f^*\left(\mathbf{y}_i \mid \boldsymbol{\beta}, \tau_i\right), \tag{7.3.12}$$

yields the first-order conditions $\Psi_{Nj}(\mathbf{y}_1, \ldots, \mathbf{y}_N \mid \hat{\boldsymbol{\beta}}, \tau_1, \tau_2, \ldots \tau_N) = 0$ for $j = 1, \ldots, K$. Solving for these functions will give a consistent estimator of the common (structural) parameter $\boldsymbol{\beta}$ under mild regularity conditions.[10]

To illustrate the conditional maximum likelihood method, we use the logit model as an example. The joint probability of $\mathbf{y}_i$ is

$$\text{Prob}(\mathbf{y}_i) = \frac{\exp\left\{\alpha_i \sum_{t=1}^{T} y_{it} + \boldsymbol{\beta}' \sum_{t=1}^{T} \mathbf{x}_{it} y_{it}\right\}}{\prod_{t=1}^{T}[1 + \exp(\boldsymbol{\beta}'\mathbf{x}_{it} + \alpha_i)]}. \tag{7.3.13}$$

It is clear that $\sum_{t=1}^{T} y_{it}$ is a minimum sufficient statistic for α_i. The conditional probability for $\mathbf{y}_i$, given $\sum_{t=1}^{T} y_{it}$, is

$$\text{Prob}\left(\mathbf{y}_i \,\middle|\, \sum_{t=1}^{T} y_{it}\right) = \frac{\exp\left[\boldsymbol{\beta}' \sum_{t=1}^{T} \mathbf{x}_{it} y_{it}\right]}{\sum_{D_{ij} \in \tilde{B}_i} \exp\left\{\boldsymbol{\beta}' \sum_{t=1}^{T} \mathbf{x}_{it} d_{ijt}\right\}}, \tag{7.3.14}$$

where $\tilde{B}_i = \{D_{ij} = (d_{ij1}, \ldots, d_{ijT}) \mid d_{ijt} = 0 \text{ or } 1 \text{ and } \sum_{t=1}^{T} d_{ijt} = \sum_{t=1}^{T} y_{it} = s,\ j = 1, 2, \ldots, \frac{T!}{s!(T-s)!}\}$ is the set of all possible distinct sequences $(d_{ij1}, d_{ij2}, \ldots d_{ijT})$ satisfying $\sum_{t=1}^{T} d_{ijt} = \sum_{t=1}^{T} y_{it} = s$. There are $T + 1$ distinct alternative sets corresponding to $\sum_{t=1}^{T} y_{it} = 0, 1, \ldots, T$. Groups for which $\sum_{t=1}^{T} y_{it} = 0$ or T contribute zero to the likelihood function, because the corresponding conditional probability in this case is equal to 1 (with $\alpha_i = -\infty$ or ∞). So only $T - 1$ alternative sets are relevant. The alternative sets for groups with $\sum_{t=1}^{T} y_{it} = s$ have $\binom{T}{s}$ elements, corresponding to the distinct sequences of T trials with s successes.

Equation (7.3.14) is in a conditional logit form (McFadden (1974)), with the alternative sets $(\tilde{B}_i)$ varying across observations i. It does not depend on the incidental parameters α_i. Therefore, the conditional maximum likelihood estimator of $\boldsymbol{\beta}$ can be obtained by using standard maximum likelihood logit programs, and it is consistent under mild conditions. For example, with $T = 2$, the only case of interest is $y_{i1} + y_{i2} = 1$. The two possibilities are $\omega_i = 1$, if $(y_{i1}, y_{i2}) = (0, 1)$, and $\omega_i = 0$, if $(y_{i1}, y_{i2}) = (1, 0)$.

The conditional probability of $w_i = 1$ given $y_{i1} + y_{i2} = 1$ is

$$\begin{aligned}\text{Prob}(\omega_i = 1 \mid y_{i1} + y_{i2} = 1) &= \frac{\text{Prob}(\omega_i = 1)}{\text{Prob}(\omega_i = 1) + \text{Prob}(\omega_i = 0)} \\ &= \frac{\exp[\boldsymbol{\beta}'(\mathbf{x}_{i2} - \mathbf{x}_{i1})]}{1 + \exp[\boldsymbol{\beta}'(\mathbf{x}_{i2} - \mathbf{x}_{i1})]} \\ &= F[\boldsymbol{\beta}'(\mathbf{x}_{i2} - \mathbf{x}_{i1})]. \end{aligned} \tag{7.3.15}$$

Equation (7.3.15) is in the form of a binary logit function in which the two outcomes are (0, 1) and (1, 0), with explanatory variables $(\mathbf{x}_{i2} - \mathbf{x}_{i1})$. The conditional log likelihood function is

$$\begin{aligned}\log L^* = \sum_{i \in \tilde{B}_1} \{&\omega_i \log F[\boldsymbol{\beta}'(\mathbf{x}_{i2} - \mathbf{x}_{i1})] \\ &+ (1 - \omega_i) \log(1 - F[\boldsymbol{\beta}'(\mathbf{x}_{i2} - \mathbf{x}_{i1})])\},\end{aligned} \tag{7.3.16}$$

where $\tilde{B}_1 = \{i \mid y_{i1} + y_{i2} = 1\}$.

Although $\tilde{B}_1$ is a random set of indices, Chamberlain (1980) has shown that the inverse of the information matrix based on the conditional-likelihood function provides an asymptotic covariance matrix for the conditional MLE of $\boldsymbol{\beta}$ as N tends to infinity. This can be made more explicit by defining $d_i = 1$ if $y_{i1} + y_{i2} = 1$, and $d_i = 0$ otherwise, for the foregoing case in which $T = 2$. Then we have

$$\begin{aligned}J_{\tilde{B}_1} = \frac{\partial^2 \log L^*}{\partial \boldsymbol{\beta}\, \partial \boldsymbol{\beta}'} &= -\sum_{i=1}^{N} d_i F[\boldsymbol{\beta}'(\mathbf{x}_{i2} - \mathbf{x}_{i1})] \\ &\times \{1 - F[\boldsymbol{\beta}'(\mathbf{x}_{i2} - \mathbf{x}_{i1})]\}(\mathbf{x}_{i2} - \mathbf{x}_{i1}) \cdot (\mathbf{x}_{i2} - \mathbf{x}_{i1})'.\end{aligned} \tag{7.3.17}$$

The information matrix is

$$\begin{aligned}J &= E(J_{\tilde{B}_1}) \\ &= -\sum_{i=1}^{N} P_i F[\boldsymbol{\beta}'(\mathbf{x}_{i2} - \mathbf{x}_{i1})] \\ &\quad \times \{1 - F[\boldsymbol{\beta}'(\mathbf{x}_{i2} - \mathbf{x}_{i1})]\}(\mathbf{x}_{i2} - \mathbf{x}_{i1}) \cdot (\mathbf{x}_{i2} - \mathbf{x}_{i1})',\end{aligned} \tag{7.3.18}$$

where $P_i = E(d_i \mid \alpha_i) = F(\boldsymbol{\beta}'\mathbf{x}_{i1} + \alpha_i)[1 - F(\boldsymbol{\beta}'\mathbf{x}_{i2} + \alpha_i)] + [1 - F(\boldsymbol{\beta}'\mathbf{x}_{i1} + \alpha_i)]F(\boldsymbol{\beta}'\mathbf{x}_{i2} + \alpha_i)$. Because d_i are independent, with $Ed_i = P_i$, and both F and the variance of d_i are uniformly bounded, by a strong law of large numbers we have

$$\frac{1}{N} J_{\tilde{B}_1} - \frac{1}{N} J \to 0 \quad \text{almost surely as } N \to \infty$$

$$\text{if} \quad \sum_{i=1}^{N} \frac{1}{i^2} \mathbf{m}_i \mathbf{m}_i' < \infty, \tag{7.3.19}$$

where $\mathbf{m}_i$ replaces each element of $(\mathbf{x}_{i2} - \mathbf{x}_{i1})$ with its square. The condition for convergence clearly holds if $\mathbf{x}_{it}$ is uniformly bounded.

For the case of $T > 2$, there is no loss of generality in choosing the sequence $D_{i1} = (d_{i11}, \ldots, d_{i1T})$, $\sum_{t=1}^T d_{i1t} = \sum_{t=1}^T y_{it} = s$, $1 \leq s \leq T - 1$, as the normalizing factor. Hence we may rewrite the conditional probability (7.3.14) as

$$\text{Prob}\left(\mathbf{y}_i \mid \sum_{t=1}^T y_{it}\right) = \frac{\exp\left\{\boldsymbol{\beta}'\{\sum_{t=1}^T \mathbf{x}_{it}(y_{it} - d_{i1t})\}\right\}}{1 + \sum_{D_{ij}\in(\tilde{B}_i - D_{i1})} \exp\left\{\boldsymbol{\beta}' \sum_{t=1}^T \mathbf{x}_{it}(d_{ijt} - d_{i1t})\right\}}. \tag{7.3.20}$$

Then the conditional log-likelihood function takes the form

$$\begin{aligned}\log L^* = \sum_{i\in C} \Bigg\{ & \boldsymbol{\beta}' \sum_{t=1}^T \mathbf{x}_{it}(y_{it} - d_{i1t}) \\ & - \log\left[1 + \sum_{D_{ij}\in(\tilde{B}_i - D_{i1})} \exp\left\{\boldsymbol{\beta}' \sum_{t=1}^T \mathbf{x}_{it}(d_{ijt} - d_{i1t})\right\}\right]\Bigg\},\end{aligned} \tag{7.3.21}$$

where $C = \{i \mid \sum_{t=1}^T y_{it} \neq T, \sum_{t=1}^T y_{it} \neq 0\}$.

Although we can find simple transformations of linear-probability and logit models that will satisfy the Neyman–Scott principle, we cannot find simple functions for the parameters of interest that are independent of the nuisance parameters α_i for probit models. That is, there does not appear to exist a consistent estimator of $\boldsymbol{\beta}$ for the fixed-effects probit models.

7.3.1.c Some Monte Carlo Evidence

Given that there exists a consistent estimator of $\boldsymbol{\beta}$ for the fixed-effects logit model, but not for the fixed-effects probit model, and that in the binary case the probit and logit models yield similar results, it appears that a case can be made for favoring the logit specification because of the existence of a consistent estimator for the structural parameter $\boldsymbol{\beta}$. However, in the multivariate case, logit and probit models yield very different results. In this situation it will be useful to know the magnitude of the bias if the data actually call for a fixed-effects probit specification.

Heckman (1981b) conducted a limited set of Monte Carlo experiments to get some idea of the order of bias of the MLE for the fixed-effects probit models. His data were generated by the model

$$y_{it}^* = \beta x_{it} + \alpha_i + u_{it}, \qquad i = 1, 2, \ldots, N, \quad t = 1, \ldots, T, \tag{7.3.22}$$

Table 7.1. *Average values of $\hat{\beta}$ for the fixed-effects probit model*

	$\hat{\beta}$		
σ_α^2	$\beta = 1$	$\beta = -0.1$	$\beta = -1$
3	0.90	−0.10	−0.94
1	0.91	−0.09	−0.95
0.5	0.93	−0.10	−0.96

Source: Heckman (1981b, Table 4.1).

and

$$y_{it} = \begin{cases} 1 & \text{if } y_{it}^* \geq 0, \\ 0 & \text{otherwise.} \end{cases}$$

The exogenous variable x_{it} was generated by a Nerlove (1971a) process,

$$x_{it} = 0.1t + 0.5x_{i,t-1} + \epsilon_{it}, \tag{7.3.23}$$

where ϵ_{it} is a uniform random variable having mean zero and range $-1/2$ to $1/2$. The variance σ_u^2 was set at 1. The scale of the variation of the fixed effect, σ_α^2, is changed for different experiments. In each experiment, 25 samples of 100 individuals ($N = 100$) were selected for eight periods ($T = 8$).

The results of Heckman's experiment with the fixed-effects MLE of probit models are presented in Table 7.1. For $\beta = -0.1$, the fixed-effects estimator does well. The estimated value comes very close to the true value. For $\beta = -1$ or $\beta = 1$, the estimator does not perform as well, but the bias is never more than 10 percent and is always toward zero. Also, as the scale of the variation in the fixed-effects decreases, so does the bias.[11]

7.3.2 Random-Effects Models

When the individual specific effects α_i are treated as random, we may still use the fixed effects estimators to estimate the structural parameters $\boldsymbol{\beta}$. The asymptotic properties of the fixed effects estimators of $\boldsymbol{\beta}$ remain unchanged. However, if α_i are random, but are treated as fixed, the consequence, at its best, is a loss of efficiency in estimating $\boldsymbol{\beta}$, but it could be worse, namely, the resulting fixed-effects estimators may be inconsistent, as discussed in Section 7.3.1.

When α_i are independent of $\mathbf{x}_i$ and are a random sample from a univariate distribution G, indexed by a finite number of parameters $\boldsymbol{\delta}$, the log likelihood function becomes

$$\log L = \sum_{i=1}^{N} \log \int \prod_{t=1}^{T} F(\boldsymbol{\beta}'\mathbf{x}_{it} + \alpha)^{y_{it}} [1 - F(\boldsymbol{\beta}'\mathbf{x}_{it} + \alpha)]^{1-y_{it}} \, dG(\alpha \mid \boldsymbol{\delta}), \tag{7.3.24}$$

where $F(\cdot)$ is the distribution of the error term conditional on both $\mathbf{x}_i$ and α_i. Equation (7.3.24) replaces the probability function for $\mathbf{y}$ conditional on α by a probability function that is marginal on α. It is a function of a finite number of parameters $(\boldsymbol{\beta}', \boldsymbol{\delta}')$. Thus, maximizing (7.3.24), under weak regularity conditions, will give consistent estimators for $\boldsymbol{\beta}$ and $\boldsymbol{\delta}$ as N tends to infinity.

If α_i is correlated with $\mathbf{x}_{it}$, maximizing (7.3.24) will not eliminate the omitted-variable bias. To allow for dependence between α and $\mathbf{x}$, we must specify a distribution $G(\alpha \mid \mathbf{x})$ for α conditional on $\mathbf{x}$, and consider the marginal log likelihood function

$$\log L = \sum_{i=1}^{N} \log \int \prod_{t=1}^{T} F(\boldsymbol{\beta}'\mathbf{x}_{it} + \alpha)^{y_{it}} \times [1 - F(\boldsymbol{\beta}'\mathbf{x}_{it} + \alpha)]^{1-y_{it}} \, dG(\alpha \mid \mathbf{x}). \tag{7.3.24$'$}$$

A convenient specification suggested by Chamberlain (1980, 1984) is to assume that $\alpha_i = \sum_{t=1}^{T} \mathbf{a}_t'\mathbf{x}_{it} + \eta_i = \mathbf{a}'\mathbf{x}_i + \eta_i$, where $\mathbf{a}' = (\mathbf{a}_1', \ldots \mathbf{a}_T')$, $\mathbf{x}_i' = (\mathbf{x}_{i1}', \ldots, \mathbf{x}_{iT}')$, and η_i is the residual. However, there is a very important difference in this step compared with the linear case. In the linear case it was not restrictive to decompose α_i into its linear projection on $\mathbf{x}_i$ and an orthogonal residual. Now we are assuming that the regression function $E(\alpha_i \mid \mathbf{x}_i)$ is actually linear, that η_i is independent of $\mathbf{x}_i$, and that η_i has a specific probability distribution.

Given these assumptions, the log likelihood function under our random-effects specification is

$$\log L = \sum_{i=1}^{N} \log \int \prod_{t=1}^{T} F(\boldsymbol{\beta}'\mathbf{x}_{it} + \mathbf{a}'\mathbf{x}_i + \eta)^{y_{it}} \times [1 - F(\boldsymbol{\beta}'\mathbf{x}_{it} + \mathbf{a}'\mathbf{x}_i + \eta)]^{1-y_{it}} \, dG^*(\eta), \tag{7.3.25}$$

where G^* is a univariate distribution function for η. For example, if F is a standard normal distribution function and we choose G^* to be the distribution function of a normal random variable with mean 0 and variance σ_η^2, then our specification gives a multivariate probit model:

$$y_{it} = 1 \quad \text{if} \quad \boldsymbol{\beta}'\mathbf{x}_{it} + \mathbf{a}'\mathbf{x}_i + \eta_i + u_{it} > 0, \tag{7.3.26}$$

where $\mathbf{u}_i + \mathbf{e}\eta_i$ is independent normal, with mean $\mathbf{0}$ and variance–covariance matrix $I_T + \sigma_\eta^2 \mathbf{e}\mathbf{e}'$.

The difference between (7.3.25) and (7.3.24) is only in the inclusion of the term $\mathbf{a}'\mathbf{x}_i$ to capture the dependence between the incidental parameters α_i and $\mathbf{x}_i$. Therefore, the essential characteristics with regard to estimation of (7.3.24) and (7.3.25) are the same. So we shall discuss only the procedure to estimate the more general model (7.3.25).

Maximizing (7.3.25) involves integration of T dimensions, which can be computationally cumbersome. An alternative approach, which simplifies the computation of the MLE to a univariate integration is to note that conditional on α_i, the error terms $v_{it} = \alpha_i + u_{it}$ are independently normally distributed with mean α_i and variance 1, with probability density denoted by $\phi(v_{it} \mid \alpha_i)$ (Heckman (1981a)). Then

$$\begin{aligned}\Pr(y_{i1}, \ldots y_{iT}) &= \int_{c_{i1}}^{b_{i1}} \cdots \int_{c_{iT}}^{b_{iT}} \prod_{t=1}^{T} \phi(v_{it} \mid \alpha_i) G(\alpha_i \mid \mathbf{x}_i)\, d\alpha_i\, dv_{i1} \cdots dv_{iT} \\ &= \int_{-\infty}^{\infty} G(\alpha_i \mid \mathbf{x}_i) \prod_{t=1}^{T} [\Phi(b_{it} \mid \alpha_i) - \Phi(c_{it} \mid \alpha_i)]\, d\alpha_i, \qquad (7.3.27)\end{aligned}$$

where $\Phi(\cdot \mid \alpha_i)$ is the cumulative distribution function (cdf) of $\phi(\cdot \mid \alpha_i)$, $c_{it} = -\boldsymbol{\beta}'\mathbf{x}_{it}$, $b_{it} = \infty$ if $y_{it} = 1$ and $c_{it} = -\infty$, $b_{it} = -\boldsymbol{\beta}'\mathbf{x}_{it}$ if $y_{it} = 0$, and $G(\alpha_i \mid \mathbf{x}_i)$ is the probability density function of α_i given $\mathbf{x}_i$. If $G(\alpha_i \mid \mathbf{x}_i)$ is assumed to be normally distributed with variance σ_α^2, the expression (7.3.27) reduces a T-dimensional integration to a single integral whose integrand is a product of one normal density and T differences of normal cdfs for which highly accurate approximations are available. For instance, Butler and Moffit (1982) suggest using Gaussian quadrature to achieve gains in computational efficiency. The Gaussian quadrature formula for evaluation of the necessary integral is the Hermite integration formula $\int_{-\infty}^{\infty} e^{-z^2} g(z)\, dz = \sum_{j=1}^{l} w_j g(z_j)$, where l is the number of evaluation points, w_j is the weight given to the jth point, and $g(z_j)$ is $g(z)$ evaluated at the jth point of z. The points and weights are available from Abramowitz and Stegun (1965) and Stroud and Secrest (1966).

A key question for computational feasibility of the Hermite formula is the number of points at which the integrand must be evaluated for accurate approximation. Several evaluations of the integral using four periods of arbitrary values of the data and coefficients on right-hand-side variables by Butler and Moffitt (1982) show that even two-point integration is highly accurate. Of course, in the context of a maximization algorithm, accuracy could be increased by raising the number of evaluation points as the likelihood function approaches its optimum.

Although maximizing (7.3.25) or (7.3.24) provides a consistent and efficient estimator for $\boldsymbol{\beta}$, computationally it is still fairly involved. However, if both u_{it} and η_i (or α_i) are normally distributed, a computationally simple approach that avoids numerical integration is to make use of the fact that the distribution for y_{it} conditional on $\mathbf{x}_i$ but marginal on α_i also has a probit form:

$$\text{Prob}(y_{it} = 1) = \Phi\left[\left(1 + \sigma_\eta^2\right)^{-1/2} (\boldsymbol{\beta}'\mathbf{x}_{it} + \mathbf{a}'\mathbf{x}_i)\right]. \qquad (7.3.28)$$

Estimating each of t cross-sectional univariate probit specifications by maximum likelihood gives $\hat{\boldsymbol{\pi}}_t$, $t = 1, 2, \ldots, T$, which will converge to[12]

$$\Pi = \left(1 + \sigma_\eta^2\right)^{-1/2} (I_T \otimes \boldsymbol{\beta}' + \mathbf{e}\mathbf{a}') \qquad (7.3.29)$$

as N tends to infinity. Therefore, consistent estimators of $(1 + \sigma_\eta^2)^{-1/2}\boldsymbol{\beta}$ and $(1 + \sigma_\eta^2)^{-1/2}\mathbf{a}$ can be easily derived from (7.3.29). We can then follow Heckman's suggestion (1981a) by substituting these estimated values into (7.3.25) and optimizing the functions with respect to σ_η^2 conditional on $(1+\sigma_\eta^2)^{-1/2}\boldsymbol{\beta}$ and $(1+\sigma_\eta^2)^{-1/2}\mathbf{a}$.

A more efficient estimator that also avoids numerical integration is to impose the restriction (7.3.29) by $\boldsymbol{\pi} = \text{vec}(\boldsymbol{\Pi}') = \mathbf{f}(\boldsymbol{\theta})$, where $\boldsymbol{\theta}' = (\boldsymbol{\beta}', \mathbf{a}', \sigma_\eta^2)$, and use a minimum-distance estimator (see Section 3.9), just as in the linear case. Chamberlain (1984) suggests that we choose $\hat{\boldsymbol{\theta}}$ to minimize[13]

$$[\hat{\boldsymbol{\pi}} - \mathbf{f}(\boldsymbol{\theta})]'\hat{\Omega}^{-1}[\hat{\boldsymbol{\pi}} - \mathbf{f}(\boldsymbol{\theta})], \tag{7.3.30}$$

where $\hat{\Omega}$ is a consistent estimator of

$$\Omega = J^{-1}\Delta J^{-1}, \tag{7.3.31}$$

where

$$J = \begin{bmatrix} J_1 & \mathbf{0} & \cdots & \mathbf{0} \\ \mathbf{0} & J_2 & & \\ \vdots & & \ddots & \\ \mathbf{0} & & & J_T \end{bmatrix},$$

$$J_t = E\left\{\frac{\phi_{it}^2}{\Phi_{it}(1-\Phi_{it})}\mathbf{x}_i\mathbf{x}_i'\right\},$$

$$\Delta = E[\Psi_i \otimes \mathbf{x}_i\mathbf{x}_i'],$$

and where the t, s element of the $T \times T$ matrix Ψ_i is $\psi_{it} = c_{it}c_{is}$, with

$$c_{it} = \frac{y_{it} - \Phi_{it}}{\Phi_{it}(1-\Phi_{it})}\phi_{it}, \qquad t = 1, \ldots, T.$$

The standard normal distribution function Φ_{it} and the standard normal density function ϕ_{it} are evaluated at $\boldsymbol{\pi}'\mathbf{x}_i$. We can obtain a consistent estimator of Ω by replacing expectations by sample means and using $\hat{\boldsymbol{\pi}}$ in place of $\boldsymbol{\pi}$.

7.4 SEMIPARAMETRIC APPROACH TO STATIC MODELS

The parametric approach to estimating discrete choice models suffers from two drawbacks: (1) Conditional on $\mathbf{x}$, the probability law of generating (u_{it}, α_i) is known a priori, or conditional on $\mathbf{x}$ and α_i, the probability law of u_{it} is known a priori. (2) When α_i are fixed, it appears that apart from the logit and linear probability models, there does not exist a simple transformation that can get rid of the incidental parameters. The semiparametric approach not only avoids assuming a specific distribution of u_{it}, but also allows consistent estimation of $\boldsymbol{\beta}$ up to a scale, whether α_i is treated as fixed or random.

7.4.1 Maximum Score Estimator

Manski (1975, 1985, 1987) suggests a maximum score estimator that maximizes the sample average function

$$H_N(\mathbf{b}) = \frac{1}{N}\sum_{i=1}^{N}\sum_{t=2}^{T}\text{sgn}(\Delta\mathbf{x}_{it}'\mathbf{b})\Delta y_{it} \tag{7.4.1}$$

subject to the normalization condition $\mathbf{b}'\mathbf{b} = 1$, where $\Delta\mathbf{x}_{it} = \mathbf{x}_{it} - \mathbf{x}_{i,t-1}$, $\Delta y_{it} = y_{it} - y_{i,t-1}$, and $\text{sgn}(w) = 1$ if $w > 0$, 0 if $w = 0$, and -1 if $w < 0$. This is because under fairly general conditions (7.4.1) converges uniformly to

$$H(\mathbf{b}) = E[\text{sgn}(\Delta\mathbf{x}_{it}'\mathbf{b})\Delta y_{it}], \tag{7.4.2}$$

where $H(\mathbf{b})$ is maximized at $\mathbf{b} = \boldsymbol{\beta}^*$ with $\boldsymbol{\beta}^* = \frac{\boldsymbol{\beta}}{\|\boldsymbol{\beta}\|}$ and $\|\boldsymbol{\beta}\|$ the Euclidean norm $\sum_{k=1}^{K}\beta_k^2$.

To see this, we note that the binary-choice model can be written in the form

$$y_{it} = \begin{cases} 1 & \text{if } y_{it}^* > 0, \\ 0 & \text{if } y_{it}^* \leq 0, \end{cases} \tag{7.4.3}$$

where y_{it}^* is given by (7.2.1) with $v_{it} = \alpha_i + u_{it}$. Under the assumption that u_{it} is independently, identically distributed and is independent of $\mathbf{x}_i$ and α_i for given i, (i.e., $\mathbf{x}_{it}$ is strictly exogenous), we have

$$\begin{aligned} \mathbf{x}_{it}'\boldsymbol{\beta} > \mathbf{x}_{i,t-1}'\boldsymbol{\beta} \quad &\Leftrightarrow \quad E(y_{it} \mid \mathbf{x}_{it}) > E(y_{i,t-1} \mid \mathbf{x}_{i,t-1}), \\ \mathbf{x}_{it}'\boldsymbol{\beta} = \mathbf{x}_{i,t-1}'\boldsymbol{\beta} \quad &\Leftrightarrow \quad E(y_{it} \mid \mathbf{x}_{it}) = E(y_{i,t-1} \mid \mathbf{x}_{i,t-1}), \\ \mathbf{x}_{it}'\boldsymbol{\beta} < \mathbf{x}_{i,t-1}'\boldsymbol{\beta} \quad &\Leftrightarrow \quad E(y_{it} \mid \mathbf{x}_{it}) < E(y_{i,t-1} \mid \mathbf{x}_{i,t-1}). \end{aligned} \tag{7.4.4}$$

Rewriting (7.4.4) in terms of first differences, we have the equivalent representation

$$\begin{aligned} \Delta\mathbf{x}_{it}'\boldsymbol{\beta} > 0 \quad &\Leftrightarrow \quad E(y_{it} - y_{i,t-1} \mid \Delta\mathbf{x}_{it}) > 0, \\ \Delta\mathbf{x}_{it}'\boldsymbol{\beta} = 0 \quad &\Leftrightarrow \quad E(y_{it} - y_{i,t-1} \mid \Delta\mathbf{x}_{it}) = 0, \\ \Delta\mathbf{x}_{it}'\boldsymbol{\beta} < 0 \quad &\Leftrightarrow \quad E(y_{it} - y_{i,t-1} \mid \Delta\mathbf{x}_{it}) < 0. \end{aligned} \tag{7.4.5}$$

It is obvious that (7.4.5) continues to hold for any $\tilde{\boldsymbol{\beta}} = \boldsymbol{\beta}c$ where $c > 0$. Therefore, we shall only consider the normalized vector $\boldsymbol{\beta}^* = \frac{\boldsymbol{\beta}}{\|\boldsymbol{\beta}\|}$.

Then, for any $\mathbf{b}$ (satisfying $\mathbf{b}'\mathbf{b} = 1$) such that $\mathbf{b} \neq \boldsymbol{\beta}^*$,

$$\begin{aligned} H(\boldsymbol{\beta}^*) - H(\mathbf{b}) &= E\{[\text{sgn}(\Delta\mathbf{x}_{it}'\boldsymbol{\beta}^*) - \text{sgn}(\Delta\mathbf{x}_{it}'\mathbf{b})](y_{it} - y_{i,t-1})\} \\ &= 2\int_{W_b} \text{sgn}(\Delta\mathbf{x}_{it}'\boldsymbol{\beta}^*)E[y_t - y_{t-1} \mid \Delta\mathbf{x}]\,dF_{\Delta\mathbf{x}}, \end{aligned} \tag{7.4.6}$$

where $W_b = [\Delta\mathbf{x} : \text{sgn}(\Delta\mathbf{x}'\boldsymbol{\beta}^*) \neq \text{sgn}(\Delta\mathbf{x}'\mathbf{b})]$, and $F_{\Delta\mathbf{x}}$ denotes the distribution of $\Delta\mathbf{x}$. Because of (7.4.5) the relation (7.4.6) implies that for all $\Delta\mathbf{x}$,

$$\text{sgn}(\Delta\mathbf{x}'\boldsymbol{\beta}^*)E[y_t - y_{t-1} \mid \Delta\mathbf{x}] = |E[y_t - y_{t-1} \mid \Delta\mathbf{x}]|.$$

Therefore, under the assumption on the $\mathbf{x}$'s,

$$H(\boldsymbol{\beta}^*) - H(\mathbf{b}) = 2\int_{W_b} |E[y_t - y_{t-1} \mid \Delta\mathbf{x}]|\, dF_{\Delta\mathbf{x}} > 0. \tag{7.4.7}$$

Manski (1985, 1987) has shown that under fairly general conditions, the estimator maximizing the criterion function (7.4.1) yields a strongly consistent estimator of $\boldsymbol{\beta}^*$.

As discussed in Chapter 3 and early sections of this chapter, when T is small the MLE of the (structural) parameters $\boldsymbol{\beta}$ is consistent as $N \to \infty$ for the linear model and inconsistent for the nonlinear model in the presence of incidental parameters α_i, because in the former case we can eliminate α_i by differencing, while in the latter case we cannot. Thus, the error of estimating α_i is transmitted into the estimator of $\boldsymbol{\beta}$ in the nonlinear case. The semiparametric approach allows one to make use of the linear structure of the latent-variable representation (7.2.1) or (7.4.4). The individual-specific effects α_i can again be eliminated by differencing, and hence the lack of knowledge of α_i no longer affects the estimation of $\boldsymbol{\beta}$.

The Manski maximum score estimator is consistent as $N \to \infty$ if the conditional distribution of u_{it} given α_i and $\mathbf{x}_{it}, \mathbf{x}_{i,t-1}$ is identical to the conditional distribution of $u_{i,t-1}$ given α_i and $\mathbf{x}_{it}, \mathbf{x}_{i,t-1}$. However, it converges at the rate $N^{1/3}$, which is much slower than the usual speed of $N^{1/2}$ for the parametric approach. Moreover, Kim and Pollard (1990) have shown that $N^{1/3}$ times the centered maximum score estimator converges in distribution to the random variable that maximizes a certain Gaussian process. This result cannot be used in application, since the properties of the limiting distribution are largely unknown.

The objective function (7.4.1) is equivalent to

$$\max_{\mathbf{b}} H_N^*(\mathbf{b}) = N^{-1}\sum_{i=1}^{N}\sum_{t=2}^{T}[2\cdot\mathbf{1}(\Delta y_{it} = 1) - 1]\mathbf{1}(\Delta\mathbf{x}_{it}'\mathbf{b} \geq \mathbf{0}), \tag{7.4.8}$$

subject to $\mathbf{b}'\mathbf{b} = 1$, where $\mathbf{1}(A)$ is the indicator of the event A, with $\mathbf{1}(A) = 1$ if A occurs and 0 otherwise. The complexity of the maximum score estimator and its slow convergence are due to the discontinuity of the function $H_N(\mathbf{b})$ or $H_N^*(\mathbf{b})$. Horowitz (1992) suggests avoiding these difficulties by replacing $H_N^*(\mathbf{b})$ with a sufficiently smooth function $\tilde{H}_N(\mathbf{b})$ whose almost sure limit as $N \to \infty$ is the same as that of $H_N^*(\mathbf{b})$. Let $K(\cdot)$ be a continuous function of the real line into itself such that

i. $|K(v)| < M$ for some finite M and all v in $(-\infty, \infty)$,
ii. $\lim_{v\to-\infty} K(v) = 0$ and $\lim_{v\to\infty} K(v) = 1$.

The $K(\cdot)$ here is analogous to a cumulative distribution function. Let $\{\sigma_N : N = 1, 2, \ldots\}$ be a sequence of strictly positive real numbers satisfying $\lim_{N\to\infty}\sigma_N = 0$. Define

$$\tilde{H}_N(\mathbf{b}) = N^{-1}\sum_{i=1}^{N}\sum_{t=2}^{T}[2\cdot\mathbf{1}(\Delta y_{it} = 1) - 1]K(\mathbf{b}'\Delta\mathbf{x}_{it}/\sigma_N). \tag{7.4.9}$$

Horowitz (1992) defines a smoothed maximum score estimator as any solution that maximizes (7.4.9). Like Manski's estimator, $\boldsymbol{\beta}$ can be identified only up to scale. Instead of using the normalization $\|\boldsymbol{\beta}^*\| = 1$, Horowitz (1992) finds it more convenient to use the normalization that the coefficient of one component of $\Delta\mathbf{x}$, say Δx_1, is to be equal to 1 in absolute value if $\beta_1 \neq 0$, and the probability distribution of Δx_1 conditional on the remaining components is absolutely continuous (with respect to Lebesgue measure).

The smoothed maximum score estimator is strongly consistent under the assumption that the distribution of $\Delta u_{it} = u_{it} - u_{i,t-1}$ conditional on $\Delta\mathbf{x}_{it}$ is symmetrically distributed with mean equal to zero. The asymptotic behavior of the estimator can be analyzed using the Taylor series methods of asymptotic theory by taking a Taylor expansion of the first-order conditions and applying a version of the central limit theorem and the law of large numbers. The smoothed estimator of $\boldsymbol{\beta}$ is consistent and, after centering and suitable normalization, is asymptotically normally distributed. Its rate of convergence is at least as fast as $N^{-2/5}$ and, depending on how smooth the distribution of u and $\boldsymbol{\beta}'\Delta\mathbf{x}$ are, can be arbitrarily close to $N^{-1/2}$.

7.4.2 A Root-N Consistent Semiparametric Estimator

The speed of convergence of the smoothed maximum score estimator depends on the speed of convergence of $\sigma_N \to 0$. Lee (1999) suggests a root-N consistent semiparametric estimator that does not depend on a smoothing parameter by maximizing the double sums

$$\{N(N-1)\}^{-1}\sum_{i\neq j}\sum_{t=2}^{T}\operatorname{sgn}(\Delta\mathbf{x}'_{it}\mathbf{b}-\Delta\mathbf{x}'_{jt}\mathbf{b})(\Delta y_{it}-\Delta y_{jt})\Delta y_{it}^2\,\Delta y_{jt}^2$$
$$=\binom{N}{2}^{-1}\sum_{\substack{i\\ i<j,}}\ \sum_{\substack{j\\ \Delta y_{it}\neq\Delta y_{jt}}}\ \sum_{\substack{t=2\\ \Delta y_{it}\neq 0,\ \Delta y_{jt}\neq 0}}^{T}\operatorname{sgn}(\Delta\mathbf{x}'_{it}\mathbf{b}-\Delta\mathbf{x}'_{jt}\mathbf{b})(\Delta y_{it}-\Delta y_{jt}) \tag{7.4.10}$$

with respect to $\mathbf{b}$. The consistency of the Lee estimator $\hat{\mathbf{b}}$ follows from the fact that although $\Delta y_{it} - \Delta y_{jt}$ can take five values $(0, \pm 1, \pm 2)$, the event that $(\Delta y_{it} - \Delta y_{jt})\Delta y_{it}^2\,\Delta y_{jt}^2 \neq 0$ excludes $(0, \pm 1)$ and thus makes $\Delta y_{it} - \Delta y_{jt}$ binary (2 or $-$ 2). Conditional on given j, the first average over i and t converges to

$$E\left\{\operatorname{sgn}(\Delta\mathbf{x}'\mathbf{b}-\Delta\mathbf{x}'_j\mathbf{b})(\Delta y-\Delta y_j)\Delta y^2\,\Delta y_j^2 \,\middle|\, \Delta\mathbf{x}_j, \Delta y_j\right\}. \tag{7.4.11}$$

The $\sqrt{N}$ speed of convergence follows from the second average of the smooth function (7.4.10).

Normalizing $\beta_1 = 1$, the asymptotic covariance matrix of $\sqrt{N}(\tilde{\mathbf{b}}-\tilde{\boldsymbol{\beta}})$ is equal to

$$4\cdot(E\nabla_2\boldsymbol{\tau})^{-1}(E\nabla_1\boldsymbol{\tau}\,\nabla_1\boldsymbol{\tau}')(E\nabla_2\boldsymbol{\tau})^{-1}, \tag{7.4.12}$$

where $\tilde{\boldsymbol{\beta}} = (\beta_2, \ldots, \beta_K)'$, $\tilde{\mathbf{b}}$ is its estimator,

$$\tau(\Delta y_j, \Delta \mathbf{x}_j, \tilde{\mathbf{b}}) \equiv E_{i|j}\{\text{sgn}(\Delta \mathbf{x}_i' \mathbf{b} - \Delta \mathbf{x}_j' \mathbf{b})(\Delta y_i - \Delta y_j)\Delta y_i^2 \Delta y_j^2\}, \quad i \neq j,$$

with $E_{i|j}$ denoting the conditional expectation of $(\Delta y_i, \Delta \mathbf{x}_i')$ conditional on $(\Delta y_j, \Delta \mathbf{x}_j')$, and $\nabla_1 \boldsymbol{\tau}$ and $\nabla_2 \boldsymbol{\tau}$ denote the first- and second-order derivative matrices of $\tau(\Delta y_j, \Delta \mathbf{x}_j, \tilde{\mathbf{b}})$ with respect to $\tilde{\mathbf{b}}$.

The parametric approach requires the specification of the distribution of u. If the distribution of u is misspecified, the MLE of $\boldsymbol{\beta}$ is inconsistent. The semiparametric approach does not require the specification of the distribution of u and permits its distribution to depend on $\mathbf{x}$ in an unknown way (heteroscedasticity of unknown form). It is consistent up to a scale, whether the unobserved individual effects are treated as fixed or correlated with $\mathbf{x}$. However, the step of differencing $\mathbf{x}_{it}$ eliminates time-invariant variables from the estimation. Lee's (1999) root-N consistent estimator takes the additional differencing across individuals, $\Delta \mathbf{x}_i - \Delta \mathbf{x}_j$, and further reduces the dimension of estimable parameters by eliminating "period individual-invariant" variables (e.g., time dummies and macroeconomic shocks common to all individuals) from the specification. Moreover, the requirement that u_{it} and $u_{i,t-1}$ be identically distributed conditional on $(\mathbf{x}_{it}, \mathbf{x}_{it-1}, \alpha_i)$ does not allow the presence of the lagged dependent variables in $\mathbf{x}_{it}$. Neither can a semiparametric approach be used to generate the predicted probability conditional on $\mathbf{x}$ as in the parametric approach. All it can estimate is the relative effects of the explanatory variables.

7.5 DYNAMIC MODELS

7.5.1 The General Model

The static models discussed in the previous sections assume that the probability of moving (or staying) in or out of a state is independent of the occurrence or nonoccurrence of the event in the past. However, in a variety of contexts, such as in the study of the incidence of accidents (Bates and Neyman (1951)), brand loyalty (Chintagunta, Kyriazidou, and Perktold (2001)), labor-force participation (Heckman and Willis (1977); Hyslop (1999)), and unemployment (Layton (1978)), it is often noted that individuals who have experienced an event in the past are more likely to experience the event in the future than individuals who have not. In other words, the conditional probability that an individual will experience the event in the future is a function of past experience.

To analyze the intertemporal relationships among discrete variables, Heckman (1978a, 1981b) proposed a general framework in terms of a latent-continuous-random-variable crossing the threshold. He let the continuous random variable y_{it}^* be a function of $\mathbf{x}_{it}$ and past occurrence of the event:

$$y_{it}^* = \boldsymbol{\beta}' \mathbf{x}_{it} + \sum_{l=1}^{t-1} \gamma_l y_{i,t-l} + \phi \sum_{s=1}^{t-1} \prod_{l=1}^{s} y_{i,t-l} + v_{it},$$

$$i = 1, \ldots, N, \quad t = 1, \ldots, T, \qquad (7.5.1)$$

and

$$y_{it} = \begin{cases} 1 & \text{if } y_{it}^* > 0, \\ 0 & \text{if } y_{it}^* \leq 0. \end{cases} \tag{7.5.2}$$

The error term v_{it} is assumed to be independent of $\mathbf{x}_{it}$ and is independently distributed over i, with a general intertemporal variance–covariance matrix $E\mathbf{v}_i\mathbf{v}_i' = \Omega$. The coefficient γ_l measures the effect of experience of the event l periods ago on current values of y_{it}^*. The coefficient ϕ measures the effect of the cumulative recent spell of experience in the state, for those still in the state, on the current value of y_{it}^*.

Specifications (7.5.1) and (7.5.2) accommodate a wide variety of stochastic models that appear in the literature. For example, let $\mathbf{x}_{it} = 1$, and let v_{it} be independently identically distributed. If $\gamma_l = 0,\ l = 2, \ldots, T-1$, and $\phi = 0$, equations (7.5.1) and (7.5.2) generate a time-homogenous first-order Markov process. If $\gamma_l = 0, l = 1, \ldots, T-1$, and $\phi \neq 0$, a renewal process is generated. If $\gamma_l = 0, l = 1, \ldots, T-1$, and $\phi = 0$, a simple Bernoulli model results. If one allows v_{it} to follow an autoregressive moving-average scheme, but keeps the assumption that $\gamma_l = 0, l = 1, \ldots, T-1$, and $\phi = 0$, the Coleman (1964) latent Markov model emerges.

As said before, repeated observations of a given group of individuals over time permit us to construct a model in which individuals may differ in their propensity to experience the event. Such heterogeneity is allowed by decomposing the error term v_{it} as

$$v_{it} = \alpha_i + u_{it}, \qquad i = 1, \ldots, N, \quad t = 1, \ldots, T, \tag{7.5.3}$$

where u_{it} is independently distributed over i with arbitrary serial correlation, and α_i is individual-specific and can be treated as a fixed constant or as random. Thus, for example, if the previous assumptions on the Markov process

$$\gamma_l = 0, \quad l = 2, \ldots, T-1, \quad \text{and} \quad \phi = 0$$

hold, but v_{it} follows a "components-of-variance" scheme (7.5.3), then a compound first-order Markov process, closely related to previous work on the mover–stayer model (Goodman (1961); Singer and Spilerman (1976)), is generated.

Specifications (7.5.1)–(7.5.3) allow for three sources of persistence (after controlling for the observed explanatory variables $\mathbf{x}$). Persistence can be the result of serial correlation in the error term u_{it}, or the result of "unobserved heterogeneity" α_i, or the result of true state dependence through the term $\gamma y_{i,t-l}$ or $\phi \sum_{s=1}^{t-l} \prod_{l=1}^{s} y_{i,t-l}$. Distinguishing the sources of persistence is important because a policy that temporarily increases the probability that $y = 1$ will have different implications about future probabilities of experiencing an event.

When the conditional probability of an individual staying in a state is a function of past experience, two new issues arise. One is how to treat the initial observations. The second is how to distinguish true state dependence from spurious state dependence in which the past value appears in the specification merely as a proxy for the unobserved individual effects. The first issue is crucial in deriving consistent estimators for a given model. The second issue is important because the time dependence among observed events could be arising either from the fact that the actual experience of an event has modified individual behavior, or from unobserved components that are correlated over time, or from a combination of both.

7.5.2 Initial Conditions

When dependence among time-ordered outcomes is considered, just as in the dynamic linear-regression model, the problem of initial conditions must be solved before parameters generating the stochastic process can be estimated. In order to focus the discussion on the essential aspects of the problem of initial conditions and its solutions, we assume that there are no exogenous variables and that the observed data are generated by a first-order Markov process. Namely,

$$\begin{aligned} y_{it}^* &= \beta_0 + \gamma y_{i,t-1} + v_{it}, \\ y_{it} &= \begin{cases} 1 & \text{if } y_{it}^* > 0, \\ 0 & \text{if } y_{it}^* \leq 0. \end{cases} \end{aligned} \tag{7.5.4}$$

For ease of exposition we shall also assume that u_{it} is independently normally distributed, with mean zero and variance σ_u^2 normalized to be equal to 1. It should be noted that the general conclusions of the following discussion also hold for other types of distributions.

In much applied work in the social sciences, two assumptions for initial conditions are typically invoked: (1) the initial conditions or relevant presample history of the process is assumed to be truly exogenous, or (2) the process is assumed to be in equilibrium. Under the assumption that y_{i0} is a fixed nonstochastic constant for individual i, the joint probability of $\mathbf{y}_i' = (y_{i1}, \ldots, y_{iT})$, given α_i, is

$$\prod_{t=1}^{T} F(y_{it} \mid y_{i,t-1}, \alpha_i) = \prod_{t=1}^{T} \Phi\{(\beta_0 + \gamma y_{i,t-1} + \alpha_i)(2y_{it} - 1)\}, \tag{7.5.5}$$

where Φ is the standard normal cumulative distribution function. Under the assumption that the process is in equilibrium, the limiting marginal probability for $y_{i0} = 1$ for all t, given α_i, is (Karlin and Taylor (1975))[14]

$$P_i = \frac{\Phi(\beta_0 + \alpha_i)}{1 - \Phi(\beta_0 + \gamma + \alpha_i) + \Phi(\beta_0 + \alpha_i)}, \tag{7.5.6}$$

and the limiting probability for $y_{i0} = 0$ is $1 - P_i$. Thus the joint probability of $(y_{i0}, \ldots, y_{iT})$, given α_i, is

$$\prod_{t=1}^{T} \Phi\{(\beta + \gamma y_{i,t-1} + \alpha_i)(2y_{it} - 1)\} P_i^{y_{i0}} (1 - P_i)^{1-y_{i0}}. \tag{7.5.7}$$

If α_i is random, with distribution $G(\alpha)$, the likelihood function for the random-effects model under the first assumption is

$$L = \prod_{i=1}^{N} \int \prod_{t=1}^{T} \Phi\{(\beta_0 + \gamma y_{i,t-1} + \alpha)(2y_{it} - 1)\}\, dG(\alpha). \tag{7.5.8}$$

The likelihood function under the second assumption is

$$L = \prod_{i=1}^{N} \int \prod_{t=1}^{T} \Phi\{(\beta_0 + \gamma y_{i,t-1} + \alpha)(2y_{it} - 1)\} \times P_i^{y_{i0}}(1 - P_i)^{1-y_{i0}}\, dG(\alpha). \tag{7.5.9}$$

The likelihood functions (7.5.8) and (7.5.9) under both sets of assumptions about initial conditions are in closed form. When α_i is treated as random, the MLEs for β_0, γ, and σ_α^2 are consistent if N tends to infinity or if both N and T tend to infinity. When α_i is treated as a fixed constant (7.5.5), the MLEs for β_0, γ, and α_i are consistent only when T tends to infinity. If T is finite, the MLE is biased. Moreover, the limited results from Monte Carlo experiments suggest that, contrary to the static case, the bias is significant (Heckman (1981b)).

However, the assumption that initial conditions are fixed constants may be justifiable only if the disturbances that generate the process are serially independent and if a genuinely new process is fortuitously observed at the beginning of the sample. If the process has been in operation prior to the time it is sampled, or if the disturbances of the model are serially dependent as in the presence of individual-specific random effects, the initial conditions are not exogenous. The assumption that the process is in equilibrium also raises problems in many applications, especially when time-varying exogenous variables are driving the stochastic process.

Suppose that the analyst does not have access to the process from the beginning; then the initial state for individual i, y_{i0}, cannot be assumed fixed. The initial state is determined by the process generating the panel sample. The sample likelihood function for the fixed-effects model is

$$L = \prod_{i=1}^{N} \prod_{t=1}^{T} \Phi\{(\beta_0 + \gamma y_{i,t-1} + \alpha_i)(2y_{it} - 1)\} f(y_{i0} \mid \alpha_i), \tag{7.5.10}$$

and the sample likelihood function for the random-effects model is

$$L = \prod_{i=1}^{N} \int_{-\infty}^{\infty} \prod_{t=1}^{T} \Phi\{(\beta_0 + \gamma y_{i,t-1} + \alpha)(2y_{it} - 1)\} f(y_{i0} \mid \alpha)\, dG(\alpha), \tag{7.5.11}$$

where $f(y_{i0} \mid \alpha)$ denotes the marginal probability of y_{i0} given α_i. Thus, unless T is very large, maximizing (7.5.5) or (7.5.8) yields inconsistent estimates.[15]

Because y_{i0} is a function of unobserved past values, besides the fact that the marginal distribution of $f(y_{i0} \mid \alpha)$ is not easy to derive, maximizing (7.5.10) or

(7.5.11) is also considerably involved. Heckman (1981b) therefore suggested that we approximate the initial conditions for a dynamic discrete choice model by the following procedure:

1. Approximate the probability of y_{i0}, the initial state in the sample, by a probit model, with index function
$$y_{i0}^* = Q(\mathbf{x}_i) + \epsilon_{i0}, \tag{7.5.12}$$
and
$$y_{i0} = \begin{cases} 1 & \text{if } y_{i0}^* > 0, \\ 0 & \text{if } y_{i0}^* \leq 0, \end{cases} \tag{7.5.13}$$
where $Q(\mathbf{x}_i)$ is a general function of $\mathbf{x}_{it}$, $t = 0, \ldots, T$, usually specified as linear in $\mathbf{x}_{it}$, and ϵ_{i0} is assumed to be normally distributed, with mean zero and variance 1.
2. Permit ϵ_{i0} to be freely correlated with v_{it}, $t = 1, \ldots, T$.
3. Estimate the model by maximum likelihood without imposing any restrictions between the parameters of the structural system and parameters of the approximate reduced-form probability for the initial state of the sample.

Heckman (1981b) conducted Monte Carlo studies comparing the performance of the MLEs when assumptions on initial y_{i0} and α_i conform with the true data generating process, an approximate reduced-form probability for y_{i0}, and false fixed y_{i0} and α_i for a first-order Markov process. The data for his experiment were generated by the random-effects model

$$\begin{aligned} y_{it}^* &= \beta x_{it} + \gamma y_{i,t-1} + \alpha_i + u_{it}, \\ y_{it} &= \begin{cases} 1 & \text{if } y_{it}^* > 0, \\ 0 & \text{if } y_{it}^* \leq 0, \end{cases} \end{aligned} \tag{7.5.14}$$

where the exogenous variable x_{it} was generated by (7.3.23). He let the process operate for 25 periods before selecting samples of 8 (=T) periods for each of the 100 (=N) individuals used in the 25 samples for each parameter set. Heckman's Monte Carlo results are shown in Table 7.2.

These results show that, contrary to the static model, the fixed-effects probit estimator performs poorly. The greater the variance of the individual effects (σ_α^2), the greater the bias. The t statistics based on the estimated information matrix also lead to a misleading inference by not rejecting the false null hypotheses of $\gamma = \beta = 0$ in the vast majority of samples.

By comparison, Heckman's approximate solution performs better. Although the estimates are still biased from the true values, their biases are not significant, particularly when they are compared with the ideal estimates. The t statistics based on the approximate solutions are also much more reliable than in the fixed-effects probit model, in that they lead to a correct inference in a greater proportion of the samples.

Table 7.2. *Monte Carlo results for first-order Markov process*

γ		$\sigma_\alpha^2 = 3$			$\sigma_\alpha^2 = 1$		
		$\beta = -0.1$	$\beta = 1$	$\beta = 0$	$\beta = -0.1$	$\beta = 1$	$\beta = 0$
Values of $\hat{\gamma}$ and $\hat{\beta}$ for the random-effects estimator with known initial conditions[a]							
0.5	$\hat{\gamma}$	n.a.[c]	0.57	n.a.[c]			
	$\hat{\beta}$	n.a.[c]	0.94	—[d]			
0.1	$\hat{\gamma}$	0.13	0.12	0.14			
	$\hat{\beta}$	−0.11	1.10	—			
Values of $\hat{\gamma}$ and $\hat{\beta}$ for the approximate random-effects estimation[a]							
0.5	$\hat{\gamma}$	0.63	0.60	0.70	n.a.[c]	0.54	0.62
	$\hat{\beta}$	−0.131	0.91	—	n.a.[c]	0.93	—
0.1	$\hat{\gamma}$	0.14	0.13	0.17	0.11	0.11	0.13
	$\hat{\beta}$	−0.12	0.92	—	−0.12	0.95	—
Values of $\hat{\gamma}$ and $\hat{\beta}$ for the fixed-effects estimator[b]							
0.5	$\hat{\gamma}$	0.14	0.19	0.03	n.a.[c]	0.27	0.17
	$\hat{\beta}$	−0.07	1.21	—	n.a.[c]	1.17	—
0.1	$\hat{\gamma}$	−0.34	−0.21	−0.04	−0.28	−0.15	−0.01
	$\hat{\beta}$	−0.06	1.14	—	−0.08	1.12	—

[a] $N = 100; T = 3$.
[b] $N = 100; T = 8$.
[c] Data not available because the model was not estimated.
[d] Not estimated.
Source: Heckman (1981b, Table 4.2).

Heckman's Monte Carlo results also point to a disquieting feature. Namely, the MLE produces a biased estimator even under ideal conditions with a correctly specified likelihood function. Because a panel with 100 observations of three periods is not uncommon, this finding deserves serious consideration.

7.5.3 A Conditional Approach

The likelihood approach cannot yield a consistent estimator when T is fixed and N tends to infinity if the individual effects are fixed. If the individual effects are random and independent of $\mathbf{x}$, the consistency of the MLE depends on the correct formulation of the probability distributions of the effects and initial observations. A semiparametric approach cannot be implemented for a dynamic model, because the strict exogeneity condition of explanatory variables is violated with the presence of lagged dependent variables as explanatory variables. When that condition is violated, $E(\Delta u_{it} \mid \mathbf{x}_{it}, \mathbf{x}_{i,t-1}, y_{i,t-1}, y_{i,t-2}) \neq 0$. In other words, the one-to-one correspondence relation of the form (7.4.4) is violated.

Hence, the Manski (1985) maximum score estimator cannot be implemented. Neither can the (unrestricted) conditional approach be implemented. Consider the case of $T = 2$. The basic idea of the conditional approach is to consider the probability of $y_{i2} = 1$ or 0 conditional on explanatory variables in both periods and conditonal on $y_{i1} \neq y_{i2}$. If the explanatory variables of $\text{Prob}(y_{i2} = 1)$ include y_{i1}, then the conditional probability is either 1 or 0 according as $y_{i1} = 0$ or 1, and hence provides no information about γ and $\boldsymbol{\beta}$.

However, in the case that $T \geq 3$ and $\mathbf{x}_{it}$ follows a certain special pattern, Honoré and Kyriazidou (2000a) show that it is possible to generalize the conditional-probability approach to consistently estimate the unknown parameters for the logit model or to generalize the maximum score approach without the need of formulating the distribution of α_i or the probability distribution of the initial observations for certain types of discrete choice models. However, the estimators converge to the true values at the speed considerably slower than the usual $\sqrt{N}$ rate.

Consider the model (7.5.4) with the assumption that u_{it} is logistically distributed. Then the model of $(y_{i0}, \ldots y_{iT})$ is of the form

$$P(y_{i0} = 1 \mid \alpha_i) = P_0(\alpha_i), \tag{7.5.15}$$

$$P(y_{it} = 1 \mid \alpha_i, y_{i0}, \ldots, y_{i,t-1}) = \frac{\exp(\gamma y_{i,t-1} + \alpha_i)}{1 + \exp(\gamma y_{i,t-1} + \alpha_i)} \quad \text{for} \quad t = 1, 2, \ldots, T. \tag{7.5.16}$$

When $T \geq 3$, Chamberlain (1993) shows that the inference on γ can be made independent of α_i by using a conditional approach.

For ease of exposition, we shall assume that $T = 3$. Consider the events

$$A = \{y_{i0}, y_{i1} = 0, y_{i2} = 1, y_{i3}\},$$
$$B = \{y_{i0}, y_{i1} = 1, y_{i2} = 0, y_{i3}\},$$

where y_{i0} and y_{i3} can be either 1 or 0. Then

$$P(A) = P_0(\alpha_i)^{y_{i0}}[1 - P_0(\alpha_i)]^{1-y_{i0}} \cdot \frac{1}{1 + \exp(\gamma y_{i0} + \alpha_i)} \times \frac{\exp(\alpha_i)}{1 + \exp(\alpha_i)} \cdot \frac{\exp[(\gamma + \alpha_i)y_{i3}]}{1 + \exp(\gamma + \alpha_i)}, \tag{7.5.17}$$

and

$$P(B) = P_0(\alpha_i)^{y_{i0}}[1 - P_0(\alpha_i)]^{1-y_{i0}} \cdot \frac{\exp(\gamma y_{i0} + \alpha_i)}{1 + \exp(\gamma y_{i0} + \alpha_i)} \times \frac{1}{1 + \exp(\gamma + \alpha_i)} \cdot \frac{\exp(\alpha_i y_{i3})}{1 + \exp(\alpha_i)}. \tag{7.5.18}$$

Hence,

$$P(A \mid A \cup B) = P(A \mid y_{i0}, y_{i1} + y_{i2} = 1, y_{i3}) = \frac{\exp(\gamma y_{i3})}{\exp(\gamma y_{i3}) + \exp(\gamma y_{i0})} = \frac{1}{1 + \exp[\gamma(y_{i0} - y_{i3})]}, \tag{7.5.19}$$

and

$$P(B \mid A \cup B) = P(B \mid y_{i0}, y_{i1} + y_{i2} = 1, y_{i3}) = 1 - P(A \mid A \cup B) = \frac{\exp[\gamma(y_{i0} - y_{i3})]}{1 + \exp[\gamma(y_{i0} - y_{i3})]}. \tag{7.5.20}$$

Equations (7.5.19) and (7.5.20) are in the binary logit form and do not depend on α_i. Let $d_i = 1$ if A occurs and 0 if B occurs. The conditional log likelihood

$$\log \tilde{L} = \sum_{i=1}^{N} \mathbf{1}(y_{i1} + y_{i2} = 1) \times \{y_{i1}[\gamma(y_{i0} - y_{i3})] - \log[1 + \exp\gamma(y_{i0} - y_{i3})]\} \tag{7.5.21}$$

is in the conditional logit form. Maximizing (7.5.21) yields a $\sqrt{N}$-consistent estimator of γ, where $\mathbf{1}(A) = 1$ if A occurs and 0 otherwise.

When exogenous variables $\mathbf{x}_{it}$ also appear as explanatory variables in the latent response function

$$y_{it}^* = \boldsymbol{\beta}'\mathbf{x}_{it} + \gamma y_{i,t-1} + \alpha_i + u_{it}, \tag{7.5.22}$$

we may write

$$P(y_{i0} = 1 \mid \mathbf{x}_i, \alpha_i) = P_0(\mathbf{x}_i, \alpha_i), \tag{7.5.23}$$

$$P(y_{it} = 1 \mid \mathbf{x}_i, \alpha_i, y_{i0}, \ldots, y_{i,t-1}) = \frac{\exp(\mathbf{x}_{it}'\boldsymbol{\beta} + \gamma y_{i,t-1} + \alpha_i)}{1 + \exp(\mathbf{x}_{it}'\boldsymbol{\beta} + \gamma y_{i,t-1} + \alpha_i)}, \quad t = 1, \ldots, T. \tag{7.5.24}$$

In general, $P(A \mid \mathbf{x}_i, \alpha_i, A \cup B)$ will depend on α_i. However, if $\mathbf{x}_{i2} = \mathbf{x}_{i3}$, Honoré and Kyriazidou (2000a), using the same conditioning method, show that

$$P(A \mid \mathbf{x}_i, \alpha_i, A \cup B, \mathbf{x}_{i2} = \mathbf{x}_{i3}) = \frac{1}{1 + \exp[(\mathbf{x}_{i1} - \mathbf{x}_{i2})'\boldsymbol{\beta} + \gamma(y_{i0} - y_{i3})]}, \tag{7.5.25}$$

which does not depend on α_i. If $\mathbf{x}_{it}$ is continuous, it may be rare that $\mathbf{x}_{i2} = \mathbf{x}_{i3}$.

Honoré and Kyriazidou (2000a) propose estimating β and γ by maximizing

$$\sum_{i=1}^{N} \mathbf{1}(y_{i1}+y_{i2}=1)K\left(\frac{\mathbf{x}_{i2}-\mathbf{x}_{i3}}{\sigma_N}\right)\log\left\{\frac{\exp[(\mathbf{x}_{i1}-\mathbf{x}_{i2})'\mathbf{b}+\gamma(y_{i0}-y_{i3})]^{y_{i1}}}{1+\exp[(\mathbf{x}_{i1}-\mathbf{x}_{i2})'\mathbf{b}+\gamma(y_{i0}-y_{i3})]}\right\} \tag{7.5.26}$$

with respect to $\mathbf{b}$ and γ (over some compact set) if $P(\mathbf{x}_{i2}=\mathbf{x}_{i3})>0$. Here $K(\cdot)$ is a kernel density function which gives appropriate weight to observation i, while σ_N is a bandwidth which shrinks to zero as N tends to infinity at a speed that is also a function of the dimension of $\mathbf{x}$. The asymptotic theory will require that $K(\cdot)$ be chosen so that a number of regularity conditions are satisfied, such as $|K(\cdot)|<M$ for some constant M, $K(v)\to 0$ as $|v|\to\infty$, and $\int K(v)\,dv=1$. For instance, $K(v)$ is often taken to be the standard normal density function, and $\sigma_N=cN^{-1/5}$ for some constant c when there is only one regressor. The effect of the factor $K((\mathbf{x}_{i2}-\mathbf{x}_{i3})/\sigma_N)$ is to give more weight to observations for which $\mathbf{x}_{i2}$ is close to $\mathbf{x}_{i3}$. Their estimator is consistent and asymptotically normal, although their rate of convergence is only $\sqrt{N\sigma_N^k}$, which is considerably slower than $\sqrt{N}$, where k is the dimension of $\mathbf{x}_{it}$.

The conditional approach works for the logit model, but it does not seem applicable for general nonlinear models. However, if the nonlinearity can be put in the single-index form $F(a)$ with the transformation function F being a strictly increasing distribution function, then Manski's (1987) maximum score estimator for the static case can be generalized to the case where the lagged dependent variable is included in the explanatory variable set by considering

$$\begin{aligned}
&P(A\mid \mathbf{x}_i,\alpha_i,\mathbf{x}_{i2}=\mathbf{x}_{i3})\\
&\quad= P_0(\mathbf{x}_i,\alpha_i)^{y_{i0}}[1-P_0(\mathbf{x}_i,\alpha_i)]^{1-y_{i0}}\\
&\qquad\times[1-F(\mathbf{x}_{i1}'\boldsymbol{\beta}+\gamma y_{i0}+\alpha_i)]\times F(\mathbf{x}_{i2}'\boldsymbol{\beta}+\alpha_i)\\
&\qquad\times[1-F(\mathbf{x}_{i2}'\boldsymbol{\beta}+\gamma+\alpha_i)]^{1-y_{i3}}\times F(\mathbf{x}_{i2}'\boldsymbol{\beta}+\gamma+\alpha_i)^{y_{i3}},
\end{aligned} \tag{7.5.27}$$

and

$$\begin{aligned}
&P(B\mid \mathbf{x}_i,\alpha_i,\mathbf{x}_{i2}=\mathbf{x}_{i3})\\
&\quad= P_0(\mathbf{x}_i,\alpha_i)^{y_{i0}}[1-P_0(\mathbf{x}_i,\alpha_i)]^{1-y_{i0}}\\
&\qquad\times F(\mathbf{x}_{i1}'\boldsymbol{\beta}+\gamma y_{i0}+\alpha_i)\times[1-F(\mathbf{x}_{i2}'\boldsymbol{\beta}+\gamma+\alpha_i)]\\
&\qquad\times[1-F(\mathbf{x}_{i2}'\boldsymbol{\beta}+\alpha_i)]^{1-y_{i3}}\times F(\mathbf{x}_{i2}'\boldsymbol{\beta}+\alpha_i)^{y_{i3}}.
\end{aligned} \tag{7.5.28}$$

If $y_{i3}=0$, then

$$\begin{aligned}
&\frac{P(A\mid \mathbf{x}_i,\alpha_i,\mathbf{x}_{i2}=\mathbf{x}_{i3})}{P(B\mid \mathbf{x}_i,\alpha_i,\mathbf{x}_{i2}=\mathbf{x}_{i3})}\\
&\qquad=\frac{1-F(\mathbf{x}_{i1}'\boldsymbol{\beta}+\gamma y_{i0}+\alpha_i)}{1-F(\mathbf{x}_{i2}'\boldsymbol{\beta}+\alpha_i)}\times\frac{F(\mathbf{x}_{i2}'\boldsymbol{\beta}+\alpha_i)}{F(\mathbf{x}_{i1}'\boldsymbol{\beta}+\gamma y_{i0}+\alpha_i)}\\
&\qquad=\frac{1-F(\mathbf{x}_{i1}'\boldsymbol{\beta}+\gamma y_{i0}+\alpha_i)}{1-F(\mathbf{x}_{i2}'\boldsymbol{\beta}+\gamma y_{i3}+\alpha_i)}\times\frac{F(\mathbf{x}_{i2}'\boldsymbol{\beta}+\gamma y_{i3}+\alpha_i)}{F(\mathbf{x}_{i1}'\boldsymbol{\beta}+\gamma y_{i0}+\alpha_i)},
\end{aligned} \tag{7.5.29}$$

where the second equality follows from the fact that $y_{i3} = 0$. If $y_{i3} = 1$, then

$$
\begin{aligned}
&\frac{P(A \mid \mathbf{x}_i, \alpha_i, \mathbf{x}_{i2} = \mathbf{x}_{i3})}{P(B \mid \mathbf{x}_i, \alpha_i, \mathbf{x}_{i2} = \mathbf{x}_{i3})} \\
&\quad = \frac{1 - F(\mathbf{x}'_{i1}\boldsymbol{\beta} + \gamma y_{i0} + \alpha_i)}{1 - F(\mathbf{x}'_{i2}\boldsymbol{\beta} + \gamma + \alpha_i)} \times \frac{F(\mathbf{x}'_{i2}\boldsymbol{\beta} + \gamma + \alpha_i)}{F(\mathbf{x}'_{i1}\boldsymbol{\beta} + \gamma y_{i0} + \alpha_i)} \\
&\quad = \frac{1 - F(\mathbf{x}'_{i1}\boldsymbol{\beta} + \gamma y_{i0} + \alpha_i)}{1 - F(\mathbf{x}'_{i2}\boldsymbol{\beta} + \gamma y_{i3} + \alpha_i)} \times \frac{F(\mathbf{x}'_{i2}\boldsymbol{\beta} + \gamma y_{i3} + \alpha_i)}{F(\mathbf{x}'_{i1}\boldsymbol{\beta} + \gamma y_{i0} + \alpha_i)}, \qquad (7.5.30)
\end{aligned}
$$

where the second equality follows from the fact that $y_{i3} = 1$, so that $\gamma y_{i3} = \gamma$. In either case, the monotonicity of F implies that

$$
\frac{P(A)}{P(B)} \begin{cases} > 1 & \text{if } \mathbf{x}'_{i2}\boldsymbol{\beta} + \gamma y_{i3} > \mathbf{x}'_{i1}\boldsymbol{\beta} + \gamma y_{i0}, \\ < 1 & \text{if } \mathbf{x}'_{i2}\boldsymbol{\beta} + \gamma y_{i3} < \mathbf{x}'_{i1}\boldsymbol{\beta} + \gamma y_{i0}. \end{cases}
$$

Therefore,

$$
\begin{aligned}
&\operatorname{sgn}[P(A \mid \mathbf{x}_i, \alpha_i, \mathbf{x}_{i2} = \mathbf{x}_{i3}) - P(B \mid \mathbf{x}_i, \alpha_i, \mathbf{x}_{i2} = \mathbf{x}_{i3})] \\
&\quad = \operatorname{sgn}[(\mathbf{x}_{i2} - \mathbf{x}_{i1})'\boldsymbol{\beta} + \gamma(y_{i3} - y_{i0})]. \qquad (7.5.31)
\end{aligned}
$$

Hence, Honoré and Kyriazidou (2000) propose a maximum score estimator that maximizes the score function

$$
\sum_{i=1}^{N} K\left(\frac{\mathbf{x}_{i2} - \mathbf{x}_{i3}}{\sigma_N}\right)(y_{i2} - y_{i1})\operatorname{sgn}[(\mathbf{x}_{i2} - \mathbf{x}_{i1})'\boldsymbol{\beta} + \gamma(y_{i3} - y_{i0})] \qquad (7.5.32)
$$

with respect to $\boldsymbol{\beta}$ and γ. Honoré and Kyriazidou's estimator is consistent (up to a scale) if the density $f(\mathbf{x}_{i2} - \mathbf{x}_{i3})$ of $\mathbf{x}_{i2} - \mathbf{x}_{i3}$ is strictly positive at zero $[f(0) > 0]$. (This assumption is required for consistency.)

We have discussed the estimation of panel data dynamic discrete-choice models assuming that $T = 3$. It can be easily generalized to the case of $T > 3$ by maximizing the objective function that is based on sequences where an individual switches between alternatives in any two of the middle $T - 1$ periods. For instance, for the logit model (7.5.24), the objective function becomes:

$$
\begin{aligned}
&\sum_{i=1}^{N} \sum_{1 \le s \le t \le T-1} \mathbf{1}\{y_{is} + y_{it} = 1\} K\left(\frac{\mathbf{x}_{i,t+1} - \mathbf{x}_{i,s+1}}{\sigma_N}\right) \\
&\quad \times \log\left(\frac{\exp[(\mathbf{x}_{is} - \mathbf{x}_{it})'\boldsymbol{\beta} + \boldsymbol{\gamma}(y_{i,s-1} - y_{i,t+1}) + \boldsymbol{\gamma}(y_{i,s+1} - y_{i,t-1})\mathbf{1}(t - s \ge 3)]^{y_{is}}}{1 + \exp[(\mathbf{x}_{is} - \mathbf{x}_{it})'\boldsymbol{\beta} + \boldsymbol{\gamma}(y_{i,s-1} - y_{i,t+1}) + \boldsymbol{\gamma}(y_{i,s+1} - y_{i,t-1})\mathbf{1}(t - s \ge 3)]}\right). \\
&\qquad (7.5.33)
\end{aligned}
$$

The conditional approach does not require modeling of the initial observations of the sample. Neither does it make any assumptions about the statistical relationship of the individual effects with the observed explanatory variables or with the initial conditions. However, it also suffers from the limitation that $\mathbf{x}_{is} - \mathbf{x}_{it}$ has support in a neighborhood of 0 for any $t \neq s$, which rules out time dummies as explanatory variables.[16] The fact that individual effects cannot be estimated also means that it is not possible to make predictions or compute elasticities for individual agents at specified values of the explanatory variables.

7.5.4 State Dependence versus Heterogeneity

There are two diametrically opposite explanations for the often observed empirical regularity with which individuals who have experienced an event in the past are more likely to experience that event in the future. One explanation is that as a consequence of experiencing an event, preferences, prices, or constraints relevant to future choices are altered. A second explanation is that individuals may differ in certain unmeasured variables that influence their probability of experiencing the event but are not influenced by the experience of the event. If these variables are correlated over time and are not properly controlled, previous experience may appear to be a determinant of future experience solely because it is a proxy for such temporally persistent unobservables. Heckman (1978a, 1981a, 1981c) has termed the former case *true state dependence* and the latter case *spurious state dependence*, because in the former case, past experience has a genuine behavioral effect in the sense that an otherwise identical individual who has not experienced the event will behave differently in the future than an individual who has experienced the event. In the latter case, previous experience appears to be a determinant of future experience solely because it is a proxy for temporally persistent unobservables that determine choices.

The problem of distinguishing between true and spurious state dependence is of considerable substantive interest. To demonstrate this, let us consider some work in the theory of unemployment. Phelps (1972) argued that current unemployment has a real and lasting effect on the probability of future unemployment. Hence, short-term economic policies that alleviate unemployment tend to lower aggregate unemployment rates in the long run by preventing the loss of work-enhancing market experience. On the other hand, Cripps and Tarling (1974) maintained the opposite view in their analysis of the incidence and duration of unemployment. They assumed that individuals differ in their propensity to experience unemployment and in their unemployment duration times and that those differences cannot be fully accounted for by measured variables. They further assumed that the actual experience of having been unemployed or the duration of past unemployment does not affect future incidence or duration. Hence, in their model, short-term economic policies have no effect on long-term unemployment.

Because the unobserved individual effects α_i persist over time, ignoring these effects of unmeasured variables (heterogeneity) creates serially correlated residuals. This suggests that we cannot use the conditional probability, given past occurrence not equal to the marginal probability alone [$\text{Prob}(y_{it} \mid y_{i,t-s}, \mathbf{x}_{it}) \neq \text{Prob}(y_{it} \mid \mathbf{x}_{it})$], to test for true state dependence against spurious state dependence, because this inequality may be a result of past information on y yielding information on the unobserved specific effects. A proper test for dependence should control for the unobserved individual-specific effects.

When, conditional on the individual effects α_i, the error term u_{it} is serially uncorrelated, a test for state dependence can be easily implemented by controlling the individual effects and testing for the conditional probability equal to the marginal probability,[17]

$$\text{Prob}(y_{it} \mid y_{i,t-s}, \mathbf{x}_{it}, \alpha_i) = \text{Prob}(y_{it} \mid \mathbf{x}_{it}, \alpha_i). \tag{7.5.34}$$

If the conditional distribution $G(\alpha \mid \mathbf{x})$ of α_i given $\mathbf{x}_i$ is known, a more powerful test is to use an unconditional approach. Thus, one may test true state dependence versus spurious state dependence by testing the significance of the MLE of γ of the log likelihood

$$\sum_{i=1}^{N} \log \int \prod_{t=1}^{T} \{F(\mathbf{x}'_{it}\boldsymbol{\beta} + \gamma y_{i,t-1} + \alpha_i)^{y_{it}}[1 - F(\mathbf{x}'_{it}\boldsymbol{\beta} + \gamma y_{i,t-1} + \alpha_i)]^{1-y_{it}}$$
$$\times P_0(\mathbf{x}_i, \alpha)^{y_{i0}}[1 - P(\mathbf{x}_i, \alpha)]^{1-y_{i0}}\} G(\alpha \mid \mathbf{x}_i)\, d\alpha. \tag{7.5.35}$$

When, conditional on the individual effects α_i, the error term u_{it} remains serially correlated, the problem becomes more complicated. The conditional probability $\text{Prob}(y_{it} \mid y_{i,t-l}, \alpha_i)$ might fail to be equal to the marginal probability $\text{Prob}(y_{it} \mid \alpha_i)$ because of past y_{it} containing information on u_{it}. A test for state dependence cannot simply rely on the multinomial distribution of the sequence $(y_{i1}, \ldots, y_{iT})$. The general framework (7.5.1) and (7.5.2) proposed by Heckman (1978a, 1981a, 1981b) accommodates very general sorts of heterogeneity and structural dependence. It permits an analyst to combine models and test among competing specifications within a unified framework. However, the computations of maximum likelihood methods for the general models are quite involved. It would be useful to rely on simple methods to explore data before employing the computationally cumbersome maximum likelihood method for a specific model.

Chamberlain (1978b) suggested a simple method to distinguish true state dependence from spurious state dependence. He noted that just as in the continuous models, a key distinction between state dependence and serial correlation is whether or not there is a dynamic response to an intervention. This distinction can be made clear by examining (7.5.1). If $\gamma = 0$, a change in $\mathbf{x}$ has its full effect immediately, whereas if $\gamma \neq 0$, one has a distributed-lag response to a change in $\mathbf{x}$. The lag structure relating y to $\mathbf{x}$ is not related to the serial correlation in u. If $\mathbf{x}$ is increased in period t and then returned to its former level, the probability of $y_{i,t+1}$ is not affected if $\gamma = 0$, because by assumption the distribution of u_{it} was not affected. If $\gamma \neq 0$, then the one-period shift in $\mathbf{x}$ will have lasting effects. An intervention that affects the probability of y in period t will continue to affect the probability of y in period $t + 1$, even though the intervention was presented only in period t. In contrast, an interpretation of serial correlation is that the shocks (u) tend to persist for more than one period and that y_{it} is informative only in helping to infer u_{it} and hence to predict u_{it}. Therefore, a test that should not be very sensitive to functional form is to simply include lagged xs without lagged y. After conditioning on the individual-specific effect α_i, there may be two outcomes. If there is no state dependence, then

$$\text{Prob}(y_{it} = 1 \mid \mathbf{x}_{it}, \mathbf{x}_{i,t-1}, \ldots, \alpha_i) = \text{Prob}(y_{it} = 1 \mid \mathbf{x}_{it}, \alpha_i), \quad (7.5.36)$$

and if there is state dependence, then

$$\text{Prob}(y_{it} = 1 \mid \mathbf{x}_{it}, \mathbf{x}_{i,t-1}, \ldots, \alpha_i) \neq \text{Prob}(y_{it} = 1 \mid \mathbf{x}_{it}, \alpha_i). \quad (7.5.37)$$

While the combination of (7.5.34), (7.5.36), and (7.5.37) provides a simple form to distinguish pure heterogeneity, state dependence, and serial correlation, we cannot make further distinctions with regard to different forms of state dependence, heterogeneity, and serial correlation. Models (7.5.1) and (7.5.2) will have to be used to further narrow down possible specifications.

7.5.5 Two Examples

The control of heterogeneity plays a crucial role in distinguishing true state dependence from spurious state dependence. Neglecting heterogeneity and the issue of initial observations can also seriously bias the coefficient estimates. It is important in estimating dynamic models that the heterogeneity in the sample be treated correctly. To demonstrate this, we use the female-employment models estimated by Heckman (1981c) and household brand choices estimated by Chintagunta, Kyriazidou, and Perktold (2001) as examples.

7.5.5.a Female Employment

Heckman (1981c) used the first three-year sample of women aged 45–59 in 1968 from the Michigan Panel Survey of Income Dynamics to study married women's employment decisions. A woman is defined to be a market participant if she works for money any time in the sample year. The set of explanatory variables is as follows: the woman's education; family income, excluding the wife's earnings; number of children younger than six; number of children at home; unemployment rate in the county in which the woman resides; the wage of unskilled labor in the county (a measure of the availability of substitutes for a woman's time in the home); the national unemployment rate for prime-age males (a measure of aggregate labor-market tightness); and two types of prior work experience: within-sample and presample. The effect of previous work experience is broken into two components, because it is likely that presample experience exerts a weaker measured effect on current participation decisions than more recent experience. Furthermore, because the data on presample work experience are based on a retrospective question and therefore are likely to be measured with error, Heckman replaces them with predicted values based on a set of regressors.

Heckman fitted the data with various multivariate probit models of the form (7.5.1) and (7.5.2) to investigate whether or not work experience raises the probability that a woman will work in the future (by raising her wage rates) and to investigate the importance of controlling for heterogeneity in utilizing panel data. Maximum likelihood coefficient estimates for the state-dependent models under the assumptions of stationary intertemporal covariance matrix

$$\Omega = \begin{bmatrix} 1 & \rho_{12} & \rho_{13} \\ & 1 & \rho_{23} \\ & & 1 \end{bmatrix},$$

first-order Markov process ($v_{it} = \rho v_{i,t-1} + u_{it}$), and no heterogeneity ($v_{it} = u_{it}$) are presented in columns 1, 2, and 3, respectively, of Table 7.3.[18] Coefficient estimates for no state dependence with general stationary intertemporal correlation, first-order Markov process, conventional error-component formulation [$v_{it} = \alpha_i + u_{it}$, equivalent to imposing the restriction that $\rho_{12} = \rho_{13} = \rho_{23} = \sigma_\alpha^2/(\sigma_u^2 + \sigma_\alpha^2)$], and no heterogeneity are presented in columns 4, 5, 6, and 7, respectively. A Heckman–Willis (1977) model with time-invariant exogenous variables and conventional error-component formulation was also estimated and is presented in column 8.

Likelihood-ratio test statistics (twice the difference of the log likelihood value) against the most general model (column 1 of Table 7.3) indicate the acceptance of recent labor-market experience as an important determinant of current employment decision, with unobservables determining employment choices following a first-order Markov process (column 2 of Table 7.3) as a maintained hypothesis, and the statistics clearly reject all other formulations. In other words, the study found that work experience, as a form of general and specific human-capital investment, raises the probability that a woman will work in the future, even after allowing for serial correlation of a very general type. It also maintained that there exist unobserved variables that affect labor participations. However, initial differences in unobserved variables tend to be eliminated with the passage of time. But this homogenizing effect is offset in part by the effect of prior work experience, which tends to accentuate initial differences in the propensity to work.

Comparison of the estimates of the maintained hypothesis with estimates of other models indicates that the effect of recent market experience on employment is dramatically overstated in a model that neglects heterogeneity. The estimated effect of recent market experience on current employment status recorded in column 3 of Table 7.3, overstates the effect by a factor of 10 (1.46 versus 0.143)! Too much credit will be attributed to past experience as a determinant of employment if intertemporal correlation in the unobservables is ignored. Likewise for the estimated effect of national unemployment on employment. On the other hand, the effect of children on employment is understated in models that ignore heterogeneity.

Comparisons of various models' predictive performance on sample-run patterns (temporal employment status) are presented in Table 7.4. It shows that dynamic models ignoring heterogeneity underpredict the number of individuals who work all of the time and overpredict the number who do not work at all. It also overstates the estimated frequency of turnover in the labor force. In

Table 7.3. *Estimates of employment models for women aged 45–59 in 1968*[a]

Variable	(1)	(2)	(3)
Intercept	−2.576 (4.6)	1.653 (2.5)	0.227 (0.4)
No. of children aged<6	−0.816 (2.7)	−0.840 (2.3)	−0.814 (2.1)
County unemployment rate (%)	−0.035 (1.5)	−0.027 (1.0)	−0.018 (0.57)
County wage rate ($/h)	0.104 (0.91)	0.104 (0.91)	0.004 (0.02)
Total no. of children	−0.146 (4.3)	−0.117 (2.2)	−0.090 (2.4)
Wife's education (years)	0.162 (6.5)	0.105 (2.8)	0.104 (3.7)
Family income, excluding wife's earnings	-0.363×10^{-4} (4.8)	-0.267×10^{-4} (2.7)	-0.32×10^{-4} (3.6)
National unemployment rate	−0.106 (0.51)	−0.254 (1.4)	−1.30 (6)
Recent experience	0.143 (0.95)	0.273 (1.5)	1.46 (12.2)
Predicted presample experience	0.072 (5.8)	0.059 (3.4)	0.045 (3.4)
Serial-correlation coefficient:			
ρ_{12}	0.913	—	—
ρ_{13}	0.845		
ρ_{23}	0.910		
ρ	—	0.873 (14.0)	—
$\sigma_\alpha^2/(\sigma_u^2+\sigma_\alpha^2)$	—	—	—
Log likelihood	−237.74	−240.32	−263.65

[a] Asymptotic normal test statistics in parentheses; these statistics were obtained from the estimating information matrix.

fact, comparing the performance of the predicted run patterns for the dynamic and static models without heterogeneity (columns 3 and 7 of Table 7.3, and columns 3 and 4 of Table 7.4) suggests that introducing lagged employment status into a model as a substitute for a more careful treatment of heterogeneity is an imperfect procedure. In this case, it is worse than using no proxy at all. Nor does a simple static model with a components-of-variance scheme (column 8 of Table 7.3, column 5 of Table 7.4) perform any better. Dynamic models that neglect heterogeneity (column 3 of Table 7.4) overestimate labor-market turnover, whereas the static model with a conventional variance-components formulation (column 5 of Table 7.4) overstates the extent of heterogeneity and the degree of intertemporal correlation. It overpredicts the number who never work during these three years and underpredicts the number who always work.

This example suggests that considerable care should be exercised in utilizing panel data to discriminate among the models. Improper control for heterogeneity can lead to erroneous parameter estimates and dramatically overstate the effect of past experience on current choices.

Table 7.3. *(cont.)*

(4)	(5)	(6)	(7)	(8)
−2.367 (6.4)	−2.011 (3.4)	−2.37 (5.5)	−3.53 (4.6)	−1.5 (0)
−0.742 (2.6)	−0.793 (2.1)	−0.70 (2.0)	−1.42 (2.3)	−0.69 (1.2)
−0.030 (1.5)	−0.027 (1.2)	−0.03 (1.6)	−0.059 (1.3)	0.046 (11)
0.090 (0.93)	0.139 (1.5)	0.13 (1.4)	0.27 (1.1)	0.105 (0.68)
−0.124 (4.9)	−0.116 (2.2)	−0.161 (4.9)	−0.203 (3.9)	−0.160 (6.1)
0.152 (7.3)	0.095 (2.5)	0.077 (3)	0.196 (4.8)	0.105 (3.3)
-0.312×10^{-4} (5.2)	-0.207×10^{-4} (2.3)	-0.2×10^{-4} (2.6)	-0.65×10^{-4} (5.1)	-0.385×10^{-4} (20)
−0.003 (0.38)	−0.021 (0.26)	0.02 (3)	1.03 (0.14)	−0.71 (0)
—[b]	—	—	—	—
0.062 (0.38)	0.062 (3.5)	0.091 (7.0)	0.101 (5.4)	0.095 (11.0)
0.917	—	—	—	—
0.873	—	—	—	—
0.946	—	—	—	—
—	−0.942 (50)	—	—	—
—	—	0.92 (4.5)	—	0.941 (4.1)
−239.81	−243.11	−244.7	−367.3	−242.37

[b] Not estimated.
Source: Heckman (1981c, Table 3.2).

7.5.5.b Household Brand Choices

Chintagunta, Kyriazidou, and Perktold (2001) use the A.C. Nielson data on yogurt purchases in Sioux Falls, South Dakota between September 17, 1986 and August 1, 1988 to study yogurt brand loyalty. They focus on the 6 oz packages of the two dominant yogurt brands, Yoplait and Nordica, for the analysis. These brands account for 18.4 and 19.5 percent of yogurt purchases by weight. Only data for households that have at least two consecutive purchases of either one of the two brands are considered. This leaves 737 households and 5,618 purchase occasions, out of which 2,718 are for Yoplait and the remaining 2,900 for Nordica. The panel is unbalanced.[19] The minimum number of purchase occasions per household is 2, and the maximum is 305. The mean number of purchases is 9.5, and the median is 5.

The model they estimate is given by

$$\operatorname{Prob}(y_{it} = 1 \mid \mathbf{x}_{it}, y_{i0}, \ldots, y_{i,t-1}, \alpha_i) = \frac{\exp(\mathbf{x}_{it}'\boldsymbol{\beta} + \gamma y_{i,t-1} + \alpha_i)}{1 + \exp(\mathbf{x}_{it}'\boldsymbol{\beta} + \gamma y_{i,t-1} + \alpha_i)}, \tag{7.5.38}$$

Table 7.4. *Comparisons of employment models using run data: Women aged 45–59 in 1968*

	(1)	(2)	(3)	(4)	(5)
Run pattern	Actual number	Number predicted from state-dependent model with heterogeneity (column 2 of Table 7.3)	Probit model that ignores heterogeneity (column 3 of Table 7.3)	Probit model that ignores heterogeneity and recent-sample state dependence (column 7 of Table 7.3)	Number predicted from Heckman–Willis model (column 8 of Table 7.3)
0,0,0	96	94.2	145.3	36.1	139.5
0,0,1	5	17.6	38.5	20.5	4.1
0,1,0	4	1.8	1.9	20.2	4.1
1,0,0	8	2.6	0.35	20.6	4.1
1,1,0	5	1.4	0.02	21.2	3.6
1,0,1	2	2.4	1.38	21.1	3.6
0,1,1	2	16.4	8.51	21.7	3.6
1,1,1	76	61.5	2.05	36.6	34.9
$\chi^{2\ c}$	—	48.5	4,419	221.8	66.3

[a]Data for 1971, 1972, and 1973, three years following the sample data, were used to estimate the model.
[b]0 corresponds to not working; 1 corresponds to working; thus, 1,1,0 corresponds to a woman who worked the first two years of the sample and did not work in the final year.
[c]This is the standard chi-square statistic for goodness of fit. The higher the value of the statistic, the worse the fit.
Source: Heckman (1981c).

where $y_{it} = 1$ if household i chooses Yoplait in period t and $y_{it} = 0$ if household i chooses Nordica. The exogenous variables in $\mathbf{x}_{it}$ are the difference in the natural logarithm of the price (coefficient denoted by β_P) and the differences in the dummy variables for the two brands that describe whether the brand was displayed in the store and featured in an advertisement that week (coefficients denoted by β_D and β_F respectively). Among the many models they estimated, Table 7.5 presents the results of:

1. The pooled logit model with the lagged choice treated as exogenous, assuming there are no individual-specific effects (PLL).
2. The Chamberlain (1982) conditional logit approach with the lagged choice treated as exogenous (CLL).
3. The pooled logit approach with normally distributed random effects with mean μ and variance σ_α^2, with the initial choice treated as exogenous (PLLHET).
4. The pooled logit approach with normally distributed random effects and the initial probability of choosing 1 given $(\mathbf{x}_i, \alpha_i)$ assumed at the

Table 7.5. *Estimates of brand choices using various approaches (standard errors in parentheses)*

Model	β_p	β_d	β_f	γ	μ_α	σ_α
CLL	−3.347	0.828	0.924	−0.068		
	(0.399)	(0.278)	(0.141)	(0.140)		
PLL	−3.049	0.853	1.392	3.458	−0.333	
	(0.249)	(0.174)	(0.091)	(0.084)	(0.102)	
PLLHET	−3.821	1.031	1.456	2.126	0.198	1.677
	(0.313)	(0.217)	(0.113)	(0.114)	(0.150)	(0.086)
PLLHETE	−4.053	0.803	1.401	1.598	0.046	1.770
	(0.274)	(0.178)	(0.115)	(0.115)	(0.133)	(0.102)
HK05	−3.477	0.261	0.782	1.223		
	(0.679)	(0.470)	(0.267)	(0.352)		
HK10	−3.128	0.248	0.759	1.198		
	(0.658)	(0.365)	(0.228)	(0.317)		
HK30	−2.644	0.289	0.724	1.192		
	(0.782)	(0.315)	(0.195)	(0.291)		
PLLHET-S[a]	−3.419	1.095	1.291	1.550	0.681	1.161
	(0.326)	(0.239)	(0.119)	(0.117)	(0.156)	(0.081)

[a]The PLLHET estimates after excluding those households that are completely loyal to one brand.
Source: Chintagunta, Kyriazidou, and Perktold (2001, Table 3).

steady state, which is approximated by

$$\frac{F(\bar{\mathbf{x}}_i'\boldsymbol{\beta} + \alpha_i)}{1 - F(\bar{\mathbf{x}}_i'\boldsymbol{\beta} + \gamma + \alpha_i) + F(\bar{\mathbf{x}}_i'\boldsymbol{\beta} + \alpha_i)}, \tag{7.5.39}$$

where $F(a) = \exp(a)/(1 + \exp(a))$ and $\bar{\mathbf{x}}_i$ denotes the individual time-series mean of $\mathbf{x}_{it}$ (PLLHETE).

5. The Honoré–Kyriazidou (2000) approach where $\sigma_N = c \cdot N^{-1/5}$ with $c = 0.5$ (HK05), 1.0 (HK10), and 3.0 (HK30).

Table 7.5 reveals that almost all procedures yield statistically significant coefficients with the expected signs. An increase in the price of a brand reduces the probability of choosing the brand, and the presence of a store display or of a feature advertisement for a brand makes purchase of that brand more likely. Also, apart from CLL, all methods produce positive and statistically significant estimates for γ, i.e., a previous purchase of a brand increases the probability of purchasing the same brand in the next period. The lagged choice is found to have a large positive effect in brand choice for pooled methods assuming no heterogeneity: The PLL estimate of γ is 3.5. However, introducing heterogeneity lowers it substantially to 2.1 (PLLHET). The estimate of γ further drops to 1.598 (PLLHETE) when the initial observations are treated as endogenous, and drops to about 1.2 using the Honoré–Kyriazidou estimator. Nevertheless, the results do indicate that after controlling for the effects of α_i, a previous purchase of a brand increases the probability of purchasing the same brand in the next period, although their effect is substaintially reduced from the case of assuming no heterogeneity. There is also an indication of substantial heterogeneity in the sample. All methods that estimate random effects give high values for the standard deviation of the household effects, σ_α, about 1.7, bearing in mind that σ_u is normalized to 1 only.

In general, the size of the estimated parameters varies considerably across estimation methods. There is also some sensitivity in the HK point estimates of all coefficients with respect to the bandwidth choice. To investigate this issue further and identify situations where the different methods are most reliable in producing point estimates, Chintagunta, Kyriazidou, and Perktold (2001) further conducted Monte Carlo studies. Their results indicate that the conditional likelihood procedures are the most robust in estimating the coefficients on the exogenous variables. However, the coefficient on the lagged dependent variable is significantly underestimated. The pooled procedures are quite sensitive to model misspecification, often yielding large biases for key economic parameters. The estimator proposed by Honoré and Kyriazidou (2000 a) performs quite satisfactory despite a loss of precision because their method de facto only uses substantially smaller number of observations than other methods, due to the use of the weighting scheme $K((\mathbf{x}_{it} - \mathbf{x}_{is})/\sigma_N)$.

CHAPTER 8

Truncated and Censored Data

8.1 INTRODUCTION

In economics, the ranges of dependent variables are often constrained in some way. For instance, in his pioneering work on household expenditure on durable goods, Tobin (1958) used a regression model that specifically took account of the fact that the expenditure (the dependent variable of his regression model) cannot be negative. Tobin called this type of model the model of limited dependent variables. It and its various generalization are known as *Tobit* models because of their similarities to probit models.[1] In statistics they are known as truncated or censored regression models. The model is called *truncated* if the observations outside a specific range are totally lost, and is called *censored* if we can at least observe some of the explanatory variables.

Consider a latent response function,

$$y^* = \boldsymbol{\beta}'\mathbf{x} + u, \tag{8.1.1}$$

where $\mathbf{x}$ is a $K \times 1$ vector of exogenous variables and u is the error term that is independently, identically distributed (i.i.d.) with mean 0 and variance σ_u^2. Without loss of generality, suppose that the observed y are related to y^* by

$$y = \begin{cases} y^* & \text{if} \quad y^* > 0, \\ 0 & \text{if} \quad y^* \leq 0. \end{cases} \tag{8.1.2}$$

Models of the form (8.1.1) and (8.1.2) are called censored regression models because the data consist of those points of the form $(y_i^*, \mathbf{x}_i)$ if $y_i^* > 0$ and $(0, \mathbf{x}_i)$ if $y_i^* \leq 0$ for $i = 1, \ldots, N$. The truncated data only consist of points of the form $(y_i^*, \mathbf{x}_i)$ where $y_i^* > 0$.

The conditional expectation of y given $\mathbf{x}$ for truncated data is equal to

$$E(y \mid y > 0) = E(y^* \mid y^* > 0) = \mathbf{x}'\boldsymbol{\beta} + E(u \mid u > -\mathbf{x}'\boldsymbol{\beta}). \tag{8.1.3}$$

The conditional expectation of y given $\mathbf{x}$ for censored data is equal to

$$\begin{aligned} E(y \mid \mathbf{x}) &= \text{Prob}(y = 0) \cdot 0 + \text{Prob}(y > 0 \mid \mathbf{x}) \cdot E(y \mid y > 0, \mathbf{x}) \\ &= \text{Prob}(u \leq -\mathbf{x}'\boldsymbol{\beta}) \cdot 0 + \text{Prob}(u > -\mathbf{x}'\boldsymbol{\beta}) E(y^* \mid \mathbf{x}; u > -\mathbf{x}'\boldsymbol{\beta}) \\ &= \text{Prob}(u > -\mathbf{x}'\boldsymbol{\beta})[\mathbf{x}'\boldsymbol{\beta} + E(u \mid u > -\mathbf{x}'\boldsymbol{\beta})]. \end{aligned} \tag{8.1.4}$$

If u is independently normally distributed with mean 0 and variance σ_u^2, then

$$\text{Prob}(u > -\mathbf{x}'\boldsymbol{\beta}) = 1 - \Phi\left(\frac{-\mathbf{x}'\boldsymbol{\beta}}{\sigma_u}\right) = \Phi\left(\frac{\mathbf{x}'\boldsymbol{\beta}}{\sigma_u}\right), \tag{8.1.5}$$

and

$$E(u \mid u > -\mathbf{x}'\boldsymbol{\beta}) = \sigma_u \cdot \frac{\phi\left(\frac{\mathbf{x}'\boldsymbol{\beta}}{\sigma_u}\right)}{\Phi\left(\frac{\mathbf{x}'\boldsymbol{\beta}}{\sigma_u}\right)}, \tag{8.1.6}$$

where $\phi(\cdot)$ and $\Phi(\cdot)$ are standard normal density and cumulative (or integrated) normal, respectively. Equations (8.1.3) and (8.1.4) show that truncation or censoring of the dependent variables introduces dependence between the error term and the regressors for the model

$$y = \mathbf{x}'\boldsymbol{\beta} + \epsilon, \tag{8.1.7}$$

where the error

$$\epsilon = \nu + E(y \mid \mathbf{x}) - \mathbf{x}'\boldsymbol{\beta}. \tag{8.1.8}$$

Although $\nu = y - E(y \mid \mathbf{x})$ has $E(\nu \mid \mathbf{x}) = 0$, we have $E(\epsilon \mid \mathbf{x}) \neq 0$. Therefore, the least-squares estimator of (8.1.7) is biased and inconsistent.

For a sample of N independent individuals, the likelihood function of the truncated data is equal to

$$L_1 = \prod_1 [\text{Prob}(y_i > 0 \mid \mathbf{x}_i)]^{-1} f(y_i), \tag{8.1.9}$$

where $f(\cdot)$ denotes the density of y_i^* (or u_i), and $\prod_1$ means the product over those i for which $y_i > 0$. The likelihood function of the censored data is equal to

$$\begin{aligned} L_2 &= \left\{\prod_0 \text{Prob}(y_i = 0 \mid \mathbf{x}_i) \cdot \prod_1 \text{Prob}(y_i > 0 \mid \mathbf{x}_i)\right\} \\ &\quad \times \left\{\prod_1 [\text{Prob}(y_i > 0 \mid \mathbf{x}_i)]^{-1} f(y_i)\right\} \\ &= \prod_0 \text{Prob}(y_i = 0 \mid \mathbf{x}_i) \prod_1 f(y_i), \end{aligned} \tag{8.1.10}$$

where $\prod_0$ means the product over those i for which $y_i^* \leq 0$. In the case that u_i is independently normally distributed with mean 0 and variance σ_u^2, we have $f(y_i) = (2\pi)^{-\frac{1}{2}}\sigma_u^{-1} \exp\{-(1/2\sigma_u^2)(y_i - \mathbf{x}_i'\boldsymbol{\beta})^2\}$ and $\text{Prob}(y_i = 0 \mid \mathbf{x}_i) = \Phi(-\mathbf{x}_i'\boldsymbol{\beta}/\sigma_u) = 1 - \Phi(\mathbf{x}_i'\boldsymbol{\beta}/\sigma_u)$.

Maximizing (8.1.9) or (8.1.10) with respect to $\boldsymbol{\theta}' = (\boldsymbol{\beta}', \sigma_u^2)$ yields the maximum likelihood estimator (MLE). The MLE, $\hat{\boldsymbol{\theta}}$, is consistent and is asymptotically normally distributed. The asymptotic covariance matrix of the MLE, asy $\text{cov}[\sqrt{N}(\hat{\boldsymbol{\theta}} - \boldsymbol{\theta})]$, is equal to the inverse of the information matrix, $[-E(1/N)\partial^2 \log L_j/\partial\boldsymbol{\theta}\,\partial\boldsymbol{\theta}']^{-1}$, which may be approximated by

$[-(1/N)\partial^2 \log L_j/\partial\boldsymbol{\theta}\,\partial\boldsymbol{\theta}' \mid_{\boldsymbol{\theta}=\hat{\boldsymbol{\theta}}}]^{-1}$, $j = 1, 2$. However, the MLE is highly nonlinear. A Newton–Raphson iterative scheme may have to be used to obtain the MLE. Alternatively, if u is normally distributed, Heckman (1976a) suggests the following two-step estimator:

1. Maximize the first factor in braces in the likelihood function (8.1.10) by probit MLE with respect to $\boldsymbol{\delta} = (1/\sigma_u)\boldsymbol{\beta}$, yielding $\hat{\boldsymbol{\delta}}$.
2. Substitute $\hat{\boldsymbol{\delta}}$ for $\boldsymbol{\delta}$ into the truncated model

$$\begin{aligned} y_i &= E(y_i \mid \mathbf{x}_i; y_i > 0) + \eta_i \\ &= \mathbf{x}_i'\boldsymbol{\beta} + \sigma_u \frac{\phi(\mathbf{x}_i'\boldsymbol{\delta})}{\Phi(\mathbf{x}_i'\boldsymbol{\delta})} + \eta_i \quad \text{for those } i \text{ such that } y_i > 0, \end{aligned} \tag{8.1.11}$$

where $E(\eta_i \mid \mathbf{x}_i) = 0$, $\text{Var}(\eta_i \mid \mathbf{x}_i) = \sigma_u^2[1 - (\mathbf{x}_i'\boldsymbol{\delta})\lambda_i - \lambda_i^2]$, and $\lambda_i = \phi(\mathbf{x}_i'\boldsymbol{\delta})/\Phi(\mathbf{x}_i'\boldsymbol{\delta})$. Regress y_i on $\mathbf{x}_i$ and $\phi(\mathbf{x}_i'\hat{\boldsymbol{\delta}})/\Phi(\mathbf{x}_i'\hat{\boldsymbol{\delta}})$ by least squares, using only the positive observations of y_i.

The Heckman two-step estimator is consistent. The formula for computing the asymptotic variance–covariance matrix of Heckman's estimator is given by Amemiya (1978b). But the Heckman two-step estimator is not as efficient as the MLE.

Both the MLE of (8.1.10) and the Heckman two-step estimator (8.1.11) are consistent only if u is independently normally distributed with constant variance. Of course, the idea of the MLE and the Heckman two-step estimator can still be implemented with proper modification if the identically distributed density function of u is correctly specified. A lot of times an investigator does not have the knowledge of the density function of u, or u is not identically distributed. Under the assumption that it is symmetrically distributed around 0, Powell (1986) proves that applying the least-squares method to the symmetrically censored or truncated data yields a consistent estimator which is robust to the assumption of the probability density function of u and heteroscedasticity of the unknown form.

The problem of censoring or truncation is that conditional on $\mathbf{x}$, y is no longer symmetrically distributed around $\mathbf{x}'\boldsymbol{\beta}$ even though u is symmetrically distributed around zero. Data points for which $u_i \leq -\mathbf{x}_i'\boldsymbol{\beta}$ are either censored or omitted. However, we can restore symmetry by censoring or throwing away observations with $u_i \geq \mathbf{x}_i'\boldsymbol{\beta}$ or $y_i \geq 2\mathbf{x}_i'\boldsymbol{\beta}$, as shown in Figure 8.1, so that the remaining observations fall between $(0, 2\mathbf{x}'\boldsymbol{\beta})$. Because of the symmetry of u, the corresponding dependent variables are again symmetrically distributed about $\mathbf{x}'\boldsymbol{\beta}$ (Hsiao (1976)).

To make this approach more explicit, consider first the case in which the dependent variable is truncated at zero. In such a truncated sample, data points for which $u_i \leq -\mathbf{x}_i'\boldsymbol{\beta}$ are omitted. But if data points with $u_i \geq \mathbf{x}_i'\boldsymbol{\beta}$ are also excluded from the sample, then any remaining observations would have error terms lying within the interval $(-\mathbf{x}_i'\boldsymbol{\beta}, \mathbf{x}_i'\boldsymbol{\beta})$. (Any observations for which $\mathbf{x}_i'\boldsymbol{\beta} \leq 0$ are automatically deleted.) Because of the symmetry of the distribution

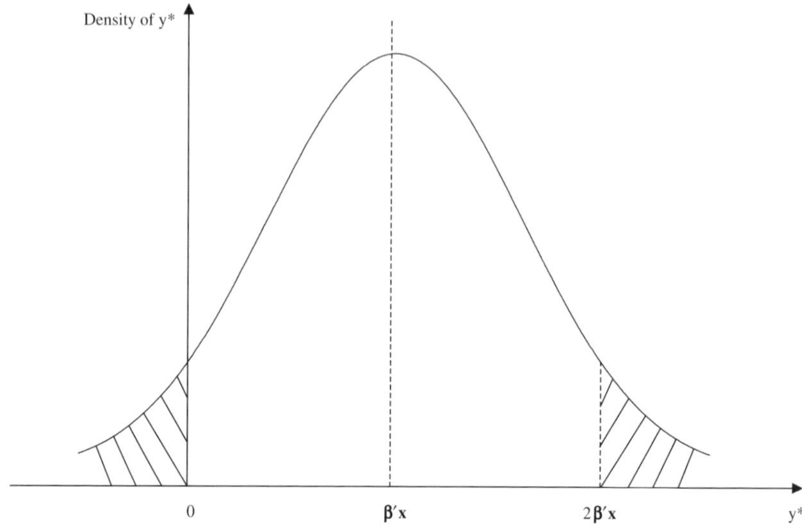

Fig. 8.1 Density of y^* censored or truncated at 0.

of u, the residuals for the symmetrically truncated sample will also be symmetrically distributed about zero. The corresponding dependent variable would take values between zero and $2\mathbf{x}_i'\boldsymbol{\beta}$ as shown in the region AOB of Figure 8.2. In other words, points b and c in Figure 8.2 are thrown away (point a is not observed).

Definition of the symmetrically trimmed estimator for a censored sample is similarly motivated. The error terms of the censored regression model are of the form $u_i^* = \max\{u_i, -\mathbf{x}_i'\boldsymbol{\beta}\}$ (i.e., point a in Figure 8.2 is moved to the corresponding circle point a'). *Symmetric censoring* would replace u_i^* with $\min\{u_i^*, \mathbf{x}_i'\boldsymbol{\beta}\}$ whenever $\mathbf{x}_i'\boldsymbol{\beta} > 0$, and would delete the observation otherwise. In other words, the dependent variable $y_i = \max\{0, y_i^*\}$ is replaced with $\min\{y_i, 2\mathbf{x}_i'\boldsymbol{\beta}\}$ as the points a,b,c in Figure 8.2 have been moved to the corresponding circle points (a', b', c').

Applying the least-squares principle to the symmetrically trimmed truncated data is equivalent to requiring the observations falling in the region AOB to satisfy the following first-order condition:

$$\frac{1}{N}\sum_{i=1}^{N} 1(y_i < 2\boldsymbol{\beta}'\mathbf{x}_i)(\mathbf{y}_i - \boldsymbol{\beta}'\mathbf{x}_i)\mathbf{x}_i = \mathbf{0}, \tag{8.1.12}$$

in the limit, where $1(A)$ denotes the indicator function of the event A, which takes the value 1 if A occurs and 0 otherwise. Applying the least-squares principle to the symmetrically censored data is equivalent to requiring the observations in the region AOB and the boundary OA and OB (the circle points in Figure 8.2) to satisfy the first-order condition,

$$\frac{1}{N}\sum_{i=1}^{N} 1(\boldsymbol{\beta}'\mathbf{x}_i > 0)(\min\{y_i, 2\boldsymbol{\beta}'\mathbf{x}_i\} - \boldsymbol{\beta}'\mathbf{x}_i)\mathbf{x}_i = \mathbf{0}, \tag{8.1.13}$$

in the limit. Therefore, Powell (1986) proposes the symmetrically trimmed least-squares estimator as the $\hat{\boldsymbol{\beta}}$ that minimizes

$$R_N(\boldsymbol{\beta}) = \sum_{i=1}^{N} \left\{ y_i - \max\left(\tfrac{1}{2} y_i, \mathbf{x}_i' \boldsymbol{\beta}\right) \right\}^2 \tag{8.1.14}$$

for the truncated data, and

$$\begin{aligned} S_N(\boldsymbol{\beta}) = &\sum_{i=1}^{N} \left\{ y_i - \max\left(\tfrac{1}{2} y_i, \boldsymbol{\beta}' \mathbf{x}_i\right) \right\}^2 \\ &+ \sum_{i=1}^{N} 1(y_i > 2\mathbf{x}'\boldsymbol{\beta}) \left\{ \left(\tfrac{1}{2} y_i\right)^2 - [\max(0, \mathbf{x}_i' \boldsymbol{\beta})]^2 \right\} \end{aligned} \tag{8.1.15}$$

for the censored data. The motivation for $R_N(\boldsymbol{\beta})$ is that if $y > 2\boldsymbol{\beta}'\mathbf{x}$, it will have zero weight in the first-order condition (8.1.12) for the truncated sample. The motivation for $S_N(\boldsymbol{\beta})$ is that observations greater than $2\boldsymbol{\beta}'\mathbf{x}_i$ if $\boldsymbol{\beta}'\mathbf{x} > 0$ and all observations corresponding to $\mathbf{x}'\boldsymbol{\beta} < 0$ will have zero weight in the first-order condition (8.1.13) for the censored sample. Powell (1986) shows that the symmetrically trimmed least-squares estimator is consistent and asymptotically normally distributed as $N \to \infty$.

The exogenously determined limited-dependent-variable models can be generalized to consider a variety of endogenously determined sample selection issues. For instance, in Gronau (1976) and Heckman's (1976a) female-labor-supply model the hours worked are observed only for those women who decide to participate in the labor force. In other words, instead of being exogenously given, the truncating or censoring value is endogenously and stochastically

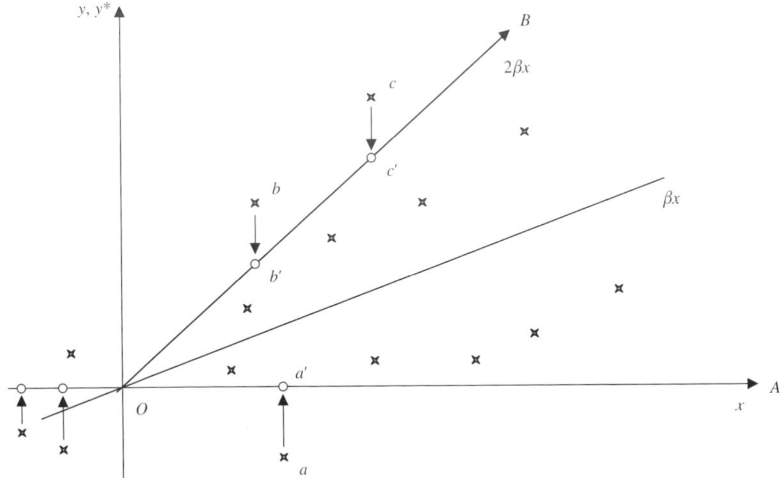

Fig. 8.2 Distribution of y and y^* under symmetric trimming.

determined by a selection equation (e.g. Duncan (1980))

$$d_i^* = \mathbf{w}_i'\mathbf{a} + v_i, \qquad i = 1, \ldots, N, \tag{8.1.16}$$

where $\mathbf{w}_i$ is a vector of exogenous variables, $\mathbf{a}$ is the parameter vector, and v_i is the random error term, assumed to be i.i.d. with mean 0 and variance normalized to 1. The samples (y_i, d_i), $i = 1, \ldots, N$, are related to y_i^* and d_i^* by the rule

$$d = \begin{cases} 1 & \text{if} \quad d^* > 0, \\ 0 & \text{if} \quad d^* \leq 0, \end{cases} \tag{8.1.17}$$

$$y = \begin{cases} y^* & \text{if} \quad d = 1, \\ 0 & \text{if} \quad d = 0. \end{cases} \tag{8.1.18}$$

The model (8.1.1), (8.1.16)–(8.1.18) is called the type II Tobit model by Amemiya (1985). Then

$$E(y_i \mid d_i = 1) = \mathbf{x}_i'\boldsymbol{\beta} + E(u_i \mid v_i > -\mathbf{w}_i'\mathbf{a}). \tag{8.1.19}$$

The likelihood function of (y_i, d_i) is

$$\begin{aligned} L &= \prod_c \text{Prob}(d_i = 0) \prod_{\bar{c}} f(y_i^* \mid d_i = 1) \text{Prob}(d_i = 1) \\ &= \prod_c \text{Prob}(d_i = 0) \prod_{\bar{c}} \text{Prob}(d_i^* > 0 \mid y_i)\, f(y_i), \end{aligned} \tag{8.1.20}$$

where $c = \{i \mid d_i = 0\}$ and $\bar{c}$ denotes its complement. If the joint distribution of (u, v) is specified, one can estimate this model by the MLE. For instance, if (u, v) is jointly normally distributed with mean (0, 0) and covariance matrix

$$\begin{pmatrix} \sigma_u^2 & \sigma_{uv} \\ \sigma_{vu} & 1 \end{pmatrix},$$

then

$$E(u \mid v > -\mathbf{w}'\mathbf{a}) = \sigma_{uv} \frac{\phi(\mathbf{w}'\mathbf{a})}{\Phi(\mathbf{w}'\mathbf{a})}, \tag{8.1.21}$$

$$\text{Prob}(d = 0) = [1 - \Phi(\mathbf{w}'\mathbf{a})] = \Phi(-\mathbf{w}'\mathbf{a}), \tag{8.1.22}$$

$$\text{Prob}(d_i = 1 \mid y_i) = \Phi \left\{ \mathbf{w}'\mathbf{a} + \frac{\sigma_{uv}}{\sigma_u}(y - \mathbf{x}'\boldsymbol{\beta}) \right\}. \tag{8.1.23}$$

Alternatively, Heckman's (1979) two-stage method can be applied: First, estimate $\mathbf{a}$ by a probit MLE of d_i, $i = 1, \ldots, N$. Evaluate $\phi(\mathbf{a}'\mathbf{w}_i)/\Phi(\mathbf{a}'\mathbf{w}_i)$ using the estimated a. Second, regress y_i on $\mathbf{x}_i$ and $\phi(\hat{\mathbf{a}}'\mathbf{w}_i)/\Phi(\hat{\mathbf{a}}\mathbf{w}_i)$ using data corresponding to $d_i = 1$ only.

Just as in the standard Tobit model, the consistency and asymptotic normality of the MLE and Heckman two-stage estimator for the endogenously determined selection depend critically on the correct assumption of the joint probability distribution of (u, v). When the distribution of (u, v) is unknown, the coefficients of $\mathbf{x}$ which are not overlapping with $\mathbf{w}$ can be estimated by a semiparametric method.

For ease of exposition, suppose that there are no variables appearing in both $\mathbf{x}$ and $\mathbf{w}$. Then, as noted by Robinson (1988b), the model (8.1.1), (8.1.17), (8.1.18) conditional on $d_i = 1$ becomes a partially linear model of the form

$$y_i = \boldsymbol{\beta}'\mathbf{x}_i + \lambda(\mathbf{w}_i) + \epsilon_i, \tag{8.1.24}$$

where $\lambda(\mathbf{w}_i)$ denotes the unknown selection factor. The expectation of y_i conditional on $\mathbf{w}_i$ and $d_i = 1$ is equal to

$$E(y_i \mid \mathbf{w}_i, d_i = 1) = \boldsymbol{\beta}' E(\mathbf{x}_i \mid \mathbf{w}_i, d_i = 1) + \lambda(\mathbf{w}_i). \tag{8.1.25}$$

Subtracting (8.1.25) from (8.1.24) yields

$$y_i - E(y_i \mid \mathbf{w}_i, d_i = 1) = \boldsymbol{\beta}'(\mathbf{x}_i - E(\mathbf{x}_i \mid \mathbf{w}_i, d_i = 1)) + \epsilon_i, \tag{8.1.26}$$

where $E(\epsilon_i \mid \mathbf{w}_i, \mathbf{x}_i, d_i = 1) = 0$. Thus, Robinson (1988b) suggests estimating $\boldsymbol{\beta}$ by

$$\begin{aligned}\hat{\boldsymbol{\beta}} = \{&E[\mathbf{x} - E(\mathbf{x} \mid \mathbf{w})][\mathbf{x} - E(\mathbf{x} \mid \mathbf{w})]'\}^{-1} \\ &\times E[(\mathbf{x} - E(\mathbf{x} \mid \mathbf{w}))][y - E(y \mid \mathbf{w})],\end{aligned} \tag{8.1.27}$$

using the truncated sample.

The first-stage conditional expectation for the estimator (8.1.27) can be estimated by the nonparametric method. For instance, one may use the kernel method to estimate the density of y at y_a (e.g., Härdle (1990); Robinson (1989)):

$$\hat{f}(y_a) = \frac{1}{N h_N} \sum_{i=1}^{N} k\left(\frac{y_i - y_a}{h_N}\right), \tag{8.1.28}$$

where h_N is a positive number, called the *bandwidth* or *smoothing parameter*, that tends to zero as $N \to \infty$, and $k(u)$ is a kernel function that is a bounded symmetric probability density function (pdf) that integrates to 1. Similarly, one can construct a kernel estimator of a multivariate pdf at $\mathbf{w}_a$, $f(\mathbf{w}_a)$ by

$$\hat{f}(\mathbf{w}_a) = \frac{1}{N\,|H_m|} \sum_{i=1}^{N} k_m\big(H_m^{-1}(\mathbf{w}_i - \mathbf{w}_a)\big), \tag{8.1.29}$$

where $\mathbf{w}$ is a $m \times 1$ vector of random variables, k_m is a kernel function on m-dimensional space, and H_m is a positive definite matrix. For instance, $k_m(\mathbf{u})$ can be the multivariate normal density function, or one can have $k_m(\mathbf{u}) = \prod_{j=1}^{m} k(u_j)$, $\mathbf{u}' = (u_1, \ldots, u_m)$, $H_m = \operatorname{diag}(h_{1N}, \ldots, h_{mN})$.

Kernel estimates of a conditional pdf $f(y_a \mid \mathbf{w}_a)$ or conditional expectations $Eg(y \mid \mathbf{w}_a)$ may be derived from the kernel estimates of the joint pdf and marginal pdf. Thus, the conditional pdf may be estimated by

$$\hat{f}(y_a \mid \mathbf{w}_a) = \frac{\hat{f}(y_a, \mathbf{w}_a)}{\hat{f}(\mathbf{w}_a)}, \tag{8.1.30}$$

and the conditional expectation by

$$E\hat{g}(y \mid \mathbf{w}_a) = \frac{1}{N\,|H_m|}\sum_{i=1}^{N} g(y_i)k_m\left(H_m^{-1}(\mathbf{w}_i - \mathbf{w}_a)\right)/\hat{f}(\mathbf{w}_a). \tag{8.1.31}$$

Robinson's (1988b) approach does not allow the identification of the parameters of variables that appear both in the regression equation ($\mathbf{x}$) and in the selection equation ($\mathbf{w}$). When there are variables appearing in both $\mathbf{x}$ and $\mathbf{w}$, Newey (1999) suggests a two-step series method of estimating $\boldsymbol{\beta}$ provided that the selection correction term of (8.1.25), $\lambda(\mathbf{w}_i, d_i = 1)$, is a function of the single index $\mathbf{w}_i'\mathbf{a}$:

$$\lambda(\mathbf{w}, d = 1) = E[u \mid v(\mathbf{w}'\mathbf{a}), d = 1]. \tag{8.1.32}$$

The first step of Newey's method uses the distribution-free methods discussed in Chapter 7 and in Klein and Spady (1993) to estimate $\mathbf{a}$. The second step consists of a linear regression of $d_i y_i$ on $d_i \mathbf{x}_i$ and the approximations of $\lambda(\mathbf{w}_i)$. Newey suggests approximating $\lambda(\mathbf{w}_i)$ by either a polynomial function of $(\mathbf{w}_i'\hat{\mathbf{a}})$ or a spline function $\mathbf{P}_N^K(\mathbf{w}'\mathbf{a}) = (P_{1K}(\mathbf{w}'\mathbf{a}), P_{2K}(\mathbf{w}'\mathbf{a}), \ldots, P_{KK}(\mathbf{w}'\mathbf{a}))'$ with the property that for large K, a linear combination of $\mathbf{P}_N^K(\mathbf{w}'\mathbf{a})$ can approximate an unknown function of $\lambda(\mathbf{w}'\mathbf{a})$ well. Newey (1999) shows that the two-step series estimation of $\boldsymbol{\beta}$ is consistent and asymptotically normally distributed when $N \to \infty$, $K \to \infty$, and $\sqrt{N}K^{-s-t+1} \to 0$, where $s \geq 5$, and where $K^7/N \to 0$ if $P_N^K(\mathbf{w}'\mathbf{a})$ is a power series or $m \geq t - 1$, $s \geq 3$, and $K^4/N \to 0$ if $P^K(\mathbf{w}'\mathbf{a})$ is a spline of degree m in $(\mathbf{w}'\mathbf{a})$.[2]

If the selection factor $\lambda(\mathbf{w}_i)$ is a function of a *single index* $\mathbf{w}_i'\mathbf{a}$, and the components of $\mathbf{w}_i$ are not a subset of $\mathbf{x}_i$, then instead of subtracting (8.1.26) from (8.1.25) to eliminate the unknown selection factor $\lambda(\mathbf{w}_i)$, Ahn and Powell (1993) note that for those individuals with $\mathbf{w}_i'\mathbf{a} = \mathbf{w}_j'\mathbf{a}$, one has $\lambda(\mathbf{w}_i'\mathbf{a}) = \lambda(\mathbf{w}_j'\mathbf{a})$. Thus, conditional on $\mathbf{w}_i'\mathbf{a} = \mathbf{w}_j'\mathbf{a}$, $d_i = 1, d_j = 1$,

$$(y_i - y_j) = (\mathbf{x}_i - \mathbf{x}_j)'\boldsymbol{\beta} + (\epsilon_i - \epsilon_j), \tag{8.1.33}$$

where the error term $(\epsilon_j - \epsilon_j)$ is symmetrically distributed around zero. They show that if λ is a sufficiently "smooth" function and $\hat{\mathbf{a}}$ is a consistent estimator of $\mathbf{a}$, observations for which the difference $(\mathbf{w}_i - \mathbf{w}_j)'\hat{\mathbf{a}}$ is close to zero should have $\lambda(\mathbf{x}_i'\hat{\mathbf{a}}) - \lambda(\mathbf{w}_j'\hat{\mathbf{a}}) \simeq 0$. Therefore, Powell (2001) proposes a two-step procedure. In the first step, consistent semiparametric estimates of the coefficients of the *selection* equation are obtained. The result is used to obtain estimates of the single index $(\mathbf{x}_i'\mathbf{a})$ variables characterizing the selectivity bias in the equation of interest. The second step of the approach estimates the parameters of the interest by a weighted least-squares (or instrumental) variables regression of pairwise differences in dependent variables in the sample on the corresponding differences in explanatory variables:

$$\hat{\boldsymbol\beta}_{\text{AP}} = \left[\sum_{i=1}^{N-1}\sum_{j=i+1}^{N} K\left(\frac{(\mathbf{w}_i - \mathbf{w}_j)'\hat{\mathbf{a}}}{h_N}\right)\cdot(\mathbf{x}_i - \mathbf{x}_j)(\mathbf{x}_i - \mathbf{x}_j)'\,d_i\,d_j\right]^{-1}$$
$$\times\left[\sum_{i=1}^{N-1}\sum_{j=i+1}^{N} K\left(\frac{(\mathbf{w}_i - \mathbf{w}_j)'\hat{\mathbf{a}}}{h_N}\right)\cdot(\mathbf{x}_i - \mathbf{x}_j)(y_i - y_j)\,d_i\,d_j\right], \tag{8.1.34}$$

where $K(\cdot)$ is a kernel density weighting function that is bounded, is symmetric, and tends to zero as the absolute value of its argument increases, and h_N is a positive constant (or bandwidth) that decreases to zero such that $N(h_N)^6 \to 0$, and $N(h_N)^8 \to 0$ as $N \to \infty$. Often, standard normal density is used as a kernel function. The effect of multiplying by $K(\cdot)$ is to give more weights to observations with $(1/h_N)(\mathbf{w}_i - \mathbf{w}_j)'\hat{\mathbf{a}} \simeq 0$ and less weight to observations for which $\mathbf{w}_i'\hat{\mathbf{a}}$ is different from $\mathbf{w}_j'\hat{\mathbf{a}}$, so that in the limit only observations with $\mathbf{w}_i'\mathbf{a} = \mathbf{w}_j'\mathbf{a}$ are used in (8.1.34), and (8.1.34) converges to a weighted least-squares estimator for the truncated data,

$$\hat{\boldsymbol\beta}_{\text{AP}} \to \{E\{f(\mathbf{w}'\mathbf{a})[\mathbf{x} - E(\mathbf{x}\mid\mathbf{w}'\mathbf{a})][\mathbf{x} - E(\mathbf{x}\mid\mathbf{w}'\mathbf{a})]'\}\}^{-1}$$
$$\times\{E\{f(\mathbf{w}'\mathbf{a})[\mathbf{x} - E(\mathbf{x}\mid\mathbf{w}'\mathbf{a})][y - E(y\mid\mathbf{w}'\mathbf{a})]\}\}, \tag{8.1.35}$$

where $f(\mathbf{w}'\mathbf{a})$ denotes the density function of $\mathbf{w}'\mathbf{a}$, which is assumed to be continuous and bounded above.

Both the Robinson (1988b) semiparametric estimator and the Powell-type pairwise differencing estimator converge to the true value at the speed of $N^{-1/2}$. However, neither method can provide estimate of the intercept term, because differencing the observation conditional on $\mathbf{w}$ or $\mathbf{w}'\mathbf{a}$, although it eliminates the selection factor $\lambda(\mathbf{w})$, also eliminates the constant term, nor can $\mathbf{x}$ and $\mathbf{w}$ be identical. Chen (1999) notes that if (u, v) are jointly symmetrical and $\mathbf{w}$ includes a constant term,

$$E(u\mid v > -\mathbf{w}'a)\,\text{Prob}(v > -\mathbf{w}'a) - E(u\mid v > \mathbf{w}'\mathbf{a})\,\text{Prob}(v > \mathbf{w}'\mathbf{a})$$
$$= \int_{-\infty}^{\infty}\int_{-\mathbf{w}'\mathbf{a}}^{\infty} uf(u,v)\,du\,dv - \int_{-\infty}^{\infty}\int_{\mathbf{w}'\mathbf{a}}^{\infty} uf(u,v)\,du\,dv$$
$$= \int_{-\infty}^{\infty}\int_{-\mathbf{w}'\mathbf{a}}^{\mathbf{w}'\mathbf{a}} uf(u,v)\,du\,dv = 0, \tag{8.1.36}$$

where, without loss of generality, we let $\mathbf{w}'\mathbf{a} > 0$. It follows that

$$E[d_i y_i - d_j y_j - (d_i\mathbf{x}_i - d_j\mathbf{x}_j)'\boldsymbol\beta \mid \mathbf{w}_i'\mathbf{a} = -\mathbf{w}_j'\mathbf{a}, \mathbf{w}_i, \mathbf{w}_j]$$
$$= E[d_i u_i - d_j u_j \mid \mathbf{w}_i'\mathbf{a} = -\mathbf{w}_j'\mathbf{a}, \mathbf{w}_i, \mathbf{w}_j] = 0. \tag{8.1.37}$$

Because $\quad E[d_i - d_j \mid \mathbf{w}_i'\mathbf{a} = -\mathbf{w}_j'\mathbf{a}, \mathbf{w}_i, \mathbf{w}_j] = 2\text{Prob}(d_i = 1\mid \mathbf{w}_i'\mathbf{a}) - 1 \neq 0$

and the conditioning is on $\mathbf{w}_i'\mathbf{a} = -\mathbf{w}_j'\mathbf{a}$, not on $\mathbf{w}_i'\mathbf{a} = \mathbf{w}_j'\mathbf{a}$, the moment condition (8.1.37) allows the identification of the intercept and the slope parameters without the need to impose the exclusion restriction that at least one component of $\mathbf{x}$ is excluded from $\mathbf{w}$. Therefore, Chen (1999) suggests a $\sqrt{N}$-consistent instrumental variable estimator for the intercept and the slope parameters as

$$\hat{\boldsymbol{\beta}}_c = \left[\sum_{i=1}^{N-1}\sum_{j=i+1}^{N} K\left(\frac{(\mathbf{w}_i + \mathbf{w}_j)'\hat{\mathbf{a}}}{h_N}\right)(d_i\mathbf{x}_i - d_j\mathbf{x}_j)(\mathbf{z}_i - \mathbf{z}_j)'\right]^{-1} \times \left[\sum_{i=1}^{N-1}\sum_{j=i+1}^{N} K\left(\frac{(\mathbf{w}_i + \mathbf{w}_j)'\hat{\mathbf{a}}}{h_N}\right)(\mathbf{z}_i - \mathbf{z}_j)'(d_i y_i - d_j y_j)\right], \tag{8.1.38}$$

where $\mathbf{z}_i$ are the instruments for $d_i\mathbf{x}_i$. In the case when y are unobservable, but the corresponding $\mathbf{x}$ are observable, the natural instrument will be $E(d \mid \mathbf{w}'\mathbf{a})\mathbf{x}$. An efficient method for estimating binary-choice models that contain an intercept term, suggested by Chen (2000), can be used to obtain the first-stage estimate of $\mathbf{a}$.

8.2 AN EXAMPLE – NONRANDOMLY MISSING DATA

8.2.1 Introduction

Attrition is a problem in any panel survey. For instance, by 1981, all four of the national longitudinal surveys started in the 1960s had lost at least one-fourth of their original samples. In the Gary income maintenance project, 206 of the sample of 585 Black, male-headed households, or 35.2 percent, did not complete the experiment. In Section 9.2 we shall discuss procedures to handle randomly missing data. However, the major problem in econometrics is not simply missing data, but the possibility that they are missing for a variety of self-selection reasons. For instance, in a social experiment such as the New Jersey or Gary negative-income-tax experiments, some individuals may decide that keeping the detailed records that the experiments require is not worth the payment. Also, some may move or may be inducted into the military. In some experiments, persons with large earnings receive no experimental-treatment benefit and thus drop out of the experiment altogether. This attrition may negate the randomization in the initial experiment design. If the probability of attrition is correlated with experimental response, then traditional statistical techniques will lead to biased and inconsistent estimates of the experimental effect. In this section we show how models of limited dependent variables [e.g., see the surveys of Amemiya (1984); Heckman (1976a); and Maddala (1983)] can provide both the theory and the computational techniques for analyzing nonrandomly missing data (Griliches, Hall, and Hausman (1978); Hausman and Wise (1979)).[3]

8.2.2 A Probability Model of Attrition and Selection Bias

Suppose that the structural model is

$$y_{it} = \boldsymbol{\beta}'\mathbf{x}_{it} + v_{it}, \qquad \begin{aligned} i &= 1, \ldots, N, \\ t &= 1, \ldots, T, \end{aligned} \tag{8.2.1}$$

where the error term v_{it} is assumed to follow a conventional error-components formulation $v_{it} = \alpha_i + u_{it}$. For ease of exposition, we assume that $T = 2$.

If attrition occurs in the second period, a common practice is to discard those observations for which y_{i2} is missing. But suppose that the probability of observing y_{i2} varies with its value, as well as the values of other variables; then the probability of observing y_{i2} will depend on v_{i2}. Least squares of (8.2.1) based on observed y will lead to biased estimates of the underlying structural parameters and the experimental response.

To formalize the argument, let the indicator variable $d_i = 1$ if y_{i2} is observed in period 2, and $d_i = 0$ if y_{i2} is not observed; in other words, attrition occurs. Suppose that y_{i2} is observed ($d_i = 1$) if the latent variable

$$d_i^* = \gamma y_{i2} + \boldsymbol{\theta}'\mathbf{x}_{i2} + \boldsymbol{\delta}'\mathbf{w}_i + \epsilon_i^* \geq 0, \tag{8.2.2}$$

where $\mathbf{w}_i$ is a vector of variables that do not enter the conditional expectation of y but affect the probability of observing y; $\boldsymbol{\theta}$ and $\boldsymbol{\delta}$ are vectors of parameters; and (v_i, ϵ_i^*) are jointly normally distributed. Substituting for y_{i2} leads to the reduced-form specification

$$\begin{aligned} d_i^* &= (\gamma\boldsymbol{\beta}' + \boldsymbol{\theta}')\mathbf{x}_{i2} + \boldsymbol{\delta}'\mathbf{w}_i + \gamma v_{i2} + \epsilon_i^* \\ &= \boldsymbol{\pi}'\mathbf{x}_{i2} + \boldsymbol{\delta}'\mathbf{w}_i + \epsilon_i \\ &= \mathbf{a}'R_i + \epsilon_i, \end{aligned} \tag{8.2.3}$$

where $\epsilon_i = \gamma v_{i2} + \epsilon_i^*$, $R_i = (\mathbf{x}_{i2}', \mathbf{w}_i')'$, and $\mathbf{a}' = (\boldsymbol{\pi}', \boldsymbol{\delta}')$. We further assume that v_{it} are also normally distributed, and we normalize the variance σ_ϵ^2 of ϵ_i to 1. Then the probabilities of retention and attrition are probit functions given, respectively, by

$$\begin{aligned} \text{Prob}(d_i = 1) &= \Phi(\mathbf{a}'R_i), \\ \text{Prob}(d_i = 0) &= 1 - \Phi(\mathbf{a}'R_i), \end{aligned} \tag{8.2.4}$$

where $\Phi(\cdot)$ is the standard normal distribution function.

Suppose we estimate the model (8.2.1) using only complete observations. The conditional expectation of y_{i2}, given that it is observed, is

$$E(y_{i2} \mid \mathbf{x}_{i2}, \mathbf{w}_i, d_i = 1) = \boldsymbol{\beta}'\mathbf{x}_{i2} + E(v_{i2} \mid \mathbf{x}_{i2}, \mathbf{w}_i, d_i = 1). \tag{8.2.5}$$

From $v_{i2} = \sigma_{2\epsilon}\epsilon_i + \eta_i$, where $\sigma_{2\epsilon}$ is the covariance between v_{i2} and ϵ_i, and η_i

is independent of ϵ_i (Anderson (1958, Chapter 2)), we have

$$
\begin{aligned}
E(v_{i2} \mid \mathbf{w}_i, d_i = 1) &= \sigma_{2\epsilon} E(\epsilon_i \mid \mathbf{w}_i, d_i = 1) \\
&= \frac{\sigma_{2\epsilon}}{\Phi(\mathbf{a}'R_i)} \int_{-\mathbf{a}'R_i}^{\infty} \epsilon \cdot \frac{1}{\sqrt{2\pi}} e^{-\epsilon^2/2}\, d\epsilon \\
&= \sigma_{2\epsilon} \frac{\phi(\mathbf{a}'R_i)}{\Phi(\mathbf{a}'R_i)},
\end{aligned}
\tag{8.2.6}
$$

where $\phi(\cdot)$ denotes the standard normal density function. The last equality of (8.2.6) follows from the fact that the derivative of the standard normal density function $\phi(\epsilon)$ with respect to ϵ is $-\epsilon\phi(\epsilon)$. Therefore,

$$
E(y_{i2} \mid \mathbf{x}_{i2}, \mathbf{w}_i, d_i = 1) = \boldsymbol{\beta}'\mathbf{x}_{i2} + \sigma_{2\epsilon} \frac{\phi(\mathbf{a}'R_i)}{\Phi(\mathbf{a}'R_i)}. \tag{8.2.7}
$$

Thus, estimating (8.2.1) using complete observations will lead to biased and inconsistent estimates of $\boldsymbol{\beta}$ unless $\sigma_{2\epsilon} = 0$. To correct for selection bias, one can use either Heckman's two-stage method (1979) (see Section 8.1) or the maximum likelihood method.

When $d_i = 1$, the joint density of $d_i = 1$, y_{i1}, and y_{i2} is given by

$$
\begin{aligned}
f(d_i = 1, y_{i1}, y_{i2}) &= \text{Prob}(d_i = 1 \mid y_{i1}, y_{i2}) f(y_{i1}, y_{i2}) \\
&= \text{Prob}(d_i = 1 \mid y_{i2}) f(y_{i1}, y_{i2}) \\
&= \Phi \left\{ \frac{\mathbf{a}'R_i + \left(\frac{\sigma_{2\epsilon}}{\sigma_u^2 + \sigma_\alpha^2}\right)(y_{i2} - \boldsymbol{\beta}'\mathbf{x}_{i2})}{\left[1 - \frac{\sigma_{2\epsilon}^2}{\sigma_u^2 + \sigma_\alpha^2}\right]^{1/2}} \right\} \\
&\quad \times \left[2\pi\sigma_u^2(\sigma_u^2 + 2\sigma_\alpha^2)\right]^{-1/2} \\
&\quad \times \exp \left\{ -\frac{1}{2\sigma_u^2} \left[\sum_{t=1}^{2} (y_{it} - \boldsymbol{\beta}'\mathbf{x}_{it})^2 - \frac{\sigma_\alpha^2}{\sigma_u^2 + 2\sigma_\alpha^2} \right.\right. \\
&\qquad \left.\left. \times \left(\sum_{t=1}^{2} (y_{it} - \boldsymbol{\beta}'\mathbf{x}_{it}) \right)^2 \right] \right\},
\end{aligned}
\tag{8.2.8}
$$

where the first factor follows from the fact that the conditional density of $f(\epsilon_i \mid v_{i2})$ is normal, with mean $[\sigma_{2\epsilon}/(\sigma_u^2 + \sigma_\alpha^2)]v_{i2}$ and variance $1 - \sigma_{2\epsilon}^2/(\sigma_u^2 + \sigma_\alpha^2)$. When $d_i = 0$, y_{i2} is not observed and must be integrated out. In this instance, the joint density of $d_i = 0$ and y_{i1} is given by

$$
\begin{aligned}
f(d_i = 0, y_{i1}) = &\ \text{Prob}(d_i = 0 \mid y_{i1}) f(y_{i1}) \\
= &\left\{ 1 - \Phi \left[\frac{\mathbf{a}'R_i + \frac{\sigma_{1\epsilon}}{\sigma_u^2 + \sigma_\alpha^2}(y_{i1} - \boldsymbol{\beta}'\mathbf{x}_{i1})}{\left[1 - \frac{\sigma_{1\epsilon}^2}{\sigma_u^2 + \sigma_\alpha^2}\right]^{1/2}} \right] \right\}
\end{aligned}
$$

$$\times \left[2\pi\left(\sigma_u^2+\sigma_\alpha^2\right)\right]^{-1/2}$$
$$\times \exp\left\{-\frac{1}{2(\sigma_u^2+\sigma_\alpha^2)}(y_{i1}-\boldsymbol{\beta}'\mathbf{x}_{i1})^2\right\}. \qquad (8.2.9)$$

The second equality of (8.2.9) follows from the fact that $f(\epsilon_i \mid v_{i1})$ is normal, with mean $[\sigma_{1\epsilon}/(\sigma_u^2+\sigma_\alpha^2)]v_{i1}$ and variance $1-\sigma_{1\epsilon}^2/(\sigma_u^2+\sigma_\alpha^2)$, where $\sigma_{1\epsilon}$ is the covariance between v_{i1} and ϵ_i, which is equal to $\sigma_{2\epsilon}=\sigma_\alpha^2/(\sigma_u^2+\sigma_\alpha^2)$.

The likelihood function follows from (8.2.8) and (8.2.9). Order the observations so that the first N_1 observations correspond to $d_i=1$, and the remaining $N-N_1$ correspond to $d_i=0$; then the log likelihood function is given by

$$\begin{aligned}
\log L = {} & -N\log 2\pi - \frac{N_1}{2}\log\sigma_u^2 - \frac{N_1}{2}\log\left(\sigma_u^2+2\sigma_\alpha^2\right)\\
& - \frac{N-N_1}{2}\log\left(\sigma_u^2+\sigma_\alpha^2\right)\\
& - \frac{1}{2\sigma^2}\sum_{i=1}^{N_1}\left\{\sum_{t=1}^{2}(y_{it}-\boldsymbol{\beta}'\mathbf{x}_{it})^2 - \frac{\sigma_\alpha^2}{\sigma_u^2+2\sigma_\alpha^2}\left[\sum_{t=1}^{2}(y_{it}-\boldsymbol{\beta}'\mathbf{x}_{it})\right]^2\right\}\\
& + \sum_{i=1}^{N_1}\log\Phi\left\{\frac{\mathbf{a}'R_i+\frac{\sigma_{2\epsilon}}{\sigma_u^2+\sigma_\alpha^2}(y_{i2}-\boldsymbol{\beta}'\mathbf{x}_{i2})}{\left[1-\frac{\sigma_{2\epsilon}^2}{\sigma_u^2+\sigma_\alpha^2}\right]^{1/2}}\right\}\\
& - \frac{1}{2(\sigma_u^2+\sigma_\alpha^2)}\sum_{i=N_1+1}^{N}(y_{i1}-\boldsymbol{\beta}'\mathbf{x}_{i1})^2\\
& + \sum_{i=N_1+1}^{N}\log\left\{1-\Phi\left[\frac{\mathbf{a}'R_i+\frac{\sigma_{1\epsilon}}{\sigma_u^2+\sigma_\alpha^2}(y_{i1}-\boldsymbol{\beta}'\mathbf{x}_{i1})}{\left[1-\frac{\sigma_{1\epsilon}^2}{\sigma_u^2+\alpha_\alpha^2}\right]^{1/2}}\right]\right\}. \qquad (8.2.10)
\end{aligned}$$

The critical parameter for attrition bias is $\sigma_{2\epsilon}$. If $\sigma_{2\epsilon}=0$, so does $\sigma_{1\epsilon}$. The likelihood function (8.2.10) then separates into two parts. One corresponds to the variance-components specification for y. The other corresponds to the probit specification for attrition. Thus, if attrition bias is not present, this is identical with the random missing-data situations. Generalized least-squares techniques used to estimate (8.2.1) will lead to consistent and asymptotically efficient estimates of the structural parameters of the model.

The Hausman–Wise two-period model of attrition can be extended in a straightforward manner to more than two periods and to simultaneous-equations models with selection bias, as discussed in Section 8.2. When $T>2$, an attrition equation can be specified for each period. If attrition occurs, the individual does not return to the sample; then a series of conditional densities analogous to (8.2.8) and (8.2.9) result. The last period for which the individual appears in the sample gives information on which the random term in the attrition equations is conditioned. For periods in which the individual remains in the sample, an equation like (8.2.8) is used to specify the joint probability of no attrition and the observed values of the dependent variables.

In the case of simultaneous-equations models, all the attrition model does is to add an equation for the probability of observing an individual in the sample. Then the joint density of observing in-sample respondents becomes the product of the conditional probability of the observation being in the sample, given the joint dependent variable **y**, and the marginal density of **y**. The joint density of incomplete respondents becomes the product of the conditional probability of the observation being out of the sample, given the before-dropping-out values of **y**, and the marginal density of the previous periods' **y**. The likelihood function is simply the product of these two joint densities; see Griliches, Hall, and Hausman (1978) for a three-equation model.

The employment of probability equations to specify the status of individuals can be very useful in analyzing the general problems of changing compositions of the sample over time, in particular when changes are functions of individual characteristics. For instance, in addition to the problem of attrition in the national longitudinal surveys' samples of young men, there is also the problem of sample accretion, that is, entrance into the labor force of the fraction of the sample originally enrolled in school. The literature on switching regression models can be used as a basis for constructing behavioral models for analyzing the changing status of individuals over time.[4]

8.2.3 Attrition in the Gary Income-Maintenance Experiment

The Gary income-maintenance project focused on the effect of alternative sets of income-maintenance structures on work–leisure decisions. The basic project design was to randomly divide individuals into two groups: *controls* and *experimentals*. The controls were not on an experimental-treatment plan, but received nominal payments for completing periodic questionnaires. The experimentals were randomly assigned to one of several income-maintenance plans. The experiment had four basic plans defined by an income guarantee and a tax rate. The two guarantee levels were \$4,300 and \$3,300 for a family of four and were adjusted up for larger families and down for smaller families. The two marginal tax rates were 0.6 and 0.4. Retrospective information of individuals in the experiments was also surveyed for a preexperimental period (normally just prior to the beginning of the experimental period) so that the behavior of experimentals during the experiment could be compared with their own preexperimental behavior and also compared with that of the control group to obtain estimates of the effects of treatment plans.

Two broad groups of families were studied in the Gary experiment: Black female-headed households and black male-headed households. There was little attrition among the first group, but the attrition among male-headed families was substantial. Of the sample of 334 experimentals used by Hausman and

Wise (1979), the attrition rate was 31.1 percent. Among the 251 controls, 40.6 percent failed to complete the experiment.

If attrition is random, as will be discussed in Section 9.2, it is not a major problem. What matters is that data are missing for a variety of self-selection reasons. In this case it is easy to imagine that attrition is related to endogenous variables. Beyond a breakeven point, experimentals receive no benefits from the experimental treatment. The breakeven point occurs when the guarantee minus taxes paid on earnings (wage rate times hours worked) is zero. Individuals with high earnings receive no treatment payment and may be much like controls with respect to their incentive to remain in the experiment. But because high earnings are caused in part by the unobserved random term of the structural equation (8.2.1), attrition may well be related to it.

Hausman and Wise (1979) estimated structural models of earnings with and without correcting for attrition. The logarithm of earnings was regressed against time trend, education, experience, union membership, health status, and the logarithm of nonlabor family income. To control for the effects of the treatment, they also used a dummy variable that was 1 if for that period the household was under one of the four basic income-maintenance plans, and 0 otherwise. Because hourly wages for experimentals and controls did not differ, the coefficient of this variable provided a reasonable indicator of the effect of experimental treatment on hours worked.

Because only three observations were available during the experiment, each for a one-month period, they concentrated on a two-period model: a period for the preexperiment average monthly earnings and a period for the average earning of the three monthly observations of the experimental period. Their generalized-least-squares estimates of the structural parameters that were not corrected for attrition and the maximum likelihood estimates that incorporated the effects of attrition, (8.2.1) and (8.2.3), are presented in Table 8.1.

The attrition-bias parameter $\sigma_{2\epsilon}/(\sigma_u^2 + \sigma_\alpha^2)$ was estimated to be -0.1089. This indicates a small but statistically significant correlation between earnings and the probability of attrition. The estimate of the experimental effect was very close whether or not the attrition bias was corrected for. However, the experimental-effect coefficient did increase in magnitude from -0.079 to -0.082, an increase of 3.6 percent. Some of the other coefficients showed more pronounced changes. The effect of nonlabor family income on earnings (hence hours worked) decreased by 23 percent from the generalized-least-squares estimates, and the effect of another year of education increased by 43 percent. These results demonstrate that attrition bias was a potentially important problem in the Gary experiment. For other examples, see Ridder (1990), Nijman and Verbeek (1992), and Verbeek and Nijman (1996).

The Hausman–Wise (HW) model assumes that the contemporaneous values affect the probability of responding. Alternatively, the decision on whether to respond may be related to past experiences – if in the first period the effort in responding was high, an individual may be less inclined to respond in the second period. When the probability of attrition depends on lagged but not on contemporaneous variables, individuals are *missing at random* (MAR) (Rubin (1976); Little and Rubin (1987)) and the missing data are ignorable. (This case is sometimes referred to as selection on observables, e.g., Moffitt, Fitzgerald, and Gottschalk (1997)).

Both sets of models are often used to deal with attrition in panel data sets. However, they rely on fundamentally different restrictions on the dependence of the attrition process on time path of the variables and can lead to very different inferences. In a two-period model one cannot introduce dependence on y_{i2} in the MAR model, or dependence on y_{i1} in the HW model, without relying heavily on functional-form and distributional assumptions. However, when missing data are augmented by replacing the units who have dropped out with new units randomly sampled from the original population, called refreshment samples by Ridder (1992), it is possible to test between these two types of models nonparametrically as well as to estimate more general models (e.g., Hirano et al. (2001)).

8.3 TOBIT MODELS WITH RANDOM INDIVIDUAL EFFECTS

The most typical concern in empirical work using panel data has been the presence of unobserved heterogeneity.[5] Thus, a linear latent response function is often written in the form

$$y_{it}^* = \alpha_i + \boldsymbol{\beta}'\mathbf{x}_{it} + u_{it}, \qquad i = 1, \ldots, N, \quad t = 1, \ldots, T, \tag{8.3.1}$$

where the error term is assumed to be independent of $\mathbf{x}_{it}$ and is i.i.d. over time and across individuals. The observed value y_{it} is equal to y_{it}^* if $y_{it}^* > 0$ and is unobserved for $y_i^* \leq 0$ when data are truncated, and is equal to zero when data are censored. Under the assumption that α_i is randomly distributed with density function $g(\alpha)$ (or $g(\alpha \mid \mathbf{x})$), the likelihood function of the standard Tobit model for the truncated data is of the form

$$\prod_{i=1}^{N} \int \left[\prod_{t=1}^{T} [1 - F(-\boldsymbol{\beta}'\mathbf{x}_{it} - \alpha_i)]^{-1} f(y_{it} - \boldsymbol{\beta}'\mathbf{x}_{it} - \alpha_i) \right] g(\alpha_i)\, d\alpha_i, \tag{8.3.2}$$

where $f(\cdot)$ denotes the density function of u_{it} and $F(a) = \int_{-\infty}^{a} f(u)\, du$. The likelihood function of the censored data takes the form

$$\prod_{i=1}^{N} \int \left[\prod_{t \epsilon c_i} F(-\boldsymbol{\beta}'\mathbf{x}_{it} - \alpha_i) \prod_{t \epsilon \bar{c}_i} f(y_{it} - \alpha_i - \boldsymbol{\beta}'\mathbf{x}_{it}) \right] g(\alpha_i)\, d\alpha_i, \tag{8.3.3}$$

Table 8.1. *Parameter estimates of the earnings-function structural model with and without a correction for attrition*

Variables	With attrition correction: maximum likelihood estimates (standard errors)		Without attrition correction: Generalized-least-squares estimates (standard errors):
	Earnings-function parameters	Attrition parameters	earnings-function parameters
Constant	5.8539 (0.0903)	−0.6347 (0.3351)	5.8911 (0.0829)
Experimental effect	−0.0822 (0.0402)	0.2414 (0.1211)	−0.0793 (0.0390)
Time trend	0.0940 (0.0520)	—[a] —	0.0841 (0.0358)
Education	0.0209 (0.0052)	−0.0204 (0.0244)	0.0136 (0.0050)
Experience	0.0037 (0.0013)	−0.0038 (0.0061)	0.0020 (0.0013)
Nonlabor income	−0.0131 (0.0050)	0.1752 (0.0470)	−0.0115 (0.0044)
Union	0.2159 (0.0362)	1.4290 (0.1252)	0.2853 (0.0330)
Poor health	−0.0601 (0.0330)	0.2480 (0.1237)	−0.0578 (0.0326)
	$\hat{\sigma}_u^2 = \underset{(0.0057)}{0.1832}$ $\frac{\hat{\sigma}_\alpha^2}{\hat{\sigma}_u^2 + \hat{\sigma}_\alpha^2} = \underset{(0.0391)}{0.2596}$	$\frac{\hat{\sigma}_{2\epsilon}}{\hat{\sigma}_u^2 + \hat{\sigma}_\alpha^2} = \underset{(0.0429)}{-0.1089}$	$\hat{\sigma}_u^2 = 0.1236$ $\frac{\hat{\sigma}_\alpha^2}{\hat{\sigma}_u^2 + \hat{\sigma}_\alpha^2} = 0.2003$

[a]Not estimated.
Source: Hausman and Wise (1979, Table IV).

where $c_i = \{t \mid y_{it} = 0\}$ and $\bar{c}_i$ denotes its complement. Maximizing (8.3.2) or (8.3.3) with respect to unknown parameters yields consistent and asymptotically normally distributed estimators.

Similarly, for the type II Tobit model we may specify a sample selection equation

$$d_{it}^* = \mathbf{w}_{it}'\mathbf{a} + \eta_i + \nu_{it}, \tag{8.3.4}$$

with the observed (y_{it}, d_{it}) following the rule $d_{it} = 1$ if $d_{it}^* > 0$ and zero otherwise, as in (8.1.17), and $y_{it}^* = y_{it}$ if $d_{it} = 1$ and unknown otherwise, as in (8.1.18). Suppose that the joint density of (α_i, η_i) is given by $g(\alpha, \eta)$. Then the likelihood function of the type II Tobit model takes the form

$$\begin{aligned}
&\prod_{i=1}^{N} \int \Bigg[\prod_{t \in c_i} \text{Prob}(d_{it} = 0 \mid \mathbf{w}_{it}, \alpha_i) \prod_{t \in \bar{c}_i} \text{Prob}(d_{it} = 1 \mid \mathbf{w}_{it}, \alpha_i) \\
&\qquad \times f(y_{it} \mid \mathbf{x}_{it}, \mathbf{w}_{it}, \alpha_i, \eta_i, d_{it} = 1) \Bigg] g(\alpha_i, \eta_i)\, d\alpha_i\, d\eta_i \\
&= \prod_{i=1}^{N} \int \Bigg[\prod_{t \in c_i} \text{Prob}(d_{it} = 0 \mid \mathbf{w}_{it}, \alpha_i) \prod_{t \in \bar{c}_i} \text{Prob}(d_{it} = 1 \mid \mathbf{w}_{it}, \eta_i, \alpha_i, y_{it}, \mathbf{x}_{it}) \\
&\qquad \times f(y_{it} \mid \mathbf{x}_{it}, \alpha_i) \Bigg] g(\alpha_i, \eta_i)\, d\alpha_i\, d\eta_i.
\end{aligned} \tag{8.3.5}$$

Maximizing the likelihood function (8.3.2), (8.3.3), or (8.3.5) with respect to unknown parameters yields consistent and asymptotically normally distributed estimator of $\boldsymbol{\beta}$ when either N or T or both tend to infinity. However, the computation is quite tedious even with a simple parametric specification of the individuals effects α_i and η_i, because it involves multiple integration.[6] Neither is a generalization of the Heckman (1976a) two-stage estimator easily implementable (e.g., Nijman and Verbeek (1992); Ridder (1990); Vella and Verbeek (1999); Wooldridge (1999)). Moreover, both the MLE and the Heckman two-step estimators are sensitive to the exact specification of the error distribution. However, if the random effects α_i and η_i are independent of $\mathbf{x}_i$, then the Robinson (1988b) and Newey (1999) estimators ((8.1.27) and (8.1.32)) can be applied to obtain consistent and asymptotically normally distributed estimators of $\boldsymbol{\beta}$. Alteratively, one may ignore the randomness of α_i and η_i and apply the Honoré (1992) fixed-effects trimmed least-squares or least-absolute-deviation estimator for the panel data censored and truncated regression models, or the Kyriazidou (1997) two-step semiparametric estimator for the panel data sample selection model, to estimate $\boldsymbol{\beta}$ (see Section 8.4).

8.4 FIXED-EFFECTS ESTIMATOR

8.4.1 Pairwise Trimmed Least-Squares and Least-Absolute-Deviation Estimators for Truncated and Censored Regressions

When the effects are fixed and if $T \to \infty$, the MLEs of $\boldsymbol{\beta}'$ and α_i are straightforward to implement and are consistent. However, panel data often involve many individuals observed over few time periods, so that the MLE, in general, will be inconsistent as described in Chapter 7. In this section, we consider the pairwise trimmed least-squares (LS) and least-absolute-deviation (LAD) estimators of Honoré (1992) for panel data censored and truncated regression models that are consistent without the need to assume a parametric form for the disturbances u_{it}, nor homoscedasticity across individuals.

8.4.1.a Truncated Regression

We assume a model (8.3.1) and (8.1.2) except that now the individual effects are assumed fixed. The disturbance u_{it} is again assumed to be independently distributed over i and i.i.d. over t conditional on $\mathbf{x}_i$ and α_i.

We note that when data are truncated or censored, first-differencing does not eliminate the individual-specific effects from the specification. To see this, suppose that the data are truncated. Let

$$y_{it} = E(y_{it} \mid \mathbf{x}_{it}, \alpha_i, y_{it} > 0) + \epsilon_{it}, \tag{8.4.1}$$

where

$$E(y_{it} \mid \mathbf{x}_{it}, \alpha_i, y_{it} > 0) = \alpha_i + \mathbf{x}_{it}'\boldsymbol{\beta} + E(u_{it} \mid u_{it} > -\alpha_i - \mathbf{x}_{it}'\boldsymbol{\beta}). \tag{8.4.2}$$

Since $\mathbf{x}_{it} \neq \mathbf{x}_{is}$, in general,

$$\begin{aligned} &E(y_{it} \mid \mathbf{x}_{it}, \alpha_i, y_{it} > 0) - E(y_{is} \mid \mathbf{x}_{is}, \alpha_i, y_{is} > 0) \\ &\quad = (\mathbf{x}_{it} - \mathbf{x}_{is})'\boldsymbol{\beta} + E(u_{it} \mid u_{it} > -\alpha_i - \mathbf{x}_{it}'\boldsymbol{\beta}) \\ &\qquad - E(u_{is} \mid u_{is} > -\alpha_i - \mathbf{x}_{is}'\boldsymbol{\beta}). \end{aligned} \tag{8.4.3}$$

In other words,

$$\begin{aligned} (y_{it} - y_{is}) = {} & (\mathbf{x}_{it} - \mathbf{x}_{is})'\boldsymbol{\beta} + E(u_{it} \mid u_{it} > -\alpha_i - \mathbf{x}_{it}'\boldsymbol{\beta}) \\ & - E(u_{is} \mid u_{is} > -\alpha_i - \mathbf{x}_{is}'\boldsymbol{\beta}) + (\epsilon_{it} - \epsilon_{is}). \end{aligned} \tag{8.4.4}$$

The truncation correction term, $E(u_{it} \mid u_{it} > -\alpha_i - \mathbf{x}_{it}'\boldsymbol{\beta})$, which is a function of the individual specific effects α_i, remains after first-differencing. However, we may eliminate the truncation correction term through first-differencing if we restrict our analysis to observations where $y_{it} > (\mathbf{x}_{it} - \mathbf{x}_{is})'\boldsymbol{\beta}$ and $y_{is} >$

$-(\mathbf{x}_{it} - \mathbf{x}_{is})'\boldsymbol{\beta}$. To see this, suppose that $(\mathbf{x}_{it} - \mathbf{x}_{is})'\boldsymbol{\beta} < 0$. Then

$$\begin{aligned} &E(y_{is} \mid \alpha_i, \mathbf{x}_{it}, \mathbf{x}_{is}, y_{is} > -(\mathbf{x}_{it} - \mathbf{x}_{is})'\boldsymbol{\beta}) \\ &\quad = \alpha_i + \mathbf{x}'_{is}\boldsymbol{\beta} + E(u_{is} \mid u_{is} > -\alpha_i - \mathbf{x}'_{is}\boldsymbol{\beta} - (\mathbf{x}_{it} - \mathbf{x}_{is})'\boldsymbol{\beta}). \end{aligned} \tag{8.4.5}$$

Since u_{it} conditional on $\mathbf{x}_i$ and α_i is assumed to be i.i.d.,

$$E(u_{it} \mid u_{it} > -\alpha_i - \mathbf{x}'_{it}\boldsymbol{\beta}) = E(u_{is} \mid u_{is} > -\alpha_i - \mathbf{x}'_{it}\boldsymbol{\beta}). \tag{8.4.6}$$

Similarly, if $(\mathbf{x}_{it} - \mathbf{x}_{is})'\boldsymbol{\beta} > 0$,

$$\begin{aligned} &E(u_{it} \mid u_{it} > -\alpha_i - \mathbf{x}'_{it}\boldsymbol{\beta} + (\mathbf{x}_{it} - \mathbf{x}_{is})'\boldsymbol{\beta}) \\ &\quad = E(u_{it} \mid u_{it} > -\alpha_i - \mathbf{x}'_{is}\boldsymbol{\beta}) \\ &\quad = E(u_{is} \mid u_{is} > -\alpha_i - \mathbf{x}'_{is}\boldsymbol{\beta}). \end{aligned} \tag{8.4.7}$$

Therefore, by confining our analysis to the truncated observations where $y_{it} > (\mathbf{x}_{it} - \mathbf{x}_{is})'\boldsymbol{\beta}$, $y_{is} > -(\mathbf{x}_{it} - \mathbf{x}_{is})'\boldsymbol{\beta}$, $y_{it} > 0$, $y_{is} > 0$, we have

$$(y_{it} - y_{is}) = (\mathbf{x}_{it} - \mathbf{x}_{is})'\boldsymbol{\beta} + (\epsilon_{it} - \epsilon_{is}), \tag{8.4.8}$$

which no longer involves the incidental parameters α_i. Since $E[(\epsilon_{it} - \epsilon_{is}) \mid \mathbf{x}_{it}, \mathbf{x}_{is}] = 0$, applying least squares to (8.4.8) will yield a consistent estimator of $\boldsymbol{\beta}$.

The idea of restoring symmetry of the error terms of the pairwise differencing equation $(y_{it} - y_{is})$ by throwing away observations, where $y_{it} < (\mathbf{x}_{it} - \mathbf{x}_{is})'\boldsymbol{\beta}$ and $y_{is} < -(\mathbf{x}_{it} - \mathbf{x}_{is})'\boldsymbol{\beta}$ can be seen by considering the following graphs, assuming that $T = 2$. Suppose that the probability density function of u_{it} is of the shape shown in Figure 8.3. Since u_{i1} and u_{i2} are i.i.d. conditional on $(\mathbf{x}_{i1}, \mathbf{x}_{i2}, \alpha_i)$, the probability density of y^*_{i1} and y^*_{i2} conditional on $(\mathbf{x}_{i1}, \mathbf{x}_{i2}, \alpha_i)$ should have the same shape except for the location. The top and bottom graphs of Figure 8.4 postulate the probability density of y^*_{i1} and y^*_{i2} conditional on $(\mathbf{x}_{i1}, \mathbf{x}_{i2}, \alpha_i)$, respectively, assuming that $\Delta\mathbf{x}'_i\boldsymbol{\beta} < 0$, where $\Delta\mathbf{x}_i = \Delta\mathbf{x}_{i2} = \mathbf{x}_{i2} - \mathbf{x}_{i1}$. The truncated data correspond to those sample points where y^*_{it} or $y_{it} > 0$. Because $\mathbf{x}'_{i1}\boldsymbol{\beta} \neq \mathbf{x}'_{i2}\boldsymbol{\beta}$, the probability density of y_{i1} is different from that of y_{i2}. However, the probability density of y^*_{i1} given $y^*_{i1} > -\Delta\mathbf{x}'_i\boldsymbol{\beta}$ (or y_{i1} given $y_{i1} > -\Delta\mathbf{x}'_i\boldsymbol{\beta}$) is identical to the probability density of y^*_{i2} given $y^*_{i2} > 0$ (or y_{i2} given $y_{i2} > 0$) as shown in Figure 8.4. Similarly, if $\Delta\mathbf{x}'_i\boldsymbol{\beta} > 0$, the probability density of y^*_{i1} given $y^*_{i1} > 0$ (or y_{i1} given $y_{i1} > 0$) is identical to the probability density of y^*_{i2} given $y^*_{i2} > \Delta\mathbf{x}'_i\boldsymbol{\beta}$ as shown in Figure 8.5.[7] In other words, in a two-dimensional diagram of (y^*_{i1}, y^*_{i2}) as in Figure 8.6 or 8.7, (y^*_{i1}, y^*_{i2}) conditional on $(\mathbf{x}_{i1}, \mathbf{x}_{i2}, \alpha_i)$ is symmetrically distributed around the 45-degree line through $(\mathbf{x}'_{i1}\boldsymbol{\beta} + \alpha_i, \mathbf{x}'_{i2}\boldsymbol{\beta} + \alpha_i)$, or equivalently, around the 45-degree line through $(\mathbf{x}'_{i1}\boldsymbol{\beta}, \mathbf{x}'_{i2}\boldsymbol{\beta})$ or $(-\Delta\mathbf{x}'_i\boldsymbol{\beta}, 0)$, e. g., the line LL'. Since this is true for any value of α_i, the same statement is true for the distribution of (y^*_{i1}, y^*_{i2}) conditional on $(\mathbf{x}_{i1}, \mathbf{x}_{i2})$. When $\Delta\mathbf{x}'_i\boldsymbol{\beta} < 0$, the symmetry of the distribution of (y^*_{i1}, y^*_{i2}) around LL' means that the probability that (y^*_{i1}, y^*_{i2}) falls in the region $A_1 = \{(y^*_{i1}, y^*_{i2}) : y^*_{i1} > -\Delta\mathbf{x}'_i\boldsymbol{\beta},\ y^*_{i2} > y^*_{i1} + \Delta\mathbf{x}'_i\boldsymbol{\beta}\}$ equals the probability that it falls in the region $B_1 = \{(y^*_{i1}, y^*_{i2}) : y^*_{i1} > -\Delta\mathbf{x}'_i\boldsymbol{\beta},\ 0 < y^*_{i2} < y^*_{i1} + \Delta\mathbf{x}'_i\boldsymbol{\beta}\}$

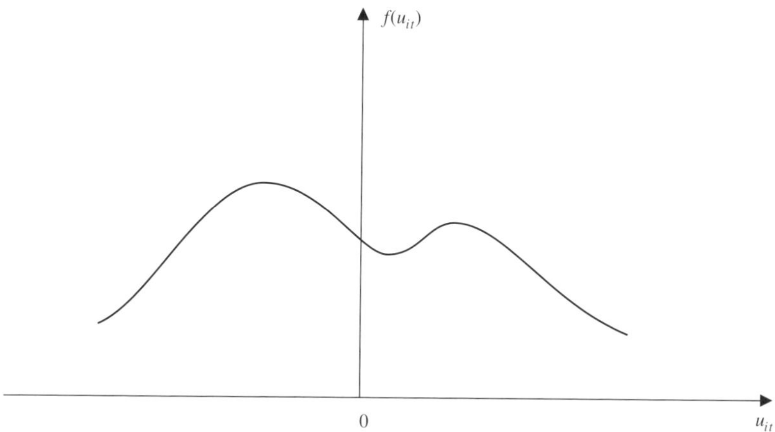

Fig. 8.3 Probability density of u_{it}.

(Figure 8.6). When $\Delta \mathbf{x}_i' \boldsymbol{\beta} > 0$, the probability that (y_{i1}^*, y_{i2}^*) falls in the region $A_1 = \{(y_{i1}^*, y_{i2}^*) : y_{i1}^* > 0,\ y_{i2}^* > y_{i1}^* + \Delta \mathbf{x}_i' \boldsymbol{\beta}\}$ equals the probability that it falls in the region $B_1 = \{(y_{i1}^*, y_{i2}^*) : y_{i1}^* > 0,\ \Delta \mathbf{x}_i' \boldsymbol{\beta} < y_{i2}^* < y_{i1}^* + \Delta \mathbf{x}_i' \boldsymbol{\beta}\}$ (Figure 8.7). That is, points in the regions A_1 and B_1 are not affected by the truncation. On the other hand, points falling into the region $(0 < y_{i1}^* < -\Delta \mathbf{x}_i' \boldsymbol{\beta},\ y_{i2}^* > 0)$ in Figure 8.6 (corresponding to points $(y_{i1} < -\Delta \mathbf{x}_i' \boldsymbol{\beta}, y_{i2})$) and $(y_{i1}^* > 0,\ 0 < y_{i2}^* < \Delta \mathbf{x}_i' \boldsymbol{\beta})$ in Figure 8.7 (corresponding to points $(y_{i1}, y_{i2} < \Delta \mathbf{x}_i' \boldsymbol{\beta})$) will have to be thrown away to restore symmetry.

Let $C = \{i \mid y_{i1} > -\Delta \mathbf{x}_i' \boldsymbol{\beta},\ y_{i2} > \Delta \mathbf{x}_i' \boldsymbol{\beta}\}$; then $(y_{i1} - \mathbf{x}_{i1}' \boldsymbol{\beta} - \alpha_i)$ and $(y_{i2} - \mathbf{x}_{i2}' \boldsymbol{\beta} - \alpha_i)$ for $i \in C$ are symmetrically distributed around zero. Therefore $E[(y_{i2} - y_{i1}) - (\mathbf{x}_{i2} - \mathbf{x}_{i1})' \boldsymbol{\beta} \mid \mathbf{x}_{i1}, \mathbf{x}_{i2},\ i \in C] = 0$. In other words,

$$
\begin{aligned}
& E[\Delta y_i - \Delta \mathbf{x}_i' \boldsymbol{\beta} \mid y_{i1} > -\Delta \mathbf{x}_i' \boldsymbol{\beta},\ y_{i2} > \Delta \mathbf{x}_i' \boldsymbol{\beta}] \\
& \quad = E[\Delta y_i - \Delta \mathbf{x}_i' \boldsymbol{\beta} \mid y_{i1}^* > 0,\ y_{i1}^* > -\Delta \mathbf{x}_i' \boldsymbol{\beta},\ y_{i2}^* > 0 \\
& \qquad y_{i2}^* > \Delta \mathbf{x}_i' \boldsymbol{\beta}] = 0,
\end{aligned} \tag{8.4.9a}
$$

and

$$
E[(\Delta y_i - \Delta \mathbf{x}_i' \boldsymbol{\beta}) \Delta \mathbf{x}_i \mid y_{i1} > -\Delta \mathbf{x}_i' \boldsymbol{\beta},\ y_{i2} > \Delta \mathbf{x}_i' \boldsymbol{\beta}] = \mathbf{0}, \tag{8.4.9b}
$$

where $\Delta y_i = \Delta y_{i2} = y_{i2} - y_{i1}$. Therefore, Honoré (1992) suggests the trimmed LAD and LS estimators $\hat{\boldsymbol{\beta}}$ and $\tilde{\boldsymbol{\beta}}$ that minimize the objective functions

$$
\begin{aligned}
Q_N(\boldsymbol{\beta}) = & \sum_{i=1}^{N} [|\Delta y_i - \Delta \mathbf{x}_i' \boldsymbol{\beta}|\, 1\{y_{i1} > -\Delta \mathbf{x}_i' \boldsymbol{\beta},\ y_{i2} > \Delta \mathbf{x}_i' \boldsymbol{\beta}\} \\
& + |y_{i1}|\, 1\{y_{i1} \geq -\Delta \mathbf{x}_i' \boldsymbol{\beta},\ y_{i2} < \Delta \mathbf{x}_i' \boldsymbol{\beta}\} \\
& + |y_{i2}|\, 1\{y_{i1} < -\Delta \mathbf{x}_i' \boldsymbol{\beta},\ y_{i2} \geq \Delta \mathbf{x}_i' \boldsymbol{\beta}\}] \\
= & \sum_{i=1}^{N} \psi(y_{i1}, y_{i2}, \Delta \mathbf{x}_i' \boldsymbol{\beta}),
\end{aligned} \tag{8.4.10}
$$

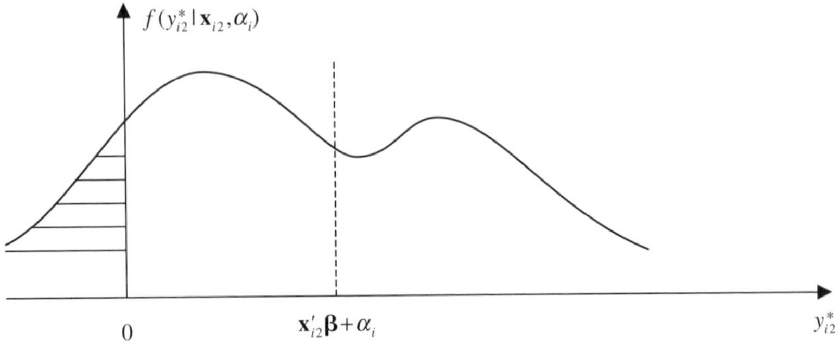

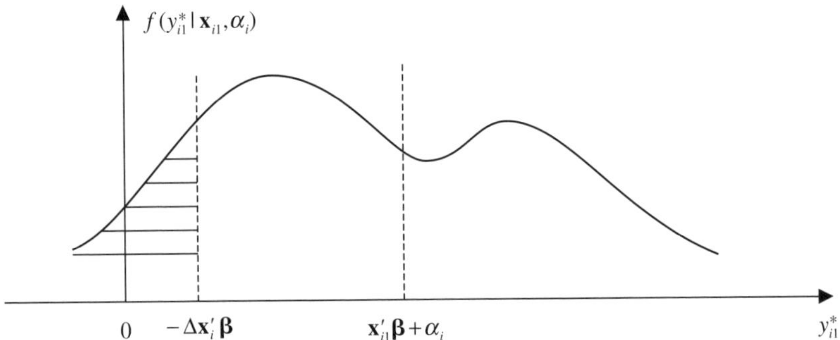

Fig. 8.4 Conditional densities of y^*_{i1} and y^*_{i2} given $(x_{i1}, x_{i2}, \alpha_i)$, assuming $\Delta x'_i \boldsymbol{\beta} < 0$.

and

$$\begin{aligned} R_N(\mathbf{b}) = \sum_{i=1}^{N} [(\Delta y_i - \Delta \mathbf{x}'_i \boldsymbol{\beta})^2 1\{y_{i1} \geq -\Delta \mathbf{x}'_i \boldsymbol{\beta},\ y_{i2} > \Delta \mathbf{x}'_i \boldsymbol{\beta}\} \\ + y_{i1}^2 1\{y_{i1} > -\Delta \mathbf{x}'_i \boldsymbol{\beta},\ y_{i2} < \Delta \mathbf{x}'_i \boldsymbol{\beta}\} \\ + y_{i2}^2 1\{y_{i1} < -\Delta \mathbf{x}'_i \boldsymbol{\beta},\ y_{i2} > \Delta \mathbf{x}'_i \boldsymbol{\beta}\}] \\ = \sum_{i=1}^{N} \psi(y_{i1}, y_{i2}, \Delta \mathbf{x}'_i \boldsymbol{\beta})^2, \end{aligned} \tag{8.4.11}$$

respectively. The function $\psi(w_1, w_2, c)$ is defined for $w_1 > 0$ and $w_2 > 0$ by

$$\psi(w_1, w_2, c) = \begin{cases} w_1 & \text{for} \quad w_2 < c, \\ w_2 - w_1 - c & \text{for} \quad -w_1 < c < w_2, \\ w_2 & \text{for} \quad w_1 < -c. \end{cases}$$

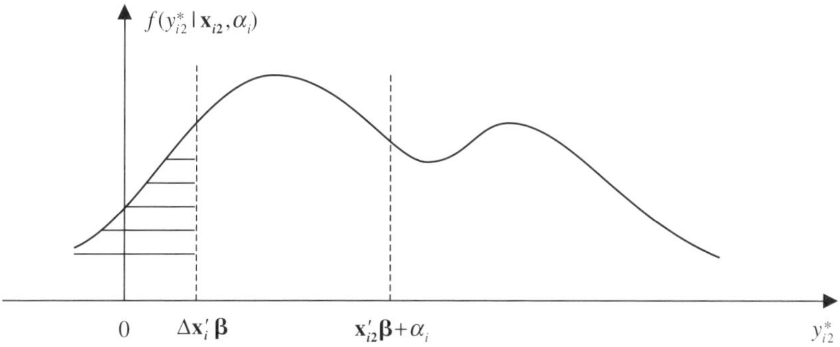

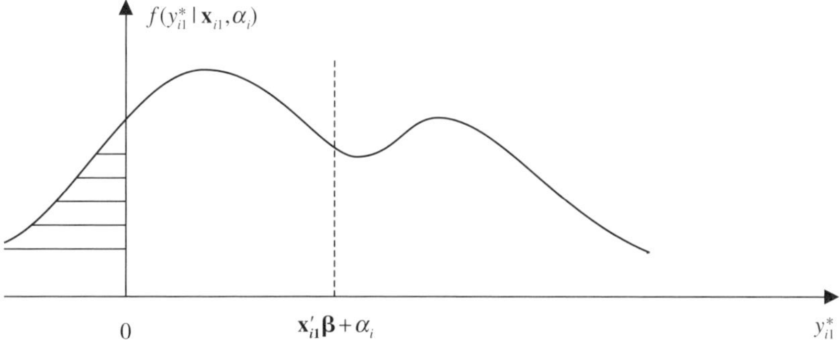

Fig. 8.5 Conditional densities of y_{i1}^* and y_{i2}^* given $(x_{i1}, x_{i2}, \alpha_i)$, assuming $\Delta x_i' \boldsymbol{\beta} > 0$.

The first-order conditions for (8.4.10) and (8.4.11) are the sample analogues of

$$E\{[P(y_{i1} > -\Delta \mathbf{x}_i' \boldsymbol{\beta},\ y_{i2} > y_{i1} + \Delta \mathbf{x}_i' \boldsymbol{\beta}) \\ - P(y_{i1} > -\Delta \mathbf{x}_i' \boldsymbol{\beta},\ \Delta \mathbf{x}_i' \boldsymbol{\beta} < y_{i2} < y_{i1} + \Delta \mathbf{x}_i' \boldsymbol{\beta})]\Delta \mathbf{x}_i'\} = \mathbf{0}', \tag{8.4.12}$$

and

$$E\{(\Delta y_i - \Delta \mathbf{x}_i' \boldsymbol{\beta})\, \Delta \mathbf{x}_i \mid (y_{i1} > -\Delta \mathbf{x}_i' \boldsymbol{\beta},\ y_{i2} > y_{i1} + \Delta \mathbf{x}_i' \boldsymbol{\beta}) \\ \cup\ (y_{i1} > -\Delta \mathbf{x}_i' \boldsymbol{\beta},\ \Delta \mathbf{x}_i' \boldsymbol{\beta} < y_{i2} < y_{i1} + \Delta \mathbf{x}_i' \boldsymbol{\beta})\} = \mathbf{0}, \tag{8.4.13}$$

respectively. Honoré (1992) proves that $\hat{\boldsymbol{\beta}}$ and $\tilde{\boldsymbol{\beta}}$ are consistent and asymptotically normally distributed if the density of u is strictly log-concave. The asymptotic covariance matrix of $\sqrt{N}(\hat{\boldsymbol{\beta}} - \boldsymbol{\beta})$ and $\sqrt{N}(\tilde{\boldsymbol{\beta}} - \boldsymbol{\beta})$ may be

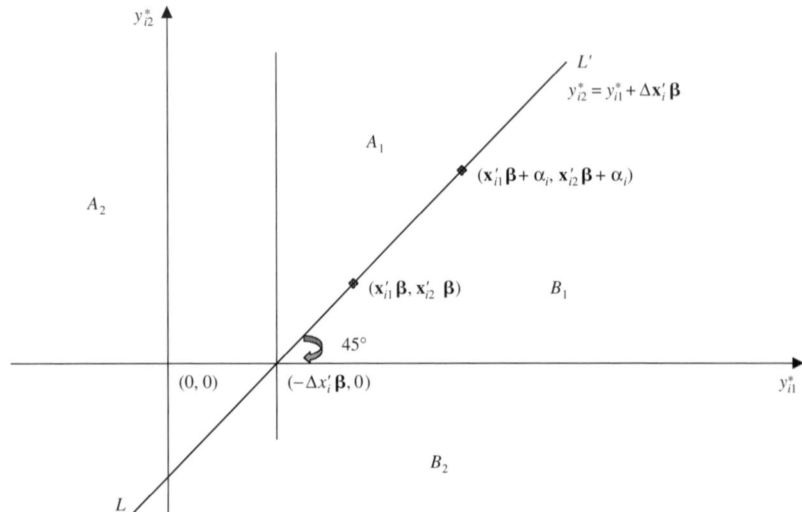

Fig. 8.6 The distribution of (y^*_{i1}, y^*_{i2}) assuming $\Delta\mathbf{x}'_i\,\beta < 0$.
$A_1 = \{(y^*_{i1}, y^*_{i2}) : y^*_{i1} > -\Delta\mathbf{x}'_i\,\boldsymbol{\beta},\ \ y^*_{i2} > y^*_{i1} + \Delta\mathbf{x}'_i\,\boldsymbol{\beta}\}$, $A_2 = \{(y^*_{i1}, y^*_{i2}) : y^*_{i1} \leq -\Delta\mathbf{x}'_i\,\boldsymbol{\beta},\ \ y^*_{i2} > 0\}$,
$B_1 = \{(y^*_{i1}, y^*_{i2}) : y^*_{i1} > -\Delta\mathbf{x}'_i\,\boldsymbol{\beta},\ 0 < y^*_{i2} < y^*_{i1} + \Delta\mathbf{x}'_i\,\boldsymbol{\beta}\}$, $B_2 = \{(y^*_{i1}, y^*_{i2}) : y^*_{i1} > -\Delta\mathbf{x}'_i\,\boldsymbol{\beta},\ \ y^*_{i2} \leq 0\}$.

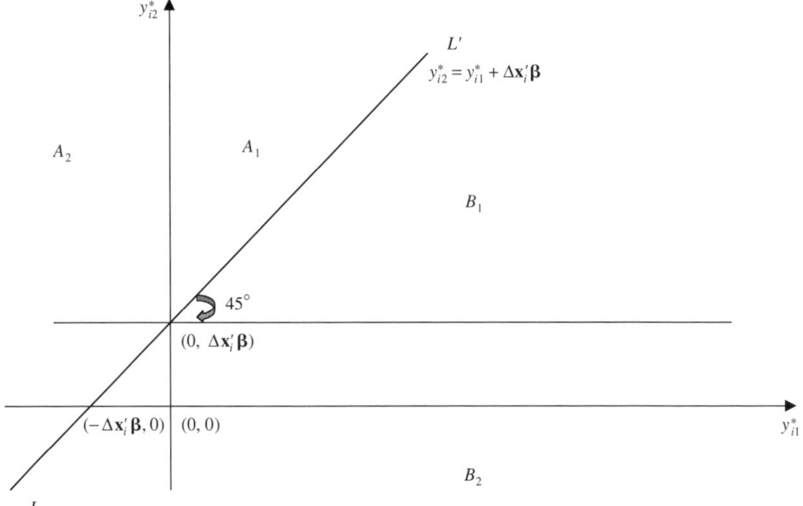

Fig. 8.7 The distribution of (y^*_{i1}, y^*_{i2}) assuming $\Delta\mathbf{x}'_i\,\boldsymbol{\beta} > 0$.
$A_1 = \{(y^*_{i1}, y^*_{i2}) : y^*_{i1} > 0,\ \ y^*_{i2} > y^*_{i1} + \Delta\mathbf{x}'_i\,\boldsymbol{\beta}\}$, $A_2 = \{(y^*_{i1}, y^*_{i2}) : y^*_{i1} \leq 0,\ \ y^*_{i2} > \Delta\mathbf{x}'_i\,\boldsymbol{\beta}\}$,
$B_1 = \{(y^*_{i1}, y^*_{i2}) : y^*_{i1} > 0,\ \ \Delta\mathbf{x}'_i\,\boldsymbol{\beta} < y^*_{i2} < y^*_{i1} + \Delta\mathbf{x}'_i\,\boldsymbol{\beta}\}$, $B_2 = \{(y^*_{i1}, y^*_{i2}) : y^*_{i1} > 0,\ \ y^*_{i2} \leq \Delta\mathbf{x}'_i\,\boldsymbol{\beta}\}$.

approximated by

$$\text{Asy Cov}(\sqrt{N}(\hat{\boldsymbol{\beta}} - \boldsymbol{\beta})) = \Gamma_1^{-1} V_1 \Gamma_1^{-1}, \tag{8.4.14}$$

and

$$\text{Asy Cov}(\sqrt{N}(\tilde{\boldsymbol{\beta}} - \boldsymbol{\beta})) = \Gamma_2^{-1} V_2 \Gamma_2^{-1}, \tag{8.4.15}$$

where V_1, V_2, Γ_1, and Γ_2 may be approximated by

$$\hat{V}_1 = \frac{1}{N} \sum_{i=1}^{N} 1\{-y_{i1} < \Delta \mathbf{x}_i' \hat{\boldsymbol{\beta}} < y_{i2}\} \Delta \mathbf{x}_i \, \Delta \mathbf{x}_i', \tag{8.4.16}$$

$$\hat{V}_2 = \frac{1}{N} \sum_{i=1}^{N} 1\{-y_{i1} < \Delta \mathbf{x}_i' \tilde{\boldsymbol{\beta}} < y_{i2}\} (\Delta y_i - \Delta \mathbf{x}_i' \tilde{\boldsymbol{\beta}})^2 \Delta \mathbf{x}_i \, \Delta \mathbf{x}_i', \tag{8.4.17}$$

$$\begin{aligned} \hat{\Gamma}_1^{(j,k)} = \frac{1}{h_N} \Bigg[& \frac{1}{N} \sum_{i=1}^{N} (1\{\Delta y_i < \Delta \mathbf{x}_i (\hat{\boldsymbol{\beta}} + h_N \mathbf{i}_k) < y_{i2}\} \\ & \quad - 1\{-y_{i1} < \Delta \mathbf{x}_i (\hat{\boldsymbol{\beta}} + h_N \mathbf{i}_k) < \Delta y_i\}) \, \Delta \mathbf{x}_i^{(j)} \\ & + \frac{1}{N} \sum_{i=1}^{N} (-1\{\Delta y_i < \Delta \mathbf{x}_i' \hat{\boldsymbol{\beta}} < y_{i2}\} \\ & \quad + 1\{-y_{i1} < \Delta \mathbf{x}_i' \hat{\boldsymbol{\beta}} < \Delta y_i\}) \, \Delta \mathbf{x}_i^{(j)} \Bigg], \end{aligned} \tag{8.4.18}$$

$$\begin{aligned} \hat{\Gamma}_2^{(j,k)} = \frac{1}{h_N} \Bigg[& \frac{1}{N} \sum_{i=1}^{N} 1\{-y_{i1} < \Delta \mathbf{x}_i' (\tilde{\boldsymbol{\beta}} + h_N \mathbf{i}_k) < y_{i2}\} \\ & \quad \times (\Delta y_i - \Delta \mathbf{x}_i' (\tilde{\boldsymbol{\beta}} + h_N \mathbf{i}_k)) \, \Delta \mathbf{x}_i^{(j)} \\ & - \frac{1}{N} \sum_{i=1}^{N} 1\{-y_{i1} < \Delta \mathbf{x}_i' \tilde{\boldsymbol{\beta}} < y_{i2}\} (\Delta y_i - \Delta \mathbf{x}_i' \tilde{\boldsymbol{\beta}}) \, \Delta \mathbf{x}_i^{(j)} \Bigg], \end{aligned} \tag{8.4.19}$$

where $\Gamma_\ell^{(j,k)}$ denotes the (j, k)th element of Γ_ℓ for $\ell = 1, 2$, $\Delta \mathbf{x}_i^{(j)}$ denotes the jth coordinate of $\Delta \mathbf{x}_i$, $\mathbf{i}_k$ is a unit vector with 1 in its kth place, and h_N decreases to zero with the speed of $N^{-\frac{1}{2}}$. The bandwidth factor h_N appears in (8.4.18) and (8.4.19) because Γ_ℓ is a function of densities and conditional expectations of y (Honoré (1992)).

8.4.1.b Censored Regressions

When data are censored, observations $\{y_{it}, \mathbf{x}_{it}\}$ are available for $i = 1, \ldots, N, t = 1, \ldots, T$, where $y_{it} = \max\{0, y_{it}^*\}$. In other words, y_{it} can now be either 0 or a positive number, rather than just a positive number as in the case of truncated data. Of course, we can throw away observations of $(y_{it}, \mathbf{x}_{it})$ that correspond to $y_{it} = 0$ and treat the censored regression model as the truncated regression model using the methods of Section 8.4.1.a. But this will lead to a loss of information.

In the case that data are censored, in addition to the relations (8.4.9a,b), the joint probability of $y_{i1} \leq -\boldsymbol{\beta}'\Delta\mathbf{x}_i$ and $y_{i2} > 0$ is identical to the joint probability of $y_{i1} > -\boldsymbol{\beta}'\Delta\mathbf{x}_i$ and $y_{i2} = 0$ when $\boldsymbol{\beta}'\Delta\mathbf{x}_i < 0$, as shown in Figure 8.6, regions A_2 and B_2, respectively. When $\boldsymbol{\beta}'\Delta\mathbf{x}_i > 0$, the joint probability of $y_{i1} = 0$ and $y_{i2} > \boldsymbol{\beta}'\Delta\mathbf{x}_i$ is identical to the joint probability of $y_{i1} > 0$ and $y_{i2} \leq \boldsymbol{\beta}'\Delta\mathbf{x}_i$, as shown in Figure 8.7. In other words, (y_{i1}^*, y_{i2}^*) conditional on $(\mathbf{x}_{i1}, \mathbf{x}_{i2}, \alpha_i)$ is symmetrically distributed around the 45-degree line through $(\mathbf{x}_{i1}'\boldsymbol{\beta} + \alpha_i, \mathbf{x}_{i2}'\boldsymbol{\beta} + \alpha_i)$ or equivalently around the 45-degree line through $(-\Delta\mathbf{x}_i'\boldsymbol{\beta}, 0)$ – the line LL' in Figure 8.6 or 8.7. Since this is true for any value of α_i, the same statement is true for the distribution of (y_{i1}^*, y_{i2}^*) conditional on $(\mathbf{x}_{i1}, \mathbf{x}_{i2})$. When $\Delta\mathbf{x}_i'\boldsymbol{\beta} < 0$, the symmetry of the distribution of (y_{i1}^*, y_{i2}^*) around LL' means that the probability that (y_{i1}^*, y_{i2}^*) falls in the region $A_1 = \{(y_{i1}^*, y_{i2}^*) : y_{i1}^* > -\Delta\mathbf{x}_i'\boldsymbol{\beta},\ y_{i2}^* > y_{i1}^* + \Delta\mathbf{x}_i'\boldsymbol{\beta}\}$ equals the probability that it falls in the region $B_1 = \{(y_{i1}^*, y_{i2}^*) : y_{i1}^* > -\Delta\mathbf{x}_i'\boldsymbol{\beta},\ 0 < y_{i2}^* < y_{i1}^* + \Delta\mathbf{x}_i'\boldsymbol{\beta}\}$. Similarly, the probability that (y_{i1}^*, y_{i2}^*) falls in the region $A_2 = \{(y_{i1}^*, y_{i2}^*) : y_{i1}^* < -\Delta\mathbf{x}_i'\boldsymbol{\beta},\ y_{i2}^* > 0\}$ equals the probability that it falls in the region $B_2 = \{(y_{i1}^*, y_{i2}^*) : y_{i1}^* > -\Delta\mathbf{x}_i'\boldsymbol{\beta}, y_{i2}^* \leq 0\}$ as shown in Figure 8.6. When $\Delta\mathbf{x}_i'\boldsymbol{\beta} > 0$, the probability that (y_{i1}^*, y_{i2}^*) falls in the region $A_1 = \{(y_{i1}^*, y_{i2}^*) : y_{i1}^* > 0,\ y_{i2}^* > y_{i1}^* + \Delta\mathbf{x}_i'\boldsymbol{\beta}\}$ equals the probability that it falls in the region $B_1 = \{(y_{i1}^*, y_{i2}^*) : y_{i1}^* > 0,\ \Delta\mathbf{x}_i'\boldsymbol{\beta} < y_{i2}^* < y_{i1}^* + \Delta\mathbf{x}_i'\boldsymbol{\beta}\}$, and the probability that it falls in the region $A_2 = \{(y_{i1}^*, y_{i2}^*) : y_{i1}^* \leq 0,\ y_i^* > \Delta\mathbf{x}_i'\boldsymbol{\beta}\}$ equals the probability that it falls in the region $B_2 = \{(y_{i1}^*, y_{i2}^*) : y_{i1}^* > 0,\ y_{i2}^* \leq \Delta\mathbf{x}_i'\boldsymbol{\beta}\}$, as seen in Figure 8.7. Therefore, the probability of (y_{i1}^*, y_{i2}^*) conditional on $(\mathbf{x}_{i1}, \mathbf{x}_{i2})$ falling in $A = (A_1 \cup A_2)$ equals the probability that it falls in $B = (B_1 \cup B_2)$. As neither of these probabilities is affected by censoring, the same is true in the censored sample. This implies that

$$E\left[(1\{(y_{i1}, y_{i2}) \in A\} - 1\{(y_{i1}, y_{i2}) \in B\})\,\Delta\mathbf{x}_i\right] = \mathbf{0}. \tag{8.4.20}$$

In other words, to restore symmetry of censored observations around their expected values, observations corresponding to $(y_{i1} = 0,\ y_{i2} < \Delta\mathbf{x}_i'\boldsymbol{\beta})$ or $(y_{i1} < -\Delta\mathbf{x}_i'\boldsymbol{\beta},\ y_{i2} = 0)$ will have to be thrown away.

By the same argument, conditional on $(\mathbf{x}_{i1}, \mathbf{x}_{i2})$, the expected vertical distance from a (y_{i1}, y_{i2}) in A to the boundary of A equals the expected horizontal distance from a (y_{i1}, y_{i2}) in B to the boundary of B. For (y_{i1}, y_{i2}) in A_1, the vertical distance to LL' is $(\Delta y_i - \Delta\mathbf{x}_i'\boldsymbol{\beta})$. For (y_{i1}, y_{i2}) in B_1, the horizontal distance to LL' is $y_{i1} - (y_{i2} - \Delta\mathbf{x}_i'\boldsymbol{\beta}) = -(\Delta y_i - \Delta\mathbf{x}_i'\boldsymbol{\beta})$. For (y_{i1}, y_{i2}) in A_2, the vertical distance to the boundary of A_2 is $y_{i2} - \max(0, \Delta\mathbf{x}_i'\boldsymbol{\beta})$. For (y_{i1}, y_{i2})

in B_2, the horizontal distance is $y_{i1} - \max(0, -\Delta\mathbf{x}_i'\boldsymbol{\beta})$. Therefore

$$\begin{aligned} E[(1\{(y_{i1}, y_{i2}) \in A_1\}(\Delta y_i - \Delta\mathbf{x}_i'\boldsymbol{\beta}) + 1\{(y_{i1}, y_{i2}) \in A_2)\} \\ \times (y_{i2} - \max(0, \Delta\mathbf{x}_i'\boldsymbol{\beta})) - 1\{(y_{i1}, y_{i2}) \in B_1\}(\Delta y_i - \Delta\mathbf{x}_i'\boldsymbol{\beta}) \\ - 1\{y_{i1}, y_{i2} \in B_2\}(y_{i1} - \max(0, -\Delta\mathbf{x}_i'\boldsymbol{\beta})))\Delta\mathbf{x}_i] = \mathbf{0}. \end{aligned} \quad (8.4.21)$$

The pairwise trimmed LAD and LS estimators, $\hat{\boldsymbol{\beta}}^*$ and $\tilde{\boldsymbol{\beta}}^*$, for the estimation of the censored regression model proposed by Honoré (1992) are obtained by minimizing the objective functions

$$\begin{aligned} Q_N^*(\boldsymbol{\beta}) &= \sum_{i=1}^{N}[1 - 1\{y_{i1} \le -\Delta\mathbf{x}_i'\boldsymbol{\beta},\ y_{i2} \le 0\}] \\ &\qquad \times [1 - 1\{y_{i2} \le \Delta\mathbf{x}_i'\boldsymbol{\beta},\ y_{i1} \le 0\}]|\Delta y_i - \Delta\mathbf{x}_i'\boldsymbol{\beta}| \\ &= \sum_{i=1}^{N} \psi^*(y_{i1}, y_{i2}, \Delta\mathbf{x}_i'\boldsymbol{\beta}), \end{aligned} \quad (8.4.22)$$

$$\begin{aligned} R_N^*(\boldsymbol{\beta}) &= \sum_{i=1}^{N}\{[\max\{y_{i2}, \Delta\mathbf{x}_i'\boldsymbol{\beta}\} - \max\{y_{i1}, -\Delta\mathbf{x}_i'\boldsymbol{\beta}\} - \Delta\mathbf{x}_i'\boldsymbol{\beta})]^2 \\ &\qquad - 2 \times 1\{y_{i1} < -\Delta\mathbf{x}_i'\boldsymbol{\beta}\}(y_{i1} + \Delta\mathbf{x}_i'\boldsymbol{\beta})y_{i2} \\ &\qquad - 2 \times 1\{y_{i2} < \Delta\mathbf{x}_i'\boldsymbol{\beta}\}(y_{i2} - \Delta\mathbf{x}_i'\boldsymbol{\beta})y_{i1}\} \\ &= \sum_{i=1}^{N} \chi(y_{i1}, y_{i2}, \Delta\mathbf{x}_i'\boldsymbol{\beta}), \end{aligned} \quad (8.4.23)$$

where

$$\psi^*(w_1, w_2, c) = \begin{cases} 0 & \text{for} \quad w_1 \le \max\{0, -c\} \text{ and } w_2 \le \max(0, c), \\ |\, w_2 - w_1 - c\,| & \text{otherwise,} \end{cases}$$

and

$$\chi(w_1, w_2, c) = \begin{cases} w_1^2 - 2w_1(w_2 - c) & \text{for} \quad w_2 \le c, \\ (w_2 - w_1 - c)^2 & \text{for} \quad -w_1 < c < w_2, \\ w_2^2 - 2w_2(c + w_1) & \text{for} \quad w_1 \le -c. \end{cases}$$

The first-order conditions for (8.4.22) and (8.4.23) are the sample analogues of (8.4.20) and (8.4.21), respectively. For instance, when $(y_{i1}, y_{i2}) \in (A_1 \cup B_1)$, the corresponding terms in R_N^* become $(\Delta y_i - \Delta\mathbf{x}_i'\boldsymbol{\beta})^2$. When $(y_{i1}, y_{i2}) \in A_2$, the corresponding terms become $y_{i2}^2 - 2 \times 1\{y_{i1} < -\Delta\mathbf{x}_i'\boldsymbol{\beta}\}(y_{i1} + \Delta\mathbf{x}_i'\boldsymbol{\beta})y_{i2}$. When $(y_{i1}, y_{i2}) \in B_2$, the corresponding terms become $y_{i1}^2 - 2 \times 1\{y_{i2} < \Delta\mathbf{x}_i'\boldsymbol{\beta}\}(y_{i2} - \Delta\mathbf{x}_i'\boldsymbol{\beta})y_{i1}$. The partial derivative of the first term with respect to $\boldsymbol{\beta}$ converges to $E\{[1\{(y_{i1}, y_{i2}) \in A_1\}(\Delta y_i - \Delta\mathbf{x}_i'\beta) - 1\{(y_{i1}, y_{i2}) \in B_1\}(\Delta y_i - \Delta\mathbf{x}_i'\boldsymbol{\beta})]\,\Delta\mathbf{x}_i\}$. The partial derivatives of the second and third terms with respect to $\boldsymbol{\beta}$ yield $-2E[1\{(y_{i1}, y_{i2}) \in A_2\}y_{i2}\,\Delta\mathbf{x}_i - 1\{(y_{i1}, y_{i2}) \in B_2\}y_{i1}\,\Delta\mathbf{x}_i]$.

Because $Q_N^*(\boldsymbol{\beta})$ is piecewise linear and convex and $R_N^*(\boldsymbol{\beta})$ is continuously differentiable and convex and twice differentiable except at a finite number of points, the censored pairwise trimmed LAD and LS estimators, $\hat{\boldsymbol{\beta}}^*$ and $\tilde{\boldsymbol{\beta}}^*$, are computationally simpler than the truncated estimators $\hat{\boldsymbol{\beta}}$ and $\tilde{\boldsymbol{\beta}}$.

Honoré (1992) shows that $\hat{\boldsymbol{\beta}}^*$ and $\tilde{\boldsymbol{\beta}}^*$ are consistent and asymptotically normally distributed. The asymptotic covariance matrix of $\sqrt{N}(\hat{\boldsymbol{\beta}}^* - \boldsymbol{\beta})$ is equal to

$$\text{Asy Cov}(\sqrt{N}(\hat{\boldsymbol{\beta}}^* - \boldsymbol{\beta})) = \Gamma_3^{-1} V_3 \Gamma_3^{-1}, \tag{8.4.24}$$

and of $\sqrt{N}(\tilde{\boldsymbol{\beta}}^* - \boldsymbol{\beta})$ is equal to

$$\text{Asy Cov}(\sqrt{N}(\tilde{\boldsymbol{\beta}}^* - \boldsymbol{\beta})) = \Gamma_4^{-1} V_4 \Gamma_4^{-1}, \tag{8.4.25}$$

where V_3, V_4, Γ_3, and Γ_4 may be approximated by

$$\hat{V}_3 = \frac{1}{N}\sum_{i=1}^{N} 1\{[\Delta \mathbf{x}_i' \hat{\boldsymbol{\beta}}^* < \Delta y_i,\ y_{i2} > \max(0, \Delta \mathbf{x}_i' \hat{\boldsymbol{\beta}}^*)] \cup [\Delta y_i < \Delta \mathbf{x}_i' \hat{\boldsymbol{\beta}}^*,\ y_{i1} > \max(0, -\Delta \mathbf{x}_i' \hat{\boldsymbol{\beta}}^*)]\}\, \Delta \mathbf{x}_i\, \Delta \mathbf{x}_i', \tag{8.4.26}$$

$$\hat{V}_4 = \frac{1}{N}\sum_{i=1}^{N} \left[y_{i2}^2 1\{\Delta \mathbf{x}_i' \tilde{\boldsymbol{\beta}}^* \leq -y_{i1}\} + y_{i1}^2 1\{y_{i2} \leq \Delta \mathbf{x}_i' \tilde{\boldsymbol{\beta}}^*\}\right] + (\Delta y_i - \Delta \mathbf{x}_1' \tilde{\boldsymbol{\beta}}^*)^2 1\{-y_{i1} < \Delta \mathbf{x}_i' \tilde{\boldsymbol{\beta}}^* < y_{i2}\}]\, \Delta \mathbf{x}_i\, \Delta \mathbf{x}_i', \tag{8.4.27}$$

$$\begin{aligned}\hat{\Gamma}_3^{(j,k)} = \frac{-1}{h_N}\Bigg\{ & \frac{1}{N}\sum_{i=1}^{N}[1\{y_{i2} > 0,\ y_{i2} > y_{i1} + \Delta \mathbf{x}_i'(\hat{\boldsymbol{\beta}}^* + h_N \mathbf{i}_k)\} \\ & - 1\{y_{i1} > 0,\ y_{i1} > y_{i2} - \Delta \mathbf{x}_i'(\hat{\boldsymbol{\beta}}^* + \omega_n \mathbf{i}_k)\}]\, \Delta \mathbf{x}_i^{(j)} \\ & - \frac{1}{N}\sum_{i=1}^{N}[1\{y_{i2} > 0,\ y_{i2} > y_{i1} + \Delta \mathbf{x}_i' \hat{\boldsymbol{\beta}}^*\} \\ & - 1\{y_{i1} > 0,\ y_{i1} > y_{i2} - \Delta \mathbf{x}_i' \hat{\boldsymbol{\beta}}^*\}]\, \Delta \mathbf{x}_i^{(j)} \Bigg\},\end{aligned} \tag{8.4.28}$$

and

$$\hat{\Gamma}_4 = \frac{1}{N}\sum_{i=1}^{N} 1\{-y_{i1} < \Delta \mathbf{x}_i' \tilde{\boldsymbol{\beta}}^* < y_{i2}\}\, \Delta \mathbf{x}_i \Delta \mathbf{x}_i'. \tag{8.4.29}$$

Both the truncated and censored estimators are presented assuming that $T = 2$. They can be easily modified to cover the case where $T > 2$. For instance,

(8.4.23) can be modified to be the estimator

$$\tilde{\boldsymbol{\beta}}^* = \arg\min \sum_{i=1}^{N}\sum_{t=2}^{T} \chi(y_{i,t-1}, y_{it}, (\mathbf{x}_{it} - \mathbf{x}_{it-1})'\boldsymbol{\beta}), \tag{8.4.30}$$

when $T > 2$.

8.4.2 A Semiparametric Two-Step Estimator for the Endogenously Determined Sample Selection Model

In this subsection, we consider the estimation of the endogenously determined sample selection model in which the sample selection rule is determined by the binary-response model (8.3.4) and (8.1.17) for the linear regression model (8.3.1), where $y_{it}^* = y_{it}$ if $d_{it} = 1$ and y_{it}^* is unknown if $d_{it} = 0$, as in (8.1.18). We assume that both (8.3.1) and (8.3.4) contain unobserved fixed individual-specific effects α_i and η_i that may be correlated with the observed explanatory variables in an arbitrary way. Following the spirit of Heckman's (1976a), two-step estimation procedure for the parametric model, Kyriazidou (1997) proposes a two-step semiparametric method for estimating the main regression of interest, (8.3.1). In the first step, the unknown coefficients of the selection equation (8.3.4), $\mathbf{a}$, are consistently estimated by some semiparametric method. In the second step, these estimates are substituted into the equation of interest, (8.3.1), conditional on $d_{it} = 1$, and estimate it by a weighted least-squares method. The fixed effect from the main equation is eliminated by taking time differences on the observed y_{it}. The selection effect is eliminated by conditioning time-differencing of y_{it} and y_{is} on those observations where $\mathbf{w}_{it}'\hat{\mathbf{a}} \simeq \mathbf{w}_{is}'\hat{\mathbf{a}}$, because the magnitude of the selection effect is the same if the effect of the observed variables determining selection remains the same over time.

We note that without sample selectivity, that is, $d_{it} = 1$ for all i and t, or if u_{it} and ν_{it} are uncorrelated conditional on α_i and $\mathbf{x}_{it}$, then (8.3.1) and (8.1.18) correspond to the standard variable intercept model for panel data discussed in Chapter 3 with balanced panel or randomly missing data.[8] If u_{it} and ν_{it} are correlated, sample selection will arise because $E(u_{it} \mid \mathbf{x}_{it}, \mathbf{w}_{it}, \alpha_i, d_{it} = 1) \neq 0$. Let $\lambda(\cdot)$ denote the conditional expectation of u conditional on $d = 1, \mathbf{x}, \mathbf{w}, \alpha$, and η; then (8.3.1) and (8.1.19) conditional on $d_{it} = 1$ can be written as

$$y_{it} = \alpha_i + \boldsymbol{\beta}'\mathbf{x}_{it} + \lambda(\eta_i + \mathbf{w}_{it}'\mathbf{a}) + \epsilon_{it}, \tag{8.4.31}$$

where $E(\epsilon_{it} \mid \mathbf{x}_{it}, \mathbf{w}_{it}, d_{it} = 1) = 0$.

The form of the selection function $\lambda(\cdot)$ is derived from the joint distribution of u and ν. For instance, if u and ν are bivariate normal, then we have the

Heckman sample selection correction

$$\lambda(\eta_i + \mathbf{a}'\mathbf{w}_{it}) = \frac{\sigma_{uv}}{\sigma_v} \frac{\phi\left(\frac{\eta_i + \mathbf{w}_{it}'\mathbf{a}}{\sigma_v}\right)}{\Phi\left(\frac{\eta_i + \mathbf{w}_{it}'\mathbf{a}}{\sigma_v}\right)}.$$

Therefore, in the presence of sample selection or attrition with short panels, regressing y_{it} on $\mathbf{x}_{it}$ using only the observed information is invalidated by two problems – first, the presence of the unobserved effects α_i, which introduces the incidental-parameter problem, and second, the selection bias arising from the fact that

$$E(u_{it} \mid \mathbf{x}_{it}, \mathbf{w}_{it}, d_{it} = 1) = \lambda(\eta_i + \mathbf{w}_{it}'\mathbf{a}).$$

The presence of individual specific effects in (8.4.23) is easily obviated by time-differencing those individuals that are observed for two time periods t and s, i.e., who have $d_{it} = d_{is} = 1$. However, the sample selectivity factors are not eliminated by time-differencing. But conditional on given i, if (u_{it}, v_{it}) are stationary and $\mathbf{w}_{it}'\mathbf{a} = \mathbf{w}_{is}'\mathbf{a}$, then $\lambda(\eta_i + \mathbf{w}_{it}\mathbf{a}) = \lambda(\eta_i + \mathbf{w}_{is}'\mathbf{a})$. Then the difference in (8.4.31) between t and s if both y_{it} and y_{is} are observable no longer contains the individual-specific effects α_i or the selection factor $\lambda(\eta_i + \mathbf{w}_{it}'\mathbf{a})$:

$$\Delta y_{its} = y_{it} - y_{is} = (\mathbf{x}_{it} - \mathbf{x}_{is})'\boldsymbol{\beta} + (\epsilon_{it} - \epsilon_{is}) = \Delta\mathbf{x}_{its}'\boldsymbol{\beta} + \Delta\epsilon_{its}. \tag{8.4.32}$$

As shown by Ahn and Powell (1993), if λ is a sufficiently smooth function, and $\hat{\mathbf{a}}$ is a consistent estimator of $\mathbf{a}$, observations for which the difference $(\mathbf{w}_{it} - \mathbf{w}_{is})'\hat{\mathbf{a}}$ is close to zero should have $\lambda_{it} - \lambda_{is} \simeq 0$. Therefore, Kyriazidou (1997) generalizes the pairwise difference concept of Ahn and Powell (1993) and propose to estimate the fixed-effects sample selection models in two steps: In the first step, estimate $\mathbf{a}$ by either Andersen (1970) and Chamberlain's (1980) conditional maximum likelihood approach or Horowitz (1992) and Lee's (1999) smoothed version of the Manski (1975) maximum score method discussed in Chapter 7. In the second step, the estimated $\hat{\mathbf{a}}$ is used to estimate $\boldsymbol{\beta}$ based on pairs of observations for which $d_{it} = d_{is} = 1$ and for which $(\mathbf{w}_{it} - \mathbf{w}_{is})'\hat{\mathbf{a}}$ is close to zero. This last requirement is operationalized by weighting each pair of observations with a weight that depends inversely on the magnitude of $(\mathbf{w}_{it} - \mathbf{w}_{is})'\hat{\mathbf{a}}$, so that pairs with larger differences in the selection effects receive less weight in the estimation. The Kyriazidou (1997) estimator takes the form

$$\begin{aligned}\hat{\boldsymbol{\beta}}_K = &\left\{\sum_{i=1}^{N} \frac{1}{T_i - 1} \sum_{1 \leq s < t \leq T_i} (\mathbf{x}_{it} - \mathbf{x}_{is})(\mathbf{x}_{it} - \mathbf{x}_{is})' K\left[\frac{(\mathbf{w}_{it} - \mathbf{w}_{is})'\hat{\mathbf{a}}}{h_N}\right] d_{it}\, d_{is}\right\}^{-1} \\ &\times \left\{\sum_{i=1}^{N} \frac{1}{T_i - 1} \sum_{1 \leq s < t < T_i} (\mathbf{x}_{it} - \mathbf{x}_{is})(\mathbf{y}_{it} - \mathbf{y}_{is})' K\left[\frac{(\mathbf{w}_{it} - \mathbf{w}_{is})'\hat{\mathbf{a}}}{h_N}\right] d_{it}\, d_{is}\right\},\end{aligned} \tag{8.4.33}$$

where T_i denotes the number of positively observed y_{it} for the ith individual, K is a kernel density function which tends to zero as the magnitude of its argument increases, and h_N is a positive constant or bandwidth that decreases to zero as $N \to \infty$. The effect of multiplying the kernel function $K(\cdot)$ is to give more weight to observations with $(1/h_N)(\mathbf{w}_{it} - \mathbf{w}_{is})'\hat{\mathbf{a}} \simeq 0$ and less weight to those with $\mathbf{w}_{it}\hat{\mathbf{a}}$ different from $\mathbf{w}_{is}\hat{\mathbf{a}}$, so that in the limit only observations with $\mathbf{w}_{it}\mathbf{a} = \mathbf{w}'_{is}\mathbf{a}$ are used in (8.4.33). Under appropriate regularity conditions (8.4.33) is consistent, but the rate of convergence is proportional to $\sqrt{Nh_N}$, much slower than the standard square root of the sample size.

When $T = 2$, the asymptotic covariance matrix of the Kyriazidou (1997) estimator (8.4.33) may be approximate by the Eicker (1963) and White's (1980) formulae for the asymptotic covariance matrix of the least-squares estimator of the linear regression model with heteroscedasticity,

$$\left(\sum_{i=1}^{N} \hat{\mathbf{x}}_i \hat{\mathbf{x}}_i'\right)^{-1} \sum_{i=1}^{N} \hat{\mathbf{x}}_i \hat{\mathbf{x}}_i \, \Delta\hat{e}_i^2 \left(\sum_{i=1}^{N} \hat{\mathbf{x}}_i \hat{\mathbf{x}}_i\right)^{-1}, \tag{8.4.34}$$

where $\hat{\mathbf{x}}_i = K(\Delta\mathbf{w}_i' \hat{\mathbf{a}}/h_N)^{1/2} \, \Delta\mathbf{x}_i(d_{i2}\, d_{i1})$ and $\Delta\hat{e}_i$ is the estimated residual of (8.4.32).

In the case that only a truncated sample is observed, the first-stage estimation of $\hat{\mathbf{a}}$ cannot be implemented. However, a sufficient condition to ensure that only observations with $\Delta\mathbf{w}'_{its}\,\mathbf{a} = 0$ are used is to replace $K[\Delta\mathbf{w}_{its}\,\hat{\mathbf{a}}/h_N]$ by a multivariate kernel function $K((\mathbf{w}_{it} - \mathbf{w}_{is})/h_N)$ in (8.4.33). However, the speed of convergence of (8.4.33) to the true $\boldsymbol{\beta}$ will be $\sqrt{Nh_N^k}$, where k denotes the dimension of $\mathbf{w}_{it}$. This is much slower than $\sqrt{Nh_N}$, since h_N converges to zero as $N \to \infty$.

8.5 AN EXAMPLE: HOUSING EXPENDITURE

Charlier, Melenberg, and van Soest (2001) use Dutch Socio-Economic Panel (SEP) 1987–89 waves to estimate the following endogenous switching regression model for the share of housing expenditure in total expenditure:

$$d_{it} = 1(\mathbf{w}'_{it}\mathbf{a} + \eta_i + \nu_{it} > 0), \tag{8.5.1}$$

$$y_{1it} = \boldsymbol{\beta}'_1\mathbf{x}_{it} + \alpha_{1i} + u_{1it} \qquad \text{if} \quad d_{it} = 1, \tag{8.5.2}$$

$$y_{2it} = \boldsymbol{\beta}'_2\mathbf{x}_{it} + \alpha_{2i} + u_{2it} \qquad \text{if} \quad d_{it} = 0, \tag{8.5.3}$$

where d_{it} denotes the tenure choice between owning and renting, with 1 for owners and 0 for renters; y_{1it} and y_{2it} are the budget shares spent on housing for owners and renters, respectively; $\mathbf{w}_{it}$ and $\mathbf{x}_{it}$ are vectors of explanatory variables; $\eta_i, \alpha_{1i}, \alpha_{2i}$ are unobserved household-specific effects; and $\nu_{it}, u_{1it}, u_{2it}$ are the error terms. The budget share spent on housing is defined as the fraction of total expenditure spent on housing. Housing expenditure for renters is just the rent paid by a family. The owners' expenditure on housing consists of net interest costs on mortgages, net rent paid if the land is not owned, taxes on owned housing, costs of insuring the house, opportunity cost of housing equity (which is set at 4 percent of the value of house minus the mortgage value), and maintenance cost, minus the increase of the value of the house. The explanatory variables considered are the education level of the head of household (DOP), age of the head of the household (AGE), age squared (AGE2), marital status (DMAR), logarithm of monthly family income (LINC), its square (L2INC), monthly total family expenditure (EXP), logarithm of monthly total family expenditure (LEXP), its square (L2EXP), number of children (NCH), logarithm of constant-quality price of rental housing (LRP), logarithm of constant-quality price of owner-occupied housing after tax (LOP), and LRP – LOP. The variables that are excluded from the tenure choice equation (8.5.1) are DOP, LEXP, L2EXP, LRP, and LOP. The variables excluded from the budget share equations ((8.5.2) and (8.5.3)) are DOP, LINC, L2INC, EXP, NCH, and LRP – LOP.

The random-effects and fixed-effects models with and without selection are estimated. However, since **x** includes LEXP and L2EXP and they could be endogenous, Charlier, Melenberg, and van Soest (2001) also estimate this model by the instrumental-variable (IV) method. For instance, the Kyriazidou (1997) weighted least-squares estimator is modified as

$$\hat{\boldsymbol{\beta}}_{KN} = \left\{ \sum_{i=1}^{N} \sum_{1 \le s < t \le T_i} (\mathbf{x}_{it} - \mathbf{x}_{is})(\mathbf{z}_{it} - \mathbf{z}_{is})' K \left[\frac{(\mathbf{w}_{it} - \mathbf{w}_{is})'\hat{\mathbf{a}}}{h_N} \right] d_{it}\, d_{is} \right\}^{-1} \times \left\{ \sum_{i=1}^{N} \sum_{1 \le s < t \le T_i} (\mathbf{z}_{it} - \mathbf{z}_{is})(y_{it} - y_{is}) K \left[\frac{(\mathbf{w}_{it} - \mathbf{w}_{is})'\hat{\mathbf{a}}}{h_N} \right] d_{it}\, d_{is} \right\}, \tag{8.5.4}$$

to take account of the potential endogeneity of LEXP and L2EXP, where $\mathbf{z}_{it}$ is a vector of instruments.

Tables 8.2 and 8.3 present the fixed-effects and random-effects estimation results for the budget share equations without and with correction for selection, respectively. The Kyriazidou (1997) estimator is based on the first-stage logit estimation of the tenure choice equation (8.5.1). The random-effects estimator is based on Newey's (1989) series expansion method (Charlier, Melenberg, and van Soest (2000)). The differences among these formulations are quite substantial. For instance, the parameters related to AGE, AGE2, LEXP, L2EXP, and the prices are substantially different from their random-effects counterparts based on IV. They also lead to very different conclusions on the elasticities of interest. The price elasticities for the average renters and owners are about −0.5 in the random-effects model, but are close to −1 for owners and −0.8 for renters in the fixed-effects models.

The Hausman specification tests for endogeneity of LEXP and L2EXP are inconclusive. But a test for the presence of selectivity bias based on the difference between the Kyriazidou IV and linear panel data estimates have test statistics of 88.2 for owners and 23.7 for renters, which are significant at the 5 percent level for the chi-square distribution with seven degrees of freedom.

Table 8.2. *Estimation results for the budget share equations without correction for selection (standard errors in parentheses)*[a]

Variable	Pooled random effects	Pooled IV random effects	Linear model fixed effects	Linear model IV[b] fixed effects
Owners				
Constant	4.102** (0.238)	4.939** (0.712)		
AGE	0.045** (0.009)	0.029** (0.010)	−0.073 (0.041)	−0.063 (0.044)
AGE2	−0.005** (0.001)	−0.003** (0.001)	0.009** (0.004)	0.009* (0.004)
LEXP	−0.977** (0.059)	−1.271** (0.178)	−0.769** (0.049)	−1.345** (0.269)
L2EXP	0.052** (0.003)	0.073** (0.011)	0.036** (0.003)	0.070** (0.016)
DMAR	0.036** (0.004)	0.027** (0.005)		
Dummy87			−0.001 (0.003)	−0.000 (0.004)
Dummy88			−0.002 (0.001)	−0.001 (0.002)
LOP	0.068** (0.010)	0.108** (0.010)	0.065** (0.016)	0.050** (0.018)
Renters				
Constant	2.914** (0.236)	3.056** (0.421)		
AGE	0.038** (0.007)	0.027** (0.007)	0.114** (0.034)	0.108** (0.035)
AGE2	−0.004** (0.000)	−0.003** (0.001)	−0.009* (0.004)	−0.009* (0.004)
LEXP	−0.772** (0.055)	−0.820** (0.106)	−0.800** (0.062)	−0.653** (0.219)
L2EXP	0.040** (0.003)	0.045** (0.006)	0.039** (0.004)	0.031* (0.014)
DMAR	0.011** (0.002)	0.001** (0.003)		
Dummy87			−0.004 (0.003)	−0.003 (0.003)
Dummy88			−0.002 (0.002)	−0.002 (0.002)
LRP	0.119* (0.017)	0.112** (0.017)	0.057** (0.020)	0.060** (0.020)

[a]* means significant at the 5 percent level; ** means significant at the 1 percent level.
[b]In IV estimation AGE, AGE2, LINC, L2INC, Dummy87, Dummy88, and either LOP (for owners) or LRP (for renters) are used as instruments.
Source: Charlier, Melenberg, and van Soest (2001, Table 3).

Table 8.3. *Estimation results for the budget share equations using panel data models taking selection into account (standard errors in parentheses)*[a]

Variable	Pooled random effects[b]	Pooled IV random effects[c]	Kyriazidou OLS estimates	Kyriazidou IV[d] estimates
Owners				
Constant	2.595[e]	3.370[e]		
AGE	−0.040** (0.013)	−0.020 (0.015)	0.083 (0.083)	0.359** (0.084)
AGE2	0.004** (0.001)	0.002 (0.001)	−0.008 (0.008)	−0.033** (0.009)
LEXP	−0.594** (0.142)	−0.821 (0.814)	−0.766** (0.102)	−0.801** (0.144)
L2EXP	0.026** (0.008)	0.042 (0.050)	0.036** (0.006)	0.036** (0.008)
DMAR	0.006 (0.007)	0.012 (0.007)		
LOP	0.126** (0.012)	0.121** (0.011)	0.006 (0.030)	0.001 (0.029)
Dummy87			−0.006 (0.007)	−0.013 (0.007)
Dummy88			−0.004 (0.004)	−0.008 (0.004)
Renters				
Constant	2.679[d]	1.856[d]		
AGE	−0.037** (0.012)	−0.027* (0.012)	0.127* (0.051)	0.082 (0.080)
AGE2	0.004** (0.001)	0.003* (0.001)	−0.018** (0.006)	−0.014 (0.007)
LEXP	−0.601** (0.091)	−0.417 (0.233)	−0.882** (0.087)	−0.898** (0.144)
L2EXP	0.027** (0.005)	0.016 (0.015)	0.044** (0.005)	0.044** (0.009)
DMAR	−0.021** (0.005)	−0.019** (0.005)		
LRP	0.105** (0.016)	0.106** (0.016)	0.051 (0.028)	0.024 (0.030)
Dummy87			−0.024** (0.007)	−0.023 (0.013)
Dummy88			−0.009* (0.004)	−0.012 (0.007)

[a] * means significant at the 5 percent level; ** means significant at the 1 percent level.
[b] series approximation using single index ML probit in estimating the selection equation.
[c] IV using AGE, AGE2, LINC, L2INC, DMAR and either LOP (for owners) or LRP (for renters) as instruments.
[d] In IV estimation AGE, AGE2, LINC, L2INC, Dummy87, and Dummy88 are used as instruments.
[e] Estimates include the estimate for the constant term in the series approximation.
Source: Charlier, Melenberg, and van Soest (2001, Table 4).

This indicates that the model that does not allow for correlation between the error terms in the share equations ((8.5.2) and (8.5.3)) and the error term or fixed effect in the selection equation (8.5.1) is probably misspecified.

The Hausman (1978) specification test of no correlation between the household-specific effects and the **x**s based on the difference between the Newey IV and the Kyriazidou IV estimates have test statistics of 232.1 for owners and 37.8 for renters. These are significant at the 5 percent level for the chi-square distribution with five degrees of freedom, thus rejecting the random-effects model that does not allow for correlation between the household-specific effects and the explanatory variables. These results indicate that the linear panel data models or random-effects linear panel models, which only allow for very specific selection mechanisms (both of which can be estimated with just the cross-sectional data), are probably too restrictive.

8.6 DYNAMIC TOBIT MODELS

8.6.1 Dynamic Censored Models

In this section we consider censored dynamic panel data models of the form[9]

$$y_{it}^* = \gamma y_{i,t-1}^* + \boldsymbol{\beta}'\mathbf{x}_{it} + \alpha_i + u_{it}, \tag{8.6.1}$$

$$y_{it} = \begin{cases} y_{it}^* & \text{if} \quad y_{it}^* > 0, \\ 0 & \text{if} \quad y_{it}^* \leq 0. \end{cases} \tag{8.6.2}$$

where the error u_{it} is assumed to be i.i.d. across i and over t. If there are no individual specific effects α_i (or $\alpha_i = 0$ for all i), panel data actually allow the possibility of ignoring the censoring effects in the lagged dependent variables by concentrating on the subsample where $y_{i,t-1} > 0$. Since if $y_{i,t-1} > 0$ then $y_{i,t-1} = y_{i,t-1}^*$, (8.6.1) and (8.6.2) with $\alpha_i = 0$ become

$$\begin{aligned} y_{it}^* &= \gamma y_{i,t-1}^* + \boldsymbol{\beta}'\mathbf{x}_{it} + u_{it} \\ &= \gamma y_{i,t-1} + \boldsymbol{\beta}'\mathbf{x}_{it} + u_{it}. \end{aligned} \tag{8.6.3}$$

Thus, by treating $y_{i,t-1}$ and $\mathbf{x}_{it}$ as predetermined variables that are independent of the error u_{it}, the censored estimation techniques for the cross-sectional static model discussed in Section 8.1 can be applied to the subsample where (8.6.3) hold.

When random individual-specific effects α_i are present in (8.6.1), y_{is}^* and α_i are correlated for all s even if α_i can be assumed to be uncorrelated with $\mathbf{x}_i$. To implement the MLE approach, not only does one have to make assumptions on the distribution of individual effects and initial observations, but computation may become unwieldy. To reduce the computational complexity, Arellano, Bover, and Labeaga (1999) suggest a two-step approach. The first step estimates the reduced form of y_{it}^* by projecting y_{it}^* on all previous $y_{i0}^*, y_{i1}^*, \ldots, y_{i,t-1}^*$ and $\mathbf{x}_{i1}, \ldots, \mathbf{x}_{it}$. The second step estimates $(\gamma, \boldsymbol{\beta}')$ from the reduced-form parameters of the y_{it}^* equation, $\boldsymbol{\pi}_t$, by a minimum-distance estimator of the form (3.8.14). To avoid the censoring problem in the first step, they suggest that for the ith individual, only the string $(y_{is}, y_{i,s-1}, \ldots, y_{i0})$, where $y_{i0} > 0, \ldots, y_{i,s-1} > 0$ be used. However, in order to derive the estimates of $\boldsymbol{\pi}_t$, the conditional distribution of y^*_{it} given $y^*_{i0}, \ldots, y^*_{i,t-1}$ will have to be assumed. Moreover, the reduced-form parameters $\boldsymbol{\pi}_t$ are related to $(\gamma, \boldsymbol{\beta}')$ in a highly nonlinear way. Thus, the second-stage estimator is not easily derivable. Therefore, in this section we shall bypass the issue of fixed or random α_i and only discuss the trimmed estimator due to Honoré (1993) and Hu (1999).

Consider the case where $T = 2$ and y_{i0} are available. In Figures 8.8 and 8.9, let the vertical axis measure the value of $y^*_{i2} - \gamma y^*_{i1} = \tilde{y}^*_i(\gamma)$ and horizontal axis measure y^*_{i1}. If u_{i1} and u_{i2} are i.i.d. conditional on $(y^*_{i0}, \mathbf{x}_{i1}, \mathbf{x}_{i2}, \alpha_i)$, then y^*_{i1} and $y^*_{i2} - \gamma y^*_{i1} = \tilde{y}^*_{i2}(\gamma)$ are symmetrically distributed around the line (1), $\tilde{y}^*_{i2}(\gamma) = y^*_{i1} - \gamma y^*_{i0} + \boldsymbol{\beta}'\Delta\mathbf{x}_{i2}$ (which is the 45-degree line through $(\gamma y^*_{i0} + \boldsymbol{\beta}'\mathbf{x}_{i1} + \alpha_i, \boldsymbol{\beta}'\mathbf{x}_{i2} + \alpha_i)$ and $(\gamma y^*_{i0} - \boldsymbol{\beta}'\Delta\mathbf{x}_{i2}, 0)$). However, censoring destroys this symmetry. We only observe

$$\begin{aligned} y_{i1} &= \max(0, y^*_{i1}) \\ &= \max(0, \gamma y^*_{i0} + \boldsymbol{\beta}' x_{i1} + \alpha_i + u_{i1}) \end{aligned}$$

and $y_{i2} = \max(0, \gamma y^*_{i1} + \boldsymbol{\beta}'\mathbf{x}_{i2} + \alpha_i + u_{i2})$ or $\tilde{y}_{i2}(\gamma) = \max(-\gamma y^*_{i1}, y^*_{i2} - \gamma y^*_{i1})$. That is, observations are censored from the left at the vertical axis, and for any $y_{i1} = y^*_{i1} > 0$, $y_{i2} = y^*_{i2} > 0$ implies $y^*_{i2} - \gamma y^*_{i1} > -\gamma y^*_{i1}$. In other words, observations are also censored from below by $\tilde{y}_{i2}(\gamma) = -\gamma y_{i1}$, which is line (2) in Figures 8.8 and 8.9. As shown in Figure 8.8, the observable range of y^*_{i1} and $y^*_{i2} - \gamma y^*_{i1}$ conditional on $(\mathbf{x}_{i1}, \mathbf{x}_{i2}, y^*_{i0})$ are not symmetric around line (1), which we have drawn with $\gamma \geq 0$, $\gamma y^*_{i0} - \boldsymbol{\beta}'\Delta\mathbf{x}_{i2} > 0$. To restore symmetry, we have to find the mirror images of these two borderlines – the vertical axis and line (2) – around the centerline (1), and then symmetrically truncate observations that fall outside these two new lines.

The mirror image of the vertical axis around line (1) is the horizontal line $\tilde{y}^*_{i2}(\gamma) = -\gamma y^*_{i0} + \boldsymbol{\beta}'\Delta\mathbf{x}_{i2}$, line (3) in Figure 8.8. The mirror image of line (2) around line (1) has slope equal to the reciprocal of that of line (2), $-\frac{1}{\gamma}$. Therefore, the mirror image of line (2) is the line $\tilde{y}^*_{i2}(\gamma) = -\frac{1}{\gamma} y^*_{i1} + c$ that passes through the intersection of line (1) and line (2). The intersection of line (1) and line (2) is given by $\bar{\tilde{y}}^*_{i2}(\gamma) = \bar{y}^*_{i1} - (\gamma y^*_{i0} - \boldsymbol{\beta}'\Delta\mathbf{x}_{i2}) = -\gamma \bar{y}^*_{i1}$. Solving for $(\bar{y}^*_{i1}, \bar{\tilde{y}}^*_{i2}(\gamma))$, we have $\bar{y}^*_{i1} = \frac{1}{1+\gamma}(\gamma y^*_{i0} - \boldsymbol{\beta}'\Delta\mathbf{x}_{i2})$, $\bar{\tilde{y}}^*_{i2}(\gamma) = -\frac{\gamma}{1+\gamma}(\gamma y^*_{i0} - \boldsymbol{\beta}'\Delta\mathbf{x}_{i2})$. Substituting $\tilde{y}^*_{i2}(\gamma) = \bar{\tilde{y}}^*_{i2}(\gamma)$ and $y^*_{i1} = \bar{y}^*_{i1}$ into the equation $\tilde{y}^*_{i2}(\gamma) = -\frac{1}{\gamma} y^*_{i1} + c$, we have $c = \frac{1-\gamma}{\gamma}(\gamma y^*_{i0} - \boldsymbol{\beta}'\Delta\mathbf{x}_{i2})$. Thus the mirror image of line (2) is $\tilde{y}^*_{i2}(\gamma) = -\frac{1}{\gamma}(y^*_{i1} - \gamma y^*_{i0} + \boldsymbol{\beta}'\Delta\mathbf{x}_{i2}) - (\gamma y^*_{i0} - \boldsymbol{\beta}'\Delta\mathbf{x}_{i2})$, line (4) in Figure 8.8.

In Figure 8.9 we show the construction of the symmetrical truncation region for the case when $\gamma y^*_{i0} - \boldsymbol{\beta}'\Delta\mathbf{x}_{i2} < 0$. Since observations are truncated at the vertical axis from the left and at line (2) from below, the mirror image of the vertical axis around line (1) is given by line (3). Therefore, if we truncate observations at line (3) from below, then the remaining observations will be symmetrically distributed around line (1).

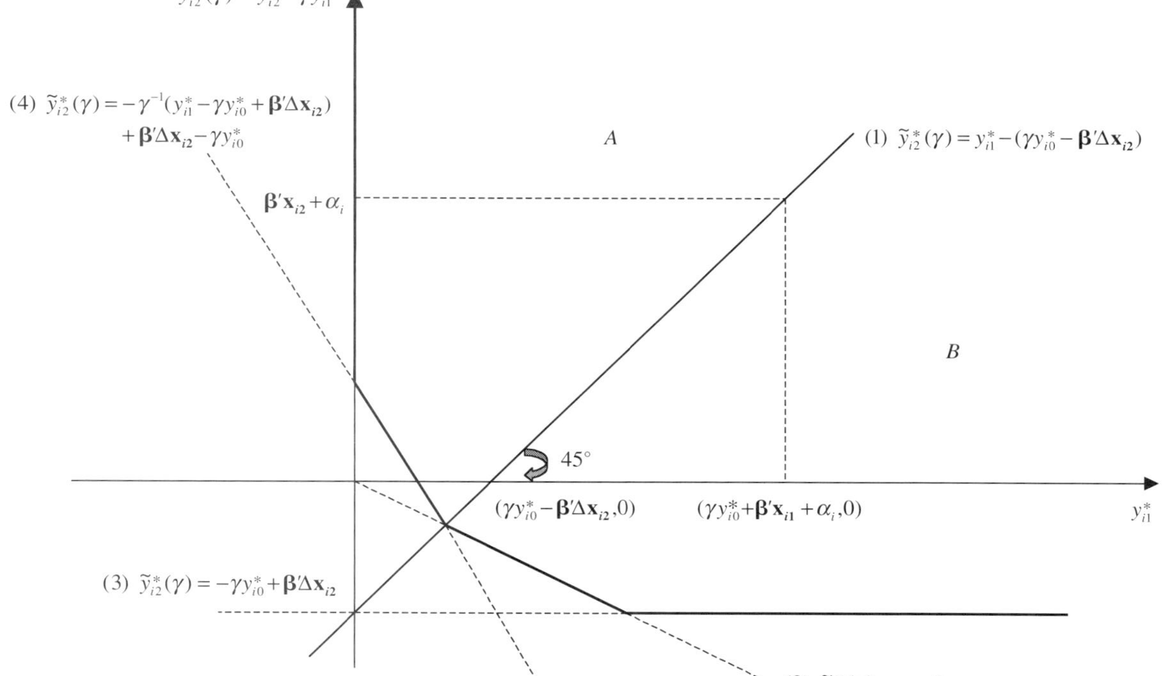

Fig. 8.8 $\gamma > 0$, $\gamma y_{i0}^* - \boldsymbol{\beta}'\Delta\mathbf{x}_{i2} > 0$.

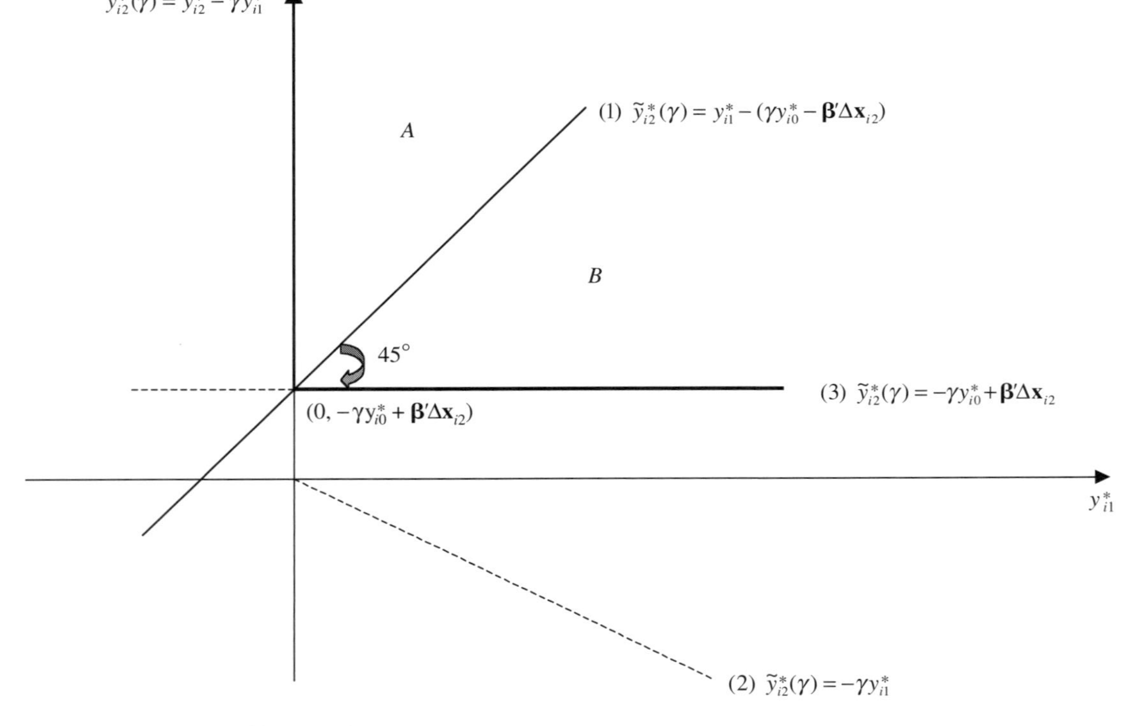

Fig. 8.9 $\gamma > 0$, $\gamma y^*_{i0} - \boldsymbol{\beta}'\Delta\mathbf{x}_{i2} > 0$.

The observations of $(y_{i1}, \tilde{y}_{i2}(\gamma))$ falling to the northeast direction of the region bordered by the lines (2), (3), and (4) in Figure 8.8 or by the vertical axis and line (3) in Figure 8.9 are symmetrically distributed around line (1) (the 45-degree line through $(\gamma y_{i0}^* - \boldsymbol{\beta}'\Delta\mathbf{x}_{i2}, 0)$). Denote the region above the 45-degree line by A and the region below it by B. Then

$$\begin{aligned}
A \cup B \equiv \{(y_{i1}, \tilde{y}_{i2}(\gamma)) : {} & y_{i1} > 0,\ \ \tilde{y}_{i2}(\gamma) > -\gamma y_{i1}, \\
& y_{i1} > \gamma y_{i0}^* - \boldsymbol{\beta}'\Delta\mathbf{x}_{i2} - \gamma(\tilde{y}_{i2}(\gamma) + \gamma y_{i0}^* - \boldsymbol{\beta}\Delta\mathbf{x}_{i2}), \\
& \tilde{y}_{i2}(\gamma) > -\gamma y_{i0}^* + \boldsymbol{\beta}'\Delta\mathbf{x}_{i2}\} \\
= \{(y_{i1}, \tilde{y}_{i2}(\gamma)) : {} & y_{i1} > 0,\ \ y_{i2} > 0, \\
& y_{i1} > \gamma y_{i0}^* - \boldsymbol{\beta}'\Delta\mathbf{x}_{i2} - \gamma(\tilde{y}_{i2}(\gamma) + \gamma y_{i0}^* - \boldsymbol{\beta}'\Delta\mathbf{x}_{i2}), \\
& \tilde{y}_{i2}(\gamma) > -\gamma y_{i0}^* + \boldsymbol{\beta}'\Delta\mathbf{x}_{i2}\}.
\end{aligned} \tag{8.6.4}$$

Symmetry implies that conditional on $y_{i0} > 0$, $y_{i1} > 0$, $y_{i2} > 0$, and $\mathbf{x}_{i1}$, $\mathbf{x}_{i2}$, the probability of an observation falling in region A equals the probability of it falling in region B. That is,

$$\begin{aligned}
& E\{(y_{i1}, \tilde{y}_{i2}(\gamma)) \in A \cup B\} \cdot [1\{y_{i1} - \tilde{y}_{i2}(\gamma) - \gamma y_{i0} + \boldsymbol{\beta}'\Delta\mathbf{x}_{i2} > 0\} \\
& \quad -1\{y_{i1} - \tilde{y}_{i2}(\gamma) - \gamma y_{i0} + \boldsymbol{\beta}'\Delta\mathbf{x}_{i2} < 0\}] = 0.
\end{aligned} \tag{8.6.5}$$

Another implication of symmetry is that conditional on $y_{i0} > 0$, $y_{i1} > 0$, $y_{i2} > 0$, and $\mathbf{x}_{i1}$, $\mathbf{x}_{i2}$, the expected vertical distance from a point in region A to the line (1), $\tilde{y}_{i2}(\gamma) - y_{i1} + \gamma y_{i0} - \boldsymbol{\beta}'\Delta\mathbf{x}_{i2}$, equals the expected horizontal distance from a point in region B to that line, $y_{i1} - \tilde{y}_{i2}(\gamma) - \gamma y_{i0} + \boldsymbol{\beta}'\Delta\mathbf{x}_{i2} = -(\tilde{y}_{i2}(\gamma) - y_{i1} + \gamma y_{i0} - \boldsymbol{\beta}'\Delta\mathbf{x}_{i2})$. Therefore,

$$E[1\{(y_{i1}, \tilde{y}_{i2}(\gamma)) \in A \cup B\}(y_{i1} - \tilde{y}_{i2}(\gamma) - \gamma y_{i0} + \boldsymbol{\beta}'\Delta\mathbf{x}_{i2})] = 0. \tag{8.6.6}$$

More generally, for any function $\xi(\cdot,\cdot)$ satisfying $\xi(e_1, e_2) = -\xi(e_2, e_1)$ for all (e_1, e_2), we have the orthogonality condition

$$\begin{aligned}
& E[1\{(y_{i1}, \tilde{y}_{i2}(\gamma)) \in A \cup B\} \cdot \xi(y_{i1} - \gamma y_{i0} + \boldsymbol{\beta}'\Delta\mathbf{x}_{i2}, \tilde{y}_{i2}(\gamma)) \\
& \qquad \times h(y_{i0}, \mathbf{x}_{i1}, \mathbf{x}_{i2})] = 0,
\end{aligned} \tag{8.6.7}$$

for any function $h(\cdot)$, where

$$\begin{aligned}
& 1\{(y_{i1}, \tilde{y}_{i2}(\gamma)) \in A \cup B\} \equiv 1\{y_{i0} > 0,\ \ y_{i1} > 0,\ \ y_{i2} > 0\} \\
& \quad \times [1\{\gamma y_{i0} - \boldsymbol{\beta}'\Delta\mathbf{x}_{i2} > 0\} \cdot 1\{y_{i1} > \gamma y_{i0} - \boldsymbol{\beta}'\Delta\mathbf{x}_{i2} - \gamma(\tilde{y}_{i2}(\gamma) \\
& \qquad + \gamma y_{i0} - \boldsymbol{\beta}'\Delta\mathbf{x}_{i2})\} \cdot 1\{\tilde{y}_{i2}(\gamma) > -\gamma y_{i0} + \boldsymbol{\beta}'\Delta\mathbf{x}_{i2}\} \\
& \qquad + 1\{\gamma y_{i0} - \boldsymbol{\beta}'\Delta\mathbf{x}_{i2} < 0\} \cdot 1\{\tilde{y}_{i2}(\gamma) > -\gamma y_{i0} + \boldsymbol{\beta}'\Delta\mathbf{x}_{i2}\}].
\end{aligned} \tag{8.6.8}$$

If one chooses $h(\cdot)$ to be a constant, the case $\xi(e_1, e_2) = \text{sgn}(e_1 - e_2)$ corresponds to (8.6.5), and $\xi(e_1, e_2) = e_1 - e_2$ corresponds to (8.6.6).

If $T \geq 4$, one can also consider any pair of observations y_{it}, y_{is} with $y_{i,t-1} > 0$, $y_{it} > 0$, $y_{i,s-1} > 0$, and $y_{is} > 0$. Note that conditional on $\mathbf{x}_{it}, \mathbf{x}_{is}$, the variables $(\alpha_i + u_{it})$ and $(\alpha_i + u_{is})$ are identically distributed. Thus, let

$$\begin{aligned} W_{its}(\boldsymbol{\beta}', \gamma) &= \max\{0, (\mathbf{x}_{it} - \mathbf{x}_{is})'\boldsymbol{\beta}, y_{it} - \gamma y_{i,t-1}\} - \mathbf{x}'_{it}\boldsymbol{\beta} \\ &= \max\{-\mathbf{x}'_{it}\boldsymbol{\beta}, -\mathbf{x}'_{is}\boldsymbol{\beta}, \alpha_i + u_{it}\}, \end{aligned} \tag{8.6.9}$$

and

$$\begin{aligned} W_{ist}(\boldsymbol{\beta}', \gamma) &= \max\{0, (\mathbf{x}_{is} - \mathbf{x}_{it})'\boldsymbol{\beta}, y_{is} - \gamma y_{i,s-1}\} - \mathbf{x}'_{is}\boldsymbol{\beta} \\ &= \max\{-\mathbf{x}'_{is}\boldsymbol{\beta}, -\mathbf{x}'_{it}\boldsymbol{\beta}, \alpha_i + u_{is}\}. \end{aligned} \tag{8.6.10}$$

Then $W_{its}(\boldsymbol{\beta}, \gamma)$ and $W_{ist}(\boldsymbol{\beta}, \gamma)$ are distributed symmetrically around the 45-degree line conditional on $(\mathbf{x}_{it}, \mathbf{x}_{is})$. This suggests the orthogonality condition

$$\begin{aligned} &E[1\{y_{it-1} > 0,\ \ y_{it} > 0,\ \ y_{i,s-1} > 0,\ \ y_{is} > 0\} \\ &\quad \times \xi(W_{its}(\boldsymbol{\beta}', \gamma), W_{ist}(\boldsymbol{\beta}', \gamma)) \cdot h(\mathbf{x}_{it}, \mathbf{x}_{is})] = 0 \end{aligned} \tag{8.6.11}$$

for any function $h(\cdot)$. When $T \geq 3$, the symmetric trimming procedure (8.6.11) requires weaker assumptions than the one based on three consecutive uncensored observations, since the conditioning variables do not involve the initial value y_{i0}. However, this approach also leads to more severe trimming.

Based on the orthogonality conditions (8.6.7) or (8.6.11), Hu (1999) suggests finding a GMM estimator of $\boldsymbol{\theta} = (\boldsymbol{\beta}', \gamma)'$ by minimizing $\mathbf{m}_N(\boldsymbol{\theta})' A_N \mathbf{m}_N(\boldsymbol{\theta})$, where $\mathbf{m}_N(\boldsymbol{\theta})$ is the sample analogue of (8.6.7) or (8.6.11), and A_N is a positive definite matrix that converges to a constant matrix A as $N \to \infty$. The GMM estimator will have a limiting distribution of the form

$$\sqrt{N}(\hat{\boldsymbol{\theta}}_{\text{GMM}} - \boldsymbol{\theta}) \to N(\boldsymbol{\theta}, (\Gamma' A \Gamma)^{-1}[\Gamma' A V A \Gamma](\Gamma' A \Gamma)^{-1}), \tag{8.6.12}$$

where $\Gamma = \frac{\partial}{\partial \boldsymbol{\theta}} E[\mathbf{m}(\boldsymbol{\theta})]$, $V = E[\mathbf{m}(\boldsymbol{\theta})\mathbf{m}(\boldsymbol{\theta})']$. When the optimal weighting matrix $A = V^{-1}$ is used, the asymptotic covariance matrix of $\sqrt{N}(\hat{\boldsymbol{\theta}}_{\text{GMM}} - \boldsymbol{\theta})$ becomes $(\Gamma' V^{-1} \Gamma)^{-1}$.

However, the orthogonality conditions (8.6.5)–(8.6.7) or (8.6.11) can be trivially satisfied when the parameter values are arbitrarily large. To see this, note that for a given value of γ, when the value of $\delta_{it} = \mathbf{x}'_{it}\boldsymbol{\beta}$ goes to infinity, the number of observations falling in the (nontruncated) region $A \cup B$ in Figures 8.7 and 8.8 approaches zero. Thus, the moment conditions can be trivially satisfied. To overcome this possible lack of identification of GMM estimates based on the minimization of the criterion function, Hu (1999) suggests using a subset of the moments that exactly identify $\boldsymbol{\beta}$ for given γ to provide the estimates of $\boldsymbol{\beta}$, then test whether the rest of the moment conditions are satisfied by these estimates for a sequence of γ values ranging from 0 to 0.9 with an increment of 0.01. Among the values of γ at which the test statistics are not rejected,

Table 8.4. *Estimates of AR(1) coefficients of log real annual earnings (in thousands)*[a]

Linear GMM (assuming no censoring)		Nonlinear GMM with correction for censoring	
Black	White	Black	White
0.379	0.399	0.210	0.380
(0.030)	(0.018)	(0.129)	(0.051)

[a]Standard errors in parenthesis.
Source: Hu (1999).

the one which yields the smallest test statistic is chosen as the estimate of γ. Hu (1999) uses this estimation method to study earnings dynamics, using matched data from the Current Population Survey and Social Security Administration (CPS–SSA) Earnings Record for a sample of men who were born in 1930–1939 and living in the South during the period of 1957–1973. The SSA earnings are top-coded at the maximum social security taxable level, namely, $y_{it} = \min(y_{it}^*, c_t)$, where c_t is the social security maximum taxable earnings level in period t. This censoring at the top can be easily translated into censoring at zero by considering $\tilde{y}_{it} = c_t - y_{it}$, then $\tilde{y}_{it} = \max(0, c_t - y_{it}^*)$.

Table 8.4 presents the estimates of the coefficient of the lagged log real annual earnings coefficient of an AR(1) model based on a sample of 226 black and 1883 white men with and without correction for censoring. When censoring is ignored, the model is estimated by the linear GMM method. When censoring is taken into account, Hu uses an unbalanced panel of observations with positive SSA earnings in three consecutive time periods. The estimated γ are very similar for black and white men when censoring is ignored. However, when censoring is taken into account, the estimated autoregressive parameter γ is much higher for white men than for black men. The higher persistence of the earnings process for white men is consistent with the notion that white men had jobs that had better security and were less vulnerable to economic fluctuation than black men in the period 1957–1973.

8.6.2 Dynamic Sample Selection Models

When the selection rule is endogenously determined as given by (8.2.4) and y_{it}^* is given by (8.6.1), with $\mathbf{w}_{it}$ and $\mathbf{x}_{it}$ being nonoverlapping vectors of strictly exogenous explanatory variables (with possibly common elements), the model under consideration has the form[10]

$$y_{it} = d_{it} y_{it}^*, \tag{8.6.13}$$

$$d_{it} = 1\{\mathbf{w}_{it}'\mathbf{a} + \eta_i + \nu_{it}\}, \qquad i = 1, \ldots, N, \quad t = 1, \ldots, T, \tag{8.6.14}$$

where $(d_{it}, \mathbf{w}_{it})$ is always observed, and $(y_{it}^*, \mathbf{x}_{it})$ is observed only if $d_{it} = 1$. For notational ease, we assume that d_{i0} and y_{i0} are also observed.

In the static case of $\gamma = 0$, Kyriazidou (1997) achieves the identification of $\boldsymbol{\beta}$ by relying on the conditional pairwise exchangeability of the error vector (u_{it}, v_{it}), given the entire path of the exogenous variables $(\mathbf{x}_i, \mathbf{w}_i)$ and the individual effects (α_i, η_i). However, the consistency of Kyriazidou estimator (8.4.33) breaks down in the presence of the lagged dependent variable in (8.6.1). The reason is the same as in linear dynamic panel data models where first-differencing generates nonzero correlation between $y_{i,t-1}^*$ and the transformed error term (see Chapter 4). However, just as in the linear case, estimators based on linear and nonlinear moment conditions on the correlation structure of the unobservables with the observed variables can be used to obtain consistent estimators of γ and $\boldsymbol{\beta}$.

Under the assumption that $\{u_{it}, v_{it}\}$ is independently, identically distributed over time for all i conditional on $\boldsymbol{\xi}_i \equiv (\mathbf{w}_i', \alpha_i, \eta_i, y_{i0}^*, d_{i0})$, where $\mathbf{w}_i = (\mathbf{w}_{i1}', \dots, \mathbf{w}_{iT})'$, Kyriazidou (2001) notes that by conditioning on the event that $\Delta\mathbf{w}_{it}'\mathbf{a} = 0$, the following moment conditions hold:[11]

$$E(d_{it}\, d_{i,t-1}\, d_{i,t-2}\, d_{i,t-j}\; \Delta u_{it} \mid \Delta\mathbf{w}_{it}'\mathbf{a} = 0) = \mathbf{0}, \qquad j = 2, \dots, t, \tag{8.6.15}$$

and

$$E(d_{is} d_{it} d_{i,t-1} d_{i,t-2}\, \mathbf{x}_{is}\; \Delta u_{it} \mid \Delta\mathbf{w}_{it}'\mathbf{a} = 0) = 0 \quad \text{for} \quad t = 2, \dots, T, \quad s = 1, \dots, T. \tag{8.6.16}$$

This is because, for an individual i, with the selection index $\mathbf{w}_{it}'\mathbf{a} = \mathbf{w}_{i,t-1}'\mathbf{a}$, the magnitude of the sample selection effects in the two periods, $\lambda(\eta_i + \mathbf{w}_{it}'\mathbf{a})$ and $\lambda(\eta_i + \mathbf{w}_{i,t-1}'\mathbf{a})$, will also be the same. Thus by conditioning on $\Delta\mathbf{w}_{it}'\,\mathbf{a} = 0$, the sample selection effects and the individual effects are eliminated by first-differencing.

Let $\boldsymbol{\theta} = (\gamma, \boldsymbol{\beta}')'$, $\mathbf{z}_{it}' = (y_{i,t-1}, \mathbf{x}_{it}')$, and

$$m_{1it}(\boldsymbol{\theta}) = d_{it} d_{i,t-1} d_{i,t-2} d_{i,t-j}\, y_{i,t-j} (\Delta y_{it} - \Delta\mathbf{z}_{it}'\boldsymbol{\theta}), \quad t = 2, \dots, T, \quad j = 2, \dots, t, \tag{8.6.17}$$

$$m_{2it,k}(\boldsymbol{\theta}) = d_{is} d_{it} d_{i,t-1} d_{i,t-2}\, x_{is,k} (\Delta y_{it} - \Delta\mathbf{z}_{it}'\boldsymbol{\theta}), \quad t = 2, \dots, T, \quad s = 1, \dots, T, \quad k = 1, \dots, K. \tag{8.6.18}$$

Kyriazidou (2001) suggests a kernel-weighted generalized method-of-moments estimator (KGMM) that minimizes the following quadratic form:

$$\hat{G}_N(\boldsymbol{\theta})' A_N \hat{G}_N(\boldsymbol{\theta}), \tag{8.6.19}$$

where A_N is a stochastic matrix that converges in probability to a finite nonstochastic limit A, and $\hat{G}_N(\boldsymbol{\theta})$ is the vector of stacked sample moments with rows of the form

$$\frac{1}{N}\sum_{i=1}^{N}\frac{1}{h_N}K\left(\frac{\Delta\mathbf{w}_{it}'\hat{\mathbf{a}}}{h_N}\right)m_{\ell it}(\boldsymbol{\theta}), \tag{8.6.20}$$

where $K(\cdot)$ is a kernel density function, $\hat{\mathbf{a}}$ is some consistent estimator of $\mathbf{a}$, and h_N is a bandwidth that shrinks to zero as $N \to \infty$. Under appropriate conditions, Kyriazidou (2001) proves that the KGMM estimator is consistent and asymptotically normal. The rate of convergence is the same as in univariate nonparametric density- and regression-function estimation, i.e., at speed $\sqrt{Nh_N}$.

CHAPTER 9

Incomplete Panel Data

Thus far our discussions have been concentrated on situations in which the sample of N cross-sectional units over T time periods is sufficient to identify a behavioral model. In this chapter we turn to the issues of incomplete panel data. We first examine the problems of estimating dynamic models when the length of time series is shorter than the maximum order of the lagged variables included in the equation. We then discuss the issues when some individuals are dropped from the experiment or survey. We note that when individuals are followed over time, there is a high probability that this will occur. Since the situations where individuals are missing for a variety of behavioral reasons have been discussed in Chapter 8 in this chapter we only distinguish three situations: (1) individuals are missing randomly or are being rotated; (2) a series of independent cross sections are observed over time; (3) only a single set of cross-sectional data is available in conjunction with the aggregate time-series observations. We briefly sketch how statistical methods developed for analyzing complete panel data can be generalized to analyze incomplete panel data.

9.1 ESTIMATING DISTRIBUTED LAGS IN SHORT PANELS[1]

9.1.1 Introduction

Because of technical, institutional, and psychological rigidities, often behavior is not adapted immediately to changes in the variables that condition it. In most cases this adaptation is progressive. The progressive nature of adaptations in behavior can be expressed in various ways. Depending on the rationale behind it, we can set up an autoregressive model, with the current value of y being a function of lagged dependent variables and exogenous variables, or we can set up a distributed-lag model, with the current value of y being a function of current and previous values of exogenous variables. Although usually a linear distributed-lag model can be expressed in an autoregressive form, and similarly, as a rule, any stable linear autoregressive model can be transformed into a distributed-lag model,[2] the empirical determination of time lags is very important in applied economics. The roles of many economic measures can be correctly understood only if we know when they will begin to take effect and when their effects will be fully worked out. Therefore, we would like to distinguish these two types of dynamic models when a precise specification (or reasoning) is possible. In Chapter 4, we discussed the issues of estimating autoregressive models with panel data. In this section we discuss estimation of distributed-lag models (Pakes and Griliches (1984)).

A general distributed-lag model for a single time series of observations is usually written as

$$y_t = \mu + \sum_{\tau=0}^{\infty} \beta_\tau x_{t-\tau} + u_t, \qquad t = 1, \ldots, T, \tag{9.1.1}$$

where, for simplicity, we assume that there is only one exogenous variable, x, and, conditional on $\{x_t\}$, the u_t are independent draws from a common distribution function. When no restrictions are imposed on the lag coefficients, one cannot obtain consistent estimates of β_τ even when $T \to \infty$, because the number of unknown parameters increases with the number of observations. Moreover, the available samples often consist of fairly short time series on variables that are highly correlated over time. There is not sufficient information to obtain precise estimates of any of the lag coefficients without specifying, a priori, that all of them are functions of only a very small number of parameters (Koyck lag, Almon lag, etc.) (Dhrymes (1971); Malinvaud (1970)).

On the other hand, when there are N time series, we can use cross-sectional information to identify and estimate (at least some of the) lag coefficients without having to specify a priori that the sequence of lag coefficients progresses in a particular way. For instance, consider the problem of using panel data to estimate the model (9.1.1), which for a given t we rewrite as

$$y_{it} = \mu + \sum_{\tau=0}^{t-1} \beta_\tau x_{i,t-\tau} + b_{it} + u_{it}, \qquad i = 1, \ldots, N, \tag{9.1.2}$$

where

$$b_{it} = \sum_{\tau=0}^{\infty} \beta_{t+\tau} x_{i,-\tau} \tag{9.1.3}$$

is the contribution of the unobserved presample x values to the current values of y, to which we shall refer as the truncation remainder. Under certain assumptions about the relationships between the unobserved b_{it} and the observed x_{it}, it is possible to obtain consistent estimates of β_τ, $\tau = 0, \ldots, t-1$, by regressing (9.1.2) cross-sectionally. Furthermore, the problem of collinearity among $x_t, x_{t-1}, \ldots,$ in a single time series can be reduced or avoided by use of the cross-sectional differences in individual characteristics.

9.1.2 Common Assumptions

To see under what conditions the addition of a cross-sectional dimension can provide information that cannot be obtained in a single time series, first we consider the case that the lag coefficients vary across individuals ($\{\beta_{i\tau}\}_{\tau=0}^{\infty}$ for $i = 1, \ldots, N$). If there is no restriction on the distribution of these sequences over members of the population, then each time series contains information on only a single sequence of coefficients. The problem of lack of information remains for panel data. Second, even if the lag coefficients do not vary across individuals ($\beta_{i\tau} = \beta_\tau$ for $i = 1, \ldots, N$ and $\tau = 0, 1, 2, \ldots$), the (often very significant) increase in sample size that accompanies the availability of panel data is entirely an increase in cross-sectional dimension. Panel data sets, in fact, usually track their observations over only a relatively short time interval. As a result, the contributions of the unobserved presample x values to the current values of y (the truncation remainders b_{it}) are likely to be particularly important if we do not wish to impose the same type of restrictions on the lag coefficients as we often do when a single time-series data set is used to estimate a distributed-lag model. Regression analysis, ignoring the unobserved truncation-remainder term, will suffer from the usual omitted-variable bias.

Thus, in order to combine N time series to estimate a distributed-lag model, we have to impose restrictions on the distribution of lag coefficients across cross-sectional units and/or on the way the unobserved presample terms affect current behavior. Pakes and Griliches (1984) considered a distributed-lag model of the form

$$y_{it} = \alpha_i^* + \sum_{\tau=0}^{\infty} \beta_{i\tau} x_{i,t-\tau} + u_{it}, \qquad i = 1, \ldots, N, \qquad t = 1, \ldots, T, \tag{9.1.4}$$

where u_{it} is independent of x_{is} and is independently, identically distributed, with mean zero and variance σ_u^2. The coefficients of α_i^* and $\beta_{i\tau}$ are assumed to satisfy the following assumptions.

Assumption 9.1.1. $E(\beta_{i\tau}) = \beta_\tau$.

Assumption 9.1.2. Let $\tilde{\beta}_{i\tau} = \beta_{i\tau} - \beta_\tau$, $\xi_{it} = \sum_{\tau=0}^{\infty} \tilde{\beta}_{i\tau} x_{i,t-\tau}$, and $\boldsymbol{\xi}_i' = (\xi_{i1}, \ldots, \xi_{iT})$; then $E^*[\boldsymbol{\xi}_i \mid \mathbf{x}_i] = \mathbf{0}$.

Assumption 9.1.3. $E^*(\alpha_i^* \mid \mathbf{x}_i) = \mu + \mathbf{a}'\mathbf{x}_i$.

Here $E^*(Z_1 \mid Z_2)$ refers to the minimum-mean-squared-error linear predictor (or the projection) of Z_1 onto Z_2; $\mathbf{x}_i$ denotes the vector of all observed x_{it}. We assume that there are $\ell + 1$ observations on x before the first observation on y, and the $1 \times (\ell + 1 + T)$ vector $\mathbf{x}_i' = [x_{i,-\ell}, \ldots, x_{iT}]$ is an independent draw from a common distribution with $E(\mathbf{x}_i\mathbf{x}_i') = \Sigma_{xx}$ positive definite.[3]

A sufficient condition for Assumption 9.1.2 to hold is that differences in lag coefficients across individuals are uncorrelated with the $\mathbf{x}_i$ [i.e., $\beta_{i\tau}$ is a random variable defined in the sense of Swamy (1970), or see Chapter 6]. However, Assumption 9.1.3 does allow for individual-specific constant terms (the α_i^*) to be correlated with $\mathbf{x}_i$. The combination of Assumptions 9.1.1–9.1.3 is sufficient to allow us to identify the expected value of the lag-coefficient sequence $\{\beta_\tau\}$ if both N and T tend to infinity.

If T is fixed, substituting Assumptions 9.1.1 and 9.1.2 into equation (9.1.4), we rewrite the distributed-lag model as

$$y_{it} = \alpha_i^* + \sum_{\tau=0}^{t+\ell} \beta_\tau x_{i,t-\tau} + b_{it} + \tilde{u}_{it}, \qquad \begin{array}{l} i = 1, \ldots, N, \\ t = 1, \ldots, T, \end{array} \tag{9.1.5}$$

where $b_{it} = \sum_{\tau=\ell+1}^{\infty} \beta_{t+\tau} x_{i,-\tau}$ is the truncation remainder for individual i in period t, and $\tilde{u}_{it} = \xi_{it} + u_{it}$ is the amalgamated error term satisfying $E^*[\tilde{\mathbf{u}}_i \mid \mathbf{x}_i] = \mathbf{0}$. The unobserved truncation remainders are usually correlated with the included explanatory variables. Therefore, without additional restrictions, we still cannot get consistent estimates of any of the lag coefficients β_τ by regressing y_{it} on $x_{i,t-\tau}$, even when $N \to \infty$.

Because the values of the truncation remainders (b_{it}) are determined by the lag coefficients and the presample x values, identification requires constraints either on the lag coefficients or on the stochastic process generating these x values. Because there usually are many more degrees of freedom available in panel data, this allows us to use prior restrictions of different kind than in the usual approach of constraining lag coefficients to identify truncation remainders (e.g., Dhrymes (1971)). In the next two subsections we illustrate how various restrictions can be used to identify the lag coefficients.

9.1.3 Identification Using Prior Structure of the Process of the Exogenous Variable

In this subsection we consider the identification of a distributed-lag model using a kind of restriction different from that in the usual approach of constraining lag coefficients. Our interest is focused on estimating at least some of the population parameters $\beta_\tau = E(\beta_{i\tau})$ for $\tau = 0, 1, \ldots,$ without restricting β_τ to be a function of a small number of parameters. We consider a lag coefficient identified if it can be calculated from the matrix of coefficients obtained from the projection of $\mathbf{y}_i$ onto $\mathbf{x}_i$, a $T \times (T + \ell + 1)$ matrix called Π, where $E^*(\mathbf{y}_i \mid \mathbf{x}_i) = \boldsymbol{\mu}^* + \Pi\mathbf{x}_i$, $\boldsymbol{\mu}^* = (\mu_1^*, \ldots, \mu_T^*)'$, and $\mathbf{y}_i' = (y_{i1}, \ldots, y_{iT})$ is a $1 \times T$ vector.

Equation (9.1.5) makes it clear that each row of Π will contain a combination of the lag coefficients of interest and the coefficients from the projections of the two unobserved components, α_i^* and b_{it}, on $\mathbf{x}_i$. Therefore, the problem is to separate out the lag coefficients from the coefficients defining these two projections.

Using equation (9.1.5), the projection of $\mathbf{y}_i$ onto $\mathbf{x}_i$ and α_i^* is given by[4]

$$E^*(\mathbf{y}_i \mid \mathbf{x}_i, \alpha_i^*) = [B + W]\mathbf{x}_i + [\mathbf{e} + \mathbf{c}]\alpha_i^*, \tag{9.1.6}$$

where B is the $T \times (T + \ell + 1)$ matrix of the lag coefficients

$$B = \begin{bmatrix} \beta_{\ell+1} & \beta_{\ell} & \cdots & \beta_1 & \beta_0 & 0 & 0 & \cdots & 0 & 0 \\ \beta_{\ell+2} & \beta_{\ell+1} & \cdots & \beta_2 & \beta_1 & \beta_0 & 0 & \cdots & 0 & 0 \\ \vdots & \vdots & & \vdots & \vdots & \vdots & \vdots & & \vdots & \vdots \\ \beta_{T+\ell-1} & \beta_{t+\ell-2} & \cdots & \beta_{T+1} & \beta_T & \beta_{T-1} & \beta_{T-2} & \cdots & \beta_0 & 0 \\ \beta_{T+\ell} & \beta_{T+\ell-1} & \cdots & \beta_T & \beta_{T-1} & \beta_{T-2} & \beta_{T-3} & \cdots & \beta_1 & \beta_0 \end{bmatrix}.$$

W and $\mathbf{c}$ are defined by the unconstrained projection of $\mathbf{b}_i = (b_{i1}, \ldots, b_{iT})'$ onto $\mathbf{x}_i$ and α_i^*,

$$E^*[\mathbf{b}_i \mid \mathbf{x}_i, \alpha_i^*] = W\mathbf{x}_i + \mathbf{c}\alpha_i^*. \tag{9.1.7}$$

Equation (9.1.6) and the fact that $E^*\{E^*(\mathbf{y}_i \mid \mathbf{x}_i, \alpha_i^*) \mid \mathbf{x}_i\} = E^*[\mathbf{y}_i \mid \mathbf{x}_i] = (\mathbf{e} + \mathbf{c})\mu + \Pi\mathbf{x}_i$ imply that

$$\Pi = B + [W + (\mathbf{e} + \mathbf{c})\mathbf{a}'], \tag{9.1.8}$$

where $\mathbf{a}$ is defined by the unconstrained projection of α_i^* onto $\mathbf{x}_i$, $[E^*(\alpha_i^* \mid \mathbf{x}_i) = \mu + \mathbf{a}'\mathbf{x}_i]$.

Clearly, if the $T \times (T + \ell + 1)$ matrix W is unrestricted, we cannot separate out the lag coefficients B and the effect of the truncation-remainder term from the matrix Π. But given that $\mathbf{ca}'$ is a matrix of rank 1, we may be able to identify some elements of B if there are restrictions on W. Thus, in order to identify some of the lag coefficients from Π, we shall have to restrict W. W will be restricted if it is reasonable to assume that the stochastic process generating $\{x_{it}\}_{t=-\infty}^{T}$ restricts the coefficients of $\mathbf{x}_i$ in the projection of the presample $x_{i,-j}$ values onto the in-sample $\mathbf{x}_i$ and α_i^*. The particular case analyzed by Pakes and Griliches (1984) is given by the following assumption.[5]

Assumption 9.1.4. For $q \geq 1$, $E^*[x_{i,-\ell-q} \mid \mathbf{x}_i, \alpha_i^*] = c_q\alpha_i^* + \sum_{j=1}^{p} \rho_j^{(q)} \times x_{i,-\ell+j-1}$. That is, in the projection of the unseen presample x values onto $\mathbf{x}_i$ and α_i^*, only $[x_{i,-\ell}, x_{i,-\ell+1}, \ldots, x_{i,-\ell+p-1}]$ have nonzero coefficients.

If $c_q = 0$, a sufficient condition for Assumption 9.1.4 to hold is that x is generated by a pth-order autoregressive process.[6]

Because each element of $\mathbf{b}_i$ is just a different linear combination of the same presample x values, the addition of Assumption 9.1.4 implies that

$$E^*[b_{it} \mid \mathbf{x}_i, \alpha_i^*] = c_t\alpha_i^* + \sum_{j=1}^{p} w_{t,j-\ell-1}x_{i,j-\ell-1}, \qquad i = 1, \ldots, N, \quad t = 1, \ldots, T, \tag{9.1.9}$$

where $w_{t,j-\ell-1} = \sum_{q=1}^{\infty} \beta_{t+\ell+q}\rho_j^{(q)}$, $j = 1, \ldots, p$, and $c_t = \sum_{q=1}^{\infty} \beta_{t+l+q}c_q$. This determines the vector $\mathbf{c}$ and the matrix W in (9.1.7). In particular, it implies that W can be partitioned into a $T \times (T + \ell - p + 1)$ matrix of zeros and a

$T \times p$ matrix of free coefficients,

$$W = \left[\underset{T\times p}{\tilde{W}} \vdots \underset{T\times(T+\ell-p+1)}{\mathbf{0}} \right]. \tag{9.1.10}$$

Substituting (9.1.10) into (9.1.8) and taking partial derivatives of Π with respect to the leading $(T + \ell - p + 1)$ lag coefficients, we can show that the resulting Jacobian matrix satisfies the rank condition for identification of these coefficients (e.g., Hsiao (1983, Theorem 5.1.2)). A simple way to check that the leading $(T + \ell - p + 1)$ lag coefficients are indeed identified is to show that consistent estimators for them exist. We note that by construction, cross-sectional regression of $\mathbf{y}_i$ on $\mathbf{x}_i$ yields consistent estimates of Π. For the special case in which $\alpha_i^* = 0$, the projections of each period's value of y on all in-sample values of $\mathbf{x}$ are[7]

$$\begin{aligned}
E^*(y_{i1} \mid \mathbf{x}_i) &= \mu + \sum_{j=1}^{p} \phi_{1,j-\ell-1} x_{i,j-\ell-1},\\
E^*(y_{i2} \mid \mathbf{x}_i) &= \mu + \beta_0 x_2 + \sum_{j=1}^{p} \phi_{2,j-\ell-1} x_{i,j-\ell-1},\\
E^*(y_{i3} \mid \mathbf{x}_i) &= \mu + \beta_0 x_3 + \beta_1 x_2 + \sum_{j=1}^{p} \phi_{3,j-\ell-1} x_{i,j-\ell-1},\\
&\vdots\\
E^*(y_{iT} \mid \mathbf{x}_i) &= \mu + \beta_0 x_T + \cdots + \beta_{T+\ell-p} x_{p-\ell}\\
&\quad + \sum_{j=1}^{p} \phi_{T,j-\ell-1} x_{i,j-\ell-1},
\end{aligned} \tag{9.1.11}$$

where $\phi_{t,j-\ell-1} = \beta_{t+\ell+1-j} + w_{t,j-\ell-1}$ for $t = 1, \ldots, T$ and $j = 1, \ldots, p$, and for simplicity we have let $p = \ell + 2$. The first p values of $\mathbf{x}_i$ in each projection have nonzero partial correlations with the truncation remainders (the b_{it}). Hence, their coefficients do not identify the parameters of the lag distribution. Only when $(t + \ell - p + 1) > 0$ are the leading coefficients in each equation in fact estimates of the leading lag coefficients. As t increases, we gradually uncover the lag structure.

When $c_q \neq 0$, the finding of consistent estimators (hence identification) for the leading $T + \ell - p + 1$ lag coefficients is slightly more complicated. Substituting (9.1.9) into (9.1.7), we have

$$\begin{aligned}
E^*(y_{it} \mid \mathbf{x}_i, \alpha_i^*) &= (1 + c_t)\alpha_i^* + \sum_{\tau=0}^{t+\ell-p} \beta_\tau x_{i,t-\tau}\\
&\quad + \sum_{j=1}^{p} \phi_{t,j-\ell-1} x_{i,j-\ell-1}, \qquad t = 1, \ldots, T,
\end{aligned} \tag{9.1.12}$$

where again (for simplicity) we have assumed $p = \ell + 2$. Conditioning this equation on $\mathbf{x}_i$, and passing through the projection operator once more, we obtain

$$\begin{aligned}
E^*(y_{i1} \mid \mathbf{x}_i) &= \mu(1 + c_1) + (1 + c_1) \sum_{t=p-\ell}^{T} a_t x_{it} \\
&\quad + \sum_{j=1}^{p} [(1 + c_1) a_{j-\ell-1} + \phi_{1,j-\ell-1}] x_{i,j-\ell-1}, \\
E^*(y_{i2} \mid \mathbf{x}_i) &= \mu(1 + c_2) + \beta_0 x_2 + (1 + c_2) \sum_{t=p-\ell}^{T} a_t x_{it} \\
&\quad + \sum_{j=1}^{p} [(1 + c_2) a_{j-\ell-1} + \phi_{2,j-\ell-1}] x_{i,j-\ell-1}, \qquad (9.1.13) \\
&\;\;\vdots \\
E^*(y_{iT} \mid \mathbf{x}_i) &= \mu(1 + c_T) + \sum_{\tau=0}^{T+\ell-p} \beta_\tau x_{i,t-\tau} + (1 + c_T) \sum_{t=p-\ell}^{T} a_t x_{it} \\
&\quad + \sum_{j=1}^{p} [(1 + c_T) a_{j-\ell-1} + \phi_{T,j-\ell-1}] x_{i,j-\ell-1}.
\end{aligned}$$

Multiplying y_{i1} by $\tilde{c}_t$ and subtracting it from y_{it}, we produce the system of equations

$$y_{it} = \tilde{c}_t y_{i1} + \sum_{\tau=0}^{t+\ell-p} \beta_\tau x_{i,t-\tau} + \sum_{j=1}^{p} \tilde{\phi}_{t,j-\ell-1} x_{i,j-\ell-1} + \nu_{it} \qquad (9.1.14)$$

for $t = 2, \ldots, T$, where

$$\tilde{c}_t = \frac{1 + c_t}{1 + c_1}, \qquad \tilde{\phi}_{t,j-\ell-1} = \phi_{t,j-\ell-1} - \tilde{c}_t \phi_{1,j-\ell-1},$$

and

$$\nu_{it} = y_{it} - \tilde{c}_t y_{i1} - E^*(y_{it} - \tilde{c}_t y_{i1} \mid \mathbf{x}_i).$$

By construction, $E^*(\nu_{it} \mid \mathbf{x}_i) = 0$.

For given t, the only variable on the right-hand side of (9.1.14) that is correlated with ν_{it} is y_{i1}. If we know the values of $\{\tilde{c}_t\}_{t=2}^{T}$, the system (9.1.14) will allow us to estimate the leading $(T + \ell - p + 1)$ lag coefficients consistently by first forming $\tilde{y}_{it} = y_{it} - \tilde{c}_t y_{i1}$ (for $t = 2, \ldots, T$) and then regressing this sequence on in-sample x_{it} values cross-sectionally. In the case in which all c_t values are identical, we know that the sequence $\{\tilde{c}_t\}_{t=2}^{T}$ is just a sequence of ones. In the case in which α_i^* have a free coefficient in each period of the sample, we have unknown $(1 + c_t)$. However, we can consistently estimate $\tilde{c}_t$, β_τ, and $\tilde{\phi}_{t,j}$ by the instrumental-variable method, provided there is at least one x_{is} that is excluded from the determinants of $y_{it} - \tilde{c}_t y_{i1}$ and that is correlated with y_{i1}. If $T \geq 3$, then $x_{i3}, \ldots, x_{iT}$ are excluded from the equation determining $(y_{i2} - \tilde{c}_2 y_{i1})$, and provided that not all of a_3 to a_T are zero, at least one of them will have the required correlation with y_{i1}.

We have shown that under Assumptions 9.1.1–9.1.4, the use of panel data allows us to identify the leading $T + \ell - p + 1$ lag coefficients without imposing any restrictions on the sequence $\{\beta_\tau\}_{\tau=0}^{\infty}$. Of course, if $T + \ell$ is small relative to p, we shall not be able to build up much information on the tail of the lag distribution. This simply reflects the fact that short panels, by their very nature, do not contain unconstrained information on that tail. However, the early coefficients are often of significant interest in themselves. Moreover, they may provide a basis for restricting the lag structure (to be a function of a small number of parameters) in further work.

9.1.4 Identification Using Prior Structure of the Lag Coefficients

In many situations we may know that all β_τ are positive. We may also know that the first few coefficients β_0, β_1, and β_2 are the largest and that β_τ decreases with increasing τ, at least after a certain value of τ. In this subsection we show how the conventional approach of constraining the lag coefficients to be a function of a finite number of parameters can be used and generalized for identification of a distributed-lag model in the panel data context. Therefore, we drop Assumption 9.1.4. Instead, we assume that we have prior knowledge of the structure of lag coefficients. The particular example we use here is the one assumed by Pakes and Griliches (1984), where the sequence of lag coefficients, after the first few free lags, has an autoregressive structure. This restriction is formalized as follows:

Assumption 9.1.5

$$\beta_\tau = \begin{cases} \beta_\tau & \text{for } \tau \leq k_1, \\ \sum_{j=1}^{J} \delta_j \beta_{\tau-j} & \text{otherwise,} \end{cases}$$

where the roots of the characteristic equation $1 - \sum_{j=1}^{J} \delta_j L^j = 0$, say $\lambda_1^{-1}, \ldots, \lambda_J^{-1}$, lie outside the unit circle.[8] For simplicity, we assume that $k_1 = \ell + 1$, and that $\lambda_1, \ldots, \lambda_J$ are real and distinct.

Assumption 9.1.5 implies that β_τ declines geometrically after the first k_1 lags. Solving the Jth-order difference equation

$$\beta_\tau - \delta_1 \beta_{\tau-1} - \cdots - \delta_J \beta_{\tau-J} = 0, \qquad (9.1.15)$$

we obtain the general solution (e.g., Box and Jenkins (1970, Chapter 3))

$$\beta_\tau = \sum_{j=1}^{J} A_j \lambda_j^\tau, \tag{9.1.16}$$

where A_j are constants to be determined by the initial conditions of the difference equation.

Substituting (9.1.16) into (9.1.5), we write the truncation-remainder term b_{it} as

$$\begin{aligned} b_{it} &= \sum_{\tau=\ell+1}^{\infty} \left(\sum_{j=1}^{J} A_j \lambda_j^{t+\tau} \right) x_{i,-\tau} \\ &= \sum_{j=1}^{J} \lambda_j^t \left(A_j \sum_{\tau=\ell+1}^{\infty} \lambda_j^\tau x_{i,-\tau} \right) \\ &= \sum_{j=1}^{J} \lambda_j^t b_{ij}, \end{aligned} \tag{9.1.17}$$

where $b_{ij} = A_j \sum_{\tau=\ell+1}^{\infty} \lambda_j^\tau x_{i,-\tau}$. That is, we can represent the truncation remainder b_{it} in terms of J unobserved initial conditions $(b_{i1}, \ldots, b_{iJ})$. Thus, under Assumptions 9.1.1–9.1.3 and 9.1.5, the distributed-lag model becomes a system of T regressions with $J+1$ freely correlated unobserved factors $(\alpha_i^*, b_{i1}, \ldots, b_{iJ})$ where the impact of last J of them decay geometrically over time.

Because the conditions for identification of a model in which there are $J+1$ unobserved factors is a straightforward generalization from a model with two unobserved factors, we deal first with the case $J = 1$ and then point out the extensions required for $J > 1$.

When $J = 1$, it is the familiar case of a modified Koyck (or geometric) lag model. The truncation remainder becomes an unobserved factor that follows an exact first-order autoregression (i.e., $b_{it} = \delta b_{i,t-1}$). Substituting this result into (9.1.5), we have

$$y_{it} = \alpha_i^* + \sum_{\tau=0}^{\ell+1} \beta_\tau x_{i,t-\tau} + \beta_{\ell+1} \sum_{\tau=\ell+2}^{t+\ell} \delta^{\tau-(\ell+1)} x_{i,t-\tau} + \delta^{t-1} b_i + \tilde{u}_{it}, \tag{9.1.18}$$

where $b_i = \beta_{\ell+1} \sum_{\tau=1}^{\infty} \delta^\tau x_{i,-\tau-\ell}$.

Recall from the discussion in Section 9.1.3 that to identify the lag parameters we require a set of restrictions on the projection matrix $E^*(\mathbf{b}_i \mid \mathbf{x}_i) = [W + \mathbf{c}\mathbf{a}']\mathbf{x}_i$ [equation (9.1.7)]. The Koyck lag model implies that $b_{it} = \delta b_{i,t-1}$, which implies that $E^*(b_{it} \mid \mathbf{x}_i) = \delta E^*(b_{i,t-1} \mid \mathbf{x}_i)$; that is, $w_{tr} = \delta w_{t-1,r}$ for $r = 1, \ldots, T+\ell+1$ and $t = 2, \ldots, T$. It follows that the matrix Π has the form

$$\Pi = B^* + \boldsymbol{\delta}^* \mathbf{w}^{*\prime} + \mathbf{e}\mathbf{a}', \tag{9.1.19}$$

where $\boldsymbol{\delta}^{*\prime} = [1, \delta, \ldots, \delta^{T-1}]$, $\mathbf{w}^*$ is the vector of coefficients from the projection of b_i on $\mathbf{x}_i$ [i.e., $E^*(b_i \mid \mathbf{x}_i) = \sum_{t=-\ell}^{T} w_t^* x_{it}$], and

$$B^* = \begin{bmatrix} \beta_{\ell+1} & \cdots & \beta_1 & \beta_0 & 0 & \cdots & 0 & 0 & \cdots & 0 & 0 \\ \delta\beta_{\ell+1} & \cdots & \beta_2 & \beta_1 & \beta_0 & \cdots & 0 & 0 & \cdots & 0 & 0 \\ \vdots & & \vdots & \vdots & \vdots & & \vdots & \vdots & & \vdots & \vdots \\ \delta^{T-1}\beta_{\ell+1} & \cdots & \delta^{T-\ell}\beta_{\ell+1} & \delta^{T-\ell-1}\beta_{\ell+1} & \delta^{T-\ell-2}\beta_{\ell+1} & \cdots & \delta\beta_{\ell+1} & \beta_{\ell+1} & \cdots & \beta_1 & \beta_0 \end{bmatrix}.$$

Taking partial derivatives of (9.1.19) with respect to unknown parameters, it can be shown that the resulting Jacobian matrix satisfies the rank condition for identification of the lag coefficients, provided $T \geq 3$ (e.g., Hsiao (1983, Theorem 5.1.2)). In fact, an easy way to see that the lag coefficients are identified is to note that (9.1.18) implies that

$$\begin{aligned} &(y_{it} - y_{i,t-1}) - \delta(y_{i,t-1} - y_{i,t-2}) \\ &\quad = \beta_0 x_{it} + [\beta_1 - \beta_0(1+\delta)]x_{i,t-1} \\ &\qquad + \sum_{\tau=2}^{\ell}[\beta_\tau - (1+\delta)\beta_{\tau-1} + \delta\beta_{\tau-2}]x_{i,t-\tau} + v_{it}, \quad i = 1, \ldots, N, \\ &\hspace{22em} t = 1, \ldots, T, \end{aligned} \tag{9.1.20}$$

where $v_{it} = \tilde{u}_{it} - (1+\delta)\tilde{u}_{i,t-1} + \delta\tilde{u}_{i,t-2}$, and $E^*[\boldsymbol{v}_i \mid \mathbf{x}_i] = \mathbf{0}$. Provided $T \geq 3$, $x_{i3}, \ldots, x_{iT}$ can serve as instruments for cross-sectional regression of the equation determining $y_{i2} - y_{i1}$.

In the more general case, with $J > 1$, $\boldsymbol{\delta}^*\mathbf{w}^{*\prime}$ in (9.1.19) will be replaced by $\sum_{j=1}^{J} \boldsymbol{\lambda}_j^* \mathbf{w}_j^{*\prime}$, where $\boldsymbol{\lambda}_j^{*\prime} = [1, \lambda_j, \ldots, \lambda_j^{T-1}]$, and $\mathbf{w}_j^*$ is the vector of coefficients from the projection of b_{ij} on $\mathbf{x}_i$. Using a similar procedure, we can show that the matrix Π will identify the lag coefficients if $T \geq J + 2$.

Of course, if in addition to Assumption 9.1.5 we also have information on the structure of process x, there will be more restrictions on the Π matrices than in the models in this subsection. Identification conditions can consequently be relaxed.

9.1.5 Estimation and Testing

We can estimate the unknown parameters of a distributed-lag model using short panels by first stacking all T period equations as a system of reduced-form equations:

$$\underset{T\times 1}{\mathbf{y}_i} = \boldsymbol{\mu}^* + [I_T \otimes \mathbf{x}_i']\boldsymbol{\pi} + \boldsymbol{\nu}_i, \qquad i = 1, \ldots, N, \tag{9.1.21}$$

where $\boldsymbol{\nu}_i = \mathbf{y}_i - E^*[\mathbf{y}_i \mid \mathbf{x}_i]$ and $\boldsymbol{\pi}' = [\boldsymbol{\pi}_1', \ldots, \boldsymbol{\pi}_T']$, where $\boldsymbol{\pi}_j'$ is the jth row of the matrix Π. By construction, $E(\boldsymbol{\nu}_i \otimes \mathbf{x}_i) = \mathbf{0}$. Under the assumption that the N vectors $(\mathbf{y}_i', \mathbf{x}_i')$ are independent draws from a common distribution, with finite fourth-order moments and with $E\mathbf{x}_i\mathbf{x}_i' = \Sigma_{xx}$ positive definite, the least-squares estimator $\hat{\boldsymbol{\pi}}$ of $\boldsymbol{\pi}$ is consistent, and $\sqrt{N}(\hat{\boldsymbol{\pi}} - \boldsymbol{\pi})$ is asymptotically normally distributed, with mean zero and variance–covariance matrix Ω, which is given by (3.9.11).

The models of Sections 9.1.3 and 9.1.4 imply that $\boldsymbol{\pi} = \mathbf{f}(\boldsymbol{\theta})$, where $\boldsymbol{\theta}$ is a vector of the model's parameters of dimensions $m \leq (T + \ell + 1)$. We can impose these restrictions by a minimum-distance estimator that chooses $\hat{\boldsymbol{\theta}}$ to minimize

$$[\hat{\boldsymbol{\pi}} - \mathbf{f}(\boldsymbol{\theta})]'\hat{\Omega}^{-1}[\hat{\boldsymbol{\pi}} - \mathbf{f}(\boldsymbol{\theta})], \tag{9.1.22}$$

where $\hat{\Omega}$ is a consistent estimator of (3.9.11). Under fairly general conditions, the estimator $\hat{\boldsymbol{\theta}}$ is consistent, and $\sqrt{N}(\hat{\boldsymbol{\theta}} - \boldsymbol{\theta})$ is asymptotically normally distributed, with asymptotic variance–covariance matrix

$$(F'\Omega^{-1}F)^{-1}, \tag{9.1.23}$$

where $F = \partial\mathbf{f}(\boldsymbol{\theta})/\partial\boldsymbol{\theta}'$. The identification condition ensures that F has rank m. The quadratic form

$$N[\hat{\boldsymbol{\pi}} - \mathbf{f}(\hat{\boldsymbol{\theta}})]'\Omega^{-1}[\hat{\boldsymbol{\pi}} - \mathbf{f}(\hat{\boldsymbol{\theta}})] \tag{9.1.24}$$

is asymptotically chi-square-distributed with $T(T + \ell + 1) - m$ degrees of freedom.

Equation (9.1.24) provides us with a test of the $T(T + \ell + 1) - m$ constraints $\mathbf{f}$ placed on $\boldsymbol{\pi}$. To test nested restrictions, consider the null hypothesis $\boldsymbol{\theta} = \mathbf{g}(\boldsymbol{\omega})$, where $\boldsymbol{\omega}$ is a k-dimensional vector ($k \leq m$) of the parameters of the restricted model. Let $\mathbf{h}(\boldsymbol{\omega}) = \mathbf{f}[\mathbf{g}(\boldsymbol{\omega})]$; that is, $\mathbf{h}$ embodies the restrictions of the constrained model. Then, under the null hypothesis,

$$N[\hat{\boldsymbol{\pi}} - \mathbf{h}(\hat{\boldsymbol{\omega}})]'\Omega^{-1}[\hat{\boldsymbol{\pi}} - \mathbf{h}(\hat{\boldsymbol{\omega}})] \tag{9.1.25}$$

is asymptotically chi-square-distributed with $T(T + \ell + 1) - k$ degrees of freedom, where $\hat{\boldsymbol{\omega}}$ minimizes (9.1.25). Hence, to test the null hypothesis, we can use the statistic[9]

$$N[\hat{\boldsymbol{\pi}} - \mathbf{h}(\hat{\boldsymbol{\omega}})]'\hat{\Omega}^{-1}[\hat{\boldsymbol{\pi}} - \mathbf{h}(\hat{\boldsymbol{\omega}})] - N[\hat{\boldsymbol{\pi}} - \mathbf{f}(\hat{\boldsymbol{\theta}})]'\hat{\Omega}^{-1}[\hat{\boldsymbol{\pi}} - \mathbf{f}(\hat{\boldsymbol{\theta}})], \tag{9.1.26}$$

which is asymptotically chi-square-distributed, with $m - k$ degrees of freedom.

To illustrate the method of estimating unconstrained distributed-lag models using panel data, Pakes and Griliches (1984) investigated empirically the issues of how to construct the "stock of capital (G)" for analysis of rates of return. The basic assumption of their model is that there exists a stable relationship between earnings (gross or net profits) (y) and past investments (x), and firms or industries differ only in the level of the yield on their past investments, with the time shapes of these yields being the same across firms and implicit in the assumed depreciation formula. Namely,

$$E^*[y_{it} \mid G_{it}, \alpha_i^*] = \alpha_i^* + \gamma G_{it}, \tag{9.1.27}$$

and

$$G_{it} = \sum_{\tau=1}^{\infty} \beta_{i\tau} x_{it-\tau}. \tag{9.1.28}$$

Substituting (9.1.28) into (9.1.27), we have a model that consists in regressing the operating profits of firms on a distributed lag of their past investment expenditures.

Using a sample of 258 manufacturing firms' annual profit data for the years 1964–1972 and investment data for the years 1961–71, and assuming that p in Assumption 9.1.4 equals three,[10] they found that the estimated lag coefficients rose over the first three periods and remained fairly constant over the next four or five. This pattern implies that the contribution of past investment to the capital stock first "appreciates" in the early years as investments are completed, shaken down, or adjusted to. This is distinctly different from the pattern implied by the commonly used straight-line or declining-balance depreciation formula to construct the "stock of capital." Both formulae imply that the lag coefficients decline monotonically in τ, with the decline being the greatest in earlier periods for the second case.

9.2 ROTATING OR RANDOMLY MISSING DATA

In many situations we do not have complete time-series observations on cross-sectional units. Instead, individuals are selected according to a *rotating* scheme that can be briefly stated as follows: Let all individuals in the population be numbered consecutively. Suppose the sample in period 1 consists of individuals $1, 2, \ldots, N$. In period 2, individuals $1, \ldots, m_1$ $(0 \leq m_1 \leq N)$ are replaced by individuals $N+1, \ldots, N+m_1$. In period 3, individuals $m_1+1, \ldots, m_1+m_2$ $(0 \leq m_2 \leq N)$ are replaced by individuals $N+m_1+1, \ldots, N+m_1+m_2$, and so on. This procedure of dropping the first m_{t-1} individuals from the sample selected in the previous period and augmenting the sample by drawing m_{t-1} individuals from the population so that the sample size remains the same continues through all periods. Hence, for T periods, although the total number of observations remains at NT, we have observed $N + \sum_{t=1}^{T-1} m_t$ individuals.

Rotation of a sample of micro units over time is quite common. It can be caused by deliberate policy of the data-collecting agency (e.g., the Bureau of the Census) because of the worry that if the number of times respondents have been exposed to a survey gets large, the data may be affected and behavioral changes may even be induced. Or it can arise because of the consideration of optimal sample design so as to gain as much information as possible from a given budget (e.g., Aigner and Balestra (1988); Nijman, Verbeek, and van Soest (1991)). It can also arise because the data-collecting agency can neither force nor persuade randomly selected individuals to report more than once or twice, particularly if detailed and time-consuming reporting is required. For example, the Survey of Income and Program Participation, which began field work in October 1983, has been designed as an ongoing series of national panels, each consisting of about 20,000 interviewed households and having a duration of 2.5 years. Every four months the Census Bureau will interview each individual of age 15 years or older in the panel. Information will be collected on a monthly basis for most sources of money and nonmoney income, participation in various governmental transfer programs, labor-force status, and household composition.

Statistical methods developed for analyzing complete panel data can be extended in a straightforward manner to analyze rotating samples if rotation is by design (i.e., random dropping and addition of individuals) and if a model is static and the error terms are assumed to be independently distributed across cross-sectional units. The likelihood function for the observed samples in this case is simply the product of the $N + \sum_{t=1}^{T-1} m_t$ joint densities of $(y_{it_i}, y_{i,t_i+1}, \ldots, y_{iT_i})$,

$$L = \prod_{i=1}^{N+\sum_{t=1}^{T-1} m_t} f\left(y_{it_i}, \ldots, y_{iT_i}\right), \tag{9.2.1}$$

where t_i and T_i denote first and last periods during which the ith individual was observed. Apart from the minor modifications of t_i for 1 and T_i for T, (9.2.1) is basically of the same form as the likelihood functions for the complete panel data.

As an illustration, we consider a single-equation error-components model (Biørn (1981)). Let

$$y_{it} = \boldsymbol{\beta}'\mathbf{x}_{it} + v_{it}, \tag{9.2.2}$$

where $\boldsymbol{\beta}$ and $\mathbf{x}_{it}$ are $k \times 1$ vectors of parameters and explanatory variables, respectively, and

$$v_{it} = \alpha_i + u_{it}. \tag{9.2.3}$$

The error terms α_i and u_{it} are independent of each other and are independently distributed, with zero means and constant variances σ_α^2 and σ_u^2, respectively. For ease of exposition, we assume that α_i and u_{it} are uncorrelated with $\mathbf{x}_{it}$.[11] We also assume that in each period a fixed number of individuals are dropped from the sample and the same number of individuals from the population are added back to the sample (namely, $m_t = m$ for all t). Thus, the total number of individuals observed is

$$H = (T-1)m + N. \tag{9.2.4}$$

Denote the number of times the ith individual is observed by q_i; then $q_i = T_i - t_i + 1$. Stacking the time-series observations for the ith individual in vector form, we have

$$\mathbf{y}_i = X_i\boldsymbol{\beta} + \mathbf{v}_i, \tag{9.2.5}$$

where

$$\underset{q_i\times 1}{\mathbf{y}_i} = \left(y_{it_i}, \ldots, y_{iT_i}\right)', \qquad \underset{q_i\times k}{X_i} = (\mathbf{x}_{it}'),$$

$$\mathbf{v}_i = \left(\alpha_i + u_{it_i}, \ldots, \alpha_i + u_{iT_i}\right)'.$$

The variance–covariance matrix of v_i is

$$V_i = \sigma_u^2 + \sigma_\alpha^2 \qquad \text{if} \quad q_i = 1 \tag{9.2.6a}$$

and is

$$V_i = E\mathbf{v}_i\mathbf{v}_i' = \sigma_u^2 I_{qi} + \sigma_\alpha^2 J_i \qquad \text{if} \quad q_i > 1, \tag{9.2.6b}$$

where J_i is a $q_i \times q_i$ matrix with all elements equal to 1. Then, for $q_i = 1$,

$$V_i^{-1} = \left(\sigma_u^2 + \sigma_\alpha^2\right)^{-1}, \tag{9.2.7a}$$

and for $q_i > 1$,

$$V_i^{-1} = \frac{1}{\sigma_u^2}\left[I_{qi} - \frac{\sigma_\alpha^2}{\sigma_u^2 + q_i\sigma_\alpha^2} J_i\right]. \tag{9.2.7b}$$

Because $\mathbf{y}_i$ and $\mathbf{y}_j$ are uncorrelated, the variance–covariance matrix of the stacked equations $(\mathbf{y}_1', \ldots, \mathbf{y}_{N+(T-1)m}')'$ is block-diagonal. Therefore, the GLS estimator of $\boldsymbol{\beta}$ is

$$\hat{\boldsymbol{\beta}}_{\text{GLS}} = \left[\sum_{i=1}^{N+(T-1)m} X_i' V_i^{-1} X_i\right]^{-1} \left[\sum_{i=1}^{N+(T-1)m} X_i' V_i^{-1} \mathbf{y}_i\right]. \tag{9.2.8}$$

The GLS estimation of $\boldsymbol{\beta}$ is equivalent to first premultiplying the observation matrix $[\mathbf{y}_i, X_i]$ by P_i, where $P_i' P_i = V_i^{-1}$, and then regressing $P_i\mathbf{y}_i$ on $P_i X_i$ (Theil (1971, Chapter 6)). In other words, the least-squares method is applied to the data transformed by the following procedure: For individuals who are observed only once, multiply the corresponding ys and $\mathbf{x}$s by $(\sigma_u^2 + \sigma_\alpha^2)^{-1/2}$. For individuals who are observed q_i times, subtract from the corresponding ys and $\mathbf{x}$s a fraction $1 - [\sigma_u/(\sigma_u^2 + q_i\sigma_\alpha^2)^{1/2}]$ of their group means, $\bar{y}_i$ and $\bar{\mathbf{x}}_i$, where $\bar{y}_i = (1/q_i)\sum_t y_{it}$ and $\bar{\mathbf{x}}_i = (1/q_i)\sum_t \mathbf{x}_{it}$, and then divide them by σ_u.

To obtain separate estimates σ_u^2 and σ_α^2 we need at least one group for which $q_i > 1$. Let Θ denote the set of those individuals with $q_i > 1$, $\Theta = \{i \mid q_i > 1\}$, and let $H^* = \sum_{i\in\Theta} q_i$. Then σ_u^2 and σ_α^2 can be consistently estimated by

$$\hat{\sigma}_u^2 = \frac{1}{H^*}\sum_{i\in\Theta}\sum_{t=t_i}^{Ti}[(y_{it} - \bar{y}_i) - \hat{\boldsymbol{\beta}}'(\mathbf{x}_{it} - \bar{\mathbf{x}}_i)]^2, \tag{9.2.9}$$

and

$$\hat{\sigma}_\alpha^2 = \frac{1}{N + (T-1)m}\sum_{i=1}^{N+(T-1)m}\left[(\bar{y}_i - \hat{\boldsymbol{\beta}}'\bar{\mathbf{x}}_i)^2 - \frac{1}{q_i}\hat{\sigma}_u^2\right]. \tag{9.2.10}$$

Similarly, we can apply the MLE by maximizing the logarithm of the likelihood function (9.2.1):

$$\begin{aligned}\log L &= -\frac{NT}{2}\log 2\pi - \frac{1}{2}\sum_{i=1}^{N+(T-1)m}\log|V_i| \\ &\quad - \frac{1}{2}\sum_{i=1}^{N+(T-1)m}(\mathbf{y}_i - X_i\boldsymbol{\beta})'V_i^{-1}(\mathbf{y}_i - X_i\boldsymbol{\beta}) \\ &= -\frac{NT}{2}\log 2\pi - \frac{1}{2}\left[\sum_{i=1}^{N+(T-1)m}(q_i - 1)\right]\log\sigma_u^2 \\ &\quad - \frac{1}{2}\sum_{i=1}^{N+(T-1)m}\log\left(\sigma_u^2 + q_i\sigma_\alpha^2\right) \\ &\quad - \frac{1}{2}\sum_{i=1}^{N+(T-1)m}(\mathbf{y}_i - X_i\boldsymbol{\beta})'V_i^{-1}(\mathbf{y}_i - X_i\boldsymbol{\beta}). \end{aligned} \tag{9.2.11}$$

Conditioning on σ_u^2 and σ_α^2, the MLE is the GLS (9.2.8). Conditioning on $\boldsymbol{\beta}$, the MLEs of σ_u^2 and σ_α^2 are the simultaneous solutions of the following equations:

$$\begin{aligned}\frac{\partial\log L}{\partial\sigma_u^2} &= -\frac{1}{2\sigma_u^2}\left[\sum_{i=1}^{N+(T-1)m}(q_i - 1)\right] \\ &\quad - \frac{1}{2}\left[\sum_{i=1}^{N+(T-1)m}\frac{1}{\sigma_u^2 + q_i\sigma_\alpha^2}\right] \\ &\quad + \frac{1}{2\sigma_u^4}\sum_{i=1}^{N+(T-1)m}(\mathbf{y}_i - X_i\boldsymbol{\beta})'Q_i(\mathbf{y}_i - X_i\boldsymbol{\beta}) \\ &\quad + \frac{1}{2}\sum_{i=1}^{N+(T-1)m}\frac{q_i}{\left(\sigma_u^2 + q_i\sigma_\alpha^2\right)^2}(\bar{y}_i - \bar{\mathbf{x}}_i'\boldsymbol{\beta}) = 0, \end{aligned} \tag{9.2.12}$$

and

$$\begin{aligned}\frac{\partial\log L}{\partial\sigma_\alpha^2} &= -\frac{1}{2}\sum_{i=1}^{N+(T-1)m}\left[\frac{q_i}{\sigma_u^2 + q_i\sigma_\alpha^2} - \frac{q_i^2}{\left(\sigma_u^2 + q_i\sigma_\alpha^2\right)^2}(\bar{y}_i - \bar{\mathbf{x}}_i'\boldsymbol{\beta})^2\right], \\ &= 0, \end{aligned} \tag{9.2.13}$$

where $Q_i = I_{qi} - (1/q_i)\mathbf{e}_{qi}\mathbf{e}_{qi}'$, and $\mathbf{e}_{qi}$ is a $q_i \times 1$ vector of ones. Unfortunately, because q_i are different for different i, (9.2.12) and (9.2.13) cannot be put in the simple form of (3.3.25) and (3.3.26). Numerical methods will have to be used to obtain a solution. However, computation of the MLEs of $\boldsymbol{\beta}$, σ_u^2, and σ_α^2 can be simplified by switching iteratively between (9.2.8) and (9.2.12)–(9.2.13).

This principle of modifying complete-panel-data estimation methods for the incomplete-panel-data case can be extended straightforwardly to dynamic models and multiple-equation models. However, with dynamic models there is a problem of initial conditions.[12] Different assumptions about initial conditions will suggest different ways of incorporating new observations with those already in the sample. It would appear a reasonable approximation in this case is to modify the methods based on the assumption that initial observations are correlated with individual effects and have stationary variances (Chapter 4, case IVc or IVc′). Alternatively, instrumental variable methods proposed for the analysis of dynamic models from repeated cross-section data (e.g., Collado (1997); Moffit (1993)) can be implemented with proper modification. However, the assumption imposed on the model will have to be even more restrictive.

When data are randomly missing, a common procedure is to focus on the subset of individuals for which complete time-series observations are available. However, the subset of incompletely observed individuals also contains some information about unknown parameters. A more efficient and computationally somewhat more complicated way is to treat randomly missing samples in the same way as rotating samples. For instance, the likelihood function (9.2.1), with the modification that $t_i = 1$ for all i, can also be viewed as the likelihood function for this situation: In time period 1 there are $N + \sum_{t=1}^{T-1} m_t$ individuals; in period 2, m_1 of them randomly drop out, and so on, so that at the end of T periods there are only N individuals remaining in the sample. Thus, the procedure for obtaining the GLS or MLE for unknown parameters with all the observations utilized is similar to the situation of rotating samples.

9.3 PSEUDOPANELS (OR REPEATED CROSS-SECTIONAL DATA)

When repeated observations on the same individuals are not available, it is not possible to control the effect of unobserved individual characteristics in a linear model of the form

$$y_{it} = \boldsymbol{\beta}'\mathbf{x}_{it} + \alpha_i + u_{it} \tag{9.3.1}$$

if α_i and $\mathbf{x}_{it}$ are correlated by the fixed-effects estimator discussed in Chapter 3. However, several authors have argued that with some additional assumptions $\boldsymbol{\beta}$ may be identified from a single cross section or a series of independent cross sections (e.g., Blundell, Browning, and Meghir (1994); Deaton (1985); Heckman and Robb (1985); Moffit (1993)).

Deaton (1985) suggests using a cohort approach to obtain consistent estimators of $\boldsymbol{\beta}$ of (9.3.1) if repeated cross-sections data are available. Cohorts are defined as groups of individuals sharing common observed characteristics, such as age, sex, education or socioeconomic background. Suppose that one can divide the sample into C cohorts where all individuals within the cohort have identical α_c, $c = 1, \ldots, C$. Then aggregation of all observations to cohort level results in

$$\bar{y}_{ct} = \bar{\mathbf{x}}'_{ct}\boldsymbol{\beta} + \alpha_c + \bar{u}_{ct}, \qquad c = 1, \ldots, C, \quad t = 1, \ldots, T, \tag{9.3.2}$$

where $\bar{y}_{ct}$ and $\bar{\mathbf{x}}_{ct}$ are the averages of all observed y'_{it}s and $\mathbf{x}'_{it}$s in cohort c at time period t. The resulting data set is a pseudopanel with repeated observations on C cohorts over T time periods. If $\bar{\mathbf{x}}_{ct}$ are uncorrelated with $\bar{u}_{ct}$, the within estimator (3.2.8) can be applied to the pseudopanel

$$\hat{\boldsymbol{\beta}}_w = \left(\sum_{c=1}^{C}\sum_{t=1}^{T}(\bar{\mathbf{x}}_{ct} - \bar{\mathbf{x}}_c)(\bar{\mathbf{x}}_{ct} - \bar{\mathbf{x}}_c)'\right)^{-1}\left(\sum_{c=1}^{C}\sum_{t=1}^{T}(\bar{\mathbf{x}}_{ct} - \bar{\mathbf{x}}_c)(\bar{y}_{ct} - \bar{y}_c)\right), \tag{9.3.3}$$

where $\bar{\mathbf{x}}_c = \frac{1}{T}\sum_{t=1}^{T}\bar{\mathbf{x}}_{ct}$, and $\bar{y}_c = \frac{1}{T}\sum_{t=1}^{T}\bar{y}_{ct}$.

In the case that $\mathbf{x}_{it}$ contains the lagged dependent variables, then $\bar{\mathbf{x}}_{ct}$ will introduce the well-known measurement error problem because y_{it} is supposed to depend on one's own past value $y_{i,t-1}$, not some averaged value. In the case that the observed cohort means $\bar{y}_{ct}$ and $\bar{\mathbf{x}}_{ct}$ are error-ridden, Deaton (1985) suggests estimating $\boldsymbol{\beta}$ by[13]

$$\boldsymbol{\beta}_D = \left(\frac{1}{CT}\sum_{c=1}^{C}\sum_{t=1}^{T}(\bar{\mathbf{x}}_{ct} - \bar{\mathbf{x}}_c)(\bar{\mathbf{x}}_{ct} - \bar{\mathbf{x}}_c)' - \Omega_x\right)^{-1} \times \left(\frac{1}{CT}\sum_{c=1}^{C}\sum_{t=1}^{T}(\bar{\mathbf{x}}_{ct} - \bar{\mathbf{x}}_c)(\bar{y}_{ct} - \bar{y}) - \boldsymbol{\omega}\right), \tag{9.3.4}$$

where Ω_x denotes the variance–covariance matrix of the measurement errors in $\bar{\mathbf{x}}_{ct}$, and $\boldsymbol{\omega}$ denotes the covariance of the measurement errors of $\bar{y}_{ct}$ and $\bar{\mathbf{x}}_{ct}$.

Although the cohort approach offers a useful framework to make use of independent cross-sectional information, there are problems with some of its features. First, the assertion of intracohort homogeneity appears very strong, particularly in view of the fact that the cohort classification is often arbitrary. Second, grouping or aggregating individuals may result in the loss of information or the heteroscedasticity of the errors of the cohort equation (9.3.2). Third, the practice of establishing the large-sample properties of econometric estimators and test statistics by assuming that the number of cohorts, C, tends to infinity is not satisfactory. There is often a physical limit beyond which one cannot increase the number of cohorts. The off-cited example of date-of-birth cohorts is a case in point.

9.4 POOLING OF A SINGLE CROSS-SECTIONAL AND A SINGLE TIME-SERIES DATA SET

9.4.1 Introduction

In this section we consider the problem of pooling when we have a single cross-sectional and a single time-series data set. Empirical studies based solely on time-series data often result in very inaccurate parameter estimates because of the high collinearity among the explanatory variables. For instance, income and price time series can be highly correlated. On the other hand, a cross-sectional data set may contain good information on household income, but not on price, because the same price is likely to be faced by all households. Thus, each data set contains useful information on some of the variables, but not on all the variables so as to allow accurate estimates of all the parameters of interest. A classic example of this is provided in a study (Stone (1954)) of aggregate-demand systems in which there was no cross-sectional variation in commodity prices and inadequate time-series variation in real incomes.

To overcome the problem of lack of information on interesting parameters from time-series or cross-sectional data alone, one frequently estimates some parameters from cross-sectional data, then introduces these estimates into time-series regression to estimate other parameters of the model. For instance, Tobin (1950) calculated income elasticity from cross-sectional data, then multiplied it by the time-series income variable and subtracted the product from the annual time series of quantity demand to form a new dependent variable. This new dependent-variable series was then regressed against the time series of the price variable to obtain an estimate of the price elasticity of demand.

The purpose of pooling here, as in the cases analyzed earlier, is to get more efficient estimates for the parameters that are of interest. In a time series, the number of observations is usually limited, and variables are highly correlated. Moreover, an aggregate data set or a single individual time-series data set does not contain information on microsociodemographic variables that affect economic behavior. Neither are cross-sectional data more structurally complete. Observations on individuals at one point in time are likely to be affected by prior observations. These raise two fundamental problems: One is that the source of estimation bias in cross-sectional estimates may be different from that in time-series estimates. In fact, many people have questioned the suitability and comparability of estimates from different kinds of data (micro or aggregate, cross section or time series), e.g., Kuh (1959) and Kuh and Meyer (1957). The second is, if pooling is desirable, what is the optimal way to do it? It turns out that both problems can be approached simultaneously in the framework of an analysis of the likelihood functions (Maddala (1971b))[14] or with a Bayesian approach (Hsiao, Mountain, and Ho-Illman (1995)).

The likelihood function provides a useful way to extract the information contained in the sample provided that the model is correctly specified. Yet a model is a simplification of complex real-world phenomena. To be most useful, a model must strike a reasonable balance between realism and manageability. It should be realistic in incorporating the main elements of the phenomena being represented and at the same time be manageable in eliminating extraneous influences. Thus, when specifying a regression equation, it is common to assume that the numerous factors that affect the outcome of the dependent variable, but are individually unimportant or unobservable, can be appropriately summarized by a random-disturbance term. However, the covariations of these omitted variables and the included explanatory variables in a cross-sectional regression may be different from those in a time-series regression. For example if high income is associated with high consumption and is also correlated with age, the cross-sectional regression of consumption on income will yield an income coefficient that measures the joint effects of age and income on consumption, unless age is introduced as another explanatory variable. But the age composition of the population could either be constant or be subject only to gradual, slow change in aggregate time series. Hence, the time-series estimate of the income elasticity, ignoring the age variable, could be smaller than the cross-sectional estimates because of the negligible age–income correlation.

Another reason that cross-sectional and time-series estimates in demand analysis may differ is that cross-sectional estimates tend to measure long-run behavior and time-series estimates tend to measure short-run adjustment (Kuh (1959); Kuh and Meyer (1957)). The assumption is that the majority of the observed families have enjoyed their present positions for some time, and the disequilibrium among households tends to be synchronized in response to common market forces and business cycles. Hence, many disequilibrium effects wash out (or appear in the regression intercept), so that the higher cross-sectional slope estimates may be interpreted as long-run coefficients. However, this will not be true for time-series observations. Specifically, changes over time usually represent temporary shifts. Recipients or losers from this change probably will not adjust immediately to their new levels. A incompletely adjusted response will typically have a lower coefficient than the fully adjusted response.

These observations on differential cross-sectional and time-series behavior suggest that the effects of omitted variables can be strikingly different in time series and cross sections. Unless the assumption that the random term (representing the omitted-variables effect) is uncorrelated with the included explanatory variables holds, the time-series and cross-sectional estimates of the common coefficients can diverge. In fact, if the time-series and cross-sectional estimates differ, this is an indication that either or both models are misspecified. In Chapter 3, we discussed specification tests without using extraneous information. We now discuss a likelihood approach when extraneous information in the form of cross-sectional data for the time-series model, or time-series data for the cross-sectional model, is available.

9.4.2 The Likelihood Approach to Pooling Cross-Sectional and Time-Series Data

Assume that we have a single cross-section consisting of N units and a time series extending over T time periods. Suppose that the cross-sectional model is

$$\mathbf{y}_c = Z_1\boldsymbol{\delta}_1 + Z_2\boldsymbol{\delta}_2 + \mathbf{u}_c, \tag{9.4.1}$$

where $\mathbf{y}_c$ is an $N \times 1$ vector of observations on the dependent variable, Z_1 and Z_2 are $N \times K$ and $N \times L$ matrices of independent variables, and $\boldsymbol{\delta}_1$ and $\boldsymbol{\delta}_2$ are $K \times 1$ and $L \times 1$ vectors of parameters, respectively. The $N \times 1$ error term $\mathbf{u}_c$ is independently distributed, with variance–covariance matrix $\sigma_u^2 I_N$.

The time-series model is

$$\mathbf{y}_T = X_1\boldsymbol{\beta}_1 + X_2\boldsymbol{\beta}_2 + \mathbf{v}_T, \tag{9.4.2}$$

where $\mathbf{y}_T$ is a $T \times 1$ vector of observations on the dependent variable, X_1 and X_2 are $T \times K$ and $T \times M$ matrices of observations on the independent variables, $\boldsymbol{\beta}_1$ and $\boldsymbol{\beta}_2$ are $K \times 1$ and $M \times 1$ vectors of parameters, and $\mathbf{v}_T$ is a $T \times 1$ vector of disturbances.[15] For simplicity, we assume that $\mathbf{v}_T$ is uncorrelated with $\mathbf{u}_c$ and is serially uncorrelated, with variance–covariance matrix $E\mathbf{v}_T\mathbf{v}_T' = \sigma_v^2 I_T$.

The null hypothesis here is that $\boldsymbol{\delta}_1 = \boldsymbol{\beta}_1$. So with regard to the question whether or not to pool, we can use a likelihood-ratio test. Let L_1^* and L_2^* denote the maxima of the log joint likelihood functions for (9.4.1) and (9.4.2) with and without the restriction that $\boldsymbol{\delta}_1 = \boldsymbol{\beta}_1$. Then, under the null hypothesis, $2(L_2^* - L_1^*)$ is asymptotically chi-square-distributed, with K degrees of freedom. The only question is: What is the appropriate level of significance? If the costs of mistakenly accepting the pooling hypothesis and rejecting the pooling hypothesis are the same, Maddala (1971b) suggested using something like a 25 to 30 percent level of significance, rather than the conventional 5 percent, in our preliminary test of significance.

The specifications of the maximum likelihood estimates and their variance–covariances merely summarize the likelihood function in terms of the location of its maximum and its curvature around the maximum. It is possible that the information that the likelihood function contains is not fully expressed by these. When the compatibility of cross-sectional and time-series estimates is investigated, it is useful to plot the likelihood function extensively. For this purpose, Maddala (1971b) suggested that one should also tabulate and plot the relative maximum likelihoods of each data set,

$$R_M(\delta_1) = \frac{\max\limits_{\boldsymbol{\theta}} L(\boldsymbol{\delta}_1, \boldsymbol{\theta})}{\max\limits_{\boldsymbol{\delta}_1, \boldsymbol{\theta}} L(\boldsymbol{\delta}_1, \boldsymbol{\theta})}, \tag{9.4.3}$$

where $\boldsymbol{\theta}$ represents the set of nuisance parameters, $\max_{\boldsymbol{\theta}} L(\boldsymbol{\delta}_1, \boldsymbol{\theta})$ denotes the maximum of L with respect to $\boldsymbol{\theta}$ given $\boldsymbol{\delta}_1$, and $\max_{\boldsymbol{\delta}_1, \boldsymbol{\theta}} L(\boldsymbol{\delta}_1, \boldsymbol{\theta})$ denotes the maximum of L with respect to both $\boldsymbol{\delta}_1$ and $\boldsymbol{\theta}$. The plot of (9.4.3) summarizes almost all the information contained in the data on $\boldsymbol{\delta}_1$. Hence, the shapes and locations of the relative maximum likelihoods will reveal more information about the compatibility of the different bodies of data than a single test statistic can.

If the hypothesis $\boldsymbol{\delta}_1 = \boldsymbol{\beta}_1$ is acceptable, then, as Chetty (1968), Durbin (1953), and Maddala (1971b) have suggested, we can stack (9.4.1) and (9.4.2) together as

$$\begin{bmatrix} \mathbf{y}_c \\ \mathbf{y}_t \end{bmatrix} = \begin{bmatrix} Z_1 \\ X_1 \end{bmatrix} \boldsymbol{\delta}_1 + \begin{bmatrix} Z_2 \\ \mathbf{0} \end{bmatrix} \boldsymbol{\delta}_2 + \begin{bmatrix} \mathbf{0} \\ X_2 \end{bmatrix} \boldsymbol{\beta}_2 + \begin{bmatrix} \mathbf{u}_c \\ \mathbf{v}_T \end{bmatrix}. \tag{9.4.4}$$

It is clear that an efficient method of estimating of $\boldsymbol{\delta}_1$, $\boldsymbol{\delta}_2$, and $\boldsymbol{\beta}_2$ is to apply the maximum likelihood method to (9.4.4). An asymptotically equivalent procedure is to first apply least squares separately to (9.4.1) and (9.4.2) to obtain consistent estimates of σ_u^2 and σ_v^2, then substitute the estimated σ_u^2 and σ_v^2 into the equation

$$\begin{bmatrix} \frac{1}{\sigma_u} \mathbf{y}_c \\ \frac{1}{\sigma_v} \mathbf{y}_T \end{bmatrix} = \begin{bmatrix} \frac{1}{\sigma_u} Z_1 \\ \frac{1}{\sigma_v} X_1 \end{bmatrix} \boldsymbol{\delta}_1 + \begin{bmatrix} \frac{1}{\sigma_u} Z_2 \\ \mathbf{0} \end{bmatrix} \boldsymbol{\delta}_2 + \begin{bmatrix} \mathbf{0} \\ \frac{1}{\sigma_v} X_2 \end{bmatrix} \boldsymbol{\beta}_2 + \begin{bmatrix} \frac{1}{\sigma_u} \mathbf{u}_c \\ \frac{1}{\sigma_v} \mathbf{v}_T \end{bmatrix} \tag{9.4.5}$$

and apply the least-squares method to (9.4.5).

The conventional procedure of substituting the cross-sectional estimates $\hat{\boldsymbol{\delta}}_{1c}$ of $\boldsymbol{\beta}_1$ into the time-series model

$$\mathbf{y}_T - X_1 \hat{\boldsymbol{\delta}}_{1c} = X_2 \boldsymbol{\beta}_2 + \mathbf{v}_T + X_1(\boldsymbol{\beta}_1 - \hat{\boldsymbol{\delta}}_{1c}), \tag{9.4.6}$$

then regressing $(\mathbf{y}_T - X_1 \hat{\boldsymbol{\delta}}_{1c})$ on X_2, yields only conditional estimates of the parameters $\boldsymbol{\beta}_2$ – conditional on the estimates obtained from the cross-sectional data.[16] However, there is also some information about $\boldsymbol{\beta}_1$ in the time-series sample, and this should be utilized. Moreover, one should be careful in the use of two-step procedures. Proper evaluation of the asymptotic variance–covariance matrix of $\boldsymbol{\beta}_2$ should take account of the uncertainty (variance) in substituting $\hat{\boldsymbol{\delta}}_{1c}$ for $\boldsymbol{\beta}_1$. [For details, see Chetty (1968); Hsiao, Mountain, and Ho-Illman (1995); Jeong (1978); and Maddala (1971b).]

9.4.3 An Example

To illustrate application of the likelihood approach to pooling, Maddala (1971b) analyzed a simple econometric model relating to the demand for food in the United States. The model and the data were taken from Tobin (1950).

The cross-sectional demand equation is

$$y_{1i} = \delta_0 + \delta_1 z_{1i} + \delta_2 z_{2i} + u_i, \qquad i = 1, \ldots, N, \tag{9.4.7}$$

where y_{1i} is the logarithm of the average food consumption of the group of families at a point in time, and z_{1i} and z_{2i} are the logarithms of the average income of the ith family and the average family size, respectively. The time-series demand function is

$$y_{2t} = \beta_0 + \beta_1(x_{1t} - \beta_2 x_{2t}) + \beta_3(x_{2t} - x_{2,t-1}) + v_t, \qquad t = 1, \ldots, T, \quad (9.4.8)$$

where y_{2t}, x_{1t}, and x_{2t} are the logarithms of the food price index, per capita food supply for domestic consumption, and per capita disposable income, respectively. The income elasticity of demand, δ_1, was assumed common to both regressions, namely, $\delta_1 = \beta_2$. The error terms u_i and v_t were independent of each other and were assumed independently normally distributed, with zero means and constant variances σ_u^2 and σ_v^2, respectively.

The results of the cross-sectional estimates are

$$\hat{y}_{1i} = 0.569 + \underset{(0.0297)}{0.5611} z_{1i} + \underset{(0.0367)}{0.2540} z_{2i}, \quad (9.4.9)$$

where standard errors are in parentheses. The results of the time-series regression are

$$\hat{y}_{2t} = 7.231 + \underset{(0.0612)}{1.144} x_{2t} - \underset{(0.0906)}{0.1519} (x_{2t} - x_{2,t-1}) - \underset{(0.4010)}{3.644} x_{1t}. \quad (9.4.10)$$

The implied income elasticity, δ_1, is 0.314.

When the cross-sectional estimate of δ_1, 0.56, is introduced into the time-series regression, the estimated β_1 is reduced to -1.863, with a standard error of 0.1358. When δ_1 and β_1 are estimated simultaneously by the maximum likelihood method, the estimated δ_1 and β_1 are 0.5355 and -1.64, with a covariance

$$\begin{bmatrix} 0.00206 & 0.00827 \\ & 0.04245 \end{bmatrix}.$$

Although there is substantial improvement in the accuracy of the estimated coefficient using the combined data, the likelihood-ratio statistic turns out to be 17.2, which is significant at the 0.001 level with one degree of freedom. It strongly suggests that in this case we should not pool the time-series and cross-sectional data.

Figure 9.1 reproduces Maddala's plot of the relative maximum likelihood $R_M(\delta_1)$ for the parameter δ_1 (the income elasticity of demand) in the Tobin model from cross-sectional data alone, from time-series data alone, and from the pooled sample. The figure reveals that the information on δ_1 provided by the time-series data is almost as precise as that provided by the cross-sectional data (otherwise the likelihood function would be relatively flat). Furthermore, there is very little overlap between the likelihood functions from time-series and cross-sectional data. Again, this unambiguously suggests that the data should not be pooled.[17]

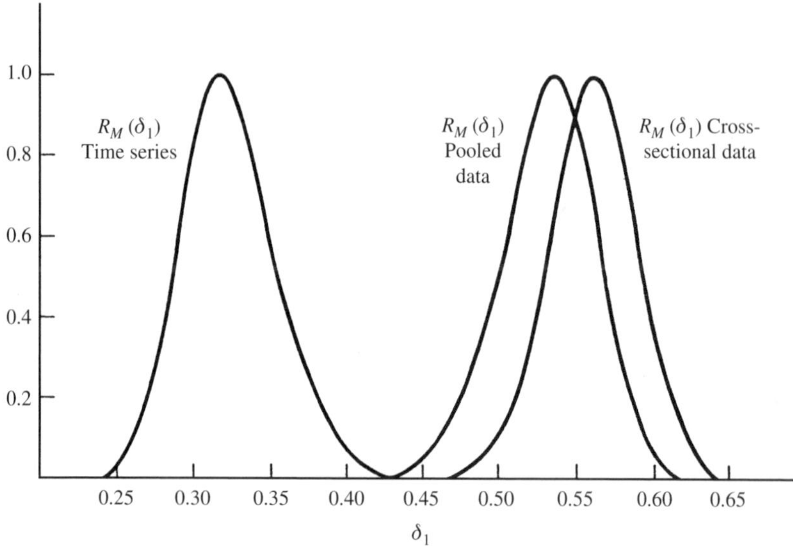

Fig. 9.1 Relative likelihoods for the parameter δ_1.
Source: Maddala (1971b, Figure 1).

Given that the time-series data arise by aggregating some microeconomic process, there cannot possibly be a conflict between the time-series and cross-sectional inferences if individual differences conditional on explanatory variables are viewed as chance outcomes. Thus, whenever the empirical results differ systematically between the two, as in the foregoing example, this is an indication that either or both models may be misspecified. The existence of supporting extraneous information in the form of cross-sectional or time-series data provides an additional check on the appropriateness of a model specification that cannot be provided by a single cross-section or time-series data set, because there may be no internal evidence of this omitted-variable bias. However, until a great deal is learned about the relation between cross-sectional and time-series estimates, there appears to be no substitute for completeness of information. Sequential observations on a number of individuals or panel data are essential for a full understanding of the systematic interrelations at different periods of time.

CHAPTER 10

Miscellaneous Topics

In this chapter we briefly consider some miscellaneous topics. We shall first consider statistical inference using simulation methods (Section 10.1). We shall then consider panels with both large N and large T (Section 10.2), leading to the discussion of the specific issue of unit-root tests (Section 10.3). Section 10.4 will discuss panels with more than two dimensions. Section 10.5 considers issues of measurement errors and indicates how one can take advantage of the panel structure to identify and estimate an otherwise unidentified model. Finally, we discuss proposals for relaxing the cross-section independence assumption apart from the specification of the individual-invariant time-varying factors.

10.1 SIMULATION METHODS

Panel data contain two dimensions – a cross-sectional dimension and a time dimension. Models using panel data also often contain unobserved heterogeneity factors. To transform a latent variable model involving missing data, random coefficients, heterogeneity, etc., into an observable model often requires the integration of latent variables over multiple dimensions (e.g., Hsiao (1989, 1991b, 1992c)). The resulting panel data model estimators can be quite difficult to compute. Simulation methods have been suggested to get around the complex computational issues involving multiple integrations (e.g., Gourieroux and Monfort (1996); Hsiao and Wang (2000); Keane (1994); McFadden (1989); Pakes and Pollard (1989)).

The basic idea of the simulation approach is to rely on the law of large numbers to obtain the approximation of the integrals through taking the averages of random drawings from a known probability distribution function. For instance, consider the problem of computing the conditional density function $f(\mathbf{y}_i \mid \mathbf{x}_i; \boldsymbol{\theta})$ of $\mathbf{y}_i$ given $\mathbf{x}_i$, or some conditional moments $\mathbf{m}(\mathbf{y}_i, \mathbf{x}_i; \boldsymbol{\theta})$, say $E(\mathbf{y}_i \mid \mathbf{x}_i; \boldsymbol{\theta})$ or $E(\mathbf{y}_i\mathbf{y}_i' \mid \mathbf{x}_i; \boldsymbol{\theta})$, where $\boldsymbol{\theta}$ is the vector of parameters characterizing these functions. In many cases, it is difficult to compute these functions because they do not have closed forms. However, if the conditional density or moments conditional on $\mathbf{x}$ and another vector $\boldsymbol{\eta}$, namely $f^*(\mathbf{y}_i \mid \mathbf{x}_i, \boldsymbol{\eta}; \boldsymbol{\theta})$ or $\mathbf{m}(\mathbf{y}, \mathbf{x} \mid \boldsymbol{\eta}; \boldsymbol{\theta})$, have closed forms and the probability distribution $P(\boldsymbol{\eta})$ of $\boldsymbol{\eta}$ is known, then from

$$f(\mathbf{y}_i \mid \mathbf{x}_i; \boldsymbol{\theta}) = \int f^*(\mathbf{y}_i \mid \mathbf{x}_i, \boldsymbol{\eta}; \boldsymbol{\theta})\, dP(\boldsymbol{\eta}), \tag{10.1.1}$$

and

$$\mathbf{m}(\mathbf{y}_i, \mathbf{x}_i; \boldsymbol{\theta}) = \int \mathbf{m}^*(\mathbf{y}_i, \mathbf{x}_i \mid \boldsymbol{\eta}; \boldsymbol{\theta})\, dP(\boldsymbol{\eta}), \tag{10.1.2}$$

we may approximate (10.1.1) and (10.1.2) by

$$\tilde{f}_H(\mathbf{y}_i \mid \mathbf{x}_i; \boldsymbol{\theta}) = \frac{1}{H} \sum_{h=1}^{H} f^*(\mathbf{y}_i \mid \mathbf{x}_i, \boldsymbol{\eta}_{ih}; \boldsymbol{\theta}), \tag{10.1.3}$$

and

$$\tilde{\mathbf{m}}_H(\mathbf{y}_i, \mathbf{x}_i; \boldsymbol{\theta}) = \frac{1}{H} \sum_{h=1}^{H} \mathbf{m}^*(\mathbf{y}_i, \mathbf{x}_i \mid \boldsymbol{\eta}_{ih}; \boldsymbol{\theta}), \tag{10.1.4}$$

where $(\boldsymbol{\eta}_{i1}, \ldots, \boldsymbol{\eta}_{iH})$ are H random draws from $P(\boldsymbol{\eta})$.

For example, consider the random-effects panel probit and Tobit models defined by the latent response function

$$y_{it}^* = \boldsymbol{\beta}'\mathbf{x}_{it} + \alpha_i + u_{it}, \tag{10.1.5}$$

where α_i and u_{it} are assumed to be independently normally distributed with mean 0 and variance σ_α^2 and 1, respectively, and are mutually independent. The probit model assumes that the observed y_{it} takes the form

$$y_{it} = \begin{cases} 1 & \text{if } y_{it}^* > 0, \\ 0 & \text{if } y_{it}^* \leq 0. \end{cases} \tag{10.1.6}$$

The Tobit model assumes that

$$y_{it} = \begin{cases} y_{it}^* & \text{if } y_{it}^* > 0, \\ 0 & \text{if } y_{it}^* \leq 0. \end{cases} \tag{10.1.7}$$

We note that the density function of α_i and u_{it} can be expressed as transformations of some standard distributions (here, standard normal), so that the density function of $\mathbf{y}_i' = (y_{i1}, \ldots, y_{iT})$ becomes an integral of a conditional function over the range of these standard distributions:

$$f(\mathbf{y}_i \mid \mathbf{x}_i; \boldsymbol{\theta}) = \int f^*(\mathbf{y}_i \mid \mathbf{x}_i, \eta; \boldsymbol{\theta})\, dP(\eta) \tag{10.1.8}$$

with $p(\eta) \sim N(0, 1)$. For instance, in the case of the probit model,

$$f^*(\mathbf{y}_i \mid \mathbf{x}_i, \eta; \boldsymbol{\theta}) = \sum_{t=1}^{T} \Phi(\mathbf{x}_{it}'\boldsymbol{\beta} + \sigma_\alpha \eta_i)^{y_{it}} [1 - \Phi(\mathbf{x}_{it}'\boldsymbol{\beta} + \sigma_\alpha \eta_i)]^{1-y_{it}}, \tag{10.1.9}$$

and in the case of the Tobit model,

$$f^*(\mathbf{y}_i \mid \mathbf{x}_i, \eta; \boldsymbol{\theta}) = \prod_{t\in\Psi_1} \phi(y_{it} - \mathbf{x}'_{it}\boldsymbol{\beta} - \sigma_\alpha \eta_i) \times \prod_{t\in\Psi_0} \Phi(-\mathbf{x}'_{it}\boldsymbol{\beta} - \sigma_\alpha \eta_i), \tag{10.1.10}$$

where $\phi(\cdot)$ and $\Phi(\cdot)$ denote the standard normal density and integrated normal, respectively, and $\Psi_1 = \{t \mid y_{it} > 0\}$ and $\Psi_0 = \{t \mid y_{it} = 0\}$. Because conditional on $\mathbf{x}_{it}$ and each of the H random draws η_{ih}, $h = 1, \ldots, H$, of η from a standard normal distribution, the conditional density function (10.1.9) or (10.1.10) is well defined in terms of $\boldsymbol{\beta}$ and σ_α^2, the approximation of $f(\mathbf{y}_i \mid \mathbf{x}_i; \boldsymbol{\beta}, \sigma_\alpha^2)$ can be obtained by taking their averages as in (10.1.3).

More complicated forms of $f(\mathbf{y}_i \mid \mathbf{x}_i; \boldsymbol{\theta})$ can also be approximated by a relatively simple simulator. For instance, if $\mathbf{u}_i = (u_{i1}, \ldots, u_{iT})'$ has a multivariate normal distribution with mean $\mathbf{0}$ and covariance matrix Σ, we can let $\mathbf{u}_i = \Lambda\boldsymbol{\eta}_i^*$, where $\boldsymbol{\eta}_i^*$ is from a standard multivariate normal with mean 0 and covariance matrix I_T, and Λ is a lower triangular matrix such that $\Sigma = \Lambda\Lambda'$. Thus, if u_{it} in the above example follows a first-order autoregressive process

$$u_{it} = \rho u_{i,t-1} + \epsilon_{it}, \qquad |\rho| < 1, \tag{10.1.11}$$

then we can rewrite (10.1.5) as

$$y_{it}^* = \boldsymbol{\beta}'\mathbf{x}_{it} + \sigma_\alpha \eta_i + \sum_{\tau=1}^{t} a_{t\tau}\eta_{i\tau}^*, \tag{10.1.12}$$

where $\eta_{i\tau}^*$, $\tau = 1, \ldots, T$ are random draws from independent $N(0, 1)$, and $a_{t\tau}$ are the entries of the lower triangular matrix Λ. It turns out that here $a_{t\tau} = (1-\rho^2)^{-\frac{1}{2}}\rho^{t-\tau}$ if $t \geq \tau$, and $a_{t\tau} = 0$ if $t < \tau$.

Using the approach described above, we can obtain an unbiased, differentiable and positive simulator of $f(\mathbf{y}_i \mid \mathbf{x}_i; \boldsymbol{\theta})$, $\boldsymbol{\theta} = (\boldsymbol{\beta}', \sigma_\alpha, \rho)'$, in the probit case by considering the following drawings:

η_{ih} is drawn from $N(0,1)$;
η_{i1h}^* is drawn from $N(0, 1)$ restricted to

$$[-(\boldsymbol{\beta}'\mathbf{x}_{i1} + \sigma_\alpha\eta_{ih})/a_{11}, \infty] \qquad \text{if} \quad y_{i1} = 1$$

or

$$[-\infty, -(\boldsymbol{\beta}'\mathbf{x}_{i1} + \sigma_\alpha\eta_{ih})/a_{11}] \qquad \text{if} \quad y_{i1} = 0;$$

η_{i2h}^* is drawn from $N(0, 1)$ restricted to

$$[-(\boldsymbol{\beta}'\mathbf{x}_{i2} + \sigma_\alpha\eta_{ih} + a_{21}\eta_{i1h}^*)/a_{22}, \infty] \qquad \text{if} \quad y_{i2} = 1$$

and

$$[-\infty, -(\boldsymbol{\beta}'\mathbf{x}_{i2} + \sigma_\alpha\eta_{ih} + a_{21}\eta_{i1h}^*)/a_{22}] \qquad \text{if} \quad y_{i2} = 0;$$

and so on. The simulator of $f(\mathbf{y}_i \mid \mathbf{x}_i; \boldsymbol{\theta})$ is

$$\tilde{f}_H(\mathbf{y}_i \mid \mathbf{x}_i; \boldsymbol{\theta}) = \frac{1}{H} \sum_{h=1}^{H} \prod_{t=1}^{T} \Phi\left[(-1)^{1-y_{it}} \left(\boldsymbol{\beta}'\mathbf{x}_{it} + \sigma_\alpha \eta_{ih} + \sum_{\tau=1}^{t-1} a_{t\tau}\eta^*_{i\tau h}\right) \Big/ a_{tt}\right], \tag{10.1.13}$$

where for $t = 1$, the sum over τ disappears.

In the Tobit case, the same kind of method can be used. The only difference is that the simulator of $f(\mathbf{y}_i \mid \mathbf{x}_i; \boldsymbol{\theta})$ becomes

$$\tilde{f}_H(\mathbf{y}_i | \mathbf{x}_i; \boldsymbol{\theta}) = \frac{1}{H} \sum_{h=1}^{H} \left[\prod_{t \in \Psi_1} \frac{1}{a_{tt}} \phi\left(\left[y_{it} - \left(\boldsymbol{\beta}'\mathbf{x}_{it} + \sigma_\alpha \eta_{ih} + \sum_{\tau=1}^{t-1} a_{t\tau}\eta^*_{i\tau h}\right)\right] \Big/ a_{tt}\right)\right.$$
$$\left. \times \prod_{t \in \Psi_0} \Phi\left[-\left(\boldsymbol{\beta}'\mathbf{x}_{it} + \sigma_\alpha \eta_{ih} + \sum_{\tau=1}^{t-1} a_{t\tau}\eta^*_{i\tau h}\right) \Big/ a_{tt}\right]\right]. \tag{10.1.14}$$

The simulated maximum likelihood estimator (SMLE) is obtained from maximizing the simulated log likelihood function. The simulated generalized method-of-moments (SGMM) estimator is obtained from the simulated (4.3.37). The simulated least-squares (SLS) estimator is obtained if we let $\mathbf{m}(\mathbf{y}_i, \mathbf{x}_i; \boldsymbol{\theta}) = E(\mathbf{y}_i \mid \mathbf{x}_i; \boldsymbol{\theta})$ and minimize $\sum_{i=1}^{N} [\mathbf{y}_i - E(\mathbf{y}_i \mid \mathbf{x}_i; \boldsymbol{\theta})]^2$.

Although we need $H \to \infty$ to obtain consistent simulators of $f(\mathbf{y}_i \mid \mathbf{x}_i; \boldsymbol{\theta})$ and $\mathbf{m}(\mathbf{y}_i, \mathbf{x}_i; \boldsymbol{\theta})$, it is shown by McFadden (1989) that when a finite number H of vectors $(\boldsymbol{\eta}_{i1}, \ldots, \boldsymbol{\eta}_{iH})$ are drawn by simple random sampling and independently for different i from the marginal density $P(\boldsymbol{\eta})$, the simulation errors are independent across observations; hence the variance introduced by simulation will be controlled by the law of large numbers operating across observations, making it unnecessary to consistently estimate each theoretical $\mathbf{m}(\mathbf{y}_i, \mathbf{x}_i; \boldsymbol{\theta})$ for the consistency of the SGMM $\hat{\boldsymbol{\theta}}_{\text{SGMM}}$ as $N \to \infty$.

The asymptotic covariance matrix of $\sqrt{N}(\hat{\boldsymbol{\theta}}_{\text{SGMM}} - \boldsymbol{\theta})$ obtained by simulating the moments in (4.3.37) that can be approximated by

$$(R'AR)^{-1} R'AG_{NH}AR(R'AR)^{-1}, \tag{10.1.15}$$

where

$$R = \frac{1}{N} \sum_{i=1}^{N} W_i' \frac{\partial \tilde{\mathbf{m}}_H(\mathbf{y}_i, \mathbf{x}_i; \boldsymbol{\theta})}{\partial \boldsymbol{\theta}'},$$
$$G_{NH} = \frac{1}{N} \sum_{i=1}^{N} W_i \left(\Omega + \frac{1}{H}\Delta_H\right) W_i', \tag{10.1.16}$$
$$\Omega = \text{Cov}(\mathbf{m}_i(\mathbf{y}_i, \mathbf{x}_i; \boldsymbol{\theta})),$$
$$\Delta_H = \text{Cov}[\tilde{\mathbf{m}}_H(\mathbf{y}_i, \mathbf{x}_i; \boldsymbol{\theta}) - \mathbf{m}(y_i, \mathbf{x}_i; \boldsymbol{\theta})].$$

It is clear that as $H \to \infty$, the SGMM has the same asymptotic efficiency as the GMM. However, even with finite H, the relative efficiency of the SGMM is quite high. For instance, for the simple frequency simulator, $\Delta_H = \Omega$, one draw per observation gives 50 percent of the asymptotic efficiency of the corresponding GMM estimator, and nine draws per observation gives 90 percent relative efficiency.

However, for the consistency of SMLE or SLS we shall need $H \to \infty$ as $N \to \infty$. With a finite H, the approximation error of the conditional density or moments is of order H^{-1}. This will lead to the asymptotic bias of $O(1/H)$ (e.g., Gourieoux and Monfort (1996); Hsiao, Wang, and Wang (1997)). Nevertheless, with a finite H it is still possible to propose an SLS estimator which is consistent and asymptotically normally distributed as $N \to \infty$ by noting that for the sequence of $2H$ random draws $(\boldsymbol{\eta}_{i1}, \ldots, \boldsymbol{\eta}_{iH}, \boldsymbol{\eta}_{i,H+1}, \ldots, \boldsymbol{\eta}_{i,2H})$ for each i, we have

$$E\left[\frac{1}{H}\sum_{h=1}^{H}\mathbf{m}^*(\mathbf{y}_i, \mathbf{x}_i \mid \boldsymbol{\eta}_{ih}; \boldsymbol{\theta})\right] = E\left[\frac{1}{H}\sum_{h=1}^{H}\mathbf{m}^*(\mathbf{y}_i, \mathbf{x}_i \mid \boldsymbol{\eta}_{i,H+h}; \boldsymbol{\theta})\right], \\ = \mathbf{m}(\mathbf{y}_i, \mathbf{x}_i; \boldsymbol{\theta}), \tag{10.1.17}$$

and

$$E\left[\mathbf{y}_i - \frac{1}{H}\sum_{h=1}^{H}\mathbf{m}^*(\mathbf{y}_i, \mathbf{x}_i \mid \boldsymbol{\eta}_{ih}; \boldsymbol{\theta})\right]'\left[\mathbf{y}_i - \frac{1}{H}\sum_{h=1}^{H}\mathbf{m}^*(\mathbf{y}_i, \mathbf{x}_i \mid \boldsymbol{\eta}_{i,H+h}; \boldsymbol{\theta})\right] \\ = E\left[\mathbf{y}_i - \mathbf{m}(\mathbf{y}_i, \mathbf{x}_i; \boldsymbol{\theta})\right]'\left[\mathbf{y}_i - \mathbf{m}(\mathbf{y}_i, \mathbf{x}_i; \boldsymbol{\theta})\right], \tag{10.1.18}$$

because of the independence between $(\boldsymbol{\eta}_{i1}, \ldots, \boldsymbol{\eta}_{iH})$ and $(\boldsymbol{\eta}_{i,H+1}, \ldots, \boldsymbol{\eta}_{i,2H})$. Then the SLS estimator that minimizes

$$\sum_{i=1}^{N}\left[\mathbf{y}_i - \frac{1}{H}\sum_{h=1}^{H}\mathbf{m}^*(\mathbf{y}_i, \mathbf{x}_i \mid \boldsymbol{\eta}_{ih}; \boldsymbol{\theta})\right]'\left[\mathbf{y}_i - \frac{1}{H}\sum_{h=1}^{H}\mathbf{m}^*(y_i, \mathbf{x}_i \mid \boldsymbol{\eta}_{i,H+h}; \boldsymbol{\theta})\right] \tag{10.1.19}$$

is consistent as $N \to \infty$ even H is fixed (e.g., Gourieoux and Monfort (1996); Hsiao and Wang (2000)).

10.2 PANELS WITH LARGE N AND T

Most of this monograph has been concerned with panels with large N and small T. However, some of the panel data sets, like the Penn–World tables, cover different individuals, industries, and countries over long time periods. In some cases, the orders of magnitude of the cross section and time series are similar. These large-N, large-T panels call for the use of large-N and -T asymptotics rather than just large-N asymptotics. Moreover, when T is large, there is a need to consider serial correlations more generally, including both short-memory and persistent components. In some panel data sets like the Penn–World Table, the time-series components also have strongly evident nonstationarity. It turns out that panel data in this case can sometimes offer additional insights into the data-generating process than a single time series or a cross-section data set.

In regressions with large-N, large-T panels most of the interesting test statistics and estimators inevitably depend on the treatment of the two indexes, N and T, which tend to infinity together. Several approaches are possible. These are:

a. *Sequential limits.* A sequential approach is to fix one index, say N, and allow the other, say T, to pass to infinity, giving an intermediate limit. Then, by letting N pass to infinity subsequently, a sequential limit theory is obtained.
b. *Diagonal-path limits.* This approach is to allow the two indexes, N and T, to pass to infinity along a specific diagonal path in the two-dimensional array, say $T = T(N)$ as the index $N \to \infty$.
c. *Joint limits.* A joint limit theory allows both indexes, N and T, to pass to infinity simultaneously without placing specific diagonal path restrictions on the divergence, although it may still be necessary to exercise some control over the rate of expansion of the two indexes in order to get definitive results.

In many applications, sequential limits are easy to derive and helpful in extracting quick asymptotics. However, sometimes sequential limits can give misleading asymptotic results.[1] A joint limit will give a more robust result than either a sequential limit or a diagonal-path limit, but will also be substantially more difficult to derive and will usually apply only under stronger conditions, such as the existence of higher moments, that will allow for uniformity in the convergence arguments. Phillips and Moon (1999) have given a set of sufficient conditions that ensures that sequential limits are equivalent to joint limits.

In general, if an estimator is consistent in the fixed-T, large-N case, it will remain consistent if both N and T tend to infinity, irrespective of how they do so. Moreover, even in the case that an estimator is inconsistent for fixed T and large N, (say, the least-squares estimator for a dynamic random-coefficient model discussed in Chapter 6), it can become consistent if T also tends to infinity. The probability limit of an estimator, in general, is identical no matter which limits one takes. However, the properly scaled limiting distribution may depend on how the two indexes, N and T, tend to infinity (e.g., Levin and Lin (1993); Hahn and Kuersteiner (2000)).

For instance, consider the linear regression model

$$y = E(y \mid x) + v = \beta x + v. \tag{10.2.1}$$

The least-squares estimator $\hat{\beta}$ of β gives the same interpretation irrespective of whether y and x are stationary or integrated of order 1 (i.e., the first difference is stationary). In the case that y and x are bivariate normally distributed as $N(\mathbf{0}, \Sigma)$ with

$$\Sigma = \begin{pmatrix} \Sigma_{yy} & \Sigma_{yx} \\ \Sigma_{xy} & \Sigma_{xx} \end{pmatrix}, \tag{10.2.2}$$

then plim $\hat{\beta} = \Sigma_{yx}\Sigma_{xx}^{-1}$. In a unit-root framework of the form

$$\begin{pmatrix} y_t \\ x_t \end{pmatrix} = \begin{pmatrix} y_{t-1} \\ x_{t-1} \end{pmatrix} + \begin{pmatrix} u_{yt} \\ u_{xt} \end{pmatrix}, \tag{10.2.3}$$

where the errors $\mathbf{u}_t = (u_{yt}, u_{xt})'$ are stationary, then

$$\text{plim } \hat{\beta} = \Omega_{yx}\Omega_{xx}^{-1}, \tag{10.2.4}$$

where Ω_{yx}, Ω_{xx} denote the long-run covariance between u_{yt} and u_{xt} and the long-run variance of x_t, defined by

$$\begin{aligned} \Omega &= \lim_{T\to\infty} E\left[\left(\frac{1}{\sqrt{T}}\sum_{t=1}^{T}\mathbf{u}_t\right)\left(\frac{1}{\sqrt{T}}\sum_{t=1}^{T}\mathbf{u}_t'\right)\right] \\ &= \sum_{\ell=-\infty}^{\infty} E(\mathbf{u}_0\mathbf{u}_\ell') = \begin{pmatrix} \Omega_{yy} & \Omega_{yx} \\ \Omega_{xy} & \Omega_{xx} \end{pmatrix}. \end{aligned} \tag{10.2.5}$$

When cross-sectional units have heterogeneous long-run covariance matrices Ω_i for (y_{it}, x_{it}), $i = 1, \ldots, N$, with $E\Omega_i = \Omega$, Phillips and Moon (1999) extend this concept of a long-run average relation among cross-sectional units further:

$$\beta = E(\Omega_{yx,i})(E\Omega_{xx,i})^{-1} = \Omega_{yx}\Omega_{xx}^{-1}. \tag{10.2.6}$$

They show that the resulting least-squares estimator converges to (10.2.6) as $N, T \to \infty$.

This generalized concept of average relation between cross-sectional units covers both the cointegrated case (Engle and Granger (1987)) in which β is a cointegrating coefficient in the sense that the particular linear combination $y_t - \beta x_t$ is stationary, and the correlated but noncointegrated case, which is not available for a single time-series. To see this point more clearly, suppose that the two nonstationary time-series variables have the following relation:

$$\begin{aligned} y_t &= f_t + w_t, \\ x_t &= f_t, \end{aligned} \tag{10.2.7}$$

with

$$\begin{pmatrix} w_t \\ f_t \end{pmatrix} = \begin{pmatrix} w_{t-1} \\ f_{t-1} \end{pmatrix} + \begin{pmatrix} u_{wt} \\ u_{ft} \end{pmatrix}, \tag{10.2.8}$$

where u_{ws} is independent of u_{ft} for all t and s and has nonzero long-run variance. Then f_t is a nonstationary common factor variable for y and x, and u_w is a nonstationary idiosyncratic factor variable. Since w_t is nonstationary over time, it is apparent that there is no cointegrating relation between y_t and x_t. However, since the two nonstationary variables y_t and x_t share a common contributory nonstationary source in u_{ft}, we may still expect to find evidence of long-run correlation between y_t and x_t, and this is what is measured by the regression coefficient β in (10.2.6).

Phillips and Moon (1999, 2000) show that for large-N and -T panels, the regression coefficient β converges to the long-run average relation so defined. However, if N is fixed, then as $T \to \infty$, the least-squares estimator of β is a nondegenerate random variable that is a functional of Brownian motion that does not converge to β (Phillips and Durlauf (1986)). In other words, with a single time series or a fixed number of time series, the regression coefficient β will not converge to the long-run average relation defined by (10.2.6) if only $T \to \infty$.

Therefore, if we define a spurious regression as one yielding nonzero β for the two independent variables, then, contrary to the case of time-series regression of involving two linearly independent $I(1)$ variables (Phillips and Durlauf (1986)), the issue of spurious regression will not arise for the panel estimates of $N \to \infty$ (e.g., Kao (1999)).

10.3 UNIT-ROOT TESTS

Panels with large cross-sectional dimension and long time periods have also been used by applied economists to examine the income-convergence hypothesis in growth theory (e.g. Bernard and Jones (1996)) and the purchasing-power parity hypothesis in exchange-rate determination (e.g., Frankel and Rose (1996)). While the time-series property of a variable is of significant interest to economists, the statistical properties of time-series estimators actually depend on whether the data are stationary or nonstationary.[2] If the variables are stationary, the limiting distributions of most estimators will be approximately normal when $T \to \infty$. Standard normal and chi-square tables can be used to construct confidence intervals or test hypotheses. If the data are nonstationary, or contain unit roots, standard estimators will have nonstandard distributions as $T \to \infty$. The conventional Wald test statistics cannot be approximated well by t or chi-square distributions (e.g., Dickey and Fuller (1979, 1981); Phillips and Durlauf (1986)). Computer simulations will have to be used to find the critical values under the null. However, with panel data one can exploit information from cross-sectional dimensions to infer stationarity versus nonstationarity using normal or t-distribution approximations by invoking central limit theorems across cross-sectional dimensions.

Since Quah (1994), many people have suggested panel unit-root test statistics when N and T are large (e.g., Binder, Hsiao, and Pesaran (2000); Choi (2002); Harris and Tzaralis (1999); Im, Pesaran, and Shin (1997); Levin and Lin (1993); Levin, Lin, and Chu (2002); Maddala and Wu (1999)). Here we shall only discuss the tests of Levin and Lin (LL) (1993), Im, Pesaran, and Shin (IPS) (1997), and Maddala and Wu (MW) (1999).

Following Dickey and Fuller (1979, 1981), Levin and Lin (1993), and Levin, Lin and Chu (2002), consider a panel extension of the null hypothesis that each individual time series in the panel contains a unit root against the alternative hypothesis that all individual series are stationary by considering the model

$$\Delta y_{it} = \alpha_i + \delta_i t + \gamma_i y_{i,t-1} + \sum_{\ell=1}^{p_i} \phi_{i\ell} \Delta y_{i,t-\ell} + \epsilon_{it}, \qquad i = 1, \ldots, N, \quad t = 1, \ldots, T, \tag{10.3.1}$$

where ϵ_{it} is assumed to be independently distributed across i and Δ denotes the first-difference operator, $1 - L$, with L being the lag operator that shifts the observation by one period, $Ly_{it} = y_{i,t-1}$. If $\gamma_i = 0$, then y_{it} contains a unit root. If $\gamma_i < 0$, then y_{it} is stationary. Levin and Lin (1993) specify the null hypothesis as

$$H_0 : \gamma_1 = \gamma_2 = \cdots = \gamma_N = 0, \tag{10.3.2}$$

and the alternative hypothesis as

$$H_1 : \gamma_1 = \gamma_2 = \cdots = \gamma_N = \gamma < 0. \tag{10.3.3}$$

To test H_0 against H_1, Levin and Lin (1993) suggest first regressing Δy_{it} and $y_{i,t-1}$ on the remaining variables in (10.3.1) for each i, providing the residuals $\hat{e}_{it}$ and $\hat{v}_{i,t-1}$, respectively. Then one estimates γ by running the regression of the following model:

$$\hat{e}_{it} = \gamma \hat{v}_{i,t-1} + \epsilon_{it}. \tag{10.3.4}$$

To adjust for heteroscedasticity across i in (10.3.4), they suggest first using the least-squares estimate $\hat{\gamma}$ of γ to compute the variance of $\hat{e}_{it}$,

$$\hat{\sigma}_{ei}^2 = (T - p_i - 1)^{-1} \sum_{t=p_i+2}^{T} (\hat{e}_{it} - \hat{\gamma}\hat{v}_{i,t-1})^2, \tag{10.3.5}$$

and then dividing (10.3.4) by $\hat{\sigma}_{ei}$ for each i, to obtain the heteroscedasticity-adjusted model

$$\tilde{e}_{it} = \gamma \tilde{v}_{i,t-1} + \tilde{\epsilon}_{it}, \tag{10.3.6}$$

where $\tilde{e}_{it} = \hat{e}_{it}/\hat{\sigma}_{ei}$, $\tilde{v}_{i,t-1} = \hat{v}_{i,t-1}/\hat{\sigma}_{ei}$. The t statistic for testing $\gamma = 0$ is

$$t_{\tilde{\gamma}} = \frac{\tilde{\gamma}}{sd_{\tilde{\gamma}}}, \tag{10.3.7}$$

where $\tilde{\gamma}$ is the least-squares estimates of (10.3.6),

$$sd_{\tilde{\gamma}} = \hat{\sigma}_{\epsilon}\left[\sum_{i=1}^{N}\sum_{t=p_i+2}^{T}\tilde{v}_{i,t-1}^{2}\right]^{-1/2}$$

$$\hat{\sigma}_{\epsilon}^{2} = (N\tilde{T})^{-1}\sum_{i=1}^{N}\sum_{t=p_i+2}^{T}(\tilde{e}_{it} - \tilde{\gamma}\tilde{v}_{i,t-1})^{2},$$

$$\bar{p} = \frac{1}{N}\sum_{i=1}^{N}p_i,\ \tilde{T} = (T - \bar{p} - 1).$$

Levin and Lin (1993) suggest adjusting (10.3.7) by

$$t^{*} = \frac{t_{\tilde{\gamma}} - N\tilde{T}S_{NT}\hat{\sigma}_{\epsilon}^{-2}\cdot sd_{\tilde{\gamma}}\cdot\mu_{\tilde{T}}}{\sigma_{\tilde{T}}}, \tag{10.3.8}$$

where

$$S_{NT} = N^{-1}\sum_{i=1}^{N}\frac{\hat{\omega}_{yi}}{\hat{\sigma}_{ei}}, \tag{10.3.9}$$

and $\hat{\omega}_{yi}^{2}$ is an estimate of the long-run variance of y_i, say,

$$\begin{aligned}\hat{\omega}_{yi}^{2} &= (T-1)^{-1}\sum_{t=2}^{T}\Delta y_{it}^{2} + 2\sum_{j=1}^{\bar{K}}W_{\bar{K}}(j)\\ &\quad\times\left((T-1)^{-1}\sum_{t=j+2}^{T}\Delta y_{it}\,\Delta y_{i,t-j}\right),\end{aligned} \tag{10.3.10}$$

where $W_{\bar{K}}(j)$ is the lag kernel to ensure the positivity of $\hat{\omega}_{yi}^{2}$; for instance, Newey and West (1987) suggest that

$$W_{\bar{K}}(j) = \begin{cases}1 - \dfrac{j}{T} & \text{if } j < \bar{K},\\ 0 & \text{if } j \geq \bar{K}.\end{cases} \tag{10.3.11}$$

The $\mu_{\tilde{T}}$ and $\sigma_{\tilde{T}}$ are mean and standard-deviation adjustment terms, which are computed by Monte Carlo simulation and tabulated in their paper. Levin and Lin (1993) show that provided the augmented Dickey–Fuller (1981) lag order p increases at some rate T^{p} where $0 \leq p \leq 1/4$, and the lag truncation parameter $\bar{K}$ increases at rate T^{q} where $0 < q < 1$, the panel test statistic $t_{\tilde{\gamma}}$ under the null of $\gamma = 0$ converges to a standard normal distribution as $T, N \to \infty$.

In the special case that $\alpha_i = \delta_i = \phi_{i\ell} = 0$, and ϵ_{it} is i.i.d. with mean 0 and variance σ_{ϵ}^{2}, Levin and Lin (1993) and Levin, Lin, and Chu (2002) show that under the null of $\gamma = 0$, $T\sqrt{N}\hat{\gamma}$ of the pooled least-squares estimator $\hat{\gamma}$ converges to a normal distribution with mean 0 and variance 2, and the t statistic of $\hat{\gamma}$ converges to a standard normal, as $\sqrt{N}/T \to 0$ while $N, T \to \infty$ (i.e., the time dimension can expand more slowly than the cross section).

Im, Pesaran, and Shin (1997) relax Levin and Lins' strong assumption of homogeneity for (10.3.1) under the alternative (i.e., allowing $\gamma_i \neq \gamma_j$) by postulating the alternative hypothesis as

$$H_A^* : \gamma_i < 0 \text{ for at least one } i. \tag{10.3.12}$$

Thus, instead of pooling the data, Im, Pesaran, and Shin (1997) suggest taking the average, $\bar{\tau}$, of separate unit-root tests for N individual cross-section units of the argument Dickey–Fuller (ADF) (Dickey and Fuller (1981)) t-ratios τ_i. They show that $\bar{\tau}$ converges to a normal distribution under the null with mean $E(\bar{\tau})$ and variance $\text{Var}(\bar{\tau_N})$ as $T \to \infty$ and $N \to \infty$. Since $E(\tau_i)$ and $\text{Var}(\tau_i)$ will vary as the lag length in the ADF regression varies, Im, Pesaran, and Shin (1997) tabulate $E(\tau_i)$ and $\text{Var}(\tau_i)$ for different lag lengths. They show in their Monte Carlos studies that their test is more powerful than Levin, Lin, and Chu's (2001) test in certain cases.

Implicit in Im, Pesaran, and Shin's (1997) test is the assumption that T is the same for all cross-sectional units and that the same lag length is used for all the ADF regressions for individual series. To relax these restrictions, Maddala and Wu (1996) suggest using the Fisher (1932) P_λ test to combine the evidence from several independent tests. The idea is as follows: Suppose there are N unit-root tests as in Im, Pesaran, and Shin (1997). Let P_i be the observed significance level (P value) for the ith test. Then $(-2\sum_{i=1}^{N} \log P_i)$ has a chi-square distribution with $2N$ degrees of freedom as $T_i \to \infty$ (Rao (1952, p. 44)).

The LL test is based on homogeneity of the autoregressive parameter (although it allows heterogeneity in the error variances and the serial correlation structure of the errors). Thus the test is based on pooled regressions. On the other hand, both the MW test and the IPS test are based on the heterogeneity of the autoregressive parameter under the alternative. The tests amount to a combination of different independent tests. The advantage of the MW test is that it does not require a balanced panel, nor identical lag length in the individual ADF regressions. In fact, it can be carried out for any unit-root test derived. It is nonparametric. Whatever test statistic we use for testing for a unit root for each individual unit, we can get the P-values, P_i. The disadvantage is that the P-values have to be derived by Monte Carlo simulation. On the other hand, the LL and the IPS tests are parametric. Although the use of the $t_{\hat{\gamma}}$ and the $\bar{\tau}$ statistic involves the adjustment of the mean and variance, they are easy to use because ready tables are available from their papers. However, these tables are valid only for the ADF test.

The panel unit-root tests have also been generalized to test for cointegration (Engle and Granger (1987)) by testing if the regression residual is stationary or integrated of order 1 (e.g., Breitung and Mayer (1994); Kao and Chiang (2000); McCoskey and Kao (1998)). For a survey of panel unit-root tests and cointegration, see Banerjee (1999).

10.4 DATA WITH MULTILEVEL STRUCTURES

We have illustrated panel data methodology by assuming the presence of individual and/or time effects only. However, panel data need not be restricted to two dimensions. We can have a more complicated *clustering* or *hierarchical* structure. For example, Antweiler (2001), Baltagi, Song, and Jung (2001), and Davis (1999), following the methodology developed by Wansbeek and Kapteyn (1978, 1982), consider the multiway error-components model of the form

$$y_{ij\ell t} = \mathbf{x}'_{ij\ell t}\boldsymbol{\beta} + u_{ij\ell t}, \tag{10.4.1}$$

for $i = 1, \ldots, N$, $j = 1, \ldots, M_i$, $\ell = 1, \ldots, L_{ij}$, and $t = 1, \ldots, T_{ij\ell}$. For example, the dependent variable $y_{ij\ell t}$ could denote the air pollution measured at station ℓ in city j of country i in time period t. This means that there are N countries, and each country i has M_i cities in which L_{ij} observation stations are located. At each station, air pollution is observed for $T_{ij\ell}$ periods. Then $\mathbf{x}_{ij\ell t}$ denotes a vector of K explanatory variables, and the disturbance is assumed to have a multiway error-components structure,

$$u_{ij\ell t} = \alpha_i + \lambda_{ij} + \nu_{ij\ell} + \epsilon_{ij\ell t}, \tag{10.4.2}$$

where α_i, λ_{ij}, $\nu_{ij\ell}$, and $\epsilon_{ij\ell t}$ are assumed to be i.i.d. and are mutually independent with mean zero and variances σ_α^2, σ_λ^2, σ_ν^2, and σ_ϵ^2, respectively.

In the case that the data are balanced, the variance–covariance matrix of $\mathbf{u}$ has the form

$$\begin{aligned}\Omega &= \sigma_\alpha^2(I_N \otimes J_{MLT}) + \sigma_\lambda^2(I_{NM} \otimes J_{LT}) \\ &\quad + \sigma_\nu^2(I_{NML} \otimes J_T) + \sigma_\epsilon^2 I_{LMNT},\end{aligned} \tag{10.4.3}$$

where J_s is a square matrix of dimension s with all elements equal to 1. Rewriting (10.4.3) in the form representing the spectral decomposition Ω (e.g., as in Appendix 3B), we have

$$\begin{aligned}\Omega &= MLT\sigma_\alpha^2(I_N \otimes P_{MLT}) + LT\sigma_\lambda^2(I_{NM} \otimes P_{LT}) \\ &\quad + T\sigma_\nu^2(I_{NML} \otimes P_T) + \sigma_\epsilon^2 I_{LMNT} \\ &= \sigma_\epsilon^2(I_{NML} \otimes Q_T) + \sigma_1^2(I_{NM} \otimes Q_L \otimes P_T) \\ &\quad + \sigma_2^2(I_N \otimes Q_M \otimes P_{LT}) + \sigma_3^2(I_N \otimes P_{MLT}),\end{aligned} \tag{10.4.4}$$

where $P_s \equiv \frac{1}{s}J_s$, $Q_s = I_s - P_s$, and

$$\sigma_1^2 = T\sigma_\nu^2 + \sigma_\epsilon^2, \tag{10.4.5}$$

$$\sigma_2^2 = LT\sigma_\lambda^2 + T\sigma_\nu^2 + \sigma_\epsilon^2, \tag{10.4.6}$$

$$\sigma_3^2 = MLT\sigma_\alpha^2 + LT\sigma_\lambda^2 + T\sigma_\nu^2 + \sigma_\epsilon^2, \tag{10.4.7}$$

σ_ϵ^2 being the characteristic roots of Ω. As each of the terms of (10.4.4) is orthogonal to the others and they sum to I_{NMLT}, it follows that

$$\Omega^{-1/2} = \sigma_\epsilon^{-1}(I_{NML} \otimes Q_T) + \sigma_1^{-1}(I_{NM} \otimes Q_L \otimes P_T) + \sigma_2^{-1}(I_N \otimes Q_M \otimes P_{LT}) + \sigma_3^{-1}(I_N \otimes P_{MLT}). \tag{10.4.8}$$

Expanding all the Q-matrices as the difference of Is and Ps, multiplying both sides of the equation by σ_ϵ, and collecting terms yield

$$\sigma_\epsilon \Omega^{-1/2} = I_{NMLT} - \left(1 - \frac{\sigma_\epsilon}{\sigma_1}\right)(I_{NML} \otimes P_T) - \left(\frac{\sigma_\epsilon}{\sigma_1} - \frac{\sigma_\epsilon}{\sigma_2}\right)(I_{NM} \otimes P_{LT}) - \left(\frac{\sigma_\epsilon}{\sigma_2} - \frac{\sigma_\epsilon}{\sigma_3}\right)(I_N \otimes P_{MLT}). \tag{10.4.9}$$

The generalized least-squares (GLS) estimator of (10.4.1) is equivalent to the least-squares estimator of

$$y^*_{ij\ell t} = y_{ij\ell t} - \left(1 - \frac{\sigma_\epsilon}{\sigma_1}\right)\bar{y}_{ij\ell .} - \left(\frac{\sigma_\epsilon}{\sigma_1} - \frac{\sigma_\epsilon}{\sigma_2}\right)\bar{y}_{ij..} - \left(\frac{\sigma_\epsilon}{\sigma_2} - \frac{\sigma_\epsilon}{\sigma_3}\right)\bar{y}_{i...}, \tag{10.4.10}$$

on

$$\mathbf{x}^*_{ij\ell t} = x_{ij\ell t} - \left(1 - \frac{\sigma_\epsilon}{\sigma_1}\right)\bar{\mathbf{x}}_{ij\ell .} - \left(\frac{\sigma_\epsilon}{\sigma_1} - \frac{\sigma_\epsilon}{\sigma_2}\right)\bar{\mathbf{x}}_{ij..} - \left(\frac{\sigma_\epsilon}{\sigma_2} - \frac{\sigma_\epsilon}{\sigma_3}\right)\bar{\mathbf{x}}_{i...}, \tag{10.4.11}$$

where $\bar{y}_{ij\ell .}(\bar{\mathbf{x}}_{ij\ell .})$, $\bar{y}_{ij..}(\bar{\mathbf{x}}_{ij..})$, and $\bar{y}_{i...}(\bar{\mathbf{x}}_{i...})$ indicate group averages. The application of feasible GLS can be carried out by replacing the variances in (10.4.10) and (10.4.11) by their estimates obtained from the three groupwise between estimates and the within estimate of the innermost group.

The pattern exhibited in (10.4.10) and (10.4.11) is suggestive of solutions for a higher-order hierarchy with a balanced structure. If the hierarchical structure is unbalanced, the Kronecker-product operation can no longer be applied. This introduces quite a bit of notational inconvenience into the algebra (e.g., Baltagi (1995, Chapter 9); Wansbeek and Kapteyn (1982)). Neither can the GLS estimator be molded into a simple transformation to a least-squares estimator. However, an unbalanced panel is made up of N top-level groups, each containing M_i second-level groups, the second-level groups containing the innermost L_{ij} subgroups, which in turn contain $T_{ij\ell}$ observations. The numbers of observations in the higher-level groups are thus $T_{ij} = \sum_{\ell=1}^{L_{ij}} T_{ij\ell}$ and $T_i = \sum_{j=1}^{M_i} T_{ij}$, and the total number of observations is $H = \sum_{i=1}^{N} T_i$. The number of top-level groups is N, the number of second-level groups is $F = \sum_{i=1}^{N} M_i$, and the number of bottom-level groups is $G = \sum_{i=1}^{N} \sum_{j=1}^{M_i} L_{ij}$. We can redefine the J-matrices to be block-diagonal of size $H \times H$, corresponding in structure to the groups or subgroups they represent. They can be constructed explicitly by using *group membership* matrices consisting of ones and zeros that uniquely assign each of the H observations to one of the G (or F or N) groups. Antweiler (2001) has derived the maximum likelihood estimator for panels with unbalanced hierarchy.

When data constitute a multilevel hierarchical structure, the application of a simple error-component estimation, although inefficient, remains consistent under the assumption that the error component is independent of the regressors. However, the estimated standard errors of the slope coefficients are usually biased downward.

10.5 ERRORS OF MEASUREMENT

Thus far we have assumed that variables are observed without errors. Economic quantities, however, are frequently measured with errors, particularly if longitudinal information is collected through one-time retrospective surveys, which are notoriously susceptible to recall errors. If variables are indeed subject to measurement errors, exploiting panel data to control for the effects of unobserved individual characteristics using standard differenced estimators (deviations from means, etc.) may result in even more biased estimates than simple least-squares estimators using cross-sectional data alone.

Consider, for example, the following single-equation model (Solon (1985)):

$$y_{it} = \alpha_i^* + \beta x_{it} + u_{it}, \qquad \begin{array}{l} i = 1, \ldots, N, \\ t = 1, \ldots, T, \end{array} \tag{10.5.1}$$

where u_{it} is independently identically distributed, with mean zero and variance σ_u^2, and $\text{Cov}(x_{it}, u_{is}) = \text{Cov}(\alpha_i^*, u_{it}) = 0$ for any t and s, but $\text{Cov}(x_{it}, \alpha_i^*) \neq 0$. Suppose further that we observe not x_{it} itself, but rather the error-ridden measure

$$x_{it}^* = x_{it} + \tau_{it}, \tag{10.5.2}$$

where $\text{Cov}(x_{is}, \tau_{it}) = \text{Cov}(\alpha_i^*, \tau_{it}) = \text{Cov}(u_{it}, \tau_{is}) = 0$, and $\text{Var}(\tau_{it}) = \sigma_\tau^2$, $\text{Cov}(\tau_{it}, \tau_{i,t-1}) = \gamma_\tau \sigma_\tau^2$.

If we estimate (10.5.1) by OLS with cross-sectional data for period t, the estimator converges (as $N \to \infty$) to

$$\operatorname*{plim}_{N\to\infty} \hat{\beta}_{\text{LS}} = \beta + \frac{\text{Cov}(x_{it}, \alpha_i^*)}{\sigma_x^2 + \sigma_\tau^2} - \frac{\beta \sigma_\tau^2}{\sigma_x^2 + \sigma_\tau^2}, \tag{10.5.3}$$

where $\sigma_x^2 = \text{Var}(x_{it})$. The inconsistency of the least-squares estimator involves two terms: the first due to the failure to control for the individual effects α_i^*, and the second due to measurement error.

If we have panel data, say $T = 2$, we can alternatively first-difference the data to eliminate the individual effects α_i^*,

$$y_{it} - y_{i,t-1} = \beta(x_{it}^* - x_{i,t-1}^*) + [(u_{it} - \beta\tau_{it}) - (u_{i,t-1} - \beta\tau_{i,t-1})], \tag{10.5.4}$$

and then apply least squares. The probability limit of the differenced estimator as $N \to \infty$ becomes

$$\begin{aligned}\operatorname*{plim}_{N\to\infty} \hat{\beta}_d &= \beta\left[1 - \frac{2(1-\gamma_\tau)\sigma_\tau^2}{\operatorname{Var}(x_{it}^* - x_{i,t-1}^*)}\right] \\ &= \beta - \frac{\beta\sigma_\tau^2}{[(1-\gamma_x)/(1-\gamma_\tau)]\sigma_x^2 + \sigma_\tau^2},\end{aligned} \tag{10.5.5}$$

where γ_x is the first-order serial-correlation coefficient of x_{it}. The estimator $\hat{\beta}_d$ eliminates the first source of inconsistency, but may aggravate the second. If $\gamma_x > \gamma_\tau$, the inconsistency due to measurement error is larger for $\hat{\beta}_d$ than for $\hat{\beta}_{\text{LS}}$. This occurs because if the serial correlation of the measurement error is less than that of the true x (as seems often likely to be the case), first-differencing increases the noise-to-signal ratio for the measured explanatory variable.

The standard treatment for the errors-in-variables models requires extraneous information in the form of either additional data (replication and/or instrumental variables) or additional assumptions to identify the parameters of interest (e.g., Aigner et al. (1984)). With panel data, we can use a different transformation of the data to induce different and deducible changes in the biases in the estimated parameters that can then be used to identify the importance of measurement errors and recover the "true" parameters (Ashenfelter, Deaton, and Solon (1984); Griliches and Hausman (1986)). For instance, if the measurement error τ_{it} is i.i.d. across i and t, and x is serially correlated,[3] then in the foregoing example we can use $x_{i,t-2}^*$ or $(x_{i,t-2}^* - x_{i,t-3}^*)$ as instruments for $(x_{it}^* - x_{i,t-1}^*)$ as long as $T > 3$. Thus, even though T may be finite, the resulting IV estimator is consistent when N tends to infinity.

Alternatively, we can obtain consistent estimates through a comparison of magnitudes of the bias arrived at by subjecting a model to different transformations (Griliches and Hausman (1986)). For instance, if we use a covariance transformation to eliminate the contributions of unobserved individual components, we have

$$(y_{it} - \bar{y}_i) = \beta(x_{it}^* - \bar{x}_i^*) + [(u_{it} - \bar{u}_i) - \beta(\tau_{it} - \bar{\tau}_i)], \tag{10.5.6}$$

where $\bar{y}_i$, $\bar{x}_i^*$, $\bar{u}_i$, and $\bar{\tau}_i$ are individual time means of respective variables. The LS regression of (10.5.6) converges to

$$\operatorname*{plim}_{N\to\infty} \beta_w = \beta\left[1 - \frac{T-1}{T}\frac{\sigma_\tau^2}{\operatorname{Var}(x_{it}^* - \bar{x}_i^*)}\right]. \tag{10.5.7}$$

Then consistent estimators of β and σ_τ^2 can be found from (10.5.5) and (10.5.7),

$$\hat{\beta} = \left[\frac{2\hat{\beta}_w}{\text{Var}(x_{it}^* - x_{i,t-1}^*)} - \frac{(T-1)\hat{\beta}_d}{T\ \text{Var}(x_{it}^* - \bar{x}_i^*)}\right] \times \left[\frac{2}{\text{Var}(x_{it}^* - x_{i,t-1}^*)} - \frac{T-1}{T\ \text{Var}(x_{it}^* - \bar{x}_i^*)}\right]^{-1}, \tag{10.5.8}$$

$$\hat{\sigma}_\tau^2 = \frac{\hat{\beta} - \hat{\beta}_d}{\hat{\beta}} \cdot \frac{\text{Var}(x_{it}^* - x_{i,t-1}^*)}{2}. \tag{10.5.9}$$

In general, if the measurement errors are known to possess certain structures, consistent estimators may be available from a method-of-moments and/or from an IV approach by utilizing the panel structure of the data. Moreover, the first-difference and the within estimators are not the only ones that will give us an implicit estimate of the bias. In fact, there are $T/2$ such independent estimates. For a six-period cross section with τ_{it} independently identically distributed, we can compute estimates of β and σ_τ^2 from $y_6 - y_1$, $y_5 - y_2$, and $y_4 - y_3$ using the relationships

$$\begin{aligned} \operatorname*{plim}_{N\to\infty} \hat{\beta}_{61} &= \beta - 2\beta\sigma_\tau^2/\text{Var}(x_{i6}^* - x_{i1}^*), \\ \operatorname*{plim}_{N\to\infty} \hat{\beta}_{52} &= \beta - 2\beta\sigma_\tau^2/\text{Var}(x_{i5}^* - x_{i2}^*), \\ \operatorname*{plim}_{N\to\infty} \hat{\beta}_{43} &= \beta - 2\beta\sigma_\tau^2/\text{Var}(x_{i4}^* - x_{i3}^*). \end{aligned} \tag{10.5.10}$$

Thus, there are alternative consistent estimators. This fact can be exploited to test the assumptions with regard to measurement errors, which provide the rationale for the validity of the instruments, by investigating whether or not the alternative estimates of β are mutually coherent (e.g., Griliches and Hausman (1986)). The moment conditions (10.5.5), (10.5.7), and (10.5.10) can also be combined to obtain efficient estimates of β and σ_τ^2 by the use of Chamberlain's π method (Section 3.9) or a generalized method-of-moments estimator.

For instance, transforming $\mathbf{y}$ and $\mathbf{x}$ by the transformation matrix P_s such that $P_s\mathbf{e}_T = \mathbf{0}$ eliminates the individual effects from the model (10.5.1). Regressing the transformed $\mathbf{y}$ on transformed $\mathbf{x}$ yields an estimator that is a function of $\beta, \sigma_x^2, \sigma_\tau$, and the serial correlations of x and τ. Wansbeek and Koning (1989) have provided a general formula for the estimators that are based on various transformation of the data. Letting

$$Y^* = \mathbf{e}_{NT}\mu + X^*\boldsymbol{\beta} + \mathbf{v}^*, \tag{10.5.11}$$

where $Y^* = (\mathbf{y}_1^{*\prime}, \dots, \mathbf{y}_T^{*\prime})'$, $\mathbf{y}_t^* = (y_{1t}, \dots, y_{Nt})'$, $X^* = (\mathbf{x}_1^{*\prime}, \dots, \mathbf{x}_T^{*\prime})'$, $\mathbf{x}_t^* = (\mathbf{x}_{1t}, \dots, \mathbf{x}_{Nt})'$, $\mathbf{v}^* = (\mathbf{v}_1^{*\prime}, \dots, \mathbf{v}_T^{*\prime})'$, $\mathbf{v}_t^* = (v_{1t}, \dots, v_{Nt})'$ and $v_{it} = (\alpha_i^* - \mu) + u_{it}$. Then

$$\begin{aligned} \hat{\mathbf{b}}_s &= [X^{*\prime}(Q_s \otimes I_N)X^*]^{-1}[X^{*\prime}(Q_s \otimes I_N)Y^*] \\ &= \boldsymbol{\beta} + [X^{*\prime}(Q_s \otimes I_N)X^*]^{-1}[X^{*\prime}(Q_s \otimes I_N)(\mathbf{u}^* - \boldsymbol{\tau}^*\boldsymbol{\beta})], \end{aligned} \tag{10.5.12}$$

where $Q_s = P_s'P_s$, $\mathbf{u}^* = (\mathbf{u}_1^{*\prime}, \ldots, \mathbf{u}_T^{*\prime})'$, $\mathbf{u}_t^* = (u_{1t}, \ldots, u_{Nt})'$, $\boldsymbol{\tau}^* = (\boldsymbol{\tau}_1^*, \ldots, \boldsymbol{\tau}_T^*)'$, and $\boldsymbol{\tau}_t^* = (\boldsymbol{\tau}_{1t}, \ldots, \boldsymbol{\tau}_{Nt})'$. In the case of $K = 1$ and measurement errors serially uncorrelated, Wansbeek and Koning (1989) show that the m different transformed estimators $\mathbf{b} = (b_1, \ldots, b_m)'$ converge to

$$\sqrt{N}\big(\mathbf{b} - \beta\big(\mathbf{e}_m - \sigma_\tau^2\boldsymbol{\phi}\big)\big] \sim N(\mathbf{0}, V), \tag{10.5.13}$$

where $\boldsymbol{\phi} = (\phi_1, \ldots, \phi_m)'$, $\phi_s = (\text{tr } Q_s/\text{tr } Q_s\Sigma_{x^*})$,

$$\Sigma_{x^*} = \text{Cov}(\mathbf{x}_i^*), \qquad x_i^* = (\mathbf{x}_{i1}^*, \ldots, \mathbf{x}_{iT}^*)', \tag{10.5.14}$$

$$V = F'\big\{\sigma_u^2\Sigma_{x^*} \otimes I_T + \beta^2\sigma_\tau^2\big(\Sigma_{x^*} + \sigma_\tau^2 I_T\big) \otimes I_T\big\}F, \tag{10.5.15}$$

and F is the $T^2 \times m$ matrix with the sth column $\mathbf{f}_s = \text{vec}(Q_s)/(\text{tr } Q_s\Sigma_{x^*})$, where vec$(A)$ denotes the operation of transforming an $m \times n$ matrix A into an $mn \times 1$ vector by stacking the columns of A one underneath the other (Magnus and Neudecker (1999, p. 30)). Then one can obtain an efficient estimator by minimizing

$$\big[\mathbf{b} - \beta(\mathbf{e}_m - \sigma_\tau^2\boldsymbol{\phi})\big]'V^{-1}\big[\mathbf{b} - \beta\big(\mathbf{e}_m - \sigma_\tau^2\boldsymbol{\phi}\big)\big] \tag{10.5.16}$$

with respect to β and σ_τ^2, which yields

$$\hat{\beta} = \left\{\frac{\boldsymbol{\phi}'V^{-1}\mathbf{b}}{\boldsymbol{\phi}'V^{-1}\boldsymbol{\phi}} - \frac{\mathbf{e}_m'V^{-1}\mathbf{b}}{\mathbf{e}_m'V^{-1}\boldsymbol{\phi}}\right\} \Big/ \left\{\frac{\boldsymbol{\phi}'V^{-1}\mathbf{e}}{\boldsymbol{\phi}'V^{-1}\boldsymbol{\phi}} - \frac{\mathbf{e}_m'V^{-1}\mathbf{e}_m}{\mathbf{e}_m'V^{-1}\boldsymbol{\phi}}\right\}, \tag{10.5.17}$$

and

$$\hat{\sigma}_\tau^2 = \left\{\frac{\boldsymbol{\phi}'V^{-1}\mathbf{e}_m}{\boldsymbol{\phi}'V^{-1}\mathbf{b}} - \frac{\mathbf{e}_m'V^{-1}\mathbf{e}_m}{\mathbf{e}_m'V^{-1}\mathbf{b}}\right\} \Big/ \left\{\frac{\boldsymbol{\phi}'V^{-1}\boldsymbol{\phi}}{\boldsymbol{\phi}'V^{-1}\mathbf{b}} - \frac{\mathbf{e}_m'V^{-1}\boldsymbol{\phi}}{\mathbf{e}_m'V^{-1}\mathbf{b}}\right\}. \tag{10.5.18}$$

Extensions of this simple model to serially correlated measurement errors are given by Biørn (1992) and by Hsiao and Taylor (1991). In the case of only one regressor measured with error for a linear panel data model, Wansbeek (2001) has provided a neat framework to derive the moment conditions under a variety of measurement-error assumptions by stacking the matrix of covariances between the vector of dependent variables and the regressors, then projecting out nuisance parameters. To illustrate the basic idea, consider a linear model,

$$y_{it} = \alpha_i^* + \beta x_{it} + \boldsymbol{\gamma}'\mathbf{w}_{it} + \mathbf{u}_{it}, \qquad \begin{aligned} i &= 1, \ldots, N, \\ t &= 1, \ldots, T, \end{aligned} \tag{10.5.19}$$

where x_{it} is not observed. Instead one observes x_{it}^*, which is related to $\mathbf{x}_{it}$ by (10.5.2). Suppose that the $T \times 1$ measurement-error vector $\boldsymbol{\tau}_i = (\tau_{i1}, \ldots, \tau_{iT})'$ is i.i.d. with mean zero and covariance matrix $\Omega = E(\boldsymbol{\tau}_i\boldsymbol{\tau}_i')$.

Suppose Ω has a structure of the form

$$\text{vec } \Omega = R_0\boldsymbol{\lambda}, \tag{10.5.20}$$

where vec denotes the operation that stacks the rows of a matrix one after another in column-vector form, R is a matrix of order $T^2 \times m$ with known elements, and $\boldsymbol{\lambda}$ is an $m \times 1$ vector of unknown constants. Using the covariance transformation matrix $Q = I_T - \frac{1}{T}\mathbf{e}_T\mathbf{e}_T'$ to eliminate the individual effects α_i^* yields

$$Q\mathbf{y}_i = Q\mathbf{x}_i\beta + QW_i\boldsymbol{\gamma} + Q\mathbf{u}_i, \tag{10.5.21}$$

$$Q\mathbf{x}_i^* = Q\mathbf{x}_i + Q\boldsymbol{\tau}_i, \tag{10.5.22}$$

where $\mathbf{x}_i = (x_{i1}, \ldots, x_{iT})'$, $W_i = (\mathbf{w}_{it}')$. Let

$$R \equiv (I_T \otimes Q)R_0. \tag{10.5.23}$$

From (10.5.2), we have

$$\begin{aligned} E(\boldsymbol{\tau}_i \otimes Q\boldsymbol{\tau}_i) &= (I_T \otimes Q)E(\boldsymbol{\tau}_i \otimes \boldsymbol{\tau}_i) \\ &= (I_T \otimes Q)R_0\boldsymbol{\lambda} \\ &= R\boldsymbol{\lambda}. \end{aligned} \tag{10.5.24}$$

It follows that

$$\begin{aligned} E(\mathbf{x}_i^* \otimes Q\mathbf{x}_i) &= E(\mathbf{x}_i^* \otimes Q\mathbf{x}_i^*) - E[(\mathbf{x}_i + \boldsymbol{\tau}_i) \otimes Q\boldsymbol{\tau}_i] \\ &= E(\mathbf{x}_i^* \otimes Q\mathbf{x}_i^*) - R\boldsymbol{\lambda}. \end{aligned} \tag{10.5.25}$$

Therefore,

$$E(\mathbf{x}_i^* \otimes Q\mathbf{y}_i) = E(\mathbf{x}_i^* \otimes Q\mathbf{x}_i^*)\beta + E(\mathbf{x}_i^* \otimes QW_i)\boldsymbol{\gamma} - \mathbf{R}\boldsymbol{\lambda}\beta. \tag{10.5.26}$$

Equation (10.5.26) contains the nuisance parameter $\boldsymbol{\lambda}$. To eliminate it, multiplying by $M_R = I_{T^2} - R(R'R)^{-1}R'$ on both sides of (10.5.26), we have the orthogonality conditions

$$M_R E\{\mathbf{x}_i^* \otimes Q(\mathbf{y}_i - \mathbf{x}_i^*\beta - W_i\boldsymbol{\gamma})\} = \mathbf{0}. \tag{10.5.27}$$

Combining (10.5.27) with the moment conditions $E(W_i'Q\mathbf{u}_i) = \mathbf{0}$, we have the moment conditions for the measurement error model (10.5.19):

$$EM(\mathbf{d}_i - C_i\boldsymbol{\theta}) = \mathbf{0}, \tag{10.5.28}$$

where

$$M = \begin{bmatrix} M_r & \mathbf{0} \\ \mathbf{0} & I_K \end{bmatrix}, \qquad \mathbf{d}_i = \begin{bmatrix} \mathbf{x}_i^* \otimes I_T \\ W_i' \end{bmatrix},$$

$$C_i = \begin{bmatrix} \mathbf{x}_i^* \otimes I_T \\ W_i' \end{bmatrix} Q(\mathbf{x}_i^*, W_i), \qquad \boldsymbol{\theta}' = (\beta, \boldsymbol{\gamma}').$$

A GMM estimator is obtained by minimizing

$$\frac{1}{N}\left[\sum_{i=1}^{N} M(\mathbf{d}_i - C_i\boldsymbol{\theta})\right]' A_N \left[\sum_{i=1}^{N} M(\mathbf{d}_i - C_i\boldsymbol{\theta})\right]. \tag{10.5.29}$$

An optimal GMM estimator is to let

$$A_N^{-1} = \frac{1}{N}\sum_{i=1}^{N}(\mathbf{d}_i - C_i\hat{\boldsymbol{\theta}})(\mathbf{d}_i - \mathbf{C}_i\hat{\boldsymbol{\theta}})', \tag{10.5.30}$$

where $\hat{\boldsymbol{\theta}}$ is some consistent estimator of $\boldsymbol{\theta}$ such as

$$\hat{\boldsymbol{\theta}} = \left[\left(\sum_{i=1}^{N} C_i'\right) M \left(\sum_{i=1}^{N} C_i\right)\right]^{-1}\left[\left(\sum_{i=1}^{N} C_i\right)' M \left(\sum_{i=1}^{N} \mathbf{d}_i\right)\right]. \tag{10.5.31}$$

In the case when τ_{it} is i.i.d. across i and over t, Ω is diagonal with equal diagonal elements. Then $m = 1$ and $R_0 =$ vec I_T, $R = (I_T \otimes Q)$ vec $I_T =$ vec Q, $R'R = \text{tr}\, Q = T - 1$, and $M_R = I_{T^2} - \frac{1}{T-1}(\text{vec}\, Q)\,(\text{vec}\, Q)'$. When Ω is diagonal with distinct diagonal elements, $m = T$ and $R_0 = \mathbf{i}_t\mathbf{i}_t' \otimes \mathbf{i}_t$, where $\mathbf{i}_t$ is the tth unit vector of order T. When τ_{it} is a first-order moving average process and $T = 4$,

$$\Omega = \begin{bmatrix} a & c & 0 & 0 \\ c & b & c & 0 \\ 0 & c & b & c \\ 0 & 0 & c & a \end{bmatrix};$$

then

$$R_0 = \begin{bmatrix} 1 & 0 & 0 & 0 & 0 & 0 & 0 & 0 & 0 & 0 & 0 & 0 & 0 & 0 & 0 & 1 \\ 0 & 0 & 0 & 0 & 0 & 1 & 0 & 0 & 0 & 0 & 1 & 0 & 0 & 0 & 0 & 0 \\ 0 & 1 & 0 & 0 & 1 & 0 & 1 & 0 & 0 & 1 & 0 & 1 & 0 & 0 & 1 & 0 \end{bmatrix},$$

and $\boldsymbol{\lambda} = (a, b, c)'$.

Further variations on the covariance structure of the regressor x or the disturbance term u_{it} in a linear framework can also be put in this framework. For detail, see Wansbeek (2001).

The measurement errors for nonlinear models are much more difficult to handle (e.g., Hsiao (1992c)). For dynamic models with measurement errors, see Wansbeek and Kapteyn (1982). For binary-choice models with measurement errors, see Kao and Schnell (1987a, 1987b) and Hsiao (1991b).

10.6 MODELING CROSS-SECTIONAL DEPENDENCE

Most panel studies assume that apart from the possible presence of individual-invariant but period-varying time-specific effects, the effects of omitted variables are independently distributed across cross-sectional units. However, often economic theory predicts that agents take actions that lead to interdependence among themselves. For example, the prediction that risk-averse agents will make insurance contracts allowing them to smooth idiosyncratic shocks implies dependence in consumption across individuals. Kelejian and Prucha (2001) and

Pinkse (2000) have suggested tests of cross-sectional dependence based on the spatial correlation analogue of the Durbin–Watson and Box–Pierce tests for time-series correlations; but unfortunately, contrary to the time-series data in which the time label gives a natural ordering and structure, general forms of dependence for cross-sectional dimension are difficult to formulate. Therefore, econometricians have relied on strong parametric assumptions to model cross-sectional dependence.

Often, cross-sectional dependence is modeled in terms of some distance measure between cross-section units, and a spatial analogue of an autoregressive moving-average model is used (e.g., Anselin and Griffith (1988); Case (1991)). For example, Conley (1999) suggests using the notion of *economic distance* to model proximity between two economic agents. The joint distribution of random variables at a set of points is assumed to be a function of the "economic distances" between them. In particular, the population of individuals may be assumed to reside in a low-dimensional Euclidean space, say R^2, with each individual i located at a point s_i. The sample then consists of realizations of agents' random variables at a collection of locations $\{s_i\}$ inside a sample region. If two agents' locations s_i and s_j are close, then y_{it} and y_{js} may be highly correlated. As the distance between s_i and s_j grows large, y_{it} and y_{js} approach independence. The joint distribution of random variables at a set of points is assumed to be invariant to a shift in location and is a function of the economic distances between them. Under this assumption, the dependence among cross-sectional data can be estimated using methods analogous to time-series procedures either parametrically or nonparametrically (e.g., Hall, Fisher, and Hoffman (1992); Priestley (1982); Newey and West (1987)).

While the approach of defining cross-sectional dependence in terms of economic distance allows for more complicated dependences than models with time-specific (or group-specific) effects, it also requires that the econometricians have information regarding this distance. In certain urban, environmental, development, growth, and other areas of economics, this information may be available. For instance, in the investigation of people's willingness to pay for local public goods, the relevant economic distance may be the time and monetary cost of traveling between points to use these goods. Alternatively if the amenity is air quality, then local weather conditions might constitute the major unobservable. Other examples include studies of risk sharing in rural developing economies where the primary shocks to individuals may be weather-related. If so, measures of weather correlation on farms of two individuals could be the proxy for the economic distance between them.

CHAPTER 11

A Summary View

11.1 INTRODUCTION

The preceding chapters have presented a wide variety of analytical tools developed by econometricians for estimating behavioral equations using panel data. In choosing the proper method for exploiting the richness and unique properties of panel data it is helpful to keep several factors in mind. First, what advantages do panel data offer us in investigating economic issues over data sets consisting of a single cross section or time series? Second, what are the limitations of panel data and the econometric methods that have been proposed for analyzing such data? Third, when using panel data, how can we increase the efficiency of parameter estimates? Fourth, the usefulness of panel data in providing particular answers to certain issues depends on the compatibility between the assumptions underlying the statistical inference procedures and the data-generating process.

11.2 BENEFITS AND LIMITATIONS OF PANEL DATA

The use of panel data provides major benefits for econometric estimation in at least four areas: (1) increasing degrees of freedom and reducing problems of data multicollinearity, (2) identifying economic models and discriminating between competing economic hypotheses, (3) eliminating or reducing estimation bias, and (4) providing micro foundations for aggregate data analysis. However, the special features of panel data can often create new and difficult econometric problems, particularly in nonlinear models.

11.2.1 Increasing Degrees of Freedom and Lessening the Problem of Multicollinearity

The shortage of degrees of freedom and severe multicollinearity in time-series data often frustrate economists who wish to determine the individual influence of each explanatory variable. This problem arises because the information provided by the sample is not rich enough to meet the information requirements of the model as specified. Given this situation, one must either augment the sample information or reduce the information requirements of the model (as by imposing prior restrictions on the parameters). Panel data, because they offer many more degrees of freedom and information on individual attributes, can reduce the gap between the information requirements of a model and the information provided by the data (Section 1.1 or Fujiki, Hsiao, and Shen (2002); Hsiao, Mountain, and Ho-Illman (1995)).

11.2.2 Identification and Discrimination between Competing Hypotheses

In economics, as in other branches of the social and behavioral sciences, often there are competing theories. Examples of these include the effect of collective bargaining on wages, the appropriate short-term policy to alleviate unemployment (Chapters 1, 7 and 8), the effects of schooling on earnings (Chapter 5), and the question of causal ordering. Economists on opposite sides of these issues generally have very different views on the operation of the economy and the influence of institutions on economic performance. Some economists believe unions indeed raise wages or that advertising truly generates greater sales. Adherents of the opposite view tend to regard the effects more as epiphenomena than as substantive forces and believe that observed differences are mainly due to sorting of workers or firms by characteristics (e.g., Allison (2000)).

Aggregate time-series data are not particularly useful for discriminating between hypotheses that depend on microeconomic attributes. Nor will a single individual time-series data set provide information on the effects of different sociodemographic factors. Cross-sectional data, while containing variations in microeconomic and demographic variables, cannot be used to model dynamics or causal ordering. The estimated coefficients from a single cross section are more likely to reflect interindividual or interfirm differences than intraindividual or intrafirm dynamics, unless data on variables controlling for these differences are available and are explicitly included in the chosen specification. For example, if information on worker quality is not available, a cross-sectionally estimated coefficient for union status in a wage equation may reflect either the effect of trade unions or differences in worker quality. Similarly, the finding that there exists a negative relationship between measures of self-esteem and delinquent behavior in a cross-sectional data set (Jang and Thornberry (1998)) cannot answer the question: Does delinquency lead to low self-esteem, or does low self-esteem lead to delinquency?

Panel data, by providing sequential observations for a number of individuals, often allow us to distinguish interindividual differences from intraindividual differences and to construct a proper recursive structure for studying the issue in question through a before-and-after effect (e.g., Hsiao (1979a, 1979b, 1982)). For instance, in the foregoing example, even if information on worker quality is not available, if a worker's ability stays constant or changes only slowly, the within correlation between the union-status dummy and the worker-quality variable is likely to be negligible. Thus, worker quality can be controlled through the use of within estimates. The resulting coefficient for the union-status dummy then will provide a measure of the effect of unionism (Chapters 3 and 4).

Moreover, proper recognition of the additional sources of variation can also provide very useful information for discriminating individual behavior from average behavior or for identifying an otherwise unidentified model. For example, in the income–schooling model, the availability of family groupings can provide an additional set of cross-sibling covariances via a set of common omitted variables. These additional restrictions can be combined with the conventional slope restrictions to identify what would otherwise be unidentified structure parameters (Section 5.4).

Furthermore, addition of the cross-sectional dimension to the time-series dimension provides a distinct possibility of identifying the pattern of serial correlations in the residuals and of identifying the lag adjustment patterns when the conditioning variables are changed, without having to impose prior parametric specifications (Sections 3.9 and 9.1) or identifying a model subject to measurement errors (Section 10.5).

11.2.3 Reducing Estimation Bias

A fundamental statistical problem facing every econometrician is the *specification problem*. By that we mean the selection of variables to be included in a behavioral relationship as well as the manner in which these variables are related to the variables that affect the outcome but appear in the equation only through the error term. If the effects of the omitted variables are correlated with the included explanatory variables, and if these correlations are not explicitly allowed for, the resulting estimates will be biased. In order to minimize the bias, it is helpful to distinguish four types of correlations between the included variables and the error term. The first type is due to the correlation between the included exogenous variables and those variables that should be included in the equation but are not, either because of a specification error or because of unavailability of data. The second type is due to the dynamic structure of the model and the persistence of the shocks that give rise to the correlation between lagged dependent variables and the error term. The third type is due to the simultaneity of the model, which gives rise to the correlation between the jointly dependent variables and the error terms. The fourth type is due to measurement errors in the explanatory variables. Knowing the different sources of correlations provides important information for devising consistent estimators. It also helps one avoid the possibility of eliminating one source of bias while aggravating another (e.g., Section 5.1).

11.2.3.a Omitted-Variable Bias

Empirical results are often criticized on the grounds that the researcher has not explicitly recognized the effects of omitted variables that are correlated with the included explanatory variables (in the union example, the omitted variable, worker quality, can be correlated with the included variable, union status). If the effects of these omitted variables stay constant for a given individual through time or are the same for all individuals in a given time period, the omitted-variable bias can be eliminated by one of the following three methods when panel data are available: (1) differencing the sample observations to eliminate the individual-specific and/or time-specific effects; (2) using dummy variables to capture the effects of individual-invariant and/or time-invariant variables; or (3) postulating a conditional distribution of unobserved effects, given observed exogenous variables.

For linear-regression models, any of these three methods can be used to eliminate the bias created by the omitted invariant variables (Chapter 3). Furthermore, both the dummy-variable (fixed-effects) approach and the random-effects approach of specifying a conditional distribution of the effects, given the observed exogenous variables, lead to the same covariance estimator of the slope coefficient if the component of the error term that varies across individuals and over time is i.i.d. (Section 3.4). Under other assumptions, although the covariance estimator for the slope coefficient may not be efficient, it remains unbiased and consistent. As a result, the fixed-effects approach has assumed paramount importance in empirical studies.

Unfortunately, the results for the linear model are really very special and generally are not applicable for nonlinear models. In nonlinear models, the fixed-effect and the random-effects approaches yield different estimators. Moreover, contrary to the linear case, in general, the Neyman–Scott principle of separating the estimation of the common coefficients from the estimation of the specific effects is not applicable. If the number of unknown specific effects increases at the same rate as the sample size, attempts to estimate the specific effects will create the incidental-parameter problem. Hence, the fixed-effects approach may not yield consistent estimates of the common coefficients (Chapters 7 and 8). For general nonlinear model with fixed effects there does not appear to exist a generally applicable analytical framework to obtain consistent estimators of the parameters that are common across individuals and over time (structural parameters). To devise consistent estimators of the structural parameters one has to exploit the specific structure of a nonlinear model. The three most commonly used approaches are: (i) the conditional approach, which conditions on the minimum sufficient statistics of the effects, (ii) the semiparametric approach, which exploits the latent linear structure of a model, and (iii) reparameterization of the model so that the information matrix of the reparametrized individual effects are uncorrelated with the reparameterized structural parameters (Lancaster (2001)). But none of these approaches is generally applicable for general nonlinear models. Whether they will yield consistent estimators has to be considered case by case.

On the other hand, the random-effects approach replaces the probability distribution of the dependent variables conditional on the specific effects and the exogenous variables by a probability distribution function that is conditional on the explanatory variables only. Because the probability function of the effects in general depends only on a finite number of parameters, there is no longer an incidental-parameter problem. However, between the linear and nonlinear models there is a very important difference. In linear models, we do not have to make specific assumptions. We need only to decompose the specific effects into two components: their projections on observed exogenous variables and orthogonal residuals (Section 3.9). In nonlinear models, we often have to assume that the conditional mean of the specific effects on observed exogenous variables is actually linear and that the distribution of the effects, given explanatory variables, can be specified parametrically (e.g., Chapters 7 and 8). These are restrictive assumptions, and there would be a payoff to relaxing them.

11.2.3.b Bias Induced by the Dynamic Structure of a Model

It is useful to distinguish between two sources of bias: One is ignoring the time-persistent errors that are correlated with the lagged dependent variables; the other is the incorrect modeling of initial observations (Chapter 4 and Section 7.5). The issue of correlation between the residuals and lagged dependent variables is not affected by the size of the time-series observations, T, whereas the initial-value problem arises only when there is no specific information to model the initial observation and T is small. When T is large, the weight of the initial observation in the likelihood function becomes negligible, and it is appropriate to ignore this issue. When T is small and the model and the data are such that it is appropriate to treat the initial observation as random, the correct procedure for eliminating the bias induced by the correlation between the initial observation and the residual depends on the pattern of serial dependence of the error term.

If the model is linear and the time-persistent error is the sum of two components, one being individually time-invariant and the other being independently distributed, then the individual time-invariant effects can be eliminated by differencing successive observations of an individual. We can then use lagged dependent variables (of sufficiently high order) as instruments for the transformed model to circumvent the issues of both the initial observation and the serial dependence of the residual (Sections 4.3 and 4.5).

If the error terms have arbitrary patterns of serial correlations, as long as the assumption of independence across individual attributes holds, we can stack all T period observations for a given individual's behavioral equation as T equations in a given model and condition the initial observation on all the observed exogenous variables. Consistent estimates of the coefficients and the serial covariance matrix can then be obtained by using simultaneous-equations estimation methods in the same way that one would if there were only cross-sectional data for a simultaneous-equations model (Sections 4.3 and 4.6).

For the nonlinear case, specific distributional assumptions about the initial value and the error process must be made (Sections 7.5 and 8.3). Often, given the nature of the model, estimation of the coefficients of a model and estimation of the parameters characterizing the error process cannot be separated. To obtain consistent estimates, the error process must be correctly specified or specified in a general form that encompasses the underlying process, and computationally complicated maximum likelihood estimators may have to be used. However, identification of the error process is a nontrivial job. A sequence of likelihood-ratio tests to narrow down the possible specifications cannot be performed without first obtaining maximum likelihood estimates of unknown parameters under various assumptions about the error process (e.g., Section 7.5).

11.2.3.c Simultaneity Bias

The standard approach to eliminate simultaneity bias is to use instrumental variables to purge the correlations between the joint dependent variables and the error terms. If the cross-equation correlations in the errors are unrestricted, then, just as in the case of conventional cross-sectional or time-series data, we use exogenous variables that are excluded from the equation as instruments for the jointly dependent variables that appear in the equation. If the cross-equation correlations are due to common omitted invariant variables, then, in addition to the excluded exogenous variables, we can also use included variables purged of these invariant effects as instruments (Sections 5.3 and 5.4).

11.2.3.d Bias Induced by Measurement Errors

Measurement errors in the explanatory variables create correlations between the regressors and the errors of the equation. If variables are subject to measurement errors, the common practice of differencing out individual effects eliminates one source of bias but creates another source, which may result in even more biased estimates than simple least-squares estimators. However, different transformation of the data can induce different and deducible changes in the parameters, which can be used to determine the importance of measurement errors and obtain consistent estimators of parameters of interest (Section 10.5).

11.2.4 Providing Micro Foundations for Aggregate Data Analysis

Aggregate data analysis often invokes the "representative agent" assumption. However, if micro units are heterogeneous, not only the time series properties of aggregate data can be very different from those of disaggregate data (e.g., Granger (1980); Lewbel (1992, 1994); Pesaran (1999)), policy evaluation based on aggregate data can be grossly misleading. Furthermore, the prediction of aggregate outcomes using aggregate data can be less accurate than the prediction based on micro-equations (e.g., Hsiao, Shen, and Fujiki (2002)). The variable coefficient models discussed in Chapter 6 is an attempt to make inference about the population taking account of the heterogeneity among micro units.

11.3 EFFICIENCY OF THE ESTIMATES

Because panel data usually contain a large number of observations, it might appear that the problem of efficiency is not as important a consideration as is consistency, but that is not necessarily the case. Assuming that the model is correctly specified, our example in Section 6.2 demonstrates that although the least-squares estimates ignoring the random-coefficient assumptions should be consistent, in practice they yield implausible results, as opposed to the efficient GLS estimates, which take account of the random nature of the cross-sectional units.

Intimately related to the problem of efficient use of the data is the issue of fixed-effects or random-effects inference. If the unobserved heterogeneity can be viewed as random draws from a common population, then it is more appropriate to postulate a random-effects model. If the unobserved heterogeneity is correlated with explanatory variables or comes from a heterogeneous population, then it is more appropriate to postulate a fixed-effects model. The fixed-effects formulation makes inference conditional on the specific effects; hence it has the advantage of not requiring one to postulate the distribution of the effects or (in particular, if it is complicated) the correlation pattern between the effects and included explanatory variables. However, there is also a loss of efficiency in conditional inference because of the loss of degrees of freedom in estimating the specific effects (Section 3.4; Chapters 7 and 8). Furthermore, as discussed earlier, if the model is not linear and the specific effects vary with the dimension in which the number of observations is increased, the fixed-effects inferences can create incidental-parameter problems that are likely to bias the estimates of the parameters that are common across individuals and through time (Chapters 4 and 7).

The random-effects inference, on the other hand, requires a distributional assumption with regard to the effects. If the model is nonlinear, the assumption needs to be very specific, and often the complicated maximum-likelihood method has to be used to obtain consistent estimates (Chapter 7). If the model is linear and (conditional on the explanatory variables) individual observations can be viewed as random draws from a common population, then the assumption can be in the general form of independently distributed effects, with common mean and finite variance–covariance matrix. The generalized-least-squares estimator is fairly simple to implement, provided we know the correlation pattern of the remaining residuals, and is asymptotically efficient. In the case in which T is fixed and the number of cross-sectional units, N, tends to infinity and the individual characteristics are independently distributed across cross-sectional units, we can also use the general approach of stacking an individual's behavioral equation over time periods as T equations in a given model and applying a minimum-distance procedure over cross-sectional observations to estimate common parameters. This procedure allows arbitrary serial correlation and certain forms of heteroscedasticity and yields consistent and efficient estimates when the error structure is unknown. Moreover, because the T-equation (serial) variance–covariance matrix can be consistently estimated without imposing a specific serial-dependence pattern, it also allows us to test the specific assumptions on the distribution of the error term (e.g., error-components formulation) (Chapters 3–6).

Although a panel contains both cross-sectional and time-series dimensions, most often it contains only a few observations in one dimension (usually the time dimension) and a great many observations in another dimension (usually the cross-sectional dimension). In order to obtain consistent estimates of the unknown parameters, we need the sample to increase in the dimension that yields information on the relevant parameters (Chapters 4, 7, 8; Sections 9.2–9.4). Thus, it is important to distinguish whether the panel tends to infinity in N or in T or in both N and T. On the basis of this information, one can then determine which parameters can, and which parameters cannot, be consistently estimated from a given panel data. The majority of this monograph focuses on the panels with large N and small T. Recently; panels with large N and T have gained more attentions (Sections 10.2 and 10.3). However, assumptions such as the individual specific effects stay constant over time may no longer appear as reasonable approximations to the reality when T becomes large. More realistic assumptions consistent with the data generating process will have to be postulated.

Finally, it should be noted that although panel data offer many advantages, they are not panacea. The power of panel data analysis depends critically on the compatibility of the assumptions of statistical tools with the data generating process. Otherwise, misleading inference will follow.

Notes

Chapter 1

1 For examples of marketing data, see Beckwith (1972); for biomedical data, see Sheiner, Rosenberg, and Melmon (1972); for a financial-market data base, see Dielman, Nantell, and Wright (1980).
2 Potential users interested in the ECHP can access and download the detailed documentation of the ECHP users' database (ECHP UDP) from the ECHP website: http://forum.europa.eu.int/irc/dsis/echpane/info/data/information.html.
3 This assumes that there are no other variables, such as consumption, that can act as a proxy for z_i. Most North American data sets do not contain information on consumption.
4 For a formal treatment of this, see Chapter 8.
5 Many issues discussed in Chapters 7 and 8 apply to general nonlinear models as well.

Chapter 2

1 This chapter is largely based on the work of Kuh (1963).
2 Note that even if the homogeneity hypothesis is rejected, some useful information can be found in pooling the data, as long as the source of sample variability can be identified. For details, see later chapters.
3 We assume that $T > K + 1$. For details of this, see Section 3.2.
4 See Johnston (1972, Chapter 6) for an illustration of the computation of analysis of covariance.
5 If the firm differences stay constant over time, heterogeneity among firms can be absorbed into the intercept term. Because intercepts are eliminated by first-differencing, the first-difference model (such as (2.3.1) or (2.3.3)) will be more likely to display homogeneous responses.
6 For further discussion of this issue, see Section 9.4 and Mairesse (1990).
7 For further discussion of investment expenditure behavior, see Chapter 6 or Hsiao and Tahmiscioglu (1997).

Chapter 3

1 These three different sorts of variations apply, of course, to both included and excluded variables. Throughout this monograph we shall mostly concentrate on relations between excluded individual time-invariant variables and included variables.

2 Although the notations are different, (3.2.5) is identical with (2.2.10).

3 Equation (3.2.7) can be viewed as a linear-regression model with singular-disturbance covariance matrix $\sigma_u^2 Q$. A generalization of Aitken's theorem leads to the generalized least-squares estimator

$$\hat{\boldsymbol{\beta}}_{\text{CV}} = \left[\sum_{i=1}^{N} X_i' Q' Q^- Q X_i\right]^{-1} \left[\sum_{i=1}^{N} X_i' Q' Q^- Q \mathbf{y}_i\right]$$
$$= \left[\sum_{i=1}^{N} X_i' Q X_i\right]^{-1} \left[\sum_{i=1}^{N} X_i' Q \mathbf{y}_i\right],$$

where Q^- is the generalized inverse of Q satisfying the conditions $QQ^-Q = Q$ (Theil (1971, Sections 6.6, 6.7)).

4 Because the slope coefficients are assumed the same for all i and t, for simplicity we shall not distinguish the individual mean corrected estimator and the within-group estimator as we did in Chapter 2. We shall simply refer to (3.2.8) or its equivalent as the within-group estimator.

5 Note that we follow the formulation of (3.2.10) in treating α_i and λ_t as deviations from the population mean. For ease of exposition we also restrict our attention to the homoscedastic variances of α_i and λ_t. For the heteroscedasticity generalization of the error-component model, see Section 3.7 or Mazodier and Trognon (1978) and Wansbeek and Kapteyn (1982). For a test of individual heteroscedasticity, see Holly and Gardiol (2000).

6 For details, see Section 3.3.2.

7 Equation (3.3.16) may yield a negative estimate of σ_α^2. For additional discussion on this issue, see Section 3.3.3.

8 The negative variance-components problem also arises in the two-step GLS method. As one can see from (3.3.15) and (3.3.16), there is no guarantee that (3.3.16) necessarily yields a positive estimate of σ_α^2. A practical guide in this situation is to replace a negative estimated variance component by its boundary value, zero. See Baltagi (1981b) and Maddala and Mount (1973) for Monte Carlo studies of the desirable results of using this procedure in terms of the mean squared error of the estimate. For additional discussion of the MLE of random-effects model, see Breusch (1987).

9 We note that the fixed-effects estimator, although not efficient, is consistent under the random-effects formulation (Section 3.3.1).

10 In this respect, if N becomes large, one would not be interested in the specific effect of each individual but rather in the characteristics of the population. A random-effects framework would be more appropriate.

11 If $(Y^{(1)\prime}, Y^{(2)\prime})'$ is normally distributed with mean $(\boldsymbol{\mu}^{(1)\prime}, \boldsymbol{\mu}^{(2)\prime})'$ and variance–covariance matrix

$$\begin{bmatrix} \Sigma_{11} & \Sigma_{12} \\ \Sigma_{21} & \Sigma_{22} \end{bmatrix},$$

the conditional distribution of $Y^{(1)}$ given $Y^{(2)} = \mathbf{y}^{(2)}$ is normal, with mean $\boldsymbol{\mu}^{(1)} + \Sigma_{12}\Sigma_{22}^{-1}(\mathbf{y}^{(2)} - \boldsymbol{\mu}^{(2)})$ and covariance matrix $\Sigma_{11} - \Sigma_{12}\Sigma_{22}^{-1}\Sigma_{21}$ (e.g., Anderson (1958, Section 2.5)).

12 When ψ^* is unknown, we replace it with an estimated value and treat (3.5.1) as having an approximate F distribution.

13 For proof, see Hausman (1978) or Rao (1973, p. 317).

14 Strictly speaking, Hausman's test is a test of $\sum_t \mathbf{x}'_{it}\mathbf{a}_t = 0$ versus $\sum_t \mathbf{x}'_{it}\mathbf{a}_t \neq 0$. It is obvious that $\mathbf{a}_t = 0$ implies that $\sum_t \mathbf{x}'_{it}\mathbf{a}_t = 0$, but not necessarily the reverse. For a discussion of the general relationship between Hausman's specification testing and conventional testing procedures, see Holly (1982).

15 We use $\otimes$ to denote the Kronecker product of two matrices (Theil (1971, Chapter 7)). Suppose that $A = (a_{ij})$ is an $m \times n$ matrix and B is a $p \times q$ matrix; $A \otimes B$ is defined as an $mp \times nq$ matrix

$$\begin{bmatrix} a_{11}B & a_{12}B & \dots & a_{1n}B \\ \vdots & \vdots & & \vdots \\ a_{m1}B & a_{m2}B & \dots & a_{mn}B \end{bmatrix}.$$

16 This is because Q sweeps out α_i from (3.6.1).

17 See Li and Hsiao (1998) for a test of whether the serial correlation in the error is caused by an individual-specific, time-invariant component or by the inertia in the shock, and Hong and Kao (2000) for testing for serial correlation of unknown form.

18 If $E(\alpha_i^* \mid \mathbf{x}_i)$ is linear, $E^*(y_i \mid \mathbf{x}_i) = E(y_i \mid \mathbf{x}_i)$.

19 Of course, we can obtain the least-squares estimate of $\boldsymbol{\pi}$ by imposing the restriction that all T equations have identical intercepts μ. But this only complicates the algebraic equation of the least-squares estimate without a corresponding gain in insight.

20 For details, see White (1980) or Chamberlain (1982).

21 For proof, see Appendix 3A, Chamberlain (1982), Chiang (1956), or Malinvaud (1970).

22 If $E(\alpha_i^* \mid \mathbf{x}_i) \neq E^*(\alpha_i^* \mid \mathbf{x}_i)$, then there will be heteroscedasticity, because the residual will contain $E(\alpha_i^* \mid \mathbf{x}_i) - E^*(\alpha_i^* \mid \mathbf{x}_i)$.

23 For fitting model (3.9.20) to panel data, see Chapter 5.

24 This follows from examining the partitioned inverse of (3.9.25).

25 If $\hat{\boldsymbol{\pi}}^*$ is another estimator of $\boldsymbol{\pi}$ with asymptotic variance–covariance matrix Ω^*, then the minimum-distance estimator of $\boldsymbol{\theta}$ obtained by choosing $\hat{\boldsymbol{\theta}}^*$ to minimize $[\hat{\boldsymbol{\pi}}^* - \mathbf{f}(\boldsymbol{\theta})]'\Omega^{*-1}[\hat{\boldsymbol{\pi}}^* - \mathbf{f}(\boldsymbol{\theta})]$ has asymptotic variance–covariance matrix $(F'\Omega^{*-1}F)^{-1}$. Suppose $\Omega - \Omega^*$ is positive semidefinite; then $F'\Omega^{*-1}F - F'\Omega^{-1}F = F'(\Omega^{*-1} - \Omega^{-1})F$ is positive semidefinite. Thus, the efficiency of the minimum-distance estimator depends crucially on the efficiency of the (unconstrained) estimator of $\boldsymbol{\pi}$.

26 For a comprehensive discussion of the Chamberlain π approach and the generalized method of moments (GMM) method, see Crépon and Mairesse (1996).

27 In fact, a stronger result can be established for the proposition that $\hat{\boldsymbol{\pi}}$ converges to $\boldsymbol{\pi}$ almost surely. In this monograph we do not attempt to distinguish the concept of convergence in probability and convergence almost surely (Rao (1973, Section 2.c)), because the stronger result requires a lot more rigor in assumptions and derivations without much gain in intuition.

Chapter 4

1 We defer the discussion of estimating distributed-lag models to Chapter 9.

2 The assumption that $|\gamma| < 1$ is made to establish the (weak) stationarity of an autoregressive process (Anderson (1971, Chapters 5, 7)). A stochastic process $\{\xi_t\}$ is *stationary* if its probability structure does not change with time. A stochastic process is *weakly stationary* if its mean $E\xi_t = m$ is a constant, independent of its time, and if the covariance of any two variables, $E(\xi_t - E\xi_t)(\xi_s - E\xi_s) = \sigma_\xi(t - s)$, depends only on their distance apart in time. The statistical properties of a least-squares estimator for the dynamic model depend on whether or not $|\gamma| < 1$ when $T \to \infty$ (Anderson (1959)). When T is fixed and $N \to \infty$, it is not necessary to assume that $|\gamma| < 1$ to establish the asymptotic normality of the least-squares estimator (Anderson (1978), Goodrich and Caines (1979)). We keep this conventional assumption for simplicity of exposition and also because it allows us to provide a unified approach toward various assumptions about the initial conditions discussed in Section 4.3.

3 This does not mean that we have resolved the issue of whether or not the effects are correlated with the exogenous variables. It only means that for estimation purposes we can let α_i stand for ω_i and treat (4.3.1) as a special case of (4.3.2).

4 For details, see Section 4.3.2 or Sevestre and Trognon (1982).

5 The presence of the term $\boldsymbol{\beta}'\mathbf{x}_{it}$ shows that the process $\{y_{it}\}$ is not generally stationary. But the statistical properties of the process $\{y_{it}\}$ vary fundamentally when $T \to \infty$ according to whether or not $\{y_{it}\}$ converges to a stationary process when the sequence of $\mathbf{x}_{it}$ is identically zero. As stated in footnote 2, we shall always adopt the first position by letting $|\gamma| < 1$.

6 V is the same as (3.3.4).

7 Bhargava and Sargan (1983) get around the issue of incidental parameters associated with the initial value y_{i0} by projecting y_{i0} on $\mathbf{x}_i$ under the assumption that α_i and $\mathbf{x}_i$ are uncorrelated. Chamberlain (1984) and Mundlak (1978a) assume that the effects α_i are correlated with $\mathbf{x}_i$ and get around the issue of incidental parameters by projecting α_i on $\mathbf{x}_i$. In either case if N is not much larger than KT, the resulting estimator will have better finite sample properties if y_{i0} or α_i is projected on $\bar{\mathbf{x}}_i$ rather than $\mathbf{x}_i$.

8 Strictly speaking, from (4.3.21), the nonstationary analogue of case IVd would imply that

$$\text{Var}(v_{i0}) = \sigma^2_{\omega 0} + \frac{\sigma^2_\alpha}{(1-\gamma)^2},$$

and

$$\text{Cov}(v_{i0}, v_{it}) = \frac{\sigma^2_\alpha}{1-\gamma}, \qquad t = 1, \ldots, T.$$

However, given the existence of the prediction-error term ϵ_{i0}, it is not possible to distinguish this case from case IVc′ based on the information of y_{i0} alone. So we shall follow Bhargava and Sargan (1983) in treating case IVd′ as the nonstationary analogue of case IVd.

9 Previously we combined the intercept term and the time-varying exogenous variables into the vector $\mathbf{x}_{it}$ because the property of the MLE for the constant is the same as that of the MLE for the coefficients of time-varying exogenous variables. Now we have incorporated the constant term as an element in the time-invariant variable $\mathbf{z}_i$ to avoid having the constant term appearing more than once in (4.3.21).

10 For the formula of the constrained estimator, see Theil (1971, p. 285, equation (8.5)).
11 See Chapter 5.
12 See Section 3.5 for another approach.
13 Note that we let $\mathbf{z}_i = 0$ for ease of exposition. When $\mathbf{z}_i$ is present, the first-differencing step of (4.3.38) eliminates $\mathbf{z}_i$ from the specification; hence the moment conditions (4.3.39) remain valid. However, for $E\bar{v}_i = 0$ to hold requires the assumption of stationarity in the mean (Blundell and Bond (1998)).
14 For ease of notation, we again assume that $\mathbf{z}_i = \mathbf{0}$.
15 Bhargava and Sargan (1983) did not report the significance level of their tests. Presumably they used the conventional 5 percent significance level.
16 We do not know the value of the GLS estimates when the initial observations are treated as endogenous. My conjecture is that it is likely to be close to the two-step GLS estimates with fixed initial observations. As mentioned in Section 4.3, Sevestre and Trognon (1982) have shown that even the initial values are correlated with the effects; the asymptotic bias of the two-step GLS estimator under the assumption of fixed initial observations is still smaller than the OLS or the within estimator. Moreover, if Bhargava and Sargan's simulation result is any indication, the order of bias due to the wrong assumption about initial observations when T is greater than 10 is about one standard error or less. Here, the standard error of the lagged dependent variable for the two-step GLS estimates with fixed initial values is only 0.037.
17 For additional discussions on the contribution of initial observations, see Blundell and Bond (1998) and Hahn (1999).
18 We say that $\mathbf{y}_t$ is stationary if $E\mathbf{y}_t = \boldsymbol{\mu}$, $E[(\mathbf{y}_t - \boldsymbol{\mu})(\mathbf{y}_{t-s} - \boldsymbol{\mu})'] = E[(\mathbf{y}_{t+q} - \boldsymbol{\mu})(\mathbf{y}_{t+q-s} - \boldsymbol{\mu})']$. We say that $\mathbf{y}_t$ is integrated of order d, $I(d)$, if $(1 - L)^d\mathbf{y}_t$ is stationary, $I(0)$. If $\mathbf{y}_t \sim I(d)$ but $\boldsymbol{\beta}'\mathbf{y}_t \sim I(d - c)$, say $d = 1, c = 1$, then y_t is cointegrated of order c. The maximum number of linearly independent vectors $\boldsymbol{\beta}$ is called the rank of cointegration. For any $m \times 1$ $I(d)$ process, the cointegration rank can vary between 0 and $m - 1$ (e.g., Engle and Granger (1987), Intriligator, Bodkin, and Hsiao (1996)).
19 $\text{Vec}(ABC) = (C' \otimes A)\,\text{vec}(B)$; see Magnus and Neudecker (1999).

Chapter 5

1 Namely, the family effect A_i has the same meaning as α_i in Chapters 3–4.
2 The asymptotic property of a fixed-effects linear simultaneous-equations model is the same as the single-equation fixed-effects linear static model (see Chapter 3). The MLE of $\boldsymbol{\alpha}_i$ is consistent only when T tends to infinity. The MLE of $\boldsymbol{\lambda}_t$ is consistent only when N tends to infinity. However, just as in the linear static model, the MLEs of $\boldsymbol{\Gamma}$ and $\mathbf{B}$ do not depend on the MLEs of $\boldsymbol{\alpha}_i$ and $\boldsymbol{\lambda}_t$. They are consistent when either N or T or both tend to infinity (Schmidt (1984)).
3 Note that the meaning of these asterisks has been changed from what it was in previous chapters.
4 By allowing X to be different, the discussion of estimation of reduced-form equations can proceed in the more general format of seemingly unrelated regression models (Avery (1977); Baltagi (1980)).
5 One can check that (5.2.7) is indeed the inverse of (5.2.6) by repeatedly using the formulas for the Kronecker products: $(B + C) \otimes A = B \otimes A + C \otimes A$, $(A \otimes B)(C \otimes D) = AC \otimes BD$, provided the products exist (Theil (1971, Section 7.2)).

6 If only the first M out of G equations have nonzero intercepts, we estimate the first M intercepts by $\{[I_M, (V_4^{MM})^{-1}V_4^{M(G-M)}] \otimes (1/NT)\mathbf{e}'_{NT}\}(\mathbf{y} - X\boldsymbol{\pi})$ and estimate $\boldsymbol{\pi}$ by $[X'V^{*-1}X]^{-1}[X'V^{*-1}\mathbf{y}]$, where I_M is the M-rowed identity matrix, V_4^{MM} and $V_4^{M(G-M)}$ are the corresponding $M \times M$ and $M \times (G - M)$ partitioned matrices of

$$V_4^{-1} = \begin{bmatrix} V_4^{MM} & V_4^{M(G-M)} \\ V_4^{(G-M)M} & V_4^{(G-M)(G-M)} \end{bmatrix},$$

and

$$V^{*-1} = \tilde{V}^{-1} + \begin{bmatrix} \mathbf{0} & \mathbf{0} \\ \mathbf{0} & V_4^{(G-M)(G-M)} - V_4^{(G-M)M}\left(V_4^{MM}\right)^{-1}V_4^{M(G-M)} \end{bmatrix} \otimes \frac{1}{NT}J.$$

For details, see Prucha (1983).

7 See Chapter 3, footnote 22.

8 As indicated earlier, we have assumed here that all variables are measured as deviations from their respective overall means. There is no loss of generality in this formulation, because the intercept μ_g is estimated by $\hat{\mu}_g = (1/NT)\mathbf{e}'_{NT}(\mathbf{y}_g - W_g\hat{\boldsymbol{\theta}}_g)$. Because $C'_h\mathbf{e}_{NT} = \mathbf{0}$ for $h = 1, 2, 3$, the only terms pertinent to our discussion are C_h for $h = 1, 2, 3$.

9 Again, we ignore $C_4 = \mathbf{e}_{NT}/\sqrt{NT}$ because we have assumed that there is an intercept for each equation and because $C'_h\mathbf{e}_{NT} = \mathbf{0}$ for $h = 1, 2, 3$.

10 For the derivations of (5.4.36) and (5.4.37), see Appendix 5A.

11 From $V \cdot V^{-1} = I_{GT}$ we have $-\Lambda\mathbf{cc}' - T\mathbf{aa}'\mathbf{cc}' + \mathbf{aa}'\Lambda^{-1} = \mathbf{0}$. Premultiplying this equation by $\mathbf{c}'$, we obtain $(b_1 + Tb_2^2)\mathbf{c}' = b_2\mathbf{a}'\Lambda^{-1}$, where $b_1 = \mathbf{c}'\Lambda\mathbf{c}$ and $b_2 = \mathbf{c}'\mathbf{a}$. In Appendix 5A we give the values of b_1 and b_2 explicitly in terms of the eigenvalue of $|\mathbf{aa}' - \lambda\Lambda| = 0$.

12 We make use of the formula $\partial \log|\Lambda|/\partial\Lambda^{-1} = -\Lambda'$ and $\partial(\mathbf{c}'\Lambda\mathbf{c})/\partial\Lambda^{-1} = -\Lambda\mathbf{cc}'\Lambda$ (Theil (1971, pp. 32–33)).

13 See Appendix 5A, equation (5A.7), in which ψ_1 is positive.

14 Finding the largest root of (5.4.43) is equivalent to maximizing (5.4.49). If we normalize $\mathbf{c}'R\mathbf{c} = 1$, then to find the maximum of (5.4.49) we can use Lagrangian multipliers and maximize $\mathbf{c}'\bar{R}\mathbf{c} + \lambda(1 - \mathbf{c}'R\mathbf{c})$. Taking partial derivatives with respect to $\mathbf{c}$ gives $(\bar{R} - \lambda R)\mathbf{c} = \mathbf{0}$. Premultiplying by $\mathbf{c}'$, we have $\mathbf{c}'\bar{R}\mathbf{c} = \lambda$. Thus, the maximum of (5.4.49) is the largest root of $|\bar{R} - \lambda R| = 0$, and $\mathbf{c}$ is the characteristic vector corresponding to the largest root.

Chapter 6

1 See Mehta, Narasimhan, and Swamy (1978) for another example to show that using error-components formulation to allow for heterogeneity does not always yield economically meaningful results.

2 Alternatively, we can postulate a separate regression for each time period, so $y_{it} = \boldsymbol{\beta}'_t\mathbf{x}_{it} + u_{it}$.

3 See Chamberlain (1992) for an extension of the Mundlak–Chamberlain approach of conditioning the individual effects on the conditioning variables to models with individual-specific slopes that may be correlated with conditioning variables. An

instrumental-variable estimator is proposed within a finite-dimensional method-of-moments framework.

4 Repeatedly using the formula $(A + BDB')^{-1} = A^{-1} - A^{-1}B(B'A^{-1}B + D^{-1})^{-1}B'A^{-1}$ (Rao (1973, Chapter 1)), we have

$$\begin{aligned} X_i'\Phi_i^{-1}X_i &= X_i'\left[\sigma_i^2 I + X_i \Delta X_i'\right]^{-1} X_i \\ &= X_i'\left\{\frac{1}{\sigma_i^2} I_T - \frac{1}{\sigma_i^2} X_i \left[X_i'X_i + \sigma_i^2\Delta^{-1}\right]^{-1} X_i'\right\} X_i \\ &= \frac{1}{\sigma_i^2}\left[X_i'X_i - X_i'X_i\left\{(X_i'X_i)^{-1} - (X_i'X_i)^{-1}\right.\right. \\ &\quad \left.\left. \times \left[(X_i'X_i)^{-1} + \frac{1}{\sigma_i^2}\Delta\right]^{-1} (X_i'X_i)^{-1}\right\} X_i'X_i\right] \\ &= \left[\Delta + \sigma_i^2 (X_i'X_i)^{-1}\right]^{-1}. \end{aligned}$$

5 Equation (6.2.9) follows from the relation that $\hat{\boldsymbol{\beta}}_i = \boldsymbol{\beta}_i + (X_i'X_i)^{-1}X_i'\mathbf{u}_i$ and $E(\hat{\boldsymbol{\beta}}_i - \bar{\boldsymbol{\beta}})(\hat{\boldsymbol{\beta}}_i - \bar{\boldsymbol{\beta}})' = \Delta + \sigma_i^2(X_i'X_i)^{-1}$.

6 We use the notation $O(N)$ to denote that the sequence $N^{-1}a_N$ is bounded (Theil (1971, p. 358)).

7 We call this a transformed Lagrange-multiplier test because it is derived by maximizing the log likelihood function of $\bar{y}_i/\sigma_i$ rather than maximizing the log likelihood function of y_{it}/σ_{it}.

8 Let

$$\left(T\hat{\omega}_i^2 - 1\right) = \frac{1}{\sigma_i^2}\left[\sum_{i=1}^{K}\sum_{i'=1}^{K} \bar{x}_{ki}\bar{x}_{k'i}\hat{\sigma}_{\alpha kk'}^2\right]$$

be the least-squares predicted value of $(T\hat{\omega}_i^2 - 1)$; then the predicted sum of squares is

$$\sum_{i=1}^{N}\left(T\hat{\omega}_i^2 - 1\right)^2.$$

9 We did not impose similar restrictions in Section 6.2.1 because we did not separate $\boldsymbol{\beta}$ from $\boldsymbol{\alpha}_i$.

10 It has been shown (Hsiao (1975)) that the Hildreth–Houck estimator is the minimum-norm quadratic unbiased estimator of Rao (1970).

11 Let $(y_{it} - \bar{y})$ be the deviation of the sample mean, and let $(\widehat{y_{it} - \bar{y}})$ be its least-squares prediction. Then the explained sum of squares is $\sum(\widehat{y_{it} - \bar{y}})^2$.

12 Note here that the first term $\dot{x}_{1it} = 1$. So the null hypothesis is $(\sigma_{\lambda 2}^2, \ldots, \sigma_{\lambda K}^2) = (0, \ldots, 0)$.

13 This section is largely drawn from the work of Chow (1983, Chapter 10).

14 Note that under the alternative, u_t^* is serially correlated. Hence, the Breusch–Pagan test may not be powerful against the alternative.

15 According to Bayes' theorem, the probability of B given A, written as $P(B \mid A)$, equals $P(B \mid A) = P(A \mid B)P(B)/P(A)$, which is proportional to $P(A \mid B)P(B)$.

16 When u_{it} is serially correlated, see Baltagi and Li (1992). For the asymptotic mean squared error when the coefficients and error-component parameters are estimated, see Baille and Baltagi (1999).

17 We are only concerned with the estimation of the short-run adjustment coefficient $\bar{\gamma}$. For discussion of estimating the long-run coefficient, see Pesaran and Smith (1995), Pesaran and Zhao (1999), Pesaran, Shin, and Smith (1999), and Phillips and Moon (1999, 2000).

18 The strict exogeneity condition (6.7.4) on $\mathbf{x}_{it}$ is crucial in the identification of a dynamic random-coefficients model. Chamberlain (1993) has given an example of the lack of identification of γ in a model of the form

$$y_{it} = \gamma y_{i,t-1} + \beta_i x_{it} + \alpha_i + u_{it},$$

where x_{it} takes either 0 or 1. Since $E(\alpha_i \mid \mathbf{x}_i, \mathbf{y}_{i,-1})$ is unrestricted, the only moments that are relevant for the identification of γ are

$$E\left(\Delta y_{it} - \gamma \Delta y_{i,t-1} \middle| \mathbf{x}_i^{t-1},\ \mathbf{y}_i^{t-2}\right) = E\left(\beta_i \Delta x_{it} \middle| \mathbf{x}_i^{t-1},\ \mathbf{y}_i^{t-2}\right), \qquad t = 2, \ldots, T,$$

where $\mathbf{x}_i^t = (x_{i1}, \ldots, \mathbf{x}_{it})$, $\mathbf{y}_i^t = (y_{i0}, \ldots, y_{it})$. Let $\mathbf{w}_i^t = (\mathbf{x}_i^t, \mathbf{y}_i^t)$, the above expression is equivalent to the following two conditions:

$$\begin{aligned} &E\left(\Delta y_{it} - \gamma \Delta y_{i,t-1} \,\middle|\, \mathbf{w}_i^{t-2},\ \mathbf{x}_{i,t-1} = 0\right) \\ &\quad = E\left(\beta_i \,\middle|\, \mathbf{w}_i^{t-2},\ \mathbf{x}_{i,t-1} = 0\right) P\left(x_{it} = 1 \,\middle|\, \mathbf{x}_i^{t-2},\ x_{i,t-1} = 0\right), \end{aligned}$$

and

$$\begin{aligned} &E\left(\Delta y_{it} - \gamma \Delta y_{i,t-1} \,\middle|\, \mathbf{x}_i^{t-2},\ x_{i,t-1} = 1\right) \\ &\quad = -E\left(\beta_i \,\middle|\, \mathbf{w}_i^{t-2},\ x_{i,t-1} = 1\right) P\left(x_{it} = 0 \,\middle|\, \mathbf{w}_i^{t-2},\ x_{i,t-1} = 1\right) \end{aligned}$$

If $E(\beta_i \mid \mathbf{w}_i^{t-2}, x_{i,t-1} = 0)$ and $E(\beta_i \mid \mathbf{w}_i^{t-2}, x_{i,t-1} = 1)$ are unrestricted and T is fixed, the autoregressive parameter γ cannot be identified from the above two equations.

19 We assume that T (>3) is large enough to identify γ and β. For an example of lack of identification when $T = 3$ and y_{it} is binary, see Chamberlain (1993) or Arellano and Honoré (2001); see also Chapter 7.

20 The values $\Psi^{-1} = 0$, $\rho = 2$, and R equal to the Swamy estimate of Δ are used to implement the hierarchical Bayes estimator.

Chapter 7

1 For a survey of the minimum-chi-square method, see Hsiao (1985b).

2 The variable y_{i0} is sometimes omitted from the specification because it is determined by $y_{i0} = 1 - \sum_{j=1}^{m} y_{ij}$. For instance, a dichotomous model is often simply characterized by a single binary variable y_i, $i = 1, \ldots, N$.

3 It should be noted that in generalizing the results of the binary case to the multiresponse case, we should allow for the fact that although y_{ij} and $y_{i'j}$ are independent for $i \neq i'$, y_{ij} and $y_{ij'}$ are not, because $\mathrm{Cov}(y_{ij}, y_{ij'}) = -F_{ij}F_{ij'}$.

4 For a random-coefficient formulation of probit models, see Hausman and Wise (1978).

5 Note that, in general, because $F(\boldsymbol{\beta}'\mathbf{x} + \alpha)$ is nonlinear, $\int F(\boldsymbol{\beta}'\mathbf{x} + \alpha)\, dH(\alpha \mid \mathbf{x}) \neq F[\boldsymbol{\beta}'\mathbf{x} + E(\alpha \mid \mathbf{x})]$.

6 Note that for notational ease, we now use only α_i instead of both α_i and α_i^*. Readers should bear in mind that whenever α_i are treated as fixed, they are not viewed as the deviation from the common mean μ; rather, they are viewed as the sum of μ and the individual deviation. On the other hand, when α_i are treated as random, we assume that $E\alpha_i = 0$.

7 The number of individuals with $y_{i1} + y_{i2} = 0$ is $N - n_1 + n_2$.

8 We call $\boldsymbol{\beta}$ the structural parameter because the value of $\boldsymbol{\beta}$ characterizes the structure of the complete sequence of random variables. It is the same for all i and t. We call α_i an incidental parameter to emphasize that the value of α_i may change when i changes.

9 Suppose that the observed random variables $\mathbf{y}$ have a certain joint distribution function that belongs to a specific family $\mathcal{J}$ of distribution functions. The statistic $S(\mathbf{y})$ (a function of the observed sample values $\mathbf{y}$) is called a sufficient statistic if the conditional expectation of any other statistic $H(\mathbf{y})$, given $S(\mathbf{y})$, is independent of $\mathcal{J}$. A statistic $S^*(\mathbf{y})$ is called a minimum sufficient statistic if it is function of every sufficient statistic $S(\mathbf{y})$ for $\mathcal{J}$. For additional discussion, see Zacks (1971, Chapter 2).

10 When u_{it} are independently normally distributed, the LSDV estimator of $\boldsymbol{\beta}$ for the linear static model is the conditional MLE (Cornwell and Schmidt (1984)).

11 Similar results also hold for the MLE of the fixed-effects logit model. Wright and Douglas (1976), who used Monte Carlo methods to investigate the performance of the MLE, found that when $T = 20$, the MLE is virtually unbiased, and its distribution is well described by a limiting normal distribution, with the variance–covariance matrix based on the inverse of the estimated-information matrix.

12 In the case in which α_i are uncorrelated with $\mathbf{x}_i$, we have $\mathbf{a} = \mathbf{0}$ and $\sigma_\eta^2 = \sigma_\alpha^2$.

13 Ω is the asymptotic variance–covariance matrix of $\hat{\boldsymbol{\pi}}$ when no restrictions are imposed on the variance–covariance matrix of the $T \times 1$ normal random variable $\mathbf{u}_i + \mathbf{e}\eta_i$. We can relax the serial-independence assumption on u_{it} and allow $E\mathbf{u}_i\mathbf{u}_i'$ to be arbitrary except for scale normalization. In this circumstance, $\Pi = \operatorname{diag}\{(\sigma_{u1}^2 + \sigma_\eta^2)^{-1/2}, \ldots, (\sigma_{uT}^2 + \sigma_\eta^2)^{-1/2}\}[I_T \otimes \boldsymbol{\beta}' + \mathbf{e}\mathbf{a}']$.

14 The transition-probability matrix of our homogeneous two-state Markov chain is

$$\mathcal{P} = \begin{bmatrix} 1 - \Phi(\beta_0 + \alpha_i) & \Phi(\beta_0 + \alpha_i) \\ 1 - \Phi(\beta_0 + \gamma + a_i) & \Phi(\beta_0 + \gamma + \alpha_i) \end{bmatrix}.$$

By mathematical induction, the n-step transition matrix is

$$\begin{aligned} \mathcal{P}^n = & \frac{1}{1 - \Phi(\beta_0 + \gamma + \alpha_i) + \Phi(\beta_0 + \alpha_i)} \\ & \times \left\{ \begin{bmatrix} 1 - \Phi(\beta_0 + \gamma + \alpha_i) & \Phi(\beta_0 + \alpha_i) \\ 1 - \Phi(\beta_0 + \gamma + \alpha_i) & \Phi(\beta_0 + \alpha_i) \end{bmatrix} \right. \\ & + [\Phi(\beta_0 + \gamma + \alpha_i) - \Phi(\beta_0 + \alpha_i)]^n \\ & \left. \times \begin{bmatrix} \Phi(\beta_0 + \alpha_i) & -\Phi(\beta_0 + \alpha_i) \\ -[1 - \Phi(\beta_0 + \gamma + \alpha_i)] & 1 - \Phi(\beta_0 + \gamma + \alpha_i) \end{bmatrix} \right\}. \end{aligned}$$

15 This can be easily seen by noting that the expectation of the first-derivative vector of (7.5.5) or (7.5.8) with respect to the structural parameters does not vanish at the true parameter value when the expectations are evaluated under (7.5.10) or (7.5.11).

16 See Arellano and Carrasco (2000) for a GMM approach to estimate the dynamic random-effects probit model.

17 Let $P_{it} = \text{Prob}(y_{it} \mid \mathbf{x}_{it}, \alpha_i)$ and $P_{it}^* = \text{Prob}(y_{it} \mid y_{i,t-\ell}, \mathbf{x}_{it}, \alpha_i)$. Let $\hat{P}_{it}$ and $\hat{P}_{it}^*$ be the MLEs obtained by maximizing $\mathcal{L} = \prod_i \prod_t P_{it}^{y_{it}}(1 - P_{it})^{1-y_{it}}$ and $\mathcal{L}^* = \prod_i \prod_t P_{it}^{*y_{it}}(1 - P_{it}^*)^{1-y_{it}}$ with respect to unknown parameters, respectively. A

likelihood-ratio test statistic for the null hypothesis (7.5.34) is $-2\log[\mathcal{L}(\hat{P}_{it})/\mathcal{L}(\hat{P}^*_{it})]$. When conditional on $\mathbf{x}_{it}$ and $\boldsymbol{\alpha}_i$, there are repeated observations; we can also use the Pesaran chi-square goodness-of-fit statistic to test (7.5.34). For details, see Bishop, Fienberg, and Holland (1975, Chapter 7). However, in the finite-T case, the testing procedure cannot be implemented, since the α_is are unknown and cannot be consistently estimated.

18 A nonstationary model was also estimated by Heckman (1981c). But because the data did not reject stationarity, we shall treat the model as having stationary covariance.

19 One can modify the estimator (7.5.33) by replacing T with T_i.

Chapter 8

1 See Amemiya (1985) and Maddala (1983) for extensive discussions of various types of Tobit models.

2 For instance, a spline of degree m in $(\mathbf{w}'\hat{\mathbf{a}})$ with L evenly spaced knots on $[-1, 1]$ can be based on

$$\begin{aligned} P_{kK} &= (\mathbf{w}'\mathbf{a})^{k-1} \qquad (1 \le k \le m+1) \\ &= \left\{\left[\mathbf{w}'\mathbf{a} + 1 - 2\frac{(k-m-1)}{L+1}\right]_+\right\}^m, \qquad m+2 \le k \le m+1+L \equiv K, \end{aligned}$$

where $b_+ \equiv 1(b > 0) \cdot b$.

3 Another example is the analysis of event histories in which responses are at unequally spaced points in time (e.g., Heckman and Singer (1984); Lancaster (1990)). Some people choose to model event histories in discrete time using sequences of binary indicators. Then the subject becomes very much like the discrete panel data analysis discussed in Chapter 7.

4 See Quandt (1982) for a survey of switching regression models.

5 In this chapter we only consider the case involving the presence of individual-specific effects. For some generalization to the estimation of a random-coefficient sample selection model, see Chen (1999).

6 A potentially computationally attractive alternative is to simulate the integrals; see Gourieroux and Monfort (1996), Keane (1994), Richard (1996), or Section 10.3.

7 I owe this exposition to the suggestion of J.L. Powell.

8 Linear panel data with randomly missing data will be discussed in Section 9.2.

9 See Honoré (1993) for a discussion of the model $y^*_{it} = \gamma y_{i,t-1} + \boldsymbol{\beta}'\mathbf{x}_{it} + \alpha_i + u_{it}$.

10 The assumption that $\mathbf{x}_{it}$ and $\mathbf{w}_{it}$ do not coincide rules out the censored regression model as a special case of (8.6.13) and (8.6.14).

11 Kyriazidou (2001) shows that these moment conditions also hold if $d^*_{it} = \phi d_{i,t-1} + \mathbf{w}'_{it}\mathbf{a} + \eta_i + \nu_{it}$.

Chapter 9

1 The material in this section is adapted from Pakes and Griliches (1984) with permission.

2 We must point out that the errors are also transformed when we go from one form to the other (e.g., Malinvaud (1970, Chapter 15)).

3 Note that assuming that there exist $\ell + 1$ observations on x before the first observation on y is not restrictive. If x_{it} does not exist before time period 0, we can always let $\ell = -1$. If ℓ has to be fixed, we can throw away the first $\ell + 1$ observations of y.

4 Note that we allow the projection of presample $x_{i,-\tau}$ on in-sample $\mathbf{x}_i$ and α_i^* to depend freely on the α_i^* by permitting each element of the vector $\mathbf{c}$ to be different.

5 One can use various model-selection criteria to determine p (e.g., Amemiya 1980a).

6 We note that $c_q = 0$ implies that α_i^* is uncorrelated with presample x_i.

7 The coefficient of (9.1.11) is another way of writing Π (9.1.8).

8 The condition for the roots of the characteristics equation to lie outside the unit circle is to ensure that $\boldsymbol{\beta}_\tau$ declines geometrically as $\tau \to \infty$ (e.g., Anderson (1971, Chapter 5)), so that the truncation remainder term will stay finite for any reasonable assumption on the x sequence.

9 See Neyman (1949) or Hsiao (1985b).

10 Thus, they assume that this year's investment does not affect this year's profits and that there are two presample observations ($\ell = 1$) on investment.

11 If α_i are correlated with $\mathbf{x}_{it}$, we can eliminate the linear dependence between α_i and $\mathbf{x}_{it}$ by assuming $\alpha_i = \sum_t \mathbf{a}_t' \mathbf{x}_{it} + \epsilon_i$. For details, see Chapter 3 or Mundlak (1978a).

12 For details, see Chapters 4 and 6.

13 See Verbeek (1992) for the discussion of the case when $(1/N_c)\sum_{i \in c} \alpha_i = \alpha_{ct}$ depends on t, and Collado (1997), Girma (2000), and Moffit (1993) for the analysis of a dynamic cohort model by treating sample averages as error-ridden observations on typical individuals, with a GMM method, and with a two-stage least-squares approach, respectively.

14 See Chetty (1968) for a Bayesian approach.

15 If the cross-sectional data consist of all individuals in the population, then in the year in which cross-sectional observations are collected, the sum across individual observations of a variable should be equal to the corresponding aggregate time-series variable. Because in most cases cross-sectional samples consist of a small portion of the population, we shall ignore this relation and assume that the variables are unrelated.

16 In the Bayesian framework this is analogous to making inferences based on the conditional distribution of $\boldsymbol{\beta}_2$, $f(\boldsymbol{\beta}_2 \mid \boldsymbol{\beta}_1 = \boldsymbol{\delta}_{1c})$, whereas it is the marginal distribution of $\boldsymbol{\beta}_2$ that should be used whenever $\boldsymbol{\beta}_1$ is not known with certainty. For details see Chetty (1968).

17 It should be noted that the foregoing results are based on the assumption that both u_i and v_t are independently normally distributed. In practice, careful diagnostic checks should be performed before exploring the pooling issue, using the likelihood-ratio test or relative maximum likelihoods. In fact, Izan (1980) redid the analysis by allowing v_t to follow a first-order autoregressive process. The likelihood-ratio test after allowing for autocorrelation resulted in accepting the pooling hypothesis.

Chapter 10

1 See Phillips and Moon (2000) for an example.

2 For an introductory discussion, see Intriligator, Bodkin, and Hsiao (1996).

3 The following results remain fundamentally unchanged when τ_{it} contains an individual time-invariant component and an independently identically distributed component.

References

Abramowitz, M., and J. Stegun (1965). *Handbook of Mathematical Functions with Formulas, Graphs and Mathematical Tables*. New York: Dover.

Abrevaya, J. (1999). "Leapfrog Estimation of a Fixed-Effects Model with Unknown Transformation of the Dependent Variable," *Journal of Econometrics*, 93, 203–228.

(2000). "Rank Estimation of a Generalized Fixed-Effects Regression Model," *Journal of Econometrics*, 95, 1–24.

Ahn, H., and J.L. Powell (1993). "Semiparametric Estimation of Censored Selection Models with a Nonparametric Selection Mechanism," *Journal of Econometrics*, 58, 3–30.

Ahn, S.C., and H.R. Moon (2001). "On Large-N and Large-T Properties of Panel Data Estimators and the Hausman Test." Mimeo, University of Southern California.

Ahn, S.C., and P. Schmidt (1995). "Efficient Estimation of Models for Dynamic Panel Data," *Journal of Econometrics*, 68, 5–27.

Aigner, D.J., and P. Balestra (1988). "Optimal Experimental Design for Error Components Models," *Econometrica*, 56, 955–972.

Aigner, D.J., C. Hsiao, A. Kapteyn, and T. Wansbeek (1984). "Latent Variable Models in Econometrics," in *Handbook of Econometrics*, vol. II, edited by Z. Griliches and M. Intriligator, pp. 1322–1393. Amsterdam: North-Holland.

Akaike, H. (1973). "Information Theory and an Extension of the Maximum Likelihood Principle," in *Proceedings of the 2nd International Symposium on Information Theory*, edited by B.N. Petrov and F. Csaki, pp. 267–281. Budapest: Akademiai Kiado.

Allison, P. (2000). "Inferring Causal Order from Panel Data," paper presented at the 9th International Conference on Panel Data, Geneva, Switzerland.

Amemiya, T. (1971). "The Estimation of the Variance in a Variance-Component Model," *International Economic Review*, 12, 1–13.

(1974). "Bivariate Probit Analysis: Minimum Chi-Square Methods," *Journal of the American Statistical Association*, 69, 940–944.

(1976). "The Maximum Likelihood, the Minimum Chi-Square and the Nonlinear Weighted Least Squares Estimator in the General Qualitative Response Model," *Journal of the American Statistical Association*, 71, 347–351.

(1978a). "The Estimation of a Simultaneous Equation Generalized Probit Model," *Econometrica*, 46, 1193–1205.

(1978b). "A Note on a Random Coefficients Model," *International Economic Review*, 19, 793–796.

(1980a). "Selection of Regressors," *International Economic Review*, 21, 331–354.

(1980b). "The n^{-2}-Order Mean Squared Errors of the Maximum Likelihood and the Minimum Logit Chi-Square Estimator," *Annals of Statistics*, 8, 488–505.

(1981). "Qualitative Response Models: A Survey," *Journal of Economic Literature*, 19, 1483–1536.

(1983). "Nonlinear Regression Models," in *Handbook of Econometrics*, vol. I, edited by Z. Griliches and M. Intriligator, pp. 333–89. Amsterdam: North-Holland.

(1984). "Tobit Models: A Survey," *Journal of Econometrics*, 24, 3–62.

(1985). *Advanced Theory of Econometrics*. Cambridge, MA: Harvard University Press.

Amemiya, T., and W.A. Fuller (1967). "A Comparative Study of Alternative Estimators in a Distributed-Lag Model," *Econometrica*, 35, 509–529.

Amemiya, T., and T.E. MaCurdy (1986). "Instrumental Variable Estimation of an Error Components Model," *Econometrica*, 54, 869–880.

Andersen, E.B. (1970). "Asymptotic Properties of Conditional Maximum Likelihood Estimators," *Journal of the Royal Statistical Society, Series B*, 32, 283–301.

(1973). *Conditional Inference and Models for Measuring*. Köbenhavn: Mentalhygiejnish Farlag.

Anderson, T.W. (1958). *An Introduction to Multivariate Analysis*. New York: Wiley.

(1959). "On Asymptotic Distributions of Estimates of Parameters of Stochastic Difference Equations," *Annals of Mathematical Statistics*, 30, 676–687.

(1969). "Statistical Inference for Covariance Matrices with Linear Structure," in *Multivariate Analysis*, vol. 2, edited by P.R. Krishnaiah, pp. 55–66. New York: Academic Press.

(1970). "Estimation of Covariance Matrices Which Are Linear Combinations or Whose Inverses Are Linear Combinations of Given Matrices," in *Essays in Probability and Statistics*, edited by R.C. Bose, pp. 1–24. Chapel Hill: University of North Carolina Press.

(1971). *The Statistical Analysis of Time Series*. New York: Wiley.

(1978). "Repeated Measurements on Autoregressive Processes," *Journal of the American Statistical Association*, 73, 371–378.

Anderson, T.W., and C. Hsiao (1981). "Estimation of Dynamic Models with Error Components," *Journal of the American Statistical Association*, 76, 598–606.

(1982). "Formulation and Estimation of Dynamic Models Using Panel Data," *Journal of Econometrics*, 18, 47–82.

Angrist, J.D., and J. Hahn (1999). "When to Control for Covariates? Panel-Asymptotic Results for Estimates of Treatment Effects," NBER Technical Working Paper 241.

Anselin, L., and D.A. Griffith (1988). "Do Spatial Effects Really Matter in Regression Analysis?" *Papers of the Regional Science Association*, 65, 11–34.

Antweiler, W. (2001). "Nested Random Effects Estimation in Unbalanced Panel Data," *Journal of Econometrics*, 101, 295–313.

Arellano, M., and S. Bond (1991). "Some Tests of Specification for Panel Data: Monte Carlo Evidence and an Application to Employment Equations," *Review of Economic Studies*, 58, 277–297.

Arellano, M., and O. Bover (1995). "Another Look at the Instrumental Variable Estimation of Error-Components Models," *Journal of Econometrics*, 68, 29–51.

Arellano, M., O. Bover, and J. Labeaga (1999). "Autoregressive Models with Sample Selectivity for Panel Data," in *Analysis of Panels and Limited Dependent Variable*

Models, edited by C. Hsiao, K. Lahiri, L.F. Lee and M.H. Pesaran, pp. 23–48. Cambridge: Cambridge University Press.

Arellano, M., and R. Carrasco (2000). "Binary Choice Panel Data Models with Predetermined Variables," *Journal of Econometrics*, (forthcoming).

Arellano, M., and B. Honoré (2001). "Panel Models: Some Recent Development," in *Handbook of Econometrics*, vol. 5, edited by J. Heckman and E. Leamer, Amsterdam: North Holland (forthcoming).

Ashenfelter, O. (1978). "Estimating the Effect of Training Programs on Earnings," *Review of Economics and Statistics*, 60, 47–57.

Ashenfelter, O., A. Deaton, and G. Solon (1984). "Does It Make Sense to Collect Panel Data in Developing Countries?" Mimeo. World Bank.

Ashenfelter, O., and G. Solon (1982). "Longitudinal Labor Market Data – Sources, Uses and Limitations," in *What's Happening to American Labor Force and Productivity Measurements?* pp. 109–126. Proceedings of a June 17, 1982, conference sponsored by the National Council on Employment Policy, W.E. Upjohn Institute for Employment Research.

Avery, R.B. (1977). "Error Components and Seemingly Unrelated Regressions," *Econometrica*, 45, 199–209.

Baille, R.T., and B.H. Baltagi (1999). "Prediction from the Regression Model with One-Way Error Components," in *Analysis of Panels and Limited Dependent Variable Models*, edited by C. Hsiao, K. Lahiri, L.F. Lee, and M.H. Pesaran, pp. 255–267. Cambridge: Cambridge University Press.

Balestra, P., and M. Nerlove (1966). "Pooling Cross-Section and Time Series Data in the Estimation of a Dynamic Model: The Demand for Natural Gas," *Econometrica*, 34, 585–612.

Baltagi, B.H. (1980). "On Seemingly Unrelated Regressions with Error Components," *Econometrica*, 48, 1547–1551.

(1981a). "Simultaneous Equations with Error Components," *Journal of Econometrics*, 17, 189–200.

(1981b). "Pooling: An Experimental Study of Alternative Testing and Estimation Procedures in a Two-Way Error Components Model." *Journal of Econometrics*, 17, 21–49.

(1995). *Econometric Analysis of Panel Data*. New York: Wiley.

Baltagi, B.H., and J.M. Griffin (1983). "Gasoline Demand in the OECD: An Application of Pooling and Testing Procedures," *European Economic Review*, 22, 117–137.

Baltagi, B.H., and Q. Li (1991). "A Transformation That Will Circumvent the Problem of Autocorrelation in an Error Component Model," *Journal of Econometrics*, 48, 385–393.

(1992). "A Monotonic Property for Iterative GLS in the Two-Way Random Effects Model," *Journal of Econometrics*, 53, 45–51.

Baltagi, B.H., S. Song, and B. Jung (2001). "The Unbalanced Nested Error Component Regression Model," *Journal of Econometrics*, 101, 357–381.

Banerjee, A. (1999). "Panel Data Unit Roots and Cointegration: An Overview," *Oxford Bulletin of Economics and Statistics*, 61, 607–630.

Barro, R., and X. Sala-i-Martin (1995). *Economic Growth*. New York: McGraw-Hill.

Barth, J., A. Kraft, and J. Kraft (1979). "A Temporal Cross-Section Approach to the Price Equation," *Journal of Econometrics*, 11, 335–351.

Bates, G., and J. Neyman (1951). "Contributions to the Theory of Accident Proneness. II: True of False Contagion," *University of California Publications in Statistics*, 215–253.

Becketti, S., W. Gould, L. Lillard, and F. Welch (1988). "The Panel Study of Income Dynamics after Fourteen Years: An Evaluation," *Journal of Labor Economics*, 6, 472–492.

Beckwith, N. (1972). "Multivariate Analysis of Sales Response of Competing Brands to Advertising," *Journal of Marketing Research*, 9, 168–176.

Ben-Porath, Y. (1973). "Labor Force Participation Rates and the Supply of Labor," *Journal of Political Economy*, 81, 697–704.

Berkson, J. (1944). "Application of the Logistic Function to Bio-assay," *Journal of the American Statistical Association*, 39, 357–365.

(1955). "Maximum Likelihood and Minimum χ^2 Estimates of the Logistic Function," *Journal of the American Statistical Association*, 50, 130–162.

(1957). "Tables for Use in Estimating the Normal Distribution Function by Normit Analysis," *Biometrika*, 44, 411–435.

(1980). "Minimum Chi-Square, Not Maximum Likelihood!" *Annals of Statistics*, 8, 457–487.

Bernard, A., and C. Jones (1996). "Productivity Across Industries and Countries: Time Series Theory and Evidence," *Review of Economics and Statistics*, 78, 135–146.

Bhargava, A., and J.D. Sargan (1983). "Estimating Dynamic Random Effects Models from Panel Data Covering Short Time Periods," *Econometrica*, 51, 1635–1659.

Binder, M., C. Hsiao, and M.H. Pesaran (2000). "Estimation and Inference in Short Panel Vector Autoregression with Unit Roots and Cointegration." Mimeo, Cambridge University.

Biørn, E. (1981). "Estimating Economic Relations from Incomplete Cross-Section/Time Series Data," *Journal of Econometrics*, 16, 221–236.

(1992). "Econometrics of Panel Data with Measurement Errors," in *Econometrics of Panel Data: Theory and Applications*, edited by L. Mátyás and P. Sevestre, pp. 152–195. Kluwer.

Bishop, Y.M.M., S.E. Fienberg, and P.W. Holland (1975). *Discrete Multivariate Analysis, Theory and Practice*. Cambridge, MA: MIT Press.

Blanchard, P. (1996). "Software Review," in *The Econometrics of Panel Data*, 2nd edition, edited by L. Matyas and P. Sevestre, pp. 879–913. Dordrecht: Kluwer Academic.

Blundell, R., and S. Bond (1998). "Initial Conditions and Moment Restrictions in Dynamic Panel Data Models," *Journal of Econometrics*, 87, 115–143.

Blundell, R., M. Browning, and C. Meghir (1994). "Consumer Demand and the Life Cycle Allocation of Household Expenditure," *Review of Economic Studies*, 61, 57–80.

Blundell, R., and R.J. Smith (1991). "Conditions Initiales et Estimation Efficace dans les Modèles Dynamiques sur Données de Panel," *Annals d'Economies et de Statistique*, 20–21, 109–124.

Bond, S., and C. Meghir (1994). "Dynamic Investment Models and the Firm's Financial Policy," *Review of Economic Studies*, 61, 197–222.

Borus, M.E. (1981). "An Inventory of Longitudinal Data Sets of Interest to Economists." Mimeo. Ohio State University.

Box, G.E.P., and G.M. Jenkins (1970). *Time Series Analysis: Forecasting and Control*. San Francisco: Holden-Day.

Box, G.E.P., and G.C. Tiao (1968). "Bayesian Estimation of Means for the Random Effects Model," *Journal of the American Statistical Association*, 63, 174–181.

(1973). *Bayesian Inference in Statistical Analysis*. Reading, MA: Addison-Wesley.

Brainard, W.C., and J. Tobin (1968). "Pitfalls in Financial Model Building," *American Economic Review*, 58, 99–122.

Breitung, J., and W. Mayer (1994). "Testing for Unit Roots in Panel Data: Are Wages on Different Bargaining Levels Cointegrated," *Applied Economics*, 26, 353–361.

Breusch, T.S. (1987). "Maximum Likelihood Estimation of Random Effects Models," *Journal of Econometrics*, 36, 383–389.

Breusch, T.S., G.E. Mizon, and P. Schmidt (1989). "Efficient Estimation Using Panel Data," *Econometrica*, 51, 695–700.

Breusch, T.S., and A.R. Pagan (1979). "A Simple Test for Heteroscedasticity and Random Coefficient Variation," *Econometrica*, 47, 1287–1294.

Butler, J.S., and R. Moffitt (1982). "A Computationally Efficient Quadrature Procedure for the One Factor Multinominal Probit Model," *Econometrica*, 50, 761–764.

Cameron, A.C., and P.K. Trevedi (1998). *Regression Analysis of Count Data*. Cambridge: Cambridge University Press.

Canova, F. (1999). "Testing for Convergence Clubs in Income Per Capita: A Predictive Density Approach," Mimeo, Universitat Pompeu Fabra.

Case, A.C. (1991). "Spatial Patterns in Household Demand," *Econometrica*, 59, 953–965.

Chamberlain, G. (1976). "Identification in Variance Components Models," Discussion Paper No. 486. Harvard Institute of Economic Research.

(1977a). "Education, Income, and Ability Revisited," in *Latent Variables in Socio-Economic Models*, edited by D.J. Aigner and A.S. Goldberger, pp. 143–161. Amsterdam: North-Holland.

(1977b). "An Instrumental Variable Interpretation of Identification in Variance-Components and MIMIC Models," in *Kinometrics: Determinents of Social–Economic Success Within and Between Families*, edited by P. Taubman, pp. 235–254. Amsterdam: North-Holland.

(1978a). "Omitted Variable Bias in Panel Data: Estimating the Returns to Schooling," *Annales de l'INSEE* 30-1, 49–82.

(1978b). "On the Use of Panel Data," paper presented at the Social Science Research Council Conference on Life-Cycle Aspects of Employment and the Labor Market, Mt. Kisco, N.Y.

(1980). "Analysis of Covariance with Qualitative Data," *Review of Economic Studies*, 47, 225–238.

(1982). "Multivariate Regression Models for Panel Data," *Journal of Econometrics*, 18, 5–46.

(1984). "Panel Data," in *Handbook of Econometrics*, vol. II, edited by Z. Griliches and M. Intriligator, pp. 1247–1318. Amsterdam: North-Holland.

(1992). "Efficiency Bounds for Semiparametric Regression," *Econometrica*, 60, 567–596.

(1993). "Feedback in Panel Data Models," Mimeo. Department of Economics, Harvard University.

Chamberlain, G., and Z. Griliches (1975). "Unobservables with a Variance-Components Structure: Ability, Schooling and the Economic Success of Brothers," *International Economic Review*, 16, 422–450.

Charlier, E., B. Melenberg, and A. van Soest (2000). "Estimation of a Censored Regression Panel Data Model Using Conditional Moment Restrictions Efficiently," *Journal of Econometrics*, 95, 25–56.

(2001). "An Analysis of Housing Expenditure Using Semiparametric Models and Panel Data," *Journal of Econometrics*, 101, 71–108.

Chen, S. (1999). "Distribution-Free Estimation of the Random Coefficient Dummy Endogenous Variable Model," *Journal of Econometrics*, 91, 171–199.

(2000). "Efficient Estimation of Binary Choice Models under Symmetry," *Journal of Econometrics*, 96, 183–199.

Chesher, A.D. (1983). "The Information Matrix Test: Simplified Calculation via a Score Test Interpretation," *Economics Letters*, 13, 45–48.

(1984). "Testing for Neglected Heterogenity," *Econometrica*, 52, 865–872.

Chesher, A.D., and T. Lancaster (1983). "The Estimation of Models of Labor Market Behavior," *Review of Economic Studies*, 50, 609–624.

Chetty, V.K. (1968). "Pooling of Time Series and Cross-Section Data," *Econometrica*, 36, 279–290.

Chiang, C.L. (1956). "On Regular Best Asymptotically Normal Estimates," *Annals of Mathematical Statistics*, 27, 336–351.

Chintagunta, P., E. Kyriazidou, and J. Perktold (2001). "Panel Data Analysis of Household Brand Choices," *Journal of Econometrics*, 103, 111–153.

Choi, In, (2002) "Instrumental Variable Estimation of a Nearly Nonstationary, Heterogeneous Error Components Model," *Journal of Econometrics*, 109, 1–32.

Chow, G.C. (1983). *Econometrics*. New York: McGraw-Hill.

Coleman, J.S. (1964). *Models of Change and Response Uncertainty*. Englewood Cliffs, NJ: Prentice-Hall.

Collado, M.D. (1997). "Estimating Dynamic Models from Time Series of Independent Cross-Sections," *Journal of Econometrics*, 82, 37–62.

Conley, T.G. (1999). "GMM Estimation with Cross-sectional Dependence," *Journal of Econometrics*, 92, 1–45.

Cooley, T.F., and E.C. Prescott (1976). "Estimation in the Presence of Stochastic Parameter Variation," *Econometrica*, 44, 167–84.

Cornwell, C., and P. Schmidt (1984). "Panel Data with Cross-Sectional Variation in Slopes as Well as Intercepts," Mimeo. Michigan State University.

Cox, D.R. (1957). "Note on Grouping," *Journal of the American Statistical Association*, 52, 543–547.

(1962). "Further Results on Tests of Separate Families of Hypotheses," *Journal of the Royal Statistical Society, Series B*, 24, 406–424.

(1970). *Analysis of Binary Data*. London: Methuen.

Crépon, B., and J. Mairesse (1996). "The Chamberlain Approach," in *The Econometrics of Panel Data: A Handbook of the Theory with Applications*, edited by L. Matyas and P. Sevestre, pp. 323–391. Dordrecht: Kluwer Academic.

Cripps, T., and R. Tarling (1974). "An Analysis of the Duration of Male Unemployment in Great Britain, 1932–1973," *Economic Journal*, 84, 289–316.

Davis, P. (1999). "Estimating Multi-way Error Components Models with Unbalanced Data Structures," Mimeo. MIT Sloan School.

Deaton, A. (1985). "Panel Data from Time Series of Cross-Sections," *Journal of Econometrics*, 30, 109–126.

DeFinetti, B. (1964). "Foresight: Its Logical Laws, Its Subjective Sources," in *Studies in Subjective Probability*, edited by H.E. Kyburg, Jr., and H.E. Smokler, pp. 93–158. New York: Wiley.

Dhrymes, P. (1971). *Distributed Lags: Problems of Estimation and Formulation*. San Francisco: Holden-Day.

Dickey, D.A., and W.A. Fuller (1979). "Distribution of the Estimators for Autoregressive

Time Series with a Unit Root," *Journal of the American Statistical Association*, 74, 427–431.

(1981). "Likelihood Ratio Statistics for Autoregressive Time Series with a Unit Root," *Econometrica*, 49, 1057–1072.

Dielman, T., T. Nantell, and R. Wright (1980). "Price Effects of Stock Repurchasing: A Random Coefficient Regression Approach," *Journal of Financial and Quantitative Analysis*, 15, 175–189.

Duncan, G.M. (1980). "Formulation and Statistical Analysis of the Mixed Continuous/Discrete Dependent Variable Model in Classical Production Theory," *Econometrica*, 48, 839–852.

Durbin, J. (1953). "A Note on Regression When There Is Extraneous Information about One of the Coefficients," *Journal of the American Statistical Association*, 48, 799–808.

(1960). "Estimation of Parameters in Time-Series Regression Models," *Journal of the Royal Statistical Society, Series B*, 22, 139–153.

Durlauf, S.N. (2001). "Manifesto for Growth Econometrics," *Journal of Econometrics* (forthcoming).

Durlauf, S.N., and P. Johnson (1995). "Multiple Regimes and Cross-Country Growth Behavior," *Journal of Applied Econometrics*, 10, 365–384.

Durlauf, S., and D. Quah (1999). "The New Empirics of Economic Growth," in *Handbook of Macroeconomics*, edited by J. Taylor and M. Woodford. Amsterdam: North-Holland.

Eicker, F. (1963). "Asymptotic Normality and Consistency of the Least Squares Estimators for Families of Linear Regression," *Annals of Mathematical Statistics*, 34, 447–456.

Engle, R.F., and C.W.J. Granger (1987). "Cointegration and Error Correction: Representation, Estimation, and Testing," *Econometica*, 55, 251–276.

Eurostat (1996). *European Community Household Panel (ECHP)*. Office for Official Publications of the European Communities, Luxembourg.

Fazzari, S.M., R.G. Hubbard, and B.C. Petersen (1988). "Financing Constraints and Corporate Investment," *Brookings Papers on Economic Activity*, 1, 141–195.

Ferguson, T.S. (1958). "A Method of Generating Best Asymptotically Normal Estimates with Application to the Estimation of Bacterial Densities," *Annals of Mathematical Statistics*, 29, 1046–162.

Fisher, R.A. (1932). *Statistical Methods for Research Workers*, 4th edition. Edinburgh: Oliver and Boyd.

Flinn, C., and J. Heckman (1982). "New Methods for Analyzing Structural Models of Labour Force Dynamics," *Journal of Econometrics*, 8, 115–168.

Florens, J.P., D. Fougére, and M. Mouchart (1996). "Duration Models," in *The Econometrics of Panel Data*, 2nd edition, edited by L. Matyas and P. Sevestre, pp. 491–536. Dordrecht: Kluwer Academic.

Fougére, D., and T. Kamionka (1996). "Individual Labour Market Transitions," in *The Econometrics of Panel Data: A Handbook of the Theory with Applications*, 2nd edition, edited by L. Matyas and P. Sevestre, pp. 771–809. Dordrecht: Kluwer Academic.

Frankel, J.A., and A.K. Rose (1996). "A Panel Project on Purchasing Power Parity: Mean Revesion Between and Within Countries," *Journal of International Economics*, 40, 209–244.

Freeman, R.B., and J.L. Medoff (1981). "The Impact of Collective Bargaining: Illusion or Reality?" Mimeo. Harvard University.

Friedman, M. (1953). *Essays in Positive Economics*. Chicago: University of Chicago Press.

Fujiki, H., C. Hsiao, and Y. Shen (2002). "Is There a Stable Money Demand Function Under the Low Interest Rate Policy? – A Panel Data Analysis," *Monetary and Economic Studies*, Bank of Japan (forthcoming).

Fuller, W.A., and G.E. Battese (1974). "Estimation of Linear Models with Cross-Error Structure," *Journal of Econometrics*, 2, 67–78.

Gelfand, A.E., and A.F.M. Smith (1990). "Sampling-Based Approaches to Calculating Marginal Densities," *Journal of the American Statistical Association*, 85, 398–409.

Girma, S. (2000). "A Quasi-differencing Approach to Dynamic Modelling from a Time Series Independent Cross-Sections," *Journal of Econometrics*, 98, 365–383.

Goldberger, A.S. (1964). *Econometric Theory*. New York: Wiley.

(1972). "Maximum Likelihood Estimation of Regressions Containing Unobservable Independent Variables," *International Economic Review*, 13, 1–15.

Goodman, L.A. (1961). "Statistical Methods for the Mover–Stayer Model," *Journal of the American Statistical Association*, 56, 841–68.

Goodrich, R.L., and P.E. Caines (1979). "Linear System Identification from Nonstationary Cross-Sectional Data," *IEEE Transactions on Automatic Control*, AC-24, 403–11.

Gorseline, D.E. (1932). *The Effect of Schooling upon Income*. Bloomington: Indiana University Press.

Gourieroux, C., and J. Jasiak (2000). "Nonlinear Panel Data Models with Dynamic Heterogenity," in *Panel Data Econometrics*, edited by J. Krishnakumar and E. Ronchetti, pp. 127–148. Amsterdam: North-Holland.

Gourieroux, C., and A. Monfort (1996). *Simulation-Based Econometric Methods*. Oxford: Oxford University Press.

Graybill, F.A. (1969). *Introduction to Matrices with Applications in Statistics*. Belmont, CA: Wadsworth.

Granger, C.W.J. (1980). "Long Memory Relationships and the Aggregation of Dynamic Models," *Journal of Econometrics*, 14, 227–238.

Griliches, Z. (1957). "Specification Bias in Estimates of Production Functions," *Journal of Farm Economics*, 39, 8–20.

(1977). "Estimating the Returns to Schooling: Some Econometric Problems," *Econometrica*, 45, 1–22.

(1979). "Sibling Models and Data in Economics: Beginning of a Survey," *Journal of Political Economy* 87 (Supplement 2), S37–S64.

Griliches, Z., B. Hall, and J.A. Hausman (1978). "Missing Data and Self-selection in Large Panels," *Annales de l'INSEE* 30-1, 137–176.

Griliches, Z., and J.A. Hausman (1986). "Errors-in-Variables in Panel Data," *Journal of Econometrics*, 31, 93–118.

Gronau, R. (1976). "The Allocation of Time of Israeli Women," *Journal of Political Economy*, 84, 4, Part II.

Grunfeld, Y. (1958). "The Determinants of Corporate Investment." Unpublished PhD thesis. University of Chicago.

Hahn, J. (1998). "On the Role of the Propensity Score in Efficient Semiparametric Estimation of Average Treatment Effects," *Econometrica*, 66, 315–331.

(1999). "How Informative is the Initial Condition in a Dynamic Panel Model with Fixed Effects?" *Journal of Econometrics*, 93, 309–326.

Hahn, J., and G. Kuersteiner (2000). "Asymptotically Unbiased Inference for a Dynamic Panel Model with Fixed Effects When Both N and T are Large." Mimeo.

Hall, P., N.I. Fisher, and B. Hoffman (1992). "On the Nonparametric Estimation of Covariance Functions." Working Paper. Australian National University.

Hansen, B. (1982). "Efficient Estimation and Testing of Cointegrating Vectors in the Presence of Deterministic Trends," *Journal of Econometrics*, 53, 87–121.

Härdle, W. (1990). *Applied Nonparametric Regression*. Cambridge: Cambridge University Press.

Harris, R.D.F., and E. Tzaralis (1999). "Inference for Unit Roots in Dynamic Panels Where the Time Dimension is Fixed," *Journal of Econometrics*, 91, 201–226.

Hartley, H.O., and J.N.K. Rao (1967). "Maximum Likelihood Estimation for the Mixed Analysis of Variance Model," *Biometrika*, 54, 93–108.

Harvey, A.C., (1978). "The Estimation of Time-Varying Parameters from Panel Data," *Annales de l'INSEE*, 30-1, 203–206.

Harvey, A.C., and G.D.A. Phillips (1982). "The Estimation of Regression Models with Time-Varying Parameters," in *Games, Economic Dynamics, and Time Series Analysis*, edited by M. Deistler, E. Fürst, and G.S. Schwödiauer, pp. 306–321. Cambridge, MA: Physica-Verlag.

Hausman, J.A. (1978). "Specification Tests in Econometrics," *Econometrica*, 46, 1251–1371.

Hausman, J.A., and D. McFadden (1984). "Specification Tests for the Multinomial Logit Models," *Econometrica*, 52, 1219–1240.

Hausman, J.A., and W.E. Taylor (1981). "Panel Data and Unobservable Individual Effects," *Econometrica*, 49, 1377–1398.

Hausman, J.A., and D. Wise (1977). "Social Experimentation, Truncated Distributions, and Efficient Estimation," *Econometrica*, 45, 919–938.

(1978). "A Conditional Probit Model for Qualitative Choice: Discrete Decisions Recognizing Interdependence and Heterogeneous Preferences," *Econometrica*, 46, 403–426.

(1979). "Attrition Bias in Experimental and Panel Data: The Gary Income Maintenance Experiment," *Econometrica*, 47, 455–473.

Hayashi, F. (1982). "Tobin's Marginal q and Average q: A Neoclassical Interpretation," *Econometrica*, 50, 213–224.

Heckman, J.J. (1976a). "The Common Structure of Statistical Models of Truncation, Sample Selection, and Limited Dependent Variables and a Simple Estimator for Such Models," *Annals of Economic and Social Measurement*, 5, 475–492.

(1976b). "Simultaneous Equations Models with Continuous and Discrete Endogenous Variables and Structural Shifts," in *Studies in Nonlinear Estimation*, edited by S.M. Goldfeld and R.E. Quandt, pp. 235–272. Cambridge, MA: Ballinger.

(1978a). "Simple Statistical Models for Discrete Panel Data Developed and Applied to Test the Hypothesis of True State Dependence against the Hypothesis of Spurious State Dependence," *Annales e l'INSEE*, 30-1, 227–269.

(1978b). "Dummy Endogenous Variables in a Simultaneous Equation System," *Econometrica*, 46, 931–959.

(1979). "Sample Selection Bias as a Specification Error," *Econometrica*, 47, 153–161.

(1981a). "Statistical Models for Discrete Panel Data," in *Structural Analysis of Discrete Data with Econometric Applications*, edited by C.F. Manski and D. McFadden, pp. 114–178. Cambridge, MA: MIT Press.

(1981b). "The Incidental Parameters Problem and the Problem of Initial Conditions in Estimating a Discrete Time–Discrete Data Stochastic Process," in *Structural Analysis of Discrete Data with Econometric Applications*, edited by C.F. Manski and D. McFadden, pp. 179–195. Cambridge, MA: MIT Press.

(1981c). "Heterogeneity and State Dependence," in *Studies in Labor Markets*, edited by S. Rosen, pp. 91–139. University of Chicago Press.

(2001). "Econometric Evaluation of Social Programs," in *Handbook of Econometrics*, vol. 5. Amsterdam: North-Holland (forthcoming).

Heckman, J.J., and G. Borjas (1980). "Does Unemployment Cause Future Unemployment? Definitions, Questions and Answers from a Continuous Time Model of Heterogeneity and State Dependence," *Economica*, 47, 247–283.

Heckman, J.J., H. Ichimura, and P. Todd (1998). "Matching as an Econometric Evaluations Estimator," *Review of Economic Studies*, 65, 261–294.

Heckman, J.J., and R. Robb (1985). "Alternative Methods for Evaluating the Impact of Interventions," in *Longitudinal Analysis of Labor Market Data*, edited by J. Heckman and B. Singer. New York: Cambridge University Press.

Heckman, J.J., and B. Singer (1982). "The Identification Problem in Econometric Models for Duration Data," in *Advances in Econometrics*, edited by W. Hildenbrand, pp. 39–77. Cambridge: Cambridge University Press.

(1984). "Econometric Duration Analysis," *Journal of Econometrics*, 24, 63–132.

Heckman, J.J., and E.J. Vytlacil (2001). "Local Instrumental Variables," in *Nonlinear Statistical Inference*, edited by C. Hsiao, K. Morimune, and J.L Powell. New York: Cambridge University Press.

Heckman, J.J., and R. Willis (1977). "A Beta-Logistic Model for the Analysis of Sequential Labor Force Participation by Married Women," *Journal of Political Economy*, 85, 27–58.

Henderson, C.R., Jr. (1971). "Comment on 'The Use of Error Components Models in Combining Cross-Section with Time Series Data'," *Econometrica*, 39, 397–401.

Hendricks, W., R. Koenker, and D.J. Poirier (1979). "Residential Demand for Electricity: An Econometric Approach," *Journal of Econometrics*, 9, 33–57.

Hildreth, C., and J.P. Houck (1968). "Some Estimators for a Linear Model with Random Coefficients," *Journal of the American Statistical Association*, 63, 584–595.

Hirano, K., G.W. Imbens, and G. Ridder (2000). "Efficient Estimation of Average Treatment Effects Using the Estimated Propensity Score," Mimeo, University of California, Los Angeles.

Hirano, K., G.W. Imbens, and G. Ridder, and D.B. Rubin (2001). "Combining Panel Data Sets with Attrition and Refreshment Samples," *Econometrica*, 69, 1645–1660.

Hoch, I. (1962). "Estimation of Production Function Parameters Combining Time-Series and Cross-Section Data," *Econometrica*, 30, 34–53.

Holly, A. (1982). "A Remark on Hausman's Specification Test," *Econometrica*, 50, 749–759.

Holly, A., and L. Gardiol (2000). "A Score Test for Individual Heteroscedasticity in a One-Way Error Components Model," in *Panel Data Econometrics*, edited by J. Krishnakumar and E. Ronchetti, pp. 199–211. Amsterdam: North-Holland.

Holtz-Eakin, D., W. Newey, and H.S. Rosen (1988). "Estimating Vector Autoregressions with Panel Data," *Econometrica*, 56, 1371–1395.

Hong, Y., and C. Kao (2000). "Wavelet-Based Testing for Serial Correlation of Unknown Form in Panel Models," Mimeo, Cornell University.

Honoré, B.E. (1992). "Trimmed LAD and Least Squares Estimation of Truncated and Censored Regression Models with Fixed Effects," *Econometrica*, 60, 533–567.

(1993). "Orthogonality Conditions for Tobit Models with Fixed Effects and Lagged Dependent Variables," *Journal of Econometrics*, 59, 35–61.

Honoré, B.E., and E. Kyriazidou (2000a). "Panel Data Discrete Choice Models with Lagged Dependent Variables," *Econometrica*, 68, 839–874.

(2000b). "Estimation of Tobit-Type Models with Individual Specific Effects," *Econometrics Review*, 19.

Honoré, B.E., and J.L. Powell (1994). "Pairwise Difference Estimators of Censored and Truncated Regression Models," *Journal of Econometrics*, 64, 241–278.

Horowitz, J.L. (1992). "A Smoothed Maximum Score Estimator for the Binary Response Model," *Econometrica*, 60, 505–531.

(1996). "Semiparametric Estimation of a Regression Model with an Unknown Transformation of the Dependent Variable," *Econometrica*, 64, 103–137.

Hsiao, C. (1974a). "Statistical Inference for a Model with Both Random Cross-Sectional and Time Effects," *International Economic Review*, 15, 12–30.

(1974b). "The Estimation of Labor Supply of Low Income Workers – Some Econometric Considerations," Working Paper 970-1. The Urban Institute, Washington, D.C.

(1975). "Some Estimation Methods for a Random Coefficients Model," *Econometrica*, 43, 305–25.

(1976). "Regression Analysis with Limited Dependent Variable," 1P-186. IBER and CRMS, University of California, Berkeley.

(1979a). "Causality Tests in Econometrics," *Journal of Economic Dynamics and Control*, 1, 321–346.

(1979b). "Autoregressive Modelling of Canadian Money and Income Data," *Journal of the American Statistical Association*, 74, 553–560.

(1982). "Autoregressive Modelling and Causal Ordering of Economic Variables," *Journal of Economic Dynamics and Control*, 4, 243–259.

(1983). "Identification," in *Handbook of Econometrics*, vol. I, edited by Z. Griliches and M. Intriligator, pp. 223–283. Amsterdam: North-Holland.

(1985a). "Benefits and Limitations of Panel Data," *Econometric Reviews*, 4, 121–174.

(1985b). "Minimum Chi-Square," in the *Encyclopedia of Statistical Science*, vol. 5, edited by S. Kotz and N. Johnson, pp. 518–522. New York: Wiley.

(1989). "Consistent Estimation for Some Nonlinear Errors-in-Variables Models," *Journal of Econometrics*, 41, 159–185.

(1991a). "A Mixed Fixed and Random Coefficients Framework for Pooling Cross-Section and Time Series Data," paper presented at the Third Conference on Telecommunication Demand Analysis with Dynamic Regulation, Hilton Head, S.C., in *New Development in Quantitative Economics*, edited by J.W. Lee and S.Y. Zhang. Beijing: Chinese Academy of Social Science.

(1991b). "Identification and Estimation of Latent Binary Choice Models Using Panel Data," *Review of Economic Studies*, 58, 717–731.

(1992a). "Random Coefficients Models," in *The Econometrics of Panel Data*, edited by L. Matyas and P. Sevestres, Kluwer: 1st edition, pp. 223–241; 2nd edition (1996), pp. 410–428.

(1992b). "Logit and Probit Models," in *The Econometrics of Panel Data*, edited by L. Matyas and P. Sevestre, pp. 223–241. Dordrecht: Kluwer Academic.

(1992c). "Nonlinear Latent Variables Models," in *Econometrics of Panel Data*, edited by L. Matyas and P. Sevestre, pp. 242–261. Kluwer.

(1995). "Panel Analysis for Metric Data," in *Handbook of Statistical Modelling in the Social and Behavioral Sciences*, edited by G. Arminger, C.C. Clogg, and M.Z. Sobel, pp. 361–400. Plenum.

(2000). "Economic Panel Data Methodology," in *International Encyclopedia of the Social and Behavioral Sciences*, edited by N.J. Snelser and P.B. Bates. Oxford: Elsevier (forthcoming).

Hsiao, C., T.W. Appelbe, and C.R. Dineen (1993). "A General Framework for Panel Data Analysis – with an Application to Canadian Customer Dialed Long Distance Service," *Journal of Econometrics*, 59, 63–86.

Hsiao, C., K. Lahiri, L.F. Lee, and M.H. Pesaran (1999). *Analysis of Panel Data and Limited Dependent Variable Models*. Cambridge: Cambridge University Press.

Hsiao, C., and D.C. Mountain (1994). "A Framework for Regional Modeling and Impact Analysis – An Analysis of the Demand for Electricity by Large Municipalities in Ontario, Canada," *Journal of Regional Science*, 34, 361–385.

Hsiao, C., D.C. Mountain, and K.F. Ho-Illman (1995). "Bayesian Integration of End-Use Metering and Conditional Demand Analysis," *Journal of Business and Economic Statistics*, 13, 315–326.

Hsiao, C., D.C. Mountain, K.Y. Tsui, and M.W. Luke Chan (1989). "Modeling Ontario Regional Electricity System Demand Using a Mixed Fixed and Random Coefficients Approach," *Regional Science and Urban Economics*, 19, 567–587.

Hsiao, C., K. Morimune, and J.L. Powell (2001). *Nonlinear Statistical Inference*. New York: Cambridge University Press.

Hsiao, C., M.H. Pesaran, and A.K. Tahmiscioglu (1999). "Bayes Estimation of Short-Run Coefficients in Dynamic Panel Data Models," in *Analysis of Panels and Limited Dependent Variables Models*, edited by C. Hsiao, L.F. Lee, K. Lahiri, and M.H. Pesaran, pp. 268–296. Cambridge: Cambridge University Press.

Hsiao, C., M.H. Pesaran, and A.K. Tahmiscioglu (2002). "Maximum Likelihood Estimation of Fixed Effects Dynamic Panel Data Models Covering Short Time Periods," *Journal of Econometrics*, 109, 107–150.

Hsiao, C., and B.H. Sun (2000). "To Pool or Not to Pool Panel Data," in *Panel Data Econometrics: Future Directions, Papers in Honor of Professor Pietro Balestra*, edited by J. Krishnakumar and E. Ronchetti. Amsterdam: North Holland.

Hsiao, C., and A.K. Tahmiscioglu (1997). "A Panel Analysis of Liquidity Constraints and Firm Investment," *Journal of the American Statistical Association*, 92, 455–465.

Hsiao, C., and G. Taylor (1991). "Some Remarks on Measurement Errors and the Identification of Panel Data Models," *Statistica Neerlandica*, 45, 187–194.

Hsiao, C., and K.Q. Wang (2000). "Estimation of Structural Nonlinear Errors-in-Variables Models by Simulated Least Squares Method," *International Economic Review*, 41, 523–542.

Hsiao, C., L.Q. Wang, and K.Q. Wang (1997). "Estimation of Nonlinear Errors-in-Variables Models – An Approximate Solution," *Statistical Papers*, 38, 1–28.

Hsiao, C., Y. Shen, and H. Fujiki (2002). "Aggregate vs. Disaggregate Data Analysis – A Paradox in the Estimation of Money Demand Function of Japan Under the Low Interest Rate Policy," Mimeo, University of Southern California.

Hsiao, C., J. Nugent, I. Perrigne, and J. Qiu (1998). "Shares versus Residual Claimant Contracts: The Case of Chinese TVEs," *Journal of Comparative Economics*, 26, 317–337.

Hu, L. (1999). "Estimating a Censored Dynamic Panel Data Model with an Application to Earnings Dynamics," Mimeo. Department of Economics, Princeton University.
Hurwicz, L. (1950). "Systems with Nonadditive Disturbances," in *Statistical Inference in Dynamic Economic Models*, edited by T.C. Koopmans, pp. 330–372. New York: Wiley.
Hyslop, D. (1999). "State Dependence, Serial Correlation and Heterogeneity in Intertemporal Labor Force Participation of Married Women," *Econometrica*, 52, 363–389.
Im, K.S., M.H. Pesaran, and Y. Shin (1997). "Testing for Unit Roots in Heterogeneous Panels," Mimeo. University of Cambridge.
Imbens, G.W., and J.D. Angrist (1994). "Identification and Estimation of Local Average Treatment Effects," *Econometrica*, 62, 467–475.
Intriligator, M.D., R.G. Bodkin, and C. Hsiao (1996). *Econometric Models, Techniques, and Applications*. Upper Saddle River, NJ: Prentice-Hall.
Izan, H.Y. (1980). "To Pool or not to Pool? A Reexamination of Tobin's Food Demand Problem," *Journal of Econometrics*, 13, 391–402.
Jang, S.J., and T.P. Thornberry (1998). "Self Esteem, Delinquent Peers, and Delinquency: A Test of Self-Enhancement Thesis," *American Sociological Review*, 63, 586–598.
Janz, N., G. Ebling, S. Gottshalk, and H. Niggemann (2001). "The Mannheim Innovation Panels (MIP and MIP-S) of the Centre for European Economic Research (ZEW), *Schmollers Jahrbuch*, 121, 123–129.
Jeong, K.J. (1978). "Estimating and Testing a Linear Model When an Extraneous Information Exists," *International Economic Review*, 19, 541–543.
Johansen, S. (1995). *Likelihood Based Inference on Cointegration in the Vector Autoregressive Model*. Oxford: Oxford University Press.
Johnston, J. (1972). *Econometric Methods*, 2nd edition. New York: McGraw-Hill.
Jorgenson, D.W. (1971). "Econometric Studies of Investment Behavior: A Survey," *Journal of Economic Literature*, 9, 1111–1147.
Jorgenson, D.W., and T.M. Stokes (1982). "Nonlinear Three Stage Least Squares Pooling of Time Series and Cross Section Data." Discussion Paper No. 952. Harvard Institute of Economic Research.
Judge, G., W.E. Griffiths, R. Hill, and T. Lee (1980). *The Theory and Practice of Econometrics*. New York: Wiley.
Judson, R.A., and A.L. Owen (1999). "Estimating Dynamic Panel Data Models: A Guide for Macroeconomists," *Economic Letters*, 65, 9–15.
Juster, T. (2000). "Economics/Micro Data," in *International Encyclopedia of Social Sciences* (forthcoming).
Kalman, R.E. (1960) "A New Approach to Linear Filtering and Prediction Problems," *Transactions of the ASME, Series D, Journal of Basic Engineering*, 82, 35–45.
Kao, C. (1999). "Spurious Regression and Residual-Based Tests for Cointegration in Panel Data," *Journal of Econometrics*, 90, 1–44.
Kao, C., and M.H. Chiang (2000). "On the Estimation and Inference of a Cointegrated Regression in Panel Data," *Advances in Econometrics*, 15, 179–222.
Kao, C., and J.F. Schnell (1987a). "Errors in Variables in Panel Data with Binary Dependent Variable," *Economic Letters*, 24, 45–49.
(1987b). "Errors-in-Variables in a Random Effects Probit Model for Panel Data," *Economic Letters*, 24, 339–342.
Karlin, S., and H. Taylor (1975). *A First Course in Stochastic Processes*, 2nd edition. New York: Academic Press.

Kaufman, G.M. (1977). "Posterior Inference for Structural Parameters Using Cross Section and Time Series Data," in *Studies in Bayesian Econometrics and Statistics, in Honor of L. J. Savage*, vol. 2, edited by S. Fienberg and A. Zellner, pp. 73–94. Amsterdam: North-Holland.

Keane, M.P. (1994). "A Computationally Practical Simulation Estimator for Panel Data," *Econometrica*, 62, 95–116.

Kelejian, H.H. (1977). "Random Parameters in Simultaneous Equation Framework: Identification and Estimation," *Econometrica*, 42, 517–527.

Kelejian, H.H., and I.R. Prucha (2001). "On the Asymptotic Distribution of the Moran I Test Statistic with Application," *Journal of Econometrics*, 104, 219–257.

Kelejian, H.H., and S.W. Stephan (1983). "Inference in Random Coefficient Panel Data Models: A Correction and Clarification of the Literature," *International Economic Review*, 24, 249–254.

Kiefer, N.M. (1979). "Population Heterogeneity and Inference from Panel Data on the Effects of Vocational Education," *Journal of Political Economy*, 87 (pt. 2), S213–S226.

(1980). "Estimation of Fixed Effects Models for Time Series of Cross-Sections with Arbitrary Intertemporal Covariance, *Journal of Econometrics*, 14, 195–202.

(1988). "Economic Duration Data and Hazard Functions," *Journal of Economic Literature*, 26, 646–679.

Kim, J., and D. Pollard (1990). "Cube Root Asymptotics," *Annals of Statistics*, 18, 191–219.

Kiviet, J.F. (1995). "On Bias, Inconsistency, and Efficiency in Various Estimators of Dynamic Panel Data Models," *Journal of Econometrics*, 68, 53–78.

Kiviet, J.F., and G.D.A. Phillips (1993). "Alternative Bias Approximation with Lagged Dependent Variables," *Econometric Theory*, 9, 62–80.

Klein, L.R. (1953). *A Textbook of Econometrics*. Evanston, IL.: Row Peterson.

(1988). "The Statistical Approach to Economics," *Journal of Econometrics*, 37, 7–26.

Klein, R., and R. Spady (1993). "An Efficient Semiparametric Estimator for Binary Response Models," *Econometrica*, 61:2, 387–342.

Krishnakumar, J., and E. Ronchetti (2000). *Panel Data Econometrics: Future Directions, Papers in Honor of Professor Pietro Balestra*. Amsterdam: North Holland.

Kuh, E. (1959). "The Validity of Cross Sectionally Estimated Behavior Equations in Time Series Applications," *Econometrica* 27, 197–214.

(1963). *Capital Stock Growth: A Micro-Econometric Approach*. Amsterdam: North-Holland.

Kuh, E., and J.R. Meyer (1957). "How Extraneous Are Extraneous Estimates?" *Review of Economics and Statistics*, 39, 380–393.

Kyriazidou, E. (1997). "Estimation of a Panel Data Sample Selection Model," *Econometrica*, 65, 1335–1364.

(2001). "Estimation of Dynamic Panel Data Sample Selection Models," *Review of Economic Studies*, 68, 543–572.

Lancaster, T. (1984). "The Covariance Matrix of the Information Matrix Test," *Econometrica*, 52, 1051–1053.

(1990). *The Econometric Analysis of Transition Data*. New York: Cambridge University Press.

(2001). "Some Econometrics of Scarring," in *Nonlinear Statistical Inference*, edited by C. Hsiao, K. Morimune, and J.L. Powell, pp. 393–402. New York: Cambridge University Press.

Layton, L. (1978). "Unemployment over the Work History." PhD dissertation. Department of Economics, Columbia University.

Lewbel, A. (1992). "Aggregation with Log-Linear Models," *Review of Economic Studies*, 59, 635–642.

(1994). "Aggregation and Simple Dynamics," *American Economic Review*, 84, 905–918.

Lee, L.F. (1978a). "Unionism and Wage Rates: A Simultaneous Equations Model with Qualitative and Limited Dependent Variables," *International Economic Review*, 19, 415–434.

(1978b). "On the Issues of Fixed Effects vs. Random Effects Econometric Models with Panel Data," Discussion Paper 78–101. University of Minnesota.

(1979). "Efficient Estimation of Dynamic Error Components Models with Panel Data," Discussion Paper No. 79–118. Center for Economic Research, University of Minnesota.

(1982). "Specification Error in Multinominal Logit Models: Analysis of the Omitted Variable Bias," *Journal of Econometrics*, 20, 197–209.

(1987). "Nonparametric Testing of Discrete Panel Data Models," *Journal of Econometrics*, 34, 147–178.

Lee, L.F., and W.E. Griffiths (1979). "The Prior Likelihood and Best Linear Unbiased Prediction in Stochastic Coefficient Linear Models," Working Papers in Econometrics and Applied Statistics, No. 1. University of New England.

Lee, M.J. (1999). "A Root-*N* Consistent Semiparametric Estimator for Related Effects Binary Response Panel Data," *Econometrica*, 67, 427–433.

Levin, A., and C. Lin (1993). "Unit Root Tests in Panel Data: Asymptotic and Finite Sample Properties," Mimeo, University of California, San Diego.

Levin, A., C. Lin, and J. Chu (2002). "Unit Root Tests in Panel Data: Asymptotic and Finite-Sample Properties," *Journal of Econometrics*, 108, 1–24.

Li, Q., and C. Hsiao (1998). "Testing Serial Correlation in Semi-parametric Panel Data Models," *Journal of Econometrics*, 87, 207–237.

Lillard, L.A., and Y. Weiss (1979). "Components of Variation in Panel Earnings Data: American Scientists 1960–1970," *Econometrica*, 47, 437–54.

Lillard, L.A., and R. Willis (1978). "Dynamic Aspects of Earnings Mobility," *Econometrica*, 46, 985–1012.

Lindley, D.V., and A.F.M. Smith (1972). "Bayes Estimates for the Linear Model," and Discussion, *Journal of the Royal Statistical Society, Series B*, 34, 1–41.

Little, R.J.A., and D.B. Rubin (1987). *Statistical Analysis with Missing Data*. New York: Wiley.

Liu, L.M., and G.C. Tiao (1980). "Random Coefficient First-Order Autoregressive Models," *Journal of Econometrics*, 13, 305–25.

MaCurdy, T.E. (1981). "An Empirical Model of Labor Supply in a Life Cycle Setting," *Journal of Political Economy*, 89, 1059–85.

(1982). "The Use of Time Series Processes to Model the Error Structure of Earnings in a Longitudinal Data Analysis," *Journal of Econometrics*, 18, 83–114.

Maddala, G.S. (1971a). "The Use of Variance Components Models in Pooling Cross Section and Time Series Data," *Econometrica*, 39, 341–58.

(1971b). "The Likelihood Approach to Pooling Cross-Section and Time Series Data," *Econometrica*, 39, 939–53.

(1983). *Limited Dependent and Qualitative Variables in Econometrics*. Cambridge: Cambridge University Press.

Maddala, G.S., and T.D. Mount (1973). "A Comparative Study of Alternative Estimators for Variance Components Models Used in Econometric Applications," *Journal of the American Statistical Association*, 68, 324–8.

Maddala, G.S., and S. Wu (1999). "A Comparative Study of Unit Root Tests with Panel Data and a New Simple Test," *Oxford Bulletin of Economics and Statistics*, 61, 631–652.

Magnus, J.R., and H. Neudecker (1999). *Matrix Differential Calculus with Applications in Statistics and Econometrics*, revised edition. New York: Wiley.

Mairesse, J. (1990). "Time-Series and Cross-sectional Estimates on Panel Data: Why are They Different and Why Should They Be Equal?" in *Panel Data and Labor Market Studies*, edited by J. Hartog, G. Ridder, and J. Theeuwes, pp. 81–95. Amsterdam: North-Holland.

Malinvaud, E. (1970). *Statistical Methods of Econometrics*, 2nd edition. Amsterdam: North-Holland.

Mankiew, N.G., D. Romer, and D. Weil (1992). "A Contribution to the Empirics of Economic Growth," *Quarterly Journal of Economics*, 107, 407–437.

Manski, C.F. (1975). "Maximum Score Estimation of the Stochastic Utility Model of Choice," *Journal of Econometrics*, 3, 205–228.

(1985). "Semiparametric Analysis of Discrete Response: Asymptotic Properties of the Maximum Score Estimator," *Journal of Econometrics*, 27, 313–333.

(1987). "Semiparametric Analysis of Random Effects Linear Models from Binary Panel Data," *Econometrica*, 55, 357–362.

Matyás, L., and P. Sevestre (1996). "The Econometrics of Panel Data: A Handbook of the Theory with Applications," 2nd edition. Dordrecht: Kluwer Academic.

Mazodier, P., and A. Trognon (1978). "Heteroscedasticity and Stratification in Error Components Models," *Annales de l'INSEE*, 30-1, 451–482.

McCoskey, S., and C. Kao (1998). "A Residual-Based Test of the Null of Cointegration in Panel Data," *Econometric Reviews*, 17, 57–84.

McFadden, D. (1974). "Conditional Logit Analysis of Qualitative Choice Behavior," in *Frontiers in Econometrics*, edited by P. Zarembka, pp. 105–142. New York: Academic Press.

(1976). "Quantal Choice Analysis: A Survey," *Annals of Economic and Social Measurement*, 5, 363–390.

(1984). "Econometric Analysis of Qualitative Response Models," in *Handbook of Econometrics*, vol. II, edited by Z. Griliches and M. D. Intriligator, pp. 1395–1457. Amsterdam: North-Holland.

(1989). "A Method of Simulated Moments for Estimation of Discrete Response Models without Numerical Integration," *Econometrica*, 57, 995–1026.

Mehta, J.S., G.V.L. Narasimham, and P.A.V.B. Swamy (1978). "Estimation of a Dynamic Demand Function for Gasoline with Different Schemes of Parameter Variation," *Journal of Econometrics*, 7, 263–279.

Meyer, J.R., and E. Kuh (1957). *The Investment Decision: An Empirical Study*. Cambridge, MA: Harvard University Press.

Miller, J.J. (1977). "Asymptotic Properties of Maximum Likelihood Estimates in the Mixed Model of the Analysis of Variance," *Annals of Statistics*, 5, 746–62.

Miller, M.H., and F. Modigliani (1961). "Dividend Policy, Growth and the Valuation of Shares," *Journal of Business*, 34, 411–433.

Min, C.K., and A. Zellner (1993). "Bayesian and Non-Bayesian Methods for Combining Models and Forecasts with Applications to Forecasting International Growth Rate," *Journal of Econometrics*, 56, 89–118.

Modigliani, F., and M.H. Miller (1958). "The Cost of Capital, Corporation Finance, and the Theory of Investment," *American Economic Review*, 48, 261–297.

Moffitt, R. (1993). "Identification and Estimation of Dynamic Models with a Time Series of Repeated Cross-Sections," *Journal of Econometrics*, 59, 99–123.

Moffitt, R., J. Fitzgerald, and P. Gottschalk (1997). "Sample Selection in Panel Data: The Role of Selection on Observables," Mimeo, Johns Hopkins University.

Mundlak, Y. (1961). "Empirical Production Function Free of Management Bias," *Journal of Farm Economics*, 43, 44–56.

(1978a). "On the Pooling of Time Series and Cross Section Data," *Econometrica* 46, 69–85.

(1978b). "Models with Variable Coefficients: Integration and Extension," *Annales de l'INSEE* 30-1, 483–509.

Nerlove, M. (1965). *Estimation and Identification of Cobb–Douglas Production Functions*. Chicago: Rand McNally.

(1967). "Experimental Evidence on the Estimation of Dynamic Economic Relations from a Time Series of Cross Sections," *Economic Studies Quarterly*, 18, 42–74.

(1971a). "Further Evidence on the Estimation of Dynamic Economic Relations from a Time Series of Cross Sections," *Econometrica*, 39, 359–82.

(1971b). "A Note on Error Components Models," *Econometrica*, 39, 383–96.

(2000). "An Essay on the History of Panel Data Econometrics," paper presented at 2000 Panel Data Conference in Geneva.

Newey, W. (1999). "Two Step Series Estimation of Sample Selection Models," Mimeo, MIT.

Newey, W., and K. West (1987). "A Simple Positive Semi-Definite, Heteroscedasticity and Autocorrelation Consistent Covariance Matrix," *Econometrica*, 50, 703–708.

Neyman, J. (1949). "Contribution to the Theory of the χ^2 Test," in *Proceedings of the First Berkeley Symposium on Mathematical Statistics and Probabilities*, edited by J. Neyman, pp. 230–270. Berkeley: University of California Press.

Neyman, J., and E.L. Scott (1948). "Consistent Estimates Based on Partially Consistent Observations," *Econometrica*, 16, 1–32.

Nicholls, D.F., and B.G. Quinn (1982). *Random Coefficient Autoregressive Models: An Introduction*. Berlin: Springer-Verlag.

Nickell, S. (1979). "Estimating the Probability of Leaving Unemployment," *Econometrica*, 47, 1249–1266.

(1981). "Biases in Dynamic Models with Fixed Effects," *Econometrica*, 49, 1399–1416.

Nijman, T.H.E., and M. Verbeek (1992). "Nonresponse in Panel Data: The Impact on Estimates of a Life Cycle Consumption Function," *Journal of Applied Econometrics*, 7, 243–257.

Nijman, T.H.E., M. Verbeek, and A. van Soest (1991). "The Efficiency of Rotating Panel Designs in an Analysis of Variance Model," *Journal of Econometrics*, 49, 373–399.

Pakes, A., and Z. Griliches (1984). "Estimating Distributed Lags in Short Panels with an Application to the Specification of Depreciation Patterns and Capital Stock Constructs," *Review of Economic Studies*, 51, 243–62.

Pakes, A., and D. Pollard (1989). "Simulation and the Asymptotics of Optimization Estimators," *Econometrica*, 57, 1027–1057.

Pagan, A. (1980). "Some Identification and Estimation Results for Regression Models with Stochastically Varying Coefficients," *Journal of Econometrics*, 13, 341–364.

Peracchi, F. (2000). "The European Community Household Panel: A Review," paper presented at the Panel Data Conference in Geneva.

Pesaran, M.H. (1999). "On Aggregation of Linear Dynamic Models," Mimeo, University of Southern California and University of Cambridge.

Pesaran, M.H., Y. Shin, and R.J. Smith (1999). "Pooled Mean Group Estimation of Dynamic Heterogeneous Panels," *Journal of the American Statistical Association*, 94, 621–634.

Pesaran, M.H., Y. Shin, and R.J. Smith (2000). "Structural Analysis of Vector Error Correction Models with Exogenous $I(1)$ Varibles," *Journal of Econometrics*, 97, 293–343.

Pesaran, M.H., and R. Smith (1995). "Estimation of Long-Run Relationships from Dynamic Heterogeneous Panels," *Journal of Econometrics*, 68, 79–114.

Pesaran, M.H., and Z. Zhao (1999). "Bias Reduction in Estimating Long-Run Relationships from Dynamic Heterogeneous Panels," in *Analysis of Panels and Limited Dependent Variables*, edited by C. Hsiao, K. Lahiri, L.F. Lee, and M.H. Pesaran, pp. 297–322. Cambridge: Cambridge University Press.

Phelps, E. (1972). *Inflation Policy and Unemployment Theory: The Cost Benefit Approach to Monetary Planning*. London: Macmillan.

Phillips, P.C.B. (1991). "Optimal Inference in Cointegrated Systems," *Econometrica*, 59, 283–306.

Phillips, P.C.B., and S.N. Durlauf (1986). "Multiple Time Series Regression with Integrated Processes," *Review of Economic Studies*, 53, 473–495.

Phillips, P.C.B., and H.R. Moon (1999). "Linear Regression Limit Theory for Nonstationary Panel Data," *Econometrica*, 67, 1057–1111.

(2000). "Nonstationary Panel Data Analysis: An Overview of Some Recent Developments," *Econometrics Review*, 19, 263–286.

Pinkse, J. (2000). "Asymptotic Properties of Moran and Related Tests and Testing for Spatial Correlation in Probit Models," Mimeo, University of British Columbia.

Powell, J.L. (1986). "Symmetrically Trimmed Least Squares Estimation for Tobit Models," *Econometrica*, 54, 1435–1460.

Powell, J.L. (2001). "Semiparametric Estimation of Censored Selection Models," in *Nonlinear Statistical Inference*, edited by C. Hsiao, K. Morimune, and J.L. Powell, New York: Cambridge University Press, 165–196.

Powell, J.L., J.H. Stock, and T. Stoker (1989). "Semiparametric Estimation of Index Coefficients," *Econometrica*, 57, 1403–1430.

Priestley, M.B. (1982). *Spectral Analysis and Time Series*, vols. I and II. New York: Academic Press.

Prucha, I.R. (1983). "Maximum Likelihood and Instrumental Variable Estimation in Simultaneous Equation Systems with Error Components," Working Paper No. 83–6. Department of Economics, University of Maryland.

Quah, D. (1994). "Exploiting Cross-Section Variations for Unit Root Inference in Dynamic Data," *Economic Letters*, 44, 9–19.

Quandt, R.E. (1982). "Econometric Disequilibrium Models," *Econometric Reviews*, 1, 1–64.

Raj, B., and A. Ullah (1981). *Econometrics, A Varying Coefficient Approach*. London: Croom Helm.

Rao, C.R. (1952). *Advanced Statistical Methods in Biometric Research*. New York: Wiley.

(1970). "Estimation of Heteroscedastic Variances in Linear Models," *Journal of the American Statistical Association*, 65, 161–172.

(1972). "Estimation of Variance and Covariance Components in Linear Models," *Journal of the American Statistical Association*, 67, 112–115.

(1973). *Linear Statistical Inference and Its Applications*, 2nd edition. New York: Wiley.

Richard, J.F. (1996). "Simulation Techniques," in *The Econometrics of Panel Data*, 2nd edition, edited by L. Matyas and P. Sevestre, pp. 613–638. Dordrecht: Kluwer Academic.

Ridder, G. (1990). "Attrition in Multi-wave Panel Data," in *Panel Data and Labor Market Studies*, edited by J. Hartog, G. Ridder, and J. Theeuwes. Amsterdam: North-Holland.

(1992). "An Empirical Evaluation of Some Models for Non-random Attrition in Panel Data," *Structural Change and Economic Dynamics*, 3, 337–335.

Robinson, P.M. (1988a). "Semiparametric Econometrics: A Survey," *Journal of Applied Econometrics*, 3, 35–51.

(1988b). "Root-N-Consistent Semiparametric Regression," *Econometrica*, 56, 931–954.

(1989). "Notes on Nonparametric and Semiparametric Estimation," Mimeo. London School of Economics.

Rosenberg, B. (1972). "The Estimation of Stationary Stochastic Regression Parameters Reexamined," *Journal of the American Statistical Association*, 67, 650–654.

(1973). "The Analysis of a Cross-Section of Time Series by Stochastically Convergent Parameter Regression," *Annals of Economic and Social Measurement*, 2, 39–428.

Rothenberg, T.J. (1973). *Efficient Estimation with a Priori Information*. New Haven: Yale University Press.

Rubin, D.B. (1976). "Inference and Missing Data," *Biometrica*, 63, 581–592.

Sant, D. (1977). "Generalized Least Squares Applied to Time-Varying Parameter Models," *Annals of Economic and Social Measurement*, 6, 301–14.

Scheffé, H. (1959). *The Analysis of Variance*. New York: Wiley.

Schmidt, P. (1984). "Simultaneous Equation Models with Fixed Effects," Mimeo. Michigan State University.

Schwarz, G. (1978). "Estimating the Dimension of a Model," *Annals of Statistics*, 6, 461–464.

Searle, S.R. (1971). *Linear Models*. New York: Wiley.

Sevestre, P., and A. Trognon (1982). "A Note on Autoregressive Error Component Models." #8204. Ecole Nationale de la Statistique et de l'Administration Economique et Unité de Recherche.

Sheiner, L., B. Rosenberg, and K. Melmon (1972). "Modeling of Individual Pharmacokinetics for Computer-Aided Drug Dosage," *Computers and Biomedical Research*, 5, 441–459.

Sims, C. (1980). "Macroeconomics and Reality," *Econometrica*, 48, 1–48.

Sims, C., J.H. Stock, and M.W. Watson (1990). "Inference in Linear Time Series Models with Some Unit Roots," *Econometrica*, 58(1), 113–144.

Singer, B., and S. Spilerman (1974). "Social Mobility Models for Heterogeneous Populations," in *Sociological Methodology 1973–1974*, edited by H.L. Costner, pp. 356–401. San Francisco: Jossey-Bass.

(1976). "Some Methodological Issues in the Analysis of Longitudinal Surveys," *Annals of Economic and Social Measurement*, 5, 447–474.

Singh, B., A.L. Nagar, N.K. Choudhry, and B. Raj (1976). "On the Estimation of Structural Changes: A Generalization of the Random Coefficients Regression Model," *International Economic Review*, 17, 340–361.

Small, K., and C. Hsiao (1985). "Multinominal Logit Specification Tests," *International Economic Review*, 26, 619–627.

Solon, G. (1985). "Comment on 'Benefits and Limitations of Data' by C. Hsiao," *Econometric Reviews*, 4, 183–186.

Smith, A.F.M. (1973). "A General Bayesian Linear Model," *Journal of the Royal Statistical Society, B*, 35, 67–75.

Stiglitz, J.E., and A. Weiss (1981), "Credit Rationing in Markets with Imperfect Information," *American Economic Review*, 71, 393–410.

Stone, R. (1954). *The Measurement of Consumers' Expenditure and Behavior in the United Kingdom, 1920–1938*. Cambridge: Cambridge University Press.

Stroud, A.H., and D. Secrest (1966). *Gaussian Quadrature Formulas*. Englewood, NJ: Prentice Hall.

Summers, L.H. (1981). "Taxation and Corporate Investment: A q-theory Approach," *Brookings Papers on Economic Activity*, 1, 67–127.

Swamy, P.A.V.B. (1970). "Efficient Inference in a Random Coefficient Regression Model," *Econometrica*, 38, 311–323.

(1971). *Statistical Inference in Random Coefficient Regression Models*. Berlin: Springer-Verlag.

(1974). "Linear Models with Random Coefficients," in *Frontiers in Econometrics*, edited by P. Zarembka, pp. 143–168. New York: Academic Press.

Swamy, P.A.V.B., and J.S. Mehta (1973). "Bayesian Analysis of Error Components Regression Models," *Journal of the American Statistical Association*, 68, 648–658.

(1977). "Estimation of Linear Models with Time and Cross-Sectionally Varying Coefficients," *Journal of the American Statistical Association*, 72, 890–898.

Swamy, P.A.V.B., and P.A. Tinsley (1977). "Linear Prediction and Estimation Method for Regression Models with Stationary Stochastic Coefficients." Special Studies Paper No. 78. Federal Reserve Board Division of Research and Statistics, Washington, DC.

Taub, A.J. (1979). "Prediction in the Context of the Variance-Components Model," *Journal of Econometrics*, 10, 103–107.

Taylor, W.E. (1980). "Small Sample Consideration in Estimation from Panel Data," *Journal of Econometrics*, 13, 203–223.

Temple, J. (1999). "The New Growth Evidence," *Journal of Economic Literature*, (1999), 37(1), 112–156.

Theil, H. (1954). *Linear Aggregation of Economic Relations*. Amsterdam: North-Holland.

(1971). *Principles of Econometrics*. New York: Wiley.

Theil, H., and L.B.M. Mennes (1959). "Conception Stochastique de Coefficients Multiplicateurs dans l'Adjustment Linéaire des Séries Temporelles," *Publications de l'Institut de Statistique de l'Université de Paris*, 8, 211–227.

Tobin, J. (1950). "A Statistical Demand Function for Food in the U.S.A.," *Journal of the Royal Statistical Society, Series A*, 113, 113–141.

(1958). "Estimation of Relationships for Limited Dependent Variables," *Econometrica*, 26, 24–36.

(1969). "A General Equilibrium Approach to Monetary Policy," *Journal of Money, Credit and Banking*, 1, 15–29.

Trognon, A. (1978). "Miscellaneous Asymptotic Properties of Ordinary Least Squares and Maximum Likelihood Estimators in Dynamic Error Components Models," *Annales de L'INSEE*, 30-1, 631–657.

(2000). "Panel Data Econometrics: A Successful Past and a Promising Future," paper presented at the 2000 Panel Data Conference in Geneva.

Quah, D. (1994). "Exploiting Cross-Section Variations for Unit Root Inference in Dynamic Data," *Economic Letters*, 44, 9–19.

Vella, F., and M. Verbeek (1999). "Two-Step Estimation of Panel Data Models with Censored Endogenous Variables and Selection Bias," *Journal of Econometrics*, 90, 239–264.

Verbeek, M. (1992). "The Design of Panel Surveys and the Treatment of Missing Observations." PhD Dissertation. Tilburg University.

Verbeek, M., and TH.E. Nijman (1996). "Incomplete Panels and Selection Bias," in the *Econometrics of Panel Data*, 2nd edition, edited by L. Matyas and P. Sevester. Dordercht: Kluwer Academic.

Wachter, M.L. (1970). "Relative Wage Equations for U.S. Manufacturing Industries 1947–1967," *Review of Economics and Statistics*, 52, 405–10.

Wallace, T.D., and A. Hussain (1969). "The Use of Error Components Models in Combining Cross-Section with Time Series Data," *Econometrica*, 37, 55–72.

Wansbeek, T.J. (2001). "GMM Estimation in Panel Data Models with Measurement Error," *Journal of Econometrics*, 104, 259–268.

Wansbeek, T.J., and P.A. Bekker (1996). "On IV, GMM and ML in a Dynamic Panel Data Model," *Economic Letters*, 51, 145–152.

Wansbeek, T.J., and A. Kapteyn (1978). "The Separation of Individual Variation and Systematic Change in the Analysis of Panel Data," *Annales de l'INSEE*, 30-31, 659–680.

(1982). "A Class of Decompositions of the Variance–Covariance Matrix of a Generalized Error Components Model," *Econometrica*, 50, 713–24.

Wansbeek, T.J., and R.H. Koning (1989). "Measurement Error and Panel Data," *Statistica Neerlandica*, 45, 85–92.

White, H. (1980). "A Heteroscedasticity-Consistent Covariance Matrix Estimator and a Direct Test for Heteroscedasticity," *Econometrica*, 48, 817–838.

(1982). "Maximum Likelihood Estimation of Misspecified Models," *Econometrica*, 50, 1–25.

Wooldridge, J.M. (1999). "Distribution-Free Estimation of Some Nonlinear Panel Data Models," *Journal of Econometrics*, 90, 77–98.

Wright, B.D., and G. Douglas (1976). "Better Procedures for Sample-Free Item Analysis," Research Memorandum 20. Statistical Laboratory, Department of Education, University of Chicago.

Zacks, S. (1971). *The Theory of Statistical Inference*. New York: Wiley.

Zellner, A. (1962). "An Efficient Method of Estimating Seemingly Unrelated Regressions and Tests for Aggregation Bias," *Journal of the American Statistical Association*, 57, 348–368.

(1966). "On the Aggregation Problem: A New Approach to a Troublesome Problem," in *Economic Models, Estimation and Risk Programming: Essays in Honor of Gerhard Tintner*, edited by K. Fox, pp. 365–374. Berlin: Spinger-Verlag.

(1970). "Estimation of Regression Relationships Containing Unobservable Variables," *International Economic Review*, 11, 441–454.

Zellner, A., C. Hong, and C.K. Min (1991). "Forecasting Turning Points in International Output Growth Rates Using Bayesian Exponentially Weighted Autoregression, Time Varying Parameter and Pooling Techniques," *Journal of Econometrics*, 49, 275–304.

Zellner, A., and H. Theil (1962). "Three Stage Least Squares: Simultaneous Estimation of Simultaneous Equations," *Econometrica*, 30, 54–78.

Ziliak, J.P. (1997). "Efficient Estimation with Panel Data When Instruments Are Predetermined: An Empirical Comparison of Moment-Condition Estimators," *Journal of Business and Economic Statistics*, 15, 419–431.

Author Index

Subject Index